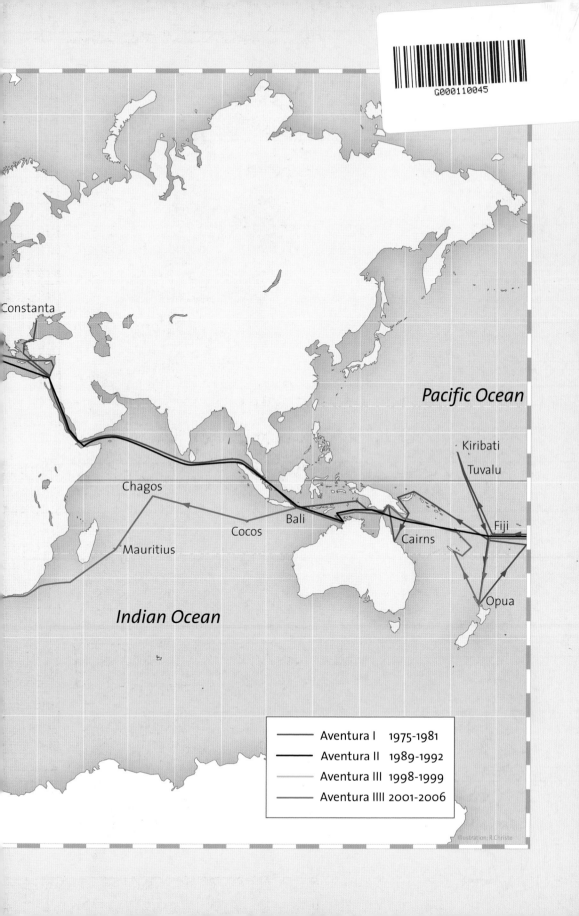

Constanta

Pacific Ocean

Kiribati

Tuvalu

Chagos

Cocos

Bali

Fiji

Cairns

Mauritius

Opua

Indian Ocean

——	Aventura I	1975-1981
——	Aventura II	1989-1992
——	Aventura III	1998-1999
——	Aventura IIII	2001-2006

Illustration: R.Christe

Jimmy Cornell

A Passion for the Sea

Reflections on three circumnavigations

Jimmy Cornell

A Passion for the Sea

Reflections on three circumnavigations

Noonsite

Published 2007 by Noonsite
P O Box 165, London, WC1B 3XA, Great Britain
www.noonsite.com

ISBN 978-0-9556396-0-9   A Passion for the Sea:
Reflections on Three Circumnavigations

Printed by Girzig & Gottschalk GmbH
Hannoversche Strasse 64
28309 Bremen, Germany
Design: Ursula und Jürgen Duscha
Photos: Jimmy Cornell
Photo page 28 ©Li Erben
Diagram page 218 ©Cruising World Magazine
Photo page 472 ©Servizio Fotografico de "L´O.R."

This book is dedicated to Abdul Waheed Sheikh,
Fahdel Sheikh, Dr Aziz Ur Rehman and the entire staff
of the Aadil Hospital in Lahore, Pakistan for their
helpfulness and concern for my wellbeing.

I am equally grateful to Dr Paul Sweny and the nursing
staff at the Renal Unit of the Royal Free Hospital in
London for their excellent care and unfailing patience.

Table of Contents

Introduction

If I have a philosophy in life it's this:
get born, live your life, die. Don't worry
about anything in between because
it's just a waste of time.

Jeremy Clarkson

In the winter of 2006, shortly after completing my latest circumnavigation, I had to undergo an operation. Lying in my hospital bed during long sleepless nights my mind was meandering wildly, bringing up forgotten memories of my early life, thoughts about my family and friends, flashbacks from my sailing days as well as images of the current state of the world which had been deteriorating since the fall of communism in the early 1990s. I started putting those thoughts down on paper trying to bring them into some kind of order. Gradually they coalesced into a whole... and the result is here.

As I began writing, I realized that at sixty-six years old my life divided neatly into two distinct halves. The first thirty-three years included my childhood and youth in Romania, marriage to Gwenda, the arrival of Doina and Ivan and the hard time of settling in England. That first half of my life formed the basis of my character. Overcoming the many difficulties that crossed my path gave me the self-confidence to deal with anything life throws at me. From my Romanian ancestors I inherited a healthy dose of fatalism that teaches you that whatever is meant to happen will happen, so you might as well make the best of it. Thanks to this fatalistic trait I never panic when faced with a difficult or dangerous situation and while I can easily blow up over trivial things due to my Latin volatility, when it really matters I manage to stay calm. Growing up under a communist dictatorship made me a fairly wild young man but fortunately age has gradually rounded off some of the rougher edges of my character.

The next thirty-three years of my life have been intrinsically linked with the sea and sailing. Starting to sail only in my early thirties I was a late starter indeed. After my first offshore experience in 1973, I built our first boat, left with Gwenda, Doina and Ivan on a six-year long round the world voyage, started writing books on sailing, organized the first ARC and other cruising rallies, and completed two circumnavigations on the two subsequent Aventuras.

Starting a new life in England was a steep learning curve but I soon learnt the important lesson that in the free world everything is possible if you are determined and try hard enough. Mainly from sailing I picked up the habit of learning from my own mistakes as well as from those of others, and whenever possible to try not to repeat those mistakes. My latest round the world voyage is a good reflection of all that I have learnt over the years – five highly enjoyable years with hardly any drama and no serious mishaps. That such a long voyage could go so smoothly is one of the main reasons why I decided to write this book.

For the first time in my writing career I decided to abandon my usual style of impartial factual reporting that I employed in my previous books and is a result of my training as a BBC journalist. Instead I decided to focus primarily on my personal experience and deal with any subject from that narrower, more subjective point of view.

Looking back on over three decades of sailing, I felt that the time had come to share that hard gained practical experience with my readers. From my contacts with many sailors preparing to set off on their own voyages, whom I met either at lectures, seminars or in the rallies that I used to organize, I knew that a book dealing with all essential aspects of offshore cruising, written by someone who had done it himself, could be of great help in their own preparations.

Although my publishers insisted that cruising narratives are a thing of the past, I felt that as in recent years I had been fortunate to visit so many exciting and interesting places, from Antarctica to remote tropical islands, I simply could not cast aside all that material. How to marry happily those two very different entities, of a narrative based on my recent wanderings and a technical presentation of what offshore cruising is all about, was the greatest stumbling block, especially as I was not prepared to abandon one or the other. So the book has ended up as basically two books that are, I hope, logically interlinked with the practical side running parallel to the cruising narrative.

Much of the cruising narrative is based on my regular reports published as Letter from Aventura in the US magazine Cruising World during my five-year circumnavigation. Although I decided to base as much of this book as possible on my own sailing experience, occasionally I could not resist the temptation to refer to some of the many cruising surveys that I conducted over the years, as I had been the first to benefit from their findings. From my previous book World Cruising Survey (UK edition) or World Cruising Essentials (US edition) I took the liberty to cherrypick some of the most relevant comments and telling quotes by the highly experienced sailors who made a valuable contribution to that overview of the cruising scene. Finally I also contacted many of my sailing friends from all over the world asking for their comments on the specific subjects that I knew to be their speciality.

It must be stressed that the main aim of this book is not to give the ultimate verdict on all essential aspects of offshore cruising but rather describe how things have worked out for me. Bearing in mind all the miles I have sailed in recent years, my solutions may not be perfect but they have the great merit that they worked and, at sea, this is what counts.

As I started writing, significant incidents from my earlier non-sailing life surfaced and refused to go away. I still had doubts whether a book that is primarily about sailing would be a suitable place for such personal musings, but Gwenda pointed out that what I was writing was a memoir and that readers might well be interested in understanding who Jimmy Cornell is. As so often, she was right, as those earlier incidents do cast light on how a young boy growing up under a totalitarian regime ended up as a sailor roaming the oceans.

There is an important factor that needs to be mentioned here. All my life I have been helped by one essential ingredient: good luck. There is an almost untranslatable Romanian saying that has been my mantra throughout my life. Its basic meaning is that it doesn't matter how stupid you are as long as you're lucky. And lucky I have certainly been!

A Passion for the Sea

Growing up in Romania

A young boy is sitting in the corner of the compartment with his nose pressed to the window. With a loud screech the train slows down and starts negotiating a long bend. Suddenly a voice shouts excitedly: 'The sea, the sea! Look... the sea!'

And there, in front of our disbelieving eyes, a vast expanse of blue-grey water stretched to the far horizon. That first glimpse was the start of an abiding fascination with the sea that has lived with me to this day.

I am the little boy, the year is 1949, I am nine years old and on my way to a state-run vacation colony. A holiday by the sea seemed a beautiful dream after the traumatic events I had been through. I could not believe my luck.

Just a few weeks earlier I had bee staying with my father in a village where he was working on a road building project. Against my father's express orders, I had swum across one of Romania's swiftest rivers, probably to impress my local village friends. When my father came to fetch me and saw my little head bobbing in the middle of that brown water, he could barely control his anger. Without a word, he yanked me home and gave me a good hiding, the first and last I ever got from him.

That same night, shortly after midnight, we were woken up by loud bangs on the door and, when my father opened up, a group of secret policemen burst into the room and, in front of me and my equally terrified sister Doina, took him away. Over 100,000 political undesirables, so-called unreliable members of the ancient regime, were seized that night, each sentenced to fifteen years hard labour building the Danube-Black Sea Canal, one of Stalin's death camps that was abandoned immediately after that tyrant's death in 1953. That night raid was the first nationwide dragnet carried out by the communists after they had taken over power in Romania, expelled King Michael and imposed a ruthless dictatorship that was to last nearly half a century.

My father and other survivors were freed a few days after Stalin's death. With his health ruined and weighing only 40 kg, my father was unable to climb the stairs to our first floor flat and had to be carried up by neighbours. Although he recovered some of the lost weight, his mind and body remained scarred by those hellish experiences to his dying day.

My father's fate has been a constant inspiration for me, but in a strangely negative way, as all my life I have done my best not to follow his example. One of the first lessons along this steep learning curve happened the day after my father's arrest when my uncle came to take us home. As we stood on the platform waiting for the train, he suddenly turned and said: 'Never pee against the wind. It is just not worth it.' I may not have understood the real meaning then, but now, fifty-seven years later, I realize that I have followed that simple advice all my life, trying to navigate the best course through life and, later, across the oceans.

My uncle followed his own advice to the letter: as a social-democrat he did what most others in his situation decided to do and joined the communist party. He never went to prison, always had a well-paid job, lived happily into retirement and died in his sleep aged eighty-eight.

My father was the exact opposite; never able to compromise he put his principles above everything else including his family. His tragic fate was a relentless downward spiral that started when he was barely sixteen and his entire class were drafted into the KK Army of Austro-Hungary to which Transylvania belonged in those days. Sent to the Italian front they suffered heavy losses as his company tried to cross the river Piave but were repelled. As my father was trying to reach their side of the river, a drowning man grabbed hold of him and started dragging him down. Realizing that he did not have the strength to save his dying comrade, my father reached down and grabbing hold of the man's open mouth yanked him away sending him to a certain death. This incident had left him with a deep sense of guilt and shame. The war years made him deeply religious, he would pray every morning and evening in front of a crucifix, always stopping to pray at any church he passed.

Demobbed at nineteen he finished his schooling in his tattered uniform, then managed to get a grant and study law in Budapest. Shortly after finishing his studies, he decided to seek his fortune in South America. With interesting travel experiences but no fortune he returned home and got a job as a village notary in Eastern Transylvania. There he met my mother, they married in 1929, my sister Doina was born in 1935, and I in 1940. In 1942, the quiet notary life was swapped for a glamorous and well-paid job as administrator of a private royal estate in the village of Savarsin in Western Transylvania.

My father's fate was sealed days after the communists took over in late 1947 and forced King Michael into exile. The communists were keen to expel the entire royal entourage and were allowing anyone connected with the King to join a special train leaving for Switzerland. My mother was so convinced we were going that she

A village in the Western Carpathians where my father's family originated from

had packed four suitcases and was waiting hopefully for its arrival, but when the royal train finally arrived in Savarsin my father just went to pay his respects to the King and was the only person left behind on the platform. As he later explained to my distraught mother, he simply could not give up the great honour of staying behind and taking care of the King's estate.

For my poor mother this was the last straw. In the dying days of the war she had lost both her parents and two of their grandchildren when their refugee train was bombed by the Germans. Her younger sister had also perished in the war. She had put all her hopes on starting a new life.

I have two abiding memories of our small Transylvanian village: the wide tranquil Mures river, where I spent every summer day learning to swim like a fish (I am a Pisces of course) and an incident which I witnessed as a four year old in the closing days of the war. A Red Cross train full of injured soldiers had stopped at our station after being repeatedly strafed by the Luftwaffe. The injured men were evacuated from the train and taken in a long straggling column into the village. The pitiful crowd, some walking but most on stretchers carried by their comrades, were slowly passing our gate where I stood mesmerised next to the royal sentry. Suddenly a single Luftwaffe plane appeared, banked hard over the column and started spraying the unfortunate and helpless victims with relentless bursts of machine gun fire. Those who could run scattered like rabbits trying to hide under trees, men missing limbs ran with long bloody bandages trailing behind them, the blind running helplessly into trees, while orderlies were falling, trying to save their stretchered charges. Having reached the end of the column, the plane came back again, and then again, mowing down everyone in sight. These images have never left me, planting the seeds of a profound fatalism that makes me take with equanimity anything fate throws at me and never feel sorry for myself.

Days after the departure of the royal train and his decision not to join the King in exile, my father was visited by the local communist party chief, who told him that the new regime needed people of his calibre and would do anything for him if he agreed to cooperate.

'I'd rather be dead,' my father replied.

'I hope you realize what you are saying. You must know Lenin's words that who is not with us is against us. Take my honest advice: if not you will be in a very dangerous situation.'

'So be it.'

My father had the mandate papers empowering him to administer the estate on the King's behalf torn up in his face and was given 24 hours to leave the village. My uncle managed to get him a job as a cashier on a remote road building site. My mother and I continued to live in a small cottage in Savarsin while getting ready to join my mother's sister in Brasov, where we moved early in 1949.

Set in a picturesque valley in the bend of the Carpathians, Brasov has a long and eventful history, having been founded in the twelfth century by German settlers from Franconia, sent by a Hungarian king to defend this outpost of the empire. Mistakenly referred to as Saxons, they

Dressed in a sailor suit at four years old with my sister Doina

developed a thriving city whose wealth was founded on trade with the Orient. The Honterus gymnasium, which I attended, was the oldest school in Eastern Europe, next to the equally famous gothic Black Church.

Our dingy flat was in a four hundred year old dilapidated building, its only advantage the central location right by the Black Church and its attendant school. The flat had two rooms, the outer one having been subdivided into a day room, where my sister slept and a small kitchen where I slept in a box like contraption that doubled up as a table. My mother slept in the inner room, while the toilet was on the outside landing. I was to live there for ten years, but my mother stayed on for nearly forty bitter years until her death in 1988.

With help from a family friend, my mother had found a job at a small office dealing with hygiene and pest control. Everything under communism depended on one's contacts and friendship was the foundation of everything, which probably explains why for me having friends is, without any doubt, the most important thing in life.

My mother's meagre salary was 400 lei, which exactly covered the cost of the monthly 5kg parcel to my father in the camp and contained honey, nuts, and cigarettes, the universal prison currency. Without such life-saving parcels my father would not have survived. To supplement her earnings, pay for the flat and feed us, my mother played gin rummy. She was very good at it and although the stakes were low, she somehow always managed to win. Her sister and husband also helped and having a comfortable house it was there that we all went for the weekly bath.

Every summer from the age of twelve I got some kind of job. Being well developed and strong, one job I got was as a porter

with a vegetable wholesaler, owned like everything else in Romania by the State. After having been there for a while I started taking vegetables home to sell to neighbours. To earn more money I was doing two full shifts from 6 am to 10 pm. Before finishing my late shift I'd load in the last truck a carefully selected sack of vegetables. Out of the gate the truck had to slow down to negotiate a crossroads and it was here that I jumped off with the sack and headed for home. Each dawn before leaving for work I would have an auction among our neighbours usually taking orders for the next day. It worked well for a while until one day I was hauled in to see the boss.

'You'll end up in prison like your father.'

'My father is a political prisoner and I'm proud of it,' I replied.

'Yes and so you should, but the way you've started, you'll end up a common criminal and should be ashamed of it. You're fired!'

It was once again my advice-giving uncle who put my mind to rest.

'The state is the biggest thief. There is nothing wrong in stealing from it.'

At a loss and not daring to tell my mother that I had been dismissed (although she soon found out) I hit upon the idea of forming a team of bell ringers at the Black Church. I was already very active in its large courtyard where kids played marbles. Every now and again I'd pick a victim, gather up his shiny marbles and say 'blackbirdchick'. Those magic words sealed their change of ownership and there were always tears but my invariable reaction was, 'stop crying you wimp – just ask your dad to buy you some more'. Children with fathers at home were my natural enemy and my hatred of them knew no bounds.

I knew the young Saxon priest as he was also my choirmaster. He liked my idea of having a permanent team as he had often been stuck to find casual workers at short notice. For Sundays and weddings he offered us the generous sum of 20 lei, 16 for funerals. As foreman I divided the money fairly into two, half for me and the other half divided equally between the others. We may have been living under communism but my mind was already more in tune with capitalist principles. I only managed to put this into words when much later I read in George Orwell's

had come early for me. I was only sixteen and had no idea what I really wanted to do in life. I had started playing rugby for the local Brasov team while still at school. Rugby was perfectly suited to my aggressive character, and I was suited to rugby too as I was tough, strong and almost recklessly fearless. It certainly used up some of my excessive energy, especially once my team qualified for Romania's first division, in which I became the youngest player. That same year I was

The medieval centre of Brasov with the Gothic Black Church

Animal Farm, 'we are all equal, but some are more equal than others'.

The Black Church had a large blackboard, which listed all forthcoming funerals. I checked it several times a day, every time I saw a new entry my heart leapt with joy, 'Oh, goody, someone else had died!'

In a drive to get young people to start work as soon as possible, the communists had reduced school from twelve to ten years, so the end of school, in summer 1956,

selected for Romania's national under-18 team and played against France's under-18s in Bucharest. I was also working as a photographer, taking photos of people in parks, restaurants and a nearby mountain resort.

After leaving school, on my parents' insistence I reluctantly agreed to study forestry at the local faculty in Brasov. Having grown up in the middle of a forest on a large estate, the forest was my father's idea of heaven, and having his son a forestry engineer probably the fulfilment of his own dream. Once again, as so many times in my life, fate intervened and solved the forestry career dilemma. By the time I had reached the second year of studies I was expelled because of my social background. This was a period when universities were being cleansed of 'bourgeois' elements both among students and professors. My situation was not helped by the fact that my father had been arrested again and was now in prison at Jilava, the notorious prison for political detainees near Bucharest, where he died one year later. My life as the son of a political prisoner was now severely restricted and I knew that the future held little promise for me.

The news of my father's death came out of the blue when one of my father's sisters had written to my mother to express her condolences. Apparently, under communist bureaucracy, the prison had sent the death certificate to my father's village of birth where his death was entered next to his birth and marriage entries on the register. This is how his sisters had found out and how, by this cruel roundabout way, the news had reached my mother. She asked me to accompany her to the prison near Bucharest to try and find out more and get him re-buried. Jilava prison was a death machine from which few escaped with their lives. During 1959 there had been a temporary thaw and we somehow managed to be received by the prison governor, a colonel in the dreaded Securitate (Secret Police). He listened to my mother quite sympathetically, but explained that the body could not be released as, according to the law, it had to remain in the prisoncemetery until the expiry of my father's 15 year sentence. earing this, my mother collapsed, and I exploded:

'Having murdered this innocent man, the least you could do is let his family give him a decent burial.' I screamed at the governor.

Terrified that she might lose her son as well, my mother begged me to stop, but I would have none of it and continued shouting at the governor. For reasons I never understood, the governor gave in, told us where the cemetery was located and gave us the necessary release papers, asking us insistently to keep this to ourselves. That was the first breach in the communist terror regime that I had witnessed and showed that there were a few officials with a sliver of humanity.

In the corner of a rundown village cemetery, my father's grave was identified by a small wooden plaque: 1006/59. When the gravedigger reached his naked body it fell to me to identify him, an image that I can never forget and fills my heart with unbearable pain on the occasions when it surfaces in my mind. We took his remains to Brasov where they now rest in a beautifully quiet cemetery that overlooks the city from a lofty hill, next to my sister, who died in 1973 and my mother in 1988, the three of them passing away at almost equal fourteen year intervals. Such fateful intervals seem to have marked my entire life and, like giant milestones on destiny's road, stand out like beacons.

It was not long after the death of my father that I came across by chance some Red Cross papers issued by the missing persons office in Geneva, and saying that the named persons had not been able to be tracked down. That evening, when I confronted my mother, she broke down and sobbing uncontrollably, exploded the family myth and finally cleared up the painful lie that had haunted her. As the only Jewish family living in a remote Hungarian village, my two grandparents, who were already in their seventies and were looking after my twin four year old cousins Peter and Ivan, had been rounded up by the Hungarian Police and sent to a German death camp. Taken separately, the twins' mother, my mother's sister, had died in Auschwitz while the only survivor her husband had died of hunger or typhus on his long walk home after the liberation of his camp. Suddenly all the questions marks and suspicions that had plagued me even as a child, came into focus and became crystal clear. Not only had I Romanian, Austrian, Serb and possibly Hungarian blood, but now a hefty proportion of Jewishness as well. Funnily enough, rather than being shocked I was quite pleased and proud, I suppose a normal reaction in an air-brained teenager like I was then.

In 1997 I drove to Romania with Gwenda and Doina and we visited my grandparents' small village in Transylvania. Walking down the muddy main street we met an older man walking towards us. As this was an area entirely populated by Hungarian Szeklers, I addressed him in Hungarian.

'Good day, uncle, you look old enough to maybe remember David and Regina Neuwirth.'

'Of course I do, God bless them. I was their driver. And who are you?'

'I am their grandson, Anna's son. This is my wife and our daughter.'

'God, oh God, what a tragedy. All the village witnessed it... and it was me who the gendarmes asked to drive your grandparents and their poor grandchildren to the first camp at Sighisoara. Let's go and see Uncle Lajos. He is now in his nineties but lived across the street from them and he used to play cards with Mr David.'

He knocked loudly on a wooden gate and a sprightly old man with sparkling eyes came out and greeted us.

'Isten hozta! God brought you!'

'Uncle Lajos this is Dragos, Anna Neuwirth's son.'

He shook my hand warmly. 'So good to see you. Your mother has visited a few times but hasn't come for many years now.'

'No, she passed away in 1988.'

'Sorry to hear that. We all pass on. Even I expect to go soon. I am ninety-six and I am tired of this life.'

'Oh don't say that Uncle Lajos,' the other man exclaimed, 'you'll outlive us all.'

'The entire village witnessed their arrest. It was incomprehensible,' said the old man. ' The war was at its end, the Russians 100 km to the east and those filthy gendarmes had nothing better to do than round up these kind people who many of us didn't know, or even care, that they were Jews. As far as I know they were the only Jews in this whole area.'

'Yes, and I remember to this moment hitching up their beautiful horses, the bay on the left, the chestnut roan on the right.'

'Oh no, you didn't,' interjected the old man. 'The bay was always hitched on the right, the roan on the left.'

'Well, sorry Uncle, but I should know. I was, after all, the driver.'

'You might have been, young man, but you are dead wrong, so stop arguing.'

In spite of being churned up inside, I burst out laughing. Here we were, fifty-three years later, and these two villagers were arguing heatedly about something that they seemed to remember as vividly as if it had happened the previous summer.

'Unfortunately Mr David's house was demolished soon after the war but let's walk over to speak to the man who bought the land from your mother and her sister,' said Uncle Lajos.

A man my age who was working in front of a barn came out and greeted us warmly. When he was told who we were, he exclaimed, 'This is such a coincidence I can hardly believe it. Last week I was rummaging in that barn and came across a few things that must have belonged to your grandparents. Among them I found two small iron snow sleds that can only have belonged to...'

'Poor Ivan and Peter,' added Uncle Lajos.

'I'll go and fetch them.'

He came back with two small black sleds and I could not control myself any longer. Gwenda burst in tears too, so did Doina and the three men as well. The utter cruelty of that day, the grotesque senselessness of the entire operation hit me as never before. This was the Holocaust as I had never really understood it: taking two innocent old people in their seventies and those four year olds to their death simply because by a quirk of nature they had been born with the wrong genes.

Wishing to bring the painful scene to an end, the man handed me the two sleds.

'Take them, I have no use for them, but for you they must have a lot of meaning.'

The house where I grew up in Brasov

They do and mounted now on a wall at our house in Provence are a constant and painful reminder of my family's tiny part in the bloody history of the twentieth century.

In the summer of 1959, exactly ten years after the first of many vacations by the Black Sea, I was back there again: this time with a precise mission. My best school friend Gunter Oberth and I had come to see if we could find a way to escape to the west. Two of our early attempts to gain entrance into the commercial harbour of Constantza had failed at the first hurdle when we found that the boarding steps of every fo-reign ship was guarded by a soldier accompanied by a large guard dog. We agreed to have one last try. Having explored the vicinity of that busy port for about a week, watching the movements and routines of arriving and departing ships, we had found out that those that had no immediate place in the harbour would spend some time anchored about three miles offshore.

Early one evening we found a suitable hideaway among the large rocks of the breakwater that protected the old casino. We got undressed, hid our clothes and dove in. The most difficult part was right at the start as the bright lights from the promenade above lit up the water along a wide band. We managed to swim underwater until we hit darker water. Earlier we had located three ships at anchor and we headed for the nearest one. The night was pleasant, the water warm and we were making good progress. About halfway to the ship we saw the lights of a small coaster crossing in front of us but didn't give it a second thought. Finally we reached the ship and saw on its stern in huge letters: Anita B, Oslo.

'Perfect choice,' I said to Gunter and started screaming:

'Man overboard, man overboard!'

A small head appeared high above us, then more heads and finally a boarding ladder was lowered over the side. After we clambered up the swaying rope ladder we found the whole crew waiting for us. In my limited English I managed to explain what we had in mind so they took us to the mess, gave us dry towels and fed us like kings. The captain was called and I told him who we were, that my father was a political prisoner, and described our plan. I begged him to hide us somewhere safe, leave us in hiding while unloading and loading the ship in Constantza, then drop us off anywhere he wanted, ideally Istanbul as it was the closest non-communist port.

The captain left and we were happily chatting with the sailors when the radio officer was called away. When he came back, his face was grim and he told us that the captain had ordered us to leave the ship immediately. A ship leaving the port had seen a man in the water and had alerted the authorities who were now patrolling the area looking for him. The radio officer had received a call asking if they had seen anything suspicious. The game was up.

Reluctantly we had to say goodbye, climb down the swinging ladder and head for the shore. For a while we stayed together but I could tell from the way we were being taken sideways that there was a current setting us towards the harbour entrance and we had to fight hard to keep our course. Suddenly I realised that I had lost sight of Gunter and started shouting as loud as I dared but he was nowhere to be seen. I was the better swimmer and I was very concerned for him fearing that he might have been swept into the harbour. The lights of the casino were shining like a beacon and eventually the current eased

and I managed to make for them. As there was no sign of a patrol and I suspected that perhaps the Norwegians had lied just to get rid of us, I made for one of the corners of the building. As I was clambering over the slippery rocks I suddenly saw a soldier on the promenade above and as I dove back into the sea he loosened a spray of bullets from his automatic rifle. As I was sinking, I felt a sharp blow under my right knee, but stayed underwater and swam as far as I could parallel to the building, then climbed out quickly and made my way carefully up to the promenade. I gingerly looked around the corner but the wide street was clear, the patrol having gone down to the water expecting to find me shot. I ran across the promenade into a small park and safely reached our hideaway. Only then did I dare look at the wound, which, by now, was bleeding profusely. Fortunately it did not appear to be too serious, although I still have the scar, but if the bullet had gone half an inch deeper the story might have been very different. I used my shirt to staunch the blood, then stood shivering, wondering what had happened to my friend. Much later, when it started to get light, I heard the slap-slap of bare feet. Shaking uncontrollably and totally exhausted, Gunter told me how he had also managed to beat the current but had landed much further away. He had walked along the promenade all the way back unaware of what had happened to me.

'What has happened to you?' he asked, pointing at my bloody shirt.

I was just about to tell him, then thought otherwise. For some reason, which I still cannot understand, I felt that I'd better keep that incident to myself and although I trusted my friend, I didn't trust him enough not to divulge the source of my injury. This was one essential lesson that one learnt living under a dictatorship, never to say more than absolutely necessary and always refrain from asking questions.

'As I came out by the side of the casino, I slipped and hit something underwater. It felt like a piece of reinforcement sticking out of a concrete block. It looks worse than it is, it just needs to be disinfected.'

'OK, what now?' asked Gunter

'Three times unlucky is enough for me,' I replied, but he disagreed.

My gut feeling told me that it was time to stop. While waiting for Gunter, I kept thinking of my mother and how devastated she would be if I had been caught and sent to prison. Gunter thought otherwise. He soon found another friend and headed for the Yugoslav border trying to cross by land. They were caught at the railway station when they arrived without the required permit and could not explain what they were doing there. They were sentenced to three years hard labour. Gunter was taken to the Danube Delta where he spent all day in leech filled water up to his chest cutting reeds for a paper factory. Ironically around the same time I got a job at that same factory working as an interpreter for the East German team who were building a large extension.

My very first outing as a budding sailor happened around that time when a departing German gave me an inflatable kayak and paddle. At the end of the summer I headed straight for the Danube, got off the train at the large bridge spanning the mighty river and descended with my heavy load to the embankment below. The inflated two-man kayak nearly sank under the combined weight of myself, my stores, tent and water. I pushed off and paddled towards the middle of the river where I was caught by the current. I looked up in wonder as a train trundled over my head as I passed under the enormous bridge. The day was beautiful, sunny and warm, dragonflies were flitting over the brown waters and I was in heaven. Here I was, on my own little ship, heading into the unknown without a care in the world. The throbbing noise of an engine made me turn as a grey patrol boat came fast alongside. A uniformed guard shouted from the foredeck. 'What flag?'

'Sorry?'

'What is the national flag of your vessel?'

'I don't understand.'

'But where the hell are you from?' he shouted impatiently.

'Oh, I am Romanian all right.'

'Not all right at all! This is an international waterway and every vessel must fly its national ensign.'

'But how can I get a Romanian flag here in the middle of nowhere?'

'Well, you should have thought about it before.'

The guy at the wheel leant out of the window and beckoned for me to get closer. He came out, handed me a tatty tricolour and said, 'hang it at the stern and bon voyage, but keep out of the way and stay closer to the sides.'

Proudly flying the red, yellow and blue at the stern, I was now legal, having been instantly promoted from ordinary seaman to a fully fledged captain commanding his own vessel on an international waterway.

The onward journey was sheer joy. Much of this area of the Danube is deserted and I only occasionally passed a village and, as I approached the Danube delta, two large ports. The final days passing through the wilderness of the delta were like a dream. There were countless water birds, thick avenues of tall reeds and friendly fishermen who shared their tasty meals with me. The inhabitants of the delta are of Ukrainian origin and are called Lipoveni, burly hefty men with penetrating blue eyes and large bushy beards, who kept crossing themselves with large gestures from forehead to belly and shoulder to shoulder. They spoke Romanian with a heavy accent that I could hardly understand. They were dedicated watermen to their fingertips and handled their narrow pitch-covered craft with such ease as if they were part of their own bodies. Around that time someone had had the brilliant idea to train some younger Lipoveni and send them to the Olympic Games were they grabbed gold medals in rowing.

Having reached Tulcea and the Black Sea, I packed my gear, took the train home... and was hooked for life. I knew that this was what I wanted to do more than anything else: to roam the world on my own boat. That dream had to wait a few years to come true, but true it came and how!

Drifting in Bucharest

After the loss of my father and not wanting to return to Brasov I drifted to Bucharest where I felt there were more opportunities for an ambitious young man like me. As my identity card was issued in Brasov, I was not able to work in Bucharest, and in fact was not supposed to even be there at all. In those days people were not allowed to live anywhere except where they were registered. If you wanted to move and found a new job, you could only take it if you had accommodation there and obtained what was called a floating visa, but you could only secure rented accommodation if you were already employed in that new location. A Catch-22 situation if ever there was one.

Living illegally in Bucharest I had to keep as low a profile as possible. I found a small

attic room in the centre where no questions were asked, but without any source of income life was tough. I did the occasional portering job in the market, then one day I met a girl who introduced me to her friends... and life suddenly took a turn for the better. She was part of a group of kids belonging to the communist elite. All her friends' parents were high officials in the party, government or army, or heads of some large company. One day at a party in a sumptuous villa in an exclusive quarter of Bucharest, attended by various boss kids, a guy my age made a dramatic entrance, looked around and asked: 'Where is that provincial yokel from Brasov who has been making waves here of late?'

'Here, you creep, and what do you want?'

'First of all I want to give you a good hiding for encroaching on my territory and for you to bugger off to where you came from!'

'Suits me, let's go outside and sort it out now!'

Gwenda at Sighisoara in Transylvania the year after we had met

The long awaited moment of our civil marriage in Bucharest

As I advanced towards him meaning every word I said the local bully must have realized that he finally had met his match.

'OK, you seem to be as impatient as a virgin on her wedding night. But I like you, so let's have a drink first.'

We eventually became friends and I never had any more trouble from him or anyone else in his gang.

As the party was breaking up a boy about fourteen sidled up to me and said:

'Jimmy, I like what you did, standing up for yourself. Would you like to be my friend?'

Tudor was the son of a high official and his mother a well known actress. Being Jewish, and in spite of the status of his parents, he was constantly pestered by bullies at his school, antisemitism always having been a shameful trait among many of my countrymen. So every afternoon, I waited outside Tudor's school gates to accompany him home. Occasionally I had to put on the heavy act, but the message quickly spread and he was never taunted again. Although much younger than me, we got on well together, and I spent many afternoons at their luxurious home, being fed regally and being served by their servants. This was communism in great style. Every evening, just before his father came home and his mother left for the theatre Tudor would hand me a 100 lei note. This was a huge sum in those days and allowed me to live well and even occasionally send my mother some money.

It was almost too good to be true but gradually I got bored with this inactive hedonistic life, especially as some of my new friends started going to university, and had less time to hang out with me. I decided to try and do the same and join the newly formed faculty of foreign trade that had just opened at the Institute of Economics. I was told that due to my background I would only succeed if I could pass the tough entrance examination with highest marks, so I studied hard and managed to pass among the top three from the five hundred candidates competing for the one hundred places.

Studying economics and languages interested me and my life seemed to have settled down. Then in 1963, while on a trip to the western town of Oradea, I met some young people from England on a tour of Eastern Europe. Among them was Gwenda. After one winter of daily letters, she came back to Bucharest and we decided to get married...and that's when more problems began. As a Romanian citizen I was not allowed to marry a foreigner, so I had to make a special application to the State Council. While waiting to get married, a family friend had lent us her small flat, which looked straight out of the 1920s but made a cosy home for us. Meanwhile, Gwenda commuted by car between England and Romania, always arriving loaded with things that we could sell on the

Gwenda with Doina and baby Ivan at home in London

black market. The years went by and our marriage application was still not approved.

As soon as I had put in the application to get married, I was expelled from the university but I wasn't too bothered as I saw it as just that first step towards freedom. So as to continue being together, Gwenda managed to get a job with an English tour operator that was sending tourists to Romania. To be close to her I got a job as a barman in a small fishing village next to the Black Sea resort she was working in. After Gwenda had returned to England, my languages helped me secure the much better job as chief of reception at the old Hotel Rex, a beautiful art deco building from the 1920s. It was there that one morning I received a cable from Gwenda's mother saying that our daughter Doina had been born and that both Gwenda and the baby were well. It was one of the happiest days of my life.

While working at the Rex Hotel I met the head of foreign co-productions at the Romanian Film Studio. Romania had just started attracting large foreign productions, due mainly to the low costs and cheap rates paid to easily available extras. These were drawn primarily from the Army and were paid one dollar a day. A new production was about to start and they needed someone with languages as both the main production team and all main actors were either German or English speaking. Thus I managed to land the best job of all. The film, Battle for Rome, was an old style epic describing the dying days of the Roman Empire. The main actors were Laurence Harvey who played Celhegus, a Roman senator, Orson Welles was the Byzantine Emperor Justinian and Sylva Koscina Empress Theodora.

My own work on the film was as assistant production manager. I had to look after the foreign stars but also to find immediate solutions to the many problems that crop up in film making all the time. The job suited me like a glove, I had always been good at improvisation, got on well with people and always managed to get them to do things for me. This problem solving talent soon earned me the nickname Mr. Fix It, which I was very proud of. Now I realize just how much those talents that I developed in my work in films helped me in my life at sea where a capacity to improvise and find solutions is even more vital than on land.

The principal stars had all been put up at the Athenée Palace, Bucharest's most luxurious hotel at that time. As our small flat was only a few minutes away from the hotel, I met the stars every day for breakfast then accompanied them to the film studios some 25 km outside Bucharest. One day Laurence Harvey took me aside.

'Jimmy, maybe you can do better than this. Find me a more decent place!'

At first I didn't understand what he meant.

'You don't like the food?'

'No, not the f...ing food but this god-awful heap. Get me out of here.'

'But this is the very best...'

'Might be for you, mate, but not for me. Capito?'

I told my production boss and he seemed to understand.

'OK, go to the tourist office and see if they can help.'

Ever since my Rex days I had remained good friends with the head of one of the tourist office departments. I told her what I needed and she replied.

'We could try and get him that official residence which used to belong to a prince before the war and whose large grounds are next to the film studios.'

It sounded perfect: a mansion that was a government guest house and where both Khruschev and Tito had stayed.

When I told Laurence Harvey he was delighted.

'Oh yes,' I added quickly, 'But there may still be a problem.'

'What?'

'The price. It's extortionate...'

'How much?'

'One thousand dollars... per week.'

He burst out laughing.

'Get it now!'

Only later did I find out that he was being paid around one million dollars for his role: a sum that I could not imagine or comprehend.

'And Jimmy, I want to move in today.'

'I'll see what I can do.'

I called my friend and told her that the deal was done and that Laurence Harvey wanted to move in straightaway.

'Oh no, no, no, that is quite impossible.'

'Why not? No one is living there.'

'Oh, you obviously don't understand, just tell Mr Harvey we need two days to get the place cleaned up.'

Two days later Larry and his entire entourage moved in: girl friend, butler, driver, and a young English writer who had been brought in to re-write his role and speeches more to his liking. They picked their rooms, and as I was about to leave, Larry turned to me:

'And where the hell are you going?'

'To work.'

'No, you stay put and help us settle in. Take that corner room upstairs, I want you to be around all the time.'

That very first evening we had a celebratory dinner to which Larry had invited all the stars, including Orson Welles. During the long and boozy dinner Orson pointed his glass at the chandelier and exclaimed:

'Let's drink to the permanent glory of Mr Ceausescu and his model regime. May he end in hell, where he and his ugly wife belong.'

I froze and gave him a pleading look, but he ignored me and, with variations, kept performing for the hidden microphones all night. Everyone had guessed the probable reason for the two-day delay. That there could be trouble, especially for me, was clear but nothing ever happened. The Securitate had obviously more important things to worry about.

Gwenda was commuting between Bucharest and the mountains with her tourists and could only see one year old Doina, who was with my mother in Brasov, once a week, while I hardly got to see my daughter at all. So I asked Larry if I could bring Doina and my mother to stay with us as well.

'Of course, go ahead. The more the merrier.'

It was a perfect set-up and we fell into a pleasant routine. Only Orson wasn't happy, complaining to my boss, who told me to try and pay him more attention. One of my tasks was to make sure he got his one-pound steak each morning and to find more interesting restaurants to tickle his palate. One day, while filming and slowly

Taking part in a film on the First Crusade

working his way through his daily bottle of vodka, he asked me to join him for lunch. While waiting outside with his driver for him to finish shooting, I needed to do an urgent job so asked the driver to take me to another film location only a few minutes away. When we got back, Orson was pacing furiously like a tiger in a cage.

'This is my f...ing car and you keep away from it, you dirty rascal.'

'Sorry, Mr Welles.'

'Sorry my foot.'

He got into the Mercedes and slammed the door. The car didn't leave and he suddenly wound down the window and shouted at me:

'What's the f...ing matter with you? Didn't I tell you we'd have lunch together? Get in the f...ing car!'

He had put on the entire scene and not meant a word of it... and I loved him for it.

At one year Doina was a cute, lovable baby and everyone adored her, including Orson. When he left, having run out of his own photographs, he grabbed one of Doina's and wrote on the back: for Doina from Daddy's friend Orson Welles. This is one of our family's most treasured heirlooms, appreciated by everyone but

no-one more than Ivan, who is the only one to have gone into the film business.

In August 1968, a serious tragedy befell Eastern Europe when the Soviet army and a few Warsaw Pact allies invaded Czechoslovakia, which put an abrupt bloody end to the Prague Spring. To his credit, Ceausescu refused to commit Romanian troops but they were ordered to the border areas on standby. At a stroke we lost our extras and the film threatened to unravel, not only our own, but also the even larger production of Mayerling directed by Terence Young and starring Omar Sharif. He had just released Doctor Zhivago and had become the hottest star in the world. Being good friends with Larry he had joined our group, the two of them constantly arguing with great humour about Israel, the Middle East and the 1967 war, Omar as an Eygptian Arab and Larry as a Jew of Lithuanian origin.

While waiting for the return of the soldiers, they asked me one evening to take them to a special restaurant. All I could think of was a small place on the outskirts of Bucharest that was a favourite with the artistic community and was one of the very first private restaurants to open. When we arrived all tables were occupied and the owner could do nothing to help. I begged him, told him who my guests were but to no avail. A desperate situation demanded a desperate solution so I asked him to set a large table on the narrow pavement outside. As we finally sat down, Gwenda happily seated next to Omar Sharif, the thought suddenly struck me: here were some of the most famous celebrities in the world having a quiet dinner on a Bucharest pavement with buses driving past and none of the passers-by taking the slightest interest.

Apart from production jobs, the stars asked me to do them a variety of personal favours: find them ancient Romanian icons or old traditional blouses, or get them caviar on the black market. The latter job became my daily task early in the days of our filming when trouble erupted on the streets of Paris. This was May 1968 and all flights to Paris were cancelled, amongst them the cargo plane supplying the top Parisian restaurants and nightclubs with Romanian caviar. In those days Romania was a leading exporter of caviar from the Danube Delta. So Bucharest was flooded with caviar at knockdown prices and I snapped it up by the kilo. Gwenda had taken an instant liking to caviar and learned to eat it with a large spoon. It has remained one of her weaknesses to this day, even if now she has to go back to eating this expensive and increasingly rare delicacy almost grain by grain like any other normal mortal.

During this time, Gwenda had made the acquaintance of the actress wife of a top party official and she was charmed by Doina. One day she told Gwenda that she was going to talk to her husband to see if he could move our marriage application along. Gwenda had also lobbied her Member of Parliament in England, who promised to speak to the Foreign Secretary who was due to make an official visit to Bucharest. We will never know which was the more important contact, but that autumn after three years of waiting our marriage application was approved. I sneaked a day off from the film studios not telling anyone where I was going and we hot-footed it to the City Hall. Not even my mother was invited, but at least now we were legal. Once married, I applied to leave Romania and join my family in England, stipulating that I wanted to renounce my citizenship and leave as a stateless person.

Ever since the first arrest of my father I've had an aversion for men in uniforms, although when I started sailing I gradually learned to control this gut reaction, always trying to deal politely with officials anywhere in the world. The most memorable encounter with a uniformed official occurred in Brasov six months after we were married. I was summoned to the police and as I entered the official's office I saw on his desk a shiny new Romanian passport. He checked my name on my identity card and brusquely said:

'OK. Take it. And now get out!'

I looked at him for a second, then as politely as possible replied:

'I'm sorry Comrade Major but this is not the kind of passport I applied for?'

His face fell.

'What the hell do you mean?' he shouted. 'You want to go to your English woman don't you? So f... off before I lose my temper!'

'I'm sorry, but I have applied for a travel document to emigrate to England. I do not want to leave this country as a Romanian citizen...'

'Are you refusing this passport?' he screamed.

I remained silent and probably started to realize the enormity of my action.

'Are you?' he asked again.

'Yes, Comrade Major. I don't want this passport.'

'Then you are not going anywhere. Out with you!'

Gwenda had recently returned to England, pregnant with our second child and it was a difficult phone call for me to make, to explain to her what I had done. Although very upset, she already knew how stubborn I could be and told me she understood. A couple of months later, after yet another push from that government minister's wife, I was called to the police again. I did not see the same Major, but just a clerk who took my identity card away and this time gave me the right document. I was a free man and I had won on my own terms. I made it to England just in time to be present at the birth of my son Ivan.

A new start in London

Ten year intervals have marked my life like milestones, 1949 my father's arrest and my first encounter with the sea, 1959 my fruitless escape attempts at the Black Sea and in June 1969 ten years later I was on the plane to London. The very evening I arrived I told Gwenda I had to tell her something important that I hadn't wanted to tell her in Romania. I could tell from her shocked expression that she obviously expected the worst so I blurted out.

'I want to go to sea. I want to be a seaman. I want to see the world...'

Gwenda burst out laughing.

'What's so funny?'

'I thought you were going to tell me that you had only used me to get out, or that you have another woman, maybe even another family back in Romania.'

With Ivan, Doina and my mother at Rambouillet near Paris

'Oh no, none of that. You are and will forever be the only one... It's only that I have this urge, this life-long passion to go to sea.'

'Yes, but how are you going to do it? First you need a job, you have a family to support, one young child and another due soon. Can't the sea wait?'

She was right of course... but I did have a mistress, and eventually, albeit reluctantly, Gwenda wisely accepted this 'ménage à trois', realizing that in spite of my undoubted love for her, the sea would always compete with her for my affection.

Having passed that first hurdle, my next priority was to change my name, as I realized that with a name like Dragos Corneliu Cismasiu life in England would be difficult or, at the very least, a constant bore. Before Doina had been born, Gwenda had already changed her name to Cismasiu so the baby would have our name. As Mrs Cismasiu she hated always having to spell it and was tired of being asked by her English tourists 'Mrs Cismasiu, where did you learn to speak such good English?'

One morning I went to a lawyer, signed a few papers, paid a modest ten shillings fee and instantly became James Cornell. Gwenda and I had already agreed on Cornell as an anglicisation of my middle name and, we felt, a good surname that worked in several languages. Everyone in Bucharest already knew me as Jimmy so that was an easy choice. My nickname of Jimmy had been bestowed on me shortly after the war when an English pilot came to visit the King in Savarsin. He landed his plane at the airstrip nearby, where my father was waiting to receive him with me in tow. In typical British fashion he ignored my name Dragos, and said he'd prefer to call me Jimmy as I reminded him of his son... and Jimmy I have remained to this day.

Our name change, however, didn't turn out to be so simple as when I went to the London registry office and asked to have a new birth certificate issued in Doina's new surname, the clerk told me bluntly:

'That's impossible. She was born Cismasiu and can only change that name herself when she reaches eighteen!'

However much I insisted and begged, he was adamant. Finally, to get rid of me, he said:

'Why don't you go to the registry office where the birth was first registered. Maybe they can help you.'

For the last months of her pregnancy Gwenda had gone to stay with her mother in Cornwall, in the west of England, and so Doina had been born at the local hospital in St Austell. On our next visit to Gwenda's mother, I went to St Austell and explained our plight to the registrar. At first his reaction was the same as his London colleague, but my insistence gradually wore him down and I could see what he thought: yet another of those bloody foreigners who can't take no for an answer.

'OK, I'll tell you what I am going to do', he blurted out in exasperation. 'I'll break every law and issue your daughter a birth certificate in her new name.'

He pulled out the large register, crossed out in ink the original surname, replaced it with Cornell and issued me with a brand new certificate in the name of Doina Claire Cornell. When I went home and told Gwenda she refused to believe it.

'Jimmy, this is impossible. How on earth did you manage it?'

'Well,' I said, proudly, I was after all Mr Fix It in Romania, so what's wrong with trying to be the same over here?'

Our choice of name seems to have been so inspired that when she got married Doina decided to keep the name Cornell, and even registered her children, Nera and Dan, as Cornell as well. I suppose this is how dynasties are born.

My next real challenge was to find a job in London. I wrote and visited countless companies, most of them in the City, quite sure that with my background and languages I could find a job in exports. As a stopgap solution, I took a job as a night porter in a large hotel, the tips for one night being as much as I was paid by the hotel for a week of twelve hour night shifts. About one month after Ivan's birth I received in the same mail two offers: one from a large British paper manufacturer to work as their sales representative in Western Europe, and one from the BBC World Service as a radio announcer in the Romanian section. Having always believed that my field would be in business, and having studied economics, I instantly preferred the former, but Gwenda had other ideas. After so many years of hardship

Editing my weekly programme in a BBC studio

and separation, she wanted me to be closer to home. Head won over the wallet and I became a journalist, a choice I have never regretted.

With help from Gwenda's mother, supplemented by two thousand dollars I had managed to smuggle out of Romania, we bought a small early Victorian house in a London suburb, the absolute cheapest we could find and afford. We immediately set about making it habitable as it had no bathroom and even the toilet was out in the garden. My shift work at the BBC was very convenient, so I could spend every free moment painting and redecorating our little nest.

The sea, however, never went away, and was only put on the backburner temporarily. The BBC had both a sailing and a yacht club, so I immediately joined the former, learning to sail 14 foot Wayfarer dinghies on the Upper Thames. I soon graduated to the yacht club which had an elderly 40 foot sloop called Ariel based on the River Hamble, on England's south coast. I signed up for a sailing weekend and Charlie McLaren, a friend from BBC television news came to collect me in his bright yellow Lotus sports

car (acronym-Lots Of Trouble Usually Serious). From London we took the motorway to the south coast, cruising happily at around 100 miles per hour in a light drizzle. While overtaking a car the Lotus suddenly took off having probably hit a wet patch. The light car was airborne, with the crash barrier to one side and the other car close and slightly below me.

'Oh my God!' Charlie exclaimed doing his best to keep the car under control.

We somehow managed to land squarely, slow down and complete our journey without any further excitement. We found the rest of the crew already waiting, so the skipper told us to quickly hop on, stow our gear and help get underway. As our docking lines were being taken off by the crew, I did my best to look busy as I had no idea what to do. As the skipper pushed the tiller to clear the dock I noticed a large hawser that was running across our cockpit from the stern of a large steamer docked ahead of us. I tried to point it out to the skipper but he brushed me aside. With an almighty crack the hawser swept our flagstaff off the stern, the proud BBC yacht club ensign now floating on the murky surface.

32

'Get a boathook... quick!' the skipper ordered and Charlie, as mate, managed to retrieve our flag.

The skipper turned with a glowering look to me. 'That was quite stupid, wasn't it?'

I was about to reply that I had tried to warn him, but remembered just in time that the captain is always right.

'I am very sorry.'

'And so you should be.'

Although I had done a bit of dinghy sailing on the Thames, I knew that I was so green that I had to lie low and observe. So I offered to do the washing up and that instantly ensured my popularity.

We stopped for lunch at a pub in a small port and then the skipper suggested we sail across to the Isle of Wight and spend the night at Yarmouth. We zigzagged around a bewildering forest of buoys of different shapes and sizes, dodged fast ferries and other yachts and eventually pointed the bows towards what looked like a fairly large harbour. Just as the skipper was telling Charlie to get the crew to lower the sails, there was a crunch and Ariel came to an abrupt halt. Even I could tell that we had run aground. The skipper revved the engine hard astern, then tried to go sideways but all to no avail. We were well and truly stuck.

Heeling over at a slight angle and rocking in the swell, Charlie organised us crew to lower the sails, but before we could do so the wildly swinging boom hit one of the crew hard on the head, the violent blow splitting his scalp open. With blood gushing all over the place, we took him below and put a towel around his head. Although bleeding profusely he didn't seem in much danger so, in proper English fashion, Charlie offered to make him a cup of tea. As he was pouring the water into a mug the boat gave a sudden lurch and all the boiling water ended up in his sea boots. Screaming like mad, he ripped them off and when he pulled off his woollen socks both legs were already covered in blisters. With the situation now bordering on the desperate, and no prospect of coming off on our own, the skipper hailed a passing motoryacht, shouted across what had happened and asked them to pull us off which they did. He then contacted the Coast Guard by VHF who said it was best to head immediately across the Solent to Portsmouth where the hospital had an accident and emergency department. We motored as fast as we could across that busy waterway, while trying to make our patients as comfortable as possible. An ambulance with its blue lights flashing was waiting at the nearest dock, the two casualties were taken off and driven to hospital.

With Charlie out of action, I bade goodbye to the skipper and remaining crew and took the train back to London.

'How was your weekend?' asked Gwenda.

'Very interesting. I think I've learnt a lot. Not much about sailing, but a lot about what NOT to do on a boat.'

Building Aventura

My urge to see the world never left me, but I realized that trying to become a seaman at my age was not practical, whereas setting off on a sailing boat might be a more feasible solution. I discussed this with Gwenda over many evenings when the children had gone to bed, and slowly a plan began to coalesce. A born wanderer – after all that's how we had met in the first place – Gwenda is still convinced that she has some gypsy blood in her veins. While setting off on a small boat with two young children was not her preferred way of seeing the world, she agreed that, from the practical and

The long awaited moment of Aventura's
launch in the London docks

financial point of view, it made sense.
Once the decision was taken, we both
started making serious preparations. The
children's education was our main concern,
so Gwenda, a trained pharmacologist,
decided to go back to college and over
two years of evening courses qualified as
a teacher. During the long winter months
I joined an evening course in seamanship
and navigation and sailed a few more
times on Ariel. In 1974, with a secured
loan on our small property, we managed
to raise enough funds to order a 36 foot
fibreglass hull. All we could afford was the
bare hull but I was convinced that I could
manage to fit her out myself.

One day in spring 1974 a gleaming white
hull was wheeled into a large shed in the
Royal Albert Docks on the Thames not
far from our house. It was only then that
I was struck by the enormity of my
undertaking. I didn't even know where to
begin, but begin I did. In the huge shed
there were a lot of other dreamers, mostly
building ferrocement boats. We were

always helping each other and it was a
pleasant friendly atmosphere. With a little
help from my friends, Charlie McLaren,
Dominic a carpenter I had met on my
navigation course and a Swedish rigger
living on his boat in the docks, amazingly
Aventura started taking shape.

It was my great fortune to make friends
with Harold Valman, a typical East End
Londoner, wise, funny and extremely
kind. He was the greatest expert on diesel
engines that I have ever met. Harold had a
variety of launches and small ships, mostly
ex-Navy auxiliary craft, which he bought for
a song at auctions, cleaned up and fitted
them out, then sold for a tidy profit. My
greenness in all matters mechanical
moved Harold to tears and he became a
permanent presence by my side. He took
charge of the engine installation, decided
on fitting hydraulic steering, as this was
the cheapest and easiest option, and lent
me tools from his vast collection, which
he kept on a beautiful Admiral's launch
outside the shed.

It was chance friendships like this that
helped me finish Aventura in such record
time and it only reinforced my firm belief, I

could almost say my life philosophy, that it is always easier to achieve something if you have good friends around you. I already knew this from Romania and it was proven many times in my subsequent life, both ashore and afloat. I still value my friends more than anything else and keep in regular touch regardless of time or distance.

Rather miraculously, by July 1974, although the interior was only partially finished, Aventura was launched, and we set sail on our maiden voyage across the English Channel to France. Motoring down the Thames at the helm of my own boat was exhilarating. My crew, however, were not so enchanted. I looked into the aft cabin as we left the Thames and saw not only the protruding bolts from the unlined ceiling, lockers without doors but four children, Doina, Ivan, Marianne and Klausi rolling about like bags of potatoes in the rough swell. My sister had died the previous year in Romania and her husband Klaus and two teenage children had emigrated to

Aventura's crew in the South Pacific

Germany. Marianne and Klausi had joined us in London for a vacation, and I decided to take them back to the continent on Aventura's maiden voyage. As we hit the English Channel the weather deteriorated and soon a SW gale was upon us. We ran for shelter into Ramsgate harbour, which was already crowded with all types of craft seeking shelter. A fisherman beckoned me to come alongside his trawler, lying four deep alongside the high quay. While I was still tying the lines, a uniformed port official

popped up above me: 'That will be £2.50. Thank you!' Welcome to my first English landfall!

The weather was calmer by the following morning so we crossed over to Boulogne, being amazed and frightened in equal measure by the stream of car ferries plying between Dover and France, and the even denser pack of ships of all shapes and sizes moving equally fast at right angles, literally squeezing through the narrowest part of the English Channel. I was totally mesmerized by all the hubbub and it took all my non-existent skills to find a suitable hole and quickly cross behind the nearest threatening monster. We were, and I had little idea then, in the busiest shipping lanes in the world, but I thought that the sea was always going to be like this and it worried me.

When we arrived at Boulogne we found the small boat harbour and made our way in. Gwenda was at the helm and I was preparing fenders and ropes. We saw my brother-in-law wave frantically from the end of a pontoon so Gwenda headed that way. She saw an empty slip and pointed for its middle still seeming to advance at the same speed. I saw what was going to happen, shouted at her to slow down, but she didn't and hit the pontoon with a mighty blow while my brother-in-law tried valiantly to stop the boat. Aventura's bows had ridden right up onto the pontoon where she stopped, then gracefully slid back in. The crash must have been heard in the entire marina but apart from Klaus no one had witnessed our dramatic arrival.

'Why did you do that?' I asked Gwenda, 'why didn't you slow down?'

'I tried.'

'Tried how?'

'I put the gear in neutral...'

'And?'

'It didn't slow down much.'

'Why didn't you go astern?'

'I was just trying to.'

I then explained exactly how to stop the boat.

'You never told me that before.'

So it was my fault but, as I had already learned from my days as a BBC yacht club crew the responsibility rests squarely with the skipper, so there was no point in arguing.

We handed over Klausi and Marianne to their father and continued our summer cruise, our sights firmly set on the Channel Islands. I can no longer remember how we managed to get there, but find them we did and made our way into Guernsey's main harbour of St Peter Port. As we came in I saw a very large round buoy with rings around it and knew that this was one of those multiple mooring buoys for visitors. Gwenda made for it and when near enough I jumped with a rope tied to our stern. I landed safely on the buoy still holding the rope and while preparing to secure it, out of

the corner of the eye I saw Gwenda motor on as if that had been her intention all along. She obviously had learned nothing since Boulogne about slowing down. I quickly let go of the rope and looked in amazement as Aventura got further and further away. A harbour launch whose two occupants must have followed this incomprehensible operation pulled up alongside, told me to jump in and then gave chase and deposited me on Aventura. They pointed to an empty berth and told us to tie up there. I'd had enough so I took over the wheel from Gwenda and told her to get a bow line ready. I pointed the bows for the dock, slowed down and went close to it, telling Gwenda, 'Jump with the line. Jump!'

'I can't do it. It's too far.'

'Oh, yes you can. Just do it. Jump!'

She jumped, but missed the slippery dock, gracefully disappearing beneath the surface. She came up spluttering.

I repeated the manoeuvre while she climbed with some difficulty onto the dock, I came alongside properly this time and we were finally safely docked. We obviously still had a lot to learn about the division of tasks on our boat.

Back in London Aventura was de-rigged and craned back into her old place in the huge shed. That maiden voyage had shown up all the mistakes I had made and as she was unfinished I could easily change things. There followed a most gruelling work schedule as I was determined to get Aventura ready to sail by the following May. I'd get up at five every morning, drive to the boat and work until 10 o'clock, drive to the BBC for the afternoon shift, which finished around seven. Back to the boat for more work and finally home around midnight. By the following spring we were ready. I resigned from the BBC but had secured a contract to continue my weekly programme Aventura (adventure

Leaving London for the Mediterranean and beyond

in Romanian), a music and adventure programme for young listeners, which attracted a large audience in Romania, once estimated by the London Daily Mail newspaper as being in the millions. That this estimate may not have been too exaggerated was proven shortly before Christmas 1974, when a large sack of mail arrived from Romania all addressed to me. In the past we had received only the odd letter posted by someone who had gone abroad. The arrival in one single day of over 1500 listeners' letters from Romania got everyone at the BBC excited. It was quite clear that the sack had either slipped by the censors, or, as I prefer to believe, a friendly guy at the Romanian post office, probably one of my listeners, had put the bag into the wrong, or rather, right pile. Having launched and presented the most successful weekly programme of the Romanian Service, the boss wanted me to continue it by sending reports throughout our forthcoming voyage. I had also been asked by a couple of English language programmes to look out for interesting material from the countries we were going to visit. When I handed in my resignation the head of the personnel department warned me not to withdraw my pension contributions.

'Better leave them here, Jimmy, as you will only get whatever you had paid in yourself and that amounts to only about £500. But if you leave it here the BBC's own contributions more than double your fund.'

'I understand, but I badly need that money as otherwise I can't pay for my sails.'

Withdrawing that money was probably the worst financial decision of my life as in those days the BBC pension fund was extremely generous and had I kept that fund untouched, as I did with the one I started on my return, I would probably have received now almost the same amount as a monthly payment. And yet, I do not regret for one moment that decision. How could Aventura have set off on such a voyage without sails?

With all the hard work done, Aventura was finished and the world was waiting. The dreaded Bay of Biscay received us with a benign smile and although there was a large swell, the winds were favourable and we arrived safely in Lisbon after a few days. Soon we headed for the Mediterranean where we planned to spend one year getting acquainted with the boat and life aboard. My dream had come true.

Three Boats for Three Circumnavigations

I n the early 1970s, when I started looking for a suitable boat for our planned voyage, I knew next to nothing about boats, the ocean and what to expect. So I read voraciously every book I could lay my

Aventura I sailing off the coast of Papua New Guinea

hands on, from Joshua Slocum to Eric Hiscock, Francis Chichester to Bernard Moitessier and countless others. Those famous sailing pioneers' well-written

tales were not only fascinating but also full of excellent advice. As I ploughed through those books I made notes and listed all essential features to look out for. Later I rearranged the list in order of priorities. I also compiled a separate list of things to avoid at all cost.

In those days the choice of a suitable boat was limited. On top of that I had my own serious limitation: I did not have enough money for a completed boat, not even a good used one. So very soon I realised that the only solution was to buy the best hull I could afford and do the fitting out myself. By this stage I had not even been able to decide between a monohull or a catamaran. I was attracted by the spaciousness of a catamaran and I approached a couple of British manufacturers building fibreglass catamarans, but both refused to sell me a bare hull. I looked at the Wharram catamarans, whose plans were available as a home build kit, but I didn't have enough confidence to build a complete boat.

Aventura I

With catamarans out, the choice became somewhat easier and eventually I decided on a Van de Stadt design, the 36 foot Trintella IIIA. The builder, Tylers, was based close to London and when I visited the yard, I was impressed by the high standard of their work and also the friendly and helpful attitude of their staff. Tylers only built hulls, leaving the fitting out to outside contractors, so I immediately placed an order. Over the years Aventura proved to have been the best choice I could have made at that time. She was easy to sail, especially for a beginner, and in spite of her modest size had an aft cabin, which made it very comfortable for a family of four. Her main quality however, was that her hull was very strongly built. I found this out when we ran aground on a reef in the Turks and Caicos Islands and spent several hours pounding hard on a coral head. When we eventually came off and I had a look with a mask at the keel and hull I was amazed that there was no serious damage except a few superficial scratches. Amazed maybe, but not surprised, because while fitting out I had to cut a hole through the hull for one of the seacocks and found that the thickness in that area was one and a half inches (40 mm), the layers of fibreglass clearly marked in different colours. In those days builders did not know how to build thin flimsy hulls. That came later.

Aventura II anchored off Ilhas Desertas near Madeira

Aventura II

After that early near disaster Aventura I looked after us well for some 68,000 miles. When the time came to choose a successor, in which I also planned to set off around the world, the choice was much wider. This time, however, I had many ideas of my own based on my previous voyage and as there seemed to be nothing on the market that came close to what I wanted, I planned to have my second boat designed and built for me. I made a list of all the desirable features and went to see Bill Dixon, a young naval architect, who had already made his name as an original thinker. Bill liked my ideas and managed to produce plans that included all my essential points. Having heard about a number of total losses due to navigational errors as well as collisions with unidentified objects, Aventura II had to be as strong as possible, which in those days meant steel. An overall length of 40 feet, which I regarded then as ideal, had been easily decided upon. As I regard shallow draft to be an invaluable advantage when cruising, we came up with a design for a retractable keel operated hydraulically. Fully retracted the keel passed through a box, which ended at deck level. Inspired by the Australian victory in the America's Cup, I asked Bill to provide the keel with two large wings. They gave additional stability and when retracted rested snugly against the bottom of the hull. With the keel fully down the draft was an acceptable 1.8 m. To maintain the shallow draft of just under one metre with the keel retracted she had two rudders. Manoeuvrability was further aided by twin Perkins 28 HP engines. Each engine could power the boat on its own, which I usually did to conserve fuel, but the main advantage of this arrangement was that one engine, the more accessible one, also acted as a generating unit, having been fitted with an oversized alternator. Both engines drove MaxProp feathering propellers.

The rig was a standard cutter with an in-mast furling mainsail. The decks were clear and, unusual at that time, the boat had a stern platform. The main feature was a fixed dodger (calling it a pilot house would be an exaggeration), which not only gave good cockpit protection but also was highly attractive and gave the entire boat a beautiful overall look. The interior was also unusual, but suited us perfectly. The main accommodation was in the beamy stern, where a large table and U-shaped settee gave the crew a good view of the outside. The snug galley was forward of this to port, while to starboard a pilot berth ended as the seat of the navigator. The navigation station was located right by the steps leading down from the central cockpit. Opposite the navigation station to port was a toilet compartment with a separate shower unit. The two cabins occupied the centre of the boat and were separated by the keel box. The full width of the starboard cabin was taken up by a double bunk. The port cabin was provided with two superimposed bunks with high sides that made them very comfortable at sea. A passageway through that cabin led forward to a massive steel door provided with submarine type clamps, which turned the forepeak into a sacrificial collision or crumple zone. With so much accommodation available elsewhere this forward cabin was not used for sleeping. Instead to port there was a full size workbench, while the starboard side was left for storage that held all my diving gear, diving compressor, two inflatable dinghies, fenders, etc.

Although Aventura II sailed well in anything over 15 knots, when the winds were light I had a slight problem. Designed by Bill Dixon to be of a reasonable displacement of 12.5 tons (27,600 lbs), which in hindsight may have been rather optimistic, when she was launched in 1988 she weighed in at a mighty 17 tons (37,500 lbs). The British builder had promised to build me a solid boat and ended up building a tank. Slowly I learned to get the best out of her and she proved to be everything I had expected. She sailed around the world safely between 1989 and 1992, mostly during the first round the world rally. Before I sold her in 1995 she had sailed some 40,000 miles. The only major job that I had to do up to that point was to completely repaint the hull. If a steel hull is not extremely well prepared for the first coat application, there will be unending problems later on, as I found out to my chagrin. Fortunately in the Canaries I met a Danish painter who took the job in hand, completely stripped the hull and deck and produced what looked like a brand new boat. Her current owners, an Australian couple working in London, whom I met again several years after having sold her, are extremely happy with her.

Aventura III

By the time I started thinking seriously of a third Aventura I was rapidly approaching the age of sixty and as I had already decided that I did not want to continue working after that age, I was determined to do what I like best: sailing. Carlton DeHart, who had taken part in one of my round the world rallies, once paid me a great compliment when he commented to a group of sailors at one of my lectures in the USA, 'Jimmy Cornell forces people to realize their dreams.' I felt that the moment had now arrived for Jimmy Cornell to force himself to realize his own dreams.

In the late 1990s I was deeply involved with the annual ARC, had sailed in the first round the world rally, and had seen so many wrong choices among my participants, that I knew exactly what mistakes to avoid. One major lesson I had learnt from the period when I decided on Aventura II was to force myself not to be too influenced by my previous boat. A common mistake people make when it comes to choosing their next boat is to look back at the boating scene that they know and are familiar with, rather than be bold and find out what new

Aventura III sailing among the ice off the Antarctic Peninsula

developments have been made since they last bought a boat.

The first time I was made aware of this pitfall was when I met Eric and Susan Hiscock on their Wanderer IV while they were anchored next to us in Fiji. During a long conversation they admitted having made the mistake of ordering this large 48 foot yacht to succeed the smaller and simpler Wanderer III. They had ended up with a heavy boat that they found difficult to handle at their age, and which was also

41

too large for their needs. Eventually they sold her and had the 39 foot Wanderer V built in New Zealand, which proved to be a much more suitable boat for the closing years of their long cruising lives. I should have remembered their example when I drew up the parameters for Aventura II as the main drawback of that good design was its weight.

Fortunately the choice of Aventura III was relatively easy as I knew what I wanted, a light but robust boat that was fast and easy to sail shorthanded and that could take me anywhere in the world from icy polar regions to shallow tropical lagoons. Because I listen to my friends, especially those who know more than me, the determining factor in my final decision was the advice of my friend Erick Bouteleux. On completing his circumnavigation, some of which we had done in company, he became the agent for OVNI yachts for the French Cote d'Azur. In the 1980s OVNIs were still a novel concept and, like some Citroen cars, very original and very French. The designer was a young naval architect, Philippe Briand, who set aside all orthodox thinking and produced a functional boat, fast, easy to sail and unusual in every way. As the distinctive boats attracted a lot of attention from the moment the first was launched, the original name Sonate was changed to OVNI, Objet Volant Non Identifié, which in French means UFO i.e. unidentified flying object. The current OVNI range goes from 36 to 49 feet LOA. Regardless of length all boats share a number of basic elements: all are hard-chined, flat bottomed and have an integral centreboard and folding rudder. This means that with both rudder and centreboard up they draw very little and can dry out practically anywhere. For a 43 footer, Aventura draws three feet (slightly under one metre) with the board up and just over eight feet (2.40 m) when the board is down. In the intervening years the individual models have been greatly improved, which is quite easy to do on an aluminium boat that can easily incorporate any modifications, as opposed to a fibreglass boat whose mould cannot be changed just to accommodate some minor improvement.

From the wide range of these unmistakable boats I chose the OVNI 43 as it seemed best suited for my requirements and was not too large to be easily handled by a small crew. With a displacement of 9 tons, the OVNI 43 sails well, is easy to handle and probably is the best cruising boat I can think of to explore those remote areas of the South Pacific. One of the great advantages of her unpainted hull is that one can forget about gleaming topsides, which are such a worry when confronted by rough docks or boarded by uncaring officials who often come alongside in launches without fenders, banging into your topsides. There are many other useful features shared by OVNIs, such as the large stern platform, the open bow well, which allows easy access to the chain and spare anchors, or the distinctive stern arch. The latter not only complements the look of the boat but is very useful as a fixed davit and also for the radar radome, flag pole, wind generator and various antennas: Iridium, Inmarsat C, GPS.

One of the questions I am often asked is how safe is it to sail in a boat without a keel. Having sailed twice across the Drake Passage, being the first OVNI to sail in Antarctica, and having experienced elsewhere on at least two occasions winds of 60 knots, with waves to match, I can easily put any doubts on stability to rest. Thanks to an internal lead ballast of 3.5 tons in a boat with a displacement of 9 tons,

Aventura is as stable as any other more traditionally designed cruising boat.

The owner of Alubat, Yves Roucher, liked my proposed cruising plans and agreed to incorporate my long list of special requirements. This was a great favour as Alubat was normally reluctant to accept any but the simplest modifications to the standard design. With this in mind they offer two options for each size: a charter layout and an owner's version, but any requests for major changes are usually met with a smile and their favourite reply 'impossible'.

Aventura may have started out, on paper, as a standard OVNI 43, but ended up as the most personalized boat ever build by Alubat. The engine is a standard Volvo

A comfortable and functional navigation station on Aventura III

MD22 of 50 HP and, although I would have preferred something more powerful around 62 HP, this was one change I had to abandon as the engine room was so tight that it encompassed the designed engine like a cocoon. I have since realized that there were not many occasions when I would have needed that additional power and

that 50 HP was more than enough for a relatively light boat. Apart from a number of irritating teething problems, bearing in mind that Aventura III has covered nearly 70,000 miles since being launched in 1998, the engine has performed reasonably well.

Interior comforts

Aventura's interior is as comfortable as we could make it. The single most important alteration that we insisted upon was to install either side of the navigation table two large domestic type leather armchairs, which Gwenda had bought at IKEA. As they swivel they can be turned to either face the table or inwards towards the cabin. They are extremely comfortable at sea and I have not come across such excellent armchairs on any other boat that I have visited.

Everything on board Aventura has its own place and when we put to sea all loose items are stored away. The same applies to the galley where I always insist that dishes and plates must be washed and put away immediately after use. Never a sink full of dirty dishes on my boat!

As Aventura was built and equipped with a cold water voyage in mind the boat incorporates several alterations to the standard version. Both deck and hull have been insulated down to the waterline. While in Antarctica the boat was always comfortable and the Webasto diesel heater kept up a pleasant temperature. Later I realized that the insulation was just as useful in the tropics as it helped keep the temperature to a bearable level however hot it was outside. Now I wish the insulation could have continued right down to the bilges as in Antarctica, where the water temperature was usually close to freezing, a lot of condensation formed in the lower parts of the boat and on one occasion we even had frozen water in the bilges, although the boat was heated and the inside temperature never fell below 6°C.

The galley

Aventura's galley is simple and functional, but it is more than adequate for our needs. The gimballed cooker has two burners, an oven and grill. Being concerned about the possibility of a gas leak, I installed an electronic cut-out at the tank that turns off the gas when it is switched off from the galley, which we always do as soon as we finish cooking. Similarly, when we want to light the cooker the system has to be activated so that it opens the valve at the tank end. In this way when the cooker is not in use there is no gas between it and the tank. The tanks are stored in a special locker that is insulated from the rest of the boat and drains overboard. All burners are fitted with their own bi-metal safety cut-outs. I use the Camping Gaz type 3 kg butane tanks, which are widely used in Europe and we had them easily filled in all the countries we visited. One tank lasts on average between two and three weeks with normal cooking, so with six tanks we have an autonomy of about three months. To save gas I often use a pressure cooker, which is excellent for making stews or cooking vegetables. I also have a barbecue that can be mounted at the stern but I don't like using it while at sea and even at anchor it is getting used less and less.

Deck layout

Aventura's deck may look like a cat's cradle and, as I am ready to admit, it can be confusing to a newcomer. Knowing that I was going to sail most of the time short-handed I have dedicated lines permanently set up for each task, which means that setting up a spinnaker, for example, never takes longer than five minutes and I often do it on my own.

I was fortunate in having my friend Erick to help me not only with the choice of boat but also with the various modifications. His most important contribution, however, was that he agreed to liaise with the builders, a most frustrating experience that I had gone through when building Aventura II and an ordeal that I hope never to repeat. With Erick's experienced input Aventura's deck layout was carefully thought out for sailing in extreme conditions. All lines and halyards are brought back to the cockpit to a powerful electric winch. One further addition was that of a Walder boom brake. When its two control lines are winched in, even in an involuntary gybe the friction of those lines on the oversized block of the preventer will slow down the movement of the boom, which otherwise can be quite violent.

One major consideration was the availability of storage space for all those items that I intended to take on my planned voyage. The standard OVNI 43 is designed with two double aft cabins but knowing where I was planning to sail I sacrificed the port cabin entirely and turned it into cavernous cockpit locker, a decision that I never regretted. To give an idea of what I manage to stow in my oversized portside cockpit locker I'll list here the main items: the larger of my two inflatable dinghies (packed), folding bike, at least two of the spinnakers, a few jerrycans, all spare engine oil, hydraulic fluid, antifreeze, six large fenders, mooring lines and a lot more besides. The watermaker, day fuel tank and heater are also located in the same locker. Being unable to stow such items properly can be a serious safety hazard as invariably such items end up on deck, which not only gives the boat a messy look but also can be a potential risk in bad weather. Ever since I lost an expensive genoa overboard on a windy night off the coast of Ecuador in 1977, I never made that mistake again and always bag and stow away whatever sail is not in use. The one exception is a spinnaker bag that is well tied at the foot of the mast, which I prefer to have at the ready if the weather looks settled. As soon as there is any sign of deteriorating weather the sail goes into a locker, as does everything else.

Among the many things I asked the builders to do, was to use lifelines covered in plastic as they are nicer to the touch and are provided with gates amidships. OVNIs come with granny bars by the side of the mast as standard and although I wasn't sure about them when I got the boat, now I find them very useful and would not be without. They are a great help if I have to work at the foot of the mast in rough weather and are also useful for securing sail bags or fenders provided these don't obstruct the view from the cockpit.

Cockpit protection

The first two Aventuras had a hard dodger as one of the things both Gwenda and I enjoy is comfort at sea. I asked the French builder to do the same on Aventura III but as the OVNI 43 had passed all EU stringent stability regulations such a major external modification to the design could not be done. So I opted for an ordinary

canvas dodger but had it made higher so it gives full headroom. It has worked very well so I am no longer sure that in the future I'd insist on a hard dodger. Initially I had a small bimini with side panels that could be closed for high latitude sailing. For my latest voyage I had a larger bimini made, initially just for the tropics, but I got so used to it, and find it so useful against the dangerous effect of being exposed to the sun for long periods, that now I use it all the time.

Centreboard

Aventura's integral centreboard is a 40 mm (1$^1/_2$ inch) thick profiled aluminium plate that weighs only 100 kg (220 lbs), so its weight, as far as overall stability is

The underwater profile of Aventura III with both the centreboard and rudder fully down

concerned, is negligible. The main role of the board is to provide lift when sailing close-hauled and reduce leeway when reaching. With the board fully down the boat draws eight feet and, if sailed properly, will point almost as high as most cruising boats. Sailed properly means that when hard on the wind sail trim is critical, a good speed must be kept up and heeling too much must be avoided or she makes a lot of leeway. There is a certain technique in sailing a centreboarder efficiently, not just on the wind but off the wind as well. This is when the centreboard becomes a true asset as it allows one to reduce the wetted surface. Also, the ability to lift the board gradually as the apparent wind goes past 135° up to the point when the board is fully retracted is a great advantage as the risk of broaching is virtually eliminated. The absence of a keel to act as a pivot in a potential broaching situation means that the boat does not tend to round up when, in a similar situation, a keeled boat would do just that. It is a feature that I have blessed on many occasions and has allowed me to continue keeping the spinnaker up longer than I would have done otherwise. The board is also normally retracted when motoring in calm waters as the reduction in wetted surface provides an extra quarter to half knot of speed.

The main reason for choosing a centreboarder is primarily to increase one's cruising options and having a boat whose draft can be reduced instantly can be a great advantage. The fact that the OVNIs have a completely flat bottom means that with the board fully up the boat can dry out on any beach, tidal bay or estuary. When the tide runs out, the boat settles down comfortably, and, as the height of the stern platform is less than two feet above the dried out surface, access aboard is very easy with the aid of the swimming ladder. We have dried out on many occasions, whether to put on a quick coat of antifouling between tides while cruising the Chilean canals or to access a shallow bay in Alaska so we could watch a grizzly bear fishing for salmon.

One other advantage of having a centreboard, which is nothing more than an aluminium plate, is that one can use it as a sounding board when entering an unfamiliar shallow anchorage. It is a technique I learnt from Erick who taught me a new meaning for the term 'sounding board'. With the board fully down and the control lever on the hydraulic pump in the open position, I motor slowly into the anchorage keeping an eye on the depth sounder. If we happen to touch the bottom, there is time to stop and pump up the board. Life has become even easier since acquiring a forward looking sonar (FLS) that shows any obstructions up to about sixty metres (200 feet) ahead allowing the person at the helm to take the necessary avoiding action. But even with the FLS I continue to use the well-tried method of sounding with the board.

The centreboard and rudder are both raised by the same hydraulic pump located in the port cockpit locker right next to the steering position, so it can be accessed instantaneously. The control levers for both rudder and board are normally in the closed position that locks the hydraulic system. On collision with an obstruction, the back-pressure in the hydraulic system blows a sacrificial valve and the board or rudder are free to swing up. The sacrificial valves are thin copper disks that can be quickly replaced. In nine years of sailing I have only blown the system on about ten occasions, usually when entering an anchorage that was shallower than anticipated and we hit the bottom. Try and do that with a keeled boat!

Having a shallow drafted boat has certain advantages but not for others as I found out only hours after launching Aventura II on the river Dart in the south of England in spring 1989. The only place we could find to tie up to was on the inside of a

Aventura III dried out on a beach in Chile for a quick coat of antifouling paint

Detail of Aventura's lifting rudder

pontoon. We had hardly tidied up our lines when another yacht of similar length made a beeline for us. As the skipper was manoeuvring to come alongside us I shouted that the water was very shallow, but he gave me a dirty look and barged ahead. He came to an abrupt halt and in spite of putting on all power astern, he was stuck there until the following tide. The skipper came to the bows and shouted at me angrily: 'You should have warned me!'

'I did but you ignored me.' I shouted back.

'No, you didn't... you just sounded as if you didn't want anyone else to come alongside you.'

That was the first of many occasions when my boat seemed to attract others like bees to the honey pot. While in Antarctica, we were making for the corner of a sheltered anchorage that I knew to be shallow enough to stop any floating icebergs entering. With the centreboard halfway up we were slowly moving ahead when I looked behind and saw that fellow Millennium Odyssey yacht Risque was following us closely. I shouted that they should stop as I had the board up but they ignored me, ran hard aground, and, as they found out later, damaged the deep unprotected rudder of their Swan 57.

Rig

The first Aventura was rigged as a ketch, a decision heavily influenced by the desire for manageable sails in the absence of furling gears. Most previous ocean voyages

47

had been done in two-masted boats so the wisdom of such a rig was not even questioned. It didn't take me long to realise that at thirty-six feet Aventura's mizzen rig was of little use. Doina and Ivan adopted the mizzen mast and its sail as their own and had a lot of fun putting up the small mizzen sail. They had even more fun shinning up to the spreaders showing off as they stood spread-eagled on either side of the mast.

I had no doubt that a single taller mast would have greatly improved Aventura's performance and so, when I decided on a rig for Aventura II, I chose a straightforward cutter with a relatively high aspect mainsail. The advent of reliable furling gears had made sail handling much easier so having larger sails was no longer regarded as a problem. Under most conditions, having a large genoa on a roller furling gear seemed to be a good solution and Aventura II ended up with that setup and an in-mast furling mainsail.

By the time I had to make that decision again, I felt that only a cutter rig would do on Aventura III. The versatility and ease of handling of the combination of a high-cut yankee and staysail, both on furling gears, has proved an excellent choice under all the sailing conditions that I have met during these last nine years. As a 130% genoa had been included in the original sail wardrobe, I kept it as a spare, but when I once replaced the yankee with the genoa, it only took me a couple of days to realize just how much more efficient the yankee/staysail combination performed than the large overlapping genoa. So the genoa was taken down, packed up and sent into permanent retirement.

The standard OVNI 43 has a single backstay split at the lower end so it clears the cockpit. Obsessed as I am with having backups for everything, I asked the builder to fit two separate backstays, one of which is used as an SSB antenna. Both backstays are provided with tensioners and while I rarely tune the mast, I always release the tension when stopping anywhere for more than a day. The tensioners also come in handy when the boat has to be hauled out by travelift as it takes no time to support the mast with the runners and remove the backstays by unscrewing the tensioners completely.

At my request, the current Aventura's rigging was substantially upgraded. Being a cutter, the designer decided against backswept spreaders and in favour of running backstays. The runners have to be set up whenever I use the staysail, except in very light winds. Setting up the runners can be a bore especially when short-tacking but I have got used to it.

Mainsail

My own experience with different types of mainsail has been quite enlightening. The first Aventura had a standard mainsail, which was adequate when we started the voyage but ended up baggy and out of shape halfway through the voyage having been affected by UV light. In the early 1970s synthetic sail materials were still being developed and Dacron hadn't been around for long. Reefing in those days was usually done in the old-fashioned way, but I also had a backup as Aventura's mainsail could be furled around the boom with a winch handle. The system was simple to use even if it made the boom sag and left the sail not in very good shape when it was partly rolled up.

The second Aventura had a Hood in-mast furling mainsail that was the trend in those days and seemed the perfect solution. In many ways it was, even if the sail was not that efficient when sailing close-hauled.

There was one early incident that happened on Aventura II's maiden voyage across the Bay of Biscay and got me worried that I had chosen this type of mainsail. We had left early, and in March the weather was, as to be expected, rough. Right in the middle of that dreaded bay, with the wind increasing, I tried to furl in some of the mainsail but however hard I tried it refused to budge. Eventually I realised that it was jammed and the only solution seemed to be to put a knife to it, something I was not prepared to do to my expensive new sail. The other alternative was to carry on with full mainsail and no foresail and hope for the best. Sailing like this in over 30 knots was certainly fast and exciting, and the heavy Aventura took it surprisingly well. On my dawn watch, after a nail-biting night, I looked back and in the half-light saw right behind us at no more than twenty metres the bow of a large yacht that was advancing fast towards us riding high on a wave. The yacht veered slightly and passed within reach, the lone man at the wheel shouting a greeting.

We made it safely into Lisbon, where we docked the boat with some difficulty with the full mainsail still up. Close to us I saw the Swan 65 that had passed us and went over to speak to the crew. That same guy was sitting in the cockpit drinking a cup of coffee.

'You certainly looked a sight,' he said, 'and I was quite impressed how well you were sailing with that full mainsail up! But I only understood now, seeing you coming in with one of those stupid in-mast furling jobs, that you weren't doing it deliberately.'

'You guessed right...it's stuck. So where are you going?'

'Delivering this tub to Mallorca.'

'I suppose it takes some crew to sail such a large boat.'

'It certainly does... that's why I decided to do it on my own.'

My mouth fell open. 'On your own?'

'Yeah. Some friends let me down at the last minute and as I couldn't wait, I simply left. OK, I'd better explain that I have done a lot of singlehanding, a couple of transats and round the world races.' He then kindly offered to help me with my mainsail, asked me to hoist him to the top of the mast and found the problem.

'It's the halyard that got jammed around the swivel. I'll get some tools and fix it for you. It's an easy job... but even I admit I wouldn't have gone aloft in that weather so you were very wise to do what you did.'

When he had finished he explained exactly how to fix the problem if it ever happened again, and also what to do to prevent it. Needless to say, it never occurred again. The incident showed me the advantage of having mast steps, which I had wanted to install but was told that it could not be done, as the supporting rivet ends would damage the tightly rolled up mainsail inside the mast.

The current Aventura has a fully battened mainsail as I realized that only such an efficient sail would be able to get any performance out of a boat with a flat bottom and a centreboard. I have been happy with my choice and would choose a fully battened mainsail again provided that it has a well thought out reefing system. Also, an electric winch located in the cockpit, is a great help as it makes it easier to hoist the sail but also to take in the reefs as both the main halyard and reefing lines are led back to the cockpit. One further improvement that I made is to provide the electric winch with a remote control. First I prepare the halyard by winding it around the self-tailing winch.

Aventura's cutter rig and fully battened
mainsail

On the wind

Rather than having the
standard sail plan that
relies on a 130% genoa,
which is indeed better
suited for Mediterranean
sailing, I opted for a proper
cutter rig. The yankee and
staysail arrangement, both
on Profurl gears, backed up
by a powerful well-cut
mainsail with four reefs,
allows me to sail the boat
efficiently in virtually any
wind strength.

I then go onto the side deck and as I start
raising the mainsail with the help of the
remote control, I can check that the sail
does not get caught in the lazyjacks. If it
does, I stop the winch, sort out the mainsail,
and continue raising it. By using the electric
winch with its remote control in the same
way I can easily lift the large tender onto
the foredeck on my own.

Both the original mainsail, which I
replaced in New Zealand after 50,000 miles,
and the present one were well cut, never
suffering any serious damage, although
the old one had started losing its shape
towards the end of its life. Doyle's
Sailmakers produced, in their own words,
a bullet-proof triple-stitched mainsail that
after 20,000 miles still looks like new. From
what I know now I would always choose
this kind of mainsail if I wanted the boat
to sail well, but if comfort and convenience
became my priorities, as they very well
could with advancing age, I would probably
consider one of the more user-friendly
in-mast or in-boom systems currently
available.

Not surprisingly, bearing in mind the OV-
NI's centreboard and flat bottom, sailing on
the wind is Aventura's weakest point, so
one has to make a real effort to minimize
this problem. The cutter rig, fully battened
mainsail and medium light displacement
all help to overcome some of this drawback,
but she'll never be a Swan. Having said that,
I remember the Millennium Odyssey fleet
leaving Las Palmas bound for the South
Atlantic Ocean. Erick and Muriel had taken
over from me for that leg as I was busy with
the other Millennium Odyssey fleet, and
so I could watch the start of the leg from
the committee vessel. As the boats headed
for the start line, I watched in sheer
amazement as with perfectly set sails
Aventura was gradually overtaking all other
boats including a Swan 57. Aventura crossed
the line and sped ahead. The light wind
undoubtedly helped but it showed what an
OVNI could do when handled efficiently by
an experienced sailor like Erick. The main
reason I cannot match Erick's performance
is that at heart he is a racing sailor and by
trying to get the best out of the boat and
sails he will often put the gear under great
strain. In this respect I am much more
conservative and cautious and there is a

limit to how much pressure I am prepared to put on my gear. The concrete result is that after 70,000 miles I still have the original yankee and staysail and have never broken any essential piece of equipment.

However inefficient Aventura may be to windward we get there eventually and, in my view, that is what matters. Usually at about 14 to 16 knots I put the first reef in the mainsail and may keep the yankee full. Whenever possible, I try to reef the mainsail first as Aventura seems to prefer this. She starts slowing down when she heels too much and the ideal is to try and sail on the first chine. As the wind increases it is easy to keep things under control by rolling in some of the yankee. By about 22 knots the second reef is put in the mainsail and the yankee furled to about 50% of its surface. Up to now the staysail would have been kept full but at 25 knots, if we are still on the wind, the third reef is taken in the mainsail and the yankee completely rolled in. It is now that the staysail shows the advantage of a cutter rig. Usually we are able to continue like this to maybe 30 knots, but then the movement may become uncomfortable and normally I prefer to ease the sheets slightly and increase the wind angle. If we are on a lee shore and have no choice I grit my teeth and try to continue as close-hauled as possible but thankfully this has happened very rarely.

Reaching

When beam reaching Aventura behaves like any other boat, she is fast, dry and comfortable and the reefing stages are almost the same as when sailing on the wind. I need to stress that the figures mentioned above are primarily for the sake of simplicity and in reality I might do things differently in view of existing conditions. As most will agree, beam reaching can be the most comfortable point of sailing and Aventura is no exception. However, due to the route I had chosen, where broad reaching or running conditions prevail for most of the time, on this latest voyage I have done very little beam reaching.

Broad reaching

This is definitely Aventura's preferred point of sailing as with her displacement and flat bottom she happily gallops along. If the wind is above 14 knots the mainsail continues to do the main job, with reefs taken in at higher wind speeds: first reef at 20, second at 25, third at 30 knots. While the yankee's surface is reduced accordingly, the staysail is rarely used as it is blanketed by the mainsail. One great advantage of Aventura, which took me years to discover, is just how happy she is sailing under mainsail alone. This, I believe, is due to her configuration. Because of the need for the mast to be exactly above the centreboard on all OVNIs the mast is further forward than on most other boats. The fore triangle seems to be smaller than on other boats of this size but this could be just an illusion. The great advantage of having the mast so far forward is that the end of the boom does not reach the cockpit, which I consider to be an important safety factor.

The efficient fully battened mainsail is often used on its own allowing me to tack easily just under mainsail, Aventura behaving like an oversized dinghy. This ability to be able to sail with the mainsail alone is a great safety factor in strong winds. I never fail to make sure that the Walder boom brake is firmly set up and its two lines are well winched in the cockpit in case of an involuntary gybe. But even in a gybe, voluntary or not, the mainsail remains under control while the boom swings slowly on to the other gybe, all friction being taken up by the boom brake.

When broad reaching under benign conditions I usually hoist the spinnaker when the wind angle gets to about 125 to 130 degrees off the beam. If the wind moves further astern the sheet, guy and pole are adjusted accordingly, my favourite method of using a fixed pole making all this quick and easy. If I expect the wind to go up, rather than use a spinnaker I prefer to pole

an eighty mile passage in the Aegean between the islands of Thira, also known as Santorini, and Crete. The previous day we had visited the site of Thira's infamous volcano, whose violent eruption and subsequent tsunami in about 1500 BC destroyed the ancient Minoan civilisation on neighbouring Crete. As is often the case in summer in the Aegean, in the morning the wind was light so we started off under full sail, then as the day progressed, and the Meltemi with it, I started reducing sail, but, as the wind was almost from astern, by the time it had reached the upper 20s we were

Sailing downwind with the yankee poled out

out the yankee. With the system I use, of a fixed pole, if the wind goes up the yankee's surface can be easily reduced and if the wind goes down, the yankee is completely furled and a spinnaker is hoisted, which is quick to do as the pole is already in place.

The first time I sailed Aventura III with just the mainsail in strong winds was on

sailing under mainsail alone and were occasionally surfing at 10 knots. Reefing the mainsail under those conditions would have been rather difficult. The wind went up to 30 knots but as the boat speed increased accordingly, and thus the apparent wind remained manageable, everything looked all right. We continued sailing fast like this and reached Crete by late afternoon having covered most of the eighty miles under full mainsail at an average of eight knots.

I have used this system on several occasions since, even in 40 knots while on passage from Fiji to New Zealand. Knowing what I know now, I make sure to reef the mainsail early while it is still easy to do, as Aventura is so efficient off the wind that in strong following winds she is just as fast reefed right down. In strong following winds I usually go straight to the third reef as I know that speed will hardly suffer. Also, the autopilot is very happy with this arrangement and so is the crew.

Sailing with the full mainsail should not be taken to extremes however. Before leaving the Mediterranean, we spent a leisurely summer cruising in the Aegean. A German magazine had contacted me and asked if a photographer could join us to take some photos of Aventura under sail. The day he arrived there was very little wind and the photos could not have looked very good. While Gwenda was steering I was driving the photographer around in the dinghy for the best angles. Photo session over, we returned on board and made our way into the nearest port. By now it was late afternoon, the small quay was chock-o-block with charter boats and even the large anchorage was full. Weaving my way optimistically among the anchored boats I eventually saw what looked like an empty space close inshore in shallow water. I told Gwenda to head for it, pumped the centreboard halfway up and went on the foredeck to prepare the anchor. As we reached the chosen spot, Gwenda slowed right down, and called. 'Three metres... two...'

'OK, stop here.' I dropped the anchor, let out some chain... and when I looked up, I nearly fainted. The mainsail was still up! Fortunately it was flat calm, so I quickly released the halyard, as if it had been my intention to anchor under sail all along, and the mainsail came down nicely.

'No wonder people gave us strange looks as we passed close to them.' Gwenda said with an embarrassed smile.

'Oh, sometimes people recognize the boat...'

'Not this time, I hope!'

Although there were reasons for such an embarrassing oversight it was unquestionably an inexcusable thing to do. We had been distracted by chatting to the photographer, rather than concentrate on what we were doing, so our well-honed routine was upset. With the large bimini up the mainsail was completely masked from the cockpit and one needed to step onto the side-deck to see it. The fact that there was no wind didn't help... but while such fine points might be presented as mitigating circumstances in a court of law, whichever one looks at it, this was a silly mistake that makes me cringe even now.

Running

By the time the wind angle approaches 165° and looks like continuing that way, I start making preparations to gybe, primarily because I feel it is not fair on the autopilot to make it work hard to keep the boat on course. I don't think I have ever had a pilot induced gybe. Sailing short-handed I find it much easier when gybing a spinnaker not to do it all standing, but to douse the spinnaker, drop it on the fore deck, swap halyards so that the new one is on the leeward side, then set up the other pole for the new gybe. I usually haul in the other pole and drop its end inside the pulpit. All lines on the lazy pole are left in place as I may well have to gybe back, so the pole might as well be all set up.

If I have done the whole procedure on my own, which I often do especially when

Doina taming the large tri-radial spinnaker

sailing with only one crew, who may be resting. I set the autopilot to a cautious 150° on the new gybe, take a few turns of the sheet and guy on their cockpit winches, guessing how much to let out, then go forward and hoist the doused spinnaker from the foot of the mast. Although the spinnaker halyard is led back to the cockpit, it can also be handled from the mast, which I prefer when I do it on my own. Winching with one hand and controlling the raising spinnaker with the other I get it up to the top of the mast. If everything looks all right I pull up the douser, the spinnaker opens nicely, I have another look to make sure that everything is OK, then rush to the cockpit to adjust the sheet and guy. Once the spinnaker starts drawing well I set the pilot on the desired course, re-adjust the sheet and guy, make the necessary adjustments to the pole (all its lines come back to the cockpit), then sit down and relax. It may sound complicated but, with this well tried method, it is certainly not. It is also deeply satisfying, especially when I do it on my own in the middle of a starlit Pacific night sailing quietly through that blessed ocean away from war in Iraq,

genocide in Dafur, famine in Somalia and certainly well away from Al Qaida. Even now, writing these lines, which I am sure took me longer to jot down than it would have taken me to gybe the spinnaker, I get a tingle of excitement remembering those exquisite moments of sheer beauty.

This is perhaps the right moment to tackle the controversial subject of running sails and especially that of spinnakers on cruising boats. Downwind sails was certainly the most discussed subject in my early days of cruising and, like virtually everyone else setting off on a long voyage, I equipped the first Aventura with twin forestays so that I could hoist my hanked on twin running jibs independently of each other. The system worked reasonably well but it induced an awful rolling motion that was very hard to take for days on end. I tried to dampen the rolling with the trysail sheeted in hard but it didn't make much difference. So on the second Aventura I went straight to a spinnaker and have used spinnakers as my preferred broad reaching or running sail ever since.

For some unfathomable reason many cruising sailors have a deep aversion for spinnakers regarding them as dangerous, unfriendly and unmanageable. Some try to solve this by using a cruising chute.... and some even twin jibs! I know all this from the four round the world rallies where boats with spinnakers were usually in the minority. This aversion to something you don't know reminds me of the day I decided to buy a new car and told Gwenda that I was thinking of getting an automatic.

Gwenda's immediate reaction was that she didn't like it.

'I grew up with manual gears and I am happiest with that.'

I knew this was all nonsense as usually when I am in the USA I hire a car, automatic of course, and find them a delight to drive. So I ordered an automatic and somehow managed to persuade Gwenda to bear with me and give it a try. Gwenda soon confessed that in fifty years of driving she had never been happier than driving our new car. But she is still averse to spinnakers and is quite reluctant to keep one up during her night watch, unless the weather is very settled and the wind is not above 12 knots. In this, in spite of her experience (she has sailed well over 100,000 miles) she is not all that different from the majority of cruising sailors, many of whom suffer from this unexplainable spinnaker aversion. It is something that really puzzles me and I wish I could change it. I hope I have done my best.

Spinnakers

Aventura III started off with one tri-radial and one asymmetric spinnaker. The tri-radial is perfectly cut and I am still using it, but the asymmetric was a disappointment. In the late 1990s when I ordered my sails, asymmetric spinnakers had only just appeared on the market and their cut was still guesswork, so I kept it as a spare and later ordered a second asymmetric spinnaker, which is perfectly cut. Halfway through the voyage, while in New Zealand, I acquired one of the new ParaSailor spinnakers.

The sail was delivered to Auckland in March 2004, from China of all places, the day before I was planning to leave New Zealand for New Caledonia. Since then Aventura III has covered some 18,000 miles from New Zealand to Northern Australia, across the South Indian Ocean and Cape of

The ParaSailor spinnaker with its distinctive slot and wing

Good Hope to the Canaries and all the way to Croatia. Looking through my logbook I reckon that the ParaSailor was used for well over one third of that distance, which I guess must be at least seven thousand

The spinnaker pole is held in a fixed position by the topping lift, forward and aft guys

miles. Besides the ParaSailor, I still have the other spinnakers: a standard tri-radial and two assymetric spinnakers, all with dousers. I am probably a rather unusual cruising sailor in that the spinnaker is my favourite sail. Since getting the ParaSailor I have only used one of the asymmetrics on a couple of occasions, and never the tri-radial, as I found the ParaSailor so versatile that I use it in a much wider range of conditions than I would the tri-radial.

The main features of a ParaSailor spinnaker are the wide slot that runs from side to side about one third down from the top, and a wing below the slot, on the forward side of the sail. Once up, the ParaSailor acts just like a normal tri-radial spinnaker but this is an illusion as the slot and wing help the ParaSailor stay full even in light winds. I have used it on a few occasions in as little as 5 knots of true wind, and every time it looked like collapsing the back pressure exerted by the slot kept it full. It is in strong winds, however, that the ParaSailor comes into its own.

Normally I drop the spinnaker when the wind reaches 17 knots true, but on one occasion, on the way to New Caledonia, when I saw a squall approaching, I decided to leave it up and see what happened. From 15 knots the wind went up and up and settled at 27 knots. Aventura took it all in her stride, accelerated to nine, then ten knots and once, when it caught the right wave, surged to fourteen. Meanwhile the ParaSailor behaved as normally as before, the flap streaming ahead and the slot wide open almost visibly spilling the wind. Wonderful! Of course, one thing that must be avoided at all cost, as with any spinnaker, is not to broach. I must confess that whenever I run or broad reach I raise the centreboard. This makes it very easy to steer Aventura even in strong winds as there is no keel to act as a pivot if a mistake by the helmsman or a large wave forces the boat into a broach. With her flat bottom and no keel, Aventura acts just like a large windsurfer, with the rudder having no difficulty keeping the boat on course. I would suggest to owners of boats with a fixed keel to play it safe and drop the ParaSailor if the wind threatens to get close to 20 knots true and the risk of a broach becomes real. Although I know that the ParaSailor can be safely left up in winds of such strength as I have negotiated several squalls around 25 knots, I now prefer to douse it, mainly because if the wind continues to go up it will be a real struggle to get the spinnaker down.

It has been suggested that on long runs one should consider using the ParaSailor rigged with two poles and drop the mainsail. I am always reluctant to drop the mainsail as, in strong winds, it is so much easier to douse the spinnaker by having it masked by the mainsail. Also, hoisting the mainsail again at sea can be quite a struggle and I now prefer to keep it up even in strong winds but well reefed. On two occasions, in the South Indian Ocean, when the wind was very light (6 to 8 knots true) and no swell I did put up the ParaSailor with two poles, and it worked, but as soon as the wind got up, I dropped one pole and the ParaSailor set much better.

I normally keep the ParaSailor poled until we are sailing at 110 degrees off the wind, then, if the wind continues moving forward of the beam and the pole is about to touch the forestay, I release the pole and fly the ParaSailor from the bows by connecting the pole downhaul to the tack of the sail. As I had asked the builders to provide a non-standard longer stemhead I don't need a short bowsprit for an assymetric spi or the ParaSailor. Flown from the bows, the ParaSailor acts as an assymetric spinnaker and I can keep it up until the wind gets to 70 or even 60 degrees off, but as I have a well cut proper assymetric, I usually prefer to switch earlier.

I hope it is very clear from this that I am happy with the ParaSailor and would recommend it to anyone who is considering buying a new spinnaker. One further advantage of the ParaSailor is that it tends to stay full even if not perfectly set, so one does not have to constantly adjust sheets and guys, a chore that will not be missed by a lazy crew.

Setting up the pole

My favourite downwind technique is to set up one of the two poles independently of the sail I intend to use, so that the pole is held firmly in position by topping lift, forward and aft guys – all three lines being led back to the cockpit. Regardless of whether I decide to pole out the yankee or a spinnaker, the sheet is led through the jaws of the pole, which is then hoisted to the desired position. I have been using this simple method since 1975 when I met the Italian singlehander Mario Franchetti, who was preparing his 50 foot Coconasse for the OSTAR transatlantic race. As a singlehander he had thought of all eventualities, which resulted in a system that was both simple and safe.

Once the pole is in place and is held up firmly by the three lines, the yankee can be unfurled, or the spinnaker hoisted and its douser pulled up. With the pole being independent of the sail, the yankee can be furled partially or fully without touching the pole. This is a great advantage when sail has to be shortened quickly, usually when threatened by a squall. When the squall has passed the yankee can be easily unfurled as the pole is still in place. If sailing under spinnaker and threatened by a squall I douse the spinnaker and lower it onto the foredeck. Once the danger has passed, with the pole still in position, the spinnaker can be hoisted and its douser pulled up.

Aventura III's two spinnaker poles are kept on the side-decks rather than parked on the mast. I regard this to be a good precaution in case the mast is lost as the poles might then be lost too. In such an emergency, the two poles can be used to create an A frame to hoist a smaller sail.

Reefing

The mainsail has been provided with four reefs, only three of which are permanently set up with blocks and reefing lines. The fourth reef needs to be set up from scratch but I have only used it once, in a blow in Le Maire Strait, where perhaps the third reef would have done anyway. Initially only the first mainsail reef came back to the cockpit and to take in the second and third reefs I had to go forward. This was obviously an illogical solution as it meant having to work at the foot of the mast in strong winds. I kept changing the arrangement until I finally arrived at what I now regard as the best solution, with all one-line reefs coming back to the cockpit. Putting a reef in is very easy as the main halyard is also led back to the cockpit. While I pay out the halyard to lower the mainsail, I take in the reef with the help of the electric winch.

Safety features

As I planned to sail in high latitudes, before Aventura III was built I had put a lot of thought into safety and devised a series of backup systems in all those areas where, from past experience, I knew that things could go wrong. Some had already been tested on my previous boats, while others were not necessarily based on my own sailing experience but were learnt from other boats that had taken part in the rallies I organized and had encountered problems which, at the time, I believed could have been avoided. In line with my belt and braces philosophy, everything on Aventura that can possibly have a backup has one. The most important ones are mentioned in the chapter on engines and maintenance.

Many engine failures on cruising boats seem to be caused by dirty fuel and on many production boats the fuel supply and filtering systems are often woefully inadequate. As on both my previous boats, Aventura has a ten gallon day tank

mounted in the port cockpit locker about one metre higher than the engine so that the fuel is gravity fed to the engine. The tank is topped up every four or five hours by manually activating a fuel transfer pump. I have deliberately avoided having an automatic filling system so that the person who fills the tank needs to actually look at what is happening. The switch is placed in such a position that one can see a glass water separator while doing it

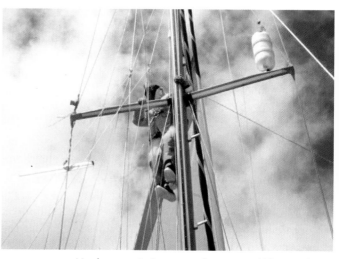

Having mast steps may have saved the mast on the way to the Falklands

thus making sure that the fuel that enters the day tank is always clean. Apart from this pre-filter, there are two more filters before the fuel reaches the engine. Every time I buy fuel, especially in tropical countries, I make sure to add a small amount of biocide.

I would also like to mention some of those little things that make life easier, such as the foot operated sea water pump for the galley which has a dual installation so it can be switched over to draw fresh water from the tanks should the electric fresh water pump fail. The folding mast steps are also a great bonus as they may have saved the mast when one of the spreaders collapsed on the way to the Falklands as it was easy to quickly climb the mast and secure the rig. The mast steps are also very useful for eyeball navigation in the tropics. The Walder boom brake is another useful feature as it ensures that even involuntary gybes do not get out of control. Finally, the stern arch, which is standard on every OVNI, fulfils a multitude of functions and also serves as a ready made davit for the dinghy, which is a great help on short cruises when I keep the larger Avon dinghy permanently inflated.

Choice of name

Over the years I have come across many unsuitable, some outright offensive, boat names and could never understand how anyone could possible sail on something called Upyours, Bloody Menace, Wet Dream or Mainshite. Those who are stuck for choice could follow the example of a couple who argued endlessly over the name of their new boat. Exasperated the man shouted, 'Oh, I give up, call it whatever.' And Whatever it has remained.

As the name of the boat will have to be spelt out on the VHF to officials who may not speak good English, this is a good reason why a simple international name (such as stars, constellations, planets, ancient gods) is a good choice. The choice of Aventura has proved to be perfect as it means adventure in many languages and is easy to spell and pronounce. Unfortunately having sold the first Aventura with her name without being aware of the British legal position on how to keep a name, by the time I came to register the second Aventura I was told that I had lost that name to the new owner. So we looked for an alternative and Gwenda had the

inspiration to call her La Aventura. The same thing happened again for the current Aventura when once again Gwenda came up with the best solution by calling her Aventura Trois (three), appropriate for a French built boat. For simplicity's sake however, I hope I will be forgiven if in this book I refer to them as Aventura I, Aventura II and Aventura III as they should have been called all along.

Preparing Aventura III for Antarctica

Aventura was built and equipped with a cold water voyage in mind and, as mentioned earlier, both deck and hull were insulated down to the waterline. Condensation was minimal, both because of the insulation and also because for Antarctica I covered the insides of all hatches with a thick layer of bubblewrap, held in place by fitted mosquito screens. This arrangement let through some light and the bubblewrap created enough of a temperature barrier to stop the worst of the condensation. The boat is heated by a Webasto diesel heater, blowing hot air through ducts leading to four outlets throughout the boat. The first, and hottest, leads to the oilskin locker, which dried gear perfectly. Generally, the heater worked well and with a consumption of 8 litres per 24 hours, it was very economical. When we were day cruising in Antarctica and spending most of the time in the cockpit or ashore, the heater only came on when we were back below. In daytime we let the temperature in the main cabin rise to 15°C, which was too hot once we became acclimatised to local temperatures, while at night we let it go down to 10°C.

There were no special provisions for the galley. Propane gas is recommended for cold climates but as Aventura is equipped with Camping Gas, which is butane, I was forced to stick with the latter. A heating element was fitted to the regulator at the tank end to stop the gas from freezing and we had no problems using butane even in the coldest weather.

The hull, being made of aluminium, did not need much preparation for occasional encounters with ice. On several occasions we had no choice but to push through large slabs of sea ice or brash ice at slow speeds, with the only visible damage being an absence of antifouling paint in the bow area. As we pushed our way through the ice, we took the engine in and out of gear to avoid damaging the Maxprop by any ice that might have been pushed under the boat, although we found that most ice was deflected sideways.

Aventura pushing her way through the ice

Regular visitors to Antarctica advise against installing a propeller guard as small bits of ice may get stuck in it making things worse than having an unprotected propeller. As a precaution I carried a spare two bladed propeller. On Aventura all seacocks had been fitted onto welded pipes to eliminate any protrusions outside the hull that may be broken off by ice, but this may have been an exaggerated precaution as shown by the fact that the B&G speedo paddlewheel was still intact at the end of the Antarctic cruise.

Among the other Millennium Odyssey yachts that sailed to Antarctica Vegewind was made of steel, so they had no ice worries, but the crew of the two fibreglass boats, Risque, a Swan 57, and Futuro, an older Swan 651, treated the ice with a great deal of respect, moving at very slow speeds and keeping contact with ice to a minimum. As some contact is practically impossible, anyone planning to sail in ice in a non-metal yacht should consider having the hull reinforced in the bow section, either with kevlar or, if feasible, a stainless steel deflecting plate.

Aventura's engine, a Volvo MD22, worked well and we used the recommended winter grade fuel. With a fuel capacity of 380 litres, we carried an additional 120 litres in jerrycans. Over a period of one month about one third of the total was used up by the heater, and as we managed to do much of our cruising under sail, the extra fuel was quite unnecessary. A second heating source would have been useful and could have been easily set up by using the cooling water from the engine to run a small radiator. One thing that I regret having overlooked was to install a warm sea water supply from the engine to the galley.

Aventura's deck layout had been carefully thought out for sailing in extreme conditions. Both the yankee and staysail are on furling gears, the control lines coming back to an electric winch in the cockpit. The cockpit was covered with a bimini (probably the wrong word for something we used extensively in Antarctica) that had windowed side panels to keep out the wind and snow. The electric winch was very useful to lift the Avon dinghy and outboard on deck, where it spent most of the time so it was not damaged by ice, or, worse still, being attacked by a leopard seal as happened to Futuro's inflatable, which was torn to shreds by a frenzied leopard seal. Sailing in those waters there should be a provision for a dinghy of adequate size to be either easily stowed on deck or in davits.

Apart from the standard electronics, a weatherfax is almost indispensable. To receive weatherfax I used a special software for my computer that was hooked up to the ICOM M710 SSB radio. Twice daily, the Chilean meteorological station at Valparaiso issued synoptic charts of the region down to the South Pole and as far west as New Zealand. They were extremely useful in assessing local weather conditions and likely wind changes, especially important when choosing an anchorage that might be encumbered by floating ice. For communications we used extensively an Inmarsat C unit, which had full coverage of the Antarctic area in those high latitudes and can be used for email or to send text messages to a computer or fax. A satellite telephone, such as my current Iridium, would have been very useful for both voice and email communications but I only acquired one on my return to Europe.

Generally I feel that Aventura had been perfectly prepared for her Antarctic voyage. She was easily handled under all conditions and was comfortable inside and out. There is no doubt that having been to Antarctica before when I sailed there on a different boat had been a great help in deciding exactly what was essential and what should be avoided.

Antarctic Interlude

'**A**ntarctica is more than an addiction, it's almost a curse.' Skip Novak had warned me when we returned to the mainland after three weeks cruising in

Sailing under spinnaker off Danco Island in Antarctica

the Antarctic Peninsula with Doina, Ivan and a couple of friends. 'You'll be back!'

Skip was right because three years later I was back, but this time on my own boat. When Ivan heard of my plans, not only to sail to Antarctica, but also to carry on all the

way to Alaska, he quit his job as systems manager at a film production company in London to accompany me as did my friends Erick and Muriel Bouteleux. The prospect of several weeks of sailing in the ice had persuaded Gwenda to stay at home. The voyage to Antarctica coincided with the sale of World Cruising Club and my gradual withdrawal from organizing rallies. This voyage to Antarctica had been on the books even before Aventura III had been launched, so the trip to the frozen continent was planned as her proper baptism, albeit by ice rather than fire.

As I regard Antarctica the most interesting cruising destination in the world I decided to start the cruising section of this book with a description of Aventura's cruise along the Antarctic Peninsula and its off-lying islands as it was blessed with some of the most exciting and satisfying moments of my entire cruising life.

The previous two Aventuras had both circled the globe along the trade wind routes, so I decided to give the well-trodden tropical route a temporary miss and do some cold water cruising instead. Having had a foretaste of Antarctic sailing on Pelagic, I drew up plans for a high latitude voyage that would take Aventura III in one year to the three cold As: Arctic, Antarctic and Alaska. Although the initial plan was to sail Aventura on her maiden voyage all the way to Spitsbergen, a delay in her delivery allowed me to get only as far as Southern Norway, somewhat short of the Arctic Circle. On her return to London, Aventura joined the Millennium Odyssey on the first leg to Portugal. This round the world rally followed two basic routes: a cold water route around the Capes, and a warm water route via the Panama and Suez Canals. I decided to join the former as it also included a trip to Antarctica before returning to the South American mainland. Sailing north from Cape Horn through the Chilean canals the route then headed for Easter Island, Pitcairn and French Polynesia. There, Aventura would leave the Millennium Odyssey to sail to Hawaii and on to Alaska and British Columbia.

Aventura's voyage south from the Canaries to the Cape Verdes, Brazil, Argentina, Falklands and finally Patagonia had gone according to plan and, like the dozen or so boats that sail to Antarctica at the start of the southern summer, we made the last preparations for the 500 mile passage to Antarctica in Puerto Williams. The main role of this small port set on the southern shore of the Beagle Channel continues to be that of a military base, with little interest in tourism or foreign visitors. As Chile continues to claim a large wedge of ocean to the south, which includes both Horn and the surrounding islands as well as much of the Antarctic Peninsula, yachts planning to visit the latter have to clear in and out of Puerto Williams. This is a base for the Chilean Navy but now that the dispute with Argentina over the Beagle Channel appears to have been settled, its military role is only symbolic. Apart from priding itself as being the southernmost settlement in the world, its only other claim to fame is a strange monument consisting of the cut-off bows of the tug Yelcho commemorating the rescue of Ernest Shackleton's crew by the Chilean Navy in 1916. A more recent wreck, that of the auxiliary ship Micalvi, has been put to more practical use as a yacht club of sorts. The walls of its bar are adorned with mementoes from Antarctic yachts whose crews never fail to stop here for a pisco sour on the way to or from the frozen continent.

Across the Drake Passage

Less than 60 miles from Cape Horn, Puerto Williams is an excellent place to wait for a weather window to cross the Drake Passage. The best time to head south is on the back of a depression, as the winds veer gradually from west to north-east. With Aventura fully provisioned for a

The first iceberg on the way to Deception Island

voyage of four weeks we didn't have long to wait before I deemed the time to be right to head south. One valuable lesson I had learnt from my previous trip was that in this part of the world if conditions look right, you go. I set a course straight across

63

the Drake Passage and as we sailed south past Cape Horn under spinnaker, my only concern was to get south of latitude 60°S as quickly as possible. A large and vicious looking low was building west of Cape Horn, and, as I followed closely the twice daily weatherfax transmissions from the Chilean meteorological office in Valparaiso, it became

The well sheltered Telefon Bay

obvious that, as usually happens, the low would track right through the middle of Drake Passage. By hurrying south we had the benefit of good winds all the way and made a satisfyingly fast passage to Deception Island off the tip of the Antarctic Peninsula.

On the fourth morning after our departure we had covered over 400 miles and were sailing fast on a beam reach. Aventura was surrounded by lots of birds: storm petrels, Mother Carey's chickens, Cape pigeons also known as painted petrels, the back of their wings akin to a checkerboard, and the first wandering albatross. It was such an overwhelming feeling to be sailing in glorious weather several hundred miles south of Cape Horn. Fifty miles from land we met our first icebergs but the visibility was so good we could easily avoid them. By mid-morning we were closing with the land and were met by three humpback whales sounding together for krill. The Antarctic plateau was by now clearly visible as were its surrounding mountain ranges. The view all around us was truly spectacular. Several blue icebergs stood out against the blinding white background of the snow-clad mountains. A school of gentoo penguins were diving ahead of us in close

formation. We passed seals and more penguins sunning themselves on smaller icebergs floated by, then we glided silently past a large glacier several hundred feet high calving smaller bergs. A stunningly beautiful introduction to an amazing world!

The crossing of the 500 mile wide Drake Passage had shown Aventura at her best as we rarely sailed below 7 knots and so managed to keep pace with our nearest rival, the American Risque, a new Swan 57 sailed with a crack crew of eight compared to our modest crew of four. Our secret weapon was Erick who had sailed virtually before he could walk and, having been involved with OVNI yachts for many years, knows these boats better than anyone else. Not only does he manage to get the best out of Aventura but, whenever anything breaks, I just smile slyly and let Erick fix it.

Deception Island 62°57'S, 60°38'W

Named in 1820 by the explorer Edward Bransfield, who must have been rather disappointed by what he found, Deception Island is a fascinating place.

The horseshoe-shaped island is the partly submerged caldera of an active volcano, which last erupted in 1991 and its unique landscape of barren volcanic slopes, steaming beaches and glaciers is covered in a thick layer of black lava dust. A narrow channel, called Neptune's Bellow, leads into the circular harbour. It is one of the few places in the world where one can sail into an active volcano. As we made our way in, the wind funnelled though the narrow entrance channel, justifying its inspired name, and we were rocked and pushed sideways by violent gusts as if Neptune was having fun pumping his bellows.

Expecting to be caught by that threatening depression we had moved into the innermost anchorage at Telefon Bay. By the time the strong winds from the low set in, we were safely tucked into a recently formed pool in the NW corner of the submerged crater of this dormant, but occasionally active, volcano. The bad

Antarctic sauna at Deception Island

weather lasted only one night, so we went looking for a famous warm water volcanic spring that gushes up near the shore. Watching the cockpit display showing the temperature of the seawater closely I saw it steadily climbing from 5°C to 12°C and settling finally at an amazing 18°C. With a mighty glacier close by on the shore it was almost impossible to believe that my instrument was telling the truth, but it was, and we had the proof when we dipped our feet in the water and it felt surprisingly warm. Further along we came across the derelict site of an abandoned Norwegian whale processing factory. The huge machinery was strewn all over the black land while in front of a building with all its windows broken stood the remnants of a small airplane. We had the entire place to ourselves and spent all morning walking around the ruins of those grim whaling days.

The Antarctic Peninsula

Deception Island is a good starting point for a cruise along the Antarctic Peninsula, also known as Graham's Land, and we started our trip along its western shore and the many offlying islands, a perfect cruising area with good protection and many sheltered anchorages. As on my previous visit I was totally overwhelmed by the sheer beauty of the scenery and the richness of its wildlife, but these were only secondary reasons for my addiction. Beyond all that natural beauty Antarctica's main attraction for me is the overpowering feeling of being a witness to a pristine world hardly touched by man, of being part of something that has remained virtually unchanged for tens of thousands of years.

A group of young male elephant seals take their siesta

The scenery of Antarctica takes centre stage, and rightly so, but there is another equally attractive dimension to the Antarctic experience and that is the wildlife. Because the animals have absolutely no fear of man, it is possible to observe them at close quarters without interfering with their day to day life. We stopped at penguin colonies almost every day but to see other animals we sometimes had to go out of our way. From my previous visit I remembered a large elephant seal colony and very close to it, a large number of giant petrels' nests. I retraced our steps from three years previously, anchored in the same spot and went ashore. I had expected the petrels to be still there, but was quite surprised to see the beach heaving with massive blubbery shapes. There were at least thirty elephant seals lying stretched out lazily in total abandonment and the first expression that sprung to mind was that even pigs couldn't have looked happier lolling about in their own... mess. They were all young males quite clearly bonding as single blokes do and enjoying a carefree summer vacation before family responsibility put an end to their hedonistic existence. The master of the congregation, a huge bull probably weighing in excess of a ton, was lying on his own right by the water's edge and growled at me unconvincingly when I stopped to take his photograph. Only later, when I had a close look at the result, did I realize that my own image was perfectly reflected in his large eyes.

Leaving the elephant seals to revert to their rudely interrupted siesta we climbed up a glacier and reached the bare summit of a hill where scores of giant petrels had their abode. Most had a young chick in the nest, but what was surprising was that at almost every nest there was also a young adult, which was last year's offspring. Apparently young petrels are not keen to face the problems of the outside world and prefer to prolong their adolescence by staying with mummy and daddy. Their indulgent parents seem happy with this arrangement and continue to provide them with food and lodging even when the youngsters have reached the size of adults, similar to some urban two-legged late starters. Just like many city teenagers they were also badly behaved and rude to strangers, receiving us with shrieks and aggressive gestures, true bullies in the making. We didn't dare go too close, as I had been warned that these petrels tend to spit at intruders, their saliva being slightly venomous. It sounded quite improbable but we kept our distance nevertheless just as most of us wise oldies do when faced with a similar situation back home.

Danco Island 64°44'S, 62°37'W

We arrived at Danco Island in brilliant sunshine and a blue sky. The island was named after Emile Danco, a geophysicist who died here during the Belgian expedition led by the explorer Adrien de Gerlache in the closing days of the nineteenth century. With our large inflatable dinghy we started exploring the immediate area and close by, on a tiny islet, we found the remains of several small whaling boats. Before whaling and fishing activities were banned south of the Antarctic Circle this area had been frequently visited by whalers during the Antarctic summer. Also on Danco Island is an old cabin belonging to the British Antarctic Survey. The unoccupied wooden hut is still maintained as an emergency shelter for scientists and has a reserve of tinned food. Later we came across several

A young giant petrel with his baby brother waiting for their parents to return with dinner

such food depots, set in prominent places and marked by a perch, which would provide survival rations to anyone lost in this wilderness.

I climbed with Ivan to the top of the 600 foot high island to visit an amazing penguin colony. There were thousands of gentoo penguins all the way to the summit. Penguins need bare soil or rock for their colonies and as such places are difficult to find on the ice covered islands, they were prepared to climb quite high to find a suitable nesting place. The adults were in continuous motion waddling up and down the mountain. To reach the sea they would slide down on their bellies through the snow and there were several parallel Cresta runs from the top to the shoreline. By late afternoon there was a continuous procession of penguins coming home to feed their chicks: a true commuter traffic at the end of the working day. It was intriguing to see how the parents recognized their own chick from among a mass of identical looking balls of fluff. The parent gave a cry, which attracted a response from several chicks, but the adult penguin ignored most and went straight to his or her own pushing the pretenders out of the way. The lucky chick stretched its head straight up and pushed its beak as far as it would go up the parent's throat to retrieve a half digested lump of krill. Watching the daily life in a penguin colony is one of the most fascinating activities in Antarctica and I could never get enough of it.

The following morning we took the dinghy to the opposite shore and started climbing up a glacier. Because of the warm weather the slopes were covered in small pools of melted water and the going was quite exhausting in the slushy heavy snow. Suddenly I fell into a crevasse up to my armpits and had it not been for my quick reaction I might have dropped to the bottom of the crevasse some forty feet below. That put an end to that kind of

The penguin colony on Danco Island

activity as at that time of year the risks were too high. On the way down I was attacked by two irate skuas protecting their nests. I braved their fury and took several photographs as they dive-bombed me. In one of the photographs a skua is right above me it swings outstretched, its eyes boring menacingly into mine. Who would blink first? It was certainly not me, but my Nikon shutter.

A penguin feeding its chick

Cuverville Island, 64°41'S, 62°38'W

We woke up in the shelter of this small island to find the boat covered in a thick coating of snow. During the short night, a blizzard had moved in from the south obliterating all visibility. Securely anchored with two anchors in tandem and four lines tied by stainless steel strops to large boulders ashore, we had nothing to fear. This anchoring technique proved to be the best answer to local conditions: rocks interspersed with patches of mud. Across

the sound, snowy peaks of the Antarctic Peninsula reared up giddily either side of a mighty glacier. Countless icebergs, which were continuously calving, were littered about, grounded in shallow water. Two icebergs, slightly larger than Aventura, had parked themselves close by during the night, their powder blue mass almost transparent in the brilliant sunshine. It was one of those Antarctic mornings, crisp and clear, that filled you with awe at nature's beauty. We had now reached nearly 65°S, but the intention was to carry on south as far as the ice would allow, but we doubted if we could get further than 66°S, where the sea was reported to be completed blocked by last winter's ice.

Antarctic glaciers calve continuously and release huge icebergs, some several miles long. Caught by winds and currents they drift aimlessly across the oceans melting slowly and thus making up for the water lost by evaporation or other reasons. Under normal climatic conditions nature keeps the balance by replacing the missing mass with the snow of the following winter. On this visit I was shocked to see the obvious changes that had occurred during a relatively short absence of only three years. Most glaciers that I remembered well from before had retreated significantly and in many places their sides were covered in green lichen, apparently the first plant to survive in that environment. I had no doubt that climatic change was on its way.

A surprise birthday present for the skipper

The smaller glaciers along the Antarctic Peninsula, or on the islands facing it, were also busy calving but their offspring rarely got far and grounded in the shallow waters. With less than one eighth of an iceberg's mass visible above the water, most of it being hidden under the surface, the largest icebergs were grounded in depths of several hundred feet, while the smaller bergs came to rest in the shallow waters close to the shores. Pushed by an onshore wind they usually ended up in one of the bays and it was imperative to be aware of this when choosing an anchorage. We always attempted to anchor in the shallowest depth possible where only the smallest bergs could follow us in. With Aventura's shallow draft this was not a problem and if the weather looked at all threatening I pumped up the centreboard and with a draft of only three feet the risk posed by visiting bergs was greatly reduced. Even so we were often woken up by the noise of a horny intruder the size of Aventura that had hopefully parked itself alongside us and was rubbing us up expectantly waiting for a response. Pushing off the unwanted visitor

A night blizzard plastered the rigging with a coating of snow

Two leopard seals have their siesta disturbed

the inflatable with its outboard on to the foredeck and started moving slowly out of the bay. Before we had time to react to the depth sounder moving speedily upwards, there was a crunch, and we were aground. 'No problem', exclaimed Erick, who was at the wheel, 'We'll lift the centreboard and come off', and that's what we did. So we sounded with the board and reached places that other boats would not even consider. This attitude, coupled with our willingness to scout ahead of the other Millennium Odyssey yachts and, where necessary, push our way through ice, turning Aventura into a mini-icebreaker, had earned us the nickname Risky, as opposed to our rival Risque. But then, we had a metal hull and they didn't.

was a waste of time, as it weighed at least twice as much as its chosen victim, so I did what I normally do in foreign lands when faced with pushy locals. I shrugged my shoulders and put up with it. After all, it was their territory we were invading.

Although these waters have been relatively well charted, landmarks often do not tally with the GPS coordinates and some small rock may have been overlooked entirely, so we had to keep a constant lookout and rely more on our eyes than on the instruments. Although we touched the ground on a few occasions, Aventura's forgiving centreboard let us get away without any damage, but other yachts found the experience quite unnerving and ended up moving very little.

Peleneau Island, 65°06'S, 64°04'W

The weatherfax from Chile at 0815 didn't show anything threatening, so we decided to move on. Having retrieved the four mooring lines and two anchors, we hoisted

Pitt Island 65°25'S, 65°29'W

There was a certain symmetry in our position, with latitude and longitude almost the same. I was tempted to go a few miles to the east where both would be equal, but that would have meant anchoring in open water. We had reached the furthest point south we could go, as from here on thick almost unbroken ice stretched to the southern horizon, more suitable for a real icebreaker.

Determined to be the yacht that reached furthest south that season, we had left Peleneau early and headed SSW. As soon as we left the protection of the islands and encountered open water, the ice started thickening and by the time we closed with the small island group we were ploughing through a lot of brash ice. The dull grey day made this bleak place even bleaker. There were hardly any animals about, except a large leopard seal that gave us a most hateful look for invading its territory. As it didn't seem bothered by our presence, after we had anchored and taken our lines to rocks ashore, we paid it a visit in the dinghy. As we got closer, with me following in the smaller dinghy and taking

Port Circumcision 65°10'S, 64°10'W

We anchored in this most delightfully protected spot on the east side of Petermann Island. The French explorer Jean-Baptise Charcot named it after the traditional day on which it was first sighted, 1 January 1909. The French expedition spent a long winter here and Aventura was anchored close to the spot where their ship Pourqoui Pas? (Why Not?) had been anchored. A plaque commemorating their

Tucked in safely in Port Circumcision with a menacing storm coming our way

photographs, it growled, then turned around and ignored us. These aggressive animals have no enemy and obviously this one didn't regard us as such. We explored the small area, found a more promising anchorage but as we were not going to stay long it wasn't worth moving. I realized that this was going to be our turning point and the thought filled me with a deep sense of regret as none of us was ready to leave this wonderful and unique world. Skip's words kept surfacing in my mind and made me understand just how addicts must feel.

stay can be seen near an Argentinean refuge hut.

With threatening weather approaching from the east we had made for this sheltered bay as it promised to give us protection from all directions. After going through the routine of anchoring and taking lines ashore, this time even more carefully than usual as I knew we were in for a blow, we landed on the nearby rocky

71

beach right in the middle of a large penguin colony. As we stepped ashore a penguin followed us closely, covered in blood and badly wounded. It had obviously been mauled by a leopard seal, but had miraculously managed to escape and was now determinedly making its way to feed its chick. I hoped it would survive but I doubted it as even if it didn't die of its wounds the skuas would probably finish the job. These aggressive predators are always to be seen on the edges of penguin colonies watching their potential prey with a beady eye. They rarely attack a healthy penguin but pounce at the first sign of weakness, their victims usually a famished chick whose parent had failed to return from a feeding expedition.

Back on board we were having a late dinner when we heard Vegewind, one of the Millenium yachts, calling us on the VHF. I looked out and saw them steaming past and heading for Lemaire Channel.

'Where are you going?' I asked the skipper Volker.

'We plan to anchor for the night just the other side of this strait.'

'But there is no protected anchorage there...and the weather doesn't look good.'

'Oh, we'll be all right.' He replied confidently.

'I wouldn't be so sure. Look, there is space in this bay and even with your draft you could make it just by the entrance.'

'No thanks, my crew want to go through the strait.'

'Silly fool'. I mumbled as I let go of the mike.

Thick low black clouds precipitated nightfall and the gradually increasing wind started pushing more and more ice into the anchorage. Having lifted the centreboard and anchored in the shallowest spot possible we were soon surrounded by a wall of ice, with only a slither of open water

around Aventura. We looked quite safe and went to bed.

When we woke up, the scenery looked even worse than the night before, but our snug location couldn't have been safer. Later in the day the wind dropped, the sun came out and the ice started retreating, so we upped anchor and headed for the strait. As we came out at its end we saw Vegewind anchored close inshore, but there was no sign of life on board, so we carried on towards the Ukrainian base on Argentine Islands.

Argentine Islands 65°15'S, 64°16'W

This large base prides itself on running the southernmost bar in the world. Located over 500 miles south of Cape Horn, this claim is beyond dispute. Also it is probably the most welcoming bar anywhere in the world. The base commander, Viktor Systov, recognised me from my previous visit on Pelagic, when we arrived only a few days after the Ukrainian Academy of Sciences had taken over the British Antarctic station Faraday, renamed Vernadsky after Ukraine's most famous physicist. Britain handed over the fully equipped station for the token payment of £1 on condition that the Ukrainians continued a number of projects started by the British, most important among these being a study of the ozone layer above Antarctica. Indeed, the Ukrainian scientists were carrying out their tasks fastidiously sending daily reports to their colleagues in Cambridge. The specialist in charge, Mykola Leonov, gave us a detailed demonstration of his work as an ozonometrist, but insisted that on present data he would not commit himself to say whether the ozone hole was getting larger or smaller. All he could say is that forty years of observations covered too short a span to be able to draw any meaningful conclusions. He did stress that the size and intensity of the ozone layer showed a remarkable seasonal variation, having a lower intensity in the Antarctic spring than at other times, which could also point to a cyclic variation that could only be measured over a number of decades, if not centuries.

For the Ukrainian scientists, playing host to the four Millennium Odyssey yachts was a highlight of their fourteen month long Antarctic sojourn, which was going to end the following month, when the eleven man team would be relieved by a new group from the Ukraine. So the party that they put on for us was also an early farewell party for their own imminent departure. True to the East European tradition of hospitality, the thirty-four Millennium guests were regally entertained and the bar was kept open from eight in the evening until three the following morning. At some point when I could still speak clearly, I made a toast to our hosts and said how happy we all were that the message of the Millennium Odyssey had reached as far as Antarctica, then handed them some Millennium souvenirs. To my shame I had not thought of setting aside a Millennium Lamp for Antarctica, as I never imagined that we would have a chance of a flame ceremony. It didn't really matter as the message of peace and friendship was what our hosts really appreciated.

The crew of Vegewind had been the first to arrive, made a beeline for the bar and hogged it for the rest of the night, putting away the Ukrainian vodka and chain-smoking the base cigarettes as if there were no tomorrow. As one younger crew passed by I asked him what they were celebrating.

'To put it briefly: our miraculous survival!'
'What happened?'

'After we came out of the strait we anchored quickly as it was getting dark, but we had hardly gone to bed when the wind came up and we started dragging. As we hadn't had time to set up any mooring lines, we were being driven fast towards the shore. Even with the powerful engine at full blast we could hardly control our drift, so we tried to set a second anchor. As we drifted into shallow water we managed to take lines ashore and just about stop the worst. The wind and ice pushed us further in, we touched the ground, but somehow that terrible night passed.'

'Sorry to hear that and even more sorry that I didn't insist more strongly that you joined us at Circumcision.'

'Yes, I overheard your chat with Volker and couldn't understand why on earth we continued. Anyway, let's drink to our amazing luck.'

Vodka was being poured out generously in ever larger glasses, accompanied by freshly baked bread covered in a thick layer of juicy red caviar. The cook Vassily, having learned that I was originally from Romania, told me that his native village was only 20 km from the Romanian border, and, in a display of regional bonding, that same night baked six large loaves of bread for the crew of Aventura. Indeed, our hosts' generosity was almost embarrassing and as they firmly refused any payment for the large hole left behind in their bar (probably larger than the ozone hole above), we tried to make up for it by buying some of the souvenirs they had made during the long Antarctic winter.

Viktor the boss came over to me and wished me the best for the continuation of the voyage.

'Jimmy, these Germans sure know how to drink!'

Coming from a Ukrainian I could only interpret this as a compliment.

'It's probably because they are sailing on a dry ship and had a most horrible night almost losing their boat.'

'Well, that makes it easier to understand, but I am still impressed.'

As several of our Ukrainian friends came from Odessa and were keen sailors at heart, they asked us to put up our sails as we left the anchorage the following morning so they could take photos and videos to show their families back home. Aventura duly obliged by running up our most colourful spinnaker, the Canaries logo of the Millennium Odyssey sponsors looking rather incongruous on a background of snow and icebergs, but it must have made an impressive picture nonetheless.

Two humpback whales cruise past us in Lemaire Channel

Lemaire Channel 65°07'S, 64°00'W

With improved visibility by mid morning we could see Cape Renard clearly at the entrance to Lemaire Channel, our day's objective at a distance of some 15 miles. Not to be confused with the strait of the same name off Staten Island, this is a five miles long narrows between Booth Island and the Antarctic Peninsula. The stunning scenery has made it the most visited site in this part of the world. In a relatively small area are concentrated all the elements that make up the grandeur of Antarctic scenery: soaring snow covered peaks, majestic glaciers, countless icebergs, large and small. As if on cue, a large cruise ship steamed into view, the passengers crowded on the upper deck taking pictures of my small sailing boat weaving her way amongst the icebergs piled up in the approaches to Lemaire Channel. With all sails up, we must have been a sight. I tuned the VHF radio to channel 16 expecting to be called in appreciation for having provided the 400 passengers with such a rare photo opportunity. We even joked among ourselves that if asked if we needed anything, we would say, 'Yes, please could we have our rubbish collected!' This is indeed a major problem as, under the terms of the Antarctic Treaty, nothing must be left behind, nor anything taken out. So all our rubbish, degradable or not, had been collecting in large plastic bags tied to the aft rail. But the ship sailed silently past, not answering our call, not even saying hello.

Photo session over, we furled the sails as slaloming between icebergs and growlers was markedly easier under power than under sail. We followed the ship into the narrows but as the ice was getting thicker and progress slower, I climbed to the first set of spreaders to eyeball a way through. Dead ahead, between two large icebergs, two grey-brown shapes were undulating in the slight swell. Every once in a while one would raise itself and blow: two humpback whales sleeping on the surface, right in the middle of Lemaire Channel. We edged closer with the engine barely ticking over. Only when we were about one boat length away did they react to our presence: they rolled over in perfect synchronisation and swam towards us. The larger of the two, probably the male, raised its head out of the water, gave us a reproachful look, then both dove under our stern. The whites of their huge flukes shimmered greenly for a long while through the clear water as they gradually disappeared from sight. From the spreaders I had had an even better view than the rest of the crew in the cockpit and we all agreed that this could be the highlight of our Antarctic trip

Back to reality we found a passage through the ice and motored slowly through the narrows. More ice had piled up at their southern end but by now our ice dodging technique was tried and tested, and we headed for the nearest anchorage behind Peleneau Island. In order to reach it, we had to pass a shallow area littered with grounded icebergs, and aptly described by daughter Doina on our previous trip as

Stark reminder of the grim times when whales were massacred in Antarctica

the "iceberg cemetery". Rain, wind and sun worked relentlessly on the stranded icebergs moulding them into shapes undreamed of even by the most inspired sculptor. We took the dinghy through this ice gallery, competing with each other in naming the shapes: a sphinx, a jumbo jet, a cathedral spire, a stranded whale.

Having once again sounded our way into the shallow corner of the Peleneau anchorage, we quickly ran through the mooring technique: put the two anchors down in tandem, lower the dinghy, run two or four lines ashore, collect some ice for a well deserved happy hour. Nothing, believe me, tastes better than a pisco sour with 20,000 year old ice!

Port Lockroy 64°49'S, 63°31'W

What turned out to be our last day in Antarctica was also the most beautiful. Perfect is, in fact, the only word to describe it. After a rendezvous with the other three Millennium Odyssey yachts at Port Lockroy, each skipper had the option to pick his own time to start the leg to Cape Horn. We all spent a highly enjoyable time at Port Lockroy, the site of the first British base in Antarctica, now a museum run by the Antarctic Heritage Trust. Two of its members spent the entire summer there, welcoming visitors both from cruise ships and yachts. The logbook kept at Port Lockroy recorded that season the arrival of 17 yachts, about half of which were regular visitors to the Antarctic Peninsula as they were engaged in charter work. Because of its strategic location and excellent shelter, every yacht stops at Port Lockroy, so the number gives a fair indication of yachts visiting the Antarctic Peninsula. If the four Millennium Odyssey boats were not included, the number of cruising boats was only about eight, which was close to the average recorded in recent years. Among recent arrivals was an Australian singlehander who had sailed nonstop from New Zealand and was planning to spend the coming winter in Antarctica having laid in stores for a stay of well over one year. Singlehanders appear to be attracted to the frozen continent as on

Slaloming between icebergs on our last day in Antarctica

the day we were leaving we heard that a Brazilian singlehander had just completed a circumnavigation of Antarctica, the first to do so, and was resting in the bay next to Port Lockroy.

Dave Burkitt and Nigel Millius were the ideal hosts at Port Lockroy and were a font of information on Antarctica. By profession a shipwright, Dave is an old Antarctic hand and had been working for the British Antarctic Survey since the early 1970s when he was in charge of a dog team. The departure of the last huskies from the Antarctic in 1994, under pressure from environmentalists, is deeply regretted as it wiped out at one stroke the true spirit of adventure of the overland explorations by sledges pulled by teams of huskies.

'They were replaced by noisy smelly skidoos – a poor replacement for the hard working huskies, and an odd way to protect Antarctica from pollution,' commented Dave with a bitter smile.

Nigel, an ornithologist, was spending his third season in Antarctica observing the life of penguin colonies, and the impact of human visitors. In spite of their steady increase, this does not seem to have affected local wildlife significantly,

although Nigel stressed the fact that keeping a check on the size of groups that were landed by the cruise ships, and the groups being always accompanied by a qualified guide, has helped minimise the potential risks.

From Port Lockroy we followed the Gerlache Strait towards the Melchior Islands, our chosen point of departure. In brilliant sunshine and on a background of towering snow-clad mountains painted onto a porcelain blue sky, the beauty of the Antarctic scenery was breathtaking. With a light breeze on the quarter we hoisted the spinnaker, gliding silently past icebergs and surprising several pairs of humpback whales feeding or resting in the calm waters of the mountain-ringed fjord. By early evening we had reached our destination, but as the weather looked nice and settled, I decided not to wait, like the others, for a weather window, but carry on without stopping. The crossing of the Drake Passage is the price one has to pay for the privilege of visiting Antarctica, so with no depression showing close to the west on the daily weatherfax, we agreed that we'd rather swallow the bitter pill sooner than later. Indeed, with depressions passing through at an average of one every three days, it is almost impossible to do the 500 miles passage to Cape Horn without getting caught by a low, a risk we were ready to take.

Return to Cape Horn

The tactic for the northbound voyage from Antarctica across the Drake Passage is

give them daily routing advice, and was taken by surprised when the skipper told everyone listening to the radio that, in view of possible deteriorating weather, he had been strongly advised to wait several days for an improvement. I butted in and explained that according to the way I read the latest weatherfax, I begged to differ, but neither Risque nor any of the other skippers listening took any notice.

We left immediately and for the first two days our gamble paid off and we made excellent progress. The strong northerly winds that had blown in the days before our departure had pushed all icebergs back

Mountainous seas on our return across the Drake Passage

to leave from as far west as possible, and also to keep some westing in hand for the intended landfall at Cape Horn, where the prevailing winds are from NW and there is also an east-setting current. The Melchior Islands are the best departure point, and there were a few other boats there waiting to cross to Cape Horn. The radio was abuzz with advice, comments and speculations as skippers defended their pet theories. I knew that Risque had commissioned a well-known offshore weather expert to

towards the Peninsula so, to our great relief, we saw not a single iceberg after we had sailed 20 miles offshore. A few hours of calm signalled a change in the weather, and when they returned, the winds had veered to the NW and by the afternoon of the third day were blowing in the high 30s. As by now we were less than 100 miles from Cape Horn and we had a good deal of westing in hand, we decided to heave to for the night. With three reefs in the mainsail and the wheel lashed to windward, Aventura took the mounting swell quite well, fore-reaching slightly but making quite a lot of leeway. By morning we had lost all our hard-earned westing and had drifted past the longitude of Cape Horn. A keen debate followed on board as to whether drifting past Cape Horn counts as having doubled the famous landmark or not.

With the wind later backing to SW, our decision to heave to proved to have been wise as it saved us from sailing over the continental shelf extending for some 50 miles south of Cape Horn, the depth between 50 and 80 metres creating hellish conditions in strong westerly winds. Our luck held as the wind obliged by backing slowly to SSW. By staying as close hauled as the strong wind would permit we gradually clawed our way back and anchored in a bay close to Horn Island almost exactly four days after leaving Antarctica. Whether we now deserved to wear an earring or not is something that didn't bother me as I never wear any jewellery, not even a wedding band. However, having passed Cape Horn from west to east, to make sure our claim was beyond dispute, we anchored in the lee of Horn Island and started preparations to actually step ashore at this famous landmark.

Practical tips for Antarctica

The boat

Safety and personal comfort are the two most important criteria. For the passage across Drake, where one can expect to encounter icebergs, a collision bulkhead forward would give peace of mind, although collisions even with the smaller growlers can be avoided by keeping a good lookout. This is not too difficult as the nights are very short and moving south get even shorter. Radar is useful in detecting and tracking the larger icebergs at night. The boat should be easily steered from a sheltered position, although the cold is not normally a major problem provided one is well dressed.

Some kind of heating for the interior of the boat is essential as the daytime temperatures rarely rise above freezing. Condensation can be a major problem if the boat is not well insulated. The worst areas are hatches and portholes, and these should be either provided with a second, transparent framed cover, or be covered in a plastic film sheet, which will cut down condensation considerably.

As many anchorages have limited swinging space, mooring is greatly facilitated by having three or four lines (floating propylene is best) of 50 metres (150 feet) to moor the boat securely while at anchor. The lines should be provided with cable strops (at least 5 m/15 ft) in circumference to be slung across rocks ashore. To ease the handling of the mooring lines they should be stored on drums installed on the fore and aft decks and provided with handles so the lines can be wound on the drums when not in use. The same mooring lines came in handy later when we were cruising the Chilean canals when often we had to moor the boat four ways.

Clothing

Adequate clothing is an essential item in cold water sailing. Personal comfort is of utmost importance when sailing in extreme conditions and I must stress that in two Antarctic voyages I had never been

Approaching
Horn Island on
our return
from Antarctica

cold, either inside or outside the boat. This makes it possible not only to enjoy the unique scenery to the full, but is also a major safety factor. There is now a wide range of good quality clothing suitable for cold climates and it is recommended to buy those that are of the breathable type. The boots should have a thick non-slip sole and should be at least two sizes larger to be able to wear two or even three additional pairs of socks. One should have between four and six pairs of fibre pile or wool socks. Gloves are just as important and should be worn in two layers, the inner fingered glove to be of wool and the outer of a waterproof material (Goretex), ideally also with fingers. One should take sufficient woollen gloves as they do get wet. A place on board is needed to dry them as well as the rest of the wet weather gear. As I could not find any good quality waterproof gloves I solved this by buying a pair of dry diving gloves, which needed talcum powder to put on but were perfect for steering or when handling wet ropes. Good head cover is also essential, such as a Polartex balaclava. Rather than a standard survival

suit, it may be more useful to acquire a dry diving suit that can be used on watch under extreme conditions and also for wet dinghy landings.

There is a so-called middle layer, which is excellent to wear under the outside wet weather gear. Some middle layers have the advantage of being able to be worn on their own when off watch. The third, innermost, layer should be some sort of thermal underwear. I found cotton suits me best as my skin is sensitive to synthetic fibres, but some people prefer silk. For walking ashore a good windproof jacket or anorak is essential. I found skiing salopettes worn with such a jacket to be perfect for shore expeditions. Also needed are good hiking boots with a non-slip sole, such as Vibram, and, if the trousers do not fit well over the boots, also gaiters. As the risk of exposure to UV light is very high, both on board and ashore it is recommended to use dark glasses as well as a strong sun block cream. As the nose is the most exposed part of the body, a nose cover made of leather or plastic and fitted to the sunglasses works well.

Walking ashore

Much time will be spent ashore, in penguin colonies, watching other animals or just exploring the shoreline and enjoying the beautiful scenery. There are two aggressive animals to be aware of; fur seals who should not be approached too closely, and skuas. The latter are in the seagull family, are very territorial and aggressive especially if they have chicks and you get too close to their nest. They will take off and dive-bomb an intruder, giving a sharp and painful peck on your scalp. The best protection is a walking or ski stick that can be held upright above your head if attacked. A stick is also very useful when walking on glaciers where it is easy to fall into a crevasse, as happened to me. Suspicious looking cracks filled with fresh snow should be explored with the stick first and, generally, when the weather starts getting warmer it is wiser not to walk on glaciers at all.

A good camera with a telephoto lens is highly recommended. Spending time ashore it is good to carry some energy fruit bars, as one gets hungry in the cold, and also water as although there is ice everywhere, melted ice water from the ground is not drinkable as it is soiled from penguin activities. A portable VHF radio to communicate with the boat is essential.

Crew changes

There are no flights to anywhere on the Antarctic Peninsula although the Chilean base on King George Island may help in a real emergency. Puerto Williams is connected by small plane to Punta Arenas and on to Santiago de Chile. A better solution for crew changes is Ushuaia, in neighbouring Argentina, which has frequent flights to Buenos Aires for onward international connections. Flights between Buenos Aires and Ushuaia are often fully booked by cruise ships passengers so bookings should be made well in advance.

Weather information

There are daily forecasts by fax from the Chilean Meteorological Institute. For the crossing of the Drake Passage it may be useful to obtain a 120 hour forecast from an international weather forecasting agency.

Tips

- Good quality high latitude foul weather gear
- Windproof trousers and jacket (light-weight Goretex) or anorak
- Middle layer clothing
- Sea boots with thick non-slip sole (two sizes larger)
- Hiking boots with Vibram soles and gaiters
- Thermal underwear
- Fibre pile jacket and trousers
- Two balaclavas or wool hats with ear protection
- Several pairs of wool or fibre pile gloves/mittens
- Rubber or Goretex overmits
- Several pairs of wool socks
- Dark glasses
- Strong sun block cream
- Small rucksack for shore trips
- Walking stick

Weather

Salesman: We have good weather on over 70% of days, so you should be able to get good use out of the boat.
Buyer (good naturedly): Are you making that statistic up? I actually happen to work for the Met Office.
Salesman: No I'm not, look, it's in the brochure!

The right attitude

I might as well start with a confession. In spite of all the years I have spent at sea my knowledge of weather forecasting is quite rudimentary. I look at the sky and clouds, see that some are white and others grey, some large, some small, some fluffy, some ragged at the edges, but rarely can I guess what they are trying to tell me. The obvious exception is a tropical squall, which announces itself so clearly that even a child could recognise it. Like every sailor I like watching sunrises and sunsets but even here I have to fall back on that old saying of red sky at night, sailors' delight, red sky in the morning, sailors' warning. As most sunsets and sunrises are usually red at sea, and they rarely seem to predict bad weather, I prefer to wait for the green flash instead.

Having said all that I hasten to add that having spent so much time observing the sea at close quarters, I seem to have developed a kind of sixth sense and I cannot explain even to myself why most of the time I sense what is going to happen. Usually I can guess how much power an approaching squall will pack, if we are going to be in for a real blow or even smell if rain is coming. This sense-based approach to weather is backed by an over-cautious

Red sky at night may show settled weather on land but has less meaning at sea

attitude, which means that I always prefer to reef early, make all necessary preparations at the first sign of impending bad weather or leave an anchorage at short notice if I deem it unsafe. Put simply, over

81

the years I have learnt never to take anything for granted and not allow wishful thinking to override commonsense.

So my approach to weather is pragmatic, in other words I take it as it comes. In fact, fatalistic is a better definition. Of course I would not leave a marina or safe harbour if there is a gale blowing outside but if the strong winds are likely to continue, and they are from the right direction, ideally on the quarter, I prefer to go. Weather tactics vary in different parts of the world. Basically, in temperate zones what matters is the direction of the wind, so if winds are predicted from an unfavourable direction one has little choice but to wait. This is why I mentioned earlier that if the direction is right, I prefer to go even if the actual strength may not be entirely to my liking. The situation is very different when sailing in the tropics where what matters is the strength of the wind as the direction, especially in trade wind areas, is normally more constant and predictable.

Strangely enough, when on passage I find it much more interesting if I do not know what to expect. As I mention in the chapter dealing with routing, I have always followed the dictum of doing my best never to be in the wrong place at the wrong time. This usually means planning a voyage that avoids known bad weather areas or seasons, particularly tropical storm seasons. With a few exceptions, I have always managed to avoid really bad weather. Furthermore I must add that I have supreme confidence in my well tried and prepared boat, which I know I can trust to take me safely anywhere, as she has shown on many occasions.

When I started cruising there were very limited sources of information on offshore weather so anyone setting off on an ocean voyage in the 1970s had little choice but to take things as they came and this became a habit. Finally, I enjoy being at sea so much and taking the weather as it comes is an intrinsic part of the mystery of the sea and one of the reasons why I am out there in the first place. But enough of philosophy, let's consider some practical examples before you start thinking I have turned into yet another weather guru.

Tropical squalls

Squalls are a very different kettle of fish altogether, as they are always preceded by an impossible to miss black cloud that has a straight bottom roughly parallel to the horizon, hence their definition as line squalls. Outside the tropics squalls are much more difficult to detect and can occasionally come out of a blue sky without any warning, hence their name of white squalls. Tropical squalls always travel with the wind, so looking regularly to windward, you should not miss one approaching. They also show up well on radar and are quite visible to the naked eye even at night. If a squall is detected in good time, and if the advancing front is small, it may be possible to avoid being in its path by altering course. Sail should be shortened promptly as by the time the squall hits it is usually too late to do much except pray that whatever sail has been left up will cope with the increased wind and that the person at the helm or the autopilot will manage to keep things under control. I avoid using the windvane in squally conditions.

Most tropical squalls generate winds of about twice the force of the current wind. As the squall strikes the wind often changes direction, so the autopilot must always be set to steer to wind, or if hand steering, the best tactic is to try and keep the wind on the quarter, enough to keep the apparent wind down but not too close astern to risk gybing. Squalls do not always bring stronger wind but are usually accompanied by rain. There is a useful German saying for this: "Kommt der Regen mit dem Wind, nimm die Segel rein geschwind; kommt der Wind und dann

time being usually too short to reef the mainsail, when sailing through a squally area it is best to use a sail combination that can be quickly reduced to about half its surface, rolling up a foresail or dousing the spinnaker being the best. The mainsail is

An approaching line squall can be clearly identified by the straight bottom of the menacing black cloud

der Regen, kann der Segler sich schlafen legen." Translated roughly it says that if the rain comes before the wind, you must reef quickly, but if the rain comes after the wind, the sailor can go to sleep. As often happens, things do get lost in translation, so occasionally my crew have turned the argument on its head and gone to sleep first, which is definitely not what I told them to do when they started their watch.

Apart from keeping a keen lookout at all times, there is nothing else that can be done to predict an approaching squall, as the barometer gives no indication. In some areas squalls occur with irritating regularity, although occasionally on some passages days can go by without a squall while at other times they can hit every hour. With

best left alone, especially as putting one or two reefs as the squall approaches may not be easy as most likely one will be broad reaching or running. Also, once the squall is gone, taking the reefs out of the mainsail is unnecessary work. On my boat I aim to have enough mainsail up for it to be able to cope on its own with a squall of any strength. Usually I prefer to leave the mainsail alone and furl up the yankee completely. My method of setting up a pole independently of the sail works perfectly in such conditions as the pole can be left untouched during the squall and, once this has passed, the furled sail, or doused spinnaker, can be returned to its pre-squall status.

Tropical squalls can be even more dangerous when they strike an anchorage, when often their arrival cannot be predicted as they approach at great speed over the land. The solution is to choose an anchorage carefully and always make sure that one is well anchored and, ideally, not too close to other boats.

Ocean weather forecasts

One of the recent improvements in ocean weather forecasting are GRIB files, which have now become extremely popular with offshore sailors. GRIB (GRIdded Binary) is a World Meteorological Organization (WMO) code used by meteorological centres for storing and exchanging meteorological charts and other data on wind, sea state, temperature, etc. The information is put into a compressed digital format that enables high-speed transmission and reception. Being able to receive such information using GSM, GPRS, satellite phone or HF radio via an internet link is an absolute bonus whether on passage or while preparing to leave. A number of servers offer this service by email to cruising sailors. The GRIB file system is a major advance on the traditional weatherfax service.

My main source of regional weather information on Aventura is via the twice daily transmissions on Inmarsat C. I have also used the five-day email forecasts provided by www.buoyweather.com. While in Antarctica I regularly consulted the daily weatherfax transmitted by the Chilean meteorological office as it provided a useful indication of impending conditions. Occasionally, on longer passages, I try to get some outside input as happened between Galapagos and Marquesas where the suggestions emailed from New Zealand by weather wizard Bob McDavitt greatly helped me in finding the best winds.

Weather windows

There are two terms, often used by sailors, which I have taken a deep dislike to: paradise and weather windows. There seem to be so many so-called paradises on earth that there appears to be no space left for hell, which unfortunately is not the case. As to that other buzz term, I once said, and I wasn't trying to be funny, that weather windows can be bad for you. Some recent examples should help bear this out.

Mediterranean, April 2006

Shortly after my return to the Mediterranean in spring 2006, we were in Menorca, in the Balearics, getting ready to hop across to Sardinia, a distance of only about two hundred miles. For this section of our cruise, Gwenda and I had been joined by Italo Masotti, an Italian friend who has spent all of his sailing life in the Mediterranean and who was very keen to sail on Aventura having followed her progress around the world. Italo is a typical Mediterranean sailor who sails mostly short distances, prefers spending nights in marinas and keeps a wary eye on the weather, which can be quite capricious. So, when on the eve of our departure from Menorca, the forecast was for 25 knots with higher gusts, he looked surprised when I declared that we were going. 'In the Med, as everywhere else, when the wind is from the right direction, you go,' I said... and off we went.

With three reefs in the mainsail and the partly furled staysail we shot out of

Mahon's narrow inlet like a cork from a champagne bottle. Past the last point of land the sea looked ugly, with a short steep swell and the occasional breaking wave. For a relatively light displacement boat, Aventura is surprisingly well-behaved in such conditions and she more than makes up in speed for the discomfort. Gwenda is very stoical when faced with rough weather and settled in her favourite corner of the cockpit while Italo was trying hard to be useful although there was nothing for him to do. He came below and found me sitting in my armchair reading a newspaper. 'Jimmy, how can you sit there so calmly...?' he asked in utter amazement.

'What do you want me to do? We are well reefed down, the boat looks happy and the pilot is doing an impeccable job. Nothing to worry about.'

With that I went back to my newspaper. I could tell that Italo was not too happy but, after all, he had insisted that he wanted to sail on Aventura so at least he could see for himself how I sailed my boat, which may not have been entirely to his taste.

The strong winds didn't abate until the mountainous outline of Sardinia punctured the eastern horizon the following morning and we made a perfect landfall. Not long afterwards, when we were tucked up in the marina, the winds turned into the east and would have been blowing hard on our nose had we left later.

French Riviera, May 2006

On the same voyage not long after we had left the boat in Tunisia and flown to our home in Provence, I went to St Raphael, which had been Aventura's base before the latest voyage. In a chandlery I bumped into my friend Patrick Canut, who keeps his Jeanneau 42 there and the previous year had sailed with me from Cape Town to the Canaries.

'Nice to see you, but what are you doing here? I thought you were in Corsica.' I greeted him.

'Well, I'm ready to leave, but the forecast is for a strong mistral and as my crew are quite green, they insisted that we wait.'

'Why wait, the wind is OK now, it may be on the increase, but it is, after all, from the right direction?'

'I know, I know, but Marie-France wasn't too happy either about leaving with such a forecast.'

'Well, good luck then, but I still feel you should be on your way.'

The summer mistral is a regular feature in the south of France with the only unaffected area being the Cote d'Azur. The north-westerly wind can occasionally get up to forty knots although the forecasts of its strength are quite reliable. Some local sailors like Erick Bouteleux think nothing of playing cat and mouse with Mr. Mistral and would go out in any weather.

Next time I met Patrick in our village, I asked him about his trip to Corsica and he burst out laughing.

'Jimmy, you were absolutely right! We left the following morning, sailed for a few hours, but about halfway to Corsica the wind died and we had to motor. Minutes after I started the engine, the alarm went off and, when I looked in the engine room, there was oil everywhere and I couldn't find the cause. As I suspected a serious problem, I decided not to restart the engine, but, after we had drifted for about an hour, my crew insisted that we call SAR in Corsica and get them to tow us in. I told them not to be stupid as we were in absolutely no danger but they panicked and, faced with such an impossible situation, I reluctantly caved in and called Corsica. A boat was sent out and towed us

A violent squall is about to break over us while sailing off the Antarctic Peninsula

into the nearest port. "Oh la la,' was all I could say, 'what an adventure. I bet that got your adrenaline going!'

'Yeah, and my wallet too as I had to pay a couple of thousand euros for the towing operation.'

'Well, at least I hope that's a lesson for you.'

'Of course, from now on I am determined to do just what you would have done.'

'So our South Atlantic trip was not an entire waste then?'

'Waste? It was one of the best things that happened to me and I'll always be grateful that you invited me to come along.'

North Carolina, November 1977

My suspicious attitude to 'weather windows' was born early in my sailing life in the autumn of 1977, when we had stopped in Beaufort, North Carolina, on our first Aventura and we were preparing for the passage to the Bahamas and Panama. The port was full of boats waiting to cross to the Bahamas or sail to the Eastern Caribbean. Every morning somebody would get the weather forecast and we would stand around in little groups discussing in great detail every aspect of it. Halloween came and went, we were still there and I was getting worried that we would never leave. After a while it dawned on me that a perfect 'weather window' might never happen and we may be stuck there for the rest of the coming winter, so I decided that if the weather was at all acceptable we would leave the following morning, which is what we did.

We had a quite unpleasant first 24 hours as we crossed the Gulf Stream in a moderate northerly that had kicked up a nasty sea as the wind was blowing against the strong current. In the middle of the night we fell off a large wave with an almighty crash but apart from the fright, we came through unscathed. We had a uneventful passage to the Bahamas and on to Panama. Nearly two years later American friends, who had been in Beaufort at the same time, caught up with us in New Zealand. They told us that we had been the only ones who had managed to get away and that the weather had deteriorated the day after our departure so that eventually everyone had been forced to make their way south along the Intracoastal Waterway. Most of them had spent the winter in Florida with only a few managing to make it to the Eastern Caribbean. It sounded as if we had caught the last of that year's weather windows. That was the first and last time that I waited for a perfect weather window to set off on a long passage. Now I set a date of departure and, if we are ready and the weather looks acceptable, we go.

Antarctica, March 1999

Refusing to wait for a favourable weather window that may never come is also what I decided to do when we reached the Melchior Islands, our chosen point of departure across the Drake Passage to Cape Horn. As the weather looked settled, I decided not to wait like the other skippers gathered there for a favourable 'weather window', but to leave immediately. It is almost impossible to avoid a low on this passage, but with no depression showing nearby on the daily weatherfax we left immediately and in the first two days made excellent progress. By the third day the winds had veered to the NW and were blowing in the high thirties, so we hove to for the night. The following day we reached Cape Horn less than four days after leaving Antarctica. Those who had decided to wait eventually left a few days after us, giving up on waiting for that elusive window. Every one of them ran into bad weather and got quite a pasting in the unforgiving Drake Passage.

The above examples should, I hope, make it quite clear that I usually prefer to follow my own nose, which, over the years I have come to trust more than that of some so-called experts. Perhaps I gave the wrong impression with my earlier statement that I know next to nothing about weather when I actually meant that my theoretical knowledge is limited whereas, thanks to the many years spent at sea, it is my intuition that makes up for that shortage.

A few days after Christmas in 1993, one week before the start of the Europa 94 round the world rally, I noticed a depression forming off Iceland. I didn't like the look of it and told Gwenda that I had the gut feeling that the low will deepen and gradually track across the Atlantic all the way to Gibraltar. Even to me this sounded rather farfetched, yet that is exactly what happened. The depression followed an unusual path and hit Gibraltar with fifty knot winds on the day of the planned start, which naturally had been postponed.

In November 2005, while in Las Palmas for the start of the twentieth ARC, I was invited to a farewell party for the ten Spanish yachts taking part in the event. With the skippers fresh from the official skippers' briefing, I was asked to make my own comments on the best tactics in the early stages of their forthcoming Atlantic crossing. I was quite reluctant to disagree with the advice given by the official meteorologist who had advised the two hundred ARC captains not to worry too much about a depression that was forming to the west of the Canaries. I disagreed and told the Spanish skippers that they should take a prudent course, sail close to the Cape Verde Islands and alter course for the Caribbean only once they had reached the latitude of the Cape Verdes. A few days later I started getting emails from some of the Spanish skippers thanking me for my advice as they had managed to make their southing without difficulty whereas much of the rest of the fleet had run into very strong head winds. But worse was still to come, even if didn't affect the ARC fleet, as that ordinary looking depression gradually turned into a tropical storm and by 2nd December it was upgraded to Hurricane Delta. This was the first ever tropical storm to hit the Canaries and caused widespread devastation in the archipelago. It was most certainly not any meteorological insight that had helped me make that inspired guess but just a simple hunch that told me that things didn't look right. I suppose that's what makes people bet on an outsider at horse races... so maybe in the future I should put my nose to better use.

Heavy Weather

Le Maire Strait, January 1999

While Cape Horn decided to show us a rarely seen smiling face for the crossing of the Drake Passage, the real test for us had come on the way down, when we were sailing through Le Maire Strait that separates mainland Tierra del Fuego from Staten Island. The sailing masters of yesteryear used to dread this treacherous stretch of water even more than doubling Cape Horn as mountainous waves can be created in the strait by a strong NW wind blowing against the fierce tides set up at the meeting point between the Pacific and Atlantic Oceans. It is therefore imperative to catch the right tide and sail through the strait on the ebb, which had been our aim ever since leaving the Falklands. With that in mind we had tried to keep some westing in hand by entering Le Maire Strait at its northern point close to the mainland coast. As we approached the strait the NW wind started increasing in strength and by the time the tide started ebbing we had 35 knots on the quarter. With wind and tide in our favour Aventura was flying at ten knots over the ground and soon we had almost reached the southern end of the strait and were breathing a satisfied, almost smug, sigh of relief. Too soon! As we approached the SE end of Tierra del Fuego, the wind backed to the west, then south-west and, funnelled by the Beagle Channel, was gusting at 50 knots. In that strong wind the Rutland wind generator was making an awful noise screeching like

a possessed devil and every now and again, when caught on its side, making a horrible deep growling sound like a propeller plane altering the pitch of its propeller as it comes in to land. Then, with a sudden high-pitched shriek, the generator started shaking so violently that the whole boat was shaking with it. With one final mortal judder it wrenched itself off its supports and flew into the sea, one of its blades hitting the stern where it left a deep indentation in the aluminium coaming. Ivan was standing in the cockpit and later, when I saw the deep gash caused by the blade, I realized that if it had hit him or anyone else it would have killed him. I have replaced the wind generator since, but now it is always disabled when I expect strong winds.

A strong wind against tide kicked up a huge swell in the Le Maire Strait before wrenching off the wind generator

Under those conditions we could neither sail nor motor in the desired direction, so we turned tail and ran back through the strait, hoping to find shelter in one of the bays on the north coast of Staten Island. With the tide still flowing in a southerly direction and the wind now blowing from the south, mountainous waves started forming within minutes. From almost a flat sea the waves had risen to at least five metres. It happened so quickly that it was almost impossible to believe that such changes could be so sudden. All four of us were huddled in the cockpit watching in awe as every now and again a massive wall of water would break over the stern and fill the cockpit. As I went below to change into something dry I saw water sloshing over the floor. When I lifted the nearest floor panel I found the bilges full of water and I shouted to Ivan to come and give me a hand. The small bilge pumps couldn't cope, but the large emergency Gusher 25 looked as if it was getting the level down. Meanwhile Ivan was doing what is often best: filling bucket after bucket and emptying them in the cockpit. I certainly saw how true it is that there is no better pump than a worried man with a bucket.

The source of all that water was still an absolute mystery so I asked Erick to have a good look when the next wave broke over us. I could already see from down below a massive wall of grey water advancing menacingly towards us. With a growling roar it broke over our stern. Over that terrible noise I heard Erick shouting 'Sacre dieux. Quelle connerie!'

I could see that water had already started pouring into the engine bilge when Erick shouted to me. 'I've got it. There are two ventilation vents for the engine room on the stern counter and somehow the water manages to find its way into the engine compartment.'

That was exactly what was happening and that one wave must have deposited at least fifty litres into the bilge. While Ivan and I were getting rid of it, Erick stuffed some rags into the vents and the problem was, at least temporarily, resolved.

At long last we reached the lee of Staten Island and made our way into the perfectly protected Hoppner Bay. At the head of the outer bay a narrow passage not much wider than Aventura's beam led into a calm pool surrounded by precipitous mountains. By the following morning, their slopes were covered in a dusting of snow reminding us that although this was the height of summer, in these latitudes, one could indeed have four seasons in one day. Later on we were joined by two other Millennium boats that had been prevented by the strength of the wind to get even close to the strait and had passed a miserable night hove to.

Hoppner Bay was the perfect place to relax after the beating we had received, and put right the damage sustained, which turned out to be much more serious as more breakages came to light, the worst being the flooded refrigerator electronics that put the whole system out of action, but as we were heading for Antarctica it was a piece of equipment that we could easily live without.

When I checked the source of that inflow of water into the engine compartment, I was amazed to find that the builders had connected each of the two vents to four-inch (100 mm) diameter plastic hoses that led into the engine compartment to provide air ventilation. This may have been an acceptable system for a boat normally used in benign conditions but was an irresponsible solution on an ocean going yacht like mine. At the first opportunity I changed the system so that the vents can be closed tightly in case of rough weather. On a few occasions I forgot to open them after the weather had passed but the engine never seemed to be starved of air with the vents closed, so it seems to have been a useless precaution.

A day later the weather improved and we sailed uneventfully through the strait and finally reached Puerto Williams, on the

A 60 knot williwaw in O'Brien Channel in Tierra del Fuego

southern shore of the Beagle Channel. One lesson I had quickly learned was that in those waters, when the conditions look right, you move, but when the prospects look doubtful you let patience prevail and wait for a break. With hindsight, we should not have attempted Le Maire in a rising wind and should have sought shelter sooner. We didn't - and paid the price!

South Indian Ocean, October 2004

Conditions were nowhere near as bad in another spell of bad weather that I encountered off Madagascar, en route to South Africa. At around 0100, during my watch, with the wind steady at 35 knots and gusting more, our speed never going below 9 knots, the pattern of the waves changed and the swell started to look menacing. I had seen higher waves in the Southern Ocean while returning from Antarctica to Cape Horn but was not expecting to see anything as bad in what I believed were the more benign waters of the Indian Ocean. In fact, the area south of Madagascar is a notorious place for its

sudden changes in weather and rough seas. They are caused by the meeting of two ocean current systems over a shallow shelf that extends about 150 miles south of the large island.

A warning received by Inmarsat C mentioned that a ship passing through that area had sighted one or more large floating logs. The threat of colliding with such a log was at the back of my mind as I stood my night watch but if you are not a fatalist, you have no business being in the middle of the ocean on a dark and windy night. With Aventura sailing fast and occasionally surfing down a large following wave we suddenly hit something so hard that it made the boat stop in its tracks. The collision sheared the pin connecting the autopilot ram to the rudder quadrant and also put the hydraulics out of action, both of which I managed to repair. Once we were under way again, I sat down in the corner of the cockpit and thought over the entire incident. In hindsight I seemed to have done everything right but this led me to think of other emergency situations that I had been through, and the advice I'd like to give to others.

The No.1 rule is not to panic. Keep calm, take a few seconds to assess the situation, draw up a plan of action and then act. Normally I am an excitable person and lose my temper quite easily, but I usually manage to keep my calm in a serious emergency situation. A similar attitude is also called for when dealing with heavy weather. Heavy weather means different things to different people but, under normal conditions, I only regard winds of over 50 knots to merit that description. With the exception of tropical storms, whose areas are fairly well defined and therefore avoiding them should be possible, spells of winds over 40 knots, especially along the usual cruising routes, are thankfully quite rare. Personally I can count the instances where I came face to face with really heavy weather on the fingers of one hand. The first instance of 50 knot winds I encountered early in my cruising life in the Bismark Sea, north of Papua New Guinea, while the most recent incident that springs to mind were the truly atrocious conditions recounted earlier that we experienced in the Strait of Le Maire off Patagonia. In between there had been a few other incidents that have taught me some valuable lessons, which are listed below, not necessarily in order of importance.

I do not have any general rules concerning the actual handling of the boat in heavy weather. So much depends on local circumstances, the type of boat and the skills of the crew. With the kind of boat Aventura is, I generally prefer to try and outsail bad weather. Above all else, the two most important things are an absolute confidence in yourself and in your boat. Any well built boat and its equipment should withstand conditions generated by winds of 50 or 60 knots. As with everything else to do with cruising, the secret is good preparation. But just as important is to keep calm, because however bad the weather may be, it will eventually come to an end. Whenever I am in a storm, at some point I remember one of my favourite songs, Dr Hook's "Storms Never Last". They never do!

Tips

- Uncluttered decks. The advent of a heavy blow is not the time to start worrying about lashing the dinghy, stowing sail bags, surfboard, jerrycans or any of the clutter that often marks the long distance cruising boat. Aventura's decks are absolutely bare with everything stowed away below or in the cockpit lockers, not just on long ocean passages but even when cruising short distances.
- A safe well protected cockpit where the crew can sit comfortably and preferably dry.
- Efficient sail handling and reefing systems so that reducing sail can be done quickly and easily, ideally from the cockpit, without putting the crew in danger.
- Good quality sails that can withstand a sudden strong gust or a squall long enough to allow the crew to reduce sail.
- A strong reliable autopilot. Especially if sailing short-handed a good pilot is absolutely essential. On many occasions in strong weather the fact that I could rely on the pilot to steer the boat allowed me to stay alert and concentrate on other things.
- Always carry a few ready meals such as tinned casseroles or stews to have a warm meal when cooking may be difficult.
- Dealing with heavy weather when it arrives is always easier if all necessary preparations have been made well in advance: foul weather gear and harnesses at the ready, a substantial meal, a hot drink in a thermos flask.

Antarctica to Alaska: A Transpacific Marathon

There is no other landmark in maritime lore to equal the awe inspiring Cape Horn.

The southernmost of a group of islands lying off Tierra del Fuego and the South American continent, the island was named Hoorn in 1616 by the Dutch navigator van Schouten. In fact there is now evidence that Sir Francis Drake landed there in 1578, but this was suppressed by the Elizabethan authorities as the discovery of a clear passage between the Atlantic and Pacific Oceans was deemed too important to be shared with other nations.

Whoever landed there first might have done so in the same spot where we landed ourselves, a small cove on the NE side of the island, close to the new lighthouse. Even in calm weather the landing is far from easy as the swell breaks over the rocky beach and the smooth stones are treacherously slippery. Having been forced to abandon a similar landing three years previously, this time I was determined to land come what may, so Ivan and I donned our survival suits, and took to our smaller dinghy, which would be easier to handle once we reached shallow water. As the bay is too deep for anchoring, Erick and Muriel stayed on board, hovering at a safe distance offshore.

The former military presence on the wind-swept island has now been replaced by a Chilean family. As the new lighthouse is automatic, the keeper's main job is to check by VHF the identity of any passing vessel. Visitors are warmly welcomed in their home, where there is a modest range of souvenirs for sale. The most sought after souvenir is the Cape Horn stamp, which now adorns Aventura's logbook and the passports of her crew. Next to the keeper's house stands a small chapel, built of driftwood and erected in memory of the countless mariners who over the centuries had lost their lives in these stormy waters. On a nearby hill stands an impressive steel sculpture of a wandering albatross, commissioned by the Cape Horners Association.

As the weather was unusually calm I asked the keeper if we could walk to Cape Horn itself. With an embarrassed smile he warned us that the path might be all right but as the entire area had been mined by the military during the conflict with Argentina, he wouldn't advise us to do so. Cape Horn mined! It was too much to bear, and so we returned to Aventura, happy to have landed there, but also disappointed to have come across such human stupidity at the very end of the world.

Back in Puerto Williams we checked in with the Chilean authorities. We then crossed the Beagle Channel to Ushuaia, in neighbouring Argentina, a busy cruise ship

Standing with Ivan by the distinctive monument erected by the Cape Horners Association

Anchored in Puerto Angusto possibly in the same spot as Joshua Slocum's Spray

anchored at the foot of mighty glaciers, we only met four cruising boats and about as many fishing boats. Indeed, from Puerto Williams to Puerto Eden, there is not one single settlement, not a farm, not even a house. Isolation is complete.

There were many more settlements once we reached the large island of Chiloe, and by the time we arrived in Valdivia, we were back in civilization. This is undoubtedly the best port on the west coast of South America to prepare the boat, either to continue into the South Pacific or for a cruise south through the Chilean canals. After weeks of wilderness it was good to finally arrive in this small town.

base and therefore the best place to stock up for the trip to either Antarctica or through the Chilean canals. I had been warned that going north absolutely nothing was available as far as Puerto Eden or Puerto Natales, a distance of some 600 miles, so we stocked up well on fuel and fresh produce.

We sailed in March from south to north, which is not the best way as the winds were almost invariably from ahead and usually very strong. Anyone planning to visit this beautiful part of the world should attempt to sail from north to south. A network of fiords and channels allows almost the entire distance to be sailed in protected waters. The south of Chile is in every respect a sailor's paradise: beautiful scenery of glaciers, tumbling waterfalls and primeval forests, countless sheltered anchorages, and not another boat in sight for hundreds of miles. It is difficult to comprehend the vastness of this country with a coastline of some 4000 miles. On a stretch of 600 miles, while we sailed through fiords and narrows,

The local authorities had pulled out all stops to make the final act of a two months stay in Chile of the Millennium Odyssey fleet an unforgettable experience for participants and locals alike. On the appointed morning the seven yachts sailed in convoy up the Valdivia river, escorted by several naval vessels, to dock in the city centre, where thousands of people had gathered to greet the bearers of the Millennium message. Non-stop coverage during the previous week in the national, local press and television had generated interest in our round the world rally, more than in any other country visited so far.

The Mayor of Valdivia welcomed us, stressing the pride of every Valdivian in having been chosen to represent the people of Chile in receiving the Millennium Flame

Flying two spinnakers in very light winds on the way to Easter Island

thousand of which had been distributed that morning. The sailors all felt, and behaved, like rock stars and thoroughly enjoyed all the attention.

For the Millennium Odyssey participants Valdivia was not only the most welcoming port in South America but also the port with the best provisioning and repair facilities. The route to Antarctica, Cape Horn and Chilean canals had put both the yachts and their crews to a great test of endurance, so the stop at Alwoplast, a boat building yard and marina operated by our host Alex Wopper, was essential to prepare men and machines for the next stage of their round the world adventure.

From Valdivia we struck out in a north-westerly direction: destination Easter Island. Erick and Muriel left us in Valdivia so this was the first long passage that Ivan and I had done on our own, and I was pleased at how well we got on. We made a good team, as Ivan liked to stay up late and get up late, whereas I always enjoy the dawn watch, which I regard as the most beautiful time of day. We worked out an ideal system: Ivan would take the first watch, immediately after dinner, around 9 p.m., until 1 or 2 a.m. I would take the rest of the night and let him sleep late as I knew that he didn't like getting up before nine, not even in London. Those night watches, alone in the cockpit, with the boat silently rushing along, were full of magic, especially the last hours: watching the sky turn slowly from black to dark blue, then start taking on all the colours of the rainbow before

and its message of peace and goodwill. He then conferred on the Millennium sailors the Freedom of the City and gave each participant a gold medallion bearing the arms of this once thriving port founded in the sixteenth century but devastated by a major earthquake in 1960. The skippers' logbooks were signed by the Military Governor of the region and then everyone went in procession into the Cathedral. Not since the Pope's visit had so many people crowded into it. The Bishop of Valdivia made a moving speech, stressing the wish of every nation to live in peace, and commending the Millennium sailors for carrying this message of hope around the world. We transferred the light from Aventura's lamp, which was one of the original lamps to have been lit in the church of the Holy Sepulchre, to a special presentation lamp, which I am told is still being kept alight in Valdivia's Cathedral. Hundreds of people waited for the crews outside the Cathedral asking them to autograph the official programme, four the sun rose over the horizon. Exquisite moments!

Between 9 and 10 I would make breakfast and on special occasions our favourite pancakes. The rest of the day was routine: we did maintenance work, read, listened to music, but as our tastes didn't mesh, we each had our own Walkman. One thing you soon learn on a small boat is to respect each other's space. We had plenty of time to talk, to comment on what we were reading, on the latest news on the BBC World Service, or Ivan's future plans. The windvane and autopilot did all the work so we hardly ever had to steer. Also, as the boat is easily handled by one person, it was very rare that I had to wake up Ivan to help me change sails, or vice versa. One dark night I managed to wrap our tri-radial spinnaker around the forestay. I had noticed what looked like a small squall approaching but had neglected or forgotten to move the autopilot from steering to compass to steering to wind, which is what I normally do when overtaken by a squall. I tried everything possible to unwrap the large spinnaker on my own but without success. Eventually I gave up and called Ivan. He offered to climb up the mast with his harness clipped to a spare halyard and then swing out to the forestay to unwrap the spinnaker, but it sounded too risky in the dark and I told Ivan that we should wait until daylight. He insisted that it should be done straight away.

'I have three spinnakers but only one son,' I retorted and sent him back to bed.

I did call him when it got light and we did save the spinnaker. It was one of the very rare moments of disagreement between us, perhaps the only time when I acted as father as well as skipper, and had the last word. The tension didn't last long as the next day we sighted Easter Island. Although we had made a reasonably fast passage

and had covered the 2,000 miles in exactly fifteen days, it had been my hope all along to arrive at Easter Island on Easter Sunday. Light winds and a blown spinnaker had scuppered my plans and in spite of our best efforts, we only managed to arrive on Easter Monday. Gwenda had been waiting for us for three days and we had a wonderful reunion after the long separation of over four months. During my long absence from home, Gwenda had completed

The anchorage off the settlement of Hangaroa on Easter Island

singlehandedly the transfer of World Cruising Club to the new owners, although the Millennium Odyssey continued to be my responsibility.

There are few places in the world more enigmatic than Easter Island, and arriving there on your own boat, making landfall at this very special island after two thousand miles of empty ocean, must be one of the most powerful experiences for any sailor. This was my second visit, having called at this Polynesian outpost of Rapa Nui on my first circumnavigation. Much had changed in the intervening years, yet much had remained the same. The anchorage off the main settlement at Hangaroa was just as precarious, the landing through the rollers just as exhilarating, and the weather just as unpredictable. The island's triangular shape offers little protection from wind or swell, so after several yachts had got into

from before. The giant statues were as awesome as when I first saw them, and so was the air of mystery that surrounded them. The experts still puzzle over how a stone age people managed to carve the enormous statues out of rock with rudimentary flint chisels and then transport them for several miles to erect them singly or in groups along the shoreline. In recent years some of the fallen statues have been re-erected onto their original platforms, albeit by using modern cranes, so now the island is ringed

A row of the mysterious giant statues face inland

difficulty and at least two lost when the wind changed direction unexpectedly and drove them ashore, the Port Captain now insisted that someone must remain onboard all the time.

Once ashore, what was immediately noticeable is how much more geared to tourism the island had become. Fortunately this first impression was confined to Hangaroa itself, because out of town, the island looked just the same wind-swept place that I remembered

with scores of statues looking inland with their backs to the sea just as they had done all those hundreds of years ago.

No less fascinating, although for very different reasons, was our next destination: Pitcairn. As this section of the Millennium Odyssey, from Valdivia to French Polynesia, was run as a pursuit race, with individual boats stopping the clock when they arrived at one of the islands, and restarting it as they left, both at Easter Island and Pitcairn there were only three Millennium boats there at the same time. Because of the very special

Millennium Odyssey participants ferried ashore in a Pitcairn Island longboat

significance of Pitcairn, the leading boats had agreed to coordinate their arrival so as to be there together. As the islanders are Seventh Day Adventists, it was decided to perform the Millennium Flame ceremony on a Sabbath. The arrival of three Millennium yachts at the same time caused such a stir in the tiny community that any other day would have done just as well.

As on Easter Island, we were strongly advised not to leave the boats unattended as, according to our concerned hosts, several boats had been lost in Bounty Bay while the crew were visiting ashore. Unbelievably, two of the incidents involved the same owner, on subsequent visits, several years apart. The joke among the islanders was that the original Bounty was finally burned by the mutineers not in order to destroy any evidence of their presence on the island but because they could not cope with moving the ship every time the wind shifted, just as visiting yachts have to nowadays. We certainly sympathized with the mutineers!

Their descendants continue to be intrepid sailors and they showed that by the impeccable manner in which they manoeuvered their longboat through the raging surf into the tiny harbour. Four men had come out to take us ashore at first light, their names sounding like a roll call of the original mutineers: Young, Warren, Brown and, as to be expected, Christian. They were too young to remember us from our previous visit but once ashore we met several old friends who greeted us warmly. Ivan met some friends of his own age whom he and Doina had joined in the tiny classroom twenty-one years previously, instantly raising the school population from seven to nine.

Once ashore, we were all loaded onto several quad bikes and whizzed up a rough track into Adamstown to be greeted at the church by what looked like the entire island's population of sixty-seven. I had kept in contact throughout the intervening years with Tom Christian, a direct descendant of Fletcher Christian, the man who started it all. Tom accepted the Millennium Flame on behalf of the small community, a gesture that I found highly symbolic listening to his comments as the heir of the best known mutineer in history. We were then treated to some beautiful singing, including two moving good-bye songs that Pitcairners normally sing to departing ships. Each crew was then adopted by a separate family, first for lunch, then for a tour of the island on one of those four-wheeled monsters. Loaded with tropical fruit we were taken back to the boats just before nightfall and, as the anchorage looked just as precarious as when we had arrived, rather than spend another rolly sleepless night we all decided to leave immediately.

Not long after our visit, the island was hit by a scandal totally out of proportion to Pitcairn's tiny size. As a British colony, the government had received a number of allegations of under age rape and sex abuse mainly from adult women now settled in New Zealand. The allegations were so grave that they could not be ignored and the British police were instructed to start an enquiry. On the conclusion of the police enquiry a legal team landed on Pitcairn where a courthouse and prison were erected. Six men were found guilty, sentenced to various prison terms and even after several appeals, the sentences were

Leaving Pitcairn just as darkness envelopes the small island

upheld by the highest court in 2006. However, the men will be released temporarily to help handle the longboats that ferry supplies to the island from passing ships.

From the local point of view, what the accused said in their defence should be looked at objectively. Accepting the reality of under age sex as a traditional feature of life in Polynesia and particularly on remote

Pitcairn does not mean condoning it, but one has to accept that in other parts of the world people do live differently to us and have different moral standards and values. If the Pitcairners manage to put this sad episode behind them and the outside world backs off, I am sure they will survive as a community, otherwise those wounds may never go away and may end up destroying the fragile fabric of this small community.

The small island stood out clearly for a long time in the gathering dusk as one by one we set our spinnakers and headed for Mangareva, 300 miles away. While the French nuclear test programme was still underway at nearby Mururoa atoll, visits by foreign vessels to the Gambier Islands, of which Mangareva is the main island, were not permitted. All that has changed now, so the Gambiers, one of French Polynesia's five groups of islands, made a perfect landfall. Being finally able to drop the anchor in a quiet, protected, tropical lagoon after so many thousand miles was sheer bliss. This was our second visit to Mangareva having spent one unforgettable month there in 1978 when, during our first voyage, we had made a long detour from Panama and had swept south to visit Easter Island and Pitcairn before making landfall there. The French nuclear programme was in full swing at Mururoa but I pleaded with the local chief of the gendarmerie who telexed Tahiti that we should be allowed to stay for health reasons, and the permission was duly granted. We stayed there for one month, Doina and Ivan went to school, and we easily integrated into the lives of the one hundred strong community. The two gendarmes, Iotua, a burly Polynesian from the island of Tahaa and his French sidekick Manu, their two wives, as well as Ivan's teacher Lucas Paeamara, became our friends. We spent every day with them, took them out fishing on Aventura outside

The craggy peaks of Rapa, the southernmost of the Austral Islands

in order to visit the Australs, the group of islands lying some 500 miles south of Tahiti. By the time we left Mangareva it was already late April and thus close to winter, so we had strong westerly winds and had to tack most of the way. Gwenda, who had been expecting tropical sailing conditions, was not impressed.

'This is about as nice as sailing in the English Channel in winter. It still beats me why you had to be so stubborn and come here.'

'I am sorry, but as you may remember we were going to come here in 1978 and I just could not resist the temptation this time.'

The history of Rapa is just as mysterious as that of its eastern namesake and there are several hilltop fortresses on the island whose origin is still under debate. Just outside the tropics the weather in Rapa is so damp and cold that there are no palm trees. These grow in abundance on Raivavae, 300 miles further north. Raivavae rates as one of the most beautiful islands we have seen anywhere and is certainly on a par with Bora Bora as the mountainous island and its lagoon are similarly ringed by a coral reef.

the lagoon, lived off the fertile land and, in hindsight, came closest to what could only be described as heaven on earth.

The island had changed a lot since our first visit. The population had diminished and the friendly laid-back atmosphere seemed to have gone. The arrival of the fortnightly supply ship, and its large supply of beer, was eagerly awaited and I could no longer detect any of the strong community feeling that I had noticed during our first visit. Lucas was now the mayor and he agreed sadly that things would never be the same again. In every sense of the word this was paradise lost.

Never content to sail in a strait line, when a detour would do as well, on leaving Mangareva I decided on just such a detour

We had better winds on our way to Tahiti, whose main port of Papeete was overflowing with sailboats when we joined the rest of the Millennium Odyssey fleet. After sailing separate routes for the last eight months, the smaller South American fleet merged here with the forty boats that had taken the Panama Canal route. It was a time of happy reunions, swapping stories and, for Aventura, of preparing for the second half of our Pacific Odyssey: Tahiti to Alaska.

There are few places in the world to better the cruising attractions of the leeward group of the Society Islands. The four islands of Huahine, Raiatea, Tahaa and Bora Bora are close to each other so that it is relatively easy to visit them all. Each has its own lagoon, except Raiatea and Tahaa which share one, the winds in winter (May to November) are the fairly reliable SE trade winds, shore facilities are of a high standard and the cuisine is French. What more can one ask?

The sustained rhythm of our long trek from Antarctica to Tahiti had left its mark on both Ivan and I so we savoured to the full a leisurely one month long interlude in French Polynesia. We had a rendezvous with the Millennium Odyssey fleet in Bora Bora, where the Millennium Flame and its symbol of peace, was accepted on behalf of his people by the Mayor of the island, Gaston Tong Son, who had hosted all the previous rallies. A lavish farewell dinner was laid on by our host while the famous Bora Bora Mamas entertained us with their well honed repertoire of nostalgic Polynesian songs.

The unmistakable silhouette of Mount Otemanu provided the perfect backdrop for the start the following morning as the large fleet tacked around a windward mark at the far end of the lagoon and then, one by one, the boats rushed through the pass into the open sea bound for Tonga and beyond. Gwenda left us here and we were joined by my niece Marianne, who was going to sail with us all the way to Hawaii. Having fulfilled our job as committee vessel, immediately after the start we tacked back to Raiatea for a symbolic stop at an ancient site reputed to be the largest religious site in Polynesia. It was from this very island, whose traditional name was Havaiki, that intrepid sailors set off to colonize the far-flung corners of the vast Polynesian triangle: Hawaii, Rapa Nui (Easter Island) and Aotearoa (New Zealand).

Our own route took us towards the apex of that magic triangle as on leaving Raiatea we headed almost due north towards distant Hawaii. We must have pleased the Polynesian gods, and in particular Tangaroa, the god of the sea, because we had excellent winds right from the start. In early June the winds were from ENE, so we were sailing on a close reach and rarely have I had a more perfect week. With winds at a constant 15 knots, Aventura rarely sailed below 7 knots, so that in one week we clocked 1100 miles, and that included stops at Flint and Malden islands. Fishing was also excellent, so the only word to describe this week was perfection.

Our first stop was at Flint, an uninhabited island, about 330 miles due north of Raiatea. We had a wet and exciting landing through the breaking surf and could well understand why the island is hardly ever

A booby and its chick on uninhabited Malden Island

visited. To get ashore we used our smaller Avon dinghy, which we rowed up to the surf line, then jumped out and waded ashore. We would probably have ruined the outboard engine if we had taken it with us as the following surf capsized the dinghy when we reached shallow water. But all the effort was justified by landing on the pristine beach obviously untouched by human feet for a long time. The island was covered in coconut trees and an impenetrable curtain of vegetation that came down to the waterline made it impossible to advance more than a very short distance inland.

Excellent winds gave us a fast passage to our next stop, the also uninhabited Malden Island, which had been used by the US military during the nuclear testing program of the 1950s. The island still bore the scars of this devastation, with rusting military equipment abandoned all over the place. We anchored on the west side out of the swell and rowed ashore but just as we approached the surf line and were getting ready to jump in we saw two large black tipped sharks cruising along. As they seemed interested in us we rowed on until we touched the bottom with the result that the surf overturned the dinghy and threw it on top of us. Fortunately our cameras had been packed in a sealed container so we escaped with just a few scratches. As at our dunking on Flint Marianne found this to be extremely hilarious and kept pointing at the black fins laughing her head off. Ashore, the landscape was punctuated by mounds of rusting drums and abandoned hardware but life was obviously returning to this devastated island, as nature was making a determined effort to reclaim the land, with bushes growing out of decaying steel drums and scores of seabirds nesting in the few trees.

The day after we crossed the equator we came to our next stop, which also had its own nuclear past. Christmas Island was used for the British nuclear

Leisurely fishing under sail off Fanning Island

tests in the 1950s and several decades later the islanders were still struggling to wipe out the consequences of this devastation. Even if radiation is said to have ceased to be a hazard, the amount of military hardware that litters the island and the lagoon is depressing. Mountains of rusting metal and huge abandoned fuel tanks lined the beaches and as the local population was either unable or unwilling to use whatever natural building materials were available, such as palm and pandanus, the main settlement, grandly called London, consisted of sad looking shacks patched together from bits of corrugated tin. Malden and Christmas are a permanent reminder of how twentieth century man has raped the environment, without any thought for the consequences of his actions. The contrast to what the Polynesians had left behind on Raiatea was not only striking, but also an unforgivable indictment of modern man's attitude to the environment. Perhaps the same rules should be applied here as in Antarctica where the former polluters are now obliged to return and clean up the mess they had left behind.

Christmas Island belongs to Kiribati, formerly the Gilbert Islands, and, for some strange reason is in the same time zone as Tarawa, the nation's capital, which lies some 2000 miles to the west across the international dateline. Undeterred by distance, the Kiribati government had decided that both islands should have the same day, so the locals proudly pointed out that, as a consequence of this clever sleight of hand, they had beaten all opposition and Christmas had managed to be the very first island in the world to greet the dawn of the new millennium.

All Fanning Island houses are made entirely from natural materials

Our general impression of Christmas Island wasn't helped by the unbending attitude of the immigration official, who, on hearing that Ivan had lost his passport, ordered him immediately back on board where he had to remain throughout our stay. Ivan had discovered the loss in Raiatea just as I was going to the gendarmerie to clear out. As we were leaving the territory the French official did not seem concerned, but we knew that we might have serious problems when we arrived in Hawaii.

The atmosphere of Christmas left us with a bitter taste and we were quite concerned that the next Line Island, Fanning, would be no different. How pleasantly surprised we were to be! As we reached the protection of the large atoll, we came across a dozen one-man outrigger canoes out in the ocean trolling for fish under sail. The perfectly formed atoll encloses a large lagoon with a narrow opening to the ocean. The pass can be easily located on the west side of the lagoon, but one can only enter at slack water as at all other times a fierce current sweeps through the narrow passage. The

locals call it "the river", as indeed the water rushes out at over 6 knots. We timed our arrival to coincide with the moon meridian passage and must have done something right because we did arrive at slack water. We made our way in and anchored off the nearest village. Although we had already cleared in at Christmas, we were supposed to complete formalities again with both police and customs. We found the policeman asleep at home and as it was a Saturday I kindly suggested that we didn't mind waiting until Monday, failing to mention Ivan's lost passport.

As the island is rarely visited by cruising boats, and even the supply ship from Tarawa only calls four times a year, the islanders were extremely welcoming. It was a pleasure to walk through the villages and be greeted warmly by everyone. Suddenly we were back in the Pacific as I knew it from before. The island was neat and tidy, and every house was made of local materials. Fanning also belongs to Kiribati and its correct name is Tabuaeran, and not Teraina, as appears on various charts and in many publications. Teraina is the correct name of

Washington, also one of the Line Islands, lying further north.

One day we borrowed the only three bikes on the island and cycled along the west side of the atoll, which is made up of several smaller islands linked by bridges or causeways. Every house was built from traditional materials of palm and pandanus and surrounded by a cleanly swept courtyard where hens were pecking in the dust. Pigs were kept in separate enclosures on the shore of the lagoon, well away from the villages. The islanders appeared to be remarkably self-sufficient, this being more than obvious in the one and only store that had only a few basic supplies, flour, rice, corned beef, the perennial Pacific staple of cabin bread, a hard rusk type biscuit and, surprisingly, canned fish. The sea, lagoon and well-tended land supported several villages, and everyone looked well nourished and healthy.

As we cycled quietly along, we heard some beautiful singing that reverberated all around us. We looked around but could see nothing. As we got closer to the source of the singing, it appeared to come from above and indeed it was as on top of a tall coconut palm we saw a man wielding his machete while singing at the top of his voice. We leant the bikes against the trunk and waited for him to climb down. In surprisingly good English he explained that he was collecting toddy and offered us some to taste. The unfermented variety is sickly sweet, but once fermented the syrup produces a potent drink. He pointed to a number of bottles suspended from the fronds of the surrounding palms, each collecting the thick sap drop by drop.

We cycled as far as we could go and only turned around when the track came to an end. On the way back we stopped in several villages to talk to people, but one memory that sticks in the mind more than any other

was that of a group of children, sitting in the middle of the dusty track... busy playing cards. We stopped, looked again and could barely believe our eyes, and just in case no one believed me, I quickly took some photos. This little incident epitomized perhaps better than anything else the carefree and relaxed existence those people were living. The land and sea provided enough food for everyone, and, from what we could see, there was little animosity among people, perhaps with the notable exception of the community being divided between Catholic and Protestant villages.

All too soon it was time to go. When the time came to leave we had to clear out and inform the policeman that Ivan had no passport. By then we had made a number of friends, Ivan had repaired the priest's CB radio and I had given a young fisherman enough material to make himself a sail for his canoe, so the policeman simply pretended not to notice. While our friends waved us off there were a few tears on both sides as "the river" got hold of us and spewed us into the ocean.

At least we knew that we wouldn't need passports at our next stop: Palmyra. We had heard on the cruising grapevine that a French sailor and former chef, Roger Dextrait, had settled on this island, which in those days was privately owned by a family from Hawaii. The owners employed Roger, who arrived here on his yacht in 1992, to keep an eye on things and make sure that visiting sailors did not overstay their welcome. The atoll had been declared a nature reserve and Roger was doing his best to correct some of the abuses of the past.

Roger led a truly Robinson Crusoe life on this large atoll, where nature was gradually returning things to normal after its devastation by the military during the second world war. Diving in the lagoon was among the best in the entire Pacific, with a profusion of tropical fish, giant manta rays, turtles and perhaps too many sharks. On land, the birds reigned supreme and there were tens of thousands of them, especially on the former airfield where one could hardly walk without risking stepping on their nests.

The future of Palmyra Atoll as a nature reserve is now guaranteed as recently it has been purchased and is now owned jointly by The Nature Conservancy (TNC) and the US Fish and Wildlife Department. All visits

Ivan and Roger brave the birds on Palmyra's airstrip

by cruising boat must be prearranged by email Palmyra@inix.com. TNC also have an office in Honolulu at 923 Nuuana Avenue. There are permanent caretakers on Palmyra and only one week stops are allowed

We left Palmyra with a heavy heart, not only because of Roger's unmatched hospitality, his heart of palm salad defies description, but also because we knew that the passage to Hawaii was likely to be hard on the wind. The accepted tactic is to make

as much easting as possible before entering the area of prevailing NE trade winds. Unfortunately that summer, the Inter-Tropical Convergence Zone (ITCZ) was virtually on top of Palmyra and strong NE winds were blowing all the way from there to Hawaii. After leaving Palmyra, we tried to keep south of the ITCZ and make some easting in lower latitudes. Then, to our great fortune, around 20 June Hurricane Adrian, the first tropical storm of the season, that was forming off the coast of Baja California, came to our help. From blowing from almost dead ahead, the winds started having some easting in them, enough to allow us to sail close hauled on course. By this time we had already managed to make some 200 miles of easting, but we still had 1,000 miles to sail hard on the wind. We managed to stay on the starboard tack all the way to Oahu and arrived in Honolulu less than nine days after leaving Palmyra. As we closed with the shore at dawn scores of surfers were bobbing up and down ahead of us trying to catch the right wave. This was Hawaii as I had always imagined it.

I had managed to get a space at the Waikiki Yacht Club and for one indulgent week we savoured the unlimited attractions of Honolulu, where everything was available and life was obviously there to be enjoyed. The entry formalities could not have been simpler. Thanks to our Inmarsat C we had been able to fax the British consulate in Los Angeles about Ivan's lost passport. The consulate had informed the relevant US officials, so when we

At rest off Johns Hopkins Glacier on completion of the voyage from Antarctica to Alaska

arrived in Honolulu the immigration official could not have been nicer. He fined Ivan $170 and gave him a temporary landing permit. Ivan eventually got a new passport flown out to Alaska.

My old friend, Alan Sitt, who had sailed with us from Peru to Easter Island in 1978, was now living on the west coast of Oahu, having built himself a large house right on the beach with reputedly the best surfing conditions in the world. His title as surfing champion had been taken over by his elder son and Alan was working as a pilot towing up gliders from a nearby airstrip. We arrived in great style, in a Jaguar XK8 convertible, a treat to myself as this was my favourite car but appreciated even more by Marianne, who insisted on jumping in and out without opening the door as she had seen done in Hollywood films. Alan took us up in turn in his plane to see Oahu from above and treated each of us to a glider lesson.

Marianne left us here and, in preparation for the long trek to Alaska, we moved to the island of Hanalei from where in early July we set off on the 2,500 miles passage to Sitka in Alaska. A huge North Pacific high was generating strong NE winds, so we sailed as close to the wind as possible on a course that pointed dead north along the meridian of Hanalei (159°W), and thus kept to the west of the high pressure area. While we were sailing fast to the north, the high pressure area started moving west, so by the time we had reached 29°N we were right inside the high, and, not surprisingly, the wind fell to almost nothing and soon we were totally becalmed. We had no choice but to motor through this calm patch and by the time we reached 33°N we started picking up SW winds. For a while they were light but good enough for our large spinnaker. By 38°N the winds had gone miraculously into the SE and remained there as far as 46°N before veering to SW. Most of the time we had only 10 knots of true wind, so we kept changing from our tri-radial to the asymmetric spinnaker and back again, making consistently good progress. As we moved into colder waters, the fog came down and we had to rely on radar as visibility dropped to a boat's length. We encountered several fishing boats, mostly Japanese, and had to avoid them as they took no notice of us. For several days the fog was so thick that we could see absolutely nothing, so we set the radar alarm with a guard at 6 miles... and carried on sailing blindly into the milky void. A very eerie feeling! By 53°N the wind started going to WNW, and although the fog and occasional rain were still with us, with 15 to 18 knots of wind we were sailing fast. We arrived in Sitka 17 days after leaving Hanalei, managing this time to get there one day before Gwenda joined us from London.

Sitka is undoubtedly the best place to make landfall in SE Alaska as it has excellent facilities. The next five weeks were spent cruising SE Alaska and British Columbia. The scenery is in many ways a mirror image of the Chilean fiordland with the notable exception of the busy traffic of cruise ships, fishing and pleasure boats. By keeping away from some of the most popular spots we managed to have some places to ourselves, the highlights of our Alaskan cruise were seeing salmon jump an almost vertical waterfall, having an unexpected encounter with a grizzly bear and its cub in a shallow bay where we had dried out overnight, and the picture postcard beauty of Glacier Bay where we were surrounded by a large pod of killer whales, while in British Columbia we liked best the wild grandeur of Princess Louise Inlet.

Having achieved my objective of sailing in one season from Antarctica to Alaska, covering 15,000 miles in only four months, I had to admit that if I carried on with the original plan and continued to California, I would find it impossible to manage the complex programme of the Millennium Odyssey by email. As I felt that my first responsibility lay with that event I decided to return to Europe. In Vancouver, BC, I took the easy option and loaded Aventura on to a Dutch transporter ship for the long trip to the Mediterranean. These special ships, which now ply regularly between Europe, the Caribbean, the west and east coasts of the US, as well as the South Pacific, are similar to a floating dry dock. Behind the bridge there is a vast dockbay, which takes up almost the entire length of the ship. This is filled with water by sinking the ship to the required depth so that the motorboats and sailing vessels can drive in through the open stern like into a marina. Once the docking operation is completed, the huge chambers are emptied of water and the yachts settle down in previously prepared cradles. On arrival, the operation is carried out in reverse, the ship sinks, the dockbay is filled with water, you untie your lines and float out. An amazingly simple and efficient operation! Six weeks later we unloaded Aventura in France.

Routing and Navigation

Skipper: You need to point higher. Just look at the stars! The minor, the major, whatever they are called.
Crew: Ursa Minor and Ursa Major.
Skipper: What?
Crew: Ursa Minor and Ursa Major. That's what they are called. Also known as the Big Dipper and Little Dipper.
Skipper: Well, point at them, aim for the middle.

Ocean routing

My interest in ocean routing goes back even further than my interest in sailing. As a young boy I often leafed nostalgically through an old atlas, imagining all those places where one day I would land from my own boat. Dreamily I would trace with my finger a route across an ocean that would take me to a tiny dot of an island: Fakarava or Nuku Hiva or some other such beautifully enticing name. I could not have been much older than eight when I started writing an adventure book in which I set off with my closest friends on a world voyage in a boat with the English title of Friend Ship. At least in that respect I was not a late starter.

My practical interest in ocean routing was born during our first round the world voyage when I realized, mainly from the books of previous voyagers, just how important it was for the overall safety of a voyage to plan the best route possible. Immediately after our return in 1981 I started working on the book that was to become World Cruising Routes. My research work took me from the British Museum to the Maritime Museum in Greenwich, right at the zero meridian, where I was given permission to study the original logs of many ships that roamed the oceans in the early nineteenth century. I was even allowed to look at Captain's Cook original logs and I can still feel the thrill of seeing the neat writing of the man whom I regard as the greatest navigator of all times.

My own voyaging, the lessons learnt from all those captains as well as the writings of other sailors such as Erick Hiscock, have formed the basis of my attitude to routing. Put simply, it is to always do one's best to be in the right place at the right time and, conversely, to avoid at all cost being in the wrong place at the wrong time. I have no doubt that this is the reason why in all these years of ocean sailing I have never been in really serious trouble. There may be a contradiction here between my willingness to take risks in my earlier shorebound life and this cautious attitude when sailing. Yet as I gained experience I have indeed taken some calculated risks. Some recent examples are the decision to leave Fiji for New Zealand early in the season or setting off the following year for New Caledonia when the safe season had barely started. On the other hand, the marathon that Ivan and I sailed from Antarctica to Alaska, had been carefully planned to coincide with the safest seasons and was consequently accomplished without any mishap.

Weather routing

Having done all my early sailing at a time when there were no weather forecasts for ocean passages, my offshore strategy had to be based on the actual conditions being experienced. In those days one of my favourite aids were the monthly pilot charts that showed average conditions for every month of the year: wind strength and direction, percentage of gale force winds, tropical storms and their tracks, ocean currents, etc. The charts had been compiled over a number of years and were based on observations made by ships' captains, so they presented a fairly accurate picture of what could be expected at certain times in any given area of an ocean. Plotting a hypothetical route with this kind of information at one's fingertips was not only easy but highly enjoyable and satisfying.

This is how I learnt my trade and there is nothing new in this because ever since man ventured onto the seas, he always tried to take the best advantage of existing conditions. In historic times, it is well known that the Phoenicians had an almost instinctive way of choosing the right time to sail west across the Mediterranean during spells of easterly winds, and got their timing right to sail home with favourable westerlies. The Vikings made repeated voyages from Scandinavia to what they called Vinland in present North America by taking advantage of the prevailing easterly winds of high latitudes, returning home with the westerlies that blow further south. Since ancient times Arab navigators sailed on regular trading voyages between the Gulf and East Africa, sailing south-west during the favourable NE monsoon and returning home with the equally favourable SW monsoon.

Christopher Columbus was probably the greatest opportunist among navigators, having instinctively picked the best route to sail from Europe to what was to become the New World with the prevailing NE

winds and return home the following spring with the prevailing North Atlantic westerlies. He was the first to realize that there was a logic to this Atlantic merry-go-round and there is still keen debate as to whether he could have discovered this simply by chance.

The sailing ships of the eighteenth and early nineteenth centuries are the best example of how commercial considerations were responsible for the development of some of the most effective sailing machines ever built. However well they sailed, their masters always made sure that weather conditions were in their favour. After all, what is more telling than the fact that in English those favourable winds are

Everything has a backup on Aventura with the two laptops being interchangeable

called "trade" winds. In all other languages they have a generic name to do with their regularity or seasonality such as Passat (German), Alisées (French) but only a mercantile nation like the British could think of naming winds "commercial" which, in my view, also goes for other irritating English expressions such as Boxing Day for the second day of Christmas, or Bank Holidays for what are after all public holidays for everyone, not just bankers.

As sailing vessels evolved and were no longer so dependent on being able to sail only with following winds, navigators became more daring and started bucking the trend by going against the established weather systems. However, the principle of planning long voyages to coincide with the best season was never abandoned. In this respect contemporary cruising sailors have remained highly traditional in their approach, even if today many prefer to play safe and obtain as much weather routing information as possible. The main cruising routes of the world have remained virtually unchanged and still follow the old trade wind routes from east to west across the oceans. Everything that I do and anywhere I go is strongly influenced by World Cruising Routes and in its regularly updated editions I do try to give my readers the very best information and advice on how to safely plan a voyage to almost anywhere in the world. On a few occasions I have gone against my own advice, most recently when I decided to take the shortest route from Cape Town to the Mediterranean via the Canaries, rather than the traditional but much longer route via the Caribbean, or the Azores. My gamble paid off and showed that this rarely sailed route is quite feasible. On the other hand, maybe I was, as often in the past, just plain lucky.

The tactics outlined in World Cruising Routes for specific routes all follow the basic principle not only to be in the right place at the right time but also to take the best possible advantage of prevailing weather conditions. The most frequented routes describe the best tactics for the successful completion of such classic passages as crossing the Atlantic from the Canaries to the Caribbean, from Galapagos to the Marquesas, around the Cape of Good Hope into the South Atlantic or returning from the Caribbean to the USA or Europe at the end of the winter season. In more recent editions I have also tried to help those who wish to divert from the beaten track by returning to the tropics from New Zealand via Tahiti, sailing from Micronesia to Hawaii against winds and current or, as I did myself recently, take the shortest route from South Africa to the Mediterranean.

This is a suitable moment to look at some of the reasons why people attempt to sail against the grain not just by going against the prevailing conditions but often setting off in the wrong season or along an illogical route. Most do it out of ignorance, but they soon learn that there is more to ocean routing than drawing a line along a desired track. Many such cases, some with grave consequences, have come to my knowledge over the years but I will mention only one.

While in Chagos I was approached by the American owner of a 50 foot boat who told me that he was planning to sail to Perth, in Western Australia, as he had arranged to meet his family and grandchildren there.

'Not easy at the best of times.' I warned him. 'You will be sailing against the prevailing winds and, if you do not leave soon, you risk running into the next cyclone season.'

'I can deal with both. I still have two hundred gallons of fuel and avoiding cyclones is not all that difficult if you know what you are doing.'

A few months later I got an email from another sailor whom I had met in Chagos, who told me that the American yacht did leave soon after my own departure and got back to Chagos three months later battered, exhausted, with all sails torn, only having been able to make less than one thousand miles towards its intended destination.

Routing advice

World Cruising Routes is complemented by *www.noonsite.com* where we get many queries from cruising sailors about routing and weather. Often the proposed routes are either plainly wrong or planned during the risky season, or both. My usual reaction is to say that I would not attempt such a route myself and suggest a safer alternative. Occasionally, a few months later, I get a contrite email admitting to having been wrong and wishing they had listened to my advice. In late summer 2006 I was asked by the owner of a 80 foot sailing yacht to advise him on the best route to sail from Singapore to Western Australia. Just as in the previous example, he was planning to do it close to the start of the South Indian Ocean cyclone season, so I warned him about this, and also told him that even at the best of times the voyage would be difficult or even impossible to accomplish if sailed along the proposed direct route across Indonesia to the Sunda Strait and on to Fremantle in Western Australia.

'I am sure it can be done,' he replied confidently, 'I have a good crew and a good boat. Anyway, the alternative route that you described is far too long, so I'd rather take a chance on the shortest available option.'

My advice had been to wait and sail the much longer but ultimately safer route by heading east from Singapore via the Philippines, make easting by staying close north of the equator to take advantage of the east-setting North Equatorial Counter Current, cross the Line far enough east to get a good angle across the SE trade winds

of the South Pacific, then take a long sweep so as to sail south of Australia during the narrow window at the height of the southern summer (December to February) when, with a bit of luck, there is a good chance of having a spell of easterly winds across the Great Australian Bight to reach Western Australia. The main problem with such a route is that in order to take advantage of the safest seasons on both sides of the equator (January to April in the North Pacific, May to October in the South

Aventura's functional nav station with everything close to hand

Pacific), the voyage could take as long as one year.

About a month later my worst expectations were confirmed when I received an email from my correspondent saying that I had been absolutely right. Having made it past the Sunda Strait without too much difficulty, once they hit the South Indian Ocean proper, the strong SE winds made it impossible for them to make any headway towards their goal. They took long tacks to no avail; they tried shorter tacks with the same result. Gear started to break, the crew were close to mutiny, so eventually they turned around and crept back tails between their legs to Singapore.

'You were absolutely right and now I wish I had listened to you and taken the longer route as you so wisely suggested. I realize that not only is it a much safer option but it also would give us an opportunity to do some cruising en route, both in the North and South Pacific. I assure you that once I manage to get the boat back into shape, that's exactly what I am going to do', wrote the contrite owner.

'Best of luck,' I replied. 'It's always better to be safe than sorry.'

So what are the main reasons for such illogical decisions? As I mentioned earlier, ignorance or wishful thinking is usually the main cause. Time pressure from crew or family or simply the need to deliver a boat on time are other causes. One of the worst things to do is to take on certain commitments without realizing the consequences, something that happened repeatedly among participants in the ARC. I was often amazed to hear how boats got into trouble sailing south from Europe for the start of the ARC in the Canaries by leaving too late because the skipper didn't want to set off before someone's birthday party or some other such trivial reason. Almost every year boats heading for the ARC get into serious trouble crossing the Bay of Biscay and however much skippers are warned to do this early in the summer, when conditions are usually the best, every time a boat gets into serious difficulty it is because the voyage had started too late in the season.

Many of the sailors joining the ARC have little offshore experience and although they have sailed to the start in the Canaries, they are much more concerned about the Atlantic crossing. At the pre-start briefings I always tried to make them understand the importance of a well prepared boat backed by good planning and timing. The impending crossing of an ocean can be a frightening prospect for inexperienced sailors so I tried to reason that offshore experience can only be acquired by practice and the only way is to bite the bullet and do it. The main source of anxiety was the size of the Atlantic itself. The way to cope with such immensity is to reduce it in one's mind into a number of shorter segments, thus making the task look more manageable. After all, things can go wrong even on a five mile trip down the coast. What matters is to be well prepared and that means the boat, crew, and above all, the skipper must be mentally prepared to face any challenge that the ocean may throw at him or her.

Paper charts and electronic plotters

Having been struck by lightning four times, of which three times were in a span of only seventeen days, I am a real advocate of using paper charts... or at the least to carry the essential charts as a backup

Michelle LaMontagne

One important aid to navigation that I have only acquired recently is an electronic chart plotter. The reason why I waited so long was mainly because over the years I had acquired a vast collection of paper charts that cover virtually the entire world. For my latest voyage, which in some places followed a route that I had not sailed before, I only had to buy maybe a dozen new charts.

Although most of my old charts are out of date and allowances have to be made to match them with GPS positions, they can still be used, especially on offshore

Astronavigation lesson for Ivan
on Aventura I

passages. The best way to describe my attitude to this important subject is to call it old-fashioned. Having completed a first circumnavigation with a sextant and paper charts I still find such charts useful for offshore navigation. The main reason, however, for my reluctance to move with the times is that I feel paper charts are more user-friendly as they provide a general picture and both myself and my crew enjoy watching the daily positions creep slowly towards our destination. I had great pleasure when I pulled out the chart of the Torres Strait and saw it crisscrossed with the lines of position of our two previous passages through that area.

On offshore passages I always mark the current position at noon, a leftover from my early cruising days when the daily noon sight was always something to look forward to. That routine was followed religiously every day with one sight just before the sun crossed the local meridian followed by another sight soon after the sun started its slow descent. Those two sights were the most important of the day as a simple calculation allowed me to work out both latitude and longitude. I have followed this noon routine throughout my sailing life, although

nowadays I simply plot the latest noon position from the GPS. The distance run from noon to noon is announced to the waiting crew and then it's time for lunch. Those early noon sights had played such an important role in our life that, at Ivan's suggestion, we named our website *www.noonsite.com*.

There is an obvious drawback to using old charts and that is their inaccuracy. Whereas in more frequented areas charts have been brought up to date to accord with GPS, in some remote areas charts are rarely corrected nor do they tally with GPS positions. For me this is not a serious handicap as by not expecting charts to be entirely accurate forces me to keep alert all the time. Nowadays my sextant has been confined to a locker and I use GPS for all basic navigation. GPS positions, even if they do not entirely agree with an older chart, are still a great improvement in accuracy over astronavigation.

As I stress in chapter 37 the conviction that you know exactly where you are can be quite dangerous and I know of several boat losses caused by over-reliance on GPS. While sailing in the Tuamotus in 2003, not called the Dangerous Archipelago for nothing, even the latest charts that I had bought for that trip were often inaccurate and in one notable instance I found that the true position of Makemo, one of the major atolls, was not only totally inaccurate but its western pass was several miles out.

Over the last three decades offshore navigation has taken bigger strides than in the previous three centuries. The first Aventura's navigation system was quite rudimentary as I only had a sextant, a radio direction finder (RDF) and a depth sounder. The latter may have confirmed a position if we were in shallow waters, or, hopefully, warned us of shallow waters in an unexpected place. Aventura II's system was a great improvement as by the late 1980s the first satellite navigation system Transit had come into use and profoundly revolutionized the art of navigation. I also had a radar and integrated instrumentation so life indeed became much easier. The current Aventura's system is more than adequate for my needs and I never felt the need for any additions. Aventura III also has radar and I have four GPS: one is integrated with the B&G instruments and autopilot, the Inmarsat C has its own GPS, which is a useful backup, and the two handheld units are also meant as backups. One of them is kept permanently in a specially prepared container to be grabbed in the event of abandoning ship.

Having reached the Mediterranean I came to realize the usefulness of chart plotters as there is no doubt that when cruising in confined areas they are a great improvement over paper charts so I decided to upgrade at the earliest opportunity. Soon after I started work on this book I went to the London boat show to help Ivan choose a suitable chart plotter for his new boat, which was nearing completion and was scheduled to be launched in spring 2007. Listening to the salesman on the GeoNav stand I was blown over by what those chart plotters could do. How could I have been so naïve as to shut my eyes and not get one earlier to help me negotiate those treacherous reefs in the Pacific? I am sure everyone will have guessed the outcome: we left the show with one chart plotter each and I cannot wait to try out my top of the range model when I sail this coming summer to one of the destinations of my dreams: Venice.

Early one morning, as we made landfall on Tahiti's north coast after a passage from the Tuamotus, Gwenda noticed that the beautiful engraved chart I was using had been printed in 1862. In spite of that, it was surprising that after all those years the chart was still reasonably accurate having probably been based on Captain Cook's original drawings when he had visited this same area to observe the transit of Venus. The three-year expedition on the Endeavour, his first into the Pacific, was one of the most significant journeys of European exploration. The rare transit of the planet Venus was used to calculate the distance to the sun. My venerable old chart of Tahiti now adorns the wall of the Tahiti Yacht Club in Arue, less than one mile from Point Venus where the famous explorer and his entourage spent several weeks in 1769.

Close encounters of a navigational kind

Even Captain Cook's navigation skills, or perhaps just his luck, failed him on a few occasions, so I find it quite normal that I ended up in some difficult situations myself.

Caicos Bank, February 1977

The way ahead seemed clear as we wove our way through the maze of coral heads heading for the Ambergris Cays, on the edge of the Caicos Bank. A small cloud passed over the sun suddenly drawing an opaque veil over the previously crystal clear water. We continued blindly on what I hoped was a safe course, then, with a gut-wrenching crunch, we ran aground. Neither full power ahead nor astern made any difference. We were well and truly stuck. I donned my mask, jumped overboard and was horrified to see the keel firmly wedged in a deep crack on top of a large coral head. In spite of our dire situation I was overawed by the stunning beauty of the underwater scenery. The reef was teaming with large fish looking puzzled but not frightened by this intrusion, while from their holes spiny lobsters waved their antennae invitingly. Back on board, I rowed out an anchor tied to a halyard, trying to heel the boat and thus reduce its draft, but it was to no avail and I realized that unless we got the tide to lift us up, our long dreamed of voyage was going to be over before it had hardly begun. After pounding hard for a couple of hours, a combination of rising tide and a fortuitous swell suddenly lifted Aventura and deposited her in the sheltered waters behind the reef. In spite of the battering, the strongly built fibreglass hull had only suffered a few scratches, but my self-confidence was severely scarred and it took me a long time to recover from that unpleasant incident.

Annapolis, USA, October 1977

On our way south from New York bound for Annapolis, we passed through the Delaware-Chesapeake channel but being slowed down by the tide, by the time it got dark we couldn't find any suitable anchorage so had no choice but to continue. As the breeze started getting up around midnight, I decided to go into Annapolis. I had a chart of the area, the lights were clearly marked on it, so we prepared to enter the long channel that leads into Annapolis Harbour. Eventually I identified the red light flashing every 2 seconds marking the outer approaches. Believing it to be the right place I told Gwenda to head for the light. Passing close to the buoy and leaving it to starboard (this being the USA i.e. red right returning,) we

suddenly touched the bottom and ran firmly aground right next to the flashing light. Aventura started shaking and banging in the swell, the rigging making that horrible noise that sounds much worse than it actually is. I tried to back off at full revs but we were stuck in the soft mud. I felt that we were not in serious danger and, after the really hard grounding in Caicos, knew that Aventura's strong hull could probably take it. To my surprise we were so far inshore that a busy road was running only some 200 metres away. I checked the chart and realised that we must have run aground somewhere different from where I thought we were and certainly nowhere near Annapolis.

A driver must have realised our predicament and flashed his lights repeatedly, which I understood to say that he was going to call for help. This is what he must have done because a quarter of an hour later a small USCG launch headed for us, but when the skipper realised we were in very shallow waters, stopped short and called us on his bullhorn. As we did not have a VHF radio, communication had to be carried out in this way. He first went through a lengthy procedure of identifying our boat, homeport, number of people on board and a host of other, to me, irrelevant questions. Finally he said that he would try to tow us out, but as he did not have a tender and it was quite obvious that there was no way he could get any closer, I shouted across that I would swim out a long line, an offer which he vehemently opposed. I ignored him, tied the end of a long anchor rode around my waist and dove overboard. I reached the launch without any problem, handed one end of the rope to the crew and returned to Aventura. While still a few metres short from Aventura's stern my rope came to an end and as Aventura only drew five feet and

I could stand in the soft mud I asked Gwenda to hand me another rope to make up the difference. Suddenly with a violent jerk the line tied round my waist tightened and I felt myself being yanked away. Obviously the Coast Guard skipper had presumed that I had secured the line and that we were ready to be towed off. While I was bodysurfing at great speed through the warm water, the skipper must have realised that the rope could not have been attached to Aventura so he stopped the launch and the crew looked flabbergasted when I surfaced spluttering at their side. I told them what had happened and asked them to repeat the operation provided they gave me enough time to secure my own end of the rope to Aventura. I made my way back to Aventura and attached the end of the rope to a cleat. Meanwhile a second USCG launch had arrived on the scene and was standing by. I shouted across to our helpful friends to start pulling. However hard the skipper tried nothing seemed to happen until I saw the line go slack and... someone shouted across that they had got my line around their propeller and had run aground themselves! So now there were two stranded boats and a Coast Guard officer with a very red face that I almost believed I could see shining in the dark.

The incoming tide eventually came to our help allowing me to slowly back off the bank. I motored over to the stranded launch to thank the skipper.

'Nothing to worry about, we'll come off soon as well. Just proceed into Annapolis – the entrance is about half a mile over there. Make sure you come to our office in the morning to sign a report and retrieve your line.'

I easily found the proper entrance channel into Annapolis and was puzzled to see that it was also marked by a red light flashing every 2 seconds. I realized that the strong tide had carried us south and I had picked the wrong set of lights. We anchored in the inner harbour and as soon as it got light I donned my mask and had a quick look at the hull. There didn't seem to be any damage although later I found that the repeated pounding on the grounded rudder had caused the hydraulic steering ram to be bent so it had to be replaced.

The USCG office overlooked the attractive Annapolis Bay. I was received by a different officer as our friends had finished their shift. He told me that they had managed to come off soon after we had left and handed me the neatly coiled rope.

'Tell me officer, why do you have lights with the same characteristics so close to each other?'

'Good question,' he replied 'but I don't really know the answer. Maybe the bosses have bought a whole identical batch. All I know is that it seems to cause a lot of confusion, as you are not the first boat to have made the same mistake.'

At least I had some excuse for my navigational error, but I am still puzzled by that example of incomprehensible bureaucracy.

Bali, July 2004

We had benign weather conditions for the one thousand mile passage from Darwin to Bali across the Arafura and Timor Seas that gave us one week of glorious sailing, all of it under spinnaker. The only slight hiccup occurred right at the end when a strong contrary current slowed us down so that it was already dark by the time we arrived off the entrance channel into Benoa Harbour. Having been in and out of the small port on several occasions in the past I decided to enter immediately rather than spend all night outside. I lined up the boat with the leading lights and moved slowly forward, but something didn't seem right... and suddenly the forward looking sonar showed shallow water right in front of us. I quickly swung the wheel to port but it was too late and we touched the bottom lightly with the centreboard. As always in such situations, the board's hydraulic circuit had been set in the open position, so the slight impact simply pushed the board up. One quick look around showed that the current had pushed us out of the approach channel and we had barely avoided running seriously aground. Now I knew exactly where we were and suddenly realized that this is what had got me into trouble in the first place: the fact that I thought I knew where I was. It is something that has got many other navigators into trouble as will become clear from other examples in this chapter.

Sardinia, May 1976

An unfailing thrill is to plot a new course that follows the old pencil marks that I had traced when I last sailed through the same waters on a previous occasion. This is what happened when we left Menorca for Sardinia in 2006. A strong mistral had given us a fast but bumpy ride and it took us only a little over twenty-four hours to reach our destination on the west coast of Sardinia. It was certainly a more successful landfall than thirty years previously when we had sailed almost exactly the same course but when we reached the same spot... Sardinia had disappeared! I still remember looking frantically all around and refusing to believe my eyes: where this large island should have been, the sea was absolutely empty. The overcast sky precluded the use of the sextant, so I took several running

fixes with what was in those pre-GPS days the most widely used aid to navigation: RDF (radio direction finding). Eventually I managed to plot a position that I knew was right... and it put us far to the east of Sardinia, which we must have passed well out of sight. It was quite a mystery how I had missed an island that measures some 120 miles from end to end. Quite a shock, even for the greenest of beginners!

There was obviously a reason for this, apart from my lack of experience, and it was eventually discovered. While tidying up the boat in Menorca for the forthcoming passage, Gwenda had moved our portable transistor radio into the locker situated right under the main compass. The radio's speaker had a powerful magnet that had swung the compass over 30 degrees to the right and if we'd continued in that direction we would have hit Africa. This time Sardinia was precisely where she was supposed to be and was certainly worth waiting for all these years.

Sardinia, April 2006

A more recent mistake, which could have had potentially much more serious consequences, happened the night we left Sardinia for Tunisia. Having left from the island's west coast we followed the coast closely to the SW corner, which we had to clear before we could set a course for Tunisia. There were no dangers close to our course and I was ticking off the lights as we sailed passed them. Before turning the corner we had to pass between an islet and the main island and as there seemed to be clear water between them I didn't alter the course and headed straight for the middle of the narrow gap. As the rocky islet loomed out of the dark to starboard I suddenly glimpsed a dark shape right ahead of me.

Waypoints should be set well clear of reefs surrounding low lying islands

I dashed to the wheel, switched off the autopilot and turned the wheel sharply to port. From the corner of my eye I saw a rocky pinnacle surrounded by frothing water that we passed by a few feet, the sounder showing a depth of only three meters. It all happened so quickly that I hadn't even had time to worry nor probably breathe either. With the boat sailing at six knots if I had not taken that avoiding action we would have hit the rock square on and I doubt that even Aventura's strong hull would have escaped unscathed. And all this close to the end of my voyage. How could I have been so careless?

Later I had a closer look at the chart. I hasten to add that it was not an old chart but the most recent one that I had bought for this very occasion. As I looked closely at the area we had just passed I saw that in the narrow gap between the main island and the offlying islet there was indeed a tiny dot but, as it was almost entirely obscured by some writing, I had not noticed it. What's worse is that before going off watch, Gwenda had told me that I should look out for a dangerous rock that lay close to our course and I had reassured her that naturally I would be careful, imagining that she had meant the off-lying islet, not some other rock. I had committed a gross error, of that there is no doubt, but being on watch and also quite vigilant had saved us and that is what mattered.

GPS: A false sense of security?

The danger I see is that more and more cruisers rely blindly on GPS navigation.

Luc Callebaut

Two months after leaving Ecuador Aventura was tethered to a pontoon at the Tahiti Yacht Club. This was the fourth time I had come to Tahiti on my own boat but this time the satisfaction of just being there

117

was accompanied by a sense of relief after the anxious moments we had experienced in the Tuamotus. Although we were never in any danger, there had been times when things could have got worse and I agreed with Gwenda that cruising the Dangerous Archipelago demanded a high price and was definitely not for the faint hearted. We had avoided the Tuamotus on all our previous trips, initially by force as in the 1970s much of the area was out of bounds because of the French nuclear tests, or by choice, preferring to spend longer in the Marquesas or Gambiers.

We were certainly not alone, as many of the boats that had arrived in French Polynesia in 2003 had visited the Tuamotus en route to Tahiti. Over the radio and from people we met we started hearing stories of boats getting into trouble and it made me wonder if perhaps GPS was to blame for giving navigators a false sense of security. In fact, the question had been answered already by my friend Antti Louhija who had sailed with me from Ecuador to the Marquesas. While in the Red Sea, 600 miles short of completing his circumnavigation, Antti lost his 36 foot Pegasos on a reef off the coast of Sudan. In his own words: 'During the darkness of a moonless night we hit a coral reef 40 miles offshore. We had been heading for a GPS waypoint and the course had been laid so as to bypass the small islet and reef of Barra Musa Kebir by two miles. We struck the reef where it should not have been, and the boat was eventually a total loss. Luckily nobody on board was hurt. GPS is a wonderful tool but do not trust the charts.'

In my own experience as a rally organizer I witnessed several instances when boats were damaged or even lost due to a navigational error caused by over-reliance on GPS. The worst case was that of a delivery crew who ran their boat onto the east coast of Barbados having set a landfall waypoint on the opposite side of the island.

The more I thought about it, the more incidents came to mind, so I decided to widen the scope of my enquiry and contact some friends sailing in other oceans. My poll by email brought forth a host of incidents, with entering an unfamiliar port or anchorage at night being one of the principal cases. Often the problem was compounded when GPS was used in conjunction with the autopilot, and the navigator relied slavishly on both. I remember sailing on a friend's boat from Crosshaven to Kinsale in Southern Ireland. It was a bright clear day, with no wind, and we were motoring under autopilot. We seemed to take a long way round a headland and I asked my friend why he didn't cut the corner, as there were no dangers closer inshore. He told me that he had already pre-programmed a route to the next port and didn't want to interfere with the autopilot as it was doing such an excellent job.

Sailing to a waypoint, often on autopilot, and not keeping a proper watch appears to be the most common cause of groundings, and one of my correspondents mentioned the case of a French yacht that ran aground at Cayo Hollandes in San Blas and was lost. Apparently the skipper had tried to find his way at night into an unfamiliar anchorage solely by GPS relying on his electronic charts and the waypoints someone else had given him. He failed because even the latest electronic charts for some parts of the world, the San Blas included, may be inaccurate especially if not updated and do not entirely agree with current GPS positions.

This is the reason why the waypoints indicated in World Cruising Routes are set at a safe distance offshore because I don't want anyone to take that term "landfall" too literally. Unfortunately, some navigators do, and one of the first to reply to my survey was Nick Wardle of the Bahamas Search and Rescue Association (BASRA) who described the case of a large motor yacht whose captain went for a nap and asked the mate to set a waypoint for the NW Channel light. The mate did such a good job of steering for that waypoint that he actually crashed into the light, the large tower landing on the foredeck. Nick mentioned other similar incidents when reliance on GPS caused navigators to set waypoints too close to the intended landfall, occasionally with dire consequences.

World Cruising Routes

When I started planning my first voyage in the early 1970s there was only one book dealing specifically with ocean routing, the British Admiralty "Ocean Passages for the World". Aimed primarily at commercial shipping, it had very little relevant information for sailing vessels. The only sailing information that had been retained from the earlier editions described weather conditions along some of the well established trade routes such as the tea clipper route from Hong Kong to England, or the wool and grain route from Australia to Europe. While those details still made interesting reading, the routes described were very different from those sailed by cruising yachts and thus the information was quite irrelevant.

All through our voyage I gathered material on ocean routing and soon after our return to London, I started doing some serious research with the aim of writing the kind of book that I would have liked to have had myself when I was planning our

round the world voyage. World Cruising Routes was first published in 1987 and I am currently preparing its sixth edition. It has been translated into German, French and Italian and has sold well over 100,000 copies. It contains essential routing and weather information on all popular cruising routes throughout the world, with details of tropical storm seasons and areas affected by them, prevailing winds and currents, suggested landfalls, relevant waypoints, recommended cruising guides and suggestions on the best time and tactics for each particular route. Over the years, the book has gradually grown in scope so that its latest edition lists over one thousand different routes that now include a much wider selection of cruising destinations. As a companion volume to World Cruising Routes in 1991 I published World Cruising Handbook, which contains essential practical information on all maritime nations of the world, from historical background to cruising attractions, entry formalities and ports of entry, repair facilities and recommended guides for each area.

One of the most interesting comments I ever received for my book came from the most unexpected direction. One day, while in Las Palmas before the start of the ARC, a participant who I knew to have been a Commodore in the Royal Navy barged into my office and exclaimed breathlessly, 'Jimmy, you will never believe this. I have just visited a British nuclear submarine that is here on a goodwill mission and guess what? On the shelf above the nav table I saw a copy of your Routes! So I asked the captain why on earth he would carry that doorstopper of a book with him.'

'So I know where those silly yachts go and can be extra careful not to smash into one when we surface.'

I had a similar backhanded compliment from the captain of an Indonesian sail training yacht that was taking part in the Hong Kong Challenge, a round the world race that I organized in 1996 to mark the handover of Hong Kong to China. At the stopover in Japan he came to my office and told me proudly: 'Mr Jimmy, I have a copy of your book.'

'Really? Is it World Cruising Routes?'

'Yes. Look at it.'

I had already noticed the battered copy he was holding but it certainly didn't look like any of my books. He handed it over and I saw it was a poor photocopied job.

'Very nice'. I said.

'Yes, the Ministry of Maritime Affairs has made enough copies to distribute to the entire Indonesian Navy', he told me proudly.

'How very interesting,' was all I could say politely trying to hide my true feelings when faced with a pirated copy.

The biggest compliment, however, came from a British singlehander whom I met in New Zealand. One day he came over to look at my boat and before leaving said rather sheepishly. 'I want to tell you something that may amuse you.'

'Go ahead.'

'After transiting the Panama Canal, a group of us were headed for the Galapagos Islands. We soon separated and I continued on my own. I had great difficulty getting out of the Bay of Panama and, whichever way I turned, the wind and current always seemed to be against me. Rather than the hoped for eight or nine day passage, it took me sixteen days to get there. When I finally arrived, everyone told me how concerned they had been for my safety.'

'What had actually happened?' one of them asked me.

'Not much, and I told them of my ordeal.'

'But didn't you have Jimmy Cornell's book on board?'

'Yeah, I do have it but never looked at the thing.'

'Well you fool, you'd better look now as it tells you exactly where to go. We did that and got here in under eight days.'

'So, Jimmy, I do owe you an apology. I did read what you wrote and the information is very clear on the tactics on leaving Panama, where to find favourable winds and currents, the lot.'

'Well, at least I hope you're using the book now.'

'Of course. All the time, otherwise I would have never told you, as I find it so stupid and embarrassing.'

Tips

- In remote areas regard all charts, whether paper or electronic, with caution.
- Never sail to a waypoint without keeping a good lookout, especially when getting closer.
- Never set a landfall waypoint that is not at a safe offshore distance from the intended destination.
- Always allow for a generous safety margin when setting a waypoint in areas affected by strong currents and tides.
- Resist over-reliance on GPS and always double check your position if in any doubt.
- Do not trust an autopilot or windvane to steer an accurate course and check the actual position frequently to detect any deviation in good time.
- Avoid entering an unknown port or anchorage at night.

Greece Rediscovered

While at Fanning Island just north of the equator having just speared a large fish for dinner, we were sitting in the cockpit enjoying the sunset over the lagoon. Across the turquoise waters the nearest village lay hidden behind a curtain of coconut palms. A small outrigger canoe was silently gliding past us, its two occupants returning from a day of fishing in the open ocean. While sipping our Aventura cocktail, fresh coconut juice lashed with rum, we were commenting on the beauty of the setting. It was truly perfect. And yet there was something missing. We agreed that however beautiful all this was, you can only do so much diving and reef walking, eat so much fish or lobster and enjoy so many spectacular sunsets. Reluctantly we admitted that after several months of beautiful anchorages and some excellent sailing, we badly missed the cultural attractions of the European ports, their waterfront restaurants and cafes.

Exactly one year later Aventura was in Greece, which I had not visited by boat for nearly twenty years. Before our first circumnavigation we had spent two long summers in 1975 and 1976 sailing in the Aegean and we stopped there again on our return in 1981. So it was with some doubt and trepidation that we returned in the

summer of 2000 and were quite prepared to be disappointed by the changes that must have occurred since our last visit some twenty years earlier.

Early that summer, with only Gwenda as crew, we sailed from St Raphael, on the French Riviera, where Aventura had spent the previous winter, to Corsica. The logical route from the South of France to Greece

The spacious protected bay on Serifos is a favourite anchorage

leads through the Straits of Messina and Corsica is an attractive and convenient stop on this direct route. After one night at anchor in Corsica and one near Maddalena, off the east coast of Sardinia, we crossed the Tyrrhenian Sea to the Lipari Islands. This group of several islands lying close to the north of Sicily, also known by their ancient name of the Aeolian Islands, have served as ports of call for the earliest sailors of antiquity. Indeed, a fascinating museum on the island of Lipari traces the origins of Mediterranean maritime trade with objects discovered at an archaeological site going back several thousand years as well as objects found on wrecks. It was quite amazing to realize that this sea was plied by sailing ships on regular trading voyages as far back as 5,000 years ago.

History is never far away anywhere in the Mediterranean and perhaps nowhere more so than in the Messina Straits where we were sailing closely in the wake of Odysseus and his brave crew. The monsters of Scylla and Charybdis still lurk beneath the surface of this waterway, but now it is not Homer's whirlpools that have to be avoided but the fast ferries crossing between the Italian mainland and Sicily. As the straits are affected by strong tidal currents, we timed our passage to coincide with a favourable tide and thus flew south at a combined speed of nearly ten knots. Favourable winds were also with us and so it took us only two days to cross the Ionian Sea, one of the legendary seven seas of the Ancient World that we were sailing through on this voyage of rediscovery.

Rather than take the more direct route via the Corinth Canal, we decided to enter the Aegean from the SW by making landfall at Pylos, on the west coast of the Peloponnese. This small port set in a large bay was made famous by a naval battle in the early nineteenth century in which an allied Anglo-French-Russian fleet completely destroyed the Turkish fleet thus opening the door to Greek independence. At that time Pylos was still known by its Venetian name of Navarino, while the Peloponnese itself was called Morea by the Venetians, who controlled much of the Eastern Mediterranean before the Turkish ascendancy. There are still many Venetian remains in the Peloponnese, outstanding among them the well preserved fortresses of Methoni and Koroni, described as the "eyes" of the Serene Republic as they guarded the strategic routes around the Peloponnese.

It was at Methoni that we noticed the first big change that had occurred since our earlier visit: a well stocked supermarket with a wide variety of fresh food, whereas in the past we would have counted ourselves lucky to be able to buy in such a place a few tomatoes, cheese and fresh bread... or not even that as Gwenda recorded in her diary at the time:

3 August 1975

Impossible to buy any provisions in this place, not even bread! Eventually the owner of the bakery took pity on us seeing our two children and gave us her own loaf.

In the small square overlooking the harbour, where now there were several attractive restaurants and bars, one could buy all the major German or English newspapers of the day before. So things had indeed changed but what took us by surprise was the small number of cruising boats that we met as we made our way slowly around the three fingers of the Peloponnese. Although this route is away from the more popular destinations, this was, after all, the height of the summer season so it was a very pleasant surprise to find so many uncrowded ports and bays.

Our last stop in the Peloponnese was at Monemvasia, once a thriving trading centre, but at our last visit a ruined ghost town where we were the only visitors. Most of the buildings have now been restored as souvenir shops or bars catering for the large groups of tourists, which crowd its narrow streets and alleys from sunrise to sunset.

By the time we arrived at our first Aegean island, Spetses, we realized that things had changed on all fronts, and quite dramatically so. Everywhere we went we found the ports full of charter boats and we counted ourselves lucky if we found a spot to anchor. By now it was impossible to find space on a dock in any of the harbours we visited and even anchoring in some of those crowded ports was not easy. In many places we left the boat unattended while we

Boisterous sailing between the islands during the summer Meltemi

visited some site in the interior, and on two occasions came back to find that another boat must have tripped our anchor during our absence and Aventura was nowhere near the place we had left her. After that, I resorted to my well-tried method of anchoring with two anchors in tandem, a storm proof system that I had not used since Antarctica.

In late July the summer Meltemi was blowing hard and there were few days with winds under 20 knots. But at least their direction was constant, varying just a few degrees between NW and NE, so we decided to make our way slowly through the Cyclades towards Crete, sailing most of the time with the wind on the quarter.

The Meltemi is such a constant feature of summer sailing in Greece that anyone planning to be there between June and August should allow for this strong northerly wind, both when deciding on the best route among the islands and when choosing an anchorage. One of our favourites, which we visited on several occasions in 1975 and 1976, was the well-sheltered Despotiko Bay, off the island of Antiparos.

5 August 1975

What a wonderfully tranquil spot! Just a couple of houses set among the green hills and several small deserted beaches. The waters teem with fish of many colours and the snorkelling is by far the best we have had anywhere in Greece... An old man came out in a small boat to sell us figs. Later we went ashore and were invited by an old lady into her house. She served us cake, coffee and ouzo. She told us that she lives on her own, but has two daughters, one in New York, the other in Athens. The phone rang while we were there. It was her daughter from Athens. Amazing that there is a phone in such a remote place where everything has to be brought by mule from the nearest village, one hour over the hill.

Twenty-five years later Despotiko Bay was just as attractive, and we spent a peaceful night there, but there are now many more houses, several tavernas on the beach, cars on the tarmac road that leads across the hill... and hardly any fish in the clear water.

On our way south through the Cyclades, we stopped at every island on the way: Serifos, Sifnos, Paros and Antiparos, Skinousa and Ios. Last time we had visited Ios Europe was just about to start shedding its hippy image of the 1960s.

21 August 1976

The island was full of young foreigners in every state of dress: baggy Turkish trousers, nipples pointing out of seethrough blouses, blond Afro haircuts, droopy Franz Josef moustaches, rags tied around ankles, sarongs knotted around breasts, the ubiquitous money bags and faded trousers. No one looked very happy, neither visitors, nor locals.

Ios is still a favourite destination for young Europeans, and although the dress has not changed much, the islanders both here and elsewhere seem to have come to terms with this annual invasion. Everyone is now aware of the importance of tourism for the local economy and the remarkable degree of prosperity that it has engendered even in some of the poorest islands.

From Ios, a quick sail took us into the sunken crater of Thira (Santorini), where we were unpleasantly surprised to find that facilities for visiting yachts were just as nonexistent as on our previous visit. As the water is far too deep for anchoring we hung on for a while to a large mooring used by cruise ships, while we tried to figure out a safe way to leave the boat to climb the 570 steps to the town perched on the lip of the crater above. One can hire a mule for the arduous trip or do the climb in even more comfort in the newly installed cable car. There appeared no solution so we sailed to a bay on the south side of the island and visited the town by taxi.

The following morning, a strong Meltemi gave us a fast passage to Aghios Nikolaos Marina on the north coast of Crete. At last we had left the charter boats behind, there was plenty of space in the marina and most other boats were foreign cruising boats. Some were already preparing to spend the coming winter in this well-appointed marina run by friendly and helpful staff. Rather than forego the obvious attractions of Aghios Nikolaos, we decided to cruise Crete on four wheels, to revisit the Minoan sites of Phaestos and Knossos and the magnificent museum in Iraklion.

Old windmills grace the hillside on Astipalia

Although by the time we left Crete it was mid-September, the Meltemi was still blowing strongly, so we sailed north on a zigzag course. Thus we managed to sail to Astipalia on one tack and from there to Amorgos on the other tack. We continued this island hopping all the way to Lavrion, a marina near Athens, where we had arranged to leave the boat for the winter. We had some exhilerating sailing and concluded that if you have a boat that goes reasonable well to windward, and are not too worried about some windward work, one can easily pick a route that takes full advantage of the prevailing northerly winds. We followed the same routine as we had all summer: got up early, picked a destination around 30 to 40 miles away, sailed there and found an anchorage in time for lunch, had a short siesta, then, by late afternoon went ashore to visit whatever there was to see and finished the day's programme with dinner ashore. This was the kind of cruising I had dreamt of while in the Pacific and I was happy to conclude that in this respect Greece fulfilled all my expectations.

Indeed this was the reason why we returned to Greece in the spring of the following year when we retraced our steps to the island of Spetses to spend Easter with local friends, then visited some of the islands in the Saronic Gulf on our way to the Corinth Canal. En route we visited the ancient theatre at Epidavros and the impressive site at Delphi to conclude a most satisfying tour of this fascinating country.

So, what were the main conclusions after an absence of twenty years? On the positive side, I am pleased to say that although much had changed, much had remained the same. Above all, in spite of an enormous increase in tourism, we found the local people as we remembered them: friendly and welcoming. I realised this at one of our first stops, on the island of Spetses, when I went ashore to do the shopping. At the check-out I realised I had left all my money on board, so I told the owner of the small supermarket that I would have to leave my shopping there and go back to the boat for the money. He insisted that I took the

shopping with me and told me to pay him next time I came ashore. This was the first time I had been to his shop, so he had no idea who I was, and, this being the middle of summer, the port was full of yachts.

One evening we went ashore for dinner at a small restaurant in Limeni. As in previous places we had never spent more than 8,000 drachmas for dinner (about 80 euros), I only took 10,000 drachmas with me. The restaurant's speciality was fresh fish and was much more expensive than we had expected. As I didn't feel like rowing back to the boat for more money, I explained to the waiter that we only had 10,000 drachmas and asked him to make sure that the dinner, including a bottle of wine, would not come to more than that. As we were leaving the restaurant, the owner came up to us, and, having heard from the waiter that we didn't have much money, gave us a bottle of wine as a present. Obviously she felt sorry for two poor sailors!

These are just two examples of the genuine hospitality that we encountered in most places. Of course, there were exceptions, and among these I would count the behaviour of some Greek ferry operators who totally ignore the rules of the sea and can be a real danger to sailing boats. Even more frustrating is the cumbersome bureaucracy which is still applied to both EU and non-EU boats. Also on the negative side, one of the main disappointments were the inadequate docking facilities for visiting yachts in most of the ports. The few available spaces on the dock were usually taken up by charter boats with large crews, so short-handed boats such as ours had no choice but to anchor, which made leaving the boat to go sightseeing more concerning. Even in some of the more popular ports there were no facilities for visiting boats such as showers or toilets. Many ports were full of old moorings, chains and assorted garbage, so that we fouled our anchor regularly.

As to the weather, the much maligned Meltemi is in fact the best time to sail as the direction of the wind is constant and it is therefore easy to choose a safe anchorage. As the number of harbours providing all round shelter is quite limited, picking an anchorage out of season is not so easy.

My final conclusion is that Greece is a beautiful country with excellent cruising potential but there is a price to be paid. It is undoubtedly an ideal cruising ground as it has all the ingredients that make a visit successful: good winds and reliable weather conditions, short distances between destinations, plenty of ports and anchorages, never a shortage of restaurants to eat ashore and something interesting to see at every stop. My advice to anyone planning to visit Greece is to decide on a suitable route that takes into account the prevailing wind conditions, so that the chosen destinations are reached without much effort. A larger crew would make it easier to manoeuvre in the crowded ports than was the case in our own situation. There are no laid moorings and almost everywhere you have to anchor with your own anchor and bring the stern or bow to the quay. As the holding ground is often not good, the anchor should be set as far out as possible. With a strong wind blowing, and a small crew, it is often a tricky manoeuvre to bring the boat to the quay while avoiding the neighbouring boats, paying out chain all the time and having two stern lines ready to throw to someone on the quay – if any of your neighbours come to take your lines, which, I am sorry to say, is rarely the case.

At the end of our tour of Greece we decided to sail back to the South of France. We had good but strong winds all the way, and were surprised that we managed to cover almost the entire distance under sail. However, two seasons in the Mediterranean convinced me that in spite of all its attractions, this was not the kind of cruising I wanted to do for the rest of my life. Back in St Raphael I started getting Aventura ready for a return to the South Seas. After all, you can only look at so many ancient temples, have so many taverna dinners and spend so many evenings in a waterfront café watching the world go by. Bringing the boat back to the Mediterranean had not been a mistake as those two seasons were enjoyable and I had needed a dose of European culture. But I had had my fill and was ready to tackle the wide oceans again. This is, after all, the beauty of having your own boat: the luxury of changing your mind and going where the wind takes you. South Pacific, here I come!

Life Afloat

To live aboard a cruising boat you cannot bemoan what you had before or what you left behind. Face the new challenges afresh and you'll enjoy life.

Glynn Beauchamp

A comfortable life afloat has been our top priority from the beginning and even if our means were limited in those days we did make a great effort to make Aventura I as comfortable as possible. However, the rather modest personal comforts that we considered adequate in the 1970s have changed considerably over the years. In 2001, as Gwenda and I passed through Gibraltar, we were greatly surprised to see our first Aventura on her way into the Mediterranean. In spite of her 27 years, she looked in tiptop condition and much better than when I had sold her in 1982. The current owner, a cabinetmaker by profession, had ripped out the interior, got rid of all my clumsy amateur work and refitted her to the highest standard. The main thing that shocked us was how we had managed to enjoy life for six long years in such a narrow and confined space.

One lesson that I learnt from the writings of cruising pioneers was how important it was to lead as normal a life as possible. This meant having proper and regular meals, ideally seated at the table and that at least the main meal should be with all the crew together. I took this so much to heart that on our first ocean passage, while crossing the Bay of Biscay, when the time came for our first lunch I hove to and asked Gwenda to lay the table.

'You must be crazy. I can hardly hang on in all this rolling and you'll never get the kids out of their bunks.' Gwenda commented, trying to inject some realism into my harebrained idea.

'But Eric Hiscock said that you must try and keep the crew happy by....'

'Why don't you go and sail with Hiscock then?' Gwenda cut me short, 'We were sailing along so well, why do you have to spoil it now?'

The sea was indeed quite agitated so I got the boat sailing again and the movement got better. Gwenda fed the children first, then handed me a bowl of steaming stew.

'That tastes good. When did you manage to cook it?'

'Well, Susan Hiscock suggests that you prepare a nourishing dish before you set off on passage so all you have to do is heat it up.'

'You women always seem to know best.'

'Yes, and also we are usually right.'

That was probably the first time I realized that not only did I have a lot to learn from those famous predecessors but that I had a ready source of commonsense advice much closer to hand and, rather reluctantly, started listening more to my wife. Over the years I have come to appreciate and value Gwenda's judgement. Whereas by nature I am impulsive and quick to take decisions, Gwenda is very English in her manner, never rash, always calm and cool, pragmatic and open-minded. She rarely reacts immediately to whatever I suggest, but takes her time to consider the issue before expressing her views on the matter, her realism being often quite irritating although usually justified. So now I have learnt to wait and let some time pass before I implement whatever idea I had put forward, but as the outcome is often altered by Gwenda's suggestions, I hope that the time lapse makes it look as if it was exactly as I had first outlined it. I am a man after all.

On Aventura III life follows a regular pattern and after so many years spent at sea most things are now second nature. However rough it may be, I shave and wash every day and I noticed that this routine always makes me feel better. There is a convenient and easy to use shower on the stern platform that can be safely used in almost all conditions. As a skipper once pointed out, 'ample water keeps you from getting sick; daily showers keep people from fighting because they feel yucky.'

Meals

Whenever conditions are right we try to eat at the cockpit table. On Aventura this is one of those ingenious French ideas that I have not seen on another boat. When collapsed the rectangular teak grating drops down to become the cockpit floor. When raised the trestle type legs open up and bring the table up to the required height. Bearing in mind where the table spends all day (under our feet) the anti-slip tablecloth I use is marked with indelible

Preparing the evening meal in Aventura's cosy galley

pen showing the side which should be in contact with the floor and which side is the clean one.

The food is either dished out onto individual plates in the galley straight from the pot, or brought to the table in a serving dish, never in the cooking pot. The main cooked meal of the day is usually dinner that is served shortly after nightfall. Lunch is at noon and usually consists of soup and a substantial salad. Everyone, whether on watch or resting, is expected to join these two meals. For breakfast everyone has what they fancy when they get up. Usually it is breakfast cereal or toast (I have a toaster that works on top of the gas burner) and, when Antti sails with me, eggs, eggs and more fried eggs. As he is cardiologist I once asked him if he wasn't worried about the cholesterol content.

'Not at all,' he replied, 'just take your statin and stop worrying. Now that you mentioned it, can I have some eggs for breakfast?'

'The usual two?'

'How about three... sunny side up?'

Provisions

Just as I decided not to have a separate diesel generator, having witnessed so many problems with gensets on other boats, I also voted against having a freezer not so much because I suspected its reliability but because I could not see any good reason for adding another power hungry piece of equipment. After nine years I still feel the same, mainly because we prefer to eat fresh food whenever possible, so the fridge is more than adequate for our needs. I have a 220 V vacuum packer which makes it possible to keep freshly caught fish for as long as two weeks, provided it is perfectly vacuum packed and stored at the bottom of the fridge. When provisioning for a long passage I always try to buy meat that had been vacuum packed already, or ask it to be done for me. Fruit and vegetables are stored in two large hanging nets, those that are vulnerable to daylight being kept carefully separated from each other on shelves in the forward cabin. Bananas are never stored next to any other fruit or vegetable as an enzyme in the bananas accelerates the ripening process in adjacent items. I always try to buy fruit and vegetables from a farmers' market where they are not chilled. Usually I go to the market one or two days before my planned shopping trip, pick the best looking stall, explain to the owner where I am going and ask him or her to bring some fresh supplies on the agreed day. Supermarket eggs are usually chilled too, and will not keep well, and the same goes for sliced bread. This is why it is best to keep supermarket bread well wrapped up in the fridge. Eggs are also best bought from the market and kept in a dark well aired place.

The selection of non-indigenous vegetables is still limited in some places such as the islands of the South Pacific, so the sooner one learns to appreciate the local produce the better. However, in recent years there has been a great improvement in provisioning everywhere, and now tomatoes and salads are available in many places in the South Pacific, where they never were in the past.

In Ecuador I had to shop for five weeks, enough to take us via the Galapagos all the way to the Marquesas. The local supermarket agreed to individually vacuum pack for me some prime Argentinian steaks. Beef keeps best and longest, and if vacuum packed it can be kept in the coldest part of the fridge for as long as one month. One of my favourite dishes on a long passage is

Fresh fruit and vegetables should be washed and dried before stowing

beef stew with vegetables, which I prepare in the pressure cooker enough to last for two or three meals.

Once underway, I go on an inspection tour every morning checking the fruit and vegetables and picking out the ripest so that they are consumed first. Early in 1978 on passage from Peru to Easter Island we were accompanied by Alan Sitt, an American friend, who had joined us in Lima. He had brought along a large sack of avocado pears from a tree growing in his courtyard. One morning I saw him take a look at an avocado, then throw it overboard.

'What on earth are you doing?' I asked.

'It started to go bad, so I threw it out.'

'What do you mean bad?'

'It had a few black spots?'

'Hey, you don't do that at sea when the nearest avocado tree is one thousand miles away. Just cut out the spots and eat the rest.'

Ever since I upgraded my inverter to 1500 watts, I have gradually acquired a number of electric kitchen implements. Besides the vacuum packer, a liquidizer is very useful both for making soups and fruit juice. For use in marinas when shore power is available I now have a toaster and electric kettle. One further improvement is that after years of consuming instant coffee we realized just how much nicer freshly brewed coffee tasted so we now use a cafetiere to make filter coffee.

I have no strict rules about alcohol consumption at sea maybe because all my friends only drink in moderation. Under normal conditions lunch is dry, except when I have my French friends on board. A sundowner is normally served on passage, usually a glass of white wine followed by a glass of red with the evening meal.

Hanging nets are a good solution for storing fruit

Alcoholic drinks are never served if the weather looks unsettled or likely to get worse. Drinks are always served in proper glasses not plastic and I still have my favourite heavy bottomed glasses that we bought in Fiji thirty years ago that have travelled thousands of miles on every Aventura since.

Our daily bread

On the suggestion of some cruising guru, Aventura I left London with a large sack of wholemeal flour. For a while Gwenda valiantly baked bread at least once a week but eventually the flour got so infested with weevils that the sack was visibly moving. Eventually we learnt not to buy large quantities of flour or rice as the outcome was always the same. Later Gwenda switched from loaves to rolls as they were easier to bake. I once looked into buying a dedicated breadmaker but was put off by the huge amount of electricity they use. Once I opted for the next best thing and took along a baker as crew. Unfortunately Patrick, who sailed with me from Cape Town to the Canaries, refused to produce bread away from his state of the art bakery. He only managed to produce once some pitiful looking rolls that tasted fine, but he never repeated the effort. It certainly made me feel very good and set my own inadequacy as a baker in a new perspective.

A good substitute for bread is crispbread of the Ryvita or Wasa type that keeps very well on long passages. One other good supplement, and one of my favourites, is pancakes. I always carry a stock of ready made pancake mix and often treat my crew to a special breakfast.

With freshly baked bread such a no-goer, nowadays I find sliced bread bought from a supermarket perfectly adequate and my French crew did too. The wholemeal type is best as it is more nourishing and also keeps better. I usually wrap each loaf up well and store them in the fridge. It will keep for up to three weeks even if towards the end there may be mould growing on the crust, which I try to get rid of out of sight of my crew. If I feel bad all I have to do is think of what they ate on Captain Cook's ships. But at least they had some compensation as each seaman got two gallons of ale and about a pint of rum per day, so life must have been quite beautiful as most of the time they were half-drunk. I once saw the list of beverages loaded in Madeira for Captain Cook's first voyage. It included 3000 gallons of wine, a staggering amount that worked out at nearly three litres of wine per officer or gentleman per day plus one litre of spirits. One must remember that they did not have good drinking water, but I still don't suggest trying out such a regime on your crew.

Landing a large male dolphin fish better known by its Polynesian name of mahimahi

Fishing

One of my greatest pleasures while cruising is catching fish, whether trolling on passage or spearing it. Fish used to be, and still is, our main source of protein on long passages. There are various ways of getting your fish. On ocean passages trolling a line with a good lure will usually bear results. Provided it is not illegal, spearfishing is both satisfying and yields good results as long as there are no sharks about. In such a situation, line fishing is safer. I also have a gill net that I rarely use nowadays, although it has been extremely useful in the past. When trolling at sea one should always be prepared to haul in the line if there are birds about as they may mistake the lure for a fish and get hooked. The worst are boobies, of which I caught at least two and so realized how they have got their silly name. Albatrosses can be just as vulnerable and in fact there is an on-going campaign at the moment as the albatross population of the Southern Ocean has been

decimated in recent years in this way by longliners.

While we were making our way into the lagoon at Salomon in Chagos, a young boy of about ten came over in his dinghy, greeted us and asked permission to come on board. He directed us to the best spot to anchor then briefed us on all essentials. He told us that the lagoon was teeming with fish and that the tastiest were red snappers. He stressed that the best time to get them was exactly at seven o'clock in the evening. After he left I rowed to the beach, picked up a couple of hermit crabs for bait, returned to the boat and by 6.30 had set up a line and sinker with the creature wriggling on the hook. I lowered the line until I felt the hook touch the bottom some sixty feet under the boat. Nothing much happened and I felt a bit foolish sitting on the stern platform wiggling a fishing line. Even my crew saw the hilarity of it and started making fun of me. He had been more impressed on our passage from Cocos when I managed to land a large fish every time I let out the line. In spite of the ridiculousness of the situation I decided to wait until seven and, lo and behold, on the dot of seven I felt a strong tug on the line, I pulled it up and when it broke the surface I had the most beautiful snapper hooked on it. It made an excellent supper, perhaps one of the tastiest fish I had ever caught. I took that perfect timing to be just a happy coincidence but decided to have another go and disprove the theory, so around the same time the following evening I repeated the operation and at precisely seven o'clock had another large snapper on the line. QED. But I hope no one asks me to explain why.

During our first voyage, we tried to live as much as possible off the sea and land, and while in Greece I became very proficient with my speargun. Unfortunately Greek waters had been fished out over the years by the widely used barbaric method of dynamite and in those days one could still see older fishermen with missing limbs. I soon found out that fishing on a moonless night with a torch was much more productive. With a powerful torch I would scan the waters around me and if lucky would catch a fish in its beam, the stationary mesmerised creature making a perfect target. I would feed it on to a wire ring that I was carrying at my waist and continue my hunt. If I was really lucky I got a conger eel or an octopus, which, after I had learnt how to tenderise them, would provide two or three tasty protein rich meals.

Life became much easier once we reached the Caribbean where fish was plentiful and could be easily caught by day. Octopus were replaced here by crayfish or spiny lobster, which were an easy target once I had learnt how to locate their hiding places. So lobster became our staple diet until we reached the Bahamas where we didn't seem to eat anything else and Doina exclaimed one day, 'Oh Daddy, not lobster again!' I got the point and reverted to ordinary fish. However justified that massacre may have been at the time to feed my family, now that I am more aware of the depleting stocks and the destruction of the marine environment, I feel really bad about it, so on my latest voyage I only fished when sailing offshore. The fish have had their revenge as at Tikehau in the Tuamotus I speared a grouper that gave both Gwenda and me a serious dose of ciguatera fish poisoning. This is the most serious risk associated with fishing in tropical waters and is described in chapter 12.

Diving

As part of the preparations for our first voyage I enrolled in an evening course of seamanship and navigation. I also joined the British Sub-Aqua Club and qualified as a diver. I have carried a full set of diving gear on all my boats, Aventura II even having its own diving compressor. On the present Aventura I have two sets of gear with two tanks, which are always kept full. I also have a wetsuit as well as a dry diving suit that allows me to dive in cold waters and which I acquired before leaving for Antarctica in case it had to be used in an emergency. Fortunately in over three decades the only times I had to dive in an emergency was to try and find a dental brace that my friend Susie Morgenstern's daughter had dropped in the marina in Bonifacio, and to find Gwenda's beautiful necklace that she had dropped in Papeete harbour and was given to her as a parting gift by our friends in the Gambiers. The tanks were rarely used when I was younger and in better shape than now and could easily free dive to fifty feet. Even nowadays I prefer snorkelling to diving, probably because I got so used to it after years of spending hours chasing after our next dinner.

Safety rules

Over the years I have compiled a number of safety rules that have now become routine. No one is allowed to leave the cockpit except in the presence of the skipper. Similarly, if anyone is taking a shower on the stern platform, there should be another person on standby in the cockpit. Swimming in the open ocean is not advisable unless it has to be done in an emergency such as when a line or net has to be cut from the propeller. The boom must be prevented at all times when broad reaching or running. This is easily done on Aventura with the help of the Walder boom brake. Whenever climbing the mast to do a job, whether with the help of steps or being hoisted in the bosun's chair, a harness should always be worm and clipped to a secure point while working. It is best to always wear a mask when swimming from the boat while at anchor so as to see if there are any sharks about. Sharks very rarely attack without warning so if a shark is seen to be hanging about you should get back on board immediately.

Entertainment

One of the great pleasures of life afloat is reading and while ashore I rarely manage to read more than one book per month, when I am sailing I devour them virtually by the day. I always make sure that I take a good supply of books with me, as generally the ones that interest me are much harder to find away from home, especially as I am not interested in those airport blockbusters. Book swapping with other sailors rarely seems to work as tastes differ so greatly and in all these years I don't think I got more than half a dozen books in this way. As I am not too keen on novels, and prefer non-fiction, I always like to have a good stock of biographies. They are the best reads on long passages as they are easy to put down and pick up again. Much of Aventura's library is made up of reference books, such as Nigel Calder's Electrical and

Nieces Lina and Marie enjoying a good read while sailing in the Canaries

Electronic Bible, a sight reduction table for astronavigation (never used any more but it makes me feel good knowing it's there), cruising guides for the various countries we intend to visit, books on seabirds, fish, cooking and a frequently used book on knots, in which I know exactly where to find a knot that I am unable to tie, which means almost any knot except a bowline or a reef knot. My own books, such as World Cruising Routes and Handbook are also often perused. On the first Aventura we carried the complete set of the Oxford Children's Encyclopaedia, which Doina and Ivan referred to frequently. Nowadays such reference material is available on CD. Guides to specific countries are best bought in advance as often they are unavailable locally.

Music can be just as important as books and on the first Aventura we left with stacks of pre-recorded tapes that we played on one of my tape recorders. Aventura III has a proper sound system with two stereo speakers in the main cabin and two more in the cockpit. At the beginning we only had cassette tapes but have now progressed to a CD player. Our trusted Super 8 film projector has been replaced by a DVD player but neither Gwenda nor I are all that keen to spend our time glued to a flickering screen while anchored in a beautiful bay so we decided against getting a proper television set and play the occasional DVD on one of my laptops.

Our preferred pastime is listening to the BBC World Service on the SSB radio although sometimes listening to grim news bulletins can hardly be described as a pastime. Short wave radio is quickly becoming a thing of the past and there are now various satellite radio as well as television services that it is possible to subscribe to.

Communications

From nothing to virtually everything is how the change from the first Aventura to the current one can be described. When we

The Iridium satellite phone can be useful on long passages as it has worldwide coverage

first set off we did not even have a VHF radio although towards the end of the voyage we did acquire an SSB radio. Aventura III has the whole range of communications, VHF and SSB transceivers, Inmarsat C for text and email, and an Iridium satellite phone for voice and email. My two laptops have been programmed to be interchangeable. For communicating by Inmarsat C, although not for receiving weather information, one must set up an account with a service provider. In the case of the Iridium phone one can either have a permanent account with a monthly subscription fee with calls being charged as per their duration, or one can buy minutes in bulk that are valid for a certain period i.e. 500 minutes for 12 months.

Email has become my main means of communication and although I normally use the Iridium phone to send messages I can also use the Inmarsat C as a backup. I use *www.uuplus.com* as a service provider. They specialise in satellite communications and provide a prompt and helpful service to their customers. The system has worked very well although some might find the use of the satellite phone to be expensive. I estimate my email costs to be around $5 per day. Mainly for this reason many cruising sailors use one of the radio based systems that are much more economical, even if slower and not suitable for volume users such as myself.

Mobile phones are nowadays extremely useful and while cruising in the Mediterranean I realized that most marinas no longer use VHF radio but expect to be contacted by phone. GSM is now the accepted standard and is used in most countries. I have almost global coverage with my tri-band model that covers two digital frequencies, 900 and 1800 MHz, and one analogue 1900 MHz. It works everywhere in Europe and also in some US cities and South American countries. In the Caribbean it only works in the French islands, which are on GSM, but not in some Anglophone islands where they use different frequencies. As the roaming charges and costs of making calls while abroad can be extremely high, it is well worth buying a local SIM card if staying longer in a certain country. Recently I acquired an international SIM card that I use when travelling abroad as it cuts the cost of calls by up to 75% and incoming calls are free.

For distant communications SSB radios were very useful in the not so distant past when I often used to make calls home via one of the relay stations. Most of these have now been closed down bringing to an end over a century of ship-to-shore communications, initially by telegraph, later by radio. My own use of the SSB radio has gone down dramatically and most of the time I only switch it on to listen to the news. Occasionally I have joined in one of the cruisers' radio nets that have proliferated in every corner of the world but I must admit that when I am in the middle of the ocean I don't like to keep the radio on for too

long nor am I all that interested in other people's chatter. This chatter has seriously undermined the nets' initial role of providing a means of reporting one's position, getting updates on weather and having a place to appeal to in case of trouble. Some radio nets have become almost as bad as mobile phones with the verbal diarrhoea making my hair stand on end.

In the old days snail-mail was virtually the only means of communication between sailors and their families as international phone calls were ridiculously expensive. Most sailors used holding addresses en route such as poste restante/general delivery or local yacht clubs, and often had to wait for weeks for mail to catch up with them. I remember my friends Erick and Muriel Bouteleux waiting for weeks in some port to receive the next batch of school assignments for Sidonie and Fabien as the French system insisted that students' work was completed in a timely fashion. For those who are still dependent on the mail system the most reliable holding addresses continue to be yacht clubs or marinas. It is advisable to contact them in advance to ask permission to use their services and also to give them an ETA and tell them to hold your mail until arrival.

Pets

Obviously it is better to have a small pet on a big boat than a large pet on a small boat.

Luc Callebaut

We have never had pets on any of our boats, nor at home for that matter, although Doina got a puppy for Nera and Dan recently so I'd better be careful what I say. Knowing how strongly some

Titus with Jeannette and Jean-François Delvaux of Alkinoos

people feel about this subject I am quite reluctant to be too outspoken on the subject of cruising pets. My main objection is of a practical nature. The restrictions applied to pets are similar to those concerning firearms and there are a few countries where importing a pet illegally is considered no lesser crime than trying to hide a gun from customs. Regulations concerning cruising pets are extremely stringent in some countries and this is the main reason why the number of cruising boats with pets is still very low, probably less than five per cent. To have or not to have a pet is a difficult question and anyone considering having a pet should think very carefully before setting off on a long voyage. I feel that especially in the case of large dogs confining them on a boat is both selfish and cruel. Small dogs or cats may be a different matter.

A German couple whom we met in many places during our first voyage, and who had a delightful poodle whom Doina and Ivan adored, admitted that having a dog with them during their voyage around the world had been a major mistake mainly because their freedom of movement had been severely restricted. Luc Callebaut disagrees. 'Cruising with a pet on board is

so nice that we plan to get a second one so we can even start breeding Schipperke dogs.' Now that is a thought!

Pests

Uninvited pests are a very different matter and cockroaches, for instance, can be a real nuisance in the tropics especially as once they are in residence they are almost impossible to get rid of. This is why it is so important to avoid being gate-crashed by these nasty squatters by observing some basic rules: never leave food remains in the open, always clean the area around the galley thoroughly, rinse fresh fruit and vegetables, and especially stems of bananas, before being taken on board (some suggest adding one or two chlorine water purifying tablets to the rinsing water), immediately remove from the boat cartons and other packaging after unpacking. Some people even suggest removing labels from tins as they can be infested with eggs. If laying up the boat in the tropics, sprinkle anti-cockroach powder in all critical areas including the bilges. Once the boat is infested the only way to get rid of the roaches is to have the boat professionally fumigated. Because we didn't know what precautions to take, Aventura I got badly infected with cockroaches and although we regularly fumigated the interior we only managed to keep matters under control but never to get rid of that nuisance completely until we returned to temperate zones. Being now much wiser, I have never had a cockroach on Aventura III and I do make sure that my crew observe the rules outlined above.

Mosquitoes can be an even greater nuisance and in some countries also carry the risk of malaria, dengue fever and other diseases. On our first voyage we took prophylactic malaria tablets in critical areas but because of their side effects and also the fact that some malaria strains have become drug resistant, many people have stopped using them. Instead, it makes sense to avoid being bitten by mosquitoes in the first place. The first rule is to anchor far enough from the shore so as to be out of their range. Mosquito nets or screens should be fitted over all openings. Using burning coils and ultrasound devices is also recommended. When going ashore always use a good repellent spray or cream and try avoiding such critical times as dusk and early evening when mosquitoes are most active.

Flies can be bad too and in Croatia we were invaded by huge swarms of fat black flies. Sprays and sticky hanging tapes seem to work and, if one has the patience, swatters too. Also in Croatia for the first time we were on a boat pestered by some very aggressive wasps. Fortunately our friends Germaine and Arthur Beiser had thoughtfully provided us with a Zephyr, a battery operated electronic zapper obtainable from local hardware stores.

An irate skua divebombs the intruding photographer

Photography

Photography has played a major role in my voyaging and, in fact, in all my life. The first job I got after leaving school was as a roaming photographer for a studio whose owner gave me a camera and flashgun and told me to go to restaurants in the evenings, take pictures of people eating or dancing, give them a card with the address of the studio and tell them to pass by if they wanted to order the finished result. When I handed out the card I charged a small deposit, and this I could keep whereas the studio kept whatever it made out of the order. It was an easy job, I was earning well and I enjoyed it. Soon afterwards my father came home on one of his regular shuttles between prison and freedom, and I proudly took him shopping and bought him a new suit. I was only sixteen.

When Aventura I arrived in Fiji and I saw the low prices in the duty-free shops I decided to go for the best and invested in two top of the range Nikon cameras and assorted lenses. It was a wise decision because over the years they have paid handsome dividends. Excellent results followed almost immediately, which was not surprising as we were cruising in one of the most photogenic areas in the world, later to be matched by equally stunning Antarctica. I now have a large selection of colour slides from our many years of

137

cruising but last year I decided to move with the times and switch to digital photography. This means that the slides will have to be scanned, which is a daunting prospect as there must be well over ten thousand of them.

My attempts in the field of movies were more disappointing and came to an abrupt, and ultimately fortuitous, end on Easter Island. As the weather was unsettled, we could not leave the boat unattended in the open anchorage off the main settlement of Hangaroa, so first Gwenda and Ivan visited the giant statues, then Doina and I. As the site was several kilometres from the anchorage, we hired two horses from a local man. Lucia and Gloria looked quite a sorry pair but the owner assured me that they were gentle and obedient animals. We took his word and set off towards the distant quarry where the giant statues had been carved and left abandoned by the mysterious earlier inhabitants of the island. As we got to the bottom of the extinct crater I prodded Lucia to stop, which she did. I dismounted and my feet had hardly touched the ground when Lucia jerked her head violently, the bridle slipped off her head, as it had not been well tied, and my mount galloped away as if possessed by devils. Leaping wildly trying to get rid of the saddlebag I watched in horror as the bag started emptying its contents, starting with my Super 8 camera that described a high arc then crashed on to the stony ground followed by my other accoutrements. Once the bag had stopped banging against her sides, Lucia calmed down and started munching grass. Meanwhile Doina's Gloria looked on placidly with a sympathetic look in her beautiful large eyes as if saying, 'nothing to do with me, Guv.'

We tied Gloria's reins to a large boulder, left Lucia to fend for herself and climbed to the top of the Rano Raraku crater to wander among the huge half-finished statues. That place, and Easter Island generally, is a fascinating place that exudes not just the sense of mystery that one expects on that magical island but an almost palpable feeling of a further dimension, something indefinable that I felt just as strongly on my return to the island years later with Aventura III.

Sightseeing over we untied Gloria and walked gently towards her neurotic sister. As we got closer, Lucia stepped back and kept the same distance from us whatever we did. Eventually it became clear that I'd never manage to get hold of her, so we set off on the long trek to Hangaroa, Lucia walking behind at the same safe distance. It was well after dark by the time we got to the village where we found the owner blind drunk on our rental fee and incapable of understanding what had happened.

Lucia put a premature end to my amateur filming career and although I managed to get the camera repaired when we got to Tahiti, I realized that Super 8 was a very expensive hobby and, having been submitted to many excruciatingly boring presentations of "holiday films", I felt that I didn't want to join that crowd and I'd better stick with what I knew best. So I stayed with still photography and have also tried to keep away from any mode of transport with four legs.

As for practical advice, as with everything else on a boat, it is worth getting two cameras: a small compact one that fits easily in a pocket for quick trips ashore, and a serious model for important assignments, ideally SLR, with a zoom telephoto lens for action shots such as breeching whales, leaping dolphins or wheeling birds. A wide-angle lens is essential to be able to take photos of what is happening on the boat itself.

Recovering from a burn Ivan entertains children in the Solomon Islands

During our first voyage I could rig up a complete dark room on board to develop films and print photos wherever we went. I also had a film projector and screen. One item worth having nowadays is a colour printer to be able to produce photographs and give them to local people, as photographs are one of the most appreciated gifts. Another useful tip is to produce a postcard with a photo of the boat and details of the crew, which can be given to friends ashore or stuck in one of those guest albums kept by committed liveaboards.

Needless to say, one must always respect local customs and never take photographs of anyone without having asked permission first as in some places people can get very upset if photographed without their agreement. How to interact with locals is a controversial subject and one should not take it too lightly as the exaggerated generosity of some cruisers has spoilt the scene for all those who followed. It is much better to trade for local produce in exchange for such things as fishhooks, fishing line, lengths of rope, T-shirts, sugar, cooking oil, etc. Naturally if locals prefer to be paid for food or souvenirs, money is still the better answer. Giving children sweets is

not a good idea, especially on islands with no dental facilities and so we always carried enough balloons or coloured pencils to be used as gifts.

Health matters

With good nutrition and such a healthy life as most cruisers lead it is not surprising that most are in good health. During the five years of my latest voyage I was never ill and only had to use my medical chest to treat one crew for an ear infection that he had picked up while diving. The most common complaints that I came across on other boats were ear and eye infections, burns and superficial wounds, scratches or insect bites. Sailors are particularly vulnerable to skin infections caused by grazings or insect stings. The infection is normally caused by the staphylococcus bacteria of which there are various strains. As the infections may take long to heal and cannot be easily kept dry they should not be treated by standard antiseptic or antibiotic creams but one of the powders recommended for this condition.

There were two serious injuries sustained by participants in the Millennium Odyssey involving outboard engines. While swimming close to his Taratoo in the anchorage off Mustique, in the Eastern Caribbean, Fabio Colapinto was run down by a local fishing boat. Fabio was badly cut by the propeller and was rushed to the hospital in Martinique where he fully recovered. In the Maldives, a young crew fell overboard from the dinghy and sustained severe cuts from the propeller as he was not wearing the automatic shut-off lanyard that stops the outboard motor. He had to be hospitalized and rejoined the yacht in the Red Sea.

Every year there are a number of injuries in the ARC, the most serious being those caused by the boom as happened to one of the crew on my very first outing with the BBC yacht. In New Zealand I was reminded of that eventful weekend when a sailor from a boat moored next to ours had to be rushed to Whangarei Hospital. He was taken to the casualty department where the doctor surprised him by exclaiming, 'You must be off one of the yachts in the harbour.'

'Yes,' replied our neighbour, 'but how did you know?'

'Because only yachties come to us with stupid accidents like this,' said the surgeon and proceeded to stitch him up.

There is always a much higher risk of catching an infectious disease while ashore than on the boat and it is therefore essential to check what vaccinations are necessary for the countries you plan to visit. Ideally such vaccinations should be done while still at home, but if they need to be done abroad, because of such real risks as HIV Aids and hepatitis, always make sure that disposable syringes are used and, if necessary, bring your own. The same advice applies if having any blood tests done.

Alison Wicks who sailed in the Millennium Odyssey urged anyone setting off on a world voyage to take personal health matters just as seriously as the preparations of the boat. 'Everyone should have a thorough medical check-up before leaving, monitor their health throughout the voyage and get the best international health insurance available. That way you probably won't need it.'

Obtaining this type of policy may be difficult for those who are already underway, so it advisable to start buying such insurance before the planned voyage so that it can be renewed more easily once the voyage had started. A comprehensive travel insurance that covers health, emergency evacuation in serious cases, as well as such things as flight cancellations is by far the best option although often quite difficult to get.

First Aid Kit

- Cotton wool and sterile gauze
- Waterproof adhesive dressings in various sizes
- Butterfly sutures, Steristrips or plasters that pull the edges of a cut together
- Sticking plaster, sterile bandages, crepe bandages for sprains
- Non-stick sterile dressings for burns
- Small scissors, tweezers, safety pins
- Thermometer
- Disposable needles and syringes (5 ml is the most useful size)
- Sterile needles with sutures for stitching
- Skin disinfectant e.g. sulphanamide powder, antiseptic and antibiotic creams, iodine tincture

On board pharmacy

Besides a comprehensive first aid kit, having a well-equipped medical chest is of utmost importance if cruising in remote places where medical help may be impossible to reach quickly in an emergency. My friend Peter Noble, who is a consultant psychiatrist but knows more about general medicine and latest developments than most general practitioners, took charge of my medical chest when I started preparing the first Aventura for her long voyage. Peter assembled a comprehensive range of medicines to cover all eventualities and has continued to do so for every one of my subsequent boats.

Regulations regarding drugs vary enormously from country to country and some customs officials may confiscate certain strong painkillers such as morphine. In several countries however, the laws are more relaxed, and many drugs that normally are only available on prescription, such as antibiotics, can be bought over the counter. Many skippers use this opportunity to stock up their medicine chest or replace drugs that have passed their expiry date. The effectiveness of antibiotics decreases with age and storage in tropical conditions but some antibiotics can still be used after the expiry date by increasing the dosage.

All medicines should be labelled and kept in their original containers. As each preparation has a trade name and a generic name, and trade names differ from country to country, a foreign doctor may not be able to advise on the use of some medications if the generic name is not known. Except in an emergency, prescription medicine should only be used on medical advice, which may be obtained over the SSB radio, satellite telephone or Inmarsat C. Excellent information is also available on the internet. It is useful to carry a formulary or pharmacopoeia for reference on dosage and indications for use.

Families sailing with young children should have specific children's remedies. In an emergency, it may be possible to use adult medication for children if the tablets or capsule are divided carefully with a sharp knife so that the reduced children's dose, as listed in the formulary, can be administered. It is often possible to improvise. Cotton and linen clothing and sheets can be cut up to make bandages and be sterilized by boiling for five minutes. Sail battens make good splints. When setting up the medicine chest for a long voyage it is advisable to consult one's own doctor, who is the best person to give advice on what to take. Most doctors will also prescribe certain drugs, which are on the restricted list, once the reason has been explained. It may be worth doing a first aid training course and get advice on how to use scalpels, sutures and syringes should the need arise. As Gwenda is a trained pharmacist we didn't have to do this and her skills did come in useful on a few occasions.

Being able to help a sick person with medication in a remote location is of such utmost importance that it is worth carrying items that may be needed, such as sufficient antibiotic and antiseptic cream, bandages, painkillers and some broad spectrum antibiotics.

Fortunately I very rarely had to access my comprehensive pharmacy but was often able to help sailors on other yachts or people ashore. While on the island of Tanna in Vanuatu I met a local fisherman who had a horrible looking open sore on his leg. I took him back to the boat and bandaged the wound as well as I could but realized that the infection was so far advanced and if it wasn't properly treated he would probably lose his leg. I told him that he needed to go to the local hospital but he objected saying that it wasn't really necessary. I would have none of it, called a taxi and we both drove there. On the way he admitted that he had been there already but that he had been sent away as he couldn't pay the fee.

The "hospital" was a small clinic attended by an overworked nurse. I insisted that my charge was properly treated and told the nurse that I wanted his dressing to be changed every day and that I'd like to pay for the entire treatment in advance. I was amazed when the bill came only to seven dollars for seven days. This poor man could have lost a leg because when he first came to the clinic he couldn't afford to pay one dollar!

Also in Vanuatu, we anchored in Gaua Bay on the island of Vanua Lava and went ashore to pay our respects to the local chief. We found him in a darkened hut moaning with pain. He pointed to his sore legs and explained that he had been attacked by wild dogs as he was walking home from the nearest village. He managed to get hold of a low branch and pull himself up but the dogs had snapped at his legs and bitten him badly. The bites had by now gone septic, so I rowed back to Aventura and brought back my first aid kit to disinfect them. I also gave him a course of antibiotic tablets. During the time we spent there his wounds started healing and I was greatly relieved that he did not seem to have got rabies as well. One day his wife stopped me to say that she had terrible toothache, so I gave her some Paracetamol tablets, which temporarily relieved the pain. As the nearest clinic was on the other side of the island and there was no path across through the impenetrable jungle they had no choice but fend for themselves as well as they could. Before we left I gave them all the medicines I could spare. To show their gratitude on the morning of our departure they put on a show of water music for us.

Tips

- Never swim on passage except in emergencies (to clear a fouled propeller).
- Install a stern light on a separate switch from the bow navigation lights, so it can be used to shed light on the self-steering gear and stern platform making it easier to board from the dinghy or handle a fish caught in the dark.
- Keep some water from the watermaker separately in a jerrycan by the galley for drinking, making coffee or tea. It tastes better than out of the main tank and saves electricity by not having to operate the fresh water pump every time you need small amounts of water.
- LPG bottles must be stowed in a locker that empties overboard. The gas supply to the galley should have a remote automatic cut-off at the tank end, not in the galley.
- Carry a good supply of disposable gloves to be used for doing dirty jobs: cleaning the toilet or handling oil and filters when servicing the engine.
- If stopping in a place where provisioning is very good plan ahead and stock up on those items that may not be available in places you plan to visit later.
- Have a well planned medicine chest and carry sufficient antibiotic and antiseptic creams, bandages, pain killers and broad spectrum antibiotics to be able to help people living in isolated places.
- Never eat lagoon fish unless you are told by a local fisherman that there is no risk of ciguatera fish poisoning in those waters.
- Have some gifts for children such as balloons, coloured pencils but no sweets!
- Produce a postcard with a photo of your boat and details of the crew to hand over to new friends ashore and afloat.
- Invest in a good quality digital camera with wide-angle and telephoto lenses as well as a colour printer.
- Get an international roaming SIM card for your mobile phone.

The Call of the Ocean

Every voyage should be made twice;
first to make mistakes and the second
time to put those mistakes right.

John Steinbeck

There is a lot of wisdom in that saying but what reason could I have for setting off on a third voyage around the world?

The end of our first voyage in 1981 had been traumatic as I was not ready to give up the sailing life. After we returned to England I started preparing for a voyage to the Pacific, ostensibly to take up an offer of employment with the Australian Overseas Radio Service but really only an excuse to continue sailing. However I soon realised that I would not be happy away from the family and that Doina and Ivan's education was paramount, so I let reason prevail and faced up to my responsibilities. In the following years various commitments limited my freedom to sail: family, writing, building up World Cruising Club and organizing rallies.

Aventura II had been designed and built with a world voyage in mind but in reality things turned out very differently and she ended up as a convenient floating base during the first round the world rally. Nor did Aventura III bring the fulfilment of my dream any closer as I was still fully involved with organizing rallies and her initial voyage as part of the Millennium Odyssey,

although satisfying, was still far removed from my real intentions. It was only when I had sold World Cruising Club that finally I was able to put my long nurtured plan into action; to wind back the clock and leave on an open-ended voyage just like we had done with the first Aventura, to sail without any restrictions and keep going however long it might take. The realization that I had finally reached that point filled me with a deep feeling of elation. I knew that at long last I was truly free.

In the summer of 2001 Gwenda and I sailed Aventura back from the Aegean to her base on the French Riviera and started

Erick Bouteleux's Igloo side by side with Aventura before our departure from St Raphael

preparations for the forthcoming voyage. Erick took charge of the technical side of things, giving Aventura a thorough service from the bottom of the centreboard to the top of the mast. All sails were laundered, checked and serviced, the main engine and outboards overhauled, all essential equipment inspected and serviced and the medical chest checked and replenished. On the suggestion of Brookes & Gatehouse

I upgraded the autopilot to the more powerful hydraulic version.

At last everything seemed to be ready. As there was no sign of the mistral, Gwenda and I left St Raphael and headed out to sea, sailing past St Tropez and the off-lying islands, and set course for Menorca. Watching the receding coastline I was elated, Aventura III was always meant to take me on a long voyage and now, with all the time in the world, I was itching to be back in the South Seas, to visit some of my favourite places again, to meet old friends and to explore new routes.

The mistral is a round-the-year feature and affects the entire area between the mouth of the mighty Rhone River and the western edge of the Cote d'Azur. Every year boats get into trouble in the violently short seas set up by a 40 knot mistral. The Phoenicians, Greeks and Romans dreaded it and there are lots of wrecks around these coasts that are a permanent reminder of the unfortunate sailors who lost their lives only miles from their destination, usually the Greek colony of Masilia (now Marseille). There is an excellent museum on the island of Porquerolles with archaeological finds made by diving enthusiasts over the years. From the variety of the exhibits it is evident that there was a huge amount of trade in wine, olive oil and many other goods and the maritime traffic in antiquity was staggering.

'In the Mediterranean you either have too much wind or none at all, and when there is wind it is from the wrong direction.' Right? Wrong! After many years of sailing in the Med all I can say is that this oft repeated mantra probably comes from one of those sailors who leave port with the sail covers on. Our 1,500 mile trip from the French Cote d'Azur to the Canaries, during which we had excellent sailing conditions, only proved the point.

Balearic landfall

At dawn on the third morning, after a comfortable passage most of it under spinnaker, we made landfall on the NE coast of Menorca, the smaller of the two main islands in the Balearics. With a whole day ahead of us we decided to carry on to get as close as possible to Mahon, the capital and main port of Menorca. We called several marinas but all were full and as this was the height of the sailing season we expected crowded anchorages as well. Our only option seemed to be the well protected bay at Mesquida, only a few miles from Mahon. We dropped the hook in front of the small fishing village and were amazed that we had the entire bay to ourselves. We took the dinghy ashore, walked to the nearest bar, called a taxi and twenty minutes later were deposited in front of a cash machine in the centre of Mahon so we could pay the cab. What a great relief it is nowadays to no longer juggle various European currencies as all the way from Greece to France and Spain all you need is a pocketful of euros.

We walked across the main square to the tourism office and were told that we had a choice of five different cyber cafes to check our emails. Cruising in the Med could not be easier! We spent the rest of the day re-acquainting ourselves with this picturesque land-locked harbour, once the main British naval base in the Mediterranean, and now overflowing with cruising boats of all shapes and sizes. Our brief Menorcan sojourn was the perfect start to a week-long Balearic cruise which took us to every one of the four main islands of the archipelago with the exception of Cabrera. That small island is now a nature reserve where visits by cruising boats are strictly controlled and must be booked well in advance. When I called

144

the office to make a booking I was told that all places had been reserved for over one month in advance, so Cabrera had to wait until another time.

In many respects Menorca feels like Mallorca's lesser sister, something which the Romans must have noticed all those

In total contrast to elegant Palma de Mallorca, Ibiza was once renowned as the most laid back place in Europe, but the hippies have now been replaced by serious party-goers who come in droves to enjoy the countless night clubs and hot spots. The island has such a reputation in England

The well-sheltered harbour of Mahon

years ago when they differentiated between the two by calling one 'major' and the other 'minor'. The islands are indeed quite different as Menorca has maintained much of its rural character whereas Mallorca is now one of the prime tourist destinations in the world. Its yachting facilities are also the most developed of all the Balearic Islands, with several marinas and many charter companies based there. Fortunately much of the cruising is marina based so even at the height of season it was possible to find relatively uncrowded anchorages, especially in the picturesque calas, narrow rocky coves that are the main feature of Mallorca's indented coasts.

that 'to do an Ibiza' is now equivalent to having a wild party. After a quick look around Ibiza's busy port, where again we found no room, we thought neighbouring Formentera might be a better choice for a quiet night before the passage to Gibraltar, which we planned to do nonstop rather than in short hops along Spain's Costa del Sol. As we sailed into Formentera's main anchorage we could hardly believe our eyes as we estimated to be surrounded by at least two hundred yachts. Being closest to the Spanish mainland, Formentera is obviously the preferred first stop for anyone setting off on a summer cruise, although I suspected that many boats never sailed much further than here. Long before night-fall, like birds flying home to roost, most had moved into one of the marinas, and we had the peaceful anchorage almost to ourselves.

We left the following morning for Gibraltar and an easterly breeze gave us an unexpectedly fast passage allowing us to cover the 400 miles in just over two days. This was the second time since we had left Greece that the weather had been on my side and disproved Gwenda's conviction that whenever she came on board the winds were

Europa Point at the tip of Gibraltar marks the point where the Mediterranean meets the Atlantic Ocean

on the nose. Not only had we sailed most of the distance under spinnaker but we had encountered much more sea life than we had ever imagined existed in the Mediterranean. We saw several turtles, one large shark, lots of dolphins, some pilot whales and, almost impossible to believe, a pod of three sperm whales! In all my years of crisscrossing the oceans of the world I had seen plenty of whales, some too close for comfort, but never a sperm whale. It proved that after many years of neglect, the Mediterranean countries have got their act together and pollution seems to be finally under control.

Home from home in Gibraltar

The Rock of Gibraltar loomed massively on the western horizon outlined in pinks and purples by the setting sun as Aventura was giving her best to make port before nightfall. We rounded Europa Point in fading light, the coast of Africa, only seven miles across the straits, already swallowed up by darkness. We tied up to the reporting dock near the runway just as a jet was taking off with its engines screaming at full throttle. Immigration, customs and port authority were all housed in the same

office and the simple formalities, conducted in good old English, only took a few minutes. We then moved across into Marina Bay Marina and walked to one of the restaurants lining the esplanade for an excellent dinner of fresh swordfish; a perfect finale to a most enjoyable passage and a splendid way to celebrate our departure from the Mediterranean.

Next morning we walked down Main Street crowded with tourists shopping for duty-free goods. A cable car took us to the top of the Rock for a panoramic view of the surrounding area, Spain's Costa del Sol on one side, Morocco's mountainous shores on the other. As one of the ancient Pillars of Hercules (the other is Gebel Musa in Morocco), the Rock of Gibraltar (Gebel Tarik in Arabic) has always been a significant landmark for sailors and the Rock's strategic position at the crossroads of two seas and two continents has coloured its history.

Gibraltar's association with Britain that goes back three hundred years has resulted in a fiercely independent people who value their freedom to decide their fate more than anything else. Because of their long isolation during the dark years of Franco's dictatorship in neighbouring Spain, the Gibraltarians are extremely hospitable to visitors and the government gave me its wholehearted support when I suggested that the first round the world rally should start and finish here. That successful event was followed by a similar rally three years later and in the intervening years I have been fortunate in always being able to count on Gibraltar's generous support for my various projects.

the Atlantic. I turned to have a last look at the looming Rock and realized just how fond I was of this truly unique place, and wondered where else a sailor could feel so genuinely 'home from home'?

We sailed past Cape Trafalgar but instead of turning SW towards Cape Espartel that marks the NW point of Africa, I set a course for the mouth of the river Guadiana which marks the border between Spain and Portugal. A few miles before we reached our destination we passed close by the mouth of another Spanish river, the Odiel, made

The suspension bridge over the river Guadiana linking Spain and Portugal

Although part of the European Union, Gibraltar is outside the EU VAT Area and the tax-free status enjoyed by visiting tourists and yachts has many attractions as diesel fuel costs less than elsewhere and one can almost sink the boat with duty-free drinks such as whisky at five euros a bottle. It also means that, for the time being, non-EU boats can spend as long as they wish in Gibraltar without affecting the total of 18 months that can be spent in the EU.

Three days later, fuelled and provisioned, with the tide in our favour and, once again, a nice easterly breeze, we headed west into

famous by a small fleet of three caravels that set off from here on 3 August 1492 bound for what was to become the New World. In 1992, as part of the celebrations marking that significant anniversary, the 146 yachts taking part in the America 500 rally, set off from here and faithfully followed in their wake.

The Algarve coast

A firm resolution that I had made for this voyage was not to bypass any of the places I had missed before and the side trip to the Guadiana was just the first of many such detours. In the early morning mist, the

The medieval compass rose at the school of navigation at Sagres

massive bridge over the wide river looked frighteningly low and I wondered if we could manage to get under it with our 50-foot mast. Although the bridge had been built a few years earlier, it wasn't shown on my latest chart and no one in the marina at Ayamonte, where we had spent the night, could tell me its actual height. So I timed our passage when the tide was at its lowest, crossed my fingers and hoped for the best. As we edged closer moving at the slowest speed possible it looked increasingly doubtful that we'd make it. As we finally passed under what looked like the highest point of the central span, I thought I saw the VHF aerial quiver on top of the mast.

'Just your imagination,' quipped Gwenda whose heart was in her mouth just as much as mine was.

'OK, but just to be on the safe side, we'd better make sure we get back at low water again, or we'll spend all winter here.'

As this was one of Europe's corners that I had not visited before, and knowing that the river was navigable for about forty miles by shallow drafted craft, I was determined not to miss this opportunity to explore the area as it would be many years before Aventura would sail this way

again. The best time to visit is autumn, when flocks of migratory birds stop here on their way to Africa. As we moved steadily northward we saw various species of wading birds among the tall bamboos and reeds that flanked the two shores. Wherever the river narrowed, there were abandoned observation posts, invariably on the Spanish side, remnants from the time of Franco when this was a busy smuggling route. Most of the small isolated farms also looked abandoned and for miles and miles we saw not a single human soul but plenty of storks nesting in trees, fish jumping in the river and ibis wading in the shallows.

On the Spanish side a hilltop fortress loomed large above the town of Sanlucar opposite its Portuguese twin of Alcoutim. Both towns had installed pontoons for visitors but these were already taken up by a score of cruising boats. I had heard that the Guadiana had become a favourite place to spend the winter, as villages and towns on both shores had installed docks for which no charge was made, the weather was some of the mildest you could find anywhere in Europe and formalities were virtually nonexistent.

With the tide helping us along we pushed on to Pomarão, at the navigable limit of the river, only touching bottom with the centreboard as we tied to a pontoon in front of a small restaurant on the

Portuguese bank. With some Spanish and plenty of gestures I managed to get the owner to understand what we wanted. It took some time to prepare but we had one of our most memorable meals of fresh fish grilled on a wood fire, salad of tasty field-ripened tomatoes drenched in olive oil and a bottle of vinho verde, a chilled, slightly fizzy white wine.

As the tide turned, we retraced our steps and reached the bridge at the right moment. From the Guadiana in the east to Cape St Vincent in the west, the Algarve coast of Portugal has seen a lot of tourism development in recent years, and yachting facilities have followed suit. Several marinas have sprung up along the coast and they provide a convenient break for boats heading either south from Northern Europe to the Canaries or to and from the Mediterranean. We turned in for the night

Bahia de la Francesa on Graciosa's west coast

at Marina Lagos, set in a picturesque old town whose wealth was based on its trade with Africa. A reminder of those times is the former slave market that stands in its centre, now converted into an art gallery. Close by stands the monument of Prince Henry the Navigator, the visionary who inspired some of the remarkable voyages of discovery of the late 15th century. Most of the early Portuguese explorers were trained at the school of navigation set up by Prince Henry at Sagres, close to Cape St Vincent.

In the morning we tucked into a small bay right below the St Vincent lighthouse. A steep path took us to the fortress on the hill above. The massive walls of the famous medieval school of navigation were in surprisingly good condition as was the drawbridge guarding the entrance. Inside the large enclosed area, the most impressive feature was a giant compass rose measuring some one hundred feet across and intersected by thirty lines of flat stones radiating outwards in different directions. The rose was only discovered in the 1920s and no one has been able to guess its meaning. I reflected on its possible use and wondered why so many of the early voyages of discovery had started from this corner of Europe. Was it because of the proximity of the prevailing northeast trade winds and its location far enough south for the Atlantic to be less of a menace and navigation to be feasible virtually at any time of the year? Or was it due to the presence of several deep navigable rivers, so important to commerce, and the tradition of boat building that still thrives to this day on their banks? When the decision was made to build replicas of the Columbus caravels in 1992, a yard was found at the mouth of the Guadiana where boats had been built without interruption since the Middle Ages, and probably long before that. I turned my gaze to the giant compass rose and sighted down the line that seemed closest to our intended course to the Canaries. It looked as if it was going to take us safely past the African coast and I wondered how many of the early navigators might have done the same all those years ago. In the small chapel I lit a candle to the memory of Henry the Navigator and those brave souls in whose wake we gratefully follow.

Steady northerly winds stayed with us as we headed into the Atlantic sailing parallel to the African coast. Aventura was sailing fast and I was convinced she was showing me just how happy she was to be on the open ocean again. I certainly was. To cap the perfection the second day out I landed a large yellowfin tuna and so we feasted on our favourite 'poisson cru', the Polynesian dish of raw fish, and had fresh tuna steaks for the rest of the passage.

La Graciosa

At dawn on the fourth day after leaving Cape St Vincent the rocky islets of Allegranza, Montaña Clara and Roque del Oeste, that guard the northern approaches to the Canaries, rose menacingly ahead of us as we slowed down to pass between them in better light. We slid past those brooding giants, ran down La Graciosa's east coast and turned the corner into La Sociedad. Long ago some inspired soul had called the smallest of the eight Canarian islands the Gracious One where the tiny fishing community lived in The Society, while the narrow stretch of water that separates Graciosa from its larger neighbour Lanzarote, and is beset by swift tides, is called El Rio, the River. La Sociedad had visibly changed since our last visit, the port was now embraced by two breakwaters and floating pontoons had been installed for local boats and visitors. The changes ashore were even more striking as where once there was just one dusty street with a flyblown shop now there were a couple of supermarkets, ATM machines and an internet café. A fishing boat had just arrived from a night on the ocean and disgorged onto the quay a heaving carpet of quicksilver, the crew shovelling the wriggling sardines into wheelbarrows. La Graciosa is a favourite holiday retreat for other Canarians who find here what has been lost elsewhere in the archipelago, a tranquil laid-back atmosphere where the arrival of a boatful of fresh sardines brings everyone to the waterfront.

In the balmy morning air we set off across the small island walking past golden sand dunes to its northern rocky shore where the relentless surge of the Atlantic swell had carved out a natural bridge over the boiling waters. Seabirds were wheeling overhead eyeing a lone suicidal crab that was sunning itself on a nearby rock. After many years of being closely associated with the Canaries they have become a second home to me and every time I return I feel like a long departed sailor getting back to his hearth after a long absence. The affection must be mutual because a while back the island of Gran Canaria had officially declared me its adopted son, which I regard as the greatest honour that could be bestowed on anyone.

Wind Selfsteering Gears and Automatic Pilots

The sails must be properly trimmed and adjusted before handing over the steering to either autopilot or windvane

Carlton DeHart

Few other items on an offshore cruising boat have been debated more fiercely than these two stepbrothers who seem to attract love and hatred in equal measure. To avoid this controversial matter I decided to take the logical easy option and have both. In my view wind operated selfsteering gears and electronic automatic pilots do not compete but complement each other and anyone thinking otherwise not only makes a mistake but also sells himself short.

Wind operated selfsteering gears

My windvane doesn't eat, sleep or have an opinion.

Round the world skipper

When I equipped the first Aventura, wind operated selfsteering gears had been around for a decade, pioneered by those legendary early circumnavigators, the main contribution to their development having been made by Sir Francis Chichester. In his epic voyage around the world he used a large contraption that he had designed and mostly built himself. Its oversized windvane was almost as large as the small mizzen sail of his Gypsy Moth yawl. His singlehanded circumnavigation showed that such a

device not only worked but that it made such a strenuous voyage possible. As a qualified pilot Francis Chichester was able to deal with the technical problems of this ingenious device that comes closest to that mythical perpetuum mobile, a perpetual motion machine. As far as I know it is the only piece of equipment on a cruising boat that can work continuously without any visible energy input. The energy is derived from the movement of the boat through the water as well as from the wind, but I still prefer to regard it as a perpetual motion machine.

By the time Aventura I was ready to leave London I had acquired what in those days was regarded as the best and most reliable selfsteering gear. This was the British built Aries, several of which had been used in the

The Hydrovane selfsteering gear keeps Aventura II on course in boisterous conditions

OSTAR, the transatlantic singlehanded race from the UK to the USA. Mine was the second version, more robust and easier to use. The inventor and manufacturer was Nick Franklin a wizard whose help and advice was always forthcoming. Although it was possible to connect the gear to a steering wheel, I decided to stick to the original concept of such gears and lead the steering lines to a tiller. Installing an auxiliary tiller was not an easy solution as Aventura had an aft cabin so I had to use a long 1½ inch (40 mm) shaft extension that passed through the cabin from top to bottom and was connected to the rudder. At its top end it emerged in the middle of the poop deck where a large wooden tiller fitted neatly onto its square head. Although it restricted space in the aft cabin this proved to be an ideal arrangement as not only did the windvane manage to steer the boat easily but I also had a permanently installed emergency steering system.

During the following six years and some 68,000 miles I estimate that the gear steered the boat for about eighty per cent of the time. It didn't always keep the most accurate course but it saved us the enormous drudge of steering by hand, a worthwhile consolation on a short-handed boat that included two young children. When sailing downwind the gear made Aventura meander about twenty degrees each side of the desired course but it didn't bother me too much at the time, although later I realised that those extra miles had added at least two days to our slow 26 day crossing of the Atlantic.

Unfortunately when this perpetual motion machine reverts to its natural state and is idle i.e. when the wind stops, there is only one solution and that is to steer by hand. On the first Aventura an autopilot would have been a godsend but we didn't have the money to buy one nor was there much choice of suitable autopilots for small boats. Some simple tiller pilots had by then appeared on the market but we only managed to get one in Singapore a few months before the completion of our voyage.

Aventura II's steering position in the centrally located cockpit was too far from the stern making it difficult to connect a windvane directly to the steering wheel. For this reason I chose a Hydrovane gear that had the advantage of being independent of the main steering system. Its large rudder was quite capable of steering a forty-foot boat on its own, provided that the sails were well trimmed and also that there was enough wind to move the large windvane, as the wind was its only source of energy. Heavy as she was Aventura II needed a lot of wind to make any progress and therefore so did the Hydrovane. Aventura II was also equipped with an automatic pilot so at long last we had the best of both worlds.

I followed the same principle on Aventura III and got what in the late 1990s was considered the best wind operated selfsteering gear, the German made Windpilot. Its Hamburg based

A stronger plywood vane was fitted to Aventura III's Windpilot to cope with the stronger winds in the Southern Ocean

inventor and manufacturer Peter Förthmann had been a regular visitor at the ARC start in Las Palmas where he came to service and repair his own products but also gave advice to those who had purchased their gears from a competitor.

Aventura's Windpilot is mounted on a special support at the stern, the two control lines being led over blocks to the steering wheel. Because Aventura's large stern arch structure tends to interfere with the windvane Peter supplied me with a custom made vane that fits perfectly under the arch. My model is the more common Pacific but there is also a Pacific Plus that has its own large steering rudder that makes it entirely independent of the boat's main steering system. I also bought a Brookes & Gatehouse automatic pilot that is integrated with the rest of the Hydra system. Just before my latest voyage it was converted fully to a hydraulic system, which significantly increased its power. The autopilot is very accurate and has worked well suffering only a couple of breakages.

To play safe Peter also supplied me with a small Navico tiller pilot that can be used as a backup for the main pilot or when the wind is too light for the windvane to operate and I want to save electricity as the main pilot consumes on average 6 AH while the Navico only 1 AH. With the small autopilot linked to the Windpilot's windvane, the Windpilot mimics the wind by moving the windvane to keep the boat on course. The movement is transmitted via the servorudder to the steering lines and the additional power derived from the movement of the boat through the water helps the small autopilot operate on very little electricity. I occasionally used this system in light winds, especially under spinnaker, when I didn't want to use the larger power hungry autopilot.

Whenever conditions are right I prefer to use the windvane and over the years I have learnt its strengths and weaknesses and we are now good friends. When the wind is light I normally revert to the automatic pilot especially when using a spinnaker. The system suits my style of sailing perfectly.

I wish I could say the same about some of my crew, especially Gwenda, who, in spite of her offshore experience, seems to be incapable of coming to terms with what she considers an uncooperative macho monster. Fortunately as with everything else on Aventura there is an easy solution to that, so as soon as Gwenda takes over her watch, on comes the automatic pilot and happiness and harmony prevail.

As the voyage progressed I have become lazier too and often preferred to push the pilot's on button than start fiddling with the Windpilot, which does need to be set up and tuned properly and also needs constant supervision. When I need to do a major sail change such as hoisting a spinnaker, I prefer to let the boat be steered by the autopilot rather than the windvane. There is a critical moment after having hoisted the spinnaker and released its douser when I need to dash to the cockpit to adjust the sheet and guy. It is then that I must be able to rely on the pilot keeping an accurate course and I always set the autopilot to steer to wind. Once the sail is properly set and the boat is moving along happily I often revert to the Windpilot, mainly to save electricity and also because it is silent.

I agree with those who argue that the advantages of a windvane outweigh its disadvantages but this is only when looking at the subject from the technical point of view. Early in this latest voyage my use of windvane versus autopilot was probably around 70 to 30, but as the voyage progressed and I was trying to sail faster, usually under spinnaker, the windvane went into semi-retirement. This was not the vane's fault but my own as being short-handed and keen on sailing the boat efficiently at all times, I found the autopilot to be more convenient to use. There is no doubt that a good autopilot, especially a top of the range one such as mine, will keep an accurate course under any conditions and not only accurate but reliable too, which is a crucial consideration.

On the wind the Windpilot steers impeccably as this is a windvane's preferred point of sailing. Reaching is also easy provided the boat is not overpowered in which case the mainsail needs to be reefed promptly to avoid too much weather-helm. Broad reaching is any windvane's weakest point and however well the sails are set, the occasional larger wave or stronger gust will push the boat off the desired course and often the gear is either incapable of bringing the boat back on course, or it takes a long time to do it. When running downwind with the sails well adjusted the windvane copes well, although because of the risk of broaching or gybing, when on this point of sailing, I never dare leave the cockpit so as to be able to intervene immediately if necessary. Running downwind wing and wing or with twin jibs is easiest on the windvane and it also works well when sailing with a spinnaker, but in the latter case I always keep a careful eye on it.

What I regard as the main disadvantage of a windvane selfsteering gear is that it keeps steering the boat to the same wind angle regardless of changes in the wind direction. Admittedly, this is also the case with autopilots if they are set to wind and not to a compass heading. While on an overnight passage between two island groups in the Chagos archipelago once we had reached the open sea I wanted to have a short rest, so I set the Windpilot and asked my crew to keep an eye on the selfsteering gear and the course we were sailing. When he called me at the end of his watch I immediately realized that we had gone badly off course and were heading towards the nearest reef. He had not noticed that the wind had changed direction and while

the sails were set as well as before we were now sailing at about 30° off our intended course. Had I come up twenty minutes later we would have run onto that reef.

Maintenance

Maintenance of a windvane is simple as most models only need to be rinsed with fresh water occasionally, the lines checked for chafe and the various nuts regularly tightened. I carry several spare vanes and servorudders and although the latter is of the sacrificial type and would break if it hit something hard, this has never happened to me. However, carrying a spare is essential, a bitter lesson learnt by a friend of mine during the maiden voyage of his boat between New Zealand and Fiji. A couple of hundred miles into the voyage, the servorudder hit something and sheared off. As they had left without a spare, he switched on the autopilot but that wasn't working either, so as there were only the two of them they returned to New Zealand. By then the season was too far advanced and they ended up spending another six months there before resuming their voyage... all because of not having a spare servorudder. On Aventura III I carry three spare servorudders and as many vanes.

Maintenance of the automatic pilot is just as simple. I regularly check the bolt and nut connecting the hydraulic ram to the rudder quadrant. I have several of these half-inch stainless steel bolts because they tend to break on average about once a year. Replacing the bolt is a straightforward operation that only takes a few minutes as Aventura's rudder quadrant and ram are easily accessible by lifting the cockpit teak grating. I also check the level of hydraulic fluid daily and always carry a gallon of it. Once a year I have the brushes of the

A small autopilot can be connected to the Windpilot as a backup

electric motor checked by an electrician, usually when I also have the brushes inspected on the other electrical appliances. As an emergency spare I carry an electric motor for the pilot's hydraulic pump. Before the system was converted to hydraulic I also carried a spare ram. The most serious autopilot breakage happened in Chile but as there were four of us on board, and we were using the windvane extensively, this was not a major inconvenience. A replacement ram was couriered to Valdivia and the system worked well for awhile but that same year, while on passage between Hawaii and Alaska, the autopilot stopped working again. At the time we were motoring across the North Pacific High in thick fog and there were lots of fishing boats around us. As there was hardly any wind we could not use the vane, so I reverted to the small Navico autopilot, which did an excellent job keeping the boat on course.The main autopilot could only be repaired once the boat was back in France.

That breakage was one reason why I decided to upgrade the system for my next voyage, but also the desire for a more powerful autopilot. The new arrangement worked well and only broke down in Malta, when the voyage was virtually completed. Neither myself nor any of the Maltese specialists could figure out the root of the problem, nor did my repeated phone calls to the manufacturers. As I still suspected the culprit to be the hydraulic ram I got in touch with its manufacturers, who couriered to Malta a replacement solenoid, but that didn't put the fault right either. Several calls later I was told to carry out a simple test... and at long last discovered that the ram had jammed and a gentle knock in the right place on its housing got it going again! Not only was I furious that I had not been advised to do this simple test earlier but also that the fault was not mentioned anywhere in the operation manual. Now I am convinced that both in Chile and en route to Alaska that kind of gentle persuasion would have got the pilot going again. I have often been annoyed at the negligence of manufacturers to supply a comprehensive fault finding chart with suggested solutions. The widespread attitude of "if in trouble contact the nearest dealer" may work when your television breaks down at home but not when you are sailing in some remote ocean with only seabirds for company.

Windvanes surveyed

Wind operated selfsteering gears have been examined in a number of surveys. A major equipment survey was conducted among the participants in the second ARC in 1987. Among the 197 yachts 43 per cent had a windvane and 67 per cent an autopilot, while 10 per cent had both. Things have changed dramatically over the years as in ARC 2004 only 25 boats (13%) had a windvane, while almost every yacht had an automatic pilot. The most common makes were Hydrovane (10) and Windpilot (10), followed by Aries (2), Monitor (1). The skippers were asked to rate their selfsteering gears on reliability, user-friendliness and value for money. The top scorer on an average of the marks given to those three features was the Monitor, followed by Hydrovane and Windpilot, but as there was only one Monitor gear that result has little statistical significance. Thirty-nine boats (23%) sailing in ARC 2005 had windvanes: Hydrovane (19), Windpilot (8), Aries (5), Monitor (4), Sailomat (2), Neptune (1). The top scorer on those three features was Sailomat.

The most significant finding of those ARC surveys, which were conducted by Yachting World magazine, is the drop in the number of yachts that are equipped with a wind selfsteering gear compared to twenty years earlier, from an average of around 50 per cent to around 20 per cent. One explanation is that most of the boats sailing in the ARC were planning to be away from home for only one year and had no intention of embarking on a long voyage. Almost invariably windvanes were present on boats planning to continue on a longer voyage after the ARC. This conclusion was confirmed by my own observations during my recent voyage when I noticed that perhaps about half the cruising boats I came across had a wind selfsteering gear mounted on their sterns. Although I could not see it, I am convinced that virtually all of them had an automatic pilot.

Autopilots surveyed

The proportion of automatic pilots on cruising boats has increased steadily over the years and currently there are hardly any boats without one. This observation was reflected in the changes that have occurred in the ARC in the last twenty years. Whereas 67 per cent of the boats had an autopilot in 1987, in the latest ARC an estimated 95 per cent had an autopilot.

Among the skippers who were interviewed in the Global Cruising Survey many expressed their concern over the electricity consumption of their pilots. Although the hourly consumption averaged 3.9 AH, in reality the figure was probably higher as several skippers admitted that they had no idea how much power their autopilots consumed. This prompted me to keep a record of my own consumption over a period of 24 hours and I ended up with an average of 6 AH, which is probably normal for a boat the size of Aventura.

The ARC 2004 survey showed that the most common make of autopilot was Raymarine with 57 Raymarine ST6000, 18 Raymarine Smartpilot 6001, 17 Raymarine Smartpilot 7001, 8 B&G Hydra, 8 Raymarine ST4000, 7 B&G Hercules, etc. The top scorer on reliability, user-friendliness and value for money was the B&G Hercules autopilot. The situation was very similar in ARC 2005 with 54 Raymarine ST6000, 45 Raymarine ST7000+, 13 B&G Hydra, 12 Raymarine Smartpilot, 9 Simrad AP20/21/22, etc., with the latter brand being the top scorer.

Although the ARC survey gave surprisingly high marks for reliability, it should be born in mind that the period under scrutiny was relatively short. In the round the world rallies I was frequently told of autopilot breakages. One of the most frequently cited causes was the fact that many autopilots were considered by their owners as insufficiently powerful to steer a boat under prolonged conditions of strong winds and high swell. For various reasons, whether because of wrong advice by the manufacturers or the

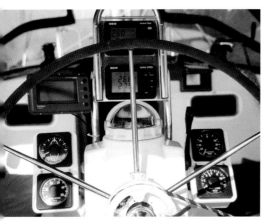

The Windpilot steering lines are brought to a drum on the steering wheel

need to save money, many sailors buy an underpowered unit, so it is not fair to put the blame on the pilot if it was being used under conditions it was not designed for. This is the reason why my own system was upgraded to the more powerful version.

Windvane or autopilot?

Looking at the general picture, as boats become faster and sailors get the taste for speed and efficient sailing, a plodding boat steered by windvane looks like a thing from the past. They were perfectly suitable when six knots was the top speed of most boats and many sailors were happy to average 120 miles per day. When I discussed this matter recently with Peter Förthmann he agreed with me only in part, pointing out that the steady sales of windvanes proved me wrong and that most cruising sailors, for whom speed is not the first priority but safety and comfort, are still happy to use the more environmentally friendly windvane than the power-hungry autopilot. In the end we agreed that we were both right and that among long distance cruising sailors my attitude was probably the exception rather than the rule.

My answer to the above question is that those who plan a long voyage and can afford it should get both a wind selfsteering gear and an autopilot. The one additional piece of advice I want to stress as forcefully as possible is not to be tempted to buy a cheap pilot just to save money. A reliable, powerful and accurate autopilot is of such vital importance to the comfort and above all safety of an offshore voyage that this is one area where only the best will do. The choice of a windvane is more complex and the final choice will depend on the configuration of the stern, the location of the steering wheel, the size and sailing characteristics of the boat and also the style of one's sailing. A good starting point is to read Peter's book on this subject, where he describes all windvane models currently available. He also deals with the main aspects of autopilots. The book is available on *www.windpilot.de*

Tips

- Always keep an eye on possible changes in wind direction when steering by windvane or when the autopilot is set to steer to wind.
- If planning to leave on a long offshore voyage consider having both an autopilot and a wind selfsteering gear.
- Make sure that you have a powerful enough autopilot to cope with long runs under strenuous conditions.
- Carry spare servorudders as well as spare vanes for the selfsteering gear.
- A small backup autopilot should be carried if planning to do long ocean passages with a short-handed crew.

Across the Ocean Sea

In the twenty years since the first ARC brought me to Las Palmas this busy port has become a second home to me and I have many close friends there. Not that it is all that difficult to make friends in Las Palmas, or in the Canaries generally, as there is a strong tradition of welcoming sailors in these islands that goes back to the time of Columbus and possibly even earlier than that as seafarers have called here since time immemorial. The Phoenicians probably visited the islands, the Romans definitely knew of them, a Norman rediscovered them in the Middle Ages and Spain took possession of the entire archipelago shortly after Columbus set off for the New World.

The Canaries, called by the Romans the Enchanted Islands, belong geographically to Africa, as the archipelago lies on the latitude of Southern Morocco, yet they are European in every other respect. Five centuries of Spanish rule has left its indelible mark, although los canarios are quite different from los peninsulares, as the locals call their mainland compatriots. Proud of their land and heritage, and fiercely autonomous, the Canarians are nonetheless the most welcoming and generous people I've met anywhere. Even Horatio Nelson, who lost the battle of Tenerife as well as his arm there, was showered with gifts on his departure.

The eight islands could safely be described as the perfect vacation destination. The climate is warm and pleasant throughout the year, the cost of living very reasonable and crime is among the lowest in Europe. An added attraction is that there is good weather all year round and the sailing season spans twelve months. The NE trade winds blow over the archipelago almost without interruption and because of this a cruise should be planned to take full advantage of the prevailing winds by starting in the NE of the archipelago, in Graciosa or Lanzarote, and zigzag to the other islands as one moves west, with the wind nearly always abaft the beam.

Every island has its own distinctive character: on tiny Graciosa you can enjoy the atmosphere of a small fishing community, Lanzarote's stark volcanic landscape provided the cinematic location for "2001: A Space Odyssey", Fuerteventura's name betrays its fame as a haven for windsurfers, Gran Canaria's unspoilt interior more than makes up for the large tourist developments along its coasts, Tenerife is dominated by the perfect volcanic cone of Mount El Teide, while neighbouring La Palma boasts the largest crater in the world, La Gomera is proud of its association with Columbus, whose favourite island it was, while charming, unspoilt El Hierro continues to feel like the end of the world, as it was regarded in days gone by.

Las Palmas preparations

The majority of yachts calling at the Canaries only use them as a convenient stepping stone on their way to the Caribbean or Brazil. The main rule for anyone intending to do this is not to leave continental Europe, and especially Northern Europe, for the Canaries too late in the season and not to leave the Canaries too early to cross the Atlantic. This means that ideally one should sail south during the summer, July and early August being the best time, and leave the boat in a marina in the Canaries unless one prefers to stay with the boat. Some people who decide to stay use the waiting time to cruise around the archipelago until it is time to sail across the Atlantic. Those who prefer to leave their boat to go home normally return by late October or early November to resume their voyage.

Responding to this trend every one of the Canarian islands now has at least one marina, so a place to leave a boat for longer periods can usually be found provided a

Juan Francisco Martin, known among friends as JuanFra

booking is made early. With so many ports to choose from it is not easy to decide which is the best place to leave from. The relative proximity to the Caribbean is hardly a factor although some sailors do like starting from one of the western islands. My opinion is that it is better to start from a port where provisioning and repair facilities are best. In this respect no island can beat Gran Canaria, especially as repair facilities are concerned. The port of Las Palmas, once notorious for its oily, dirty water, is now much cleaner and Muelle Deportivo, located in a corner of the large commercial harbour, has been miraculously converted into a well run marina with nearly 2000 berths. Repair facilities and provisioning can only be described as excellent, which, mainly thanks to the

demands of the annual ARC, is only to be expected.

Following my own advice, Gwenda and I had made the trip from the Mediterranean to the Canaries to arrive in early September so as to benefit from good winds. As I wasn't planning to leave across the Atlantic until early December I had arranged to leave Aventura in Las Palmas where my friend Juan Francisco Martin had secured me a place on a private pontoon. I had met JuanFra while preparing the first ARC and, over the years, we have become close friends. Every year JuanFra makes a point of sailing at least once on Aventura and has joined me all over the world, from the Bahamas to Vanuatu, St Lucia to Tahiti. Being so familiar with Aventura he has become very proprietary with what he regards, during my absence, as his boat and appears to get a lot of enjoyment looking after her while I am away.

Over the years I have spent a lot of time listening to tales of broken booms and masts, lost rudders, bent spinnaker poles, blown sails, recalcitrant engines and many such problems encountered by ARC participants during the Atlantic crossing. Therefore all I wanted for my third Atlantic crossing was a comfortable passage with minimal problems and hopefully no breakages. This didn't seem an unreasonable wish as Aventura had already taken me safely to Antarctica under conditions that were obviously much harder than a passage in the tropical North Atlantic during the best season.

Good preparation has always been my rule, so before my crew arrived in Las Palmas, I spent a week checking the boat from top to bottom and was surprised to discover a loose strand on one of the lower shrouds near the top swaged terminal. A local rigger promptly swaged two new cables and replaced the suspected pair. If a shroud shows signs of wear and needs to be replaced, it is safest to replace its pair as well.

In all my voyaging I have not been to a place where provisioning for an ocean passage is better than in Las Palmas. Thanks to their mild climate the Canaries produce a wide variety of fruit and vegetables and most of the early fresh produce that arrives during the winter in mainland Europe originates from there. Shopping at one

One of the fresh produce markets in Las Palmas

of the three markets in Las Palmas is an absolute delight and as everything is fresh and not refrigerated, fruit, vegetables and eggs normally outlast an Atlantic crossing. Early one morning I made a tour of the market, did all my shopping at one particularly well stocked stand and asked the owner to deliver everything to my boat, which he promptly did.

My next trip took me to El Corte Ingles, a Spanish department store whose supermarket is on a par with the best in the world. The choice was truly bewildering with a quality to match. From the ready meal counter I ordered three pre-cooked

dinners so as not to have to bother with this chore at the start of our passage. Knowing that I would not be able to find anything comparable in the Caribbean, for once I decided to ignore my dictum and loaded Aventura down with a lot of goodies. A friend of JuanFra's, who is a wholesaler for Rioja wines, supplied me with a selection of vintage wines for the coming Christmas, so that by the time we were ready to leave Aventura could easily compete with the best five star establishment.

Gwenda chose to only join me in the Caribbean, so I had asked my French publisher Gildas de Gouvello and his wife Christine to crew for the crossing. Neither had done any offshore sailing but as they had recently bought a 40 foot yacht with that in mind I invited them to come along. Although we got on very well and they tried hard, I now feel that for a long ocean crossing I should have chosen a more experienced crew, which would have made my life much easier.

By the time they joined me in Las Palmas, the boat was fully provisioned, tidy and organized and I felt that I couldn't have been better prepared. With a good long term forecast we wasted no time and left immediately, heading for that mythical point 1000 miles SW of the Canaries where the butter is supposed to melt and steady trade winds blow all year round. Long before the butter had had a chance to melt (it was in the fridge anyway) we found the NE trade winds and, as the weather looked settled, rather than carry on further south I set a direct course for St Lucia.

Atlantic tactics

The wind system of the North Atlantic is heavily influenced by the Azores High. As is well known, in the Northern hemisphere winds blow in a clockwise direction around an area of high pressure, which means that the prevailing winds north of the Azores High are westerlies, NE on its east side and easterlies south of the Azores High. Conversely, winds blow in an anti-clockwise direction around an area of low pressure, which is why SW winds are so common in the Bay of Biscay and why latecomers bound for the Canaries often get bad weather on their way to the ARC start. There is a certain logic to the North Atlantic, a sort of merry-go-round that I like to call the Atlantic Circle.

When Columbus set sail from Spain in 1492 little was known about what in those days was called the Ocean Sea stretching west from the Canaries. In fact, the limit of the known world was only a few miles away from Las Palmas, at the end of the island of El Hierro. Although a lot has been learnt about prevailing winds and weather forecasting in the intervening years, the routing suggestions made by Columbus as a result of his four voyages to the Caribbean are still valid and can hardly be improved upon. His two fastest passages took 21 days, an excellent time even by today's standards.

Every book that has been written on transatlantic voyaging has something to say about the ideal route for a trade wind crossing, although very little can be added to what Columbus found out. The first concern is to move quickly out of the region of calms and variables that surround the Canaries. The old advice to first make for a point at 25°N, 25°W needs some qualification as the winter trades seldom blow as far north as 25°N, so this suggestion is only valid for summer crossings. A more valid suggestion is to sail SSW for 1000 miles on leaving the Canaries, so as to pass between 200 and 300 miles NW of the Cape Verde Islands before turning west. Unless one has access to up-to-date weather information the suggestion to pass close to the Cape Verdes makes sense, otherwise such a longer route would not be justified. By passing relatively close to the Cape Verdes not only is there a better chance of finding steady ENE winds earlier but, as happens every year in the ARC, those who have an emergency or have burnt up their fuel can stop briefly at Mindelo, on Sao Vicente Island, to fill up with diesel.

Unfortunately there is no way to predict what the crossing will be like as weather conditions vary from year to year and in some years fast passages have been made by boats ignoring the traditional approach and sailing the shortest route across. This is why it is so important to obtain some indication of the overall weather situation that shows where the trade winds are blowing and thus allows the best route to be chosen. As one moves west the direction of the NE trade winds becomes more easterly. Their strength is not very consistent and the average force 4 on the Beaufort scale mentioned in some publications is unfortunately an average and nothing more. There is a favourable current during the crossing that makes itself felt as one leaves the Canaries and becomes stronger in the latitude of the Cape Verdes. This is the North Equatorial Current that sets westwards at 1/2 knot or more.

Although gale force winds are rarely experienced in winter, in December the trade winds usually blow at between twenty and twenty-five knots, with tropical squalls being the painful exception. As squalls always travel with the wind and are preceded by a menacing black band of cloud, they are easily detected and are visible both in daytime and at night if one looks frequently in the direction of the wind.

Atlantic crossing

Our passage south to the latitude of the Cape Verdes was rather uneventful and we managed to sail most of the time. Having steady winds from beginning to end is very rare so most sailors, myself included, prefer to motor during calm spells. Generally this is a good tactic as areas of calms are often relatively small and stationary so by motoring through them one is more likely to find better sailing conditions than by just waiting for the winds to arrive.

We only found steady trade winds when we reached latitude 14°N. The trade winds did not arrive on their own but treated us to the occasional squall. One night, having left the spinnaker up, as the winds were light at the time and the weather looked settled, I was woken up by the noise of the boat accelerating fast. By the time I got to the cockpit the squall and rain were upon us and the boat was flying at over ten knots. Fortunately this kept the apparent wind speed down and, equally fortunately, I had set the autopilot to steer to wind, so it kept the boat sailing to a steady wind angle. Even so our headlong rush into the pitch-black night was quite unnerving. There was little danger of broaching as we had been running with the centerboard fully up. While pondering what to do, I avoided looking at my frightened crew as my looks, I am sure, could have killed her. When I had passed through the cockpit I had noticed the cushions piled up comfortably in a corner. Christine had obviously been fast asleep.

There was little I could do except try to enjoy the roller coaster ride while praying between gritted teeth that the spinnaker could take it. I wasn't too worried about blowing it out as it was my spare asymmetric spinnaker but I knew that the mess of a shredded sail, some of which might end up under the boat, was something to be avoided. As the squall showed no sign of letting up I decided not to tempt fate and take the spinnaker down

Spinnaker repair during a calm patch while crossing the Atlantic

while the gods were still on our side. Well, they weren't any longer. As I tried to pull down the douser, it jammed, and now we had a full spinnaker to contend with... and another squall on our heels. It was no good pulling and yanking as the douser just wouldn't budge. Eventually with Gildas' help we managed to mask the spinnaker behind the mainsail and get it down without dousing it just as another squall loosened its fury upon us. As I was bagging the sail on the foredeck in a deluge of cold rain, I remembered a quote from a crew on one of the boats that had blown a total of twenty-eight spinnakers in a Whitbread round the world race. 'We put them up and God takes them down!' At the time

Landfall on the north coast of St Lucia

I thought it very funny but now that it almost happened to me I no longer found it quite so amusing. It was, however, a valuable lesson in what can go wrong with inexperienced crew and helped me understand how some of those ARC breakages had come about. For most ARC participants the Atlantic crossing is their first experience of tropical weather and many fall prey to those vicious squalls.

The second half of our Atlantic crossing was really pleasant. Gildas had taken over the cooking and with his French style, made a very good job of it. We caught several fish, then lost my best lure and all the line to a real monster; we enjoyed some spectacular sunsets and twice caught the green flash. Shortly before landfall in St Lucia we had the exciting company of a large killer whale, who insisted on swimming under our hull then surfacing close to the boat looking at us as if expecting to be applauded. We completed the passage in little over 18 days, which could have been bettered if we had pushed the boat just a little harder. After that disastrous night, knowing that I could no longer rely on my green crew, I only had a spinnaker up on my watch and generally sailed more prudently. Although slower than the 17 days I had set as a target, this was still considerably faster than my previous crossings of 21 days on Aventura II in 1989 and a dawdling 26 days on Aventura I in 1976. The balance of breakages would have been nil if my Iridium satellite phone had not stopped working halfway across so we could neither make calls nor send emails, but at least I had the Inmarsat C as a backup. Only later did I find out that it was in fact a fault of the satellite network and not of the phone itself. In all other respects, it was a perfect passage.

All through the crossing my thoughts kept going back to my first voyage across this mighty body of water. Then the prospect of crossing an ocean filled me with awe but I cannot remember ever being actually worried. Right from the beginning I enjoyed those wide empty spaces and felt a great sense of satisfaction from being in the middle of an ocean on my nutshell of a boat, living without a care in the world and enjoying every moment of it.

Finally, the long awaited moment arrived and the island of St Lucia came into view. We sailed along its rocky NE coast, passed though the channel that separates St Lucia from Martinique, rounded Pigeon Island and found Rodney Bay packed full with boats. The unmistakable lilting Caribbean voice of Rodney Bay Marina manager Cuthbert Didier broke through on the VHF radio. 'Welcome home, Jimmy, long time no see!'

'Thank you, Cuthbert, it certainly feels good to be back on this beautiful island.'

'God bless you, Jimmy, we are all on the main dock waiting.'

Tips

On the occasion of the twentieth ARC I was asked to list the ten most important points for a safe and enjoyable Atlantic crossing. The suggestions are probably just as relevant for any ocean passage.

- Have the boat, sails, engine and equipment thoroughly prepared and checked before leaving. This means getting to the port of departure in good time so as to have the necessary time to get everything ready.
- Choose your crew with utmost care: the single most common reason for an unsuccessful passage is tension and problems with the crew.

- Draw up a good watch system, then stick to it and make sure that there is always somebody keeping a lookout, day and night. Take every safety measure that you deem necessary: wearing harnesses, using a boom preventer, etc. Have strict rules: no one to leave the cockpit without the skipper being present, the skipper to be called if the crew on watch has any doubt about the course steered, changes in wind or weather, other ships or equipment failures.
- Provision well so as to have a good supply of fresh food and make sure that every taste is catered for.
- Get communications sorted out before the crossing. Make sure that the email works so it will be possible to communicate with your family and friends.
- Have good downwind sails, ideally at least one spinnaker.
- Check deck gear, sails and engine every day. Do not allow chafe to cause damage by protecting sails, and making sure that spinnaker poles and booms are firmly fixed and have no play.
- Have a good charging system that does not rely on only one source (main engine or generator) but have some alternate sources: wind, towing generator, solar panels.
- Get your fishing gear sorted out: a good strong line, a reel with a ratchet and some good lures.
- Finally, leave all worries behind. Crossing the Atlantic, or any other ocean, along the trade wind route is easy and safe provided that notice is taken of the above nine points.

Sailing in the Tropics

Sailing in the tropics is like married life.
When things go well life is perfect
but when things go wrong it can turn
to sheer hell.

Tom Williams

Sailing in the tropics during the safe season can be highly enjoyable as the weather conditions are generally benign and, especially on long passages, one can have days on end of trouble-free sailing without even having to touch the sails. This is trade wind sailing at its best so not surprisingly the main route passing through the South Pacific is called the milk run, or, more poetically in German, the barefoot route. However, for sailors arriving from a temperate area the tropics demand a different approach to sailing as many of the situations that may be encountered in this new environment are quite different to what they are used to.

Tropical weather

After God had created the world and its weather, he was sitting in heaven with a happy smile on his face looking very satisfied when St Peter stopped by.

'You look very happy with yourself, my Lord,' St Peter said.

'Yes, just look at what I have created. Sheer perfection.'

St Peter looked down at the Blue Planet and replied. 'It's not right. Only you can be perfect, nothing else should be, you can't launch a perfect product and then sit back and relax. You need to build in some small imperfection or people will simply take it all for granted.'

So God looked at the tropics again and, to balance things out, endowed them with two seasons, one of hurricanes, cyclones and typhoons, and left the other season unchanged so that for half the year the tropics could still be regarded as a perfect creation. And so it has remained, with the worst of the tropical storm seasons coinciding in each hemisphere with the summer and early autumn months, while the tropical winter months are normally as pleasant as God, in His wisdom, had always intended.

In spite of current anomalies in world weather, this ideal set-up has remained generally unchanged so that a voyage can still be planned to take advantage of the best and safest possible conditions. I have enjoyed close to perfect conditions on most of my long ocean passages, notably our crossing of the North Indian Ocean in February-March 1980 on Aventura I, a highly enjoyable transatlantic passage in 1989 on Aventura II and fast passages through the South Indian and Atlantic Oceans on Aventura III in 2004 and 2005. The most enjoyable passage from Galapagos to Marquesas was, at nearly 3,000 miles, also the longest in miles.

Tropical squalls

Unfortunately I am now going to throw a fly in the ointment by outlining some aspects that can spoil that attractive picture. The main culprits are undoubtedly those irritating tropical squalls, which often catch newcomers to the tropics by surprise and can cause damage to gear. While squalls at sea can usually be easily dealt with by a vigilant crew, abrupt changes in weather caused by the passing of a depression can cause havoc among boats at anchor. With the strengthening wind often changing by as much as 180° in direction, boats anchored in places that were deemed to be safe and well protected can be put suddenly on a dangerous lee shore. Combined with a violent short swell produced by several miles of fetch across a wide lagoon, a boat can easily be driven ashore. Severe damage can also be caused by the chain being caught under coral heads.

Anchoring so close in should only be done in settled weather and in daytime

The first time I got a taste of such a frightening experience was in 1978 in Bora Bora where we were anchored in the sheltered lagoon with about a dozen other cruising yachts. Around midnight I was woken up by the screaming wind and the slap of waves where until then had been a calm and quiet anchorage. From the cockpit I looked out at a situation that was straight out of hell. The sudden wind, which I estimated at between 40 and 50 knots, had turned all the boats around and we all were now hobbyhorsing violently with our sterns towards the beach. As the anchorage was over 50 feet deep, the stretched chains

already had some boats dangerously close to the fringing reef. While Gwenda powered ahead with the engine at full revs I tried to get up the anchor and chain but the anchor was well dug in and we ended up riding over the entire length of chain, narrowly missing a small Swedish yacht whose petrified crew must have thought we were going to mow them down. As we reached deeper water the anchor was finally dislodged but as I was unable to handle with the manual anchor winch the accumulated weight of all that chain hanging vertically in the water, we could only crawl into the wind at a snail's pace. Slowly, dragging the anchor and chain with us, we manoeuvred around the corner into a more protected bay and tied to a small dock. Looking back I was surprised to see that we were the only boat to have moved and by the time a few others decided to follow our example a couple of boats had been driven onto the reef already, sadly among them the well travelled yacht of Alex Du Prel. This colourful character had arrived here with his family in the early 1970s and founded the Bora Bora Yacht Club, which for many years was one of the favourite watering holes along the world cruising circuit.

Our prompt action had saved us from more serious trouble and I was to apply the same tactic throughout my cruising life. A Canadian sailing friend recently reminded me of how we had left the crowded anchorage at Honiara in the Solomon Islands when a sudden thunderstorm played havoc. He was surprised to see us pick up the anchor and spend the night hove to off the island, but he understood why after passing an anxious nail-biting night in the cockpit. Such local wind changes are usually unpredictable although warnings of unsettled weather accompanied by thunderstorms or squalls, as issued on Inmarsat C, should not be ignored. If anchored in a lagoon that does not offer all-round protection, the best solution is to use what I call the CAM system as described in chapter 16. I conceived this safer way of tropical anchoring while in Chagos where a 50 foot yacht had been driven ashore onto the reef by just such a sudden change in weather a short time before our visit.

Also worth mentioning here are the so-called reinforced trade winds that are more common in the South Pacific than in other tropical areas. It is a phenomenon that occurs throughout the winter months and is particularly frequent in French Polynesia, where it is called maramu. This phenomenon also occurs on passages between New Zealand and the tropics. One other phenomenon, again associated with the South Pacific, is the South Pacific Tropical Convergence Zone that stretches in an arc all the way from Tahiti to the Solomon Islands and can affect weather conditions throughout the area. The SPTCZ is closely monitored by local weathermen and its location is broadcast daily.

Seasons

When the end of the safe season approaches my firm opinion is that it is imperative to leave the tropics and head for an area unaffected by tropical storms. In my early days of cruising this was the accepted thing to do but over the years attitudes have changed and by the time I reached the South Pacific again in 2004 I reckoned that between one third and one half of the cruising boats remained in the tropics during the cyclone season. Most managed to find a place in a marina or boatyard and were usually left unattended. A few continued to cruise, their crews keeping a wary eye on the weather. Those who decide to take this line of action should make sure that they know of, or preferably are close to, some shelter and in chapter 23 I list the various hurricane holes in the South Pacific. The situation is similar in the Eastern Caribbean where many boats spend the hurricane season in a marina or boatyard, provided they are located south of 12°40'N as stipulated by the insurance companies. Rodney Bay Marina in St Lucia, although north of this line, is excluded from this provision because it is well protected inside a landlocked lagoon.

Probably as a sign of changing climatic conditions recently there have been some notable exceptions in those well defined tropical storm seasons with a number of storms occurring during the accepted safe season or in areas that had never experienced such storms before such as Brazil and the Canaries: Cyclone Gina that devastated Vanuatu in June 2003, tropical storm Catarina that formed off Brazil in February 2004, Cyclone Phoebe in the South Indian Ocean in July 2004 and Hurricane Delta in the Canaries in early December 2005.

Tropical tactics

The tropics demand a different approach not just to offshore sailing but to navigation as well. By their very nature many tropical destinations are remote, difficult to reach and, once there, dangerous to negotiate. Even with the help of GPS and other current aids to navigation, many tropical destinations are not accurately charted and should be approached with utmost caution. Even if some charts are not accurate and do not tally with the actual GPS positions, most passes into lagoons throughout French Polynesia are marked by beacons. Although other Pacific island nations have also improved their aids to navigation, they should not be relied on as lights and beacons are often reported to be missing.

As many tropical islands are protected to windward by massive reefs, few of which are lit, making landfall in such places can be a risky business and such difficulties are often compounded by the presence of strong, unpredictable currents. Thus it is always wise to set a landfall waypoint at a safe distance from the intended destination.

One's problems are far from over once landfall is made as entering a lagoon is rarely a simple matter of just pointing the bows for the middle of the pass. One should attempt to synchronize one's arrival at the beginning of the incoming tide, just after slack water, when there may still be a slightly contrary outflowing current. This is the time when passes are normally at their calmest. What makes the situation difficult is not just the force of the tidal streams but also the fact that lagoons are constantly filled by the seas pouring over the windward reef, as a result of which the water level in some lagoons can be several feet higher than that of the surrounding ocean. It is not uncommon for an outflowing current to reach six knots or more and in some places even double digits. All these facts must be born in mind and it is therefore essential to carry a worldwide tide table, various software versions being available.

From above coral heads are easily seen in the clear water

Eyeball navigation

Once inside, most lagoons can be crossed relatively easily in good light. Some lagoons, mainly in French Polynesia and Fiji, may be beaconed but generally one has to find one's own way. One must quickly learn the tricks of the trade, better known as eyeball navigation. Many tropical lagoons or anchorages are strewn with isolated coral heads, some of which reach up almost to the surface. In more frequented lagoons these are marked by perches, but often they are not. Depth sounders are of no help as the depths are usually quite constant and there is no early warning of the presence of such coral heads. However, in good light, they can be easily seen in the clear water. Good light means having the sun behind the observer so the timing must coincide with favourable conditions. In other words one should plan on going west through a lagoon between early and mid morning, when the sun should be behind one's head, and, conversely, move in an easterly direction in mid afternoon. With the sun ahead of the observer the surface of the lagoon turns into an impenetrable opaque mass when not even obstructions that are close to the surface are visible to the naked eye. A pair of good Polaroid glasses can help if the sun is not too low ahead of the observer. Being able to climb the mast, ideally provided with steps, can be a great advantage as the visibility from a higher point is much better than from deck level.

An absolute godsend for this kind of lagoon navigation is a forward looking sonar which shows the profile of the bottom and any dangers that may lay ahead. Depending on the model and strength of the signal, a forward looking sonar can see as far forward as 40 or 50 meters. The latest models are supposed to see between 100 and 200 metres but are a lot more expensive. Having had an Echopilot FLS throughout my latest voyage I can vouch for its usefulness as it got us out of tricky situations on several occasions. Twice in the Tuamotus we had to cross a wide lagoon studded with coral heads with the sun in our eyes. We managed to weave our way among the coral heads with Gwenda at the wheel watching the sonar while I was perched on the spreaders.

Tuamotus

The Tuamotus were until fairly recently rarely visited by cruising yachts, and for very good reason: navigation among the reefs and atolls is even in these GPS days a daunting task and calls for a high degree of alertness and vigilance. It is a price most sailors regard as worth paying as these remote atolls fit perfectly the ideal image of a tropical destination: turquoise blue lagoons, deserted islets shaded by swaying coconut palms and magnificent underwater scenery with a profusion of fish and corals. However, there are some basic rules to be followed, such as choosing an anchorage carefully and avoiding a long fetch if strong winds are expected or a front is predicted to pass. Most sailors used to cruising in the Eastern Caribbean do not expect the drastic wind changes that commonly occur in this area of the Pacific.

I had worked out the optimum times for entering a lagoon at our first arrival in the Tuamotus. After a pleasant passage from Ua Pou in the Marquesas we made landfall at Raroia. This was a symbolic stop as Thor Heyerdahl's balsa raft Kon Tiki had finished her epic journey from South America running up on the windward reef of this very island. From the way the water was gushing out through the pass it looked obvious that our timing was wrong, but as we didn't want to spend several hours waiting on the outside, I decided to go for it and with the engine at full blast we pointed for the middle of the half mile wide pass. Half an hour later we were little more than 50 metres from where we had started. Fortunately a local man who was returning home after fishing in the lagoon must have guessed our predicament, motored over with his boat powered by a large outboard and beckoned us to follow him. He headed

Spinnaker flying is one of the pleasures of sailing in the tropics

straight for the edge of the pass where obviously he knew that there was a slight counter current and within minutes we were inside. The friendly Raroian slowed down so we could catch up with him and led us to a spot close to the village where he told me to anchor then left with a wave.

Special considerations

These balmy sun-kissed tropical islands are not the healthiest places on earth as the early sailors soon found out. Now that we know so much more about UV light and other associated risks to our skins, the main concern is overexposure to the sun. A hat and if possible a long sleeved shirt should be worn, the boat should be provided with a bimini or awning and those who have a particularly delicate skin should use strong sun block cream. The skin should also be protected from bites by mosquitoes or the irritating sandflies common to some of the beaches in the Marquesas. Repellent sprays are quite useful, but better still is to avoid being ashore at the critical times around

dusk and early evening when mosquitoes are most active. Of the mosquito born diseases dengue fever is present throughout the Pacific, while malaria is the main hazard in islands west of Fiji (Vanuatu, Solomons and Papua New Guinea). In these areas prophylactics should be taken, but as several strains of malaria are now resistant to prophylactic medication the best protection is still to avoid being bitten. Not going ashore at dusk, using a strong repellent while ashore in doubtful areas, using smoking coils and screening all openings, are simple precautions that seem to work.

Swimming has its own risks and although sharks are often present in lagoons, they are rarely of danger if some simple precautions are observed. As in the case of mosquitoes, the time to avoid is around dusk at shark feeding time. If fishing with a speargun, the speared fish should be taken out of the water immediately and put in a dinghy as the blood and vibrations emitted by a wounded fish will attract any sharks that happen to be in the vicinity. One serious hazard in all tropical waters is ciguatera fish poisoning. The culprit is a toxic microscopic algae that is ingested and concentrated in their flesh by reef feeding fish.

Ciguatera fish poisoning

As in much of the Caribbean there is either little fish left or spearfishing is prohibited, so it was with great anticipation that I looked forward to the Tuamotus, where fish are still abundant and the underwater scenery is almost without equal. En route from the Marquesas to

Tahiti we stopped at various atolls, most attractive among them the uninhabited atoll of Tahanea. The pass into the large lagoon had beautiful coral formations and was teeming with fish. Although aware of the possibility of ciguatera fish poisoning I couldn't resist the temptation but only speared a couple of smaller fish. Gwenda marinated one of them in lime juice, which we ate raw in Polynesian style, and pan-fried the fillets of the other. Halfway through the afternoon, while beachcombing on a nearby motu, all hell broke loose as we were both overcome by terrible stomach cramps. By the time we got back to the boat, other symptoms were telling me clearly that after thirty years of catching and eating tropical fish, I was now on the receiving end. The first twenty-four hours were the worst but not severe enough to risk sailing the 300 miles to Tahiti for help. We chose to deal with the matter ourselves and although we felt very bad for a couple of days, we very slowly recovered although it was one month before all symptoms disappeared. The last to go was the tingling and a queer reversal of sensations when a hot drink felt cold... and ice cream burnt my mouth.

There are many different kinds of seafood poisoning, but the most prevalent type found throughout the tropics is what is now known as ciguatera. Known by the ancient Chinese, reported by Columbus on his first visit to the Caribbean, and accurately described by Pedro de Quiros during his Pacific voyage in 1606, ciguatera fish poisoning is endemic in all tropical areas and occurs regularly between latitudes 35°S and 35°N. It is estimated that every year there are about 60,000 cases worldwide, while in the Caribbean, where most cases occur north of Martinique, around 100 cases per 10,000 people are reported each year. The situation is possibly even worse in the tropical Pacific Ocean, particularly in French Polynesia and the Marshall Islands.

Over 400 different species of fish have been incriminated at one time or another, a species being toxic in one area but not in another, even within the same lagoon. This is the essence of the problem as there

Local fishermen are the best source of advice on which lagoon fish are safe to eat

is no way of telling which fish may be poisonous and which safe. However, the actual source of the toxin is now known: a dinoflagellate, Gambierdiscus toxicus, a unicellular plant similar to a micro-algae. A creature of the ocean depths, normally only a few of these algae live on the reef but under certain circumstances their number can increase dramatically. Fish feeding on coral ingest these toxic algae and so the toxin enters the food chain. These grazing fish usually live and feed in one small area so they gradually build up larger and larger amounts of toxin. A predatory snapper, grouper or barracuda then swims into the area and with one bite acquires all the toxicity its herbivorous victim had spent a lifetime collecting. These larger fish then carry the toxicity to other parts of the reef or lagoon.

Much of the early research work had been conducted in French Polynesia, where ciguatera still causes hundreds of cases every year. In the late 1970s Dr Raymond Bagnis, head of the Medical Oceanographic Research Unit in Tahiti, finally identified the cause of ciguatera. He also established that in every outbreak of ciguatera some damage to the coral reef had occurred in the preceding year or two. Sometimes this was a naturally occurring event, such as a bad storm or cyclone but more often it was caused by man's interference, from blasting a pass into a lagoon, building quays or breakwaters on live coral, to the dumping of metallic materials or other polluting debris into lagoons. The toxic algae thrive on newly exposed coral surfaces multiplying very rapidly and so the cycle leading to ciguatera poisoning begins.

Not everyone eating ciguatoxic fish has the same symptoms although diarrhoea, nausea, abdominal pain or vomiting usually occur within a few hours. Prickling in the fingers and toes as well as tingling around the mouth are other symptoms accompanied by an alteration of sensation causing cold objects or drinks to feel hot or plain water to taste like soda and a shower to feel like pin pricks of electric shocks. Other symptoms are extreme tiredness and lethargy, itching, muscle and joint pain, a weakened pulse and falling blood pressure. In very severe cases respiratory paralysis leads to death but this is very rare and mortality rates are under one per cent of cases. One of the first reported deaths was that of the Bounty's surgeon, who passed away in Tahiti after a large feast.

In most instances the symptoms subside after a few days, although the itching and alteration of sensations can last for several weeks. The symptoms are caused by the toxin acting on the body's sodium channels thereby causing changes in the electrical potential and permeability of the cells. Recently ciguatera has been treated successfully with IV mannitol. The usual dose is one gram mannitol per kilogram of body weight. The medication is infused intravenously as a twenty per cent mannitol solution. It is believed that mannitol acts at cell level by rendering the toxin inert. The earlier a victim is diagnosed and treated with IV mannitol, the more likely its success. A large number of patients treated in the Marshall Islands successfully responded to this treatment. Antihistamines, calcium gluconate, atropine and vitamin B have also been used to ameliorate the symptoms. Untreated, ciguatera can last between one to two months, although some symptoms may persist for longer. Recovery usually begins in a couple of days, but the disease does not produce any immunity so the next poisoning is usually more severe than the previous one. People repeatedly exposed to tiny amounts of ciguatera poisoning, which are usually too small to cause an outbreak, gradually become sensitised to the toxin and consuming a toxic fish will trigger an attack, while other non-sensitised people, who have consumed the same fish, may not be affected.

The risks can be minimised by gutting fish as soon as it is caught and by not eating the head, liver, roe and viscera as the toxin is concentrated in these organs. All very large fish caught inside a lagoon, or close to a reef, should be treated with suspicion, especially snappers, groupers, barracuda, jacks and moray eels. It pays to take local advice as most islanders know only too well which fish and which areas of their lagoon have to be avoided. Freezing, drying, cooking or marinating the fish does

Tackling atoll passes

Having missed the best time to leave our anchorage at Tahanea by the time we were ready to go the sun had moved into the west turning the surface of the lagoon into a shimmering silvery mirror. Crossing the three mile wide lagoon with the sun in our

Lagoon passes such as this one at Rangiroa can be swept by very strong currents

not destroy the poison and affected fish looks, smells and tastes normal. Various traditional tests have been recommended but none is truly effective. Dr Hokama of Hawaii University has perfected a test kit capable of identifying the presence of ciguatoxin in fish flesh. When used properly, Cigua-Check (TM) will test ciguatoxin at levels generally below the level that can cause clinical symptoms in humans.

One message is abundantly clear: every outbreak of ciguatera indicates that something is wrong with the reef. For interfering with the fragile ecosystem of living coral nature exacts a high price.

eyes proved to be a nightmare. Although we had crossed the lagoon in the opposite direction without any problems, we now had to dodge the numerous coral heads that littered the lagoon under the worst possible conditions. I climbed to the first set of spreaders for better visibility but even with my Polaroid glasses could only see a short distance ahead. With her eyes glued to the FLS mounted next to the wheel, Gwenda was moving cautiously ahead, frequently changing course abruptly before I could even see the reason why. After a while I realised the futility of my presence up the mast and climbed down. Gwenda and the FLS were doing an excellent job weaving a circuitous path around the coral heads. The FLS showed very clearly anything we needed to avoid and so we managed to make it to the main pass safely.

I knew that the best time to leave the lagoon was just before slack low water when the incoming tide hadn't had time to get established. It looked as if our timing was right so we lined up with the middle of the pass and with all sails set and full power forged ahead. Outside the pass the incoming tide had already created a massive wall with six foot steep waves breaking all over the place, the change from the outgoing to the incoming tide being almost instantaneous. Soon we were amidst this violent maelstrom and as we crashed from the breaking crest of a large wave the engine alarm sounded. Gwenda immediately turned off the engine and with difficulty we managed to sail through the breaking waves into deeper, relatively calmer water. When I opened the engine compartment I was confronted with black oil sprayed onto everything and could only presume that under the tremendous pressure caused by Aventura crashing from the top of that steep wave, the oil had been ejected through the air breather. While Gwenda was sailing in the lee of the large atoll I cleaned up the horrible mess as well as I could. Fortunately I always carry some oil absorbing pads and also a lot of old rags. I then filled the engine with new oil, it started as if nothing had happened and off we sailed to the next island ready to face new challenges.

Some of the above comments and observations may seem quite daunting but one should never forget that the tropics include some of the most attractive anchorages in the world. As we all know there is always a price to be paid and, however difficult it may appear to be, the islands of the South Seas are certainly worth the sacrifice.

Tips

■ While on passage the watchkeeper should keep a good lookout to windward for any approaching squalls. Sail should be shortened promptly and if on autopilot it should set to steer to wind.

■ Many charts are still inaccurate and do not agree with GPS, so islands, especially those protected by reefs to windward, should not be approached at night but given a wide berth.

■ Time the arrival to enter a lagoon just after slack water and to leave immediately before slack water.

■ Always attempt to cross a lagoon in good light by having the sun behind the observer.

■ Always have an exit strategy if anchored in a large lagoon in case a change of wind direction will put the boat on a dangerous leeshore. If the weather looks like changing leave a doubtful anchorage for the open sea while there is still time and good light.

■ Anchor in an area that is free of coral heads. Check that the anchor is well set and if possible inspect it with a mask.

■ Only eat lagoon fish if you know that no cases of ciguatera have been reported in that area.

■ A ciguatera test kit is available from the Ciguatera Hotline in Hawaii Tel. +1 808-539-2345. Email: cigua@oceanit.com http://www.cigua.com

A Caribbean Cruise

No matter how many times I crossed an ocean, every time I make landfall after a long passage it still gives me an overwhelming feeling of satisfaction. This was my third landfall on St Lucia, an island that has played a special role in my life, and my feelings went deeper than the excitement of completing another voyage safely.

We arrived in Rodney Bay on a Friday evening and the marina was bursting at the seams with some two hundreds ARC boats. Although Aventura had left Las Palmas eight days after the start of the ARC, we'd made a reasonably fast crossing, and in the last 24 hours we'd pushed hard to arrive in time for the ARC prize-giving party. Although I had stopped running the event two years earlier I still regarded the ARC as my baby. And what sailor would willingly miss a party?

St Lucia has some of the most attractive scenery in the Caribbean

The elusive Big Drum

There is only one place to be in St Lucia on a Friday night, so soon after our arrival we walked to the small village of Gros Islet. Before we got there, the air throbbed with the deep bass of reggae, the music so loud that surely it could be heard 15 miles away in neighbouring Martinique. Live bands with giant sound systems stood at every corner, their sound waves making the small wooden houses shake. All the house owners had thrown open their doors, selling beer, rum or fried chicken, and you could wander into anyone's home. Never was the expression "open house" more true.

Twenty-five years, almost to the day, had passed since my first visit to Gros Islet.

Apart from the Friday night jump-up not much had changed in this otherwise sleepy fishing village that in the intervening years had earned itself another claim to fame as it was here that Nobel prize winning author Derek Walcott had based his poem Omeros, a Caribbean version of Homer's Odyssey. My first visit had also been a kind of odyssey as I was trying to track down the African roots of the St Lucian population.

Soon after our first Caribbean landfall in Barbados, I started looking for local material, which I could use in my radio reports for the BBC African Service in London. From the start my reports recorded in various Caribbean islands became a great hit with the audience of the daily Good

Morning Africa programme. My freelance work during our first voyage is described in more detail in chapter 30.

St Lucia promised some rich pickings after I had met by chance K.K. Joseph, the High Priest of the Ke'ele cult. This was a local version of Shango whose believers worshipped the Yoruba god of thunder and fertility. Clearly impressed by my BBC credentials Mr Joseph agreed to help me but first of all we had to locate the Big Drum, which apparently played an essential role in the Ke'ele ceremony. This is how we ended up in Gros Islet looking for an old woman who held the sacred drum. It was a long and sweaty search under a scorching midday sun not made much easier by Mr Joseph insisting that we stopped at every rum shop to enquire about the old woman. At every such place we first had to pay our respects to the owner by gulping down a tot of fiery rum, only to be sent along to the next shop to resume the search for the elusive keeper of that sacred drum. Eventually we did find the keeper, a shrivelled ancient lady who looked a century old and who explained something in patois to Mr Joseph. He informed me with a happy smile that we were on the right track: the Big Drum was with her nephew Henry in Babonneau, a village in the mountains, where he was building a new house. Half a dozen rumshops later we found our way into a clearing in the forest where two men were in the midst of putting up a house. One of them was Henry, with whom Mr Joseph talked at length, repeatedly pointing at me and my taperecorder.

'Yes,' Mr Joseph told me, 'a ceremony could be arranged but would the BBC pay for a goat, or preferably a ram, that had to be sacrificed?'

'I don't know about the BBC,' I replied, 'but for the sake of recording such a unique performance of the Big Drum, I'd be happy to pay for the goat myself.'

'Record the Big Drum?' asked Mr Joseph, looking slightly embarrassed, 'For that you'd have to come back next year as the Big Drum is only used on very special occasions.'

Reluctantly I decided that the life of a poor goat was not worth sacrificing

Colourful houses line the street in a St Lucian village

without the sound of the Big Drum. I saved my journalistic cred by recording instead an interview with Dunstan St Omar, a local artist who had made a name for himself all over the Caribbean by painting a Black Christ who dominated the fresco of a newly consecrated church.

After that first visit I had been back to St Lucia on many occasions and over the years had established a special relationship with this island, so I always fancied that the old lady in Gros Islet must have cast a spell on me. She was probably instrumental in my decision to move the finish of the ARC from Barbados to St Lucia. By 1989, when I crossed the Atlantic in Aventura II, the ARC had been running for three years and while generally successful we had many complaints from the participants about the inadequate facilities that awaited them on arrival in Barbados. As Barbados had always been regarded as the logical landfall for a transatlantic passage I was reluctant to look for an alternative. It was only when I arrived there on my own boat and saw the island through the eyes of my fellow sailors that I finally had to admit that the situation was indeed unacceptable. Early in 1990 the decision was taken to move the ARC to St Lucia where it has remained ever since. The main attraction was Rodney Bay Marina, the creation of Arch Marez, a Californian who had sailed here in his Swan in the early 1980s and realizing the untapped potential of this spot decided to build a marina. In the intervening years Rodney Bay Marina has turned into one of the most popular Caribbean landfalls for transatlantic sailors and the once mosquito-ridden lagoon, where the first Aventura had anchored in complete isolation a quarter of a century earlier, is now surrounded by hotels, restaurants and elegant residences.

Exploring the Indian River in Dominica

Island hopping

Soon after completing the Atlantic crossing my crew left and I was joined by Gwenda and Ivan for a leisurely Caribbean cruise. We set off in a northerly direction and made our first stop at St Pierre in neighbouring Martinique. Exactly one century earlier the former capital of the French colony was completely destroyed by a violent eruption of Mount Pelée that wiped out its entire population, the most famous among the few who escaped with their lives being the sole occupant of the local prison, the only building to survive. The volcano is still active and its brooding presence is a permanent reminder of what the future might bring. The reality of this threat was highlighted by the recent eruption of the active volcano on the island of Montserrat.

Following in the first Aventura's wake we anchored next in Rupert's Bay in neighbouring Dominica and, just as a quarter century earlier, before we had even managed to drop the anchor we were surrounded by several young men in small boats offering their services. On our first visit this was a still a rare phenomenon in the Caribbean but now it has become a widespread source of work and income for the locals. Having been given the name of the local Capo I asked if he was among that entourage. As soon as he stepped on board the others left us alone and during our stay there we could not have had better protection. The main reason why cruisers stop here is to visit the nearby Indian River that discharges into the bay. Early the following morning our guide loaded us into his shallow drafted canoe and we set off for a break in the jungle wall that at this point reaches down to the sea. Dominica is one of the least developed of the Caribbean islands and much of its wild interior has remained largely untouched. The luxuriant rainforest at the centre of the island that is dominated by the so-called Dockyard used to be the Caribbean base of the British Royal Navy. Its decaying buildings were restored after the Second World War thanks to the efforts

Spectacular view over crowded English Harbour on Antigua

the Morne Trois Pitons volcano is now a UN World Heritage site that prides itself on having the richest biodiversity in the Lesser Antilles. As we slowly made our way up the river we were pleased to notice that nothing seemed to have changed since our previous visit. Huge gnarled trees with their aerial roots forming an almost impenetrable curtain reached down to the water that was teeming with all kinds of creatures from jumping fish to tiny turtles and skimming insects. Colourful birds were darting about in the dense canopy that enveloped the shallow river like a cocoon.

The contrast could not have been more different at our next port of call: Antigua's English Harbour, a landlocked bay that over the years has become one of the most famous yachting destinations in the world. In the eighteenth and nineteenth centuries

of Vere Nicholson, whose family continue to live in English Harbour. Most historic buildings have been preserved and have various uses, one of them known as the Admiral's House is now a museum. It is reputed to have been Horatio Nelson's residence, which is probably incorrect as when he was stationed here he was just a humble lieutenant.

In and around English Harbour are some of the best yachting facilities in the Caribbean and the Dockyard quay is always full of luxurious yachts. One other reason for Antigua's popularity is Antigua Sailing Week, which is held every year during the last weekend in April and offers some of the best racing in the world with excellent winds and keen competition. Although the patina of English Harbour increasingly smacks of commercial application there are still a few genuine traditions to keep even the most critical sailor happy. First among these is to watch the sunset from Shirley

Heights that overlook what must be one of the most picturesque sights anywhere on our planet. As the sun's upper limb is about to sink below the western horizon everyone stares expectantly hoping to see that rare green flash. I have been lucky to have had that unique experience on several of my visits to this spot although Gwenda insists that my good fortune seems to be in direct proportion to the amount of rum punch consumed.

Ever since it was discovered, with a bump, early in the sixteenth century, Barbuda has spelt disaster for sailors. Lying to windward of all its neighbours this reef-encumbered island thirty miles north of Antigua has claimed some four hundred wrecks over the years. No wonder that it was both feared and hated by sailors and even now is out of bounds for most charter boats. With Aventura drawing less than three feet with

On Barbuda Aventura has the whole of Spanish Wells to herself

the centreboard up Barbuda presented no real problems and we set about exploring her south and west coast at leisure. The best anchorage is at Spanish Point, a sheltered spot among the reefs on the SE

corner, facing a beautiful sandy beach. It was in this idyllic spot that tragedy occurred several years previously when three young Barbudians boarded the 65 ft Computacenter Challenger and murdered all four persons on board.

After passing a peaceful night all on our own in that tranquil anchorage, we took a long walk along the beach fronting the exposed east coast. Mighty rollers that had travelled unimpeded for 3,000 miles all the way from Africa were crashing on the fringing reef in an explosion of spray. The beach was littered with flotsam, a nightmarish collection of plastic in all forms and sizes and there was also a large container full of shoes, all of which were left foot. Further along, a mighty fifteen metre long tree trunk, that must have floated all the way from Africa, was stranded high up on the beach.

'God forbid anyone crashing into this monster at night,' I told Gwenda and asked her to stand against it for a photograph to better show up its huge size.

As we made our way back across the island we met a group of wild donkeys and further on a deer jumped from behind a bush, both of us being equally surprised. They were the descendants of the wild animals introduced by the Codrington family who had leased this remote island from the British government in 1685 at the cost of one fat sheep a year. As everywhere else in the Caribbean the work was done by African slaves and it is now known that the Codringtons used Barbuda not just as a hunting reserve but also as a breeding

The renowned Baths anchorage in the Virgins

station for slaves to be used on their other plantations.

A fast overnight sail took us to St Barts whose main port of Gustavia was bursting at the seams. Being told by the port captain that we needed to anchor while waiting for an empty slip we all agreed that the busy place had little attraction for us and so continued to Virgin Gorda. As the Virgins are now one of the most popular charter areas in the world, I was quite resigned to be disappointed by what we might find. While the number of boats had certainly increased, the unique beauty of those islands has not suffered any visible ill effect. A highlight of our previous visit, which we duly revisited, was the so-called Baths, huge boulders of cosmic proportions that lay tumbled about in the turquoise waters. Later that day we sailed past Norman Island that had been Robert Louis Stephenson's inspiration for Treasure Island. Ivan reminded me that when we called here with the first Aventura he and Doina had been terrified that we might be attacked by pirates. This time, the nearest we came to the disciples of Henry Morgan and John Hawkins, who had their lair here, was a fake buccaneer ship which was sporting a huge

banner proclaiming it to be the oldest bar in the Caribbean.

There were two reasons for our next stop: Puerto Rico where we had a change of crew as Ivan left us here to return to London and we were joined by Barry Esrig, a friend from New York. As we made our way into the crowded marina at San Juan I saw a lone figure waiving frantically from the end of a pontoon. It was Bill Butler who now lives here with his Puerto Rican wife Lirio. Ever since I first met Bill at the start of America 500, I had been impressed by his joie de vivre and positive attitude to life. The latter quality was undoubtedly essential for someone who had lost two of his boats and had miraculously survived to tell the tale. After we tied up next to one of those top heavy unattractive powerboats that dominated the harbour, Bill took us first to see his latest mistress: Teresa, a bullet proof creation from Admiral Dönitz's leftovers. After a brief inspection I agreed that even Bill might find it difficult to sink that mini U-Boat, but one never knows with Bill.

Caicos revisited

The strong winter trade winds gave us a fast passage from Puerto Rico to Grand Turk. Early on the third morning we made landfall off the northern tip of the island but the large breaking swell made it impossible to anchor anywhere close to the main settlement at Cockburn Town. Over the VHF the harbour master directed us to the commercial dock off the island's southern extremity where we were met by customs and immigration. Entry formalities were quick and easy and the customs officer even called a taxi to take us on a tour of Cockburn Town, the sleepy capital of this remote British colony. Its main attraction is the small museum, which exhibits items found on a Spanish ship wrecked around 1510 on nearby Molasses Reef. This is the earliest wreck discovered in the New World and the well-preserved objects provide a fascinating glimpse into life onboard an armed sailing vessel nearly five centuries ago.

Wrecks had been very much on my mind ever since our arrival, as it was near here that we nearly lost our first Aventura in 1977. Just like now, we had stopped here on our way from Puerto Rico to the Bahamas for exploring those waters. Even so, after weaving our way between the coral heads and passing close to the spot where we believed we had run aground all those years ago, I decided not too push our luck and dwell too long among those dangerous reefs. We anchored in the lee of Big Fish Cay, launched the dinghy and landed on a sandy beach. The small island was covered in the distinctively shaped Turk's head cactus that has given the islands their name. A pair of ospreys had made their nest on a rocky

Turks Head cactus on Fish Cay in the Caicos Bank

and one day decided to explore the Ambergris Cays on the edge of Caicos Bank. Poor visibility combined with my lack of experience in navigating among coral heads had stranded us on a reef from which we were very fortunate to get off with only a few scratches. Quarter of a century later we were back in the same waters trying to locate the spot of our near disaster.

This time I was far better prepared. Thanks to GPS I knew exactly where we were, while Aventura's aluminium hull and lifting centreboard were far better suited

pinnacle from where their fluffy chick uttered desperate shrieks while its parents tried to frighten us away by dive-bombing us relentlessly. We got the message and retreated.

While for Gwenda and I this trip was emotional, for Barry the reason was far more prosaic. Barry's yacht Annie B is a Baltic 51 that draws ten feet and I had asked him to join us for a cruise in this particular area so he could see how different cruising can be with a draft of three feet rather than ten. I had met Barry when he was sailing Annie B from the Med to the US and had joined one of the early ARCs for the Atlantic crossing. Over the years we met on many occasions and became close friends but I will never forget the very first time I spoke to him when he called the ARC office in Las Palmas.

'I am going to cross the Atlantic in the ARC and as I have no idea whether we can find provisions there for the crossing, I was wondering if I should bring enough freeze-dried food from the USA.'

At first I thought he was joking, 'Did you say freeze-dried food?'

'Yes, there is a very good selection of meals available for expeditions...'

'Oh, you needn't worry. Just come and you'll find everything you need here, probably even better than in the USA.'

'That I doubt, but thank you. I'll see you in two days' time.'

As soon as he arrived, I drove him to the El Corte Ingles supermarket. When Barry saw the excellent quality and huge range of goods displayed, from scores of all types of fresh cheese to row upon row of smoked Sierra hams, crispy fresh fruit and every conceivable kind of vegetable, not to speak of the best selection of Spanish wines, he turned to me laughing;

'Jimmy, I must have been mad. This is truly awesome.'

'Certainly better than crossing the Atlantic on a diet of freeze-dried food!'

Over the years I have teased Barry relentlessly about this incident but he always takes it with much laughter, having that rare quality of being able to laugh at himself. My book World Cruising Essentials is dedicated to him with these words, "To Barry, for never losing his sense of humour."

From Fish Cay we headed straight across the Caicos Bank along a thirty mile long track where the water is rarely deeper than nine feet. The weather was reasonably good and a light breeze ruffled the surface of the water slightly, making it easier to read the depths. We kept the board down but with the hydraulic lock disengaged so if we touched bottom the board simply flipped up. We did touch a couple of times when we strayed off the charted track but reached Sapodilla Bay on Providenciales, at the far end of the bank, without any problems. Barry was impressed and I wondered how he would feel about cruising when he was back on top of a ten foot fin keel. Even I could not get over how easy it all seemed and kept thinking back to our earlier traumatic experience in these waters. In hindsight, I am grateful for that experience because it taught me a lot and I am sure made me into a more cautious sailor.

Whereas at Grand Turk we had been the only boat, in Provo we were surrounded by several cruising boats as it is a popular port of call for boats plying between the Bahamas or Florida and Puerto Rico and the Virgins. The anchorage in Sapodilla Bay was open to the south and therefore not a safe place to leave the boat unattended for too long. Not that there was all that much ashore to tempt us away – just a string of shopping malls for tourists arriving by air with the distinct disadvantage that nothing was within walking distance. The two supermarkets were very well stocked, proving the point that Provo was indeed a convenient and useful place for a quick stop, but not much else. We hired a car and drove to check out Turtle Cove Marina, on the north coast, which was used primarily by powerboats because access through the shallow Sellar's Cut was difficult. Back at Sapodilla Bay we cleared out at the customs office at the nearby commercial dock and left for the Bahamas. After the emotional visit to the Ambergris Cays our next destination San Salvador was a purely symbolic pilgrimage.

Safety Afloat and Ashore

If safety becomes a serious concern then I would rather not be in such a place at all as the boat becomes like an albatross around your neck.

Skip Novak

Safety has been a major concern for seafarers from the earliest days of sailing and whereas in the old days mariners were willing to put their fate in the lap of the gods, today's sailors prefer to play safe by taking some additional precautions. It is quite uncanny that every time I start on a new chapter I invariably get to hear about some incident or disaster relevant to the subject. It happened when I was writing about the possible choice of a catamaran as an offshore cruising option, when the news broke of two separate incidents involving catamarans that had been found washed ashore on the NW coast of the USA dismasted and with their crews missing.

After starting this chapter we were contacted at noonsite and asked for help by the concerned friends of a German skipper who had been reported lost in the Red Sea. The 72 foot Anna Lisa was making its way past Eritrea when the crew noticed that the skipper had disappeared. Not being able to handle the large yacht on their own the two crew were rescued by a passing freighter and the yacht abandoned. Later it became apparent that the two hitchhikers, who had never sailed before, had been taken on as crew by Gellert Tripolszky although he had just met them. The yacht was found abandoned later but there was no sign of the missing skipper.

Thinking of this and similar incidents with fatal consequences I am tempted to believe that some people must have a death wish. What other explanation could there be for such a disastrous decision of taking on a couple of unknown people who you happened to meet on a dock? Reeling back the memories of other real or potential tragedies I am forced to conclude that in some situations sailors had brought such disasters upon themselves. This may be regarded as perhaps too bold a statement, but let me start with my own experiences. Both groundings experienced with my first Aventura could have been avoided if I had observed some simple precautions. In the first case entering a reef area in bad light was an unforgivable mistake as was my later decision to enter an unknown port at night. Later, my crew got me into trouble by getting Aventura II caught in a huge tuna net close to Gibraltar, but ultimately I, as the captain, have to take the responsibility. Relying too much on my presumed GPS position almost got me into trouble while entering Benoa Harbour in Bali with Aventura III. There were a few less dangerous incidents which I have mentioned at the relevant point in this book.

By looking at some of the total losses mentioned in these pages, it is quite remarkable that almost every one of them could have been avoided. Several boats were lost for being anchored in an unsafe place, their skippers not being prepared to leave when the weather deteriorated (Pitcairn Island, Port Resolution). As mentioned elsewhere, two of my friends lost their boats in situations that they themselves admit as having been avoidable (Pegasos in the Red Sea and New Chance in Nova Scotia). Even Bill Butler's encounter with whales in the Pacific, and the loss of Sibonney, could have been avoided if, as

Bill points out, he had realized the seriousness of the situation and had done something, such as start the engine, to chase the whales away. The recent tragedies were probably just as avoidable as no sane sailor should sail a catamaran in the middle of winter in the rough seas off the coast of Oregon.

The list of such disasters could go on, but I hope that by mentioning these avoidable tragedies the one encouraging conclusion to draw is that sailing can be quite safe. The question of how safe offshore cruising is nowadays is such an important subject that I decided to deal with it separately in chapter 37.

Doina and Ivan's soft toys were kidnapped on the way to Lake Titicaca

Personal safety

In recent years the subject of personal safety has become a major concern among cruising sailors. This is in total contrast to the situation during my early days of cruising when I can remember very few occasions when either myself or my fellow sailors expressed serious concerns about our personal safety.

In my early surveys personal safety was hardly ever mentioned, whereas now, when I give lectures or take part in cruising seminars, most questions from the audience revolve around this subject. Towards the end of a lecture in Miami I was asked by a couple who were about to set off on a long voyage how safe it was out there in the wild world.

'Quite safe,' I replied, 'in fact I'd go as far as to say that you are probably much more likely to be mugged on your way home tonight in Miami than if you were returning to your boat in a remote anchorage.'

That comment seemed to go down very well with my American audience, several of who came to see me after the lecture to say

that it was exactly what they had hoped to hear.

In all my years of sailing neither my family nor myself have ever felt seriously threatened and the few thefts that we suffered were all quite minor. There is symmetry to them as there was one for each of my boats. Having spent the winter cruising in the Eastern Caribbean, where I had been reasonably cautious when leaving the dinghy unattended, when we eventually reached Puerto Rico having thus arrived in what I believed then to be the more "civilised" world, we dropped our guard completely. One day we were beachcoming with the crew of Calao on the island of Culebrita close to the eastern tip of Puerto Rico. We saw in the distance a large power yacht anchor close to where we had left our dinghies and the crew going ashore. When we got back to the dinghies the yacht had disappeared... and so had all our snorkelling gear and everything else we had left in the dinghy.

The only time any of my boats was broken into happened in Gibraltar where I had left Aventura II to return to London. One morning I received a call from the marina to be told what had happened and that all loose gear inside the boat as well as the SSB radio had been stolen. Aventura III has fared better as the only thing that was ever stolen was the lid of our barbecue in St Raphael in the south of France, probably taken by a fellow sailor to replace what had been stolen from his boat. All in all, not a bad record for all those years and miles of cruising.

In spite of this I continue to observe basic rules such as always locking the boat when going ashore and usually, but not always, when going to visit another boat. My outboard engines on the aft rail are always kept chained and padlocked. Some people go as far as locking the boat at night when they are onboard, while others have installed alarm systems, both of the active and passive type. A simple precaution is to remove everything on deck that can be easily picked up, and to make sure that there are no tempting loose items in the cockpit when visited by locals.

In fact, as John Ellis pointed out, 'the biggest thieves are rarely the locals but other sailors. Dinghy theft seems to be more prevalent rather than theft from inside the yachts. I advise everyone to use a combination padlock on a steel cable to secure the dinghy motor and the tank, both when going ashore but also at night when the dinghy is tied to the boat. Most vulnerable items are dinghies and outboards. In suspicious area, the tender and outboard should always be brought up on deck at night.'

Travel

In spite of the widespread concern over acts of piracy or violent robberies, sailors are often more vulnerable when sightseeing ashore or travelling as ordinary tourists than when on their own boats. In such situations the precautions to be taken are the same as if arriving in another country by aeroplane or car. Most cruising sailors travel widely away from their boats and there are very few who do not take this excellent opportunity to see more of the world. The subject of cruising in stages and leaving the boat unattended while travelling inland is discussed in chapter 34.

Personal safety while travelling on land is a constant concern and we were robbed twice. Once I had my backpack skilfully sliced on a bus in Bangkok and the most valuable thing taken were our return tickets to Malaysia where we had left our boat. While travelling by train to Lake Titikaka high in the Andes a local woman, who was selling wool jumpers, managed to hide the children's bag under her wide skirts. She must have been very disappointed when she discovered that it was full of children's soft toys. Doina and Ivan were terribly upset having lost some of their oldest travelling companions but we made up for it by replacing them with their Inca relatives.

Avoiding troublesome areas

The best precaution is to avoid doubtful areas altogether. Such precautions apply equally to areas where attacks on cruising boats have been reported recently and also to countries undergoing a period of political uncertainty as happened in 2006 in both Tonga and Fiji. While there is no doubt that avoiding countries or areas with a known record of violence is highly recommended, cruising sailors are usually in little danger in countries where such acts of violence have an underlying political cause. In such cases sailors should try to keep abreast of developments by monitoring the news before arrival, staying in contact with their embassies and, if already in the country concerned, keeping a low profile. Avoiding doubtful areas is a good policy whether travelling by boat or land. Noonsite tries to keep any new information on these areas posted on the website.

Piracy and robberies

Beside personal safety when cruising, a more serious concern is that of the possibility of a piracy attack. The term piracy describes attacks against a vessel by another vessel on the high seas, so strictly speaking many recent incidents involving yachts should not be described as piracy but robbery. The much publicized death of Peter Blake was the result of a violent robbery and while this type of crime involving cruising sailors has increased, fortunately very few with fatal consequences, cases of actual piracy involving cruising yachts are still relatively rare. The areas where piracy is a real threat to yachts are well known and should be avoided. Theft and robberies from yachts are, on the other hand, much more wide-spread geographically and the best way to deal with them is to take precautionary measures similar to those one would take when travelling on land or living in a big city. Whichever way one looks at this aspect of safety, there is no doubt that the situation has deteriorated, although it must be stressed that in most areas frequented by cruising boats acts of piracy or violence are not a serious risk, as the vast majority of reported cases seem to be concentrated in known areas, such as the Gulf of Aden or, more recently, Venezuela.

A much publicized incident involved the yachts Mahdi and Gandalf that were attacked by armed pirates off the coast of Yemen in March 2005. The pirates started firing as they approached the two boats, one of them ramming Gandalf. The skipper of Mahdi, a retired US Navy officer, started shooting back and hit at least one of the attackers, after which the two boats retreated. The incident caused much debate in cruising circles and re-ignited the controversy over the wisdom of carrying guns or not.

The year 2006 was a relatively uneventful year in the previously infamous Gulf of Aden with not a single incident reported. This is undoubtedly the result of the Coalition forces patrolling the area around Somalia on a regular basis, primarily to protect the UN food relief vessels. Altogether there were a total of ten reports made to the Piracy Reporting Centre regarding attacks on yachts or robberies from yachts. Four occurred in South East Asia, where three unattended yachts were robbed on Tioman Island, Malaysia. The fourth incident was an attempted boarding of a yacht en route between Singapore and Borneo that was repelled. There was one incident in the Northern Red Sea where a yacht was boarded and an outboard motor was taken by force from the skipper. The worst incidents have been reported from Venezuela where there have been three separate attacks on cruising yachts, two involving use of guns by the attackers. There were further robberies involving cruising yachts in the Solomons and Cape Verde Islands. There is also growing concern over thefts from yachts in some of the Eastern Caribbean islands, especially Trinidad and St Lucia.

Noonsite keeps a record of piracy attacks going back to 1999. In recent years noonsite has also been instrumental in helping concerned sailors form convoys through the Gulf of Aden. There are some basic precautions that ought to be taken if sailing through such areas and these are listed at the end of this chapter.

Spitsbergen is one of the few places in the world where a gun is obligatory for self defence

From among the fatal incidents that have come to my knowledge I will mention two. The first involved a crew who had just finished the ARC and had left on a cruise of the Caribbean. While anchored in Barbuda three local men boarded the 65 foot Computacenter Challenger and murdered the British crew Ian Cridland and Thomas Williams, as well as their American guests Kathleen and William Cleaver. Shortly before he was killed, Cridland had sent a radio message saying 'This is one of the most beautiful places on the planet.' The motive was robbery and it was rumoured that the men were high on drugs. They were apprehended and two of them were sentenced to death.

New Zealander Peter Blake, America's Cup winner and one of the most successful sailors in yachting history, was killed when he and his crew were attacked by masked gunmen on their boat Seamaster. A group of armed intruders boarded the yacht as it lay at anchor at Macapa, Brazil and, in the confusion, they fatally shot Peter Blake and injured two crew members. Peter Blake had been taking part in an expedition to raise international awareness of the environment with the aim of protecting life in the oceans of the world. According to the police all the gunmen got away with were a watch and one of the 36-metre boat's outboard engines. They were all caught and sentenced to long prison terms.

Guns

I doubt I would knowingly go to a region where a couple of Uzis and a rocket launcher would be needed.

Arthur Beiser

Regulations concerning firearms vary enormously from country to country and their presence on board a cruising boat can cause certain difficulties because of the formalities involved. In some countries firearms are bonded on board but more often they are removed for the duration of the boat's sojourn in a particular port or even country. The return of the firearms on the eve of departure can sometimes lead to complications and it is advisable

187

to make the necessary arrangements in this respect when surrendering the weapons on arrival.

Among one hundred skippers questioned on this subject in an earlier survey conducted in the Caribbean and South Pacific, the majority were firmly against the idea and this included both those who had a gun and also some of those who did not. Only eleven skippers considered firearms to be essential for their protection. Six skippers, who were reluctant to carry arms, stressed nevertheless that their possession might be justified in certain parts of the world, even if not in the South Pacific, where the interviews took place. Several owners described their guns as a deterrent and not an offensive weapon. For some skippers who did not wish to carry guns, the solution to this problem was to avoid areas with a bad reputation. The most unexpected condemnation of guns on boats came from a retired officer in the French Gendarmerie, who refused to have guns on board his boat as he considered them to be more trouble than they were worth. Because of the disadvantages of having firearms on board, several people had acquired mace or pepper spray containers, which were regarded as an acceptable alternative for self-defence as being more useful against burglars and amateur intruders, which are more common than pirates. As one skipper pointed out, 'It's far better to have a potential robber crying his eyes out in the cockpit, than to discover you have shot dead the cousin of the local police chief.'

Luc Callebaut summed up the dilemma faced by those who might consider having firearms, 'If you take them out when threatened, you may scare the aggressors away or, more likely, you may encourage them to fire at you! You don't always know in advance. If taken by surprise you may not

A demonstration of a helicopter rescue put on in Las Palmas for ARC participants

have time to get your gun and you cannot have it ready every time you meet someone you don't know.'

This is exactly what went through my mind when sailing from Panama to Ecuador in March 2002. Having just left Colombian waters I was still rather apprehensive and was expecting the worst one early morning when I was approached by a large whaler type boat with three men on board. They looked quite menacing as they came at great speed towards Aventura. They slowed down a few feet away and then shouted instructions as to how to avoid their nearby fishing long lines. If I had been armed, I should have had my gun ready to fire before they got too close. Fortunately I was not armed so what turned out to be an entirely innocent incident did not have the tragic consequences it could have had. Like myself, most sailors have given the subject of firearms a great deal of thought and decided that arms and yachts are not a good combination.

There are a few instances where having a gun is justified, such as when cruising in Spitsbergen where it is in fact compulsory to always carry a gun as there have been several attacks by polar bears and a number of people, including tourists, have been killed.

The threat of an attack on the high seas is one of the reasons why some sailors prefer to join a rally as there is an element of safety in numbers as happened towards the end of the Millennium Odyssey while the yachts were crossing the Gulf of Aden. The British 50 foot Nori was menaced by a boat apparently coming from Northern Somalia. Three other Millennium yachts sailing in the vicinity were immediately alerted and closed in with the threatened yacht. The French military authorities in Djibouti, who had been monitoring the progress of the Millennium fleet, were alerted by the rally organisers and immediately dispatched a helicopter to the scene. By the time it got there the offending boat had disappeared over the horizon. The helicopter gave chase and intercepted the boat as it was making full speed towards the Somali coast.

Tips

For piracy waters

- Try to form a convoy of between three and six boats of similar speed whose crew are prepared to remain in close contact and, if necessary, slow down or help the slower boats.
- Maintain visual contact in daytime and find a way to keep in contact at night (ideally by radar) without showing masthead lights or any other lights which can be seen from beyond the range of the convoy.
- Maintain radio silence on the standard VHF channels, which can be easily monitored by other parties by scanning all channels, but keep permanently open a SSB channel on a frequency agreed and available to all other boats in the convoy.

- Have a crew member on permanent listening watch on the agreed SSB frequency and/or have the SSB radio connected to a speaker in the cockpit.
- Monitor the immediate area on radar and, if anything suspicious approaches, alert the others immediately. Even if the suspected vessel is still out of visual range, but it appears to be on an intercepting course, the convoy should close.
- At least one boat in the convoy should be equipped with a satellite telephone and have the numbers available of maritime or naval authorities in neighbouring countries as well as those of the international SAR authorities so that they can be contacted promptly in an emergency.
- Make sure that a responsible person ashore receives regular position reports from the convoy and can promptly contact the relevant authorities in an emergency.
- If the worst comes to the worst, do not resist the attackers, keep calm, hand over all valuables and follow their instructions. In all known recent cases, when the crew being attacked offered no resistance, the pirates appeared satisfied with just robbing the boat but refrained from killing or being violent to anyone.

In case of an attack

- Do not resist.
- Avoid making eye contact.
- Avoid any action that may be deemed to be aggressive.
- Hand over valuables and have some cash prepared for such eventuality even if the rest is hidden.

Collisions

*We always have someone on watch
24 hours a day. We have had to make rapid
course changes when we have overtaken
or been overtaken by a vessel with no one
on watch. A potential collision was
avoided only because we were watchful.*

Bob Hall

Collisions with ships, containers, whales or unidentified objects are probably the main cause of boat losses on the high seas. Among all those hazards I consider ships to be the greatest risk to sailing boats and although I have only had a couple of potentially dangerous encounters, there is always somebody on watch on my boat, and whenever I feel that a ship is too close for comfort, I prefer to be the first to take avoiding action.

Possibly the worst incident happened in the Bay of Biscay when I was sailing with a Portuguese friend from the Isle of Wight to Porto. During his night watch Luis Miguel called me to come up quickly and, as I stepped into the cockpit, I saw a large ship some 50 metres away and bearing down on us. As we were broad reaching with the yankee poled out, there was not enough time to gybe, so I started the engine, turned the wheel, the mainsail went over to the other gybe, and the ship missed us by not more than ten metres. As it sped by with all lights blazing we could see the crew working on deck, but no one seemed to have noticed us, although we had our masthead navigation light on. After we had sorted out the sails and gone back onto our original course, Luis Miguel explained that the ship was overtaking us

on a parallel course when it suddenly changed course, made a sharp turn and headed straight for us. The only explanation that I could think of was that it may have been on automatic pilot and, having reached its waypoint, it had automatically altered course for the next waypoint. This seemed the most plausible explanation as we were close to Cape Finisterre where ships do alter course having passed that important landmark. Whatever the reason, it was a frighteningly close call and we could have easily been run down. A similar situation, although less threatening, happened in the Indian Ocean when my crew had fallen asleep while on night watch. When I came into the cockpit entirely by chance, I saw a large ship passing us close by while my friend was snoring peacefully in a corner. The

Gwenda sizes up to a huge tree trunk on Barbuda's windward coast

officer on watch had probably seen us and had altered course to pass us at a safe distance but it was an unnerving experience nevertheless.

The one and only collision with a ship that I ever experienced still makes me angry as it should have never happened. As part of a historic anniversary of Portugal I had been invited to Horta in the Azores to take part in a race marking that event. On the morning of the start outside Horta Marina the small fleet of yachts were trying to position themselves for the line while the light wind and strong tide played havoc amongst us. Immediately after the start the committee vessel, the Portuguese sail training ship Sagres, left its position at one end of the starting line and barged through the fleet like the proverbial bull in a china shop. Taking no notice of the small boats in her path Sagres ploughed on regardless with Aventura II smack in front of her. I was unable to manoeuvre as the two engines had been sealed for the race and the situation was made worse as the big ship came so close that it blocked even what little wind there was, so a collision looked imminent. I rushed below to break the seals on the engines but it was too late and Sagres gave us a mighty side blow that damaged the bows, pulpit and also hit one of the top spreaders. While all this was happening the sailor who was stationed at the bows as a lookout was staring at us as if mesmerised and probably did not inform the bridge what was happening right in front of the big ship. Meanwhile scores of VIPs including the President of Portugal were looking down from the rail high above us as if all this was part of the show. Fortunately Aventura II had been built like a tank so I hoped that the damage was only superficial. We motored back into the marina where I assessed the damage. It was bad but we were able to cope with it.

My main concern was that the spreader had been hit and so there was a risk of

possibly losing the entire mast, but a thorough visual inspection put my mind to rest.

I have also experienced two collisions at sea, the most recent one at night off Madagascar as described in chapter 4. It happened after we had received a warning by Inmarsat C that some large logs had been seen in that area. From the shock of

Good for the photographer but otherwise it is better to keep a distance from whales

the collision, which brought Aventura III to a dead stop, I am sure we hit one of those half submerged logs but fortunately the aluminium hull sustained no damage.

The Indian Ocean seems to have it in for me because my very first collision happened while en route to the Red Sea in 1980 and it also involved a floating log. Before I took over the night watch Gwenda had asked me if it was prudent to continue under full sail.

'Oh, there is really nothing to worry about in this area,' I reassured her.

She reminded me of my over-confident statement when she was abruptly woken up by a loud bang. In the light of the torch I saw a large tree with its thick branches disappearing under our keel. 'What was that?' Gwenda asked as she rushed into the cockpit.

'It looks to me as if we have landed in a forest.'

With the twin jibs set Aventura had been stopped in her tracks, but she slowly extricated herself and we left the tree behind. A quick inspection of the bilges showed there was no water coming in and it looked as if we had not suffered any serious damage.

'Nothing to worry about?' Gwenda asked.

What could I say? I just shrugged. I let Gwenda go back to sleep and stayed on watch until it started getting light. I was looking idly ahead in the half darkness when suddenly I saw not three boat lengths ahead of us a dark shape undulating in the swell. I grabbed the wheel and managed to avoid it by a few inches. It was a large whale fast asleep on the surface. Nothing to worry about indeed!

Collisions with whales are not that uncommon and most of the time seem to occur when the whale is asleep on the surface. Before we left on our first voyage there had been two incidents in the South Pacific with cruising yachts being sunk by whales. A pod of killer whales attacked the yacht Lucette while sailing close to Galapagos in 1972. The crew of five barely managed to launch the liferaft and their dinghy before the yacht sank. After spending 38 days adrift, they were saved by a ship.

One year later, off the coast of Guatemala, the yacht Auralyn was rammed by a large whale and sunk. Earlier the yacht had passed a whaling ship and the crew were convinced that the whale might have been injured as there was a lot of blood around the yacht when it happened. Maralyn and Maurice Baily spent an incredible 117 days in their liferaft before being rescued by a Korean fishing vessel.

One of the best known cases of collision with whales is that of my friend Bill Butler. In his own words: 'On June 15, 1989, as I sailed from Panama to Hawaii, on our long way to the start of the America 500 rally, we crossed into the home boundary of a pod of pilot whales. The night was ink black. Four hours passed until the mother whales, convinced that my boat was a large whale, an intruder in their pod and a menace to the young, gave the order to kill. Twenty whales on each side relentlessly rammed the hull until it cracked and sank. We hopped into our raft to begin what would become a 66 day "small boat cruise".'

Eventually Bill and Simonne's ordeal came to an end when they were rescued close to Costa Rica. Back in Miami, and determined not to miss the start of America 500, although by now he had lost Simonne who had immediately filed for divorce, Bill got another boat, called her New Chance, crossed the Atlantic and arrived in time for the start of the Columbus anniversary rally.

I was reminded of that attack on Siboney when the yacht Risque, sailing in the Millennium Odyssey, was similarly attacked while on passage from Chile to Easter Island. A large pod of pilot whales had surrounded the 57 foot yacht and without any obvious reason started ramming the fibreglass hull. Fortunately the well built yacht sustained no damage but the experience seriously shook the crew nonetheless.

My relationship with whales is very ambivalent as I am quite concerned about bumping into one while at sea, but at the same time cannot resist the temptation to get as close as possible when the risk looks small. Being in the company of whales was one of the greatest thrills while in Antarctica where there are always large numbers of humpback whales

My friend Bill Butler, the serial boat loser

to keep them away without doing them any damage. I have certainly noticed that we never had dolphins accompany us when the FLS was on, although this could be just coincidence. Only now while writing these lines, did it cross my mind that I should test this theory by switching the unit on and off while we have dolphins in our vicinity, which I am definitely going to do next time we meet some.

that migrate south for the summer to gorge on the abundant krill. I must have met some of the same whales later in Vava'u where humpback whales come to breed.

My attitude has changed now that I sail in an aluminium hull, but whenever we encountered whales with the first Aventura I always tried to put some distance between us. Once, while cruising among the outer islands of Papua New Guinea, we were surrounded by a pod of killer whales. They didn't show any aggressive intentions but just their menacing presence was worrying enough, so I decided to use a small trick. I poured a small amount of diesel into the water that quickly spread on the surface. As soon as the smelly stuff reached their blowholes the whales instantly departed. It was a harmless and highly effective solution. Nowadays I prefer to leave my FLS (forward looking sonar) on when I am in a critical area, as the ultrasound signal emitted by the transducer probably irritates or warns a whale of our presence. Those harmless ultrasound waves are hopefully enough

Groundings

There have been two instances where the loss of my boat could have been a possibility. They both happened soon after the start of our first round the world voyage and I am sure that they served as serious warnings as I managed to avoid repeating the experience. The first and potentially more serious grounding happened in the Turks and Caicos Islands. The second incident happened later that year at night in the Chesapeake Bay when I tried to enter Annapolis in the dark. Both incidents are described in chapter 6.

Bill Butler's New Chance was the second of his boats to be lost. 'The shipwreck happened off the coast of Nova Scotia. Tired after five hours on watch, I turned the helm over to my crew, an experienced sailor and owner of a similar boat to mine. It was a clear sunny day and I told him to stay in at least fifty feet of water while I went below for a nap. An hour later a loud crunch announced we were aground. My helmsman had fallen asleep. The boat was lost.'

Bill is a survivor par excellence. After America 500 he crossed the Atlantic back to Europe, sailed through the river and canal systems up the Rhine, down the Danube and reached the Black Sea. Later he circumnavigated South America anti-clockwise, then set his eyes on some cold water cruising. Having lost two yachts anyone would have expected him to give up, but not Bill. A friend not bearing to see him without a boat gave him Teresa, a 40 foot sloop built in Germany at the end of the last war from steel destined for U-Boats. She had been built not only as strong as the proverbial tank but even stronger as a German submarine. She sounds just like the right boat for Bill Butler.

Lightning

Although I am rarely worried and certainly never frightened while at sea there are two situations that give me a distinct sensation of unease: being close to large ships whose intentions are not clear and being in the middle of a thunderstorm with lightning. One of the most violent thunderstorms that I ever experienced happened in 1978 while sailing between Tonga and Samoa. The storm lingered for a long time right over us and I was convinced that we would be struck as massive forked bolts landed all around us. An even worse storm greeted us as we crossed the doldrums on our way from Ascension to the Cape Verdes in February 2005 although by now I was less concerned as I knew that if we were struck the damage sustained by a metal hull would be less serious than to a fibreglass boat. However, I did make sure that all essential equipment was unplugged and

also that none of us touched any part of the hull or rigging while the storm was raging.

Mother Nature had yet another go at me right at the very end of my latest voyage while closing with the coast of Montenegro in July 2006. This time I was absolutely convinced that we would not escape unscathed and that somebody up there was trying to show me that no voyage is over until it is actually completed. I did my best to avoid the worst of the storm by zigzagging from the edge of one menacing black cloud to another. Fortunately luck was once again on my side but it's not an experience that I'd like to repeat. I did, however, witness a lightning strike almost first hand in Singapore. The violence of the so-called Sumatras is well known and when one of these electric storms broke over Raffles Marina, where the yachts taking part in a round the world rally were gathered, their crews were advised to leave their boats. From the control tower I had a panoramic view of the marina and from the frequency and proximity of the lightning bolts I felt that it would not be long before a boat was struck. It happened right in front of my eyes as a massive bolt of lightning smashed into the mast of a boat berthed right by the control tower. Although all electronics had been disconnected, the damage was extensive and all electrical and electronic equipment had to be replaced. The only positive side to this disaster was that we were in a place where such equipment was widely available so the boat could be quickly re-equipped and did not miss the start of the next leg of the rally. Fortunately the boat was insured for such an occurrence, which is something that should be checked as damage from lightning strikes is sometimes excluded. While sailing from Vava'u to Fiji, I heard on the radio of an incident that highlighted the limitations of modern navigation systems. A boat sailing the same route as us had been struck by lightning and had lost its computer and everything that was stored on it. The situation was exacerbated by the fact that the boat used only electronic charts for navigation and wasn't carrying any paper charts, so the crew were unable to plot a course through the reef-infested waters they needed to cross to reach a port in Fiji.

A deep crack in Aventura's rudder caused by a collision in the Indian Ocean

Fortunately they managed to get their radio to work so other sailors came to their assistance by plotting a course with the help of a series of waypoints. They managed to follow these on a handheld GPS that luckily had not been obliterated by the lightning strike that had destroyed the rest of their electronic equipment.

Dealing with emergencies

Some of the incidents mentioned earlier highlight two essential matters: the capability to deal with an emergency when it happens and to be able to put anything right that may break. While on passage from Reunion to South Africa we encountered bad weather off the southern tip of Madagascar, where sudden changes in weather can cause very rough seas. During my night watch, with the wind steady at 35 knots and gusting more, our speed never going below 9 knots, with occasional higher bursts as the boat surfed down the high following seas, the pattern of the waves changed and the swell started to look menacing. I had seen higher waves in the Southern Ocean while returning from Antarctica to Cape Horn but was not expecting to see anything as bad in what I believed should have been more benign waters. Earlier that evening there had been a warning on Inmarsat C that a ship had seen one or several large logs afloat in that area.

The threat of colliding with one of those logs was still at the back of my mind and I was savouring the thrill of seeing 12.5 knots on the speedometer as we were surfing down a big wave when, above the hiss and rumble, I thought I heard a louder noise. The boat pulled out of its slide, settled on its haunches, when another noise, loud and metallic, and coming from the direction of the steering warned me that something was not right. Almost instantly the movement of the boat changed and my first thought was that the autopilot had gone off. I grabbed the wheel and it felt heavy and unresponsive. I lifted the cockpit grating and shone the flashlight onto the steering mechanism and saw that the 12mm bolt joining the hydraulic autopilot ram to the rudder quadrant had sheared.

As the steering also appeared to be faulty, I decided to heave to. First I lowered the centreboard as it had been raised while broad reaching. As we were sailing under reefed mainsail and staysail, I hauled in both sheets and turned into the wind, the steering being very hard to handle. Hove to with the wheel lashed to windward Aventura was close-reaching slowly into the large swell.

I woke up my friend Antti, found a replacement bolt and replaced the broken one. With the job completed, we brought the boat back on course, still wondering why it was so hard to steer, and re-engaged the pilot. Only then did it occur to me to check the rudder hydraulics. I tried to pump down the rudder but it felt dead thus confirming my suspicion that this was probably the cause of our troubles. If the valves controlling the rudder or centreboard are left in the closed position, and one or the other hits something, the resulting pressure blows a safety valve that opens the hydraulic circuit. The sacrificial valve is a thin copper disc 8 mm in diameter that only took me one minute to replace. Only then did I realize that we must have hit something, maybe a log or other debris that had floated off Madagascar. Whatever it was, the boat had ridden over it and, as there was nothing under the boat to stop it, it ended up hitting the rudder. Thanks to its design, the rudder had absorbed the shock without suffering any apparent damage but one year later, when I hauled out the boat in Las Palmas, I noticed a suspicious crack in the main rudder body. The rudder had to be taken off and welded, and it could have only been a consequence of that collision, which must have been very violent to crack the massive aluminium plate.

Dealing with the emergency had not taken half an hour, not much more than it took me to describe it now. Later I heard that the upturned keel-less hull of the South African yacht Moquini had been discovered south of that area. Of its crew of six there was no sign. The 42 foot yacht had been taking part in the Mauritius to Durban race when it disappeared without a sign or signal. I am sure that they must have hit something similar as violent thunderstorms that had devastated parts of Madagascar around that time had washed out a lot of debris into the ocean.

There have been a few other breakages that had to be dealt with at sea of which I shall mention the most significant ones. By far the most dramatic occurred while sailing from the Falklands to Patagonia and we were caught by strong winds against the tide in what is probably the worst place in the world: Le Maire Strait. The incident is described in chapter 4.

Another breakage that had to be dealt with promptly was in the South Indian Ocean when a broken gooseneck pin put the boom in a precarious position as it was held up only by the mainsail. As we were running before a strong wind with three reefs in the mainsail, dropping the mainsail was not an option, so I steadied the boom with the boom break and lifted it to its normal position with the topping lift. Even so, extracting the broken 10 mm pin and replacing it was very difficult as lining up the two holes of the gooseneck with the opposite holes on the mast was quite a performance. As this was the second time the pin had broken, in Cape Town I had the entire system changed.

One of the most common failures experienced by boats taking part in the ARC is to their steering systems. Over the years a number of ARC boats had lost their rudders during the Atlantic crossing and, as mentioned elsewhere, some had to be abandoned. After two yachts had been abandoned in ARC 2006, I asked the organisers to comment on this frequently occurring problem. "Those yachts were not the only ones with rudder problems; there were many reports of steering cables and systems breaking due to the pressure on them and the amount of rudder movement

Lucky Petter Noreng who was found by another yacht 24 hours after being lost overboard

needed to keep the yacht on course. Another contributing factor is overloading; an easy mistake to make as piles of stores, water, fuel, crew gear and cruising equipment are added before departure. All this extra weight adds to the strain of steering systems, especially in heavy seas, and doubly so if the sails are incorrectly trimmed and the yacht is unbalanced. Bad trim can often go unnoticed when the autopilot is used for long periods and the crew do not hand steer. When undertaking an Atlantic crossing it is a good idea to have the boat lifted and to overhaul the steering systems and bearings. Carrying spare steering cable and tools to effect repairs is also strongly recommended."

Man overboard

The danger of losing a crew overboard is something that I dread more than anything else and, I must admit, that should something like this ever happen, I'd much prefer for me to be the one lost, because I simply could never live with the thought that I had been responsible for somebody's death. Strict rules on all of my boats have thankfully avoided any such situation but the loss of one young man in the first round the world rally had shook me to the core. That was the only life lost in any of the rallies I had organized, although there had been a few man overboard situations in the ARC, all of them with a happy ending.

One of them involved the German owner of an OVNI, a boat similar to my own Aventura III, who fell overboard while cleaning an engine filter on the aft deck. As the boat was sailing with poled out twin jibs, the skipper could not quickly turn the boat around and it took a while to take in the two poles. The engine was also out of action as it was being dealt with when the incident happened. To make things even worse, the steering was out of action as well, as the skipper had taken the wheel off as it was making an irritating noise while the boat was being steered by the autopilot. Eventually the wheel was remounted, the boat was turned around and, shortly after nightfall, the man was found and fished out of the sea.

A young Norwegian had the luckiest escape when he fell overboard from his 33 foot boat. Fortunately he was wearing a lifejacket that kept him afloat. Several ARC boats responded to the crew's Mayday and spent the next 24 hours doing a wide search. Eventually the man was found by another Norwegian boat. What is even more incredible is that the young couple had already saved a man shortly before the

Sailing in a convoy is a good precaution in a dangerous area

start of the ARC. While sailing towards Las Palmas to join the ARC, they saw something afloat that made them suspicious, so they got closer and found an exhausted African who was close to drowning. They pulled him on board and took him to Las Palmas, where he told the authorities that he had been taken on board a Ukrainian ship with a large group of other potential asylum seekers. As the ship was passing Gran Canaria, the captain ordered his crew to push all men overboard so they could make their own way to land. The young man rescued by the Norwegian yacht was the only survivor.

Abandoning ship

To my great relief my personal experience in this matter is based entirely on hearsay but as I regard the possibility of having to abandon ship as something that could happen to anyone, I have given the matter serious thought and have made the necessary preparations. I always discuss such an eventuality with new crew, preferably before leaving on a passage as I find the subject rather upsetting if broached when we are already at sea. Here are the seven separate steps that need to be dealt with promptly and in the right

order if the decision to abandon Aventura were ever taken:

■ Write down current GPS position
■ Send distress signal on Inmarsat C
■ Secure and launch liferaft
■ Activate EPIRB and secure in liferaft
■ Put survival containers in liferaft and secure lanyards
■ Take satellite telephone
■ Load extra water and easily grabbed food

I have timed the first six items and, with help from the crew, it can be done in about two minutes. The 405 MHz EPIRB, which is registered with Aventura's details, is right by the companionway so that it can be quickly activated and put in the liferaft. The liferaft itself can be easily launched from its recessed bin on the aft platform. While the crew is dealing with these matters, my job is to jot down the current position from the GPS, activate the distress button on the Inmarsat C and disconnect the satellite phone from the fixed antenna. Its portable antenna, as well as a fully charged spare battery, are permanently stowed in one of the survival containers. I regard the satellite phone as my best chance of rescue and have written in indelible pen the numbers of the US and UK Coast Guards on the lid of one of the survival containers and also on a piece of paper kept in one of the containers.

One often overlooked point is to ensure that the liferaft lanyard is secured to the yacht. This is one of the items that is checked during the safety inspection to which all yachts taking part in the ARC or other rallies are submitted and it was always a great surprise to find that as many as one third of the skippers had failed to actually secure their liferaft to a strong point.

From the suggestions made by skippers when they described the contents of their survival containers, some containing a bare minimum, while others being able to support the crew for several weeks, I compiled a list of the best ideas and most common suggestions:

Food: a mixture of dry and concentrated food, not all of which has to be reconstituted with water, food in self-heating tins, chocolate, glucose.

Medicine: first aid kit, vitamins, laxatives, sunblock cream, painkillers, anti-seasickness medication, water purification tablets, any personal medicines.

Safety: EPIRB, battery operated GPS, satellite telephone with spare battery, flares (in separate waterproof container) or flare pistol, portable VHF radio with spare batteries and aerial, dye marker, torch and batteries, signalling mirror, spare sea anchor, survival handbook.

Miscellaneous: hand operated watermaker, knife (pocket knife with various blades), drinking cup, spoon, plastic plate(s), fishing gear, can opener, sponge, repair kit with patches and adhesive, assorted plastic bags.

Personal: passports, money, paper and pencil, reading matter, playing cards, dice.

Comfort: survival suits or aluminium blankets, spare clothing, sun hats, sunglasses, folding umbrella (can be used to shelter from rain or sun, catch rain water and even as a sail, if strong enough).

Navigation: compass, plastic sextant, almanac or navigational computer, routing chart(s).

The above list is so comprehensive that one would almost need a second yacht to carry all that stuff so on Aventura I tried to reduce it to more reasonable proportions and ended up with what I regard as the most essential items necessary for survival. My two survival containers are waterproof plastic containers of the type normally used for flares with a wide mouth and screw top. Both have lanyards to make fast to the liferaft and are kept close to the companionway. As liferaft emergency packs contain very little water I always have a jerrycan of water under the helmsman seat but it is not completely full so it floats if thrown overboard. Probably the most important item to take along is a hand-operated watermaker but even if one is available some additional water should be carried as well. The contents of Aventura's two survival containers are as follows:

◼ Selection of flares (one orange smoke, two parachute, two red flares)
◼ Hand-operated PUR watermaker
◼ Plastic measuring jug
◼ Hand-held VHF Radio, GPS, torch, 48 AA alkaline batteries
◼ Charged spare battery for Iridium satellite phone, emergency telephone numbers (all in separate waterproof box)
◼ Fishing gear, hooks, monofilament line, etc
◼ Two knives, one with cork handle
◼ Leatherman compact tool kit
◼ Pliers
◼ Can opener
◼ Liferaft repair kit and adhesive
◼ Personal medication, antibiotic tablets, antibiotic cream
◼ Sunblock cream, first aid kit, anti-seasickness pills
◼ Paper and pen

The above items are meant to complement the survival contents included in the liferaft.

Passports and money are also kept where they can easily be grabbed. The EPIRB and Iridium phone would be taken separately, as would any food items that could be grabbed from the galley and the jerrycan of water kept in the cockpit for this eventuality. All battery operated items use the same alkaline AA type batteries that are rotated regularly so that those that are in the container are always the latest batch.

Tips

- Prepare an abandon ship procedure, discuss with crew and assign individual tasks.
- Prepare survival container.
- Check and rotate contents of survival container regularly.
- Keep emergency jerrycan of water in cockpit.

General Safety Tips

- Do not spend more than one night in a doubtful anchorage.
- In doubtful areas try cruising or anchoring in company with another boat and consider anchoring in tandem for the night.
- Bring dinghy and outboard on deck for the night and lock.
- On arrival in an anchorage prepare an exit strategy by noting down essential waypoints and making a sketch of the anchorage so as to be able to leave at short notice whether because of a change in weather or a perceived danger.
- If leaving the boat for travelling ashore make a mutual arrangement with another crew to look after your boat during your absence.
- Take normal precautions when going ashore, never carry too much cash, keep valuables and passport in a pouch close to the body (in some countries it is compulsory to have ID at all times).

- Be careful when hiring cars, never leave anything visible inside.
- Avoid being too aggressive to local people who offer things for sale or to do work on your boat. They need to make a living and, never forget, that you are a guest in their country.
- If you have an FLS (forward looking sonar) leave it switched on in area where you are concerned about the presence of whales (the depth sounder might work too).
- Besides the masthead tri-colour light have secondary navigation lights at deck level. Also carry a battery operated emergency bi-colour set to be used if one of the two main systems fail (low level navigation or masthead tri-colour light) possibly as a result of power failure.
- When anchored always leave a light on at night. Solar powered lights used in gardens can be used. Their great advantage is that they come on automatically at night and most batteries will last all night.
- Have a diving mask and sharp serrated knife in an easily accessible place to be able to cut free a fouled propeller.
- The boarding ladder should be lowered whenever someone is in the water.
- Have a lanyard permanently attached to the boarding ladder so that in an emergency it can be easily pulled down by someone from the water.
- If the boat is provided with mast steps always wear a harness and clip it on to a fixed point while working. For more difficult jobs have the crew hoist you in a bosun's chair.

Spiky Officials and Spiny Lobsters

As the outline of San Salvador started separating from the western horizon my thoughts went back to the young Rodrigo de Triana whose call of 'Tierra... tierra' in the early hours of 12 October 1492 marked the first sighting of the New World. Columbus's three ships stood off for the night and the Spaniards landed in the morning on the island that the natives who met them on the beach called Guanahani. Columbus promptly changed the name to that of the Saviour and claimed the land for Spain. Later the island became known as Watling but in 1926 San Salvador was finally accepted as the first landfall in the New World and the island reverted to the name bestowed upon it by the great navigator.

There is still a lingering controversy over Columbus's original landfall in spite of the fact that Samuel Eliot Morison, the famous naval historian and biographer of Columbus, declared Watling Island as Columbus's first landfall. He wrote, 'There is no longer any doubt that alone of any island in the Bahamas, Turks or Caicos groups, San Salvador fits Columbus's description.'

Personally I find the controversy both irritating and useless. Does it really matter? Columbus's achievement was in the successful voyage itself not whether he landed on this or that island. All I am interested in is that he landed somewhere and San Salvador is as good as any other. In fact I am convinced that San Salvador was the site of that historic landfall as it seems to fit the bill in various ways. The description of the island's main features are close to both those made by Columbus and other contemporary reports, while recent finds on San Salvador of Spanish coins from that era and other artefacts should, I hope, put this subject to rest.

Bahamas winter cruise

Our planned stop at San Salvador was to revisit the place that saw the culmination of America 500 in 1992. Among the various events to mark the quincentenary celebrations of Columbus's arrival in the New World, America 500

At Landfall Point on San Salvador Island where Columbus first set foot in the New World

was the only one to follow the historic route across the Atlantic. Having completed clearance formalities in Cockburn Town we sailed south and anchored as close as

A Canarian palm in George Town on
Great Exuma Island brought across during
America 500

possible to what is called Landfall Point. Over the years a number of monuments have been erected there as well as a large bronze bowl from where the Olympic Flame was transferred to Mexico in 1968 for the Olympic Games, the first to be held in Latin America.

What we had come to see were the Canarian palm trees that had been planted by the America 500 crews on the completion of their transatlantic passage. To my great disappointment I found that only a few stunted specimens had survived the hurricane that had hit the island soon after the event's departure. As I did not consider San Salvador to be safe enough to accommodate the large America 500 fleet, I had decided to hold the final celebrations on Great Exuma Island, whose main settlement George Town overlooks the landlocked Elizabeth Harbour that could easily provide shelter for our large fleet.

After paying homage to Columbus in San Salvador a leisurely cruise took us towards Great Exuma with stops at Rum Cay and Conception Island. I have visited the Bahamas in every one of my boats, Aventura I in 1977, Aventura II in 1990 and now on Aventura III. While there have been major changes in the settlements between each of those visits, the anchorages, especially those in the Outer Bahamas, were as attractive as ever and although this was January and the height of the winter season we met relatively few cruising boats. The one change that somewhat spoilt my pleasure was the ban on spear fishing. The Bahamas have such beautiful underwater scenery that must be preserved for future generations, so selfish considerations had no justification and I entirely agreed with the ban.

A narrow pass took us into Elizabeth Harbour and, as we passed Stocking Island, the main anchorage opposite George Town, I counted over one hundred boats in that sheltered spot alone. I was told later that there were over three hundred boats in the immediate area and that their number normally swells to five hundred during Regatta Week that is held every March and signals the end of the winter season.

As soon as we landed we walked towards the distinctive pink government building that had been our headquarters in December 1992, and where we had planted one of the extra Canarian saplings that had been sent across in case some of its brethren did not survive the crossing. After the disappointment in San Salvador where I felt bitter that all the efforts made to leave behind something significant for future generations had failed so miserably, I was doubly pleased to see that our palm tree had not only survived but had grown into an impressive specimen.

After a pleasant few days in the George Town area, rather than take the long roundabout way around the south-eastern tip of Great Exuma and its outlying islands, I decided to take the risk of going through the shallow Hog Cay Cut. As far as I know, no other sailing boat had dared pass through that area before and even with our board up I had to time our arrival to coincide with high water. If anyone is keen on getting a real adrenaline kick, this is it. As we skimmed over coral heads that looked as if they were breaking the surface I made for the deepest part of the narrow channel, the depth decreasing rapidly until the echo sounder was showing only 0.2 metres under the boat... and that was with the board fully up! Once we had reached deeper water, I lowered the centreboard and paid out the fishing line, as I guessed that there must be fish in that area. I had hardly let the line out when I had a hit. When I hauled in the line I landed a beautiful red snapper on the aft platform, its large eyes giving me a mournful look for having spoilt his day.

A cold front that was predicted to pass through later that day made us pick up our skirts and seek shelter at the southern end of Long Island where we tucked in between a small cay and a large sandbank. The front passed during the night but we were well anchored. Strong winds continued the following morning as we skimmed over the flat waters at great speed. We made it through the pass at Crooked Island having covered 67 miles in nine hours and anchored in a sheltered spot at French Wells. Ashore we could see ruined walls disappearing in the dense vegetation. We landed at Gun Point and, true to its name, came across a sixteenth century canon and the ruins of an old fort.

Winter sailing in the Bahamas can be a truly exhilarating experience as the waters are often sheltered and the winds rarely blow over twenty knots. On the next leg south we sailed parallel to the western shore of Long Cay, then made it into the Bight of Acklins, a large bay on the oddly-shaped island of that name. On the chart it looked as if we might be able to find a suitable place to anchor in Jamaica Bay but after we touched the bottom a couple of times I had to admit that the shallow bay was beyond even our reach and continued to the attractively named Delectable Bay. Somebody must have had fun naming these places as our anchorage was off a small place called Pompeii, of which only ruins remained, that may have inspired the choice of name. A local man was fishing at the end of the broken down pier when we landed from the dinghy. He welcomed us warmly to his island and offered to take us on a tour in his battered pickup truck. From his non-stop commentary all that stuck in my mind was that the bitter ingredient of Campari comes from the bark of a bush that grows on the island and is a major source of income for the small community.

The Cuban experience

It might have been the music of Buena Vista Social Club that made me include Cuba on this whistle-stop tour of the Caribbean, but in fact there was another reason for this detour. Having grown up under a similar regime in my native Romania, I was interested to find out how different a communist society looked under the blue Caribbean sky compared to the grey East European variety, and how this system, which had failed so miserably elsewhere, had fared there.

From Acklins Island an overnight spinnaker run took us into Baracoa on Cuba's NE coast. The attractive sixteenth century town, the earliest Spanish settlement in Cuba, was listed as an official port of entry and I had been assured by a Cuban contact that we could clear in there. As soon as we anchored, three officials boarded Aventura and told me that we couldn't stop as the regulations had changed recently and visiting cruising boats now had to proceed to an international marina. The nearest was at Santiago de Cuba, about one hundred miles away along the south coast, so reluctantly we had to up anchor and leave.

I was quite annoyed about this setback especially as this was my second attempt to visit Cuba. It started to look as if I wasn't meant to go there. My previous attempt had been eleven years earlier when I had left Key West on Aventura II heading for the Hemingway International Marina near Havana. We arrived off the Cuban coast in the late afternoon but the strong northerly wind that had given us such a fast passage was kicking up large breakers along the entire coast. Looking through the binoculars at the gap in the reef that led into the marina I could see that the breakers in the narrow entrance looked extremely dangerous. Someone from the marina came up on VHF and offered to guide us in.

'What about those breakers? Do you think it is safe to come in?' I asked.

'Don't worry, they look worse than they are.'

I don't usually worry, except when I am told by somebody else not to. I had a better look at the breakers through the powerful binoculars and the situation looked distinctively suicidal.

'Sorry, but there is no way I will take my boat through those breakers.'

'OK, why don't you make for Puerto Mariel instead? That is a large port and you can go in whatever the weather.'

My crew had followed the entire conversation and looked quite upset, all of us looking forward to the fleshpots of Havana whose tall buildings beckoned temptingly a few miles away. While sailing west parallel to the coast, a dark night fell on us and by the time the lights of Puerto Mariel came into view it was nearly midnight. Going into a strange port at night, especially one for which I had no plan or information, seemed as foolish as braving those breakers, while heaving-to for the rest of the night was equally unappealing, so I told my crew that I'd had enough of Cuba and had decided to make straight for Panama, our final destination. Soon afterwards a voice came over loudly on the VHF.

'Aventura, this is the Cuban Coast Guard, where are you?'

I gave my position and the voice came back.

'You are expected at Puerto Mariel, what is your ETA?'

'I am sorry but the weather conditions are not good, and so we have decided to continue to Panama.'

'You cannot do that. You have entered Cuban territorial waters and must proceed to the nearest international port for clearance.'

'Please understand, the weather is bad, this is a small boat, and I am not prepared to risk it and the lives of its crew.'

'You must do as you are told.'

'OK, I am altering course and heading for Puerto Mariel.'

'Very well, we are waiting.'

'Tom, switch off those navigation lights. We are going offshore into international waters. They can have Cuba to themselves!'

By dawn we had moved well offshore and had lost sight of the coast. Throughout the day at frequent intervals we could hear Aventura being called again and again by

The bay of Santiago de Cuba

the Coast Guard from stations strung along the coast, but no patrol boat came out, and we made it safely as far as Cuba's western extremity. The northerly wind had set up a horrible swell against the powerful Gulf Stream that was pushing its way through the narrow gap of the Yucatan Channel between Cuba and Mexico. As it was dark by now, I took a chance and closed with the Cuban shore, hoping to find a counter-current. The tactic worked, we hit the Caribbean Sea flying and had a fast sail all the way to Panama.

Now on Aventura III it was very tempting to vote with my feet once again and head for Jamaica, especially as on leaving Baracoa our course took us right into the teeth of the strong trade wind. This stretch of coast is Cuba's most spectacular and while we still had enough light we tacked as close as we dared to the sheer cliffs. The scenery was of a wild and primeval beauty. It took us a long time and several tacks to round Cape Maisi, Cuba's eastern extremity. The strong wind continued after we had turned the corner and, with just the

mainsail up, we were flying. Two sailboats passed close by, bashing their way under power on a reciprocal course, bound for the Windward Passage. With the prevailing contrary winds and current, Cuba's south coast is not the best route to head east. Shortly after midnight we passed within one mile of the entrance into Guantanamo Bay, where we knew that hundreds of Al Qaida suspects were held, but security seemed nonexistent although we sailed by in view of the large US base.

The mighty fort of San Pedro del Morro at the entrance into the Bay of Santiago made an impressive show in the rosy light of dawn. Inside the well-protected bay the ramshackle installations at Ponta Gorda, described as an international marina, were quite an exaggeration. There were only two broken down pontoons with a couple of visiting boats, not looking much better, tied up alongside. An attendant pointed for us to tie up to one of them but I saw on the nearer pontoon in what looked like the best berth a small racing boat, obviously local, occupying the prime spot.

"Disculpeme, amigo, pero porque no podemos tomar este mejor atraque?'

'Con mucho gusto, señor!' he replied with a wide smile and, helped by another guy, moved the boat to make space for us.

How good it was to be speaking Spanish again, which, among all the languages that I speak is by far my favourite. I like the Spanish people, and I have particular affection for the Canarians. Many Cubans are of Canarian descent and this is betrayed by the Cuban accent which sounds very much like the Spanish spoken in the Canaries. I always enjoy chatting in Spanish, especially in Latin America, where, because of the dominance of English, people always respond enthusiastically when a foreigner speaks their language.

It took all morning for the various officials to complete the lengthy formalities. Besides Aventura there were two other foreign boats, but the atmosphere among visiting sailors was subdued, similar to what we found later among the tourists in town. As my Spanish is reasonably fluent after many years of taking sailing events to the Canaries, I found it easy to communicate. What struck me immediately was how freely people discussed everything and how happy they were to talk, and that even included one of the officials who came to clear us in. Although several Cubans whom we met during the week we spent in and around Santiago complained about certain shortages no one voiced any actual criticism of the regime. On the contrary, several stressed what they regarded as the main achievements of the revolution: free education and free health care. With my background I felt that if people had real complaints they probably would have voiced them, but maybe I was wrong and they were being careful not to get into trouble. This attitude was similar to what I remembered from my own youth.

Indeed my own background put me in a rather ambivalent situation. On the one hand I disagreed with Castro and hated his dictatorship, but on the other was open-minded enough to recognize that in Cuba the communist regime had been faced with very different challenges compared to my native Romania, and, by and large, had somehow managed to put the worst things right. People had jobs of sorts, no one looked hungry, health and education were free, so all that was lacking were freedom and democracy. What impressed me most were the Cubans themselves, their friendliness, good humour and stoicism, so very different from people living under similar regimes in Eastern Europe who were often sour, impatient, rude and unfriendly.

Having been attracted to Cuba mainly by its music we missed no opportunity to get our fill. La Trova was a bar in the centre of Santiago where local bands played all afternoon and evening, and we spent most of our time there. While the music was as good as we had expected, what I found disturbing was that the drinks were all priced in US dollars and even the modest entrance fee had to be paid in greenbacks. One evening, as we were going in, a young man sidled up to me and asked if I spoke Spanish. When he heard that I did he begged me to pay his entrance ticket so he could listen to his favourite group. He joined us for a drink and told us that he was a semi-professional boxer, former champion of Cuba, and that while a lot was all right in his country there were just as many things that were bad. For a while I thought that he was trying to set me up and refrained from making any comments but after a while I realized that no secret police informer would go so far in his criticism. We spent the rest of the evening in the company of this interesting man who reminded me in some ways of my younger self.

The yacht club staff all stressed how much they appreciated having foreign visitors and were sorry to see several boats leave in irritation at the unbending attitude of the officials. The most frustrating rule was the requirement to clear in and out at a so-called international marina. We had planned to cruise some of Cuba's south coast and clear out at one of the ports along that coast but the new regulation meant that we would have to sail all the way to the city of Trinidad, which was much too far for our tight schedule. The alternative was to stay in Santiago and see as much as possible of the surrounding area by land.

One afternoon we ended up in a suburb of Santiago looking for Foco Carabalis, a local group that we had been told put on the best show for carnival. This was a rundown part of the city with low decaying houses most of which had their front door open so we could look into the bare interior of rooms with unpainted walls and a few sticks of rickety furniture. Every now and then there was a corner shop stocking a meagre selection of ration-controlled foodstuff. Suddenly Castro's Cuba no longer looked so rosy.

After many wrong directions we found the home of the dance group and explained to its leader that we were interested in Cuban music and wanted to see their show. He invited us to join them for the dress rehearsal the following afternoon when we could see the special performance they were preparing for St Valentine's Day. The venue was more like a social club that attracted many of the older women living in the area. When we arrived the following day we were given the VIP treatment and were seated in the front row where two decrepit armchairs had been prepared as if waiting for royalty. After the performance we were asked to wait for a few minutes and, from the coming and going of the old ladies, we could see that something was afoot. While the leader of the group treated us to some fiery rum, platter after platter of snacks started appearing and we realized that this whole treat had been put on for our benefit. We felt both moved and embarrassed, as we knew by now to what lengths those poor old ladies must have gone to prepare such a feast from their meagre rations. The following day being St Valentine's we were asked to join the group for the proper performance, an invitation we gladly accepted.

The shrill ring of the satellite phone woke us up early in the morning. It was Doina who told us that Gwenda's stepfather had died. As the only child Gwenda decided to return immediately to England to be with her mother. We took a taxi to the airport to see if there were any flights that connected with an international flight in Havana but it soon became apparent that it would be almost impossible to leave the country at such short notice. Instead I suggested that we leave immediately for Jamaica. Gwenda had already booked a flight from there to London as from Jamaica I was going to sail to Panama with my niece Marianne and my Canarian mate JuanFra.

We had thoroughly enjoyed our stay and felt that more than in any other country it was the people who make Cuba the interesting place it is. What I found disappointing was the blatant absence of personal freedom. Just as in other similar situations, from Soviet Russia in the early 1920s to Czechoslovakia in the late 1960s, personal freedom and a communist regime seem unable to make comfortable bedfellows, with the state always ending up in total control. In this respect Castro's Cuba was no exception:

a totalitarian regime where political dissidents were locked up just as in the old Soviet Union.

Clearing out took us almost all day but we finally got through all the formalities and could leave. I was sorry to have missed our new friends' St Valentine's Day performance and equally sad to leave Cuba before being able to see more, as we had planned to go by train to Havana. As we sailed out of Santiago Bay past the mighty fort guarding its entrance, it occurred to me that it was here that US troops and ships defeated the Spanish garrison in 1898 leading to Cuba's independence. How strange that in spite of current propaganda, Cuba's fate was still so closely intertwined with that of its mighty neighbour. As I cast a last look towards the fast receding coast, I wondered how much longer the situation could continue unchanged and whether Cuba will eventually go the same way as all former communist countries in Eastern Europe. Five years later I am still waiting for that answer.

The relatively short hop to Montego Bay close to Jamaica's western extremity went without hitch, Gwenda caught her flight home and, a few days later, I collected my new crew from the airport. JuanFra had sailed with me on several occasions, Marianne had sailed from Bora Bora to Hawaii but her partner Bernd was an absolute greenhorn. As all seemed keen to go and were not interested in staying in Jamaica longer than necessary, we got the boat ready and headed west towards Cape Negril. Around midnight we finally passed Jamaica's westernmost point and could turn south. The wind kept gradually increasing and by dawn was blowing thirty knots. Although the wind was from the north and we could run with it, the clash with the old easterly swell set up a nasty cross swell that made all my crew sick. The fault was entirely mine as I had known that we could expect strong winds from the north but as I regarded this to be a favourable direction the thought had never occurred to me to worry about anything else. Eventually the wind turned into the east and we were reaching fast but by now we had picked up a current of about two knots against us so the swell was just as bad as earlier.

My thoughts kept going back to my previous trip along the same route in Aventura II. After the fiasco in Cuba we had another bout of excitement when I plotted a course that led us briefly into Colombian territorial waters and were intercepted by the Colombian Coast Guard. I could still remember the radio conversation as if it had only happened quite recently and not eleven years previously.

'Vessel passing close to Roncador Island. This is the Colombian Coast Guard. Identify yourself.'

'Buenas noches, señor. Velero La Aventura bandera inglesa.'

'Habla bien español, que nacionalidad?'

'Ingles.'

'Usted no es ingles... Panameño?' Wow, what a compliment. I never thought my Spanish was that good.

'No, no, nacido en Rumania... pero hace muchos años.'

'How interesting... and the rest of the crew?'

'One Jamaican, two Danish, one Panamanian...'

'United Nations, no less... why do you have a Panamanian on board?'

'He is a friend.'

'What is your destination?'

'Panama.'

'OK, prepare for boarding.'

My heart froze. Even in the lee of the atoll the swell was considerable and if a vessel came alongside us it could have been a disaster.

'I am very sorry but that is quite impossible under these conditions. Do you have an inflatable?'

'Never mind that. You have entered Colombian territorial waters without having cleared in. Prepare for boarding.'

I turned to my friend Jaime as I knew that only he had a chance of getting us out if this. Not only was he a top lawyer but he had excellent connections right to the president of Panama who was a family friend.'

Kuna women display their molas in Aventura's cockpit

'Jimmy, I can't do this. It will only make it worse.'

'Jaime, nothing can be worse now. If they try to board us in this weather, we are done for.'

Reluctantly Jaime took the mike.

'Ola, this is Jaime Arias.'

'Did you say Arias? Not by any chance of the Arias family?'

Even as he was saying that, it was noticeable how the tone of the official had changed and sounded almost friendly. Jaime responded in the same vein, they chatted amicably for a few minutes and finally the Colombian captain must have realized that there was nothing suspicious about us after all and told us to proceed. But it had been a very close call.

Eleven years later we were sailing exactly the same route that cuts across the Caribbean Sea passing close to a number of dangerous reefs all of which can be safely left to starboard. The only exception, which I knew too well, was the small island of Roncador which belongs to Colombia . The island is fronted by extensive reefs that sticks out to the east. With a strong easterly

wind and high swell , I didn't fancy passing on their windward side so decided to take a risk and pass close inside them. As we got closer I was relieved that the flashing light was working and we could easily pass close to the west of the light.

'Vessel passing Roncador Island. This is the Colombian Coast Guard. Identify yourself.'

Not again! This couldn't be true. Without replying I handed over the mike to Juan Fra. 'Do your best, compañero.'

'Buenas noches. Yate velero Aventura Tres. Capitan Juan Francisco Martin Naranjo.'

I had to admit that it sounded very impressive... and it worked because after a pleasant chat we were allowed to continue on our way. Ooof!

Among the Kuna

The following day we tried hard to sail as fast as possible so as to make landfall before it got dark at Porvenir, the port of entry for San Blas, where we had to negotiate an intricate channel. By the time we got close to the small island, the light was fading fast. With nowhere else to go, I had no choice but to trust my luck... and managed to weave our way through the reefs to find a precarious spot among the half dozen anchored boats just as darkness enveloped us.

The tiny island and its airstrip are the official port of entry for the archipelago

Anchored off a tiny islet in San Blas

and all arriving boats must call there first. All officials were housed in the airport building and in the morning formalities took only minutes to complete. The immigration officer also doubled up as official representative of Kuna Yala, the autonomous regional government of the indigenous San Blas community. A unique phenomenon, the Kuna community has successfully preserved its customs and traditional way of life almost intact in spite of the onslaught of mass tourism. Hardly a day goes by without at least one huge cruise ship visiting the archipelago and

yet life on the small islands continues unperturbed. This was such a contrast to other island communities that I had visited where traditional life had been badly affected by the impact of tourism.

Cruising sailors, who now visit San Blas in ever growing numbers (at least two hundred boats call there every year), quickly adapt to the local lifestyle and I found quite remarkable the symbiosis that had evolved between islanders and most sailors. Rarely had I seen such a genuine give-and-take attitude between locals and visitors. We followed their example and on several occasions made water for families living on remote islands as the nearest source of drinking water was on the mainland – a round trip of some 40 miles by paddle canoe. The Kuna had very little apart from what they grew or caught in the sea, and supplies of any kind could only be bought on the larger islands or on the mainland. The little money they needed was earned from selling their distinctive embroideries as well as lobsters, fish or shells to sailors or tourists. Transactions were usually conducted by the women, few of whom ever left the tightly-knit communities, whereas the men occasionally went to Panama City to work and therefore spoke some Spanish. This division of tasks was reflected in their dress: the women were always traditionally clad, whereas men wore T-shirts and shorts.

Once again Aventura's shallow draft came into its own as it allowed us to reach many rarely visited spots. One of those was the tiny island of Moro Du (Turtle Island) where we spent a few days in the company of a Kuna family who were harvesting coconuts and making copra. Even smaller was Coco Bandero, a tiny sandy islet shaded by a clump of palm trees under which stood a hut made from palm fronds. As I waded ashore, I half expected to be confronted by a shipwrecked sailor gnawing on some fish bones.

Three Kuna generations at Moro Du

One day we called at the main settlement of Carti Suitupo, a large crowded village with many of its houses built over the water. There were shops, a school and also the local museum. This was also the seat of the regional assembly where we saw democracy in action, as every adult, both male and female, had the right to participate in debates where all matters of common interest were discussed and voted upon. By chance we met a young man Eulogio, who spoke fluent English and told us that he had studied in the USA but had decided to return to his ancestral place where life was much more tranquil and enjoyable than anywhere else. He took us to meet Father Ibelele Nikktiginya, the local priest and a keen amateur anthropologist, who kept us enthralled with tales of the early history of the Kuna, the significance of their myths, and the little known fact that the Kuna had a concept of ice and snow, which proved that they migrated from the High Andes to the sweltering Darien coast where the temperature never fell below 25°C.

Before arriving in San Blas I had been in regular contact by email with Doug and Judy Decker, whose Limerence sounded as if it had grown roots in San Blas. We had got to know each other via our website and their regular updates and contributions to noonsite were of the highest order. Being so close I was keen to meet them and so we arranged by VHF a rendezvous at a well-protected anchorage. When we arrived there at exactly the agreed time, they greeted us warmly and I asked them to come over for dinner that evening. By the time we had anchored, a cayuki with two Kuna men had pulled up alongside, the younger asking us if we wanted to buy lobster.

'How many do you have?' JuanFra asked.

The young man lifted a mat and pointed to small heap of hand-sized spiny lobsters. 'Fifteen.'

'How much?'

'Fifteen dollars.'

JuanFra handed over a twenty note.

The man tried to explain that he had no change but JuanFra told him to keep it.

'OK.' JuanFra told them, 'tomorrow you bring us some fish.'

'You shouldn't have done that?' I told JuanFra.

'What, ask for fish?'

'No, pay over the odds. For these guys this is a sign of stupidity. Only an idiot would pay twenty for what had been set at fifteen,

With a Kuna family on Canitupo

when in fact he would have been just as happy to get only ten.'

The Deckers rowed over and as they boarded I saw Doug clutching half a bottle of wine.

'Welcome to Aventura. But what's that?' I asked.

'Some wine for us to drink.'

'You don't mean to say that you came over to my boat which has a cellar to put Maxim's in Paris to shame and bring your own plonk with you. Is it just you or do all cruisers do it these days?'

'Everybody does it. You simply don't expect to be fed and watered.'

'Obviously I have a lot to learn as in the good old days of cruising however poor you were, and most of us were, you always had something to offer your guests.'

The lobsters were a great success and, over a copious dinner, well watered by some excellent Rioja white wine, the Deckers outlined their future plans. After several years in the Caribbean they had set their sights on the Med but from the way they were speaking I had the feeling that something was not right.

'But you sound as if you have a problem?' I asked.

'Yes, we do not feel confident enough to do the crossing.'

'Have you ever thought of shipping your boat across. I did that from British Columbia to the Med. You could probably do it for around 20k dollars. Can you afford it?'

'Of course... what a marvellous idea!'

And that's exactly what they did. They returned to Fort Lauderdale, loaded Limerence on a special transporter ship and a few weeks later she was safely lowered into Toulon Harbour. Sometimes it is good to listen to your friends' advice.

JuanFra's Kuna friends were back that evening.

'Have you got the fish?' JuanFra asked hopefully.

'No señor, all we could catch was lobster?'

'How many this time?'

'About the same as yesterday. Fifteen.'

'And how much?'

'Twenty, señor.'

JuanFra looked at me and burst out laughing.

'OK, Jimmy, you win – again!'

The last days were spent at Chichime, a popular anchorage as it was protected from all directions by the surrounding reef. We met several sailors, some of who had spent several months in San Blas, and were so happy that they didn't want to leave. In spite of my incurable wanderlust, I could well understand their feelings as I could hardly think of another place that came closer to perfection.

Anchors and Anchoring, Tenders and Outboards

I have often been amazed at just how lazy people are to re-anchor even if their anchor is obviously not holding well, or they have dropped it in the wrong place.

Klaus Girzig

In over thirty years of cruising I have used all types of anchors: CQR, Bruce, Danforth, a French FOB, very rarely a Fisherman. I have also used a Bahamian moor when anchored in rivers or tidal estuaries, also a tandem arrangement

me and I entirely agree with Don Babson's comment even if now I believe that there is no such thing as an anchor that never drags. There may be types of anchors whose holding is better than that of others but no anchor should be regarded as one hundred per cent reliable under any conditions.

Anchor types

My preferred anchor? One that doesn't drag.

Don Babson

Whereas in the early 1970s there may have been only three or four types of

Tropical anchorage in Raivavae lagoon where a sudden change in wind direction could put a boat on a lee shore

with two anchors while in Antarctica and Southern Chile. In spite of all that experience anchors are still a mystery to

anchors specifically designed for sailing yachts, there is now such a variety of anchors to choose from that it is virtually impossible to make up one's mind. Fortunately there are a number of good books dealing with this subject, one of the best among them being "The Complete

213

Anchoring Handbook" by Alain Poiraud, who, incidentally is also the inventor of the Spade and Oceane anchors. As a true professional Alain has managed to distance himself from the subject and his book provides a comprehensive overview of the various types of anchors, their main characteristics, advantages and disadvantages.

Alain sent me the following comments on anchors generally: "Out of all the equipment on today's boats the anchor is the one that attracts the least interest from sailors. They want the latest electronic equipment but many don't even know the brand of their anchor. In the time of satellite navigation many boats are still equipped with anchors that look as if they had been invented by the ancient Greeks and Romans. Even some of the "modern" anchors have been designed sixty or seventy years ago. Like all other techniques in recent times, anchors have evolved, old wisdoms have been replaced by new theories, anchors no longer have to be heavy to be efficient, anchoring rode doesn't have to be all chain and new designs are proven to be more efficient. New ideas have been successfully tested; since the introduction by Spade anchors of a blade of concave shape other new generation anchors are copying the concept. New ideas are also being tried, such as having a hollow shank or using roll bars to improve holding. There is no doubt that current design anchors improve security for those who are wise enough to try them."

With practically every cruising boat that I knew using a British designed and built CQR (se-cu-re), when it came to choosing an anchor for the first Aventura I automatically opted for a 15 kg/35 lbs anchor with 50 m/150 ft of 8 mm/ 5/16' chain. This type of plough anchor worked quite well in temperate waters but was not so good when we reached the tropics. No type of anchor is perfectly suited for anchoring among coral heads and while any anchor will hold once either itself or the chain, or both, have fouled, a plough type anchor tends to get fouled easier than most other types. Basically there is no answer to this dilemma faced by anyone cruising in the tropics. Before we left the London docks my Cockney friend Harold Valman presented me with a mighty 60 kg/140 lbs modified Admiralty type anchor that he insisted I should take along as a hurricane anchor. It was never used but it certainly made me feel good just knowing that I had it. For lack of inspiration, Aventura II also ended up with a CQR as her main anchor, this time upgraded to 20 kg/45 lbs.

In the case of Aventura III the decision was taken out of my hands as she came supplied with a French designed FOB anchor of 15 kg/35 lbs which I was assured was more than adequate for Aventura's displacement. I now carry 60 metres/200 feet of 10 mm (3/8 inch) galvanized chain, and a shorter length for a second anchor. I also bought, as a second or stern anchor, a light aluminium dismantable FOB that weighs only 8 kg/ 20 lbs but is much larger than a standard FOB of its weight. It is easy to handle and row out in the dinghy and, being provided with 6 metres/20 feet of 10 mm chain and 50 metres/150 feet of nylon rode it works reasonable well but only on soft bottoms... or when I deliberately dive down and hook it around a suitable obstruction.

For reasons that I cannot remember, once I reached the Pacific I replaced the FOB with a Bruce anchor, but it proved so disappointing that I gave it away when I reached New Zealand. I also have a small 5 kg/12 lbs Fisherman that I first used in Antarctica in a tandem arrangement with my main anchor. The Fisherman was shackled to a length of 20 feet of 10 mm chain, which was connected to the main anchor. The Fisherman was let go first, and being held down by its short length of chain, would usually settle in well firmly holding down the main anchor. We never dragged when anchored in this way and

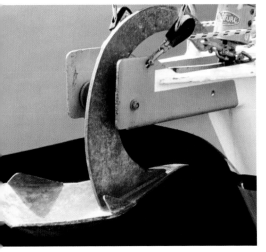

Oceane type anchor

even later whenever I was in a dubious place or planned to stay longer, I used this reliable system. Retrieving the anchors is easy as the main anchor is hauled in normally with the electric winch then, when the additional chain breaks the water, it can be either handled or grabbed with a boathook and lifted on to the foredeck. If I plan to anchor again soon, I leave the whole caboodle shackled up on the foredeck and ready to go.

While in New Zealand I was contacted by the manufacturer of Spade anchors who asked me to test the new Oceane model. The Oceane is of a similar design to the Spade but from what I gather incorporates some improvements on its successful predecessor. To test it I started making a note of the type of bottom, depth, how

much chain had been let out, etc. and so I started paying more attention to my anchoring technique than in the past. It came as a surprise to find, when I double checked, that often I was not as well anchored as I had presumed. I must admit that I have never dragged badly enough to put the boat in danger, although there have been a couple of close calls. A few times I dragged not because I had done anything wrong but because, while we were away, some other boat had dragged over our chain and pulled us away from our spot, or someone had picked up our anchor with theirs and then dropped it without any thought of what might happen to our boat. One such incident happened in Greece and could have had serious consequences had it not been for an alert taverna owner who knew our host and called us to return quickly to our boat. It probably saved my boat but ruined my Easter lunch. After that I was very reluctant to leave the boat unattended while paying long visits inshore.

Anchoring techniques

Over the years I have honed down my anchoring technique to a simple routine with a few rules that I try to observe whenever possible. The main thing is to always try to anchor in a depth where in an emergency I can free dive to retrieve the anchor or untangle the chain, or, if too deep, have diving tanks on board for just this kind of situation. My mask and snorkel are always kept by the companionway and it is surprising how often I have to dive quickly to sort out a fouled anchor, or help out someone else. In fact, the mask is kept there not so much to retrieve the anchor but to check if it had set properly. Not being able to dive on your own anchor can be a serious handicap. The very first money I earned as a sailor happened a few days after we had arrived in Greece when the skipper of a charter boat asked me if I had diving tanks on board as they had lost their anchor in deep water. He offered me the equivalent of fifty dollars if I could find their anchor so I wasted no time, donned my equipment, found the anchor, secured it with a line and not five minutes later was back on the surface all smiles. The skipper gratefully paid my fee, which in those days was a substantial sum as it was as much as I was paid by the BBC for my weekly programme. Unfortunately I was never again paid for such a job, although I have saved many anchors for other cruisers.

Our usual anchoring routine is for me to be at the bows looking for a suitable spot while Gwenda motors slowly forward keeping an eye on the depth and also on the forward looking sonar. When we reach a suitable depth, I drop the anchor and let out chain to between three and five times of the depth. I then ask Gwenda to go astern and usually the stretching chain tells me that the anchor had set. If conditions allow it I normally dive to check the anchor. I usually free dive, but I also have a full set of diving gear, a wetsuit, a complete dry suit, and always carry two full diving tanks to be used in emergencies or if the water is too deep.

Occasionally I may have to dive to re-set the anchor by hand, or ask Gwenda to pay out more chain. If I am not happy with what I find, I return on board, pick up the anchor and look for a better spot. Even with all these precautions I often end up having to repeat the procedure two or three times until I am perfectly satisfied that the job is as well done as it can be. If I am in any doubt I am prepared to re-anchor several times until I am satisfied. This is particularly important if we plan to be away from the boat and leave it unattended for any length of time. Being lazy about anchoring is simply not an option.

Ideally an anchor should do all of the following:
- It should dig in fast and bury itself deep;
- It should provide maximum holding power without dragging;
- It should resist any movement, both lateral and vertical, even if submitted to extreme loads;
- It should hold despite wind, tide or current shifts.

Anyone would admit that this is quite a tall order but having seen and heard of so many boats lost as a result of being badly anchored I cannot stress enough how seriously this matter should be taken. Basically, as Klaus Girzig comments at the start of this chapter, when it comes to anchoring properly many skippers have an entirely wrong attitude. The best example in this respect is that of a singlehander who stopped at Pitcairn Island, dropped his hook in Bounty Bay and went ashore to enjoy the hospitality of his hosts. Later that day the wind came up and the Pitcairners warned him that the wind from that direction normally backs and will blow straight into the bay thus putting his boat on a deadly lee shore. They strongly advised him to return to his boat immediately and re-anchor in a better place. Being happy ashore he refused... and lost his boat. He managed to get a lift on a passing ship and, a couple of years later, was back in Pitcairn on a new boat. Incredibly the situation repeated itself and, once again while ashore, the wind came up, he was warned to return to this boat but laughed it off saying that such things never happen twice. Well, they do... and did, and he lost his second boat in exactly the same spot as the first one!

Aventura's functional chain locker provides easy access to both chain and spare anchors

A similar fate befell a yacht anchored in Port Resolution on the island of Tanna in Vanuatu. When the wind started blowing strongly into the anchorage during the night, putting the yacht on a dangerous lee shore, the crew tried to leave in the dark. As they were making their way out with the help of the radar and GPS the yacht clipped the corner of the fringing reef and was quickly pushed onto the rocks by the large swell. The crew managed to save themselves but the boat was a total loss.

This is the kind of nightmare scenario that I fear almost more than anything else, so whenever I am anchored in a doubtful place I make sure I have an exit strategy. Usually, on arrival, I make a note of the GPS coordinates of the entrance and mark down a safe exit track. After we have anchored I jot down the coordinates of that spot. These coordinates can be useful as an indication of the boat dragging, especially at night when it is reassuring to see that the boat is still in the same position. If I feel that I might have to leave the anchorage at short notice, I set an exit track with suitable waypoints. Also to assist in a quick getaway, the end of my anchor chain is secured to the boat with a line that, in an emergency, can be quickly cut and the chain and anchor buoyed to be hopefully retrieved later. As a

rule, however, if the weather looks at all like turning, I prefer to play safe and leave the anchorage before I have to put my exit strategy into practice.

One day while in Chagos I went for a dive on the wreck of a cruising boat that had been lost on the fringing reef off Fouquet Island during a violent NW squall that caught the crew by surprise as the strong wind came from the opposite direction to the prevailing SE wind. The wreck of the fifty foot ferrocement hull lay in about twelve feet of water, a large gaping hole on its port side teeming with fish of all colours, shapes and sizes. It was a sorry sight and made me think how such a tragedy could have been prevented.

Every year boats are lost under similar conditions while anchored in a place that is protected from the prevailing winds by an island or a reef. A passing front can generate violent squalls from the opposite direction to the prevailing wind. Such an abrupt change will put a boat on a dangerous lee shore as the boat swings on its anchor and is pushed by wind and swell onto the fringing reef. If this happens suddenly, getting up the anchor and leaving is rarely possible and all one can do is pray that the anchor will hold until the squall has blown itself out. But there may be an alternative that I have tried out and will refer to it as the CAM technique.

Cornell atoll mooring

This unusual system of anchoring in the tropics is basically a modified Bahamian moor and consists of using two anchors, both streamed from the bows so that the boat swings around a relatively fixed point. CAM could be very useful when anchoring in areas where sudden changes

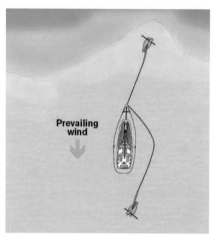

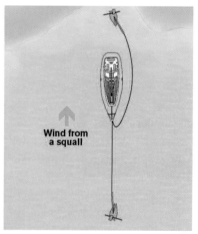

Cornell atoll mooring

of wind direction are a known phenomenon being usually caused by a passing depression or front. As this system of anchoring takes some time to set up it will appeal primarily to those planning a longer stay.

With the wind blowing from the prevailing direction, the main anchor is let go at a reasonable distance from the beach or fringing reef. The chosen spot should be far enough from the beach or reef to allow the boat to swing around safely should the wind change direction. A second anchor is then taken by dinghy and dropped into shallow water off the beach or fringing reef. Ideally this inshore anchor should be checked with a mask and if necessary set by hand. The anchor should be buoyed, the rode taken to the boat and made fast at the bows. This now becomes the holding anchor. The end of its rode should also be buoyed in case it has to be dropped in a hurry. The rode on the main anchor may have to be let out to its full length so as to be able to pick up the end of this second (inshore) rode. Both rodes are now adjusted so that the boat is held firmly by the inshore anchor. Ideally the two anchors should be in line with each other, and with the direction of the wind.

The spot where the first anchor is to be dropped can be estimated at approximately three quarters of the total length of the two anchor rodes. During my test the main anchor was dropped at a depth of 40 feet at approximately 250 feet from the fringing reef. In order to pick up the end of the second rode (150 feet of one inch nylon line plus 10 feet of chain), I had to let out all 200 feet of chain connected to the main anchor. When both anchors were set I hauled in some of the main chain and Aventura was now lying to the secondary anchor at approximately 150 feet from the reef.

Anchored in this way, if the wind swings around, the boat will swing with it and will be held by the main anchor. Hopefully this should be enough to hold the boat off the reef or beach, and ride out the squall. However, should the situation deteriorate making it necessary to leave, CAM will allow you to quickly drop the second rode and anchor (both of which had been buoyed), ride up to the main anchor, retrieve it and move into deeper water or to a more sheltered spot.

The whole idea of this technique is to be prepared for the worst, so if the wind swings to the opposite direction from the prevailing wind, and puts the boat on a lee shore, you are in a position to do something about it and not end up on the reef or beach.

Anchor winch

The first Aventura had a manual anchor winch that was not only poorly manufactured but was also not powerful enough so I ended up hauling in the chain by hand. The electric winch installed on Aventura II had been manufactured by the Global Cruising Survey among the forty skippers fourteen listed a powerful electric anchor winch among the five essential items on their ideal cruising boat. It is a view I entirely agree with, as I know from personal experience just how much easier life can be with a good quality reliable anchor winch. And

Dinghy traffic jam at Georgetown in the Bahamas

a well-known British firm but it proved to be just as bad as its predecessor. Aventura III has an Italian made Lofrans winch that has worked impeccably for nine years. It is powerful, reliable and needs minimal maintenance.

One great advantage on Aventura III is the open chain and anchor locker into which the chain drops in freely as it is hauled in by the horizontal-type winch. Being able to watch the chain while hauling it in is a great help. The chain locker is large enough to provide storage space for two spare anchors, a 150 foot long nylon rode and three chain floats.

How much importance long distance sailors attribute to the anchor winch was demonstrated by the fact that in

not just easier but also much safer as re-anchoring if necessary several times is no longer an effort so I can repeat the operation until I am satisfied that we are well anchored.

Tenders

The right choice of the type of tender for a long voyage is yet another difficult decision as it is so easy to make the wrong one. On the first Aventura we set off with a small Avon inflatable given to us as a parting gift by my BBC colleague and friend Charlie McLaren of the flying Lotus and boiling boots fame. By the time we got to Gibraltar I realized that we needed to have a larger backup to be used on longer expeditions, so we bought a larger inflatable made by a subsidiary of

Zodiac. As it was almost impossible to row I also bought a 2 HP Seagull outboard engine, a noisy, smoky and smelly affair that with its worldwide network of clones could well have been responsible for starting the current process of global warming.

In New Zealand we acquired a fibreglass dinghy, which I fitted out from a bare hull. It had a centreboard and mast and could double up as a sailing dinghy to the delight of our junior crew. The dinghy fitted well upturned on the foredeck and was a delight to row, which I like to do very much. Whenever possible I avoid using an outboard if I can row. While anchored with other yachts in the Torres Strait sheltering from a strong gale I decided to row this new dinghy to one of my neighbours to look at his weatherfax. As I was rowing against the strong wind, the skipper was watching me from his cockpit. When I reached his yacht he exclaimed. 'Jimmy, that was truly awesome. Do you realize that it is blowing a steady 40 knots and yet you managed to get here as if you were rowing in a flat calm.'

'It's really the dinghy's merit. She could almost do it on her own.' And I almost meant it.

The two dinghy configuration was repeated on both the second and the current Aventura, which has two Avons, a 2.40 metre three-person and a 3.20 metre five-person model. I also have two Honda 4-stroke outboards, a Honda 2 HP, which can be used on both dinghies, and a Honda 5 HP to be used on the larger inflatable when I have a larger crew, go diving or on longer exploratory outings. If I need to land quickly, maybe to complete formalities in a new place, I can get the smaller dinghy ready in less than ten minutes. She rows well, especially when I am on my own and I can easily lift it ashore on my own. If I am in a remote anchorage and need to go further afield for provisions or if my crew is too large for the smaller dinghy, I inflate the larger Avon. Depending on conditions I use the smaller or larger motor. On longer expeditions I always clamp the 2 HP as a backup next to the 5 HP motor. It is amazing how often the large outboard decided to pack up in the most awkward places (it has been unreliable throughout its life) and I had to quickly swap it for the smaller one, which has never let me down. As a precaution I always carry a pair of good oars with me. To avoid losing them, I have drilled holes through the oars so each can be tied with a long lanyard to the dinghy, so they stay with the dinghy when making a wet landing.

Both inflatables can be easily rowed, even the larger one, which I have also fitted with retractable wheels to make it easier to pull up the beach. As in the case of Aventura II, I chose Avon as I regard this to be the best make. Made from the durable and long lasting Hypalon material both dinghies are still in perfect condition although they are now nine years old. Having seen on many occasions the usefulness of having a backup dinghy I strongly recommend such a two tender system.

The choice of the main tender is a difficult decision and it is very much a matter of personal preference. In my case, as I insist on being able to stow all my gear in lockers, primarily for safety reasons, the tender has to be inflatable. This may not be to everyone's liking and if a RIB can be safely and adequately stowed it is probably a better choice. RIBs have a number of advantages over ordinary inflatables: they take the ground better, which is very important on rough beaches where I have to be very careful not to puncture my inflatable dinghies, they are easily driven and steered, and they have a good carrying capacity for their size. On some yachts they are stowed on the foredeck, either right way up with a well fitting cover to keep the water out, or upside down. Most boats however seem to keep them permanently in stern davits.

Other tender solutions that I have come across have been quite original: an inflatable canoe or kayak that can be used for a quick landing or to paddle around an anchorage, even a surfboard to paddle ashore with all valuables in a waterproof container. In even more extreme cases I have seen people swim ashore with the ship's documents in a sealed container. I must add that in all these cases the yachts in question also had a proper tender but had a ready solution if needing to go ashore, or to another boat, at short notice.

While in Antarctica, the skipper of one of the Millennium yachts had the uninspired urge to tease a leopard seal with an oar. These violent creatures that have no enemies are not known for having a sense of humour. Unable to retaliate against its tormentor, the enraged animal vented its fury on the nearest thing it could find, and attacked the yacht's RIB with amazing ferocity reducing it to shreds before the skipper could even say sorry. With a large charter party now stuck on board and knowing that I had two dinghies the skipper begged me to lend him one of mine until we returned to the mainland. This is but one example, albeit not a very commonly occurring one, why it pays to have a backup tender. Ideally it should be a smaller inflatable that, at a pinch, could carry the entire crew and should be easy to row.

There is a certain technique in landing from a tender. If there is surf breaking on the beach where you intend to land, as the dinghy reaches shallow water, the crew should be ready to jump out, take hold of the dingy on both sides and walk it ashore.

As the tender might be swamped in such a situation, all vulnerable possessions should be kept in a water-tight container. Ideally one should try to land on such beaches without an outboard, but if one has to use an outboard, it should be stopped before reaching shallow water. In case the boat is turned over and the outboard is swamped, the motor should be rinsed in fresh water immediately, the spark plug(s) removed and a little oil poured into the cylinder(s).

If landing on a coral reef it is advisable to wear plastic sandals or diving booties to protect the feet from the sharp coral. An inflatable dinghy must never be dragged on such beaches. Landing in extreme conditions, such as when Ivan and I visited Horn Island, wearing a survival suit or dry diving suit might be essential.

Outboard motors

If you plan to go any distance in your dinghy be sure you have enough fuel as well as a way of communicating with others.

Bob Hall

The choice of outboard motors is so vast that I wouldn't even know where to begin. With two stroke engines being gradually phased out in favour of less polluting models, if I had to make a choice now I would naturally start by looking first at an outboard motor's impact on the environment. I am seriously considering getting an electric outboard which I am sure would work well, especially as the actual time spent propelling the tender is usually of short duration and its battery can be charged between uses.

Diesel outboard motors are another option, and if they use green fuel are less polluting. Their great advantage is that they use the same fuel as the yacht and one is therefore no longer forced to carry petrol/gas, which I regard as a serious hazard. The one drawback of diesel outboards is that they are much heavier than petrol/gas models of similar power, but I am sure that if there is sufficient demand light-weight models will soon be developed.

Outboard power

The question of adequate power is, once again, a matter of personal preference. For a smaller tender a 2 HP or 2 1/2 HP model is usually sufficient and has the great advantage of being light and using little fuel. All that I can say about the outboard motors used on tenders is that in 90% of cases they are far too powerful. Consequently they may be too heavy to handle safely (some boats need a special derrick on the stern to lift or lower them), they use a lot more fuel and are also more expensive. What I cannot understand is this: if most sailors are quite happy to sail at 6 or 7 knots, why on earth do they need an outboard that pushes their dinghy at twice that speed, so that they reach the nearest beach in one and not two minutes? This is a question that puzzles and infuriates me in equal measure, watching inconsiderate sailors, often kids, zooming noisily and at great speed around a beautiful tranquil anchorage.

My advice is to resist temptation and get for your main tender the outboard that is adequate for the purpose and not the maximum power that the tender can handle. There is absolutely no need for the outboard to be powerful enough to get the tender to surf, when a steady slower speed will get you where you want to go just as well.

Whatever kind of outboard one has, it is a good idea to always carry the essential spares. On Aventura I have waterproof plastic boxes for each of my tenders with spare spark plugs, replacement shear pins and the necessary tools. While anchored in a bay in Vanuatu, we lingered too long on a beach and when we left for Aventura, anchored about half a mile away, the light was fading. In the failing light I hit an isolated coral head hard and broke the sacrificial pin on the propeller. I tried to row but we made little progress, so I headed for the nearest beach, where by the light of the torch that I fortunately had grabbed at the last moment, I managed to wrench out the sheared pin and replace it.

This is the kind of minor incident that can have serious, even fatal, consequences and I have come across several such cases and will mention one that happened while we were anchored in Abemama lagoon in Kiribati. Having spent the day and part of the evening ashore, digging into the freshly arrived supply of beer with their local friends, a couple from a yacht anchored close by, left the beach and headed for their boat. In the pitch-black night, they missed their yacht and as they lost the lee of the low island, the small outboard could no longer cope with the strong wind. They realized that they were being driven towards the wide pass and thus into the ocean, so the man made an abrupt turn for what he hoped was the nearest beach, but in doing so the outboard got swamped and it stopped. The flimsy plastic oars were even less help against the wind but with a desperate effort they managed to land on a shallow reef on one side of the pass. They dragged the dinghy over the reef, badly cutting their feet and, exhausted, spent the night on that beach. In the morning, the wind having died, they managed to row to their boat. Meanwhile none of the surrounding yachts had noticed their absence. With absolutely no land for 1,000 miles, they would certainly have lost their lives and were still in shock when I met them later that day.

There are many lessons to be learnt from their ordeal and the main ones are summarized at the end of this chapter. One crucial question that you should always ask yourself is, if faced with a similar situation, whether you could manage to row against wind and current if the outboard stopped working. Should you still be attracted to such stunts, just in case the worst comes to the worst, I suggest you add a couple of flares to that emergency tool box I mentioned earlier.

One other problem that I want to highlight here is that of serious accidents caused by outboards, two of which happened to participants in the Millennium Odyssey. In both cases the dinghy operator was on his own and fell overboard not wearing the automatic outboard cut-out on his wrist. Within seconds both were badly cut by the propeller as the dinghy was racing in tight circles out of control. Both had to be hospitalized as they suffered extensive lacerations. Unfortunately one of them was a boy of ten who had been driving his over-powered tender in ever decreasing circles, enjoying the mini-tsunamis he was creating and rocking the nearby boats while his over-indulgent parents were watching his antics from their cockpit. I gave this particular example as it is very often boys of this age who behave like this getting a kick out of driving a dinghy at the highest possible speed.

Similar accidents have also been caused by colliding either with other high-speed dinghies or with a yacht being driven around blindly while the crew are looking for a suitable place to drop the anchor.

Collisions at speed with another dinghy occur regularly in crowded anchorages such as in the Bahamas. Worst still is being run down by a local fishing boat or runabout, those fast fantail boats used all over SE Asia being the worst culprits. Just as bad are jet skiers, water-skiers, windsurfers, water-scooters or fast powerful RIBs towing a parachute. The latter can be a menace as the operators of such boats, by necessity, have to look backwards at their tow with only the occasional quick glimpse to see what is ahead of them. Tenders commuting between shore and their boats are not the only potential victims as swimmers are at even greater risk and I have been forced to take avoiding action on several occasions while swimming off my boat when I suddenly saw a fast tender heading for me. Several cruisers have been injured in this way, so this warning should not be taken lightly.

Memorable anchorages

My most memorable anchorages are a diverse lot, some remembered for their sheer beauty, others for what happened there.

Vanua Balavu, Fiji, August 1978

While spending a few months cruising in Fiji on the first Aventura, we decided to sail to the Lau Islands. This group of islands in the eastern part of Fiji continues to be closed to visitors as the government is determined to allow the local population to preserve its traditional life style without outside influence and interference. The only exception was the island of Vanua Balavu which I hoped to reach in one day's long sail.

Although we had left the last anchorage in good time, the prevailing easterly winds had delayed us and it was nearly dark by the time we had reached the lee of the large island. Having picked what looked like a good spot to spend the night in safety, I dropped the anchor, the chain rumbled for a while, then it started tugging and I knew that the anchor had fouled on a coral head. I donned my mask and snorkel and was preparing to dive from the foredeck when suddenly in the gathering dusk I saw first one, then several large sharks. Dusk is by far the most dangerous time to go swimming as this is shark feeding time.

Getting your anchor fouled is an unavoidable hazard in tropical waters and if you are not a good diver, sooner or later you may lose your ground tackle. The way to avoid this is to try to find a sandy spot to anchor and in order to be able to do this it is essential to arrive at a chosen anchorage in good light when the white sandy patches are clearly seen. One should always avoid anchoring near coral heads and it is a good idea to first have a look around with a mask so as to identify a suitable spot.

While in the Pacific, I learned a simple but efficient trick from my friend Luc Callebaut. If there are any coral heads in the vicinity of the anchoring spot, as I drop the chain I insert at regular intervals of about eight to ten metres a plastic fishing float that is tied to the chain with a one metre long line. Even if the anchor itself might get fouled, the floats stop the chain from getting entangled. I found four fishing floats of about 40cm in diameter among the debris that is found on any windward beach. For convenience I provided each line with a carbine hook so they can be quickly attached to the chain. Since using this system I have never had a fouled chain again.

The bay of chuckling waters at Vanua Balavu

As I probably presented a tasty evening meal I stayed put and we spent a rather uncomfortable but otherwise uneventful night. As soon as it got light enough I put on the mask, but first had a look under the surface. The field looked clear and there were no sharks in sight. The anchor situation was worse than I had imagined and the chain had wrapped itself around several coral heads. It took me about half an hour to entangle it before we could continue on our way.

The sleepless night off Vanua Balavu was a well justified sacrifice because when we entered the bay called poetically by another sailor, "the bay of chuckling waters", we were instantly seduced by its incredible beauty. The bay was peppered with individual rocky formations that looked like giant flowerpots with their narrow bases gnawed away by wave action. From their

Egmont Island, a tranquil anchorage of the kind that dreams are made of

narrow base each 'flower pot' flared out to sustain a dense patch of vegetation on the top. We tied Aventura four ways close to such a flower pot and spent an unforgettable week there. Doina and Ivan found a cave nearby in which they spent all day and some nights as well, while I was diving to my heart's content, fishing and gathering shells for Gwenda's ever-expanding collection.

Egmont Atoll, Chagos, September 2004

Close in beauty was the anchorage at Egmont atoll in the Chagos archipelago, which we found totally deserted. To my shame I must admit that the main pre-condition for a perfect anchorage is to have it all to myself. Egmont was in every way the typical photogenic tropical anchorage: sparkling blue waters, shallow enough to anchor close to the beach, a wide pristine beach of white coral sand overshadowed by swaying palm trees with the obligatory palm tree leaning over the water so beloved by photographers when framing their dream shot.

Soapstone Cove, Alaska, August 1999

While in Alaska with Gwenda and Ivan we headed for the night to a small landlocked bay which I knew would provide us with perfect protection. The large outer bay was crowded with salmon fishing boats, so we wove our way through the fleet and passed through the narrow entrance to drop anchor in the middle of the small bay. The spot looked quite suitable to dry out, so I pumped up both the centreboard and rudder. The tide was already running out and shortly before dark we were happily sitting on the mud with not a care in the world. Later we noticed a group of fishermen arriving on the nearby beach all gaping at us in great wonder. I understood immediately the source of their amazement. Having seen this stupid yachtsman take his sailboat into this totally unsuitable tidal bay, they had now come to have a good laugh at us spending the night heeled over like one of those photogenic palm trees. Well, the laugh was firmly on our side and I hope a great disappointment for those professional fishermen who, like their colleagues the world over, seem to hate yachtsmen with a passion. Not one of

225

Grizzly bear fishing for salmon in Soapstone Cove

them had bothered to warn us not to go into that bay.

The tide came in around midnight, we floated up with it, then it ran out and by dawn we were sitting on the ground again. As we were having an early breakfast in the cockpit, out of the corner of my eye I detected some movement on the opposite shore and there right in front of us a large grizzly bear and its cub were slowly pacing through a small stream emptying into the bay. With a sudden movement mummy bear snatched a salmon out of the water and I managed to catch the action with my camera. It was one of those exquisite moments that I will treasure forever.

Port Circumcision, Antarctica, February 1999

Picking a safe anchorage in Antarctica is of vital importance as the weather can change dramatically without warning for the worse and an onshore wind driving the ice before it can spell disaster. Perhaps the best anchorage off the Antarctic Peninsula is the strangely named Port Circumcision. It is almost landlocked with just a narrow entrance and as it was shallow we had to raise the centreboard so as to be able to anchor in its most protected part.

The weather still looked settled but black clouds started gathering on the far horizon and a falling barometer foretold of worse things to come. We had a late dinner and slept a quiet night totally unconcerned by the whistling of the increasing wind in the rigging. When we got up in the morning, the small bay and all the sea outside were blocked in solid ice, the only tiny patch of clear water was the pool where we were anchored. We stayed there until the ice cleared as we were neither able nor in any hurry to leave such a beautiful spot and would have been quite happy to spend all our Antarctic time there.

Nukulaelae, Tuvalu, October 1978

After the independence celebrations in Tuvalu's main island of Funafuti, on the way back to Fiji we decided to stop at Nukulaelae, one of Tuvalu's southern islands. We had met the island chief Tinirau during the festivities and he had warmly invited us to visit his island and its small community of some two hundred people. As the island had recently received its first ever generator, I agreed to take along some diesel fuel and light bulbs that had been left behind by the supply ship.

Nukulaelae is entirely surrounded by an enclosed lagoon with only a very shallow pass on its western side. It was totally unsuitable for Aventura so we had to anchor outside the reef in the open sea. A fleet of outrigger canoes headed for us as soon as we got nearer, among them Tinirau's son Sasau, who took matters in hand and pointed out the best place to anchor. We were then loaded onto different canoes and turned for the shore. Looking over his shoulder, Sasau patiently waited for the right wave, paddling forcefully to keep his aptly called Skyrocket under control. When the wave arrived, with a burst of powerful strokes, Sasau positioned the canoe on the wave's advancing lip and we virtually flew with the breaking wave into the calm waters beyond the fringing reef.

The entire population from the youngest to the oldest were waiting for us on the beach, they put flower garlands around our necks and accompanied us to Tinirau's airy home. Gwenda, Doina and Ivan spent the next few days there while I had to be taken to Aventura every evening as I was worried about leaving her unattended for the night, the daily return trip by canoe being even more difficult and exciting than coming in. Every dawn, just before it got light, I would get up to watch the dozen canoes silently gliding by under sail, their sole occupants hand trolling for fish of which they caught many large ones, all catch being then equally divided among the villagers.

We spent a highly enjoyable time in Nukulaelae, Doina joining the girls of her age making flower garlands, while Ivan was taken by his new friends to sail their small outrigger canoes in the calm lagoon. I managed to get the diesel generator started, which wasn't too difficult as it was based on the same Perkins 4108 engine as Aventura's own. That evening the electric lights came on for the first time in the maneapa (traditional meeting hall) and the history and daily life of this tranquil community thus took a leap into the future.

Doina learning how to make flower garlands

As this seemed to be such a time of firsts, the following evening we invited everyone to watch some of the short silent films we carried with us for this very purpose. I somehow managed to get my projector through the surf but when I switched it on the bulb had given up the ghost. I did have a spare but unfortunately had left it on board. One more dizzying trip back to the boat solved that problem while the audience waited patiently. The old Charlie Chaplin, Laurel and Hardy and similar comedies were an immediate success. What amazed me was that even sketches, which involved cars and trains, which few in

Ivan learning to sail an outrigger canoe

the audience had ever seen, were instantly understood and the jokes appreciated. It just shows the universality of humour and, if I may extrapolate, how similar and not all that different the people all over the world really are.

On Sunday we joined the community for the church service for which everyone turned out. Tinirau objected to my shorts and Gwenda and Doina's dresses and insisted on clothing us in what he regarded as suitable attire, which came out of the family trunk. We ended up looking like a bunch of beggars but our host seemed happy and was clearly very proud of our transformation.

Even the most beautiful moments must eventually come to an end, so a few days later, accompanied by the whole village, we made our way to the beach. We whizzed through the surf for the last time and were deposited with all our gifts on Aventura. As we slowly departed with tears in our eyes, we threw our flower crowns into the wake, praying for our return to those wonderful people. If there is one single experience that symbolises the beauty of the cruising life, it would be those few days we were so fortunate to spend on Nukulaelae.

Tips

- Always check that the anchor has set well, ideally with a mask.
- Ensure that the end of the anchor chain is tied to a fix point with a line that can be cut in an emergency. Tie a large fender to the chain in case it has to be left behind. Write down the GPS position of the spot.
- In choppy anchorages use a strop made from a strong line and chain hook that will take the strain off the chain.
- Never anchor too close to a reef or beach and allow sufficient space to swing should the wind turn.
- If in any doubt leave an anchorage before it is too late.
- In any doubtful anchorage prepare an exit strategy by plotting a safe track.
- Consider using the CAM technique if spending longer in a tropical anchorage.
- Avoid returning to the boat by dinghy in the dark.
- Leave a light on the boat and take a torch with you if you may be delayed ashore.
- Have proper oars that can be used for rowing and tie them securely with lanyards to the tender.
- Prepare a waterproof box with essential spares and tools for the outboard.
- Make sure the outboard engine is fitted with a safety cut-out lanyard worn by the operator on his/her wrist.
- Never tow a dinghy at sea.

Return to the South Pacific

In the last quarter of a century I have transited the Panama Canal with every one of my boats, and have persuaded some two hundred other skippers, sailing in the round the world rallies, to take this route to the Pacific. A lot has changed in Panama during these years: during my first transit in 1977, the Canal was still under US administration and there was a Panama Canal Zone. Now the entire management is under Panamanian control and, in spite of what its detractors may say, the operation is as smooth as ever. If anything, formalities for small craft are now simpler, and as transit fees are no longer based on tonnage but length, the visit of an admeasurer is used to check that the boat complies with all requirements, such as four able crew besides the helmsman, four 125 foot mooring lines, strong cleats, proper fenders, as well as the ability to maintain a minimum speed of 5 knots.

When we arrived in Cristobal, on the Caribbean side, both the pontoons at the Panama Canal Yacht Club and the yacht anchorage on the Flats were overcrowded with boats waiting to transit. Admittedly, this was the busiest time of year (early March) when boats rush out of the Caribbean to catch the favourable season in the Pacific. There was a one week waiting time for transits but the procedure was streamlined and painless. Every morning boats were inspected either at the yacht club or on the Flats, papers were issued to take to the bank and an appointment made by phone or VHF for the actual transit. At 43 feet, Aventura's fee came to $550 plus a returnable deposit of $900. The latter would be partly or wholly forfeited if the boat failed to make the

Aventura in the Miraflores Lock

transit because of engine failure or other such reason, but not if the delay was dictated by operational criteria. Our deposit was returned in full one month later.

On the appointed morning, the pilot's launch met us on the Flats and we proceeded towards the first lock. The pilot told me that we would uplock tied to a tug, which I consider the best method, as it is much easier on both the boat and its crew than centre-chamber. The latter is the usual way to lock pleasure craft and it entails the yacht being held in the centre of the lock by four long mooring lines. In the uplocks, the yacht enters the chamber behind the ship, while in the downlocks it is positioned in front of the ship. The easiest method is to have a

The crew of Aventura II is trying to gain extra speed while crossing Gatun Lake

large group of yachts transit at the same time, rafted together in nests of three. We pioneered this method with the first round the world rally in 1991, and in the Millennium Odyssey we broke a Canal record by having 21 boats locked through at the same time. However, the Panama Canal Authority is reluctant to use this method as it ties up a lock and also wastes a lot of water as the minimal displacement of the yachts, compared to that of large ships, means that a huge amount of water needs to be used to fill one of the enormous locks.

In the first Gatun Lock, a second tug tied up to our host and by the time we had rafted up on the outside, we were perilously close to the other side of the lock chamber. The filling of the lock went smoothly enough but when our lines were cast off and the nearest tug to us left the nest with full power ahead in a maelstrom of churned up water, Aventura was thrown sideways and I had great trouble avoiding being smashed against the concrete wall. In the next lock I begged the tugmaster to show some restraint, which he did, and so we reached Gatun Lake with no further excitement.

The huge artificial lake, created by damming the Chagres River, had been a stroke of genius that saved the fate of the Panama Canal as the original plan drawn up by Ferdinand de Lesseps, who had also been instrumental in building the Suez Canal, was to link the two oceans by a straightforward canal without locks. The French engineers started work in 1881 but in spite of superhuman efforts they could not overcome the impenetrable obstructions presented by the massive backbone of the continental divide and the mighty Chagres River. Furthermore, the climate with its torrential rains, incessant heat and fatal diseases, took its heavy toll in countless human lives. Eventually the assets of the French company were handed over to the USA and in 1894 work on the canal was restarted. There is no doubt that the Americans benefited from the French experience and managed to avoid many of the original problems. The saving decision was to create a series of locks that would raise ships 27 metres to the level of the Gatun Lake, then lower them on the other side via another set of locks. After ten years of unimaginable effort the canal was finally completed. The canal was officially opened on 15 August 1914 with the transit of the first ship. The entire project had cost 639 million dollars to complete and the cost in human lives was beyond comprehension as it is estimated that some 30,000 lives were lost from the 80,000 persons who had taken part in the construction work of what, at the time of its opening, was described as one of the wonders of the world.

As we entered Gatun Lake the pilot told me that if we could maintain a speed of just over 7 knots we might be able to complete the transit in one day. He seemed just as keen to avoid a second day, so he even allowed us to hoist the sails to gain an extra knot in the fresh breeze. We streaked through the fresh water lake taking several shortcuts and by late afternoon had reached the first of the downlocks at Miraflores. A webcam had been installed here so I phoned home to tell Gwenda where we were and she confirmed that she was following our progress on the internet.

Just as the mighty gates started opening in front of us in the very last lock at Pedro Miguel, the tug crew made the mistake of letting go of our bowline first and we slewed violently sideways as the strong current took hold of us. I screamed to let go astern and, with full power ahead, miraculously managed to straighten up, but it was a close thing! Never was the saying "it's not over until it's over" more true. Shortly after nightfall we tied up at the new Flamenco Marina on the Pacific side, opened a bottle of champagne and decided that next time I'd probably opt for something less exciting such as the North-West Passage.

For many years I had hoped to singlehand on an ocean passage so when the crew, who was supposed to join me for the trip to Ecuador, failed to show up in Panama, I seized the opportunity and decided to set off on my own. As Marianne, Bernd and JuanFra, who had helped me transit the Panama Canal, cast off the lines and waved me off, I made my way out of Flamenco Marina and headed into the Pacific Ocean. Although I often handle the boat as if I were on my own, and Aventura had been set up for short-handed sailing, this was the first time in my long sailing life that I was sailing alone on my boat and this realization filled me with excitement.

The Bay of Panama greeted me with steady northerly winds, but also a lot of shipping converging on the canal. The temptation to keep going at a fast clip proved irresistible, so while the autopilot kept the boat on course, I set up the spinnaker and soon I was doing a steady 8 knots. In the first 24 hours, with help from a favourable current, I managed to cover slightly over 200 miles, Aventura's best run ever. All day and night I kept the radar alarm set at six miles, so it sounded every time a ship came within that target area. I dozed in the cockpit but was too excited and also rather apprehensive to sleep for more than a few minutes.

During the second night the wind increased so the spinnaker had to come down but Aventura continued going just as fast with the poled out yankee. There were still a lot of ships and several triggered off the radar alarm at six miles so I reduced the target zone to four miles. By the third night the wind had almost disappeared so I switched on the engine. There was a reason for keeping up a good speed as I was trying to pass as quickly as possible through this stretch of Colombian waters. As I got closer to the equator, and thus to the Ecuadorean border, I was enveloped in typical doldrum weather with dull grey skies, oily seas and little wind. As I was just about to cross the Line I called Gwenda on my satellite phone and was pleased to tell her that at last I was in the middle of an empty ocean with not a ship in sight.

Up to this point, as a precaution, I had set a course that kept me well offshore but on the fourth and last night I started closing with the coast. By now I was about 30 miles off and signs of the coast's proximity became increasingly obvious. I passed through an area with lots of debris probably caused by heavy rains inland. Dodging uprooted tree trunks in the dark was quite unnerving, but as by now the wind had dropped to almost nothing it was easier to slalom under power. By dawn I was confronted by a new menace: miles of long fishing lines barely marked by floating buoys. Singlehanding under these conditions didn't seem so much fun any more, especially as first the centreboard and then the rudder got entangled with a line. I managed to get rid of the line by pumping up the rudder but had to dive to free the centreboard. As I wrote in my log: 'it's been a very long night with hardly any sleep, the occasional squall, lots of fishing boats, the sea full of floating trees, then being caught up in a fishing line that I had to dive with a mask and cut.'

As I was reflecting on the never-ending list of problems that had beset me in the last 24 hours, I noticed in the distance a boat approaching at great speed. It was a whaler-type boat about 25 foot long with three rough looking guys who, even at a distance, looked menacing. There was little I could do but wait and see. As they got closer, they started waving frantically and once I could also hear what they were shouting I understood that they were trying to guide me clear of their lines. They shouted to follow them and when we were finally clear of the lines, they waved good-bye and were gone. As they disappeared in the distance the thought occurred to me that here was a perfect example of the dilemma faced by anyone carrying a gun on board in case of being attacked by pirates: when to shoot? If one waited too long until the intentions of the possible attackers became clear, they might have got too close and using one's gun might be too late. If one shot at them when they were still at a safe distance, one might end up shooting some innocent fishermen, as in this case. So, once again, I decided that whatever the dangers involved, guns were not for me.

By mid-morning I could see the faint outline of the coast ahead and by noon I was making my way into Puerto Lucia Yacht Club marina at La Libertad. With everything stowed away, I headed for the reception dock as instructed over the VHF. As I put the engine into reverse to slow down, the boat jumped forward and continued even faster on its course. Something was terribly wrong, so I quickly took it out of gear, turned away from the fast approaching dock and decided to run aground on a nearby beach while shouting at the marina attendants to give me a hand as I was unable to manoeuvre. Weaving my way between anchored boats I saw to my great relief the marina launch catch up with me. The two men skilfully took hold of Aventura and guided us painlessly to the dock. As soon as we were tied up, I donned my mask and jumped overboard to have a look at the propeller as I realized that the problem could only be there. Indeed, the MaxProp was wound up tightly in green fishing line that had kept it jammed in the forward position. A rather exciting finish to a highly enjoyable passage of 735 miles that had taken only a little over four days to complete.

But the story doesn't end there. When I returned home and called my insurance agent to tell him that the boat was now safely stored ashore in Ecuador he replied: 'In Ecuador? How on earth did you get there without insurance? Have you forgotten that your policy was limited to the Caribbean?'

I suddenly realized, to my dismay, not only that I had sailed without insurance through the Panama Canal as well as on to Ecuador but also that singlehanding was expressly excluded from my policy.

There were several reasons why I had decided to leave Aventura for a while at this convenient marina, one of those being the opportunity to sail with Erick Bouteleux in Spitsbergen. My original plan had been to sail Aventura on her maiden voyage as far north as possible but a delay in her delivery only allowed me to go a little short of the Arctic Circle. Leaving Aventura in a safe place while I returned home for shorter or longer periods became a regular feature as my voyage progressed. I coined the term 'cruising in stages' and in chapter 34 describe in detail the attractions of this style of cruising.

From the equator to eighty degrees north

Whenever possible I try to plan my movements in such a way as to be at home in Provence during May and early June, when the weather is perfect and our large garden is at its best. Having left Aventura in Ecuador in March I could enjoy both spring in Provence and early summer in Spitsbergen. Erick and Muriel, and their friends André and Lucie, had left the Shetland Islands in early June and by mid-summer day had reached their destination. Shortly afterwards I flew north, changed planes in Oslo, and joined them in Longyearbyen, Spitsbergen's main settlement and the northernmost settlement in the world.

Our plan was to complete a circumnavigation of Spitsbergen but by midsummer the eastern shore of the large island was still encumbered by ice and the long term forecast was not good. A helicopter had just flown over the area and the pilot reported a build-up of ice in all passages. Reluctantly we activated Plan B and left Longyearbyen immediately planning to sail Igloo as far north as the weather would permit.

Spitsbergen's popularity as a tourist destination has turned Longyearbyen, with a permanent population of some 2,000 souls, into a hub of activity. There were several flights to mainland Norway every day, large cruise ships called here for reprovisioning, as did an increasing number of yachts. Like Erick's Igloo, an OVNI 39, about half the yachts were flying the French flag, and most were engaged in some kind of charter work. All yachts must obtain a permit from the Governor of Svalbard, which is the correct name of this Norwegian province that includes several islands, of which Spitsbergen is the largest. Yachts must also have adequate insurance cover in case a search and rescue operation has to be activated. Also, as polar bears have killed or mauled several people in recent years, one must always carry a gun.

Centuries of exploitation have left their indelible mark, with abandoned mines and ruined whaling stations scarring the landscape in many places but what I found most disappointing was the dearth of animals. It was quite a shock to see reindeer and whale meat on the menu in Longyearbyen, both being freely hunted by the Norwegians, who now claim to limit their whaling to five hundred minky

Walrus colony
at eighty degrees
north

whales per year. At least they don't pretend to kill them for scientific purposes as the Japanese do. The very few species that are protected, such as walrus and polar bear, have made a comeback and it is estimated that Spitsbergen has a population of some three thousand polar bears. Most prefer the ice-bound east coast, where food is more plentiful.

Compared to Antarctica, conditions in Spitsbergen are more benign at the height of summer, and we had several weeks of uninterrupted daylight. The weather was quite pleasant with little wind and as there was no threat of sudden wind changes, picking an anchorage was much more relaxing than in Antarctica. Besides its wild beauty, which is best appreciated while sailing close to the shore, Spitsbergen's main attraction is the opportunity to take long walks ashore. As there are plenty of sheltered anchorages we could leave the boat unattended without having to worry. Everywhere we stopped there was a mountain to climb, a valley to explore or a glacier to cross. This was in marked contrast to Antarctica where glaciers were crisscrossed by lethal crevasses that were difficult to detect as they were often covered by fresh snow even

in summer, which seriously limited shore expeditions.

Taking advantage of a spell of unusually warm weather we pushed north as fast as possible, the long days and permanent presence of the sun making us all weirdly hyper-active. We usually went to bed at two or three in the morning but, even with all curtains and shades drawn, found it almost impossible to sleep. One sunny morning we reached our destination: the tiny island of Moffen located at 80°01.5′N, 14°30′E. With no land between here and the North Pole we were tempted to carry on, but we knew that we wouldn't be able to get very far. A large walrus colony was in residence on the pebble beach, a couple of aggressive males swimming over to us trying to frighten us away. It was a very odd feeling to know that we were that far north and even looking at the GPS read-out it was still impossible to believe it was true.

Returning along the west coast of Spitsbergen we stopped in several sheltered bays, most of them sporting a huge glacier. We spent most of our time ashore, one of the longest treks taking us inland from Lillehöök Glacier, which measures about 5 miles across and is the widest glacier in Spitsbergen. About half a mile inland we came across the remains of a German signal station, with scores of fuel drums, marked Kriegsmarine (War Navy), radio equipment, all kinds of utensils and the detritus of a large camp. During the Second World War the Germans had several weather stations on Spitsbergen,

Grisly remains coming out of the permafrost in Spitsbergen

while its deep fiords sheltered the infamous U-Boats that menaced Allied shipping.

Further inland from the German station, on a small hill that commanded a perfect view of both the station and the fiord behind, we found hidden under a rock an old radio transmitter. Close by was a steel container used for dropping supplies, and, to our great surprise, we also found the remains of its parachute. When we returned to Longyearbyen an official told me that it was quite likely that the radio had belonged to an Allied observation post that had been keeping an eye on the activity below as well as the movement of submarines. He also confirmed that the German signal station was the only place on Spitsbergen where a battle had been actually fought, and lives were lost.

Many more lives were lost during Spitsbergen's turbulent history when early visitors had a slim chance of getting out alive. Testimony to this were the scores of graves that litter the places where whalers, sealers and trappers had made their temporary camps, and usually left their bones there too. Because of the hard permafrost, the graves were quite shallow and, presumably as a result of global warming, the permafrost was now melting and pushing up the rough coffins and their grizzly contents. Skeletons that had lain undisturbed for hundreds of years were now scattered among the spring flowers: a grim reminder of a grim past.

At Virgohamna we landed at an old whaling station from the 17th century. Nearby were the remains of two failed attempts to reach the North Pole by balloon in 1896 and 1897 by the Swede Andrée and American Wellmann. While walking on the beach I nearly stumbled over a skeleton that had escaped the confines of its rough coffin. From its size it could only have been a boy, most probably from the old Dutch whaling station.

The following day, while leaving the anchorage at Hamilton Glacier, we saw a polar bear on a small island. We lifted the centreboard and managed to get close to the rocky shore, but when the bear saw us, he trundled over to the other side. We followed him as close as we could, dodging rocks and small growlers in the shallow water, but hardly were we within telephoto

A rare encounter with a polar bear, who irritated by our presence takes to the water

distance when he turned around and disappeared back to where he had come from. Round again we went... until he obviously got fed up with this game, jumped in the water and started swimming for the opposite shore. When Igloo caught up with him, this King of the Arctic, who has no enemy, was visibly furious at our impertinence. He snorted and growled but could do little as we eased the boat next to him. He was almost eight feet long, a beautiful mature male. Photo session over, we turned away and saw him return to the island where he had probably been looking for nests with young chicks or eggs before he was so rudely interrupted.

Up to then we had been reluctant to carry the heavy hunting rifle but after this encounter we took the threat seriously and shouldered it every time we went ashore.

One afternoon, relaxing on a beach, Erick suggested that we had a competition to see who was the best shot. He set up a rusty tin can on a post, retreated about twenty meters, took aim and missed. André followed next and, although he was the owner of the gun, he missed too. I took careful aim trying to keep the heavy gun steady, pressed the trigger and to everyone's amazement, mine included, the tin flew in the air with a shrill bang.

'Very good,' Erick said, 'as the best shot you now have the honour of carrying the gun.'

Later that day as I was puffing up a slippery glacier humping the heavy rifle the thought occurred to me that I had been set up to carry it. If this was true, it made sense that they had missed the target but by what secret power had they made me hit it? As any died-in-the-wool Englishman might say, 'those guys from across the Channel are capable of anything!' Although I doubt that even such a backhanded compliment may have gone down well with an Alsatian such as André.

I left Spitsbergen to fly back to France together with André and Lucie. At the airport André was very concerned that he would not be allowed to check in his gun and probably have it confiscated. Knowing that I travel a lot, he asked me to deal with the check-in person. I tried to charm her by chatting away about what we had been doing, and when I produced the gun all she asked was if we wanted it to be checked all the way through to Paris, then handed me our boarding cards.

'Look André, nothing could be easier. Now all you have to do when you arrive in Paris, is collect the gun from the carousel, then check in for your domestic flight.'

'Jimmy, it might sound simple to you but with all those security checks after 9/11 do you seriously believe they'll simply let me handle this gun as if it were just a pair of skis?'

'All you have to do is wait and see. But if you get safely home with your gun you owe me a case of the best Alsatian wine.'

'It's a deal!'

Shortly afterwards André came down to his boat in St Raphael and called me to say he had something for me. When I met him he was all smiles.

'You'll never believe this but it happened just like you predicted. The gun arrived on the carousel, I picked it up then walked with it slung on my shoulder and the case full of

Scenic Magdalene Glacier is one of the most visited spots in Spitsbergen

bullets in my other luggage, right across Orly Airport on the busiest weekend of the year without anyone batting an eyelid, not even some menacing looking fully armed policemen. I checked in for my connecting flight to Metz… and here is your case of a special late harvest Traminer, the very best!'

Engines, Maintenance and Spares

Diesel engines are extremely reliable but are often mistreated by sailors who do not run them under load, do not let them reach their working temperature and generally treat them as a convenience and not as a friend.

Chester Norman

Diesel engines are indeed usually reliable and if they are looked after well can give years of trouble-free service. In over three decades of sailing I had few engine failures on any of my yachts but those that did occur each taught me a lesson. So, rather than start with a general discussion of engines and how to look after them, I prefer to relate those incidents as each has a tale to tell.

Corsica, October 1975

There have been many memorable moments in my sailing life but few stay as fresh in my mind as one that happened more than thirty years ago on our passage through the Bonifacio Straits between Sardinia and Corsica. In 1975 we were at the beginning of our first voyage and, after having spent the summer cruising in the Aegean, had reached Sardinia. Our Perkins engine broke down in Porto Cervo, even then the most expensive marina not just in the Mediterranean but probably in the whole world. As we couldn't possibly afford to have the engine repaired

there, the kindly mechanic suggested that we sailed to Bonifacio on neighbouring Corsica where there was a Perkins agent. He then arranged to have Aventura towed out of the marina and we were on our own.

Between us and our destination lay the Straits of Bonifacio, a treacherous stretch of water where a maze of rocks is swept by strong currents and has been the graveyard of countless ships. Light winds helped us reach the straits and just as we set a course for a distant mid-channel buoy, a school of dolphins positioned itself at the bows delighting Doina and Ivan with their gambolling. As we tacked back and forth in the narrow fairway, the dolphins kept changing direction as well, always staying in front of us, until I realized that this

With her engine out of action Aventura is towed out to sea

perfect display of synchronized swimming could not possibly be pure chance.

'Let me try out something,' I told Gwenda 'and don't worry whatever happens'. When the time came for our next tack, rather than tack back into the fairway, I steered for the nearby rocks. All of a sudden the dolphins became extremely agitated. They jumped out of the water, swam backwards and forwards as if trying to point into the safe direction we should take. Close to the rocks I altered course, we tacked into deeper water and just as suddenly the dolphins calmed down and took up their previous

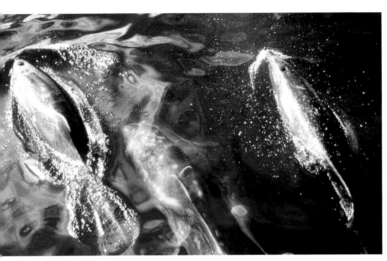

A group of dolphins helped us navigate safely through the Straits of Bonifacio

position at the bows. We repeated the test at the end of that tack, and the situation repeated itself. We finally reached the end of the straits and as soon as we got into clear water, our escort left us. Mission accomplished. It was hard to believe but the dolphins had been clearly trying to protect us.

We made it safely into Bonifacio late that night slowly tacking into the narrow canyon-like harbour. We anchored in a small bay for the rest of the night and in the morning I took the dinghy into the port. The local boatyard towed Aventura in and, having inspected the engine, the yard manager informed me that the engine had seized up and had to be completely rebuilt. As the season was far advanced that meant that we would have to spend the winter

there and postpone our cruising plans by one year. The yard did a good job and not only managed to repair the engine but the manager wrote a report to Perkins pleading our case and explaining that although the engine was out of warranty by a few months, the breakage had been caused by a manufacturing fault. Eventually Perkins agreed and we only had to pay labour costs.

New Zealand, January 1978

That same engine was put to the test again in New Zealand where, I later realized quite foolishly, I had agreed with a teacher from Whangarei, who had befriended us, to swap Aventura against his car for a month. The idea seemed very attractive as we had both our mothers visiting us at the time and this would give us the opportunity to see more of this interesting country. Without a further thought I agreed to the suggestion, explained to the car owner all that I could think of about Aventura, loaded the family into the car and set off on a complete tour of New Zealand's two main islands. The old Wolsey showed its age right at the start when it could barely splutter its way to the top of the hill overlooking Opua harbour where Aventura lay at anchor. By the time we reached the main road, there was a thick ill-smelling oily cloud pouring from the exhaust. As all the cars we had had in London had not been much better than this old lady I wasn't too concerned, so at the first station bought a supply of oil and ended up topping her up with oil in almost the same proportion as her fuel consumption.

Miraculously we made it all the way to the tip of South Island and back again although we seemed to spend as much time waiting by the side of the road for the engine to cool down as actually driving.

A final puncture close to the end of our New Zealand incident packed expedition

While we were virtually on the home stretch Mrs Wolsey decided to give us a final adrenaline kick when we heard the two grannies scream that the back of the car was on fire. With smoke pouring out of the boot, I wrenched it open and managed to put out the flames before they devoured our luggage. It was an electric fire that was put right, at some painful cost, by a local garage and with great relief we made it back to Opua and handed our friend the car keys.

'I hope it went all right,' he said, and I was convinced he must be pulling my leg.

'Well,' I said, 'it all depends how you look at it. Let's say it could have been worse, much worse.'

'That's all right then.' He said visibly relieved.

'And what about Aventura?'

He looked away rather shiftily and I expected the worst. They have wrecked my boat was the first thought to cross my mind.

'We had ... a small problem but I am sure it can be easily sorted out.'

'What's that?' I asked almost relieved.

'The engine wouldn't turn, I think the starter motor is ruined.'

'Well you could at least have had it fixed before our return.'

'Oh, I thought you'd like to deal with it yourself.'

'Thanks very much mate, I see I have no choice!'

Back on board I checked the batteries and they were low but still had enough juice to at least turn the engine but when I turned the key nothing happened. Unless the engine had seized up just as in had in the Mediterranean it could only be the starter motor.

And when do such things happen? Late on a Friday afternoon, of course. With the two grannies due to fly home two days later we didn't have much choice.

'We have to get to Whangarei?'

'Hire a car?' Gwenda asked hopefully.

'No, we'll sail there.'

'You must be joking! Not through this busy bay at a weekend, then up that winding river.'

'Now listen here, I am really surprised that after Bonifacio you don't trust my judgement.'

'That was totally different, we had no choice.'

'Well, as far as I can see it we don't have a choice now either... and by the way, I hear there are some really friendly Kiwi dolphins.'

'Fantastic, now that certainly gives me some hope!'

As it was getting late, I suggested we sailed a few miles to a bay where we had stopped before and anchor there for the night. We left immediately, reached the bay before dark and anchored far enough out to be able to sail out the following morning.

As soon as we were anchored Gwenda's very English mother piped up. 'I'd love a cup of tea, I haven't had one all day.'

'And nothing to eat either,' added my mother just to rub it in.

Emergency outboard bracket on Aventura's stern

While I was preparing to hang out a gill net for the night, Gwenda went to heat up some water. I heard her yell.

'There is no gas. Those friends of yours have used up the whole tank.'

'No problem, said I calmly, settling into my Tarzan role, 'we will make a fire on the beach.'

'And heat up the kettle?'

'No, we'll grill something.'

'Like what?'

'Like the fish that has just committed suicide in my net this very instant.'

Indeed the net was shaking as if some monster was trying to tow the entire boat away. I pulled in the net and there was a beautiful red snapper. The fire was duly lit to Ivan and Doina's delight and we had a most enjoyable picnic on that moonlit beach.

'There are compensations for everything in life,' I said as we were rowing back to the boat.

The sail down the coast took all day and we did have a school of dolphins accompany us for a while. Although one of them would occasionally lift his head and look back at Aventura, as if to make sure she was following, they didn't seem to be the navigator type. As luck would have it we reached the entrance to the Whangarei river just as night was falling.

Fortunately it was a well-lit channel with lots of bright flashing buoys, there was a little wind to help and the tide was slack. We short tacked from side to side making slow progress and by midnight had reached a spot where we could anchor out of the way and were close enough to row to the town dock. In the morning, this being helpful New Zealand, the very first boat to come out responded to my signal, and although he was on his way out for a day's fishing, the nice skipper tied up alongside and skilfully manoeuvred Aventura into her waiting slip.

'Miracles do happen', I couldn't resist saying smugly to Gwenda.

'Well, this was a lot easier than Bonifacio.'

'Well, it was... and next time it will be easier still.' And so it was to be, even if it happened quarter of a century later and half a world away.

Those early incidents had given me confidence both in Aventura's sailing capabilities and even more in my own ability to handle the boat under sail alone. From then on the prospect of not being able to use the engine never worried me. We had two more incidents in the South Pacific, when dirty fuel had put the engine out of action, and each time we managed to sail to the nearest harbour and have the problem fixed.

Malta, May 1992

Aventura II gave the least trouble with engine breakdowns, even if such an occurrence would have been no great problem because it had two engines and so there was a permanent working backup in case of an emergency. The only trouble I ever had was in Malta close to the end of her circumnavigation with the first round the world rally, when one of the transmission boxes seized up, so it wasn't really an engine failure. Repair facilities in Malta then as now were very good, so there was no problem getting the failure fixed. The mistake I made was that being there in the official capacity as organiser of that rally, I expected to be get special treatment. I could not have been more wrong because when I got the bill I nearly fainted. It came to a staggering $1500 and I could have easily bought a brand new transmission box for that. So there is a valuable lesson to be learnt in every mistake: never agree to a job, however small, without a firm estimate, preferably in writing. I have followed this rule ever since and I am sure that I have saved that $1500 several times over, but I never forgave those Maltese falcons their sharp practice.

South Africa, October 2004

Aventura III's worst engine breakdown happened in the worse possible place while on the daunting passage around the bottom of South Africa, which is notorious for its hellish conditions. An unexpected spell of good weather had persuaded me to make a dash along this aptly named Wild Coast. The start could not have been more enjoyable. With the spinnaker up and the help of the current we were doing ten knots over the ground. When the wind dropped and I guessed that the weather would probably change, I decided to make for the commercial port of East London about 70 miles away. I started the engine to motor out of the current, it ran for a while then slowed down and stopped. I tried to restart it but from the sound it made I guessed it had drawn air so I checked the day tank but it was full. I bled the engine, tried to start it but it refused to turn so I presumed that it was due to a faulty solenoid. As I had a spare and it was calm, I decided to replace it. Meanwhile we were drifting with the strong current, doing four knots over the ground but without enough wind to even fill the sails. With the new solenoid installed I turned the key but the starter still refused to budge. So what was the one essential spare I did not have on board? Of course, a starter motor.

Fortunately the wind came up later in the day, so up went the spinnaker again and we sailed well for a few hours doing six knots of boat speed plus a bonus of four knots from the current. The wind fell at night when we still had about twenty miles to go and it took us several hours to edge out of the current so as not to risk being swept past East London. Eventually we made it, but by now it was midnight and I decided not to push my luck and enter an unknown harbour at night without an engine, so we tacked up and down off the harbour entrance for the rest of the night and entered at first light. I had already installed on the stern the emergency outboard bracket, but as we had enough wind to sail we tacked into the outer harbour, then tacked... and tacked again trying to pass through the narrow gap that led into the inner harbour. The outflowing current from the Buffalo River, on whose banks the town stands, was strongest at that point and it took us ages and all my sailing skills to ease Aventura past it. More tacks took us up the narrow river until eventually we managed to drop the anchor near a spot where some yachts were docked. I put the outboard motor on its emergency bracket, it started first time, but the current was too strong and we could not even turn the boat. Meanwhile the anchor dragged in the soft river mud, we drifted slowly and hit ever so lightly... the local police launch! We proceeded to tie up to the launch trying to give the impression that this had been our intention all along. Two officers came to see what was happening and when I explained our predicament, they were very nice and told us not to worry and to stay there.

The skipper of a nearby tug, who had been following our earlier manoeuvres, came over and recommended a local electrical repair shop. Later that day the starter motor was taken off and when it was dismantled at the workshop they found that the plastic planetary gear was badly worn and had to be replaced. Unfortunately neither this part nor a complete starter motor could be found locally so it looked as if we were going to be stuck in East London for a long time. After I got my contacts in Durban and Cape Town as well as son Ivan in London lined up to help locate a replacement starter motor, I decided to have one more go, got into a taxi and started scouring

the town's electrical workshops, breakers' yards, etc. The owner of a small shop looked at my defunct starter motor and said, 'Wait a minute. I had one of those for years and don't know why I kept it. Now I know!' His was a left-hand side mount, mine a right-hand side, but the parts could be transferred... and that same afternoon I had a reconditioned starter motor.

With the engine repaired, there was nothing to keep us in East London, so as soon as the weather looked right we left and made a beeline for the axis of the Agulhas current. We eventually made it without stopping to Cape Town where the first thing I did was to order a brand new starter motor.

Croatia, August 2006

A breakdown that deserves to be mentioned happened in the summer of 2006 in Croatia as we were motoring down a river having visited the spectacular Krka waterfalls. The engine alarm sounded suddenly, I switched off the engine and found that it had overheated. Being in a river I naturally suspected that we had picked up some weed or debris but when I checked the water trap I saw instead a lot of water in the engine bilge so I realized that we had a more serious problem. I dropped the anchor where we were, which unfortunately was right in the middle of the river in the way of the numerous excursion boats but that couldn't be helped. When I lifted the covers in the aft cabin to look at the back of the engine I was met by a strong smell of exhaust fumes. The plastic exhaust mixing pot had a large hole on its side through which both exhaust and cooling water had been able to escape. While Gwenda was trying to make clear to passing excursion boats that we had not anchored there for afternoon tea but had a problem, I got a tube of underwater epoxy, rolled and mixed the two components and managed to cover the hole. We waited one hour for it to set, turned the key and the engine started up and ran happily. It was quite a minor problem that could be dealt with easily but it could have had very serious consequences. We had with us Doina and our grandchildren Nera and Dan, who slept in the aft cabin. If this problem had happened at night, when they were asleep, they could have been easily overcome by the highly poisonous carbon monoxide in the exhaust fumes, as these would have leaked out of the mixing pot long before the engine would have overheated, triggering off the alarm. Just the thought of what could have happened got me worried then and makes me shudder still.

Maintenance

One of the main observations that I made among participants in the various rallies is that the newer someone was to cruising, the less inclined they were to carry out regular maintenance work and usually waited until something broke before tackling it. This kind of attitude may be acceptable on land where people are used to being able to call for outside help, whether to fix something in the house or to get the car going again if it broke down. At sea one has to be self-sufficient and tackle the jobs as they occur. Initially I behaved in exactly the same fashion until damage from chafe and small breakages that could have been easily prevented finally made the penny drop. Once maintenance turned into routine I became almost obsessed by my daily inspection tour and all of a sudden many of those niggling problems disappeared and life became much more enjoyable. It is surprising what can be discovered by just having a good look around the boat at least once a day. Most things may be simple matters: a suspect split pin, a chafed sheet running over a block that was out of line, a sail that was rubbing against the rigging, etc. Potentially more serious problems such as one loose strand of rigging, a cracked turnbuckle or a loose rudderstock could end up with a lost mast or steering. My luckiest discovery was to find one morning one of the spinnaker poles loose on the foredeck. During the night we had had some strong winds and rough seas and the probable explanation was that, while tacking, the flapping yankee sheet had somehow opened the jaws of the pole so that it was dislodged from its usual parking position.

Bearing in mind its vital importance, the engine deserves special attention and that means a visual check every time the engine is started, having a look to see that the exhaust is discharging water, and making sure that the engine is fed clean fuel. On the current Aventura I was left without an engine twice, once off Portugal because of a blocked fuel line and once off South Africa because of a broken starter motor. Besides those two failures, Aventura III has suffered from a number of irritating problems, the worst being a recurring leaky sea water pump, which must be a manufacturing fault as it has plagued me for several years and even now, like an old man, the pump still has a slight but constant leak. To show up any leaks, I placed a sheet of aluminium cooking foil under the pump so I could see at a glance if there had been a leak. Every time I found it dry it filled my heart with joy, so even routine maintenance jobs can give satisfaction.

One of the most important things I have learnt over the years is the value of preventative maintenance. I look after my gear and the gear looks after me. Engines, after all, are similar to the human body and nowadays a good doctor would insist on preventative medicine rather than wait until the symptoms tell the bad news, which may be too late. For this reason, every year I try to find a convenient place to give the engine a thorough overhaul when injectors, compression and all other essential aspects are checked and, if necessary, put right. In spite of all the care and regular maintenance, every time the engine is opened the mechanic usually finds something wrong in its guts which would have probably ended in disaster if not detected in time. While in New Zealand I had the engine submitted to a thorough overhaul and when the engine had been dismantled the Volvo mechanic discovered that the aluminium exhaust manifold was badly corroded. Initially it looked so bad that a complete replacement seemed unavoidable but with typical Kiwi ingenuity a local metal shop managed to build up the missing aluminium, machine the manifold and make it as good as new.

One of the annual jobs on Aventura is to replace the timing belt on the front of the engine. Erick, who has the same engine on his Igloo and had dealt with countless owners of the various OVNIs he has sold, warned me that the rubber timing belt on this model tends to wear out and therefore it is better to prevent this from happening by replacing it regularly even if it looks all right. This and any other more difficult maintenance jobs I prefer to leave to the professionals but daily visual inspections and regular maintenance have probably prevented other potential problems. The few that happened couldn't have been detected by the most thorough inspection such as the burnt out exhaust pot in Croatia. They can only be put down to

bad luck but fortunately there have been very few of those.

Soon after I started running the ARC, I decided to compile at the end of each rally a list of all reported breakages. Later we went further and handed out questionnaires to all skippers not just in the ARC but also in the round the world rallies. Most of the engine failures were caused by dirty fuel and I found that on many production boats the fuel supply and filtering systems were often inadequate. To avoid such problems I asked the French builders to install a day fuel tank on Aventura III, so that the pre-filtered fuel is gravity fed to the engine.

Anodes

Regardless of the hull material, zinc anodes are essential in protecting seacocks, propellers and their shafts. Some engines may have sacrificial anodes in the heat exchanger, in the salt water system and possibly in the cooling loop of the transmission. Normally there is also an anode in the cooling system of the refrigerator. All these anodes should be inspected and replaced at least once a year. Bronze propellers are protected from electrolysis by anodes mounted either on the shaft or, as in the case of MaxProps, on the propeller. These are easy to inspect regularly with a mask. Boats with an iron keel should have at least one anode placed near it but one must be careful that the bare metal of the keel is not exposed and it is protected by its coating. The keel bolts can be vulnerable to electrolysis even if the keel itself looks fine on the outside.

Hull materials steel or aluminium both have advantages and disadvantages, their intrinsic strength being their main advantage. As for the disadvantages, in

Fitting sacrificial anodes to the shaft and propeller

affect your own boat or, hopefully, only your anodes. It happened to me in Tunisia where I had left Aventura for three months in Monastir Marina. While I was away the marina moved a large steel boat right next to mine. It had obviously run its generator much of the time as, when I returned and had Aventura hauled out to be antifouled, I was shocked to find all the anodes, which had been renewed three months earlier in the Canaries, eaten away down to their base. The propeller anode was also gone and the prop itself had taken on a sickly colour. Fortunately this was discovered in time and so the damage was only superficial but the situation could have been much worse if I had come back a couple of months later. In a way it was my fault because usually, if I have any doubts, I hang two large additional anodes from the bows and stern. This is also why whenever I leave the boat for longer periods I prefer to have her hauled out ashore.

the case of steel it is the need for the best possible preparation of the hull and decks for painting followed by careful maintenance. In the case of aluminium the almost irrational fear of electrolytic reaction that so many people continue to associate with aluminium hulls is quite unjustified. Modern alloys have taken care of that, as do the obligatory sacrificial anodes. As an added precaution, the OVNI builders provide each boat with a stray current meter that shows instantly if there is a negative or positive current leak detected in the hull. Provided the boat has a well-thought out electrical installation any possible damage caused by electrolytic action can be avoided provided a few simple precautions are taken.

There are certainly a few situations to be avoided if at all possible. Possibly the worst among them are poor electrical installations on marina docks where occasionally the wrong polarity is used or there is an accidental current leak. Equally bad is being moored next to a boat that is running its generator and/or air-conditioning unit most of the time. The stray current from either can seriously

Talking about anodes I want to mention what happened to an old friend whom I stopped to see in Southern Spain on the way to the Balearics. I had asked him to find me a place at his yacht club and when I called him on my mobile phone from a few miles offshore he told me that I could use his own berth as his boat had to be hauled out unexpectedly. Apparently the forward toilet bronze seacock had turned to cheese and when my friend checked all the others he found them also a suspicious colour. All seacocks were replaced, but as I was looking at the gleaming hull just about to be launched, I was struck by the complete absence of any anodes. Not even the propeller and shaft had been provided with zinc anodes, so I asked my friend the reason for it.

'Oh, the builder assured me that anodes are a complete waste of time on a fibreglass hull.'

'And you believed him?'

'Of course.'

'But what about the prop and shaft?'

'Same thing, not really necessary.'

'What happened to your seacocks then, or was it divine intervention?'

'Yes, the guys at the yard are puzzled, but I called the builder and he assured me that it had nothing to do with the absence of anodes, most likely some faulty seacocks which he offered to replace.'

I expressed my serious doubts on this matter but in spite of what had just happened my friend preferred to listen to his well-known Scandinavian builder rather than to commonsense. In his place I would have installed a few anodes, just in case.

Tools

The first Aventura was, at least in the first year, a floating workshop and, if I remember well, there were a few jobs that I never managed to finish before our return six years later. Probably with the same thought in mind, on the second Aventura I had sacrificed the entire forepeak and kept it as storage/workshop area. On the portside there was a full-length workbench with a vice and a wide selection of tools stored in the lockers above. On the starboard side I had a diving compressor, three tanks, and enough space to stow an inflatable dinghy. While the compressor proved to be useful in those days when I was still a keen diver, the workbench was very rarely used. As the boat had been fitted out professionally, nothing had been left "to be done later" as had been the case with its predecessor. Because of my endeavour to learn from my own mistakes, I had incorporated a lot of "useful" features in the second Aventura that I had sorely missed on the first. Many of them turned out in the end not to be really that useful. Fortunately I drew the right conclusions the next time and on the current Aventura the nearest thing that comes to a workshop is a portable vice that fits into the top of a cockpit winch.

I do carry such essential tools as a complete set of spanners and socket sets (both metric and imperial), riveting gun, woodworking tools, and a good selection of screwdrivers. Also electrical tools: drill, screwdriver, jigsaw, rope cutter, soldering gun, 12V engine oil changing pump, 12V dinghy pump. There is also a whole lot of bits and pieces that may come in useful (and often do): stainless steel plate, threaded studs, various lengths of teak, plywood, etc. All small items such as nuts and bolts, screws, solder, bulbs, blocks, tapes, toilet spares, etc. are kept in separate plastic boxes with the main destination of the contents marked on the cover.

Being prepared for the worst

As I am a firm believer in a belt and braces attitude, on Aventura III there is a backup for virtually everything that matters. This is probably the main reason for my recently completed five year long voyage being generally trouble-free. As some of these features are mentioned elsewhere in the book I shall describe here only the most relevant ones.

Rigging: I asked the builders to install two backstays, rather than the standard single backstay, so the starboard backstay also acts as a radio antenna, and the portside stay is continuous. A boat crossing the Atlantic in the ARC lost its mast when its backstay antenna insulator broke, and brought the mast down with it. They had two spinnaker poles with which they rigged a jury arrangement and managed to sail the rest of the distance to St Lucia. On Aventura I also have two spinnaker poles of equal length, which are kept on deck, so, if the mast is lost, they do not go with it and can be used to improvise an A frame. There are backup halyards for every sail.

Steering: An emergency tiller that can be fitted quickly onto the rudderstock is kept in readiness in case the Whitlock steering should fail. The hydraulic ram of the Brookes&Gatehouse autopilot is connected directly to the rudder quadrant so even if the manual steering should fail, the boat could be steered with the automatic pilot, which is totally independent of the main steering system. The autopilot is backed up by a windvane selfsteering gear. A small Navico autopilot is carried as a backup. To increase its efficiency the small autopilot can be connected to the windvane so that it derives its power from its servorudder.

Engine: In case of engine failure and the need to maneouver the boat under power, a special outboard bracket can be fitted to the stern platform so that the larger outboard motor can be used to move the boat.

Electrics: The engine is fitted with two alternators, a standard 55 AH alternator and a 120 AH alternator. The standard alternator charges the engine starting battery that also supplies power to the anchor winch. The larger alternator charges

During a routine overhaul the New Zealand mechanic discovered bad corrosion in the aluminium heat exchanger

the four gel batteries that have a total capacity of 360 AH. A switch allows the general batteries to be used to start the engine, and either alternator can charge both banks.

Communications: I have two laptop computers of which one is used mainly for email via an Iridium satellite telephone while the other is permanently connected to the Inmarsat C unit. The latter provides regional weather forecasts as well as an alternative email and text service. The two laptops have the same software installed so as to be interchangeable.

Safety: Both the 406 MHz EPIRB and the Inmarsat C can be used in a distress situation. I have four separate GPS units: the main unit is integrated with the B&G Hydra system, the Inmarsat C has its own integral GPS, plus two handheld models, one of which is kept permanently in the emergency container. More for safety than sport, I also have two sets of scuba gear and two diving tanks that are always kept full. I have a wet suit as well as a dry diving suit, and also a survival suit. I have two inflatable dinghies and two outboard motors. The smaller dinghy can be quickly inflated and easily rowed while the larger dinghy is used for longer expeditions or when I have larger crew.

Spares

Over the years I have built up a comprehensive range of spares. They are kept in various lockers, their contents being listed in alphabetical order in an address book. Each locker is identified by a code and the layout plan is drawn on the first page of the spares book. This is a useful idea in an emergency situation when one's concentration may be focused on something else and one may have to ask the crew to find something in a hurry. Similarly, all instructions manuals, lists of parts, etc are stored in alphabetical order in a concertina type folder.

■ *Engine*
- 55 AH alternator
- Regulator
- Starter motor
- Starter solenoid
- Complete seawater pump
- Seawater pump kit with impellers
- Four gallons of engine oil
- Four oil filters
- Two fuel filters
- Timing belt
- Alternator belts
- One gallon of coolant
- Outboard oil
- Fuel transfer pump
- Anodes and set screws for MaxProp propeller
- Two propeller shaft anodes
- Two bladed propeller
- Baja fuel filter
- Liquid gasket

■ *Autopilot*
- Four gallons hydraulic fluid
- Electric motor for hydraulic pump, spare brushes
- Three 12 mm bolts for pilot ram
- Hydraulic ram relay unit

■ *Electronics and electrics*
- Paddle-wheel unit for speedometer
- Printed circuit board for wind speed indicator
- Transducer for forward looking sonar
- Battery operated emergency navigation lights
- Bulbs, fuses, connectors, terminals, including spare deck light
- Three hand-held VHF radios
- Emergency SSB radio whip aerial
- Satellite phone antenna
- Satellite phone battery (always kept charged)

■ *General*
- Hand operated watermaker
- Fresh water pump
- Complete toilet (without bowl) plus spares
- Two water generator turbines with 40 metres towing lines each
- Wind generator blade, brushes
- One mast step
- Two 100 watt inverters 12VDC to 110/240VAC (for laptops)
- Two diving tanks
- Two regulators
- Two masks, snorkels and fins
- Six Camping Gaz tanks
- LPG regulator
- Two cooker burners
- Two cooker hoses
- Avon dinghy pump
- Two repair kits for the inflatable dinghies
- Two tubes of two-part underwater epoxy repair kits
- Assorted sealants, water repellent sprays, WD40, Loctite
- Complete set of spares for outboards
- One set of oars
- At least two metres of each size of plastic hose used on the boat

- Two large (1.20 x 0.50 m) Avon inflatable fenders
- Four winch handles
- Anchor winch handle
- Assorted blocks (two large ones with opening jaws)

■ *Steering*
- Sacrificial valves for hydraulic steering system
- One gallon of steering fluid
- Three windvanes
- Three servorudders

■ *Sails*
- Genoa
- Adhesive repair material for white sails and various colours for spinnakers
- Complete sewing kit, twine, needles
- Grub screws for furling gear profile
- Lazybag battens

Worth mentioning are two other items specially made for Aventura: a six foot long plank of wood provided with ropes to be used when docking against pilings or rough quays, and a teak foot rest that is fixed to the cockpit floor with butterfly nuts and serves as a brace when the boat is heeled over.

Tips

■ Carry out a visual inspection of the engine every day or every time it is started up after an idle period longer than 24 hours.
■ Check that cooling water is discharged from the exhaust every time you start the engine.
■ Regularly check the oil and coolant levels, seawater trap, look for possible leaks around injectors, filters and seawater pump.
■ Check the tightness of the alternator(s) belt(s). Fine black deposits are a first indication of wear.
■ When motorsailing and heeling regularly right up the boat so the oil gets circulated around the engine.
■ Stop the engine after having motored for a few hours, carry out a visual inspection and check the oil level.
■ Regularly check the fluid level in the transmission.
■ Regularly check for leaks from the stern gland and always inspect it when the boat is launched after a haulout. Some stern glands need to be squeezed to fill them with water after a haulout.
■ Carry all essential spares and consumables especially if setting off on a voyage to remote places.
■ Make a detailed list of all engine and parts numbers and leave a copy at home or with a reliable friend in case parts need to be ordered and shipped to the boat.
■ Add a small amount of biocide to the fuel at every fill-up, especially if sailing in warm climates.
■ Treat any fuel bought in less frequented places as suspicious and filter it is as well as possible (I carry a Baja filter).
■ Avoid completely emptying the fuel or water tanks.
■ Keep the tanks separate by closing them off so they cannot be completely emptied inadvertently.

The Longest Passage

Just as some people dream of running their own hotel, a few years ago I toyed with the idea of taking over the Bora Bora Yacht Club and running it as a meeting point for world voyagers. Other sailors have turned their dream into reality by building their own marinas, such as Pepe Calero (Puerto Calero on Lanzarote), Arch Marez (Rodney Bay Marina in St Lucia) or Dick Smith, who has been welcoming cruising boats for many years on Malololailai Island in Fiji, where visiting sailors become life-long members of his informal Musket Cove Yacht Club. The beautifully appointed Puerto Lucia Yacht Club in Ecuador, where Aventura spent several months, has been a true labour of love for Ricardo Palau, a local developer and passionate sailor, who clearly enjoys meeting long distance navigators calling at his marina. Ever since I first met him in London, he had followed my voyage closely and, once in Ecuador, had given me all possible support. On the morning of our departure he spent a couple of hours on Aventura, and, as he stepped ashore, he told me, 'I would give anything to be able to do just what you are doing now: cast off and go!'

The last thing to do before leaving was to settle my large marina bill. Ever since I had returned to the boat I had been asking the manager Galo Ortiz to prepare it for me and there had always been some delay. With only a couple of hours before our planned departure, and everything ready to go, I went to Galo's office.

'We are ready, so as soon as I have settled with you we can go.'

'Then all we need to do is wish you the very best of luck and hope that we'll see you again soon!'

The penny refused to drop.

'Oh, I'll come back, of that you can be sure. But can I have my bill now, please.'

'Jimmy, there is nothing for you to pay, Sr Palau told me that you are his personal guest.'

'But that can't be! Aventura has been here ten months, Antti and I have stayed in the hotel, signed for all our meals, wine...'

'Jimmy, please stop. You are our guest.'

'But what have I done to deserve this?'

'More than you think. Ever since you received Sr Palau at your club so kindly and offered to take him and Sra Palau around London, they have regarded you as a valued friend.'

'Galo, but that was nothing, I would do that for anyone.'

'Jimmy, you obviously do not understand. This is Latin America. We value our friends more than anything and nothing gives us more satisfaction than being able to show them just how much we appreciate their friendship. Farewell!'

Ricardo Palau was on the dock as we were leaving.

'Muchas gracias de nuevo para todo, estoy muy agradecido.'

'That's OK, just send me a postcard from time to time.'

'I certainly will. Hasta luego!'

So for the five years of Aventura's voyage Ricardo Palau has received a postcard from every one of Aventura's stops. If Latin Americans know how to appreciate their friends, so do I. After all, it has been my life philosophy for as long as I can remember.

After such a long break I was looking forward to sailing Aventura again, and the relatively short hop to Ecuador's offshore island group was a perfect way to slide back in to my offshore routine. For this section of the voyage I was joined by my Finnish friend Antti Louhija. Shortly before noon we motored out of the marina entrance and pointed west. This area of Ecuador has one of the most benign climates in the world as I was told that winds over 20 knots had never been recorded and they have never had storms of any kind. We had to motor for a while but around midnight picked up a light SSW wind and with full sails up were going well close-hauled.

The SSW winds continued and although only blowing at about 10 knots, with no swell and a freshly painted bottom Aventura was romping ahead happily doing 6 knots. We were enjoying ourselves so much just being at sea that Antti agreed to my suggestion to bypass the usual ports in the Galapagos and go straight to Puerto Villamil on Isabella. Normally visiting boats are only allowed to clear in at one of the two main ports of entry, Baquerizo Moreno or Puerto Ayora, but as we were coming from mainland Ecuador I was sure that I'd manage to persuade the port captain in Villamil to let us stop there for a few days.

Our second day at sea was followed by an equally splendid night, with a starry sky and virtually flat seas. The SW winds continued blowing at 7-8 knots and Aventura managed to make 4-5 knots herself. As the wind slowly drew more into the south up went the asymmetric spinnaker. By later afternoon the wind had gone into SSE and the asymmetric spinnaker was now in its element.

Day three followed the same pattern and as the wind drew more into the east we swapped the asymmetric for the larger tri-radial spinnaker. During the night we passed the island of Española. I remembered my visit there a few years previously when we had chartered a ten cabin excursion boat with a number of participants in the second round the world

One of the giant tortoises that gave the Galapagos their name

rally. We cruised around the archipelago for one week visiting the various islands and enjoying their unique wild life. Española has the largest colony of blue-footed boobies and I will never forget watching the gentle dance performed by courting couples. Española is also an important breeding ground for sea turtles that come to lay and bury their eggs on its sandy beaches. On that weeklong cruise among the islands we were fascinated not just by the abundance of wildlife, ashore, in the air and in the sea, but also its variety. Every island seemed to have its own resident species, penguins on San Salvador, sea iguanas on Santa Fé, land iguanas on Fernandina, frigate birds on Seymour, sea lions on San Cristobal, giant tortoises on Isabella and white-tipped sharks at Bartolome.

The following day was calm so the engine had to take over. We were visited by a school of very large dolphins, the largest I had ever seen in the Pacific. A pod of humpback whales swam close by snorting noisily but ignoring us. We passed south of Floreana, one of the four islands that have settlements on them. Floreana's past is probably the most colourful of all the Galapagos as it was a favourite pirates' lair. Later it was a convenient resting place for the crews of whalers who visited these islands to load hundreds of the giant turtles. The poor creatures were then laid on their backs in the ships' hold waiting to be slaughtered for food, their main attraction being the fact that they could survive without water or food for many months. Some of those sailors started the fashion of leaving letters for home in a barrel hoping that some kind soul would pick them up and post them, a fashion that has continued to the day. There is also a bloody side to Floreana's past

A male frigate bird displays for his mate

involving murders and suicides among its early German settlers. But nothing has contributed more to the fame of these islands than the consequences of the visit by Charles Darwin. His long stay here in 1835 resulted in the theory of evolution that profoundly affected scientific thought.

Unfortunately this unique world is in grave danger mainly as a result of its own success. Although the Ecuador authorities have made great efforts to control the number of visitors that are allowed to land at any one time on one of the nature reserve islands, they have been far too lax when it came to their own population. In recent years thousands have come

over from the mainland attracted by job opportunities that were absent back home. While one can accept the reasons for this, the consequences are now badly threatening the delicate nature of the islands and their habitat. The main settlements at Puerto Ayora and Baquerizo Moreno are growing at an exponential rate causing not just overcrowding but also serious pollution. On my last visit to Puerto Ayora I was dismayed by the changes that had occurred in the ten years since I started visiting the islands regularly. As I preferred to preserve the beautiful memories of my previous visits I decided to stop only at Puerto Villamil, as Isabella is still an oasis of peace and tranquillity in a sea of change.

Strictly from the legal point of view, unless one has an official permit, cruising boats are not allowed to stop at the Galapagos except in an emergency. How this is interpreted can depend on the port captain and the regulations have recently been applied more rigorously. Generally cruising boats continue to be allowed to stop in the islands for a few days. On arrival, boats must clear in at either Baquerizo Moreno or Puerto Ayora, and throughout their stay must not leave these ports. To visit the other islands the crews can join one of the many excursion boats, either on a day trip, or on a longer charter as we did.

Early on the fifth day after our departure from the mainland, we made our way into the sheltered anchorage in front of the small settlement at Puerto Villamil where the port captain agreed to a 48 hour emergency stop, which he later extended just as readily. Although the largest island of the archipelago, Isabella is off the beaten track with only a handful of visitors and there was only one other boat there.

On the narrow beach where visiting sailors pull up their dinghies a local fisherman Henry Segovia had set up the Little Yacht Club, a modest establishment serving drinks, snacks and offering help and advice to cruising sailors. Flags donated by sailors complement Henry's own collection of flotsam, skeletons of dolphins, turtles and swordfish, as well as weirdly shaped tree trunks found on the beach.

One day I set off with Antti on a walk to a former US airbase, which, after the Second World War had been transformed into a penal colony. For a dozen years, until 1958, the worst criminals from a number of South American countries were kept in this high

Close encounter between a land and marine iguana

security prison under extremely tough conditions. To keep them occupied they were forced to build a high stonewall, which was dismantled every time it was completed so that work on it could start again, an unending punishment worthy of the labours of the mythical Sisyphus.

Close to the main settlement was a tortoise regeneration and breeding centre. Giant tortoises are brought here from other islands to regenerate before they are returned to their place of origin. Tortoises are also bred here and kept until they are two years old so as to be large enough to

resist attacks by rats and cats, which are the biggest danger for young tortoises. It is a splendid effort to put right the wrongs of the past. Twelve different species of tortoises survive on Isabella, their large number being due to the fact that Isabella was rarely visited by pirates or whalers and was colonized very late. The largest colony is in the north of the island where there is an estimated ten thousand giant tortoises, many over one hundred years old.

Our forays ashore had whetted our appetite to see some of the interior of this largely untouched island. We agreed with a local guide to join a small group to trek on horseback to the Sierra Negra volcano that has the second largest crater in the world. My horse, called Pendientes (ear-rings), looked strong enough to carry me but what worried me was the look of the rudimentary wooden saddle. With stirrups of the old-fashioned Spanish style it felt like being back in the age of the conquistadors. It took us nearly three hours of rough going to reach the rim of the giant crater. The long walk down to the bottom of the crater ended at an area of fumaroles that were belching out steam in large clouds, the pestilential smell of sulphur pervading everything. The surrounding rocks were covered in thick layers of sickly yellow sulphur. It was almost impossible to breathe and I almost choked trying to hold my breath to take a photograph of a particularly active fumarole. The atmosphere and setting were straight out of hell and we wasted no time in returning to our horses that had been left on the rim of the crater. The return trip was even more painful as going downhill the wooden saddles dug deep into one's posterior and it took a week before I could sit down without

Trekking in Isabella's volcanic interior

wincing. After my Easter Island experience I thought I had finished with horses, so I swore that after the Isabella trek I would never again attempt to be a cowboy.

For the long passage to the Marquesas I managed to get a local farmer to supply us with some of his produce: bananas, avocados, watermelons, grapefruit, oranges and eggs. The day before departure I cooked a large stew to last us for at least three dinners. We bade goodbye to Henry and his family and headed out into the ocean. Ahead of us lay the longest unbroken stretch on any of the world cruising routes with nothing but water for nearly three thousand miles.

If there is a favourable wind soon after the start, the recommended tactic is to sail a direct course to the Marquesas. If there is no wind, one should sail southwest to around 2°S where there is a better chance of finding the wind. From there the course can be set for one's destination. An area to be avoided lies between 3°S and 8°S and 95°W and 108°W where frequent unsettled weather conditions have been reported. One should avoid making too much southing at the beginning, as better conditions are normally found closer to the equator. There is also a higher chance of getting a favourable current by staying north of 5°S in the early stages. These tactics are only recommended if there is enough wind for sailing, otherwise it makes more sense to motor along the rhumb line. Normally the winds are from SE for the first half of the passage and more easterly in the second half. Usually the weather gets better as the season progresses, with passages in March and April experiencing more unsettled weather than in May or June.

For the first time in my sailing life, on the eve of our departure I decided to get some outside advice and contacted Bob McDermitt of the New Zealand Meteorological Service who advised me on the best course to be sailed in view of impending conditions. After a slow start, the winds became steadier so up went the asymmetric spinnaker to be replaced by the tri-radial when the wind finally settled in the southeast. With over one knot of favourable current and the wind rarely blowing more than 14 knots, these were perfect conditions. We ate every meal at the cockpit table and, as the sails needed little adjusting, we split the night into two watches, so each of us could have a nice long sleep. It was almost too good to be true... until one afternoon Aventura was surrounded by a pod of several dozen pilot whales. Their blunt heads gave them a menacing look, especially when I remembered that this was the area where several boats had had unpleasant

Light winds on passage to the Marquesas

finger on it when he said, 'It's only those people who don't keep watches who never see other ships. We see them all the time.'

The day after we had passed those fishing boats the weather changed dramatically, the blue skies turned a dull menacing slate colour, we had several squalls with little wind in between them and a large confused swell. Even the temperature dropped and it felt so chilly that we could have easily believed that we were sailing in the North Sea and not some two hundred miles south of the equator. These were typical doldrums conditions and apparently a known phenomenon on this route.

After 24 hours the wind came up from the southwest and with it a lot of rain, the visibility being so bad in the pouring rain that I had to put on the radar. Right on cue, an email from Bob McDermitt advised me to alter course and move as quickly as possible to 5°S, 105°W where we should find good winds. Those promised winds arrived much sooner and were blowing steadily from the SE. With all sails up and also a favourable half-knot current Aventura picked up her skirts and was soon galloping on her way west.

After a while those winds turned out to have been a false alarm and they petered out, so we had to motorsail in a south-west direction. Gradually the winds returned, became steadier and settled at around ten knots from the SE so we could hoist the assymetric spinnaker. The sky took on the

encounters and had been rammed and sunk by whales. In the case of Bill Butler's Siboney the culprits were definitely pilot whales so with these thoughts at the back of my mind, I wasn't too thrilled by our uninvited companions. Antti, who had lost his own boat on a reef in the Red Sea a couple of years earlier and until then had greeted any sea life with great interest, looked even less excited by our escort. Fortunately the whales soon lost interest and left us alone. With a sigh of relief, I told Antti, 'Obviously aluminium wasn't on their menu!'

To our surprise, we saw more ships than we had expected. Exactly 200 miles west of Galapagos we came across several fishing boats that were obviously working on the limit of Ecuador's territorial waters. Later, we crossed tracks with a couple of cargo ships and I remembered the result of a questionnaire in the ARC when I asked crews about the number of boats they saw during the Atlantic crossing. Most hadn't seen any at all, but one skipper put his typical trade wind look with fluffy clouds around the horizon, flying fish darting ahead of us and the water temperature reaching a steady 28°C. Looking at my logbook I see that it was at that point (4°40'S, 104°W) that we picked up the proper South Pacific trade winds and our tactic appeared to have paid off.

Under those benign conditions we enjoyed a stable routine, with lunch at midday immediately after plotting our noon position and announcing the miles run in the last 24 hours. Around sunset we would have a sundowner, then I would cook dinner, which was served at 1900 while listening to the news on the BBC World Service, a habit that I have followed during all my cruising years. After dinner Antti would wash up while I did a tour of the boat checking all systems and also deciding if we should continue with the same sails during the night. Antti would start his watch at 8 p.m. while I checked my emails and then turned in.

So far we had had no breakages of any sort, the only minor ones occurring as we were approaching our halfway point. First the speedometer started giving false readings and as I was unable to recalibrate it, for the rest of the passage I had to get our speed by GPS. I also had to replace a leaky O ring on the hydraulic pump operating the lifting rudder and once again I blessed Aventura's builders for having provided such an efficient and easy to use installation.

Another pleasant night lit by a splendid full moon, while doing over seven knots in fourteen knots of wind, brought us to our halfway point. In spite of the variable conditions at the start we had managed to keep up a good average speed. I called Gwenda on the satellite phone and Antti called Nina, who is just as adverse to long passages and happily agreed to stay on her own while us boys were playing sailors. In fact I suspect that Nina, who is a well known writer in her native Finland, was probably quite happy to have Antti out of the way so she could work on her latest novel. I wondered if Gwenda felt the same.

A special occasion calls for a special dinner, so I retrieved from the bottom of the fridge the last vacuum packed steak I had bought in Ecuador, the Argentinian prime beef being the best meat I had ever bought in a supermarket. The steak was accompanied by the last bottle of vintage Rioja wine that my friend JuanFra had given me before I left Las Palmas. For dessert I used up the last of our bananas which I flambéed with a generous lashing of brandy.

As we were sailing through such an effortless area, Antti and I agreed to split the night in two, so he took the first watch from 8 p.m. to 1 a.m. and I took the rest of the night. More for my own sake, I decided to relax one of my strict night rules, that of not reading on watch because having a light on badly affects one's night vision. In this fashion, the nights passed by pleasantly, the bright starry night reflected in our equally sparkling wake being of a beauty that only those fortunate enough to experience such moments can comprehend.

That night I finished reading an excellent biography of Che Guevara. Like most people of my generation, I had been intrigued by this man whose anger at the inequalities that affected the world I could readily identify with, but whose political views I could not share, primarily because of my experience of having lived under a communist regime. My visit to Cuba had not changed my opinion, rather confirmed my view that while Fidel Castro had started off as an idealistic revolutionary, once

Spectacular anchorage at Hanavave
Bay on Fatu Hiva

the struggle had succeeded, his utopian intentions were abandoned in favour of the temptation of absolute power. Having died before arriving at such a situation, Che has ensured that his image will forever be that of a true revolutionary and an inspiration for young people everywhere. We will never know how he would have turned out in old age.

My log entry for the following day notes that sailing wing and wing with the yankee poled out and full mainsail we were going "like a train". The seas around us were full of life with lots of sooty terns darting about. Shortly after noon we saw a sail far in the distance. After we made contact on VHF we agreed to switch over to a better frequency on the SSB. The elderly New Zealand couple told me that they had left Galapagos one week before us and as their autopilot could only cope with reduced sail, they had to keep their speed down or steer by hand. I asked if they needed any help

with food, water or fuel, but they assured me they were all right and expected to take another ten days to reach the Marquesas. We altered course to pass closer and lost sight of their masthead light around midnight.

The last week passed very quickly. We lost my best lure to a monster marlin who struck with such force that I am sure it would have towed us backwards had the smoking line not parted with an almighty twang. For a long time, the large fish kept somersaulting furiously in our wake, and I felt really bad about the agony he was going through.

At noon on day 19, with only 41 miles to go to Atuona, we saw at about the same distance to the SW the island of Fatu Hiva. Located so temptingly to windward of all the Marquesas, many sailors succumb to the temptation and stop there first knowing that sailing to Fatu Hiva after having first cleared in at Hiva Oa entails a tough beat to windward. This had been quietly tolerated by the French authorities in the past but as I knew that this was no longer the case, we decided to continue as planned to Atuona and clear in properly. One important thing I have learnt after having sailed to some one hundred countries is that regulations are made to be observed, and breaking local laws just for one's convenience is not only unjustified, but may also lead to serious consequences.

With only minutes to spare before dark, we dropped anchor in the small harbour below the village of Atuona on the island of Hiva Oa. Although I had hoped to get here in eighteen days, towards the end of the passage there had been little reason to sail faster as Gwenda was not going to arrive for another five days. In every respect, it had been an extremely pleasant passage and one of my most enjoyable ocean crossings.

Having made such good time Antti and I had several days to kill before Gwenda's arrival. After resting for a couple of days, we got some fresh supplies and early one morning left for Fatu Hiva. Luck was on our side as there was no sign of the expected strong south-easterlies and we had to motor all the way in virtually calm seas. Shortly before arrival I landed a small tuna and by early afternoon dropped anchor at Hanavave, considered to be one of the most beautiful anchorages in the world. Called in French La Baie des Vierges (the Bay of Virgins) the surroundings are truly spectacular, with huge rock formations overlooking the tranquil bay. As we had arrived in the Marquesas well ahead of the annual migration, Aventura had the beautiful bay all to herself. The small village at the head of the well-protected bay now had a breakwater and short quay, which made landing from the dinghy much easier than in the past. Walking through the small village we were warmly welcomed by everyone, and, as we were the first yacht to

arrive that season, I was told several times how everyone was looking forward to the annual arrival of the cruising yachts. This was probably because many visiting sailors have helped the villagers in various ways, repairing outboards, fixing television sets or playing soccer with the youngsters.

Being in such a calm spot I decided to do some maintenance work and as I always like to start with the most difficult job first I took Antti by surprise when he found me giving the forward toilet a long delayed service.

The small port of Atuona on the island of Hiva Oa

'Jimmy, what you are doing is almost blasphemous. Have you got nothing better to do than work on your toilet here, in the most beautiful spot on earth?'

'I agree, but one thing I always make sure is that everything works on this boat when Gwenda arrives, and that means a spotless galley and a functioning toilet. So you'd better tackle the galley why I finish here.' A captain must always have the last word.

Crew and Watches

The ideal crew would be a fairly laid back character who can keep it together under pressure. Plus, someone who can fix most things on a yacht and, of course, a good cook.

Steve Spink

That sounds like quite a tall order, although Steve, who sailed as skipper on one of the Millennium yachts, and as crew in two previous round the world rallies, has all those rare qualities. Fabio Colapinto who sailed his own yacht in the same event, and who has had more than his fair share of crew problems in his long sailing life, was of the firm opinion that "nothing can spoil the pleasure of a voyage more than problems with your crew." Fabio echoed my own feelings as I am also of the firm opinion that more voyages have been abandoned because of crew problems than by the wrong choice of boat, gear failure or financial difficulties. This conclusion is not based on my personal experience but is drawn from countless examples that I have come across as organiser of cruising rallies. Even allowing for the fact that I was dealing with very large numbers of people, the proportion of boats that experienced crew problems was much higher than I would have expected or ever imagined.

The scenario is simple: you invest all your energy and probably much of your savings in the boat of your dreams and finally set off on your planned voyage. You are accompanied by people who you know well and some that you know less well. However well you know them, whether friends or even family, you know them from another dimension, a comfortable life ashore. But

the sea is different, an alien dangerous medium where a person's true character often quickly reveals itself as selfish, anxious, stubborn, lazy, mean, greedy or having a lack of consideration towards others and no sense of humour, not to speak of physical or psychological problems. On top of that they may have irritating habits as well, being noisy, demanding, untidy, eating messily, not washing, not sharing cooking, washing up and other tasks, smoking, drinking too much or worse being addicted to drugs. There may also be problems with watch keeping, crew that sleep on watch and crew that cannot be relied upon. However skilful and tolerant the skipper may be in trying to make allowances for a difficult crew member, this may work with close family but with others is often impossible. If all this sounds like a description of the crew from hell, I should point out that there are also many crew who exhibit none of these faults and are a pleasure to have on board.

Types of crew

Firstly I will deal with crew from a general point of view and then examine the same subject from my own experience. Getting crew for a long voyage is not a simple matter as I know too well from the various rallies. Basically, there are five types of crew:

■ *Paid crew:* people who are experienced and you want to trust, to tell them what to do and who are not joining your yacht just to have a good time. These people expect to be paid a salary and have all their onboard expenses taken care of.

■ *Casual crew:* people who may not be so well qualified but are willing to work for their trip. Such people need not be paid, but you still need to support their onboard living expenses. This category also includes so-called hitchhikers, often young people who hang out in ports frequented by cruising boats and are keen to do some sailing even if they may not have much experience. Usually such crew are picked up at short notice.

■ *Sharing crew:* these are often friends who join a boat for a shorter or longer period. Normally they are expected to contribute towards their living expenses and do a fair share of work.

■ *Paying crew:* people who want to join an adventure, are prepared to work the boat, and also make a contribution to the overall costs, or even pay a reasonable fee per day.

■ *Charter guests:* normally these are not expected to do much, although they may take watches and help where necessary. They expect to be fed and looked after well, so such boats need to have a full crew to do that, including a cook. As such people are usually paying substantial charter fees, their expectations are high and therefore such operations must be approached as a purely business operation.

Regardless of the type of crew, a skipper or owner has to be very careful who they take on board, what arrangements have been made (financial and otherwise) and what the skipper's responsibilities are (repatriation, health, etc). There are many hidden problems that can show up, some of them serious, so the matter must not be taken lightly.

Those who decide to go down the charter guest route, must approach that option in a

Crew briefing on route and tactics before a long passage

proper businesslike manner. One should not mix the owner's personal friends with paying guests. Many sailors hope to supplement their cruising kitty in this way, and although taking on paying guests may look like an attractive solution to finance or at least underwrite one's cruising costs, there are many pitfalls. People who pay that kind of money have high expectations, they want service, and are not prepared to compromise and make allowances. If one is still determined to go ahead, adequate preparations must be made. First of all, if the owner/skipper is not going to be onboard for the charter, a professional skipper must be employed, also a permanent crew that includes at least a cook and a deckhand.

A few cruising couples have made this a successful business, but in all cases they were both competent sailors and ran a well organised ship. A good example are John and Amanda Neal who have been running for many years their Hallberg Rassy 46 Mahina Tiare III as a navigation and sail training ship. Fee paying crews join John and Amanda for offshore training stages in ocean voyaging, seamanship and navigation, the operation being backed up by regular cruising seminars held in various locations around the USA.

Some owners, who may be put off by the complications of running a properly set up charter operation, may consider going for a mixed solution. If the owner is not going to be on the yacht for much of the time, it is better to take a chance, go only for proper charter guests, and run the boat with a permanent crew of three persons (skipper, cook and deckhand). Whatever decision is made by the owner it must be agreed with the skipper, as he will have to deal with any problem and should always have the last word when crew is chosen. Professional skippers are renowned for being extremely touchy, so owners often have to treat them with kid gloves, which many owners find difficult. This must be the reason why professional skippers seem to change jobs so frequently. In fact, although I mentioned earlier that crew can cause the biggest problems on a voyage, equally serious problems can be caused by professional skippers, who are often arrogant and difficult to get on with.

I am giving these warnings because I have seen too many bad situations caused by friction between owner and skipper, owner and crew, captain and crew, owner/captain and paying guests, etc. So anyone planning to dive into this potential quagmire must be prepared to do their best to avoid such problems. One will not be able to avoid them all, but at least one should minimize the chance of a major falling out.

One other matter to be born in mind if running a charter operation is that in some countries this is liable to various legal restrictions and chartering may be limited to locally flagged boats. Occasionally, to avoid such problems, one can say that the crew are personal friends, but this should not be overdone as the authorities soon get suspicious if there are too many crew changes.

Taking on crew

To avoid possible legal problems, the owner must make sure that everything that is agreed is very clear and ideally set out in a written agreement both with the skipper and with any crew that is taken on. I once met a skipper who usually sailed alone but would occasionally take on crew. Every time he made sure that a proper contract was drawn up and signed by both of them detailing everything, from skipper and crew's obligations to sharing costs and other financial arrangements. At the time I found this rather exaggerated but over the years I realized that it was a wise thing to do.

A similar precaution is that of asking the crew to deposit with the skipper a sum of money equivalent to their return fare home. This can be used in case the crew has to be repatriated quickly, whether in an emergency or if he or she demands this. Crew repatriation is the responsibility of the skipper. This precaution applies to both professional and casual crew. It is exactly what happened to a skipper in one of the round the world rallies. While in Ecuador he had taken on a young man not so much because he needed an extra hand but because he had taken pity on him. In Tahiti the crew got involved with a girl on another boat and both decided to leave the rally and fly to her native New Zealand. They went to immigration and demanded to be repatriated by their respective skippers. Legally this was their skippers' obligation and although the skippers asked me to help, there was little that I could do. The skipper who had taken on the young man was very distressed as he felt he was being blackmailed, so I agreed to accompany him to the immigration office. When the head of immigration asked the skippers to produce the crews' tickets before he would clear their yachts, I pointed out that whereas the New Zealand girl should return home, the young man who was British should be repatriated to London not New Zealand. The officer agreed, and the crews' scheme collapsed at the last moment as they had to fly their separate ways.

Before moving on from this complex subject I must mention what could be the main problem in such a situation, and that is neither the crew nor the skipper, but the boat itself. Too many owners who are attracted to what they believe is an easy source of earning money do not realize just how important it is that their yacht is fully adequate for the job in hand, large enough, well equipped, comfortable and safe. Starting off with an unsuitable boat and the attitude that "we'll manage somehow" is simply a recipe for disaster.

Much of the above advice is culled from a detailed report I compiled for a Belgian owner of a 53 foot yacht who was planning to set off on a world voyage and was hoping to finance it by taking on paying guests. As I was doing this consultancy work for a fee, I had to put some serious thought into it, and had to give clear advice. Unfortunately all the pitfalls that I spelt out to my client eventually came true: he had a serious falling out with his professional skipper before they had even left the Mediterranean, mixing paying crew and personal friends proved to be a disaster, and after a terrible season in the Caribbean, the owner decided to abandon the whole project, sold the yacht and gave up. What made him especially bitter was that originally he had bought the yacht for a round the world voyage with his wife and grown up sons. By tackling the project from the wrong angle, which I repeatedly tried to warn him about, he eventually ended up with nothing but bad feelings. By being obsessed with attempting to find a way for the voyage to pay for itself, while being just as keen for it to be highly enjoyable, my client fell right between those two incompatible positions. As the saying goes, one cannot have one's cake and eat it.

One of the most frequent problems is caused by skippers taking on crew they don't know. I have been often amazed during the ARC when some skippers agree to take on crew on the eve of the start, being prepared to set off on a long ocean passage with people they knew nothing about. Occasionally it worked out but there have been just as many unpleasant outcomes.

Crew competence

One important point to bear in mind when choosing crew for an ocean passage is that at least one of the crew members should be competent enough to stand in for the skipper in an emergency. Among many examples that have come to my knowledge over the years of what can go wrong when the skipper is the only person capable of handling the boat I shall mention only the most recent one. A serious incident that happened in ARC 2006 shows that just having a spare pair of hands on a long passage is not enough should there be a serious emergency. The incident is described by the ARC organisers as follows: "The skipper of a yacht was taken ill when a pre-existing mental condition reoccurred and after five days and sleepless nights the crew felt that they could not continue to sail the yacht. All were evacuated onto a superyacht that had come to their assistance and taken to Antigua. As the skipper was the only competent person to sail, the yacht had to be abandoned. This incident highlights the need to have a balance of knowledge amongst the crew, and the importance of having a capable first mate or co-skipper able of completing the voyage."

The skipper being the only competent sailor on board is just as common on boats sailed by a couple and there have been many cases when the wife was unable to handle the boat in an emergency. This subject was investigated in two surveys when I interviewed a large number of cruising couples sailing in the South Pacific. The majority of the women (92 per cent) were confident that they could sail their boats singlehanded should the skipper become incapacitated. Some admitted that they might have difficulties coping with any repairs, or with jobs that required physical strength. One quarter of the women pointed out that if they had to leave an anchorage on their own they would probably have to leave the anchor and dinghy behind as they wouldn't be able to handle them on their own. Over half (62 per cent) could not set the windvane to steer the boat and there were even three women who admitted that they wouldn't know how to set the autopilot either. Among the women interviewed two had had to cope with this kind of emergency, one when her husband was struck down by a severe case of hepatitis, the other when the skipper developed blood poisoning from a badly infected knee. Both of them managed to sail the boat on their own to a port and get their husbands attended to.

While in Chagos I heard on the daily radio net about the tragedy that had struck Robert and Sue Baker of Carefree, a couple in their sixties whom we had met a few weeks earlier in Cocos. With only one hundred miles left to Rodriguez Robert suffered a fatal heart attack. As the wind was getting stronger and not being confident that she would be able to handle the boat on her own, Sue put out a Mayday that was relayed to the Australian authorities. They in turn alerted Mauritius, and an aeroplane was sent out to ascertain the situation but could do little to help. Eventually the captain of a supply ship that happened to be in Rodriguez decided to leave port at once and come to the rescue. The Mauritius Coast Guard embarked some of its officers on the ship who transferred to Carefree and helped Sue bring the boat safely into Rodriguez.

Skipper competence

I believe firmly in democracy. On my yacht all decisions are taken by unanimity... as long as I agree with them!
Fabio Colapinto

Trying to blame problems on the crew is not fair as there is just as good a chance that the fault may lie with the skipper. Some of the bad traits I outlined earlier apply as much to the skipper as to the crew. Among the boats that I have observed in various rallies, yachts with crew or skipper problems were still in a small minority and there were many more happy boats and happy crews. It was interesting to notice that some skippers never seemed to have crew problems whoever sailed with them and on the other hand other skippers always seemed to be having problems. The greatest handicap for a skipper is lack of experience. I came across this on my very first sail in England and I have never forgotten the valuable lessons I learnt then as described in chapter 1. We were only sailing during a weekend in sheltered coastal waters, so I hate to think how a long passage with such a skipper would have turned out.

While there is little that can be done to improve a bad skipper, as far as the crew is concerned there are ways to pre-empt or deal with problems as they occur. As even the smallest yacht is, after all, a ship, some basic naval rules must apply and be seen to be applied. Discipline is not only essential but vital. Just as in the navy the surest way to achieve discipline is through routine, which must be imposed and insisted upon from the very beginning. This means having regular meals, regular watches, a fair distribution of tasks, tidiness and respect for the skipper and other crew. As a minor example, however bad the weather, I shave and wash every day. If I notice that one of the crew starts letting himself go by not washing and not shaving, which often happens on long passages, I try to point this out politely as this may be the first sign of a potentially deteriorating situation.

When a skipper is faced with a difficult crew member at the very beginning of a voyage, a quiet talk with him or her, but never in front of the others, often works. Ideally it should be done on his or her night watch when one can talk without being overheard. It normally calms down the situation but if it doesn't one may be forced to seek a drastic solution by making for the nearest port and disembark the crew. This is what happens every year in the ARC as, soon after having left the Canaries, some boats make a detour to the Cape Verdes to get rid of their troublesome crew.

Peter Noble, whose book "The Mind of the Sailor" deals with the psychological aspects of sailing and the effects on skipper and crews, comments, 'In recent years the importance of the human factor to the success of a sailing crew has been increasingly recognised. Small crews, particularly husband and wife teams, get on best. Compatibility is everything; be reluctant to sail with strangers. A small boat at sea, except possibly for the singlehander, is not an emotional "escape". People take their problems with them. The successful and happy sailor was usually successful and happy before putting to sea.'

There is no doubt that in most cases the ideal crew on a cruising boat is that of a couple or of family members. In the case of couples, sailing is often the man's dream, many wives going along just for his sake. This may not turn out to be a major problem if the couple have a healthy relationship when things usually work out. After sailing many tens of thousands of miles together, towards the latter part of my latest voyage Gwenda finally realized that she didn't like long ocean passages and made it very clear why. "I think it is important to know your interests and limitations which is the reason I didn't want to do the Atlantic crossing because I knew that I wouldn't really enjoy it. Of course I can do it if necessary because I've done it before, but if you don't enjoy something you are just a dead weight on the others."

From New Zealand onwards, Gwenda only joined me for specific cruising stages so I had to find a solution to complete my voyage and did the rest with various crew, usually one or two. By the time I completed the voyage, a total of twelve different crew had sailed with me. I am happy to say that with one notable exception it all worked out extremely well, mainly for three reasons: I chose my crew carefully, briefed them extensively beforehand on what to expect, and probably most important, had the experience not just to deal with them, but to show them by force of example that I knew all there was to know about my boat and sailing it. Obviously this is an ideal position to be in but as I am primarily writing this book for the benefit of less experienced sailors I'm afraid they may not have some of my advantages.

Dealing with crew

By nature I am a rather forceful character, but by being aware of it, I have learnt to make allowances, both in dealing with my family, friends or crew. So while I may be a potential Captain Bligh, over the years and with increasing experience I have learnt to control myself, be more tolerant and patient.

The critical parts of the voyage are the very beginning, the middle and the end. Among those three stages the start is the most important as it sets the scene for the rest. Because so much seems to depend on the initial contact, when the crew tries to suss out the skipper and vice-versa, and any small thing can be blown out of all proportion, I now have a three days rule. I explain to my crew that during this initial period whatever I say is not meant as criticism but is an attempt to make them understand how the boat functions. They must take no offence at anything I say, or how I say it, as it is not meant to tell them off. I also assure them that if they can bear this for three days, the rest will be easy.

The three day rule came in extremely useful when I was joined in Cape Town by Patrick and Marc. As both of them have their own boats and have some sailing experience, right from the start Patrick started questioning my orders. I reminded him of the three day rule, and although he didn't seem to like it, from then on he tried

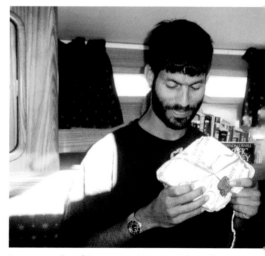

Ivan opening his present on crossing the equator

to be cooperative. Even before the three days were over both of them realized that I knew what I was doing and that it was in their own best interest to go along with what I kept reminding them, 'You are here to learn, so just do as I tell you and you won't regret it.'

Generally, by the time a passage has reached its mid point and one is in the middle of the ocean, it is not uncommon to notice among the crew a sense of anxiety, boredom and irritation with the others after a long period of close proximity. This was most certainly not the case with Patrick and Marc who by that time had settled in perfectly and were clearly enjoying the passage and life at sea. One way to deal with boredom on long ocean passages is to prepare something that the crew can look forward to. On the first Aventura we had prepared presents for everyone to be opened as we crossed another ten degrees of longitude. The children loved it and we continued doing it all around the world. It was such a simple idea that I continued using it later with adult crew too, and it is surprising how much pleasure even a simple gift can make when there is little else to look forward to.

As a passage gets close to its end the prevailing feeling is often one of impatience to arrive. If there have been previous clashes, the atmosphere can be explosive. Even simple matters like concern over a flight to catch or missing home and the family, can create a tense atmosphere. This can be the most difficult stage and there is little one can do to improve things. One thing that a skipper should do is not to allow the crew to cut it too fine when they are booking their flights home. This time pressure can have serious affects on both skipper and crew, and can often spoil an otherwise successful ocean passage. I normally insist that I am consulted on the date of a crew's return flight after a passage and, if I am in any doubt about how long it will take to reach our intended destination, I strongly advise the crew to book a flexible ticket. In these days of cheap flights crews are often tempted to buy the cheapest fare possible and by the time the skipper finds this out it is often too late and the choice is either for the crew to miss their flights or for the skipper to do everything possible to make landfall before the flight.

Firmly booked flights are one of the most common causes of friction among crew and skipper in the ARC and, having seen boats arriving in St Lucia at the end of the ARC, it never failed to amaze me how many crew had their bags packed and were ready to step off the boat before it was even properly docked. It was easy to guess what must have been going on during the crossing and what a rotten time they must have had.

Assigning tasks

I was tempted to call this subsection "Giving Orders" but that would have sounded too much like being on a navy ship. Assigning tasks is the most common source of friction for the simple reason that most people do not like being told what to do. Often this puts the skipper in an impossible situation as I know only too well as when faced with a touchy crew I often end up doing a job myself rather than trying to delegate it.

Just as the crew have to obey certain rules, so does the skipper. Paramount among these is not telling off a crew in

The crew of Duen playing music together

front of others or shouting at the crew unless the skipper makes it clear that if he raised his voice it was not in anger but because he wanted to make sure that he had been heard. I am very much aware of this problem as two of my crew have hearing problems. One of the most popular T-shirts for seawives is one that simply says in large letters on the front: DON'T SHOUT!

I am ashamed to admit that in my early sailing days I did shout at my crew and usually that meant Gwenda. My lack of experience meant that I was unsure of myself, made lots of mistakes and often ended up shouting. I know that lack of experience is hardly an excuse but I am still annoyed with myself for my attitude in those days. Not to shout at the crew is another valuable lesson that I have learnt and followed without fail to this day.

The problem with crew that are hard of hearing is that by necessity the skipper is forced to raise his voice to make himself heard, but this can be easily misinterpreted and unfortunately some deaf people are even more touchy when yelled at than people whose hearing is normal. This is why I insist that such crew wear their hearing aids at all times, and I also make it very clear, as I do to any crew, that if I need to raise my voice, this is only because I want to make sure that I am heard.

I have often wondered why people seem happy to wear glasses but are reluctant to have a hearing aid. The probable answer is that young people wear glasses too, whereas having a hearing aid is a clear sign of advancing age, which most people do not like to admit even to themselves. This is something that puzzles me as nowadays so many people, young and old, seem to have something stuck in their ears, most contraptions being a lot larger and more obvious than a discreet hearing aid. I certainly don't have that hang-up and as soon as I realized that I could no longer hear the birds chirping in our garden, I got the best hearing aid I could find.

While in Vanuatu I was joined by Dieter Walz, a friend who had sailed with me before. As we made our way into a lagoon and I was looking for a place to anchor I shouted to Dieter who was on the foredeck: 'Prepare the anchor.'

The rumble of the chain running out fast made me realize immediately what he had done and so I shouted even louder, 'Stop, stop.'

At least 100 feet of chain had already gone down and although I immediately tried to stop the boat, we had run over the chain and the anchor was now lying on the bottom somewhere behind us. We managed to retrieve the anchor, make for a better spot and re-anchor.

'What did you do that for?'

'You shouted: drop the anchor, and I did just that!'

'No, I shouted prepare the anchor and anyway we were still moving so how could I have asked you to drop it? Aren't you wearing your hearing aid?'

'Sorry, no.'

'OK, from now on please wear it all the time and, to be safe, we'll start doing things the navy way. You repeat whatever I tell you to do, so I know that you heard.'

'Yes, sir. Understood, sir!'

Next time we anchored, when everything had been tidied away I saw Dieter walk to the stern and dive in. He suddenly resurfaced screaming as if possessed and trying to swim as fast as he could back to the boat. As he grabbed hold of the boarding ladder I asked, 'What on earth happened?'

'I left my expensive hearing aids in. I hope they are not ruined.'

'I'm sorry, I know I asked you to wear them all the time, but I didn't mean it literally.'

Fortunately after being rinsed in fresh water and dried in the sun they were saved. Both incidents joined the list of things that we often had a good laugh about, which wasn't all that difficult as Dieter has a really good sense of humour. That may be about the most important quality in any crew.

My friend Antti's hearing is not that good either but in spite of that he avoids wearing his hearing aid. The day after he had arrived in Reunion for the leg to Cape Town, I hired a car and, as a special treat, drove him into the spectacular interior where I had already spent some time with Gwenda, so I knew the area well and was only doing it for Antti's sake. On the drive back, I was trying to make some small talk but as he was not responding, I asked, 'Antti can you hear what I am saying?'

'I only hear what I am interested in!'

'Well, that wasn't very nice,' I said quite annoyed that all I got for my efforts to make him welcome was this put down, but he is an old friend and I knew better than start an argument on the eve of a long passage.

After we had passed the Cape of Good Hope and were approaching Cape Town some time after midnight, we had a late dinner and, as I always try to arrive in port with a tidy boat, I told Antti, 'Why don't you wash up before we arrive.'

He was gone a long time and when he finally returned he smelt strongly of aftershave.

'Antti, what have you done?'

'Washed and shaved, as you told me.'

I burst our laughing, 'Antti, I'd never tell you that? No, I told you to wash up, to wash the dishes!'

It was his turn to laugh, 'I did think it was odd when you asked me to wash at 3 a.m., but stranger things have happened.'

One other important lesson I have learnt is not only to make sure that crew understand an order but, especially with new crew, to check that they have actually carried it out. I always try to do this as discreetly as possible. Most crew, especially if they are experienced, dislike being looked at over their shoulder, so the skipper has to be very careful not to upset them unnecessarily. On the other hand, not checking what a crew is doing, or whether an order has been carried out, can be just as bad, as I found out when sailing in Sweden with a friend, who was also an experienced sailor. With an imminent gale approaching we ran for shelter in a small port. I spotted a space by what looked like a home-built steel boat. As I eased Aventura alongside a grinding noise made me fear the worst. My friend had failed to put out any fenders! Fortunately Aventura's unpainted aluminium hull only suffered a few superficial scratches but more damage was done to my friend's ego. The mistake I had made was to trust my crew to use his own initiative, rather than tell him specifically what to do.

Crew briefing

Whenever new crew join me I make sure they get a detailed briefing on all aspects of the boat and its running routine. My first priority on the crews' arrival is to take everyone out to dinner on that first evening as this eases the atmosphere no doubt helped by a glass or two of good wine. I feel that it is essential that this introductory meeting takes place on neutral ground away from the distractions of the boat as on such an informal occasion people seem to be more relaxed to discuss matters and ask questions without inhibitions.

The following morning I take the crew around the boat and explain everything in detail. Although Aventura is very easy to handle once the sails are up, her deck layout is quite complicated with dedicated lines and blocks all over the place, which for a newcomer can be quite bewildering. Having dealt with the sailing side of things we then discuss the engine, selfsteering gear and autopilot. Safety comes next, followed by what to do or not to do if the worst comes to the worst and we have

On this jointly owned yacht all decisions are taken by consensus

to abandon ship so that everyone knows what role he or she is expected to play. Some hypothetical emergencies are also discussed such as losing the steering or the mast.

Perhaps the most important part of the briefing is left to the end as it involves on board routines. I regard enjoying a normal civilized life on passage as paramount and always make sure that the crew knows this. Having described the kind of meals I intend to provide as I enjoy doing the cooking at sea, we then go through the list of provisions with everyone being asked their likes and dislikes. We then troop to the chosen supermarket and when everything on the list has been chosen I ask everyone to pick any special treats they might like. Most of the time these are sweets or chocolates, but I was certainly taken aback once when my Danish friend Peter Ibsen put two one gallon jugs of Chlorox into the shopping trolley. Peter is a great sailor, a former dinghy champion of Denmark, but has an obsession with cleanliness. While he was sailing with me our toilet was the cleanest I had ever seen on any boat and the smell of Chlorox lingered on long after he had left. Chanel No 5 it certainly was not.

The supermarket bill and all other bills involving provisions are split equally between all of us, myself included. We also share restaurant bills, except when I take the crew out for dinner or I am the guest of my crew. Over the years I have decided that money matters can cause so much bad blood that I prefer to cover all the boat costs myself. I therefore pay for fuel, docking, any port fees and of course the cost of any spares or repairs. After all I regard my crew as my personal guests so why apply different rules at sea to when they are guests in my house. Removing this kind of financial pressure seems to give great pleasure to the crew and it certainly works well.

Crew incidents

Although most of my experience of crew comes from my latest voyage, a telling incident did take place on Aventura II. After Gwenda had to return to London from the Azores, I took two friends along for the 1000 mile passage to Gibraltar. It all passed off quite uneventfully, we sailed past Cape St Vincent and set course for Gibraltar proper. With the situation looking clear ahead and nothing much to do I decided to have a short rest so as to be ready for the forthcoming arrival, something which I always try to do before landfall after a long passage, when even a short sleep helps clear the mind. Before going below I told the crew quite clearly to call me if they saw anything at all, suspicious or not. I was woken up abruptly by a loud knock followed by a grinding noise. I jumped into the cockpit and right alongside and within reach was a flashing light on a perch. I knew immediately what it signalled and that we had run into one of those gigantic tuna nets that Spanish fishermen set in this area. My guess was confirmed when I looked over the side and saw in the light of my torch a thick cable and a heavy net hanging from it. I quickly raised the retractable keel to stop it being entangled even more and also prepared my powerful cable cutters, which I always keep in an easily accessible place. I then called Tarifa Radio as the nearest shore station, explained our predicament and said that if help was not forthcoming I would cut the cable.

'Don't do that, please don't do that,' a voice screamed in Spanish. 'Wait. We are coming immediately.'

Soon afterwards a small fishing boat headed towards us at full speed and the helmsman signalled us to follow him. First he positioned his own keel over the cable to lower it and with Aventura's keel retracted, we managed to get across both the cable and net. The boat guided us to a gate in the huge net about a couple of miles away... and we were free.

My crew had broken one of my most important rules: to inform the skipper immediately if they saw anything suspicious. Although they told me later that they had seen the flashing light but as it was so weak they had estimated it to be much further away.

A good example involving the breaking of this crucial rule is one that involved my friend Bill Butler. While sailing in New Chance off the coast of Nova Scotia and needing a short rest, he told his crew to keep an eye on the course and to make sure they stayed in deep waters. Bill was woken up by the noise of the boat running aground. His crew had fallen asleep while on watch and the yacht had strayed into shallow water. In spite of all efforts New Chance was lost.

Watch systems

Over the years I have ended up with a watch system that I consider as close to perfect as possible and which is particularly suited to boats with crew of two or three. All through our first voyage Gwenda and I were very disciplined in keeping night watches although it wasn't always easy. We were often tired, although as the children started growing up they would take an afternoon watch together so we could catch up on sleep. They could be trusted and always called one of us if they thought it necessary. In those days we only had the Aries windvane so whenever the winds were too light or we were motoring we had to steer by hand. As I had other jobs to do and often did a longer night watch, Gwenda generously took the larger share during the day and I hate to think of the many hours she spent perched on her seat trying to keep the boat on course while fighting hard not to fall asleep. An autopilot of any kind would have turned our life from beautiful into perfect.

Night watches in those days started after the evening meal at 8 p.m. local time. As I can easily go to sleep at any time and usually do so the moment my head hits the pillow, I normally slept first. If Gwenda could stay awake until midnight she would let me sleep until then, those blissful four hours being so restful that I rarely had to call her again all night. I normally had another sleep in the day, usually while Gwenda was turning from mother into teacher and the children did their daily schoolwork.

Having the person on watch fall asleep is a serious concern for me when sailing with friends but never with Gwenda as I can never remember her falling asleep on her watch. Gwenda has an incredible ability to stay awake however tired she may be.

During the long years of separation while we were waiting for permission to get married, Gwenda was regularly commuting by car between England and Romania. We once worked out that over a period of five years she had done that trip across Europe on seventeen occasions. To complete the 3,000 mile journey in the shortest time possible she would drive for fourteen hours a day, only allowing herself two overnight stops. One of her worst trips was in the spring of 1968 when she had nine month old Doina with her, who mostly slept while she drove but woke up and became active and demanding once they stopped when Gwenda was yearning for some rest. Just as bad was her last trip, exactly one year later, when she decided to drive back to England while being six months pregnant with Ivan.

On Aventura III night watches start at 8 p.m. and end at 8 a.m. I always try to get the last dawn watch as I never tire of sunrises at sea. This way I can let the crew off watch sleep in the morning until they wake up on their own. The night is divided into four three-hour periods. If there are only two of us each has to do two night watches. Whenever I am joined by new crew I explain the system and ask if they find it acceptable. Occasionally less experienced crew ask to have the watch reduced to two hours as they find three hours on their own too long on an unknown boat, but we usually revert to three hour watches when they realize that a two hour sleep is rarely sufficient.

If the crew is inexperienced or, as sometimes happened, tend to panic when they realize where they are – in the middle of a vast ocean on a dark night stuck on a small nutshell which they are unable to leave for many more days. These are probably valid reasons for anyone to break out in a cold sweat. If I notice this kind of anxiety, and I normally do as the crew usually sends out some signal or may even mention it casually, if there are three of us, I double the watch so that the crew stand watches together for three hours while I cover the rest.

My worst experience of such a situation happened while I was sailing with a friend across the Caribbean from St Lucia to the Dominican Republic. One morning he told me that when he realised we were passing Puerto Rico by only some 15 miles he was caught by a sudden attack of panic, shivering uncontrollably and being terrified that he would die. He was so desperate that at one point he was about to call Puerto Rico Coast Guard on the VHF and ask to be evacuated by helicopter. Fortunately he got himself under control, calmed down and finished his watch. He said nothing at the change of watch but told me everything over breakfast and apologized profusely. We are still good friends and that night off Puerto Rico was never mentioned again. He is just the kind of person to manage to bring himself under control as he is normally calm and composed and with a great sense of humour, which is exactly the way he described the crisis the following morning, helplessly laughing at his own stupidity. No wonder he is still one of my favourite crew.

My friend's experience taught me to be more careful with fresh crew, especially when left to do a night watch on their own. My niece Marianne, who sailed with me from Tahiti to Hawaii, expressed the same kind of feeling and admitted that she was sick with fear when sitting alone in the cockpit at night, being overcome by the vastness of the surrounding ocean and the immensity of the starry sky above. Gwenda shares this general anxiety when she is sailing offshore and it is this feeling of uneasiness that probably explains her dislike of long passages, rather than her complaint about the boredom of spending a long time at sea. I find it quite strange to be frightened when, for me, this is the most exhilarating part of offshore sailing – the feeling of being on your own small boat, far away from everything and in total control of your own fate.

Night watches

The off-watch crew sleeps in his bunk while the on-watch crew sleeps in the cockpit.

Thomas Hahn

Falling asleep on night watch is a common occurrence but few people are prepared to admit it. With the boat gliding along effortlessly, the gentle movement of the boat can be a powerful soporific. Occasionally I have dozed off myself but fortunately I always wake up, with a start, after a few minutes. Whenever it happens I make myself a coffee, walk around, check the sails, and do my best to keep awake. While I was singlehanding from Panama to Ecuador I set the radar alarm at 6 miles and the alarm clock to ring every twenty minutes, but usually I managed to wake up before the clock sounded.

I had at least two incidents that I know of when my crew fell asleep. Once I was fast asleep below and probably quite relaxed as it was a quiet night when I woke up suddenly with a distinct feeling that something was wrong. I rushed into the cockpit where my crew was happily snoring in a corner. Abeam of us a large yellow ship with lights blazing was ploughing at over 20 knots through the swell going in the same direction as us. My heart stopped as I estimated that a mere 30 metres separated

us from disaster. Everything happened so quickly that by the time my crew was fully awake the ship was already ahead of us. I realised that with our masthead light showing and Aventura's aluminium hull giving a good radar signal, the officer on watch had obviously seen us, altered course slightly and passed us at a safe distance, probably cursing us that we hadn't done it ourselves. I was so mad but somehow managed not to say anything and the matter was never mentioned again. My friend was such an experienced sailor that there was no need to dwell on such a fundamental error.

What woke me up? I have no idea, but Gwenda is convinced I have a special sixth sense. Occasionally I get a gut feeling that something is wrong, and I can usually sense the arrival of bad weather in spite of my declared ignorance of scientific weather prediction. I sometimes wake up for no clear reason and almost every time the reason soon becomes apparent. Gwenda also remarked how some of her subliminal messages miraculously seemed to get through to me while she was on watch. Just as she was thinking that she needed to call me, I would pop up in the cockpit. But I put this down simply to my being so much in tune with my boat that I detect even the tiniest changes in her behaviour.

Night rules

There are some very firm rules on Aventura, which I always apply. First among these is for the crew not to leave the cockpit for any reason whatsoever without calling the skipper. If the weather is settled I do not insist on wearing harnesses as I consider the cockpit to be very well protected. Urinating over the side is completely forbidden, even in daytime

Freshly caught fish being filleted by Marc who took over Aventura's galley on the long leg from Cape Town

problem, such as a flapping sail, a loose sheet, a strange sound from the autopilot or from the engine if motoring, whales blowing nearby and many others. If such signs are heard something can be done in time. Also, the faint sound of an engine, or more likely that of a propeller, which can travel a long way through the water, can indicate a ship somewhere in the vicinity or a submarine as happened on a night watch on Aventura I as we were sailing past the Spanish naval base at Cartagena. The regular throb increased slightly and suddenly I got a strong whiff of heavy fumes. I could not see any ship, so realized that a submarine was near us. I put on the deck lights to make it clear that we were a sailing yacht and soon the smell disappeared and the engine throb ceased.

and in fact I insist that not only do men have to use the toilet at all times but that they must also sit down. Aventura III has a second toilet right next to the companionway, which is easy to reach in the dark without disturbing the other crew.

There are two other night rules, which I have started imposing of late and I believe for very good reason: no reading and no listening to music at night. To be able to read one needs a light and that impairs one's night vision. Crew on watch occasionally put the book down to have a look around, often with the light still on, but I suspect this to be too short for their night vision to have been restored. Being able to see well at night, not just other ships, but also to look at the sails for example, is so important that I believe this rule to be justified.

I feel just as strongly that not being able to hear is similarly unacceptable. Being shut off from any outside sound can be dangerous. There are many sounds on a boat, which can foretell an impending

Cooking and washing up

Delegating cooking on Aventura is never a problem as I enjoy cooking at sea and I am happy to prepare all meals, which also puts me in better control of the provisions. Of course I am happy to opt out when I have a qualified chef on board like my friend Marc. As I am quite fussy about tidiness on the boat, what really annoys me is the absolute mess that some of my crew create in the galley by the time a meal is ready to be served, with empty dishes, various utensils and ingredients spread all over the place. I know that this is because people who are used to large kitchens with generous surfaces seem unable to adapt to a compact galley. When I cook I normally put everything back immediately, even wash some of the dishes and implements that have been used, so that by the time the meal is ready to be served, the galley looks orderly.

Among the things that I learnt from my two catering friends, Patrick and Marc, is how thoroughly they cleaned the galley when they had finished washing up. The cooker got special treatment and ended up gleaming and looking like new. I noticed because I always leave this tedious job until it can no longer be ignored. As in their professions hygiene and ultimately the reputation of their businesses is of such importance I was not really surprised but was still impressed that they took this matter so seriously.

Most of my other crew were poor cooks and did not even try to hide their lack of enthusiasm. Not surprisingly the best cooks were all French. During the Atlantic crossing Gildas, who is a dedicated, almost obsessive gourmet, proved the point that those who really like their food are the best at preparing it. So every meal was a real feast and he would spend all morning planning and preparing the midday meal and all afternoon elaborating his dinner. And elaborate affairs they always were, even if serving a simple rice salad with various ingredients mixed in.

The most delicious meals I have had at sea were between Cape Town and the Canaries when Marc took over the galley from the moment he stepped on board and miraculously managed to produce a never ending stream of original dishes. Marc is in every respect a wonderful person, easy going, funny and kind. He and his wife Corinne keep their hotel and restaurant open for six months only, then retire exhausted with their two younger children to French Polynesia where they live on a catamaran. The children go to school there which is easy as the system is the same as in mainland France. The elder

son is attending a special hotel school in the south of France so the tradition is guaranteed to continue.

Patrick is a very different person. He is robust, hardworking and adores Provence and everything Provençal, speaking French with that unmistakable accent recognizable after a couple of words wherever in the world they are spoken. He runs his bakery business with an iron fist but just like Marc he is seriously preparing for early retirement and a life of cruising. Patrick's main quality is his capacity to laugh at his own mistakes. When they joined me in Cape Town the atmosphere was rather stiff as they didn't know me well and were probably quite anxious as they had never done any offshore sailing before except a couple of trips to Corsica. As pleasantly as I could I made it clear that there were certain rules on the boat that needed to be followed, something which I knew would not be easy to be accepted readily by two successful businessmen. But they did and we had a great time together and have remained the best of friends.

I gave these examples to show that in spite of the crew problems I mentioned earlier, those were exceptions rather than the rule. As I don't want to give the impression that I have always been lucky and never had crew problems I will describe a few personal incidents that I regard as significant as each has a useful lesson embedded in it.

My very first lesson in the delicate field of human relationships happened right at the beginning of my sailing life when I decided to take Aventura I across the English Channel on a shakedown cruise to Brittany. I had a crew of four, a friend who brought along two of his colleagues from the same London hospital and Dominic, a neighbour whom I had met on a navigation course. As he was a carpenter Dominic kindly offered to spend every free weekend doing the more difficult woodwork on Aventura that I was totally incapable of. His help was one of the reasons I managed to get that boat completed in such record time.

We had hardly made it into Brest's well-sheltered inner harbour when a violent storm broke over the area. The storm continued for several days with no sign of abating. Stuck in port with no prospect of doing any sailing, the situation became terribly trying, especially in the confined space of a small boat, while the three doctors drank and played cards all day long. As the days passed and we continued to be stuck, the atmosphere deteriorated until, after another heavy bout of cards and booze, one of the doctors started blaming me for having ruined his long awaited holiday. He was so insulting and also quite obviously drunk that I couldn't take it anymore.

'If that's how you feel I think you should leave my boat immediately. You are definitely no longer welcome here.'

As they had come together they decided to leave together. My friend, who had brought his two colleagues along, apologized profusely but I assured him that I understood and that it would be all right for him to go as well. After they had left, Dominic, who had witnessed all this in complete silence, turned to me and said, 'And they call themselves educated people?'

The worst experience in my sailing life happened in the Indian Ocean. When he heard of my plans, an acquaintance, who had just bought a boat and was planning to set off with his partner on a world cruise, volunteered to join me from Darwin to Cape Town. I had some doubts about setting off with a person I hardly knew but

he was extremely keen. It was only later that he told me he had serious difficulties with his teenage son, who was living with his ex-wife, who was ill with cancer. My crew was obviously quite concerned so before we left for Darwin I suggested he dropped out and deal instead with his family problems. I told him not to worry as I could easily find a replacement crew. He refused point blank saying that he would not miss such a unique opportunity for anything. Everything went fine on the leg from Darwin to Bali but just before we arrived there his ex-wife died so he flew home for one week. Before he left I suggested strongly that now it would be even more important for him to stay with his son, and that Gwenda had offered to fly out and sail with me if necessary, but again he refused.

In Cocos Keeling, which was our next stop, and a delightful place, we spent several days in the company of other cruisers. As we were leaving for Chagos he told me that this had been the best time of his life and how grateful he was that I had taken him along. The time we spent in Chagos was just as enjoyable, one of the highlights of the entire voyage and we decided to make one final stop at the remote Egmont Atoll. While on this overnight passage, when I went off watch I left my crew precise instructions to keep an eye on the self steering gear and the course we were sailing. When he called me at the end of his watch I checked our position on the GPS and nearly froze when I saw us heading towards a reef. During his watch the wind had changed direction and we were now sailing at about thirty degrees off our intended course. I was so relieved that we had escaped with just a close shave that I decided not to make too much fuss over it. I did point out to him the seriousness of his deed but as I regarded him as a friend, and the incident was over anyway, I left it at that.

We had Egmont entirely to ourselves, without doubt one of most beautiful tropical anchorages I had ever seen. The following day, on the Inmarsat C forecast, the winds were predicted to start backing SE which was almost too good to be true. We left that same evening and were able to lay a course for Mauritius.

At dawn, as he was finishing his watch, he lingered on obviously wanting to tell me something. He eventually blurted out, 'I have decided to leave the boat in Mauritius!'

At first I could not believe my ears, so I asked, 'But what happened? It's not that long ago that you were telling me just how much you enjoyed this voyage, how happy you were to live this life.'

He didn't reply so I asked again, 'Just tell me what made you take this decision?'

'There is nothing to say. I have decided to leave the boat.'

'Very well, that is all right by me too, as with such an attitude I would most certainly not be prepared to continue sailing with you.'

We sailed the rest of the way in a frosty but civilized atmosphere and the matter was not mentioned again. The wind held and we eventually finished what under different circumstances would have been a highly satisfying leg in a creditable eight days. As soon as we arrived in Mauritius he left the boat.

What I could not understand was not so much his decision to quit, which by then I had accepted, but the abrupt change in his attitude, which I found and still find totally incomprehensible. There seemed no logical explanation for his behaviour. All I can surmise is that the problems with his son must have put him under a lot of pressure and I just happened to be the most convenient person upon whom to vent his pent-up frustrations. Understanding people's irrational behaviour is way beyond my knowledge of human psychology, so I gave up trying. It had already been arranged that Gwenda would join us in Mauritius and Reunion while my friend Antti jumped at the chance to sail with me again and at short notice joined me in Reunion for the leg to South Africa.

Tips

- Do not take on crew that you do not know well.
- On long passages there should be at least one competent crew who can stand in for the skipper in an emergency.
- It is always advisable to part company with a difficult crew early rather than hope that matters might improve.
- Never trust a new crew until he or she has proven him/herself.
- New crew should be briefed on all on board routines as well as on emergency procedures. This should be done before setting off on an offshore passage.
- All financial arrangements should be agreed and, if necessary, set down in writing.
- The skipper or owner should send joining crew a covering letter stating that he/she is joining the boat. Such a letter may be requested when checking in at the airport of departure.
- Caution should be exercised if taking on paying guests as such operations may infringe local laws and may also invalidate one's insurance.

Among the Islands of Tahiti Nui

In a place like Atuona nothing much seems to happen and the time spent there by Paul Gauguin is still mentioned as if it were recently, so it was perhaps not surprising that every living soul on the island seemed to have descended onto Hiva Oa's small airport to welcome the flight from Tahiti. Gwenda stepped off the small plane looking diminutive among the burly Marquesans returning home. After a separation of two months, I was happy to be with Gwenda again and was looking forward to the prospect of sailing together all the way to New Zealand.

Although we had visited all the Marquesas on Aventura II in 1991, we had enjoyed that cruise so much that we wanted to repeat the experience. We also wanted to spend some time on Hiva Oa, an island to which we had been a couple of times before but never had time to explore at leisure. One of the first things we did was to walk the steep road that leads up from Atuona to the small cemetery where Gauguin was laid to rest in 1903. The tomb was overshadowed by a gnarled Tiare Tahiti tree whose fragrant flowers fluttered down gently onto the simple stone grave. Nearby was the grave of Jacques Brel, a Belgian singer who had also chosen to end his days on this remote island.

Our visit coincided with the one hundredth anniversary of Gauguin's death which had galvanized Hiva Oa's small community into a burst of civic activity. The painter's Maison de Jouir (house of pleasure), which was burnt down by the villagers on his death, had been faithfully restored and now contained reproductions of the famous canvases he painted during his troubled sojourn on the island. Shunned by the locals while he lived in their midst, he was now acknowledged as a local celebrity.

Those Gauguin copies that adorned the walls of his restored studio had a story behind them worthy of the peripatetic painter himself. On my previous visit to Atuona I had met a French singlehander who had just arrived in his yacht from France. Alain had set up an easel under a

The grave of Paul Gauguin in Atuona's small cemetery

large tree that overshadowed Gauguin's former abode and was busy painting. He told me that he was planning to reproduce all Gauguin's paintings in time for the centenary celebrations of his death. The canvas he was working on looked almost identical to the reproduction he was copying from a large art catalogue and when I commented how good it looked he told me that if I was interested he would be happy to paint one for me as well. We agreed on one of my favourite Gauguins and as the price he quoted was quite acceptable, I placed an order and paid him an advance. As I had only come for a couple of days to make preparations for the arrival of the Millennium Odyssey fleet, I could not wait and arranged with Alain to give the finished canvas to one of my staff who would pay him the balance of his fee. This is what eventually happened and Alain's painting (unfortunately not the one I had ordered) now hangs on the wall of our London apartment.

Reproducing Gauguin's canvases outside the painter's restored home

This is by no means the end of the story as in the meantime I had found out that Alain was one of the most famous forgers in France who had ended up in prison after one of his many scams. When he had finished his sentence he vowed never to get into trouble again and use his undoubted talents to produce original work. Unfortunately the ever alert French tax office had other ideas. One day a taxman paid Alain a visit and presented him with an enormous bill for unpaid taxes on all the money he had made from the fake paintings he had sold over the years to various dealers. Alain promised to find the money but asked to be given some time to do so. Instead, he wasted no time in buying a 40 foot yacht and set off for the South Seas where I met him. After he finished his work in Atuona he disappeared without trace and the unforgiving French taxman is probably still looking for him.

A bumpy four-wheel drive took us to the opposite side of the island to the archaeological site at Puamau, whose centrepiece is an ancient stone tiki about three metres high and the largest of its kind in the Marquesas. Due to their isolation, the Marquesas, known by their original name as Te Henua Enata, meaning Land of Men, had developed a thriving civilisation whose death knell was sounded by the arrival of the first Europeans.

The first to call here was the Spanish navigator Alvaro de Mendaña, who arrived in 1595 and named the islands Las Islas de la Marquesa, after the Marchioness of Mendoza. Extensive ruins on each island are a sad reminder of the thriving community of at least 100,000 people that once lived here. Their massive fortification complexes proved to be of no avail against the invisible enemy in the shape of various diseases brought by those early visitors. Their tragic fate was later compounded by the forceful abduction of men to work on plantations, the infamously called blackbirding, which completed the decimation of the native population so that by the middle of the 19th century their number had been reduced to only six thousand. The Marquesans never managed to recover from those traumatic years and even today the total population of the islands is less that nine thousand.

After having spent several days in Atuona's rolly harbour we sailed across to the nearby island of Tauhata and anchored in Noe Noe Bay. The nearby golden beach looked very tempting but having made the same mistake ten years previously when the infamous Marquesan sandflies

Pointing for the island of Ua Pou's spectacular skyline

had almost eaten me alive, we preferred to enjoy the scenery from the safety of our cockpit. The last time I was anchored here was with Aventura II in the company of several yachts taking part in the first round the world rally. A local Marquesan and his son had come from the nearest village unable to understand what had brought about such a large invasion. Having explained what had brought us there, he kindly offered to go into the nearby hills to, as he put it in his simple English, 'kill some piggies with my doggies.' He did just that and the two of them returned with a piggie each on the shoulder, made a huge fire on the beach and treated us to the most delicious barbecue that I can ever remember... nor will I ever forget those nasty sandflies either, whose only role in life, I am told, is to take revenge on any outsider for the sufferings visited on the natives of these islands, who seem impervious to their attacks.

The spectacular scenery of the Marquesas with their craggy soaring peaks and lush vegetation make them among the most beautiful islands in the world. As we sailed out of Noe Noe Bay, the sharp peaks of Ua Pou pierced the sky to the south while Nuku Hiva's majestic silhouette beckoned from the north. While Hiva Oa thrives on its association with Paul Gauguin, the main island of Nuku Hiva's claim to fame is the setting of Herman Melville's Typee. Although most of the story is entirely fictional, Melville did call at the Marquesas on the whaler Acushnet in 1843, where he jumped ship with a friend. They spent some time among the people of Nuku Hiva, so his description of local people and places rings true. We decided to check this out at the village of Taipivae that inspired the title of the book. Hidden in the dense forest above the village is one of the best maraes (sacred sites) of the island. In the profound silence large stone tikis stood guard over ancient graves, the oppressive atmosphere and sultry heat almost bringing to life Melville's gruesome story.

We then drove across the island to its northern shore and halfway there stopped at two other ancient sites at Kamuihei and Hikohua. Just like on Easter Island, ceremonial demands and rivalry amongst chiefs had led to the construction of massive stone terraces, large temples and impressive statues. Close to a group of tikis, a huge mango tree had shed its golden fruit that was covering the ground in a thick fragrant layer. I could not resist the temptation to pick up a few as I find that fruit that I can gather myself always tastes better.

As I had not been able to treat Gwenda to her favourite lobster meal for a long time, at Hatiheu we stopped for lunch at a

A large Tiki stands guard over a sacred site on Nuku Hiva

small restaurant that we remembered from our previous visit. In spite of her French sounding name, the owner Yvonne was a larger than life Marquesan lady who insisted that she remembered us from before and produced a most delicious meal. Having enjoyed an excellent lunch in the open-sided restaurant set on the beach against a backdrop of lofty mountains, we both agreed that the Marquesas had once again lived up to our highest expectations.

Our last stop in the Marquesas was at Haka Hatau, a small village on the west coast of Ua Pou. Before leaving for the Tuamotus I had to go ashore to buy bread and some fruit. A large swell was breaking in a shower of spray on the small quay and the continuous surge made it difficult to land from the dinghy. Ashore, a burly Marquesan was watching my pitiful attempts to control the wild buckings of my inflatable. As I was trying to time myself to leap onto the slippery concrete steps, I felt myself grabbed under the arms and lifted onto the quay like a sack of potatoes. With a friendly smile, the man greeted me in broken English and I replied in French.

'No French,' he said, 'you must speak English to me,' and then explained that he had been sent by his teacher who had seen our English flag and wanted to invite me to their class. Nearby, in an open sided building, sat a dozen men, who were local fishermen but were learning English so as to be able to deal with the tourists who had started to arrive in increasing numbers on their island. The teacher prompted every pupil to introduce himself in English and I was then asked to describe my voyage, family and occupation. I tried to summarize the latter part of my life in a few simple words but I doubt that they understood much of it. After I had got my bread and fruit and was getting ready to board the dinghy they all came down to the quay to wave me goodbye. As I rowed back to the boat, it occurred to me that what really sets the Marquesas apart is not just the natural beauty of the islands, but also the unique beauty of their inhabitants, so magnificently portrayed in Gauguin's work.

Squally unsettled weather caused by a stationary front over the Tuamotus stayed with us for the four days that it took us to get there. After the near perfect voyage from Ecuador I felt really sorry for Gwenda who always seemed to get the worst deal. The last night we deliberately slowed down to avoid arriving too early at the island of Raroia. On my watch, I kept thinking back to the anxious moments I had passed in this same area twenty-five years earlier when we had sailed nonstop from the Gambiers to Tahiti. Our route took us right across the Tuamotus, a challenge that still fills me with satisfaction for having achieved it without any problems. With only my sextant for navigation and even that being restricted to day sights as cloudy skies made it impossible to take any star sights, we had to sail blindly throughout the hours of darkness. Knowing that the area was swept by strong currents, when I worked out my last position in late afternoon, I always allowed a margin of safety of 30 miles. Even so, I remember the absolute shock I felt one dawn when I looked ahead and saw in the grey light breakers at perhaps one mile distant. A strong current must have swept us sideways during the night and right ahead of us was this island that was supposed to be 30 miles off our course. How different things were now: I had GPS and radar, and could pinpoint my position any time I felt like it.

The serrated outline of Raroia's coconut trees were spiking the horizon as we closed with the island's northern shore at dawn. This was a highly symbolic landfall for me as it was on this atoll that the Kon Tiki raft finished its epic 101 days voyage from Peru in 1947. The Norwegian explorer Thor Heyerdahl had tried to show not only that such a voyage was possible in a balsa raft but also that it proved that people from South America had sailed a similar route to Polynesia in days gone by. A few years later Thor Heyerdahl's international bestseller, which described that great adventure, was also published in my native Romania, the book having somehow slipped past the Communist censors. I was around twelve and can still remember the excitement I felt reading that thrilling adventure and my amazement that free people could do what they liked and travel where they wanted. I have no doubt that it was that book that sowed in me the wanderlust that has never left me.

Throughout his life, Thor Heyerdahl had been involved in many similarly controversial projects, and attracted much criticism, such as this rather ungenerous quote from the author Paul Theroux: "Heyerdahl's single success was his proof, in Kon Tiki, that six middle-class Scandinavians could successfully crashland their craft on a coral atoll in the middle of nowhere." Even if the Norwegian explorer didn't prove that Easter Island had been colonized by people from South America, instead of Polynesians arriving from the west, Kon Tiki still stands out as one of the greatest adventure stories of all time.

Timing our arrival to coincide with good light was not enough in the Tuamotus as I soon found out when we came to the pass leading into the lagoon and were confronted by a strong contrary current. We eventually managed to get through but I knew I had to do better next time and pay closer attention to tides. Hardly had our anchor gone down in front of the one and only village than a small canoe left the broken down quay and headed for us. A young girl asked permission to come aboard then spread out a dozen black pearls on a towel eyeing Gwenda as a potential customer. The production of cultured black pearls is now a major industry in the Tuamotus with pearl farms in almost every lagoon. The prices must have gone up because we found them much too expensive, and declined to buy any. Later that day while walking ashore we met the girl again and when we still refused to make a deal, she picked one of the smaller pearls and gave it to me, probably thinking we were too poor to afford buying one.

An overnight passage took us to our next destination Makemo. The main village was located on the northern shore of a wide lagoon, the long fetch and the strong winds making the anchorage both uncomfortable and risky so I decided to look for better shelter at the western end of the atoll. As we sailed along the northern shore of Makemo I was puzzled that by our current GPS position we should have been level with the Tapuhiria Pass, on Makemo's west side. For a while I thought we had missed it and was even considering turning around, but when I checked with the radar I realized that something was amiss. What I saw on the radar screen did not in any way match my chart, which, for a change, was not my usual recycled lot, but a brand new corrected chart that I had recently acquired. At last the narrow break in the reef came into view and, as this time I had made sure that the tide was not against us, we got through without difficulty and anchored close to an abandoned copra shed. As we entered the pass I took down the GPS position so that I could compare it with my

chart. While the pass was located at 16°26.83'S, 143°57.99'W, on US DMA chart 83023, the coordinates of the pass were 16°21. 75'S, 143°58.60'W, a difference in latitude of close to five miles! Maybe changing the name from the Dangerous Archipelago to plain Tuamotus had been rather premature.

Our most memorable stay in the Tuamotus was at the uninhabited Tahanea atoll, now a nature reserve. One morning we saw a yellow catamaran approach our anchorage and I immediately recognized the bearded man at the helm, whom I had last met in Paris. In the 1960s Antoine was a major star on the French pop scene, and he still has lots of fans. He still gives the occasional performance but is now better known for the books and videos he produces while roaming the seas on his Banana Split. He persuaded us to up anchor and follow him to his favourite spot in the SE corner of the lagoon, which he had been visiting regularly since 1986. We did and spent a highly enjoyable time with Francette and Antoine, who regaled us with nonstop stories from his peripatetic life.

Also memorable, although for different reasons, are two incidents that also occurred at Tahanea. It was there that both Gwenda and I fell ill with ciguatera fish poisoning and, to cap it all, we had a most hairy exit as we were leaving the lagoon through the narrow pass. Both incidents were described in chapter 12.

Our next destination was Fakarava, some 40 miles from Tahanea. As by now I knew that passes into most lagoons can have very strong currents, it was essential to time both departures and arrivals carefully as the best – and often – only time to leave or enter a pass safely is just after slack low tide. With an optimum arrival time at Fakarava of 6 a.m., I decided to sail there overnight. Some Tuamotu bad spirit must have taken a dislike to me as we had such strong winds for the 40 mile passage that I had great trouble slowing Aventura down and instead of arriving there at dawn we had to heave to off the island at 2 a.m. As soon as it got light we went through the pass and dropped anchor close to a trimaran called Sloepmouche. The 46 foot Cross trimaran has been home for Jackie Lee and Luc Callebaut since 1995 when they left St Maarten in the Caribbean and headed west. Eleven years later, as I am writing these lines, they have reached Vanuatu. As Luc pointed out in one of his emails, their voyage around the world may never end, but if it eventually did it will join the competition for the slowest ever circumnavigation.

I had been in regular email contact with Luc soon after we launched our website and he generously offered to send us updates from the various places he visited. In the meantime Luc has become part of the noonsite team and our rendezvous in Fakarava was meant to finally bring us face to face. From the tone of his emails I was expecting to meet a jovial heavy-set Belgian but the guy who waved at us from the stern of his boat looked exactly the opposite, a sun tanned wiry fellow whose age was hard to guess. Jackie is originally from California and Luc from Belgium, and they met in 1984 while working as diving instructors in the Caribbean. Soon afterwards they acquired their first boat and have been cruising ever since, picking up jobs en route and enjoying life to the full. Luc's propensity at finding jobs is so impressive that I will return to it in the chapter that discusses ways of earning money while cruising.

As both Luc and Jackie are keen divers later that morning I joined them for a drift dive through the pass we had just negotiated. By now the tide was sweeping through at a good rate so it took me no time at all to fly over the amazing coral formations, a sensation that I had never experienced before and felt like watching an underwater film in fast motion. We then sailed in company across the well beaconed lagoon, past several pearl farms, to anchor close to an islet on the windward side of the lagoon. This proved to have been a very inspired move as during the night we had very strong winds with several violent squalls and would have been in real trouble if we hadn't left our previous exposed anchorage. By now I was starting to see why the Tuamotus may never become a popular cruising destination. As we already knew some of the western atolls, such as Rangiroa, from a previous visit, I suggested to Gwenda that we should sail straight to Tahiti. I could see from the relief showing on her face that she would have probably suggested this herself, but it was better if it came from me as it had been my idea all along to spend some time in the Tuamotus.

Under normal conditions the 250 miles to Tahiti should have taken us well under two days, but by the time we reached the open ocean the winter trade winds had piped up to their normal level and were blowing a steady 25 knots. With Aventura reefed right down we were still doing over six knots and it looked increasingly that rather than arrive in Tahiti at first light we would probably get there in the middle of the night. Of late, overnight passages and heaving to seemed to be the name of the game and this kind of cruising, if it can be called that, was certainly not to Gwenda's liking.

By 4 a.m. we had got as close to Tahiti's north coast as I dared go and we hove-to until it got light. The Bay of Matavai has a wide entrance between the reefs fronting Tahiti's northern shore and we passed through it soon after it got light. To our portside was the lighthouse on Point Venus, a name inspired by Captain James Cook's stay there in 1769 when he had come with a team of scientists to observe the rare phenomenon of the transit of the planet Venus across the face of the sun.

Colourful flower market in Papeete

We had hardly turned for the narrow beaconed channel that led to the Tahiti Yacht Club when a most violent squall accompanied by rain of deluge proportions overtook us from behind. Within seconds all visibility had gone and I slowed down the engine to a crawl as I had no idea where we were or where we were going. The rain was cascading so hard on the bimini that I feared it would be torn apart. The squall passed just as quickly as it had arrived and we made it into the small yacht club marina where Michel Alcon, the manager of the club, had been watching our ordeal and was waiting to take our lines.

Michel is one of the old friends that I have the good fortune of having all over the world. Many of them were made during my first voyage and I have kept in regular contact with all of them. Fortunately my work with the round the world rallies meant that I had to visit places like Tahiti about once every year or two, so these friendships hardly needed renewing. Often on my travels I feel like I am walking down the main street of that mythical global village and stop here and there to have a chat with an old friend. Having a drink on the airy yacht club terrace with Michel felt just like that.

Papeete's waterfront had greatly changed since my last visit and docking facilities for visiting yachts had been greatly improved. Papeete has one major advantage for yachts engaged in a long voyage as due to an active local yachting community its repair facilities are the best this side of New Zealand. There are a couple of well stocked chandleries and various specialist workshops. Provisioning is just as good, even if the prices are less so, as Tahiti is the most expensive place in the South Pacific. That didn't deter us from stocking up Aventura with all those French delicacies, including a good supply of wine that we knew would not be available in the places we were heading for.

Spending even a short time in Papeete was a great shock after weeks of cruising in the Tuamotus and Marquesas. The capital of French Polynesia is now a busy, noisy, polluted town, with fast traffic and impatient drivers. Gone forever is much of that unique charm that had seduced travellers in the past and had made countless dreamers abandon their home and family to run away to the South Seas. The natural beauty of the Society Islands, and that includes Tahiti's interior, still make them one of the most attractive places in the world, but whenever I return to Papeete I have a feeling that something has been lost. While the mistakes made by other Pacific nations can usually be blamed on the short-sighted attitude of local authorities, here the blame rests mostly with the French administration. The current problems are a direct result of the controversial period of nuclear tests

Craggy mountains overlook Cook's Bay on Moorea

when France had a large military presence and money was pouring into this French overseas territory. Job opportunities attracted thousands of people from the outer islands to Tahiti but when the tests were discontinued and the military presence scaled down, the demand for jobs dried up. Few people returned home but stayed on, so while Tahiti's population rose to almost quarter of a million, that of the entire Marquesan archipelago is still under ten thousand.

Although I do not agree with the current situation I cannot condemn the attitude of the French government as it treats people in the French overseas territories exactly as

it treats Frenchmen back home. All are French citizens with full rights and are entitled to all benefits just as people in mainland France. While I recognize the merits of such generosity and sense of equality, what I object to is the paternalistic overtone of such an attitude. By being spoon-fed by Paris these people will always have great difficulty to fend for themselves, and it makes me wonder if the shock therapy that was forced upon former British colonies may not turn out, in the long term, to have been a blessing in disguise. Although still muted, there are increasing calls among the people of French Polynesia for more autonomy from Paris, or eventually even independence, and the close French involvement may come to an end. If nothing else, one thing that should happen soon is to get rid of the colonial overtones of the territory's current name and change it to Tahiti Nui (Greater Tahiti) or some other acceptable name.

After the hubbub of Papeete, neighbouring Moorea, only nine miles away, is a world apart. Its natural beauty has been preserved almost intact and tourism development has not been allowed to develop unchecked. The picturesque anchorages on its north coast are still among the most beautiful on the world cruising circuit although there are now such serious concerns about the damage done to the coral and its fragile ecosystem that a law is being discussed that will prohibit cruising boats from using their own anchors. Special moorings will be provided in the most popular anchorages, which will not only protect the underwater scenery but also limit the number of visiting boats.

With Aventura safely anchored in Cook's Bay overlooked by the needle-sharp profile of Mount Mou'a Roa, one afternoon we climbed to the Belvedere, a high point that overlooks Moorea's spectacular north coast. We waited until the setting sun cast a veil of pinks and reds over the surrounding mountains, then started on the long walk down. As is usual in the tropics there was hardly any dusk and we had to make our return trip in almost complete darkness. On the way up we had stopped to say hello to Alex DuPrel, whom we had first met when Aventura I spent one month anchored in front of his welcoming Bora Bora Yacht Club. It hadn't been all that long that Alex had arrived there himself after singlehanding his 37 foot Lutetia from Hawaii. As he told me at the time, he had bought the derelict Hanna Carol ketch in 1966 but the forty year old boat was in such bad shape that, as a civil engineer, he decided to save it by covering the wooden hull in a solid skin of ferrocement. For a sociable person and born raconteur sitting idle on his boat wasn't his idea of spending the rest of his years, so he got hold of a piece of land by the lagoon and built the Bora Bora Yacht Club, which instantaneously became a popular meeting point for cruising sailors.

In those days Bora Bora was a sleepy place where nothing much ever happened, there were only a couple of small hotels and hardly any tourists at all. While we were there an Italian film crew were on the island filming a new version of the film Hurricane. One day Alex asked me bluntly 'how would you like to earn fifty dollars a day as an extra?' In those days we were living on fifty dollars a week! I accepted on the spot, and after getting rid of my bushy beard, for one week I was one of a number of US Navy sailors being filmed dancing with some beautiful Polynesian girls. Some work!

Soon after our departure Alex sold the yacht club, married a local girl and settled on her island of Moorea. He worked for a while for a local newspaper then decided to fill a gap by publishing his own magazine of news and comments on local affairs. Over the years the independent voice of Tahiti-Pacifique has made many friends and almost as many enemies, especially among government officials whose abuses and indiscretions Alex never fails to expose. He told me proudly that the government had taken him to court on more than a dozen occasions but he had won in every case. Besides his journalistic career he has published two slim volumes of short stories, which record and bemoan the disappearance of a unique Polynesian culture ground up in the maul of this materialistic world. His latest concern was focussing on environmental issues and he continues to be one of the most adamant critics of the government, his unforgiving stance going back to the almost forgotten period of French nuclear testing at Mururoa. Alex's comments on the fate of his adopted country filled me with deep sadness and I asked him if he felt that everything was lost.

'Not at all, but we are getting close to that stage. That is why I keep banging my drum, to force people to wake up and do something before it is too late.'

'And will they?'

'If you live among Polynesians you never give up hope. It is simply not in their nature.'

After my concerns over Tahiti, Alex's final comment gave me some hope, which was confirmed at our next island stop: Huahine. Once again, because of the distance involved, I decided on an overnight hop and at long last the weather

Sacred marae on the island of Raiatea, formerly known as Havaiki

cooperated and we had a perfect sail. One of the least populated of the Society Islands, Huahine was exactly as we remembered it from our first visit. Tourism development had not been allowed to destroy the island's fragile fabric, life continued to move at a tranquil pace and cruising sailors were welcome. Huahine has some of the best preserved remains in the Society Islands, although the most important marae in all of Polynesia was on neighbouring Raiatea, our next stop.

Raiatea is the site of ancient Havaiki, the symbolic centre of the Polynesian triangle whose far-flung corners stretched to Hawaii, Rapa Nui (Easter Island) and Aotearoa, the Land of the Long White Cloud (New Zealand). On her previous passage through the Pacific Aventura had touched two of that triangle's points by sailing from Easter Island to Raiatea and on to Hawaii. This time we were on our way to New Zealand, following in the wake of the intrepid Maoris whose large double-hulled canoes had left from this same spot one thousand years earlier. Standing on the sacred soil of Havaiki one cannot feel

but the deepest admiration for those Polynesian navigators who not only managed to sail their fragile craft way beyond the limits of their known world, but then sailed back and forth between their new home in New Zealand and their ancestral home.

Raiatea shares the same lagoon with her smaller sister island Tahaa and as there is deep water all around the island we made a complete circuit of Tahaa, just as we had done on our first Aventura. At first sight any changes that might have occurred in the intervening years were hardly noticeable but soon we saw one restaurant with its own dock in a bay we were passing, then another one and soon realized that even the smallest bay now sported its own restaurant and private dock, often a large banner welcoming sailors for a drink and meal. Because of its ideal setting Raiatea is now one of the major charter destinations in the Pacific, its main attractions being the sheltered waters of its lagoon and central location at the heart of the Society Islands with Bora Bora only a short sail away. To cater for the large number of charter crews every land owner on Tahaa seemed to have climbed on the bandwagon. We realized how bad the situation must have become when we stopped at a tiny island where years ago I had taken photographs of Gwenda walking on the pristine beach to show the beauty of Pacific cruising. As we got closer in the dinghy we saw a large notice in French and English nailed to a palm tree: Private Island Keep Out. A Polynesian family were having a picnic by the beach, so I ignored the sign, walked up to them and asked in French if they would allow us to walk around their little island.

'Of course, just go ahead. And would you like to join us for a drink?'

So things may not have all changed for the worst and from this brief encounter, and other similar incidents involving local people, such as the girl with the black pearl on Raroia or the fishermen on Ua Pou, I felt that in French Polynesia as everywhere else what meets the eye may not necessarily be a reflection of the true situation.

I wish I could have felt the same at Bora Bora, our last stop in French Polynesia. James Michener once described Bora Bora as the most beautiful island in the world and for many years I agreed with Michener's comment and considered Bora Bora one of my favourite cruising destinations and certainly the best in French Polynesia. Tied to one of the moorings installed by the new owners of the Bora Bora Yacht Club, we watched the ever-changing scene around us. There was certainly a lot more movement than we ever remembered with fast launches coming and going from the airport located on one of the outer islands, excursion boats taking tourists on sightseeing tours of the lagoon, and dive boats heading for a session of shark feeding or swimming with manta rays. While we were in Tahiti I had read in a local newspaper that Bora Bora's picturesque lagoon had suffered recently a drastic reduction in its live coral and fish population, which may have been caused by an unprecedented rise in water temperature. The local authorities thought otherwise and tried to put the blame on visiting yachts, and were planning to impose the same restrictions as those envisaged on Moorea. I felt that using cruising boats as a convenient scapegoat was rather hypocritical when tourist development had been allowed to mushroom unchecked with more resorts being built even on the small islets straddling Bora Bora's fringing reef. I couldn't help wondering what happened to the waste from all those hotels that was being discharged untreated into the lagoon and surrounding sea. As this question kept revolving in my mind, a large cruise ship dropped its anchor right behind us, its huge anchor probably doing in one go more damage to the coral than all the cruising boats that passed through Bora Bora in one year.

We both felt that it was high time to go and explore some of the South Pacific's less frequented areas. As we headed out through the pass and felt the gentle embrace of the ocean I realized that for the first time I could ever remember I was leaving a place without planning to return. Every time I had come back to Bora Bora in recent years I found that things had gone from bad to worse. Slowly my beautiful memories of our first visit were being erased by the sad images of the current decay. An inveterate traveller once said that one should never return to a place you had enjoyed as your first impressions can never be matched by what you may find on subsequent visits. In the case of Bora Bora that comment could not have been more true.

Offshore Routines

Electricity is the heart of your boat;
it keeps everything ticking.

Bill Butler

The findings of my surveys as well as observations made on other boats influenced me very much when I came to decide on the charging system for Aventura III. I had seen so many botched electrical systems on other boats that this is yet another area in which my advice is to leave such important decisions to the experts. Fortunately my friend Wilhelm Greiff who, with his wife Astrid sailed their 39 foot Octopus in the first round the world rally, insisted on taking charge of Aventura III's electrical system. Wilhelm is a qualified electrical engineer with an unusual, highly pragmatic approach to this tricky subject. He has a number of inventions to his name, including the Greiff intelligent regulator. In my view, his most ingenious invention to date is a multiple switch to be mounted at the wheel, that controls all lights: navigation, decks, masthead, anchor, etc. For Aventura Wilhelm devised an efficient charging system that has worked well and to which, over the years, I have made a number of additions.

Generating electricity

As I wanted to avoid having a separate diesel generator I had to make sure that I had an adequate enough system to satisfy my needs. I planned to use the engine as the main source of charging the batteries but backed up by some alternative sources: wind generator, solar panel, towing generator.

Aventura's engine is fitted with two alternators, a standard 55 AH alternator and a 120 AH model that needed to be fitted with a double pulley and two belts. The 120 AH alternator charges the house batteries whereas the standard 55 AH alternator charges the engine starting battery which also supplies power to the anchor winch as it is normally only used when the engine is running. As a useful backup either alternator can charge both banks on its own and a switch allows the house batteries to be used to start the engine. However, I do make sure that the banks are always kept separate and, in fact, I never have had to use both banks to start the engine as the engine battery is more than adequate for the limited use it gets.

An 80-watt rigid solar panel is mounted on the coachroof and provides around 5 AH on sunny days. A Rutland 930 wind generator puts in an additional 1 to 4 AH depending on the strength of wind. On all long passages I tow an Aquair water generator that is highly efficient as it provides enough power (approximately 1 AH per knot of speed) to run the autopilot and fridge. There are two disadvantages to the towing generator, one that I cannot troll a fishing line and tow the turbine at the same time, so if I want to fish, I have to haul in the turbine and its 100 foot line. This is not an easy operation if the speed of the boat is over 3 knots, and at 6 knots virtually impossible. Slowing down Aventura once she gets going, even if I am prepared to drop the sails, which I would never do, is a waste of time, so it's either no fish for dinner or, on passages where I expect to have to do some motoring at some point, as in the Mediterranean, I do not use the towing generator and as soon as we are out of port the fishing line is let out instead.

The other, more costly, disadvantage of a water generator is losing the turbine altogether and there are a couple of reasons for this: chafe or a hungry shark. The spinning whirring turbine must look and sound to a shortsighted shark like some tasty prey. In the tropics I have lost on average two turbines per year. It usually happened at night when the problem was probably compounded by the fact that the spinning turbine created so much luminescence that it was reflected on the sails. The first indication that something was amiss was the generator suddenly going silent and when I checked it I found the sacrificial connection had sheared. This plastic link between the towing line and the generator shaft is meant to break at higher loads to avoid the entire generator being wrenched off its mountings. Losing a line and turbine worth $200 is far better than a whole generator costing over $1000.

To prevent chafe I regularly check the knot at the generator end and also make sure that the line runs out without any obstructions. To prevent chafe at the turbine end I pulled a two metre length of clear plastic hose over the end of the line that connects to the turbine. In the past I found that at speeds over 7 knots, especially with high following seas, the turbine tends to leap out of the water and double up on itself, and I am sure that this is how I lost a turbine on at least a couple of occasions, but not since that simple improvement. The manufacturers recommend using a turbine with a coarser pitch for higher speeds, but swapping the turbines is probably such a hassle that I decided to continue with the standard type... and make sure that every time I fly back to the boat after a long absence I take along a couple of extra turbines. Having used the towing

generator extensively over these last five years I have the highest praise for it and, as the saying goes, would never leave home without it.

Gradually I have come to the conclusion that, depending on one's cruising area, there may not be any real need for an additional diesel generator. Personally I found that even when not going far but just moving from one anchorage to

A hydrogenerator can keep the batteries topped up on long passages

another the engine is used enough to keep the batteries charged up. With so many charging options on the current Aventura I felt there was no need for a separate diesel genset.

Two other improvements that I made while in New Zealand was to acquire a better 30 AH battery charger for the times when I am in a marina, and to upgrade the inverter to 1500 watt as the previous 1000 watt model was not able to cope with some of my electrical appliances. Whereas the previous system had a combined charger/inverter unit, the current inverter is a stand-alone model, which I installed myself. I realized that by wiring the inverter into the boat's mains power network I ran the risk of forgetting to switch off the inverter when I plugged into shore power, so I bought a large mains switch, which has three positions: 0 – all power off, 1 – inverter on, and 2 – shore power on. Simple and foolproof.

My generating system has worked satisfactorily during my long voyage and coped well with my energy requirements. The addition of a higher capacity alternator in New Zealand was a useful improvement and made it possible to bring the batteries to a full charge in a shorter time than before. The solar panel and towing generator provided a useful boost on long passages but, under those conditions, the wind generator was a disappointment. In nine years I had to replace the batteries once every three years, which is far from perfect but is probably the price I paid for leaving the boat unattended for several long periods when the batteries could not be charged under optimum conditions and had suffered as a result. I am now convinced that for my kind of sailing the system was perfectly adequate and should I ever have to make such a voyage again I would probably choose a similar system.

The surveys

The modern yacht is usually very power hungry, so wind or solar generation may not be sufficient.

John Ellis

Energy consumption has been one of the subjects that has interested me ever since my earliest surveys when I interviewed hundreds of cruising sailors on a wide range of subjects, including electricity consumption and generation. One of the main conclusions was that perhaps as many as 90% of owners, myself included, underestimate their

consumption, or overestimate their charging capability, which is saying more or less the same thing. This is the main reason why I had a larger alternator fitted in New Zealand and also replaced my flexible solar panels with a more efficient rigid one.

One of the main conclusions of the earlier surveys was that the consumption of electricity caused many skippers serious concern and often the only solution they could think of was to turn the power hungry item off. Automatic pilots are one of the pieces of equipment that can raise the consumption of electricity dramatically and several skippers were annoyed that their autopilots consumed more than they had been led to believe. This may be explained by the fact that the pilots have to work much harder to keep a yacht on course in the vigorous downwind sailing of an ocean passage, when compared to the smaller swell met with during coastal cruising. As a result, a high proportion of cruising boats are now equipped with diesel generators independent of the main engine. The increasing need for an additional source of electricity generation is virtually unavoidable on most cruising boats bearing in mind the many accessories that most sailors now regard as essential: autopilots, watermakers, freezers as well as certain items that normally run off mains power such as television sets, DVD players, washing machines, dishwashers, microwave ovens, breadmakers, etc.

One observation from my latest survey was the steep increase in energy consumption compared to earlier surveys. As electricity consumption is a cause of so much concern among those planning an ocean voyage, I asked each skipper for suggestions based on his personal experience. While the majority seemed resigned to the fact that their personal comfort could only be maintained at the price of high energy consumption, and that adequate preparations needed to be made to meet this task, a few skippers stressed that rather than be obsessed with the need to produce more electricity, one should rather try to consume less. It was these skippers who pointed out that it was a mistake to rely solely on an automatic pilot and stressed the advantage of a wind operated selfsteering gear on long passages. It is almost needless to say that the first category usually included the larger boats with more powerful engines and separate diesel generators, while the latter category were the owners of the

Two alternators will provide a more efficient charging system

smaller boats almost all of which sported wind generators and solar panels.

The skippers were asked to comment on the generating system they would have on their ideal yacht. With only two exceptions, all skippers agreed that some kind of additional source of electricity generation was not only desirable but essential. It was pointed out that before taking any decision, the first requirement is to make a realistic assessment of one's projected daily needs and then double that figure for good measure. The battery capacity should be at

least twice that amount, and the batteries should be in separate banks – one for general consumption and one dedicated to engine starting. The two banks should be separated by a switch. Consumption and battery capacity should dictate the size of the alternator, as usually the standard alternator provided with the engine is not powerful enough.

Average electricity consumption

All theory seems to go out the window when you are cruising and running all your equipment 24 hours a day. You find you use much more power than you had planned on using. My advice is to install the most battery power you can handle and a very large alternator.

Carlton DeHart

Good advice from Carlton who pointed out that, 'we had 1000 Amps of 24 Volt battery capacity charged by a 120 AH alternator. The autopilot, radar and inverter ran continuously as well as all instruments.' Certainly not on Bill Butler's boat who stated, 'I use the selfsteering gear most of the time, with the autopilot only used when we are under power. To conserve electricity, even the GPS only gets turned on briefly two or three times a day.' Two very contrasting approaches to be sure.

The average consumption derived from the Millennium Odyssey survey was between 150 and 240 Amps per 24 hours, although there were a few yachts that consumed less, and quite a number who consumed a lot more. The average consumption was almost identical to the findings of my previous survey on the same subject but I must stress that in both cases there were such huge differences between the various surveyed boats that an average consumption was irrelevant. This is very close to my own consumption, so maybe those average values should not be dismissed so easily as they could provide a useful yardstick.

Aventura's daily consumption when I am not using any alternative sources of energy is between 150 and 240 Amps. This total is greatly reduced when I am in my environmentally conscious mood, which occurs more and more frequently these days. On Aventura, when I use both the wind and towing generator the consumption on passage is quite small, as I noticed that at speeds over 5 knots the towing generator produces enough electricity to keep both the fridge and autopilot going. With the autopilot running, and without help from the towing generator, the 24 hour consumption goes up to about 160 AH, so I need to run the engine once a day to keep the batteries happy.

The average battery capacity among the boats taking part in the survey was 550 Amps. This is more than my own capacity as I have four house batteries with a total capacity of 360 Amps, as well as a 90 Amps engine starting battery. On Aventura, the state of the batteries is constantly monitored by a counter that shows the amount being consumed at the moment as well as the total amount left in the batteries both in Amps and as a percentage of their total capacity. The monitor can be programmed to sound a warning if either the voltage or the amount left has dropped below a certain level but as the monitor is mounted in a prominent position where it cannot be ignored I always know exactly what is going on and, usually, when it shows that the batteries are below 70% of their capacity, I start the engine.

Charging systems

Except for diesel generators, all other sources do not provide enough power to run a yacht full of equipment on a full time basis.

Carlton DeHart

Some kind of auxiliary charging system is almost indispensable on boats with heavy demands and a separate diesel generator is probably the best answer on boats with a consumption of over 200 Amps per day. This was certainly the case in the latest ARC in which all boats over 50 feet had a separate diesel generator and even some of the smaller boats had such a generator. A number of the smaller boats had other means of generating electricity although in all those cases the main engine was the prime source of charging the batteries.

Some skippers regarded a separate diesel generator as an alternative source of energy as they believed that should the main engine fail they would have their genset to keep them out of trouble. True and false, and I am sure that the term alternative energy was not coined with this situation in mind. While I have no doubt that in many cases a separate genset is indeed justified, I still feel that any boat, not just those fitted out for long term cruising, should also have some proper alternative source of energy, be it solar panels, wind or towing generator. Those who want to play it really safe may also consider getting a portable petrol/gasoline generator that can also be useful for power tools.

Most long distance cruising boats have some alternative source of energy and as Luc Callebaut pointed out, 'You need alternative energy sources even if just for backup.' On boats with a modest consumption, water generators appear to provide the better solution on passage

294

and wind generators in port. Provided one has sufficient deck space, solar panels might be able to cover most needs, although the demands on boats that have room to accommodate them usually surpass the modest output of the panels. On some boats that do not have sufficient space for the solar panels to be mounted permanently on deck, the panels are displayed temporarily when at anchor or in port. Solar panels are also useful on boats that are left unattended as they continue to trickle charge the batteries thus keeping them in optimum condition.

When investigating the reasons why some ARC boats ran their batteries flat during the Atlantic crossing, I found that usually the skipper was not aware of how much higher than expected the electricity consumption was and only found this out when it was too late. Such yachts rarely had an alternative way for charging their batteries, so they either had to carry on blindly (no GPS or instruments either) or ask help from another yacht. Sometimes a kind hearted skipper lent them a portable generator, not an easy operation in mid-ocean.

Water and watermakers

My water consumption dropped to less than half once I turned off the electric pump and the crew had to use the foot pump instead.

Volker Reinke

Watermakers are one improvement that has greatly enhanced the quality of cruising life. Gone are the days when I used to row

Taking a saltwater shower will help conserve fresh water

ashore with empty jerrycans begging someone to let me take some water, then lug it all into the dinghy and get it back to the boat. When spending a long time in remote anchorages we could never have a fresh water shower and most of the time water was only for drinking and cooking. On my latest voyage I don't remember filling my tanks with shore water on more than three or four occasions, and then only when we were leaving a marina and my crew were using water faster than the watermaker could make it. Not only did I enjoy this great luxury but could also let others share in it. The first time it happened was in San Blas where we met a Kuna family living on a tiny offshore island and the man had to paddle in his canoe twenty miles to the mainland to get water. I made enough water to fill several jerrycans and when I took them ashore they were so impressed that the women started crying led by the young mother of a few weeks old baby who obviously found it very hard to cope with the shortage of water. Later in the Pacific I did the same on a couple of occasions, regretting that I didn't have a watermaker with a larger output.

Being able to have a shower is one thing and, in fact, the consumption is quite modest, but in the Millennium Odyssey there were two yachts whose crew were using more water than the average hotel. On one, the owner's wife insisted on

Laundry day with the help of a rainwater tank on Direction Island

changing all bed linen and towels every day, just as she used to do at home. On that same yacht the toilets were flushed with fresh water! On another yacht, the skipper used to make 400 gallons every laundry day so his wife could do several washing loads, as on that boat clothing and linen were also changed with great frequency. Carlton DeHart made this very clear when he said, 'A large capacity watermaker is an absolute must as the quality of life aboard is directly proportional to the amount of water available.'

My own HRO watermaker is an older 12V model that produces about 20 litres per hour. It has worked well for the last nine years and its only fault is that it takes ages to go through the recommended procedure when shutting it down for more than two weeks, which, with my style of cruising, I often have to do. Current models are much more user friendly, with most functions computerized, and they are also much more efficient, producing larger quantities of water with lower energy consumption. Some of my 200 gallon a day friends cannot comprehend how I manage with one tenth of their output but I point out that 20 litres is a lot more than zero.

Among the things that I have learnt from my early days of cruising is to be economical with water, so even with a watermaker I still frown when my crew spend too long under the shower as if they were back home. It took all my willpower to control my tongue when my good friend JuanFra forgot the deck shower on and managed to completely empty one tank. Fortunately we were not in the middle of the ocean at the time and, equally fortunately, the two water tanks were separated by a valve, which had to be switched over manually so they could not be used together.

When I was fitting out the current Aventura I was sent by a manufacturer a prototype water monitor to test. It had a lot of useful functions showing the amount of water available, average daily consumption, etc. It could also be programmed to switch off the pump if consumption exceeded a certain rate or if the amount of water left had reached a critical level. It sounded almost too good to be true, and it was, because it never worked. But its menacing presence is

Loading additional water for a long passage

I feel that my own system as just described is adequate enough. What I'd like to add is that some current production boats do not have sufficiently large tanks for long ocean passages. Some people have overcome this problem by having additional tanks built in. In the ARC and round the world rallies we advised skippers of such boats to take on additional water in jerrycans for the longer passage, or just buy a number of gallon containers of water as sold in supermarkets.

still there, so, when I have crew who leave the tap running while brushing their teeth or shaving, and I hear the pump running, when they finish I tell them that the water alarm had sounded to warn us of excessive consumption. It has never failed and no one ever asked me to show them how that silent censor actually worked.

Even with a watermaker one should always leave on a long passage with full tanks. Also, as an added precaution, there should always be at least one jerrycan in the cockpit or close at hand on deck to be used either if the water in the tanks gets spoilt for any reason or one has to abandon ship. In the latter case I have a hand operated watermaker which could also be used to make water if all systems on board fail... and I do make sure to point out to the most profligate water consumer that if we run out of water he won't be too happy to pump for one hour to produce one litre of water. The message always gets through!

Whereas in the case of electricity consumption and generation I found it useful to refer to my earlier surveys as they contained much useful information on that subject, when it comes to water

Tips

- Make a realistic assessment of the estimated daily needs of electricity and then double that figure. The latter figure should dictate both the choice of an adequate charging system and battery capacity.
- Have an alternative means of charging the batteries should the main system fail.
- Water tanks should be separated by a valve so they cannot be emptied at the same time.
- On long ocean passages even if you have a watermaker always leave with full tanks and take some additional water in jerrycans.
- Always monitor the energy consumption carefully and have a charging routine on long passages.

Between Coconut Crabs and Humpback Whales

Every voyage starts as a dream, and dreams are often inspired by a book. When I first read Tom Neale's "An Island to Oneself" I could only dream that one day I would step ashore at Suwarrow, an uninhabited atoll halfway between Tahiti and Samoa. Lying off the traditional route, a visit to Suwarrow entails a long detour, and so on both my previous trips through the area I missed the chance to stop there. This time, however, I was determined to follow up a thirty year old dream, and so on leaving Bora Bora I laid a course for distant Suwarrow, 680 miles away in the Northern Cooks.

After several weeks of easy sailing among the Society Islands I was looking forward to a longer offshore passage and had promised Gwenda some nice trade winds... but once again I was wrong. Two days out of Bora Bora the western horizon turned into a menacing dark mass and I knew that we were in for a hiding. The area between French Polynesia and Tonga is known for its unsettled weather and in my previous passages through this area I had experienced some of the worst conditions I had met anywhere in the Pacific. The culprit is the South Pacific Convergence Zone, a relatively recently identified meteorological phenomenon that affects weather conditions in a vast swathe that stretches all the way from the Solomons to Tahiti. Its position and movement are updated daily by the Fiji meteorological office and broadcast both on Inmarsat C and HF radio.

As the system got closer we were swept by a series of violent squalls accompanied by black clouds shaped like gigantic anvils that were rent apart by forked tongues of lightning straight out of the Apocalypse. Reefed right down, we managed to avoid

Yachts off Anchorage Island in Suwarrow Lagoon

the worst by slaloming between those monsters, then the wind dropped, there was an eerie lull before the heavens opened with a deluge of solid water that could hardly be described as rain. By the following morning it was all over, the sun came out, the sea turned blue, flying fish were once again streaking over the wave tops and Aventura was dancing merrily towards our destination with a light wind humming sweetly in the rigging.

A week in Suwarrow

On the morning of day five a smudge on the horizon slowly coalesced into a bristling line of palm trees, then into a small island, then into a whole string of them: Suwarrow! We sailed through the pass into the sparkling lagoon, passed Anchorage Island and dropped anchor among nine other boats sheltering in this idyllic spot. Suwarrow is a typical Pacific atoll and was named by the Russian explorer who first set eyes on it after the Russian military hero General Alexander Suvorov. The spelling has undergone several versions and seems to have settled on the present Suwarrow.

The seven or eight mile wide lagoon is surrounded by a reef studded with a dozen small islands. Tom Neale had made his home on Anchorage Island, where he lived a truly Robinson Crusoe existence, fishing in the abundant lagoon, growing vegetables, and breeding chickens, some of whose descendants still roam his island. After Tom's death in 1977, Suwarrow was left to its own devices. It was occasionally visited by itinerant fishermen or a fisheries patrol boat but the only people who spent any time there were cruising sailors. In recent years, the Cook Islands government declared Suwarrow a nature reserve and a caretaker is posted there during the cruising season from May until October, but cruising boats continue to be welcomed without any restrictions. The sailors have maintained Tom's original house and have cleaned up the area around it. The special affection in which Suwarrow is held by sailors is shown by the various plaques that have been left there over the years. Some thoughtful soul had nailed a sign to a coconut tree: "Take but nothing leave but footprints", while perhaps the most famous of all Pacific wanderers, Frenchman Bernard Moitessier, who was a frequent visitor,

left his own memento made from a slab of coral that reads: "Tom Neale lived his dream on this island 1952-1977".

Next to Tom's original wooden house the Cooks government erected a solid hurricane shelter known as the yacht club and decorated with flags from visiting yachts. It was also the home of the caretakers Ioane Kaitara, or Papa John, as he was affectionately called by everyone, and his assistant Mareko Leikal, nicknamed Baker. They made us feel really welcome and asked us to sign the visitors' book, in which I counted an average fifty boats per year. We then paid the mandatory $50 that covered our entire stay – however long we wanted it to be. Never have formalities been simpler! Both caretakers were in their seventies and quite obviously enjoyed the presence of all those sailors, some of whom lingered on for several weeks. There was a truly international feeling among the boats surrounding us with every boat flying the flag of a different nation: USA, Australia, Israel, Spain, Italy, Finland, South Africa and Germany.

Anchored further out was a steel catamaran that looked like a small cargo vessel and flew the flag of the Cook Islands. The skipper told me that it had been chartered by the Cook Islands Environmental Association, some of whose members had come to Suwarrow to lay rat poison against these vermin who were decimating the bird nesting colonies. They were also assessing the possibility of having the atoll declared a fully fledged national park. To our great surprise we found out that one of the passengers was Tom Neale's daughter Stella. She hadn't been back to Suwarrow since her childhood and revisiting her father's island was a very moving experience. We talked much about her father, whom Stella described as a complex person who relished solitude to the point of neglecting his family, his absence clearly having affected her as a young girl.

Meanwhile we enjoyed this truly relaxing spot to the full. The presence of the caretakers did not seem to deter sailors from treating Anchorage Island as their own and much had been done by previous visitors to provide some simple comforts. Hammocks were slung between trees, lounge chairs had been knocked together from driftwood for comfortable reading, a barbecue had been made from an old 55 gallon drum and a pit dug for burning garbage, while a large tank next to Tom's old house held enough rain water for everyone to do their laundry. Every second night Papa John and Baker invited everyone in the anchorage to a potluck dinner. One or two large fish caught in the pass by Papa John with a traditional mother-of-pearl lure were cooked in an earth oven. Beautifully displayed on a tray plaited from coconut fronds the fish were accompanied by breadfruit fritters or tasty pancakes made from germinating coconut. The sailors' contributions were salads and highly appreciated cold beers. While Papa John strummed on his ukulele under the flickering light provided by a small generator the party stretched far into the balmy night.

One day the indefatigable Papa John invited all sailors to join him on a day's outing. Two yachts, one of them Aventura, took the party across the lagoon for a first stop at an island used for breeding by a large colony of sooty terns. As we stepped ashore, thousands of birds took squealing to the sky abandoning their nests and eggs visibly disturbed by the unexpected invasion. We repaired to a nearby island whose main attraction was hidden under our feet rather than dive-bombing us from above. Papa John had tempted us with the

foremost culinary delicacy of the Pacific: coconut crab, of which he assured us there were thousands on this island. Followed silently by a rather sceptical group of sailors he kept poking under trees and looking into cracks in the ground, but without any success. Having built up the suspense to the highest degree of anticipation, and probably realizing that we might soon lose interest, he suddenly poked his pointed stick between the roots of a tree and told us that he could feel a large crab hiding in its burrow. He started digging with both hands, throwing loose earth in all directions, then, with a deft movement, he pulled up a wriggling shape from the hole and held up a large crab for all to see. More victims followed and when it looked like there were enough to feed us all, we returned to the spot where we had left Baker. While we had been away, he had built a large fire from old coconut husks, and had also opened several green coconuts, some to drink their refreshing juice, while others had been split open for their tasty flesh. While the crabs were being roasted on the open fire and Baker was opening more nuts, Papa John was plaiting trays from palm fronds on which the cooked crabs were then served. I doubt that I had ever tasted anything more delicious or enjoyed a meal more than this kingly feast. As we sat on the ground, eating with our fingers and quenching our thirst with green nuts, I willed myself to grasp that moment and freeze it in my memory. It was, in every respect, a dream that had come true.

The pass into Suwarrow lagoon is reputed to be one of the best diving spots in the South Pacific, so one day I went to check it out for myself. The underwater scenery was indeed magnificent and teeming with fish, some quite large, but there were also many sharks. They did not take much notice of me so I spent a long time watching the activity below me through the crystal clear water. In spite of the horror stories one hears from time to time, shark attacks are quite rare and I do not know of any fatal incident involving a cruising sailor. Nevertheless, basic precautions are imperative, and while in Suwarrow we heard on the radio that a person had been attacked by a shark in Moorea. Apparently he was spearfishing on the reef, and this is indeed one of the situations when attacks are most likely as sharks are attracted by blood from an injured fish. The best tactic is to avoid spearfishing in areas where there are sharks, or to land the fish in the dinghy as soon as it had been speared, which is what I normally do. Sharks very rarely attack directly, and this is why the best protection is always to swim with a mask to be able to see what is happening around you. If a shark shows any interest and continues to stay close, it is time to beat a retreat while watching the shark all the time. Over the years I have swum and dived close to sharks on innumerable occasions and regard them as one of the most beautiful creatures of the seas, so perfectly adapted to their environment that they have remained unchanged for millions of years.

Having seen the large numbers of tasty fish swimming idly in the pass, on the morning we left Suwarrow I made sure that the fishing line was run out as we sailed through the pass. Within minutes the telltale shriek of the line running out fast heralded a strike. As I was reeling it in I could see a lot of commotion behind us and I guessed that our lunch might be feeding other hungry mouths. By the time I had reeled in the line all there was left on the hook was the sorry head of the fish, while the rest had been surgically removed by those beautiful creatures of the deep. Sharks 1 – Aventura 0.

Passage to Niue

There is only about 500 miles between Suwarrow and Niue, our next destination, so we expected to take less than four days to get there. "Only 500 miles" is the kind of distance one has to sail from one island to the next in the Pacific, and is something that those used to cruising in the Caribbean or Mediterranean find difficult to imagine. At least the weather on this leg was reasonably good and for the first two days we had light but steady winds. The large tri-radial spinnaker stayed up while the autopilot did all the work, Gwenda baked bread and I managed to catch a large mahimahi, that tastiest of pelagic tropical fish confusingly called dolphin-fish although it has nothing to do with dolphins. The beautiful creatures of the deep kept their distance this time, but then that party pooper, the South Pacific Convergence Zone, had another go at our marital harmony. A front detached itself from the SPCZ and made the wind back from ENE to WNW. As the front passed we were hit by several squalls in which the wind changed direction rapidly. Such wind shifts are hardly a problem at sea but can have serious consequences at anchor. Friends who were still at Suwarrow told us on the radio that, as that same front passed over them, the boats had to leave the anchorage to find shelter elsewhere in the lagoon, while in the Ha'apai group of Tonga a New Zealand boat was lost when caught on a lee shore by the unexpected wind shift.

By the following morning the winds had gone into the SE and we could see our destination in the distance. Niue is a very strange island indeed, a massive slab of coral that had been pushed up by tectonic activity. Surrounded by sixty foot high cliffs, it has no natural harbours and the only shelter from the prevailing winds is an indentation on the west coast where a number of moorings had been laid for the use of visiting yachts. In settled conditions this is a safe spot to leave the boat while visiting the island, although the ocean swell

A hidden oasis on Niue's rocky coast

is forever present and the constant surge makes landing a very exciting affair. Very thoughtfully, the Niueans had provided a crane for hoisting tenders onto the quay but perfect coordination is needed to hook up the tender to the waiting strop while landing on the slippery steps. Knowing what to expect, I had inflated the smaller of our dinghies so Gwenda and I had no problem dragging it behind us as we climbed the slippery steps. Having been contacted by radio, the various officials were waiting when we landed ashore and entry formalities took only minutes to complete.

Caves and chasms

As a dependency of New Zealand, Niue has a special status. Its citizens have the right to work and settle in New Zealand and as a result there has been a steady drain with more Niueans now living abroad than on the island. Although some 1400 people still live on Niue, the island had a deserted look about it, and when we rented a car and left the main settlement of Alofi we felt that we had the island almost to ourselves. Because of its unusual geological formation, Niue is riddled with underground tunnels and caves, while on the east coast, which is constantly battered by huge Pacific rollers, a number of deep chasms had been carved out of the massive coral cliffs. When we reached the bottom of one such chasm we were surprised to find a cool oasis of tall palms growing by the side of a limpid stream.

We stopped for lunch at the Washaway café, whose young owner Willie explained that he had given it this name after he had been repeatedly told that he had chosen the wrong spot and his café would end up being washed away by the waves, which obviously had not yet happened. As we were the only customers, Willie was happy to talk. He had worked for several years in New Zealand but had returned home as he felt that Niue was still the best place to live. He complained that too many Niueans were dependant on state handouts and had lost the ability to look after themselves. He felt strongly that Niue had always been self-sufficient and there was no reason why it should not be so now.

At least the Niueans who chose to stay on the island knew what was best for them, and this was what I was told when we stopped in a small village on the north coast. What had caught my eye were several dugout canoes that were been built by the side of the road. We were shown around by Taumafai Fuhiniu, who told us that he had been concerned at seeing the old skills being lost as everyone was using aluminium runabouts powered by large outboards, so he decided to teach young men how to build their own paddling outriggers or sailing canoes. Taumafai's workshop was very successful and several canoes that had been adzed out of tree trunks were nearing completion.

As the supermarket in Alofi only stocked chilled and frozen produce flown in from New Zealand we tried our luck at the nearby market but the selection of fresh vegetables was quite disappointing. A friend on another boat told me that we might have better luck at the prison, which apparently had its own vegetable garden. It sounded a bit far-fetched to me, but as we still had the rented car, I drove up to the prison. A man in blue overalls was working in a well-tended garden with rows of tasty looking vegetables. He told me that his name was Cosini and as he seemed eager to talk, I asked him how he had ended up there. Apparently there had been a family argument during which he had threatened his mother-in-law with a gun, without realizing it was loaded. The gun went off and she got killed. As even in Niue killing your mother-in-law is a crime, even if it happened by accident, he was sentenced to eight years in prison, of which he had already served three. As he had a wife and five children to support he tried to earn some money growing vegetables. At weekends his wife and children, whom he kept referring to as his "juveniles", came to help. There was another inmate in this open prison, but, as Cosini pointed out, he was a real murderer and was not at all interested in gardening, which, from Cosini's disapproving tone, he seemed to consider as the greater crime.

Driving around the island, one got the impression that Niueans liked keeping everything in the open and even family graves were erected in front of their homes rather than hidden away in a cemetery. Elaborate structures adorned with framed photographs of the dead stood by the side of the road, but it was a taller memorial that made us stop and have a closer look. The modest white obelisk commemorated the surprisingly high number of men from one the smallest nations on earth who had fallen in the first and second world wars while fighting with the New Zealand forces. A line that had been added at the bottom of the memorial mentioned five Niueans who had died in the Vietnam War. It seemed so incongruous on this small peaceful island. May all of them rest in peace.

Swimming with whales in Vava'u

Tonga's northern group of islands has been one of the most popular cruising destinations in the South Pacific for a very long time. The perfectly sheltered anchorage off the small town of Neiafu looked very different to how I remembered it from my first visit in 1978 when we had chosen it as a rendezvous with our friends Erick and Muriel on Calao. As they were in Peru and we in New Zealand, we each drew a line on a chart of the South Pacific and the lines crossed in Vava'u. We had agreed

The approaches to Refuge Harbour in the Vava'u Islands

by mail to meet the first weekend in May and both yachts arrived on the same morning.

The strategic location of Vava'u at the crossroads of several sailing routes, as well as the reputation of the main anchorage, Refuge Harbour, as a safe hurricane hole not surprisingly turned it into a busy yachting centre. Several charter companies are now based there and there is a wide range of facilities for cruising boats. Nowhere else in the South Pacific have I come across such a radical change, from a sleepy backwater with a couple of fly blown shops to a busy place with banks, supermarket, even a patisserie run by an Austrian expat and several restaurants on the waterfront catering for a busy charter fleet. Although the improvement in facilities is also of benefit to cruising sailors, there is no doubt that it is the needs and requirements of charter clients that really count. However convenient it may be to find a small restaurant in every bay you drop your anchor in, as we first noticed in Tahaa and rediscovered in Vava'u, there

comes a point when I'd rather have a place to ourselves even if we have to cook our own dinner.

Some of my comments may sound like the typical grumbles of an old man, and they probably are. In all fairness, I am the first to recognize that many of the changes have been for the better, but I am sure that I am not the only one to be disappointed to arrive at Neiafu and to find that virtually the entire bay is peppered with moorings belonging to various companies, which cruising boats are welcome to use... at a price.

In spite of all that, Vava'u continues to be a most beautiful place, its tranquil waters being the favourite destination of some travellers of a very different kind: scores of humpback whales that gather here to breed. We met them frolicking with their young throughout the islands and heard their chatter reverberate through Aventura's aluminium hull. There were several boats specializing in whale watching, taking clients to within feet of those benign giants, snorkelling with them being the latest thrill. The morning we were leaving for Fiji a large female and her newly born calf were ambling slowly next to us only metres from the shore, so I asked Gwenda to stay as close to them as possible while I donned my mask and fins. It was only when I tried to catch up with them that I realized that their idle pace was a lot faster than I could swim. Just as I managed to get reasonably close they both sounded, the sight of their disappearing tails sending me a clear message that the interest was definitely one-sided.

Melanesian landfall

Fiji is protected from the east by a string of extensive reefs, a virtually impenetrable natural barrier that separates Melanesia to the west from Polynesia to the east. Passing that difficult obstacle was until fairly recently a major challenge and many vessels, both small and large, regularly ran aground and were lost in that maze. While the challenge is still largely undiminished, the hazards are much more manageable although even with the help of GPS and radar, a high state of alert is not only advisable but unavoidable. In my previous forays through the area I always chose one of the two main shipping channels as they were both relatively wide and well lit. This time I picked the nearest pass to our direct course, planning to pass through the critical area soon after daylight. On the third night after leaving Vava'u we had to slow down so as not to arrive too early at the waypoint I had set ten miles to windward of a beacon on Bukatatanoa Island. The timing was perfect as we sighted the beacon at 0700 and by 1000 had passed the dangerous Reid Reef

and had entered the Koro Sea, the large body of water that extends between Fiji's main island of Viti Levu to the west and the Lau Group and its reef systems to the east.

Crossing the 120 mile wide Koro Sea also needed to be timed right so as to arrive at the entrance pass leading to the port of Savusavu soon after daybreak the following day. After years of indecision the Fijian authorities had finally agreed to make Savusavu an official port of entry, so boats arriving from Tonga or Samoa now had a convenient port to clear in. Two marinas, Waitui and Copra Shed, have laid moorings in the creek fronting the small town and Savusavu is regarded by cruising sailors as one of the best spots in the entire South Pacific. I understood why that was from

The well sheltered creek at Savusavu

the moment I called Waitui marina on VHF and was greeted like an old friend. Shortly afterwards, Curly Carswell, a retired Australian diver who had settled in Fiji and managed the small marina, came out in his dinghy and led us to a mooring. He also arranged for the officials to come to the boat so that formalities were over in a matter of minutes. The customs and immigration offices were across the road from the marina, and everything was within walking distance: supermarkets, bakery, post office, banks, restaurants and an excellent fresh produce market. There was an internet outlet at Copra Shed marina as well as a small chandlery with a small selection of spares. They also stocked the whole range of the excellent Fijian charts.

Both marinas had a busy programme of buffet dinners or barbecues, often enlivened by a local band, for the substantial number of cruising sailors of whom many had made their semi-permanent home there. This was not surprising as few places in the world could be more laid-back and relaxed than Savusavu. One other major attraction of the well sheltered harbour was proven the year before our arrival when tropical cyclone Ami swept through the harbour with winds of up to 100 knots. All the boats had been previously moved to cyclone-proof moorings and none sustained any significant damage.

Several boats were planning to stay in Savusavu during the next cyclone season, which now seems to be an established practice as all the way from Tahiti to Tonga and Fiji we had met boats that were going to spend the coming cyclone season in the tropics. This was a significant change from my experience of the 1970s when hardly any boats spent the summer in the critical area, most of them migrating out of the cyclone belt, usually to New Zealand or subtropical Australia. From what I was told, there were three main reasons for this change in attitude: a number of relatively benign cyclone seasons in recent years, the availability of marinas mainly in French Polynesia and Fiji, where

the boats could be left unattended, and the reluctance to undertake the passage to New Zealand. The decision to stay put is due to the fact that in recent years the 1200 mile passage had claimed a few casualties, mostly on the return voyage to the tropics, when boats had encountered very bad weather.

South Pacific hurricane shelters

For those planning to spend the cyclone season in the tropics (mid-November to April) there are a number of hurricane holes spread out across the South Pacific. Only a few are proper hurricane shelters and because of the large distances that separate the various island groups, running for shelter if a cyclone is predicted may not only be a hazardous affair, but one may also find that there is no space left when one gets there. For those who are determined to stay in the tropics, the best tactic is either to stay close to a chosen shelter, or cruise on the edges of the cyclone belt, so as to be able to possibly sail out of danger.

The risk of tropical storms increases as one moves west and while Galapagos and Easter Island are not affected by cyclones, tropical storms have reached as far east as Pitcairn, and north-east to the Marquesas, although the latter are very rarely hit by a fully-fledged cyclone. The outer island groups of French Polynesia (Gambiers and Australs) can be affected but the risk is lower than in the Tuamotus, where adequate shelter is almost impossible to find in the large exposed lagoons. The Society Islands are struck by fewer cyclones than islands further west but even so should not be considered safe during the tropical storm season. In Tahiti, Taina marina is full with local boats so the only possible shelters are the landlocked lagoon

Dick Smith and some of his staff welcome us to Musket Cove

at Port Phaeton on the south-west coast and the anchorage behind the reef at the Tahiti Yacht Club in Arue, east of Papeete. The two boatyards on the island of Raiatea normally store unattended boats on the hard but during one cyclone several boats did fall down and suffered extensive damage.

A new marina that is being built at Rarotonga in the Cook Islands may provide adequate shelter, but until that happens the Cooks are best avoided. One of the best natural shelters is Port Refuge at Neiafu in Vava'u but as the holding ground is poor a cyclone-proof mooring is essential. As I mentioned earlier, this is the permanent base of a large number of charter boats so finding a vacant mooring may not be easy. The maze-like cruising area of Vava'u has a few sheltered corners and several boats survived Cyclone Waka in January 2002 huddled in an anchorage off Tamana Island. Exactly two years later, Cyclone Heta passed close to Vava'u but caused only limited damage compared to the devastation wreaked in Niue.

In the Samoas, traditionally the best cyclone shelter is at Pago Pago, where several boats survived Cyclone Heta almost unscathed in January 2004. More hurricane shelters are to be found in neighbouring Fiji. Near the capital Suva local boats have traditionally sought shelter among the creeks and mangroves close to the Tradewinds anchorage. A few marinas were built in recent years on the west coast of Viti Levu, such as the marina at Vuda Point, which offers good protection in a circular basin that can be entirely closed off by an anti-surge barrier. Boats left on the hard have their keels dropped into a trench for added protection. A cyclone shelter has also been created in a completely landlocked basin at Musket Cove on the island of Malololailai. Further west, the landlocked natural harbour at Port Vila in Vanuatu may offer adequate protection in a cyclone as does Marina Port Moselle at Noumea in New Caledonia. In the Solomons the best shelter is reported at Tulagi opposite the capital Honiara.

The above list is by no means exhaustive and there may be other sheltered spots known only to locals. Those who decide to stay in the tropics should work out a plan of action in case a cyclone does come their way. The alternative is to pack up early and head out of the tropics to New Zealand, subtropical Australia or Papua New Guinea. Another alternative is to cross the equator and spend the southern cyclone season cruising the islands of Micronesia. Leaving the tropics is, in my view, still the wisest tactic, especially as the cyclone season seems to be getting longer, which may be due to global warming.

Long before getting to Fiji I had decided to spend the next cyclone season in New

Zealand, but before heading south I wanted to make one final stop to see my friend Dick Smith who runs a large resort on the island of Malololailai. I had first met Dick when I came to Fiji to prepare the ground for the first round the world rally. Although I had made provisional arrangements for the fleet to be hosted by the Royal Suva Yacht Club, Dick's enthusiasm persuaded me to change my plans. Dick had already made a name for himself among sailors by starting

working for a while in the hotel business he bought Malololailai Island where he set up a resort that eventually mushroomed into the current Musket Cove complex. But Dick has always remained a sailor at heart and people arriving on their own boats are welcome at his resort where visiting sailors are allowed to use all its facilities. There is a bar on the dockside where a barbecue is set up every evening for the use of sailors anchored out in the bay and drinks cost the equivalent of one US dollar. Dick is in every respect the most generous host one can imagine but even so the welcome that was put on for us at Musket Cove was quite overwhelming. Not only was Dick there to greet us but also a small group of his staff played for us. It is always a pleasure to be greeted by old friends, but when I asked one of the young girls singing our welcome if she remembered me. She replied, 'Yes, aren't you Ivan's father?' Obviously Ivan had made his mark on more than just a beam. What made our arrival even more special was that it coincided with Dick's birthday, so the party started from the moment we stepped on the dock.

The tranquil Tradewinds anchorage near Suva

the Musket Cove Yacht Club where every skipper arriving on his own yacht was made a lifetime member on payment of one Fiji dollar. As Ivan was in charge of Aventura II during the rally in 1991, it is his name and not mine that was carved into one of the overhead beams, yet another touch that makes the Musket Cove Yacht Club such a unique place.

Dick arrived in the South Pacific on his own boat in the 1960s and after cruising for a while decided that he liked the place so much that he didn't want to leave. After

Sailing as a Family

The most important and difficult action is putting your dream into practice. The highlights arrive by themselves.

Klaus Girzig

Jody and Carlton DeHart sailed around the world with their daughters Amy and Caroline

Having enjoyed six wonderful years in the closest companionship with Gwenda and our two children Doina and Ivan, we continued this happy relationship to this day, so it is little wonder that I consider the family unit as the ideal set-up on a long distance boat. Indeed there are plenty of similar examples, but among those that stand out among my sailing friends are Erick and Muriel Bouteleux who sailed with their children on Calao, the three generations on Duen, on which Albert and Dottie Fletcher, their children and grandchildren spent fourteen incredible years around the world, and Arthur and Germaine Beiser, who are now in their mid-70s and continue to sail as they have done for over fifty years.

Decision to go

Neither the boat nor the amount of gear you have really matters, just get out there and do it. Leaving is the most difficult thing we ever did.

Carlton DeHart

The decision to turn one's back on shore life in favour of a life at sea can put an enormous strain on a marriage, and even some of the most harmonious relationships may end up being seriously affected. I have come across such examples among participants in my various rallies and occasionally have been asked to advise on how to reach a mutually acceptable solution. All too often the initial idea to go sailing comes from the man and there is no doubt that the urge to explore, the love of adventure and to pit oneself against the forces of nature, is very much a male characteristic. In my own case, it was my desire to see the world in my own boat that made me take my family along. I was very fortunate that Gwenda had a keen spirit of adventure herself and had always liked travelling, so my task of persuading her to throw in everything and set off into the blue was not too difficult. From what I observed in later years, Gwenda was exceptional and many women whom I met sailing with their partners were doing it more or less reluctantly. Some were bold enough to admit that it was the price they paid to save their marriage. There were also husbands who were not prepared to abandon their dream but were equally determined to preserve their marriage, so they managed to work out a solution that satisfied both parties. In most cases it meant sailing all the long passages with friends or hired crew, to be joined by their wife for the cruising stages. Almost invariably this was a workable solution and I met several cruising boats happily sailing around the world in this way. In each of the round the world rallies there were some wives who preferred to follow their husband by flying from place to place so avoiding the longer passages. Occasionally even the best will in the world cannot overcome one or the other partner's unwillingness to compromise and I cannot think of a better example than that of an Australian participant in the Millennium Odyssey who, on reading about the round the world rally, told his wife that he would very much like to do it. The wife objected vehemently but he refused to be swayed.

'I have spent my entire life being a responsible family man, but now the children have grown up, we are well off and so I feel it is high time that I do something for myself.' To which the wife retorted, 'It's either the boat or me.'

'In that case, I am sorry, but it's the boat!' And off he went.

There are also some exceptions that I have came across, the most remarkable being that of a woman whom I met in Tahiti. All his life her husband had dreamt of going cruising so as he was nearing retirement he started building his dream boat. Unfortunately his untimely death brought that dream to a cruel end but determined not to abandon her husband's long nurtured dream, his wife decided to complete the building of the boat. When I met her, she and her teenage son were in the second year of their voyage, her husband's dream having become her own.

Never have I come across a better example of sheer determination to go against all odds than that of an ARC participant in his seventies who had been warned by his doctor not to risk an Atlantic crossing because of his heart condition. Undeterred by this he continued with his preparations but then had a skiing accident and this time his doctor insisted that he called off his voyage. 'If you are all so concerned about the state of my health,' he told his doctor, 'then you, the cardiologist and the orthopaedic surgeon must come along, because I am definitely going!' And so he did with several of his family as well as the three doctors.

A better title for this section might have been "the decision to go and continue going" as many voyages come to a premature end when one or the other partner decides that this is not the kind of life he or she is prepared to live. The importance of having a good relationship with one's partner is a major factor and one should never start off on a voyage if one has any doubts about the strength of one's relationship. For many people, the cruising life can be a cruel eye opener and makes them realize that they hardly knew their partner before. This particularly applies when the couple have both had demanding careers ashore and maybe only spent a few hours a day together. Spending twenty-four hours in close proximity can have an effect on any relationship and one woman observed cynically that life afloat is very good at pulling people apart. Often, the passive role played by some women in the initial decision can lead to problems later on, endangering not just the continuation of the voyage but the relationship itself.

I have been fortunate in being able to count on Gwenda's support throughout my life but, of late, even her boundless tolerance seemed to be getting close to being exhausted. The decision to build the second Aventura caused no problems between us as I never planned to set off on a long voyage. Even Aventura II's circumnavigation, which was done mostly as part of the first Europa round the world rally, was dictated primarily by the convenience of providing a permanent base for our staff. When Aventura III came along, and from the way she was equipped, Gwenda realized that I had some serious voyaging in mind. She was very open in telling me not to count on her full participation, which I understood and accepted. As a result she did not join me on my trip to Antarctica but when Ivan and I set off on a transpacific voyage from Chile to Alaska, Gwenda joined us in Easter Island and sailed all the way to Tahiti, and later cruised with us in Alaska and British Columbia. We had the same arrangement during Aventura's recently completed round the world voyage when Gwenda missed most ocean passages but joined me on all the cruising stages. It was a win-win situation and the ultimate merit for its success is entirely Gwenda's who, however reluctantly, wisely accepted that I was a lost cause and as I would never get the sailing bug out of my system she might as well learn to live with it.

The decision to go can have such an important bearing on one's life that I decided not to limit its discussion just to my personal experience but to bring in the comments and advice of other sailors faced with the same dilemma. As Carlton DeHart pointed out 'the most significant thing I did was to make up my mind to do it, cut all ties, get on the boat and leave. Too many people plan all their life to sail away and never go for whatever reason.'

Some of the sailors I interviewed tried to bring in a dose of realism into the argument such as Glynn Beauchamp who pointed out that passage making can be exhausting and even boring at times. In some cases, the couple decided to take on crew to help handle the boat on long passages. This worked for some, but not for others. As Anne Harsh commented, 'Our first thought was that on long passages an extra crew was a desirable safety factor in case of bad weather, illness, etc. Having made many long passages we decided that it was not really necessary and we now agree that sailing alone as a couple is preferable as we found that the crew can often be lonely and ends up feeling the "odd person out".'

Ideal age

There is no ideal age but I know
that if at all possible the best time is
now as tomorrow may be too late.

Jimmy Cornell

Although I made that statement many years ago I still stand by it and several recent examples have only reinforced its validity. Many of the round the world rallies attract retired sailors in their sixties who finally grab the opportunity to do something that they had never been able to

Saundra and Charlie Gray have sailed together all over the world

do during their busy lives. In the Millennium Odyssey we had three skippers who were diagnosed with different types of cancer within months of each other. They all returned home for treatment while their crews, with help from sailors on other boats, continued the voyage. Two of the skippers rejoined the rally while the third could only attend the final ceremony in Rome. They all admitted how happy they were to have been able to do it, but also how much they regretted not having done it a little earlier. 'Whatever you do and whenever you decide to go – don't leave it too late.' Words of wisdom from Carlton DeHart.

Although there probably isn't an ideal age, in hindsight, our decision to leave at thirty-five was probably right as both of us were in good physical shape and the age of our children also fitted in well into our six year long voyage.

Cruising couples

A boat is not the place to fix anything wrong with a relationship, whether it is with a partner, a child or a friend. If someone irritates you ashore, they will irritate you more on a boat. Some people are not emotionally geared for life aboard. They are not wrong or misfits, they are just not boat people.

Saundra Gray

Saundra has sailed for many years with her husband Charlie, they have cruised with their children, and took part in both America 500 and the Millennium Odyssey. They are one of the most exceptional cruising couples that I have met and their comments and advice to other sailors stand out for their realism and commonsense. Although earlier I highlighted some of the problems that may beset cruising couples

I must stress that there are probably many more happy stories. Among the remarkable couples that I have met are Bob and Judy Hall and Betty and Duke Marx, who, just like Saundra and Charlie also sailed in both America 500 and the Millennium Odyssey so our friendship stretches to over fifteen years during which time we have shared many enjoyable moments. All these are examples of perfect sailing couples. In Judy's words, 'we love sailing together and have a wonderful, close, loving relationship.' Lois and Don Babson who also sailed in the Millennium Odyssey commented, 'we sail as a couple and are happy with our closeness while cruising.'

Dottie and Albert Fletcher who spent fourteen years sailing with their children and grandchildren are another example of an enduring relationship. John Neal, who has sailed some 200,000 miles teaching seamanship and navigation to his students, described his wife Amanda as his 'sweet, knowledgeable darling of a partner.' Erick and Muriel Bouteleux are yet another example as are Jody and Carlton DeHart. Asked to advise other couples planning to embark on a similar life, Jody sounded a note of realism. 'One should never start off on such a voyage unless you already get on well with each other ashore.'

Marcia Davock stressed that in certain situations women have a greater capacity for endurance, while Saundra Gray admitted that there were occasions when she didn't find it easy to cope when there were just the two of them. 'We enjoy being alone on the boat but on long passages, especially during rough weather, it is nice to have extra experienced hands. However, there can be problems with additional crew as the relationship between people changes when others are introduced into the equation.'

The crews of Distant Drum and Hornblower on completion of their circumnavigation

Lack of sailing experience combined with the anxiety associated with a long passage can have serious consequences as in the case of two fathers who admitted being extremely worried about their responsibilities towards their families. One of them arrived in the Caribbean mentally and physically exhausted having stayed awake for the last few nights due to his apprehension of the impending landfall. The other skipper expressed his disillusionment as he had been looking for peace at sea but the only thing he had found was apprehension. He was therefore determined to give up. This was a painful realization for someone who had dreamt for thirty years about such a voyage but had never considered the practicalities of this dream. It was ironic that his wife, who admitted having been reluctantly dragged along on the voyage because of his dream, had come to love the cruising life and was very reluctant to give it up.

Labour division

The sharing of responsibilities is a crucial ingredient in a harmonious relationship and a fair division of labour is as important

on land as it is at sea. During the first summer on Aventura I we agreed that it made more sense for Gwenda to steer the boat, while I, being stronger, would handle the lines, docking and anchoring. Gradually Gwenda became very efficient at handling the boat and we kept this system throughout the first voyage, although we rarely saw it on other boats. While in Fiji we met Susan and Eric Hiscock and among many other things discussed over dinner on our boat Susan made some sharp comments on this very subject. 'Men are simply just macho, they want to be seen to be in control.' Indeed we came across many situations where a burly male shouted instructions from the wheel while his tiny wife struggled with a huge anchor or tried to fend the boat off the dock.

The subject of labour division interested me so much that I returned to it in the Millennium Odyssey survey. Whereas the earlier surveys showed that women were usually cast in a secondary often passive role, according to my latest survey tasks were designated more according to ability than to the traditional roles that still seem to dominate shore life.

'Some of our roles are shared and some are not, each of us doing what we like best or do best. As the female, I handle provisioning, communications, navigation, stand watches and steer the boat during emergencies when male strength is needed on deck,' commented Judy Hall.

Sailing children

At the start of our voyage Doina was seven and Ivan five, so they could take an active part in sailing and also be old enough to appreciate the places we were visiting. On our return Ivan was eleven and Doina nearly fourteen, which, in her case, was probably one or two years beyond the best age for this kind of life. I once asked Doina to comment on this subject and she pointed out that reintegration can be the most difficult problem faced by a child who has been away from shore life for a long time. 'The problem wasn't so much me having difficulty in adapting to life ashore but other children not being able to accept

Birthday celebration for Ivan and Doina

me as I was so very different to them. It was just as hard for Ivan. Other children can be very cruel.'

As children are by nature very adaptable, even the very young seem to have no difficulty in coping with life on a moving boat. Over the years I have met a number of children who were born during their parents' voyage and grew up successfully in this environment. As we found out ourselves difficulties only started when Doina reached puberty and showed that teenagers can be as much a problem afloat as ashore.

Although our experience of bringing up children on a boat was quite successful, I have come across several examples that would not fit that description. In every case the fault lay squarely with the parents who

were either too lax or had never thought seriously about what was best for their child. One such example was a young child of between one and two who sailed with his parents in one of the round the world rallies. The parents were of the 'let the child grow up without any constraints' persuasion and as a result the little boy had not been potty trained, so he was always walking around with a bare bottom, or completely naked, which caused raised eyebrows in several of the places the rally visited.

Some of the children I met were often spoilt and ill behaved and usually as inconsiderate as their parents. By far the worst were boys in their mid or late teens, who were obviously frustrated by not having the company of their peers, which is so important at that age. Usually these were also the children whose education had been neglected by their parents, either because they could not be bothered, or because not having had an education themselves they found dealing with it beyond their capacity. Probably the main disadvantage for such children is that they don't learn to socialize with groups of other children as they would in a big school.

Jody DeHart, who sailed around the world with her daughter from the age of seven to nine, felt that 'the pros outweigh the cons by such a large measure that the cons don't really count. Children on a boat learn how to entertain themselves with reading, crafts and schoolwork in a way that kids in school with a TV at home could never equal. They learn how to learn from books which benefits them for the rest of their lives, how to make friends quickly and how to interact with adults when other children are not around. They get to see their parents making difficult decisions.'

Jody was one of those parents who took their responsibility seriously. Saundra Gray, who has cruised with her own children, has seen 'some very successful parenting aboard boats and some that didn't seem to be working out so well, not far different than land based parents. A cruising family is like a pioneer or explorer family; they must be self-sufficient, independent and creative. Much maturity on the part of both partners must be exercised to make a cruising lifestyle workable with children.'

Children growing up on a cruising boat are normally self-confident and, if guided in the right direction, will grow up successfully. At our table the main topic of conversation was usually politics, which is not surprising with a journalist father fed on daily doses of BBC news to which we all listened regularly. One other major topic was the culture and the people of the country we happened to be visiting. From those days, and the often heated discussions, Doina and Ivan learnt to express their own opinions and even now, some thirty years later, a family dinner at the Cornells is never a quiet affair.

From his earliest days Ivan never ceased to amaze us with his keen sense of observation and I will never forget the embarrassed moments he caused right at the start of Aventura's first voyage. While getting ready to set off across the Bay of Biscay we had stopped for a couple of days on the river Fowey in south-west England. Local friends had come out to guide us to a mooring and we were all sitting in the cockpit busily talking. Ivan tapped me on the shoulder. 'Daddy, the boat is moving.'

'Of course it's moving, it's a boat after all, not a house,' I replied rather impatiently, returning to my conversation. A couple of minutes later, he was back again.

'Daddy, the boats are moving.'

'Boats? What boats?' I asked, and when I looked across at the other moored boats, I realised with a shock that it was us and not

them that were indeed moving. We had slipped the mooring, which our friend had not secured well, and while chatting busily we were drifting seawards on the outgoing tide. We quickly put it right but there were red faces all around and all thanks to a five year old. I never mistrusted his judgement again.

Swimming

While spending the cyclone season in Papua New Guinea, we witnessed a terrible tragedy on a neighbouring boat where an unattended toddler had fallen in the water and drowned. Ever since they were small, we had made an effort to teach Doina and Ivan to swim, and once we started sailing it became much easier. Finally, by the time we got to Bequia, Ivan managed to swim around the boat unaided and got a big prize for his achievement. Recently I used the

Doina exploring an underwater reef

same incentive for our granddaughter Nera who impressed us all when she managed to swim the entire length of the boat although the water was quite cold and, from her expression, it was clear that she was scared. But she persevered and made it as far as the anchor chain. I was quite impressed by such determination and willpower in a six year old. No doubt she takes after her mother, as Doina was always a good swimmer. Diving for shells was Doina and Ivan's favourite activity while we were in the tropics, and while in New

Ivan searching for hidden treasure

Zealand Doina won the school swimming championship. On her return to England Doina decided to join a diving club, which in those days was a very male dominated activity. The instructor told her that she would only be accepted if she could show that she could swim underwater. Doina dived into the pool, swam its entire length underwater, and when she surfaced at the far end, shouted across, 'Will that do?' It was just the kind of lesson the instructor and his macho mates deserved.

Along with anything to do with the sea I have been a passionate swimmer all my life. I know how to pace myself, never tire and can happily swim for hours, which I often did. During one of the summer vacations at the Black Sea my mother came to visit, looked for me everywhere on the beach and as she couldn't find me she asked the supervisor. 'Have you seen Dragos by any chance?'

'No, he has been away all morning as he usually is, I wouldn't be surprised if he has drowned.'

Fortunately my mother was made of strong stuff, so she just sat down on the sand and waited. After a while I emerged like Neptune from the waves, covered in red antifouling paint from having helped a fisherman prepare his boat that morning. My mother thought at first it was blood.

'What on earth happened to you? Are you injured?'

'No, don't worry, it's just paint.'

The supervisor passed by.

'Oh there you are you red devil, where have you been all this time without telling anyone?'

'I found a shallow sandbank offshore and spent the morning splashing about there.'

'You'd better warn me next time or you'll be sent home.'

'I hope that won't be necessary.' My mother quickly intervened. 'Dragos is such a sensible boy otherwise.'

'Sensible? Him? He is a born trouble-maker, that's what he is.'

Education afloat

As part of Doina and Ivan's education, whenever we arrived in a new place, Gwenda would not only read to them about its history but would also make a quick research trip to a nearby site or museum. She would then compile two worksheets which the children had to complete as part of their schoolwork. Shortly after our arrival in Iraklion, the capital of Crete, we had visited the Minoan remains at Knossos. In the ancient labyrinth beneath the Royal Palace Gwenda read out to all of us the legend of the Minotaur, the unique setting so impressing Doina and Ivan that they never forgot that special day.

The summer we spent in Greece, when Doina was eight and Ivan six, nurtured in them an interest in Greek mythology and ancient history, which Doina has kept to this day. In Iraklion Gwenda had set her sights on the museum of antiquities which houses the best frescos retrieved from Knossos and were skilfully displayed to great effect on the museum walls. One day about two hours before closing time, she took the children to the museum where they started completing their worksheets. The questions were not difficult but were meant to make them look properly at the items on display.

'Where was the fresco with dolphins located?' Ivan: in the Queen's bathroom.

'Why were the ancient Cretans so scared of the Minotaur and what did they associate it with?' Doina: earthquakes.

The children were busily copying some of the frescos, when one of the museum attendants told them that it was closing time and they had to leave the museum. At this, both of them started crying and saying they didn't want to go. Not knowing what to do, the attendant went to call her boss.

'What wonderful children you have,' he told Gwenda. 'We've had plenty of children crying in the museum but never when being asked to leave.'

Gwenda took her job very seriously and unless the weather was really bad, school was never missed. I only contributed one subject and that was navigation. If they worked hard while at sea, Doina and Ivan rarely did school work in port, which they highly appreciated. Gwenda's work paid due dividends as both children fitted easily back into the British system on our return and finished their schooling with good exam results.

While in Chagos I met an Austrian family who were already on their fourth continuous circumnavigation on their 40 foot Mapopo and were not planning to stop. We spent some pleasant days in their company anchored near a beach on which they had built from dead coral a barbecue and a bread oven. Their son Janni, who had been the first to greet us on arrival, was always with us, joining the conversation without inhibition as is often the case with such children used to being with adults and learning early to be self-confident. From the very moment when I met him I was struck by his politeness and maturity.

The skipper Hans told me that they managed to survive by picking up any job that came his way and as a professional diver with his own compressor on board, he found this to be the most lucrative. Having worked on a black pearl farm in the

Drawing Tongan carvings as part of the day's school assignment

Tuamotus where he had been paid in pearls he now had a steady source of finance as he sold pearls to other cruisers.

There came a point where Hans and Karin described their future plans and expressed their concern for Janni's formal education. They sounded obviously quite reluctant to interrupt their enjoyable and highly satisfying peripatetic life. I felt that they had brought up the subject so openly because they knew that I had been through the same situation myself. I told them that I always felt that by the time a child reached the early teens he or she should be allowed to return to a more structured life, a formal education and an environment where social contacts especially with their peers were the rule rather than the exception. Continuing with a lifestyle that suited the parents so well but was becoming entirely unsuitable for the child was, in my view, both selfish and irresponsible. I gave a few examples of children's education being neglected by their parents who could not tear themselves away from the cruising life. Usually by their mid-teens such children started having serious problems, both with their parents and with themselves, and when they did eventually return to shore life, they were often incapable of reintegrating in society. I could see that Hans and Karin did not like to hear what I was saying but they promised to consider it seriously and perhaps change their plans. I have no idea if they have done so or not but I do hope that they have put Janni's interests first.

For Gwenda and I, having to take a similar decision was never a problem as we had always planned to return to England on the completion of our voyage even if it ended up taking twice as long as we had originally envisaged. Our problems with Doina started in the South Pacific where local girls mature early and by the time they reach puberty are already regarded as ready for sex. We often saw local men making advances to Doina who was well developed for her age, so much so that when we took the train from Malaysia to Thailand to visit Bangkok and had bought two children's tickets for Ivan and Doina, the Thai conductor took a look at Doina and said 'this no child, this woman – you pay'. In spite of my protestation I did pay but when we reached Bangkok I noticed that most adult women weren't as tall as Doina was at twelve. By the time we had reached Papua New Guinea in 1980, the situation had become difficult enough for us to realise that something needed to be done, so we sat down with Doina and explained our intention. 'Doina, we feel that you are no longer happy on the boat and we thought that it would be better if you returned to England, went to stay with Granny and go to school there.' Her reaction was immediate, 'That is so unfair! I started this voyage and I want to complete it, please don't make me go'.

'As you wish.'

'Thank you.'

Then Doina added, 'but I do want to go to school, so please promise that you will get back home as quickly as possible'.

That is exactly what we did and less than one year later we were back in England.

Our six year long voyage does not seem to have greatly affected their education as both children went on to university in London, Doina to study international history at the London School of Economics and Ivan computer science at University College. Doina now lives in the west of England and manages our website *www.noonsite.com*. Ivan has followed his passion for film and, until recently, worked for a London post-production company as their systems manager. In 2006 Ivan took a year's sabbatical leave to build his own 26 foot boat, which he completed in a rented railway arch in east London only a couple of miles from where I had fitted out my own Aventura thirty-two years earlier. Chip from the old block indeed!

Out of the Tropics and Back

After a very pleasant stay at Musket Cove, we were ready for the long passage to New Zealand. Surrounded by so many cruising sailors, it was not the best place to set off from as my unorthodox approach to weather not only raises eyebrows but often generates a debate as to the rights or wrongs of the decision to go. I usually set a date for departure and if the weather looks at all acceptable, I normally leave, an attitude many find difficult to understand. This is exactly what I did in Musket Cove. The weather was not ideal but waiting for a change did not look any better, so we left. We had an unpleasant first 24 hours, with strong SSW winds that forced us to the west of our intended track. This didn't worry me too much as I knew that we would be able to make up the lost ground closer to New Zealand where the prevailing winds are from the west.

Unfortunately the easterly winds, that usually blow south of Fiji, had a lot of south in them, so we were pushed more and more to the west. By the third day we had to go on the starboard tack as I didn't want to stray too far from the direct course. The accepted tactic on this passage is to make some westing in the early stages, so as to be in a better position closer to landfall, when the winds often come from the west or even south-west. Luck was again on my side as conditions gradually improved and a low that was heading our way across the Tasman Sea began generating north-westerly winds, so we were soon broad reaching. Gradually the wind crept up to over 30 knots and frequent squalls kept me on my toes.

After the earlier SSW winds, the new wind direction had resulted in an uncomfortable swell, so Gwenda spent much of the time in her bunk. I was certainly glad that Aventura was so easy to handle on my own, without the need to leave the cockpit. Earlier in the trip, when the winds were lighter, I had left the steering to the windvane but when the winds got stronger and there was a risk of gybing, I preferred to put my trust in the autopilot. After I while, I took the wheel and was surprised how hard it was to keep the boat on course as, with just the reefed mainsail up, she was rather unbalanced. Probably the worst drawback of a fully battened mainsail is the difficulty of dropping it even in moderate following winds as the sail is plastered against the spreaders and the battens get caught in the rigging. So on long passages I normally avoid dropping the mainsail and will keep it up well reefed as long as possible. The result is that I often end up sailing with only a deeply reefed mainsail. I know that this is a rather unusual way of sailing and may not suit other boats but Aventura seems to cope well with this arrangement and I have got used to it.

By the seventh day the wind had levelled off at 35 knots with occasional stronger gusts. Every now and again I would disengage the autopilot and steer for a few minutes, enjoying every moment of it with the boat surfing down the waves, the speedometer rarely going below 10 knots. Admittedly, the movement was quite lively but at that speed keeping the boat on course with the wind on the starboard quarter wasn't too difficult. Occasionally a large following sea picked us up, lifting the stern slightly and I could feel the acceleration as the boat trembled slightly under my feet. The speedometer needle kept going up and peaked once at well over 14 knots. It stayed there for a few exhilarating moments, then the wave pulled ahead and we settled at a more sedate seven or eight knots. This went on for at least one hour, in the middle of which Gwenda put her head through the hatch and, as she later told me, saw me standing at the wheel with a huge grin on my face. 'You are absolutely crazy,' was all she said before

Most yachts make landfall in the Bay of Opua

going back to her bunk, and she repeated those words more forcefully later, when the weather had calmed down.

Halfway round the world

The day before our expected landfall, I called Taupo Radio to inform New Zealand Customs of our arrival, which all incoming vessels are required to do. I told the officer on duty that it looked as if we might arrive in the Bay of Islands after dark, so I requested permission to anchor in a bay for the night and proceed to Opua for clearance the following morning. Permission to do this was firmly denied as all boats arriving from abroad had to proceed directly to an official port for clearance.

Fortunately I knew the large bay from previous visits but even so it was not easy to follow the buoys across the bay, then make our way up the river in pitch darkness. It was near midnight when we finally tied to the quarantine dock at the new Opua marina. The trip from Fiji had taken just over eight days and with all the tacking we had sailed 1160 miles. Once again, I had

been right to leave when we did as a delay of one or two days in our departure would have put us right into the path of that depression and we would have ended up with strong SW winds for the last 200 miles rather than the exhilarating broad reaching conditions that we actually had.

In the previous six months Aventura had sailed from Ecuador to New Zealand and had covered some 8,000 miles so both Aventura and her crew were ready for a long period of R&R. Having totted up almost 50,000 miles since her launch in 1998, Aventura needed a lot more than just a well deserved rest and I was planning to give her a thorough overhaul. New Zealand was the perfect place to do it as it has some of the best yachting facilities in the South Pacific. This is one of the main reasons why hundreds of cruising sailors leave the tropics every year to spend the cyclone season in New Zealand. This is also what brought the first Aventura south in 1978, and why I returned a quarter of a century later. What I found this time around was very different to the quiet backwater of my previous visit when we arrived at a weekend and found that the whole country had virtually shut down so we could not even buy a pint of fresh milk. Now it was a vibrant modern country that during our absence seemed to have leapt from the 19th straight into the 21st century. What had not changed, however, were the Kiwis themselves whom I rate among the most welcoming and helpful people in the world.

New Zealand is, by any standard, an outstanding country and so are its people. For a nation of barely four million the Kiwis have totted up some truly remarkable achievements: the first man to climb Mount Everest, the best rugby team in the world, not to speak of winning the America's Cup as well as several victories in the Whitbread (now Volvo) round the world race. Those sailing achievements should not be too much of a surprise, as this is a nation of sailors and the Maoris, who are the original New Zealanders, made one of the most remarkable ocean voyages in the history of seafaring when they sailed their double hulled canoes in search of a new home from Havaiki (present day Raiatea) to what they called The Land of The Long White Cloud (Aotearoa).

Visiting sailors seem to prefer the top half of North Island where both facilities and the weather are generally better. Local cruising opportunities, whether to Great Barrier Island or the Bay of Islands itself are another attraction. A foray to the South Island is definitely more challenging and so most cruisers prefer to explore its spectacular beauty on four wheels. There is a wide choice of marinas and boatyards and we could have stopped at the very first place we arrived in as Opua in the Bay of Islands has a marina and full service yard as good as any. Sailing south towards Auckland we stopped at the marina at Tutukaka, which has almost no repair facilities, whereas a little further on the small town of Whangarei has everything a sailor may want, and more: a marina right in the centre of town and a full range of specialist workshops and boatyards. We had spent several months there on Aventura I when, just like this time, we completed a long list of jobs in preparation for the return voyage to Europe.

Auckland itself has several marinas, such as Westhaven, a huge marina centrally located, while on the opposite shore Bayswater marina is a favourite among liveaboards. From the two marinas located in one of the quieter suburbs, Westpark and Half Moon Bay marina, I picked the latter as it offered a full range of repair and service facilities.

First on my long list of jobs was a complete engine service that started off as a fairly routine operation but became more complicated, as well as more costly, as a host of hidden problems were uncovered. In parallel with the engine, all sails were checked, repaired and restitched. Although the mainsail was still in reasonably good condition, I decided to take advantage of the relatively low prices and ordered a new sail. The old one I gave away to a Kiwi sailor building his own boat who could not believe that someone would throw away a sail before it actually fell apart. The standing rigging was checked and tested, and I had the forestay replaced as well as the lifelines. At the same time the yankee and staysail furling gears were taken apart and serviced too. The electrical system was completely revised and the charging system, which had given me some trouble in the past, was upgraded with a new 120 AH alternator, a new solar panel and new gel batteries. The least work required was on my Brookes & Gatehouse instrumentation and autopilot, with only new brushes needed for the latter. Among the safety equipment, the liferaft had its usual service, while the 406MHz EPIRB, which needed a new set of batteries, ended up being replaced with a new unit that cost less than the set of special batteries.

Considerably poorer than when I had arrived but with a boat in top shape, by the end of the southern summer I was ready to resume my voyage. I had arranged with two Kiwi friends to sail with me on the first leg to Noumea in New Caledonia. I had first met Paul Ewing in Greece when we arrived with Aventura I on completion of her long voyage and he was about to hand over the boat that he had built and sailed from New Zealand to her new French owner. Roy was a friend of Paul's and as they were both keen sailors they sounded like the perfect crew to join me for the leg to New Caledonia.

The time to leave New Zealand for the tropics is after the end of the cyclone season, which, at least on paper, is April the first. Paul and Roy were quite amazed when I told them that we'd leave Auckland, as I had always said, on 31st March so that by the first of April we would be on our way to New Caledonia. From what I was told by the Customs officer when I cleared out of Auckland, we were the first boat to leave for the tropics that season. There was a good reason for this as I was very keen to be in Vanuatu by the end of April when I knew that there would be a land diving ceremony on the island of Pentecost. This rare occurrence was something I had missed on all of my previous visits and I was determined not to miss it this time.

We had light winds for the first three days and occasionally had to use the engine but by the fourth day we had moved sufficiently north to pick up the SE trade winds. After one day of perfect sailing with the asymmetric spinnaker we had to endure 24 hours of miserable conditions, with violent squalls and torrential rain, while the wind got stronger and stronger. I had no doubt that we were in for a bout of reinforced trade winds, which is a frequent feature in this area but at least the wind continued to blow from the right direction even if it did creep up towards the 30 knot mark.

The strong winds and large southerly swell put paid to my long nurtured plan to stop at Norfolk Island, which lies almost halfway between the top of New Zealand and New Caledonia. Once used by the British as a penal colony, in the 19th century it was turned over to settlers from Pitcairn. That tiny island, where the Bounty mutineers and their Tahitian wives managed to hide for many years from the long arm of the Royal Navy, could no longer support its hugely expanded population so the offer of Norfolk was gratefully accepted. The majority of those transferred to Norfolk settled there happily and their descendants continue to live there today, but a number of Pitcairners were consumed by nostalgia and returned to their abandoned island. Having twice visited Pitcairn I was very keen to call at Norfolk as well. The island's only harbour is on the south side, which was untenable in winds from that direction. As we came within sight of Norfolk and its verdant cliffs, course was regretfully altered as I considered it too risky to enter the exposed harbour. We sailed on all day before we lost sight of this tempting landfall. What a disappointment!

At least we had some compensation as the winds gradually eased, the sun came out, and we could hoist the brand new ParaSailor that I had received the day before our departure from Auckland. This novel type of spinnaker, which I described in chapter 2, had been advertised as the

Sunset over Havannah Pass near Noumea

best invention since sliced bread. Both this kind of statement and the comments made by those who had used such a sail in the past sounded too good to be true, so I had some serious reservations as did my crew. Hoisting the ParaSailor was no different to a standard tri-radial spinnaker and, once it was up, it didn't behave all that different either... or so I thought. After a while I noticed that in spite of the confused swell that had been left over from the previous squally night, the spinnaker remained full and stable. Roy, who was a racing sailor and a former sailing champion of New Zealand, soon realized that his tweaking and playing with the lines didn't seem to make any difference as the ParaSailor was quite happy to be left alone. After two days of perfect sailing, with the ParaSailor doing all the work, we crossed the Tropic of Cancer and, almost on cue saw the first flying fish.

Among Caldoches and Kanaks

There was a full moon on the last night as we sailed slowly up the SW coast of New Caledonia. At first light we went through Amadé Pass and followed the long beaconed channel into Port Moselle where we tied up to the visitors' dock. The dock was full of French liveaboards, most of whom had found jobs locally and seemed happy to take a break from sailing while filling up the cruising kitty. In spite of my disapproval of France hanging on to its former colonies, I must admit that the French know how to enjoy life to the full, especially in their overseas territories. One of the beneficiaries of this global network have been French sailors who can count on a "home from home" every few thousand miles. Nowhere is this more obvious than in Noumea, which is a thriving city with well stocked supermarkets, restaurants for all tastes and a distinct feeling of being somewhere in mainland France.

New Caledonia is occasionally visited by cyclones, but Port Moselle marina is well protected and those who wish to seek even more shelter can go to one of the nearby mangrove creeks. The best cruising is in the outlying islands, either the Isle of Pines or

323

the Loyalties (Maré, Lifou and Ouvea). As neither is close to Noumea, the authorities allow boats that have cleared out to sail to Vanuatu, Fiji or New Zealand, to stop at one of those islands on the way.

Having taken two weeks holiday to sail with me, Paul and Roy had to return home to go back to work, and their place was taken by Dieter Walz, a Swiss friend who had last sailed with me in the Bahamas, and Juan Francisco Martin, my Canarian friend and Aventura's adoptive father. A misjudged crew overlap meant that for a few days Aventura was rather overcrowded but the five of us had an excellent time together nonetheless. One day we hired a car to see some of the large island's interior and finished the day at a former penal camp. As in the case of neighbouring Norfolk Island, as well as Australia, the first European settlers had been convicts, France's penal colony of New Caledonia having a terrible reputation. More settlers followed to this land rich in natural resources, with a heavy influx of French colons from North Africa after Algeria's war of independence in the early 1960s. Of the current population of 200,000 about one third are of European descent, while 44 percent are Kanaks, the local Melanesian people. The rest are recent immigrants from other French territories. This imbalance was at the root of the troubles that erupted here in the 1980s and eventually came to an end when France gave the Kanaks a much better deal, with improved education and health benefits, as well as the promise of a referendum on possible independence at some point in the future.

The current situation seemed peaceful and stable, and the French administration had made an obvious effort to improve the country's infrastructure. We saw this on the island of Maré, in the Loyalties, where we made a brief stop after JuanFra had strained his back and had to see a doctor. As we were tying up to the deserted quay in the port of Tidane a car pulled up with a young Frenchman at the wheel. He offered to take us to the local hospital, where, although it was a Sunday, we saw the doctor on duty who consulted JuanFra and prescribed some medication which he then dispensed from the well stocked pharmacy. He told us that normally the consultation would have been free and that we would have to pay only for the medicines, but as the formalities were too cumbersome, we might as well have them for free as well.

The young man who had brought us to the hospital was waiting to drive us back to the boat, and on the way told us that he was a teacher who had just arrived on a two year appointment. He was accompanied by his wife, also a teacher, and they knew that when they eventually returned to France they would have saved enough money to start a family. He reminded me of a similar young teacher I had met at our first landfall in French Polynesia, in the Gambier Islands, in 1978, but that teacher had not come of his free will. He was a conscientious objector and as he had refused to do his military service, he was sent to work for three years as a teacher in French Polynesia instead. Not a bad deal!

Back to the stone age

Sailors are probably more prone than ordinary people to keep looking back nostalgically to a golden past when there were still countless unspoilt places to explore and you could sail around the world on a shoestring. It is probably true that cruising in the 1970s was generally more rewarding but there are still a few places where things have changed very little. Such a place is Vanuatu, formerly known as the Condominium of the New Hebrides once administered jointly by Britain and France. When we arrived there shortly before independence in 1979 we came across some of the most isolated and undeveloped communities that we had seen anywhere. Quarter of a century later life in the outer islands has changed very little and a way of life can still be found that has disappeared elsewhere. Stretching in a long chain from south to north the twenty-odd islands have everything one could wish for: calm anchorages, welcoming villagers and some of the most interesting sights in the Pacific. There are two highlights that stand out above all others: Yasur volcano on Tanna and the land divers of Pentecost. Having bypassed both islands on my previous visit, a pleasant overnight sail took us from Maré to Tanna where we anchored in Port Resolution named after Captain's Cook ship who was probably the first European to set his sights on these remote islands which he called the New Hebrides.

A young Ni-Vanuatu man greeted us warmly as we stepped ashore on the beach at Port Resolution. Pointing to a couple of thatched huts on the headland behind him, he exclaimed, 'Welcome to the Port Resolution Yacht Club. I'm Wherry.'

To make sailors more comfortable and encourage them to stay longer, Wherry's uncle, Chief Ronnie of the neighbouring village, had built a large hut, now adorned with flags and club burgees, to be used as a shore base by the crews of visiting yachts. Unfortunately Cyclone Ivy that hit Tanna in March 2004 with 120 knot winds, had damaged some of the buildings while devastating crops, flattening banana plantations and denuding

Young and old dancers from a custom village on Tanna

coconut trees. With no help coming from central government, the villagers were eagerly waiting for the arrival of the cruising boats that now provided their main source of income and supplies. As we were the first to arrive that season, our reserves of rice, flour, cooking oil, corned beef and fishhooks were soon exhausted.

After years of dithering the authorities had finally made Tanna a port of entry. Now boats coming from overseas can clear in here instead of being required to call first at Port Vila, the capital, and then be faced with a tough beat against the strong trade winds if they wanted to see Tanna and its main attraction, the live Yasur volcano. Unfortunately formalities had to be completed at Tanna's main settlement of

Lenakel, which is on the opposite side of the island and entailed a bone-rattling trip in a local truck. Several villages are strung along the rough track and, as we drove through one of them, I saw a scene that encompassed in one image the uniqueness of this amazing country: fixed to the trunk of a large tree was a wooden box with a telephone inside from which a man was making a call, while not twenty paces away, another man had just shot a large bird with a bow and arrow.

A public telephone was also the central feature on the village green at Port Resolution, where it stood proudly in its own thatched hut next to a solar panel and a large antenna. Two objects lying incongruously in the middle of the village green caught my attention: a large boom and a spinnaker pole. Wherry explained later that these were among the few things left from a 53 foot yacht that had been lost there the previous year.

Yasur has been active for many years and on dark nights its reddish glow can be seen a long way off, a welcome pointer in a country where lighthouses are unheard of. Wherry offered to arrange a visit to the volcano but explained that it had been reclaimed by the villagers who live on its slopes and they were the only ones allowed to guide visitors to the rim of the mighty crater. Looking shyly at the ground and speaking in a whisper, Wherry also told me, sounding almost apologetic, that the villagers made a charge for this. I told him that there was nothing wrong with that and that I was happy to pay. But I still felt that something was not right so I asked him. 'Wherry, what do other visitors do?'

'Some people are not happy to have to pay but there is nothing I can do because a custom village has the right to charge.'

'In that case there is no need to worry because, as I said, I'll pay... but can we also visit the village itself?'

'Oh no, the village is taboo, and outsiders must not see the women, but occasionally the men will put on a performance for visitors.'

By now I had realized that everything had to be extracted out of Wherry with a lot of patience.

'Very good, so why don't you tell the custom village chief that I am very interested in seeing both the volcano and the performance.'

The following day Wherry told me that the chief had agreed and was expecting us. Wherry also arranged for us to be collected by the one and only local taxi, a battered 4WD pickup truck that I knew too well from my bone crushing trip to Lenakel.

Although I had been in Vanuatu on several occasions I had never had a chance before to visit a custom village. In the narrow sense of the word this usually meant a traditional village where people had returned to the ways of their ancestors, both in their day to day life and in their animistic beliefs. The chance of meeting people from a custom village on Tanna was made even more attractive by the fact that it was here that the John Frum cargo cult originated during the Second World War. Its followers believed that all their needs would be satisfied by goods falling from the skies, their conviction probably inspired by the many aeroplanes that they saw flying over their islands. Even if those expectations have come to nothing, the movement has survived in some villages whose people had turned their backs on the doubtful benefits of the modern world.

A short walk along a narrow muddy path took us to a clearing that was hemmed in on all sides by an impenetrable jungle curtain. Through a small opening at the foot of a gigantic banyan tree, a row of chanting men emerged slowly. They were of all ages, from very young boys to gnarled old men. All were naked with the exception of a tiny skirt at the front, their private parts enclosed in a penis wrapper called a namba sheath, that once was common throughout Melanesia. Chanting and stamping the packed ground with mighty thuds they danced around in a circle, never raising their eyes. It looked straight out of the stone age and something that I had never experienced before.

At the end of the performance the men disappeared through the banyan curtain and we made our way slowly to the rim of the volcano. This was about as close as one wanted to get to a live volcano, as even at the safe distance of one hundred meters the spewing volcano was a sight to behold. Every now and again a deep rumble foretold of a more forceful eruption when large boulders were thrown sky-high. The sight was awesome and so was the pestilential smell, and it was easy to imagine where the vision of hell had originated.

A cult of the ancestors

While Captain Cook had a rather warm welcome on Tanna, at our next stop on the island of Erromango, we were told that early visitors had met with a less friendly reception. When the first two missionaries, John Williams and James Harris, stepped ashore like us at the village of Unpongkor, the locals took them to a sacred place, drew their outline on a large flat rock on which they were laid spread-eagled, then cut them up, cooked them and ate them. We had the privilege of being taken to that gruesome place by the son of the current chief, Joe Mete, who admitted that his own

Our host on Erromango with his ancestors

ancestors had quite probably feasted on the two unfortunate missionaries.

The following day Joe came on board Aventura and we sailed along the coast to Suvu, a small bay fronted by a sandy beach overshadowed by tall coconut trees. He explained that the beach was taboo and no one was allowed to land there because in a nearby cave were the remains of his family members going back several generations. We landed on the beach and made our way up a steep path, slipping on the moist soil. We stopped in front of a wide crack in the cliff face that led into the sacred cave. Before going in, Joe called into the cave, warning his ancestors that he had come to visit them with some friends, and asking their permission to enter the cave. Down in the damp and gloomy cave were piles of bones and about two dozen skulls. As we were leaving, Joe explained that until not so long ago, when an older person felt that the end was near, he or she would ask to be taken to the cave and be left to die alone.

Just as terrible as the fate of those first missionaries were the consequences for the local population of subsequent contacts with traders and missionaries. As a result of various diseases brought by outsiders, and

A land diver takes a death defying leap from a high tower

appease the gods and ensure another good harvest. An overnight sail from Port Vila brought us early one afternoon to Waliap, on the SW coast of Pentecost. Friends in Port Vila had offered to help and for several days had tried to send a message to Chief Willie, who reigned over the area and we had been assured was the only person who could help us see a land diving performance. When we landed on the beach we were met by a large reception committee made up mostly of children but among them was also Chief Willie. My friend had already been in touch with him by phone, so the chief was expecting us and told us that although we had arrived one day early the men were ready to do the land dive that same day.

Several members of Chief Willie's large family accompanied us to a nearby forest

later the widespread kidnapping of men for forced labour in neighbouring territories, the population of Erromango fell from twenty thousand inhabitants in the early 1800s to less than four hundred in 1930. The population had now increased to 1500 and, according to Joe, ten different Christian sects now lived side by side on the island, but as on Tanna, some people had abandoned Christianity, modern dress and practically any links with the outside world, and had reverted to a traditional way of life.

After a safe landing the ankle ties are cut off by a chief

The land divers of Pentecost

The best known custom village on the island of Pentecost is Bunlap, home of the famous land divers of Vanuatu. This special ceremony is normally held at the end of the yam season, a root vegetable which is a staple diet in this part of the Pacific. Young men perform this unique feat of daring to

where a tall tower stood in a clearing. Diving towers are normally only used once and take about one week to build. The divers were from Bunlap, the famous land diving village, and Chief Willie had somehow managed to persuade them to use their tower for an extra performance for our benefit.

The tower was much higher than I had expected and must have been at least eighty feet high. Pairs of lianas were hanging down from platforms inserted at various heights. There were seven divers as well as two young boys, one of who cannot have been more than seven and who looked quite terrified as he prepared to jump from one of the lower platforms.

Before jumping, the diver stood on the edge of the platform, calling out in defiance to the other villagers and, apparently, being free to shout out any indiscretion he liked. He then threw himself forward, as if into a swimming pool, the fall being surprisingly swift as the diver fell rapidly towards the ground. The impact was lessened by the lianas tied to his ankles, the green vines having enough stretch in them to slow down the fall. Even so, what I had not realized, was that the diver actually hit the ground, and, as part of the ceremony, was in fact supposed to touch the loosened soil with his forehead. How hard they hit was difficult to tell as on landing they curled up in a foetal position. A chief would quickly came to help the diver on his feet, who still looked rather stunned, and cut with a machete the vines that had been tightly bound to his ankles with strands of pandanus fibre. The diver then retook his place among the dancers at the base of the tower. Throughout the performance several dozen men, women and young boys would dance, stomp and chant, while the divers made their preparations for the jump.

Neither words nor photographs can describe the sheer excitement that I felt as a spectator, as diver after diver hurtled towards the ground, the adrenaline coursing in my veins as if it was me and not them who had taken that awesome death-defying leap.

Unexpected head winds slowed our progress as we made our way north among the islands and by the time we had reached our destination, the small island of Gaua,

it was night. Although I always try to avoid entering a bay or even a port at night, as we slowly approached Lakona Bay we found it bathed in bright light by a full moon. The forward looking sonar helped me find a good spot and we dropped the anchor in eight meters. In the morning we reanchored in shallower water closer to the shore where the solitary occupant of a small outrigger canoe paddled out to welcome us on behalf of his father, the local chief who sent his apologies for not being

Double waterfall at Sasara in Northern Vanuatu

able to come himself as he was sick. Apparently he had been attacked by some wild dogs and had been badly bitten. I asked the young man if his father needed help and he admitted that they were at a loss at what to do as the only clinic was on the opposite side of the island and there was no road across.

We found Chief Johnstar moaning softly in a darkened hut. The bites looked infected so I gave him a treatment of antibiotics and by the time we were ready to leave a few days later, the infection was on the mend and Chief Johnstar could walk around unaided. As a farewell gesture the chief's family put on a performance of water music. Standing up to their waist in

A farewell concert of water music before we leave Gaua

the shallow water they slapped the surface with slightly cupped hands then moved their hands from side to side, the resulting hum sounding like a deep organ. As we were leaving the young man who had been the first to welcome us, paddled out in his canoe that had been filled with fruit and vegetables for us.

Our last stop in Vanuatu was at Sasara, on the west coast of Vanua Lava, better known among sailors as Double Waterfall Bay. I remember it being deserted when we stopped there with Aventura I, but as we entered the bay with Aventura III, an outrigger canoe, carrying a man and several children, headed towards us. The man introduced himself as Chief Kerely and invited us ashore. We landed later in front of a cluster of houses, where all the family members were gathered and, as we stepped ashore, they all burst out singing 'Welcome to Waterfall Bay'... to the tune of God Save the Queen.

We were then welcomed into what Chief Kerely grandly described as the yacht club. He told us that having worked for several years on various islands, he decided to strike out for himself, so took over the tiny settlement that had been started by his grandparents in the early 1980s. He gradually constructed a small village, with everything built from traditional materials. Later he was joined by his brother and family and by the time of our visit the expanded family had grown to over twenty people. Kerely admitted that they depended greatly on the services they provided to visiting yachts. Indeed, the interaction with visiting sailors seemed to be more pronounced here than at other similar places I had come across, and evidently quite essential to the villagers' well-being if not survival. Various things had been done to make visiting sailors welcome and encourage them to stay longer: an airy club house, trips in outrigger canoe or jungle walks, visits to the family burial cave as well as providing meals ashore and dealing with laundry. Some services were paid for in money but trading goods were usually preferred. The previous year, as Sasara started to be visited by more and more yachts, Kerely decided to organize a sailors' get-together. The word must have spread because a total of 28 yachts showed up for the feast and virtually filled the bay, the visiting sailors being joined by people from surrounding villages who came over for a weekend of dancing, singing and games.

Sailing Friends

Friends have been a constant source of happiness throughout my life, and I regard even my closest family primarily as friends, and treat them as such. I have no doubt that my excellent relationship with Gwenda is due to the fact that we started off as friends and have continued to be best friends all our life. I regard Doina and Ivan, now that they are grown up, more as friends and equals than just my children. I treat my nephew Klaus and my niece Marianne the same way and as a result I think we have a closer relationship than they have with their own father. All through my life I have always kept in touch with my friends and, as a result, am still in regular contact with old school mates, fellow rugby players, not to speak of the many friends we made in countries all around the world while cruising on the various Aventuras.

Already as a child I realized just how important was the support of one's friends so as to survive the cruel system that I grew up in. I heard this from my father, whose survival in prison had often been thanks to his friends, and I saw how much support my mother drew from her friends during those difficult times. My family was in no way exceptional as everyone else lived and survived by the same rules. In June 2006 I drove to Romania for the celebrations marking the fiftieth anniversary of our graduation from the Honterus Gymnasium. Practically all my schoolmates had by then emigrated to Germany, but almost all of them came back to Brasov because, just like me, they felt the power of friendship.

My sailing life is no exception, so whenever I am not sailing with my family I try to sail with friends and I have rarely sailed with people I don't know well. What makes me really happy is that not only have I never had problems with any of my friends on board, but also that my friends don't seem to have any problem with me either, as every one of those who sailed with me always responds enthusiastically when I invite them to join me again.

Many of the friends I have made over the years have already been mentioned in this book, such as JuanFra Martin, Barry Esrig, Antti Louhija, Dieter Walz, Marc Martinez and Patrick Canut, all of whom sailed with me at some point during my latest voyage. I have been privileged to meet

Former ARC participants Lucy and Mirek Misayat receive a plaque for their support of the event

many interesting sailors over the last thirty years, and their stories would easily fill a book on its own, so I will only profile some of them.

Like Barry Esrig, some of my sailing friends I have met through the ARC and kept in contact afterwards. Mirek and Lucy Misayat sailed their Kaprys in one of the early ARCs and became so enthusiastic about it that they decided to sponsor one of the major prizes. On several occasions they flew over to St Lucia to present their prize, which, unfortunately was discontinued after the ARC was sold. However we have still remained friends

331

and I sailed with them on Kaprys in Scotland and Ireland.

One of the most outstanding of the ARC sailors is Ernst Torp, who sailed in the first two ARCs. Years before I met him, Ernst had been diagnosed with multiple sclerosis but he refused to give in and continued to lead as normal a life as possible. Although confined to a wheelchair he successfully completed four Atlantic crossings and, when I invited him to come to Gibraltar for the start of the first round the world rally, he drove his specially converted minibus all the way from Norway. After the start he took the ferry to Gran Canaria where his wife Brit runs a physiotherapy clinic. Although now in his seventies, Ernst continues to race in the 2-metre class, has won titles at the Paralympic Games and is a Nordic champion.

I met Pierre Ribes in Las Palmas as he was preparing his 26 foot Sphinx for yet another voyage to West Africa. Every year Pierre would load up his boat with medical equipment collected from French hospitals and take them to Senegal. To make sure that they reached the right people he would then tour the country delivering equipment, medication and used spectacles to village clinics and small hospitals. A serious work accident, which broke his spine, had left him crippled but with iron determination he taught himself to walk again. As he could no longer work as a market gardener he took up sailing and ended up running an annual delivery trip between France and West Africa. Two years ago I received the sad news that Sphinx had disappeared while crossing the Bay of Biscay.

Also in Las Palmas one day I was surprised to see a small red boat flying the Hungarian flag. On board were two young men, Jozsi Gal and Nandor Fa, who had set off to sail around the world. Knowing who I was, they asked me to give my opinion on their proposed route that would take them around the capes of Horn and Good Hope. As their 30 foot boat had been built to sail on Lake Balaton and not in the Roaring Forties, I had serious misgivings and told them that as their intention was to be the first Hungarians to sail around the world they might as well do it the easy way by the classic trade wind route. They would have none of it and took the hard route. During the following year they kept me informed of their progress and, to my great relief, managed to achieve their ambition and return to their landlocked country to a heroes' welcome. In the intervening years Nandor has taken part in several single-handed round the world races, while Jozsi is running a successful charter business.

Peter Noble

Peter is one of my oldest London friends. His children were a similar age to Doina and Ivan and attended the same school in the London suburb where we both lived. When I started work on Aventura, as a keen sailor himself, Peter took great interest in the progress of my work. He continued to support me through all my subsequent boats and each time took charge of my medical supplies.

We spent the first summer of our voyage in Greece, crisscrossing the Aegean hopping from island to island. Our favourite island was Tinos, which is the main place of pilgrimage in Greece, its church having an icon of the Madonna with miraculous healing powers and there was a continuous stream of sick and disabled people and their families arriving on the frequent ferries from Piraeus. Many of them crawled down the gangplank on their hands and knees and then proceeded to cover the

Peter Noble at the helm of Artemis

remaining kilometre up the hill to the church in the same fashion. Doina and Ivan were fascinated by this pitiful and yet moving spectacle.

Around this time Doina and Ivan had discovered the pleasure of rowing and spent hours in the small inflatable pottering about the large harbour. Early one morning, while taking advantage of a quiet spell to record one of my radio programmes, I faintly heard Doina's voice shouting for help. I jumped into the cockpit, saw that the wind had come up and the dinghy was drifting out to sea. I dove in and as I hit the water felt one of my front crowns come loose. I clamped my mouth shut and, swimming as fast as I could, reached the dinghy and rowed it back to the boat. When I tried to resume my recording I realised that without a front tooth I had a terrible lisp, so I fixed the crown back with chewing gum and completed the recording. I then took it out and carefully stowed it in a safe place.

In Tinos we had arranged to be joined by Peter, his wife Mary and a teacher that Gwenda had worked with in London. The morning of their arrival I went to look for my tooth, as I certainly did not want to look like Long John Silver when I met those two ladies. I looked everywhere but the tooth and the tissue it was wrapped in had disappeared.

'Gwenda, have you seen my tooth? You know, my precious recording tooth.'

'No, where did you put it?'

'Here in this locker, but now it's empty.'

'Oh my goodness, I tidied up all the lockers this morning and threw out everything that looked like rubbish to make space for the guests.'

'Oh no, what am I going to do? We must find it.'

But the ferry was already coming in and as we met our friends they looked puzzled to see my unsmiling face.

'What's the matter?' Peter asked.

'I've lost my front tooth,' I lisped, 'and cannot even smile.'

I was furious and not speaking to Gwenda, so Peter offered to accompany her in a taxi to the local rubbish dump in the hope of identifying our bag amongst the recent arrivals. Not surprisingly they returned later empty handed so I was stuck with my lisp.

In the early 1980s Peter bought Artemis, a Rival 34, in which he made a complete circuit of the Atlantic, crossing from the Canaries to the Caribbean, spending the winter there, and returning home via the Azores. He eventually sold Artemis, bought a larger boat, then sold her as well and, for a while gave up sailing. Recently he took me by surprise when he told me that he had managed to track down his old Artemis whose third owner had completely refitted her. As she was stored ashore in Southern Portugal, Peter bought her sight unseen. He now plans to take up cruising again. My first reaction when he told me what he had just done was of utter dismay, but later I realized that sailors are a romantic, often crazy lot, and even an eminent psychiatrist like Peter is no exception.

Mike Craggs

During Aventura III's maiden voyage, Mike Craggs, a friend from London, joined us for a cruise in Scandinavia. Mike is not only a keen sailor but also an electronics wizard with several inventions to his credit, notable among them a tiny device that can be implanted into a paraplegic person's spine and helps them control their incontinency, an ingenious solution that has dramatically improved the lives of many people. With his wide experience in designing gadgets, Mike had generously agreed to help me with a problem I had in the round the world rallies. In order to accommodate both those who join a cruising rally simply for its safety aspect, and those who are looking for a challenge and some competition, both the ARC and the round the world rallies included a racing division. Using the engine in the racing class was not allowed, but in the cruising division a limited amount of engine use was permitted, had to be declared and was taken into account when results were calculated. After two round the world rallies it became apparent that this was a major source of suspicion among skippers, as some had failed to declare the hours of engine use honestly and were clearly cheating.

Ivan had already conceived the prototype of a special hour counter that was clamped to the propeller shaft and would start counting the moment the engine was put in gear. This meant that engines could still be used for charging the batteries. It looked like the ideal solution but the system was not perfect so I asked Mike to help. He took matters in hand, managed to miniaturized the device and provide it with small, watch-type batteries. The new monitors were used in the third round the world rally and seemed to be the ideal solution... until one skipper worked out a system of attaching a magnet next to the device that stopped it working. If somebody is determined to cheat, they'll do it regardless, even in an amateur cruising rally, so I decided to give up.

By way of compensation for all of Mike's hard work, I invited him to join us for a cruise along the coasts of Sweden and Denmark. With an imminent gale approaching we ran for shelter into the small port of Mölle, spotted a space beside a home-built steel boat, and I told Gwenda and Mike to get ready to come alongside. While Gwenda was on the foredeck with a line in her hands, Mike stood on the side deck looking ready as well. I eased the boat alongside... and a grinding crunching noise made me fear the worst.

'Mike, where are the fenders?'

'Oh God, Jimmy, I'm so sorry. I honestly don't know how I could have been so stupid!'

After we managed to squeeze in the fenders, I had a look at the damage, which was minimal.

'There is nothing like an unpainted aluminium hull to save friendships and marriages,' was my heartfelt comment.

Erick and Muriel Bouteleux

Erick and Muriel have been our close friends ever since we met in La Palma, in the Canaries, in 1976 both preparing to set off on our first Atlantic crossing. As we came into the crowded port looking for a spot to anchor and row a line ashore, a dinghy detached itself from the stern of a nearby classic looking yacht and made for us, the blond guy of my age propelling it in typical French fashion by sculling.

'If you desire my dinghy and don't want to blow yours, you can have her.'

Erick and Muriel Bouteleux fishing in the Marquesas

That was the beginning of a lasting friendship and, in hindsight, the best thing that came out of that first voyage.

Soon after we arrived in the Caribbean we met Calao again and, for a while, cruised in company, Doina and Ivan getting on very well with Sidonie and Fabien, who were slightly younger. As we reached Antigua I decided to postpone our voyage to the South Pacific as I didn't want to miss the unique opportunity of first seeing the USA. When I told Erick, who was just about to turn around and head for Panama, he replied without a moment of reflection. 'That sounds great, we'll come too.'

We reached Florida via the Bahamas then sailed in company sometimes inside the Intra Coastal Waterway, sometimes outside when we got bored with motoring, all the way via New York to Camden, Maine. The appearance of the French and British flagged yachts in an area, which rarely saw foreign sailors, caused much interest and provided us with an uninterrupted supply of invitations ashore.

With the end of the hurricane season approaching, and winter on its heels, we headed back the same way, sailed through New York for the second time and finally arrived in Beaufort, NC, where we parted company. Aventura made straight for the Outer Bahamas and continued to Panama, while Calao lingered on but eventually followed the same route to Peru. By the time Calao got there Aventura was already in New Zealand where we spent the entire summer, while the cyclone season was burning itself out in the tropics. Before returning to the tropics we had agreed by letter to meet at the point where a line drawn due west from Peru would intersect with the track up from New Zealand. The point of intersection was the Vava'u group in Tonga where we were supposed to meet on a certain day in late May. Aventura arrived there on the morning of the agreed day and while we were sitting happily at anchor, around midday we saw a white sloop approaching. 'Calao' we all shouted, and indeed it was the Bouteleux family.

The day we left Vava'u for Samoa the weather looked unsettled, so I told Erick that as they had already been to Samoa, if the weather got bad it made more sense for them to go straight to Wallis where we would meet them later. We soon lost sight of them and the next day we ran into a vicious thunderstorm with incessant bolts of lightning hitting the sea all around us. We were tempted to turn tail for Wallis but I had some radio work arranged so we continued to Western Samoa. The morning after we had arrived in Apia we were surprised to see Calao sailing through the harbour entrance. I simply could not believe my eyes and shouted across.

'I was sure you would go to Wallis in that awful weather.'

'But Jimmy, you invited us to dinner at Aggie Grey's for Gwenda's birthday, you didn't imagine that we would miss out on such an invitation?'

So we spent an unforgettable evening at Aggie Grey's, one the most famous establishments in the South Pacific, celebrating not just Gwenda's birthday but also our friendship.

From Wallis we went separate ways again, Aventura sailing north to Tuvalu and Kiribati while Calao headed for Australia. Once again, we arranged a rendezvous, this time in Cairns, Queensland. On the appointed day we had almost given them up, when in the dusk we saw the unmistakeable lines of Calao coming slowly up the river being towed by Erick in his dinghy. While motoring into the river the

Fabien Bouteleux at the South Pacific Festival of Arts

engine alarm had sounded but as there had been a few false alarms before and less than a mile to go and no wind to sail, Erick decided to continue. That decision had the serious consequence of seizing up the engine completely, as the alarm had

been warning of a fall in oil pressure. We had already agreed to sail together to Papua New Guinea for the South Pacific Festival of Arts and as Erick was not one to be left behind, on the given day we towed Calao out of the harbour and she sailed engineless all the way to Port Moresby through the Great Barrier Reef and some of the most treacherous waters in the world. They arrived in time for the Festival which proved to be worth any sacrifice as it brought together all the best from the various Pacific nations during two weeks of dancing, singing and traditional canoe racing.

Having already ordered all the necessary engine parts from France, Erick proceeded to dismantle the engine and, although he had never done it before, managed to put it together again. They then caught up with us in Bali and we continued to sail together as far as Malaysia, where we parted company yet again. As we had promised Doina to return to England as soon as possible, we left Calao behind and reached the Mediterranean a few months later. Calao spent longer in the Indian Ocean but while in Port Sudan news reached them from France that Muriel's father had died and they had to return home immediately. They had no choice but leave the boat where they were, possibly one of the unsafest places in the world. Three months later, when they came back, Calao was anchored unharmed in the same place. The long exposure to the scorching sun had opened all seams on the old wooden yacht so the entire hull had to be recaulked. During their absence a freighter had run aground and the locals were busy retrieving

Dottie, Albert and Toby Fletcher on Duen

its fuel, so Erick joined them and filled his jerrycans with diesel which would come in handy for the tough beat up the Red Sea. Soon after he started the engine, it came to a stop, and when he tried to restart it he found that the fuel was so contaminated that it had ruined the injection pump. With no repair facilities available, they had no choice but to sail to Suez. What is even more astonishing is that the authorities took pity on them and allowed Calao to proceed through the Suez Canal propelled by its outboard engine. Having reached the Mediterranean, Calao sailed to Cyprus, where Erick once again dismantled his long suffering engine, got it going again, and finally made it back to their home in the south of France. They could say truly that they had SAILED around the world.

Dottie and Albert Fletcher

I cannot think of a better example of a happy cruising family that that of the crew of Duen. Among the many cruising people I have met, Dottie and Albert Fletcher have been among the most remarkable. Their boat Duen was also remarkable, a 50 ft traditional Norwegian fishing boat built in 1939 and lovingly restored by Albert. We first met them in New Zealand and our paths crossed in several places after that. As Dottie and Albert had both been married previously and each had children and even grandchildren, Duen's crew was made up of various members of their combined families. I never managed quite to work out who belonged to who as they all looked related even if they were not. None of this

seemed to make any difference and they all mixed happily together.

As Duen plodded her way around the world with time of absolutely no essence, other young people were welcomed aboard with open arms, fed and looked after, so the crew was constantly being augmented. Some stopped for days and some stayed for months. I have never seen a happier atmosphere on any other boat and put it all down to Dottie and Albert's generous and tolerant characters. Being kind to your neighbour was Albert's deep conviction and, while sailing with them in the Caribbean I was not entirely surprised when, after the evening meal, the entire crew gathered in the main cabin to listen to Albert read out a text. Its meaning was then discussed openly by everyone. When it was over, the instruments came out and, led by Albert who is an excellent guitarist and has a beautiful voice, the improvised band played the night away. Needless to say we have remained close friends and have visited them on their large property in Missouri. What is surprising is that they now live as far away from the sea as one can possible go, maybe because after their fourteen-year circumnavigation they have had their fill.

Arthur and Germaine Beiser

Marina Kremik in Croatia, where Aventura III had been waiting patiently while I was writing this book, had been recommended to me by Arthur and Germaine Beiser whose boat had been based there for several years. The two of them have been sailing for well over fifty years, ever since they got married in New York and bought their first boat. In 1960, they bought the 58 foot Abeking and Rasmussen ketch Minots Light, and accompanied by their three daughters, crossed the Atlantic to Scandinavia. The next ten years were spent mostly in the Baltic, cruising in the summer, while in the winter the girls went to school and Germaine and Arthur wrote books. Later when the girls went to university in the USA, they sold Minots Lights and purchased the Swan 47 Quicksilver. Missing the comfort of their previous yacht, they decided that only a larger yacht would do, so they purchased a Nicholson 70. On the way to the Azores, during their crossing of the Atlantic, the yacht sank as a result of shoddy work done while she was being refitted. The crew was saved by a cargo ship and eventually the yard had to settle with the insurers.

Arthur and Germaine manage to successfully divide their time between their sailing and professional lives. As a professor of physics and author of a number of college texts, Arthur spends the summers cruising and the winters revising or re-editing his many books. Apart from his scientific books, Arthur has also written books on sailing, best known among them being "The Proper Yacht". Germaine is the author or co-author of seven books on various aspects of physics.

For the last twenty years Arthur and Germaine have been cruising the Mediterranean and living a most

Germaine and Arthur Beiser on board their comfortable Ardent Spirit

comfortable life on their Ardent Spirit. The Moody 58 had been customized for their needs and has allowed them, in Arthur's words 'to enjoy comfortable, safe and happy cruising all over the Med. We cannot imagine life without her.'

Any excuse for a party

For my sixtieth birthday I invited our closest friends for a long weekend to a mountain resort above Brasov, in Romania, where I grew up. Seventy-four of them showed up and we had a most wonderful time together. If Erick and Muriel would sail through bad weather to Samoa for dinner, it is not surprising that they flew to Romania from France. Dottie and Albert plus Barry Esrig flew in from the US. Other friends came from Australia and from all over Europe, Mirek and Lucy Misayat from Spain, Antti and Nina from Finland, Dieter and Li from Germany, Mike Craggs from London and Peter and Joan Noble who have never missed a Cornell party wherever it might be held. As I am writing these lines I remember some of the moments I have spent with my friends, some afloat, others ashore, and realize just how lucky I have been.

Pacific Farewell

A ventura lay at anchor in the most delightful place located at 11°07'S, 152°20'E close to the island of Panasia, an uninhabited island in the Calvados chain in the Louisiades archipelago, a cluster of small islands in the far SE corner of Papua New Guinea. On the chart of this part of the world the tiny specks of islands look as if some flies had had a busy time.

to the boat, they hung about quietly waiting to be noticed and invariably brought a small gift. The islands themselves are a cruising paradise, probably what the Virgins looked like fifty or more years ago. There are scores of tiny islands, mostly hilly but also a few low-lying ones, with beautiful sandy beaches and lots of anchorages sheltered from the prevailing trade winds.

Some of the small communities were completely cut off from the outside world. They were very much on their own, without

Villagers come to welcome us in the Louisiades

The Louisiades are remote even by New Guinea standards, and the small villages we visited would not have looked any different if we had landed there two hundred years earlier. The few people we met were all very friendly and welcoming, and a great bonus was that almost everyone spoke English, some of them surprisingly well thanks to their missionary school education. This made it possible to have a proper conversation, to find out how they lived and what they did. Unlike some other parts of the world, the people were shy and unobtrusive, and when they paddled out

any help or interference from the local government, who I suspected didn't know what was going on in some of the remoter parts of the country. This became clear when we cleared in at the small port of Misima and I asked the chief of police if people in the neighbouring islands still lived a traditional life. He assured me quite firmly that they most certainly did not... and, a few hours after that conversation, the very first place where we dropped anchor was exactly the kind of place that I had hoped to find. What puzzled me was that the same day the police chief was setting off by launch on a tour of those same islands, but then I realized that he only went to the main settlement, met the local police chief then went back to base.

Soon after we dropped the anchor behind Bobo Eina island an outrigger canoe with two women and three children paddled out to greet us and gave us a bag of small tomatoes and a bunch of greens. Both women spoke English and asked if we had any items to trade, so I asked them what they needed. From the items they mentioned I realized that they were used to visiting yachts: paint, sealant, a diving mask, as well as the more usual requests such as fish hooks and rice. They told us that they lived with their family close by and invited us to visit.

We took up the invitation and landed on their beach later that day. Drawn up on the beach were several canoes of various sizes, the largest having a sail and being used for longer inter-island trips, the others having smaller sails or just paddles. Under a large tree a young man was hewing a small canoe out of a tree trunk, his only tool a simple adze. This versatile tool, a few pots and pans, and some plastic containers were the only items that were not made of natural materials. I was told that their extended family had moved over from one of the neighbouring villages and had made its base there: grandfather, father and mother, son, daughter-in-law and three children. Grandfather was quite old and was sitting on a shady open platform playing with a baby. The houses were all made of woven pandanus and coconut thatch. A well-tended garden had been cleared out of the bush to grow papaya, yam, taro, sweet potato, beans, pumpkins and tomatoes.

A man carving a canoe out of a tree trunk at Bobo Eina

What we found both there and in the more remote islands of Vanuatu was self-sufficiency in its purest form as people lived from the land and sea, grew and caught what they needed, and did not seem to need all that much from the outside world. Soon after the first traders arrived here the local people were either induced or decided for themselves to harvest or grow a cash crop: sandalwood, sea cucumbers, mother-of-pearl shells, copra or timber. Later, planters arrived and set up large coconut plantations providing employment for local men. So money began circulating and people were able to buy their basic supplies. This encouraged them to live in villages, with their store, school and church. In recent years, as a result of a drop in both the demand and price of copra, most plantations have been abandoned, so a reverse phenomenon was now in evidence. As there was no market for cash crops, nor any demand for work on plantations, there was no source of income so people had no choice but to become self-sufficient again. Rather than live in a village, some families moved out to live on their own. Usually they resettled on ancestral land and lived in harmony with nature just as their forbears had done. If the children needed to go to school they were usually sent to stay with relatives. For some of these isolated families trading with visiting sailors had become a way of life, and wherever I came across such examples I felt that the human contact with passing cruisers was more important than what the locals actually got out of them.

At Panasia we had the small island to ourselves. The evening of our arrival two men came over in a sailing canoe from the neighbouring island to offer us two large lobsters, which we traded for some T-shirts. The following day we were visited by a large canoe with eight men who brought some carvings, shells, eggs and a few vegetables to trade. Having recently heard of several cases of robberies in other parts of Papua New Guinea I was rather concerned to be faced with a bunch of rough looking guys with only two of us onboard. But it soon became clear that they meant no harm and were in fact just enjoying having someone different to talk to. To my shame, having automatically suspected these innocent people, I was so relieved that I only bargained with them to keep up appearances and was actually quite happy to give away all my trading goods. Their young chief, John Mwasi, told me that his Meisoga clan had recently won a court case confirming their ownership of the island and surrounding reef. He was hoping to attract more visiting boats to the area, so Panasia's deserted days might be over soon.

They left us as the sun was going down and, as I sat on deck, it occurred to me that this was my last anchorage in the Pacific so I tried to take it all in: the scenery of craggy cliffs and turquoise waters, the ring of islands on the horizon, the psychedelic colours of a tropical sunset. In the last quarter of a century I had left the South Pacific by boat three times but this was the first time that I was leaving without the certainty that I would return.

Through the Torres Strait

I had a really nice surprise when I pulled out the chart covering the approaches to the Torres Strait and saw on it the cats-cradle of position lines I had drawn on my first passage through those waters. That was in the good/bad old days of astronavigation and I can still remember vividly the feeling of anxiety as we approached these treacherous waters with nothing but a sextant and depth-sounder to tell me where we were. As soon as the sun was up I took the first of several sights hoping to pinpoint the gap in the reef that led into the buoyed shipping channel. A small islet, Bramble Cay, marks the northern edge of Bligh Entrance and would have been concrete proof that we had arrived in the right place. By mid-morning I gave a great sigh of relief as we found the first buoy and thus the main shipping channel, but I never saw Bramble Cay.

And now? My GPS told me exactly where we were so making landfall was child's play... well, almost, as I still had a knot in my stomach while setting a zigzag course among all those reefs. History repeated itself as I found the first buoy, turned the corner and... just as that first time, Bramble Cay refused to show its face! It took us all day and the following night to reach Thursday Island on the edge of the Arafura Sea.

Having completed entry formalities into Australia as well as the stringent quarantine requirements in the small port, a four knot current sent us flying into the dull green waters of the Arafura Sea, the change from the dark blue waters of the Pacific being so abrupt that it was almost painful. Even the winds felt different and after the boisterous trade winds that we had enjoyed since we had left the Louisiades, we now had light winds that felt like having a different texture. We were quite clearly entering not just a different ocean but a different world.

Those balmy ESE winds settled at around 15 knots which were ideal spinnaker conditions, the ParaSailor keeping up a steady speed of between six and seven knots. Our target was Darwin about 800 miles almost due west of Thursday Island. There are two ways to reach the port, the easier but longer route that passes west of Bathurst Island, or a shorter route through the Dundas and Clarence Straits. The latter route is usually avoided by cruising yachts as the straits are swept by strong tides and the intricate route through a maze of reefs and small islands makes for challenging navigation. In spite of, or to be honest, because of this, I was tempted to try that route. In order to be able to do this we had to catch the right tide and that meant arriving at the northern entrance into Dundas Strait at exactly the right time.

Nothing helps focus the mind better than having a rendezvous with Miss Tide on a Friday night at 9 p.m. at Cape Don some 580 miles distant. We had to keep up an average speed of six knots, which with the help of the spinnaker we manage to do although the wind later dropped to ten knots. We even managed to catch a large kingfish, one of the tastiest pelagic fish.

We arrived off Cape Don at precisely the agreed time and Miss Tide was there waiting. With a smile on her face she waved at us to follow her, so we turned Aventura's bows south and, once we were pointing in the right direction, Miss Tide gave another

Aboriginal rock painting in Kakadu reserve

wave and was gone. Fortunately she left us with a strong favourable current that helped us make fast progress. The wind had by now increased to 20 knots so we were flying, which would have been a thrilling experience in the open sea but not when I had to plot an absolutely accurate course to pass the Abbot Shoals at a safe distance, which we zipped past in the dark night doing 8 knots. The next gap to find was the entrance into Howard Channel, where we arrived just as it was getting light. As we still had the tide with us, the current in the narrow channel was 3.2 knots, and our speed over the ground 9 knots. Fortunately at this end of the channel there were a number of lit buoys, but I would have preferred to have had them earlier while it was still dark. As we shot past the last pair of buoys, having managed to do the entire shortcut on one tide, I could see far ahead the outline of Darwin's tall buildings.

The capital of Australia's Northern Territory is a pleasant modern city that has had to be re-built twice from scratch, once after it was almost pulverized in the second world war, and then in 1974 when cyclone Tracy tried to complete the unfinished job of the Japanese bombers. As the base of a large shrimping fleet, Darwin has excellent repair facilities and the new Cullen Bay marina has turned it into a popular stop for long distance cruising sailors. Darwin is also a good starting point for inland trips whether to the nearby Kakadu nature reserve or the spectacular Kimberleys. Although the Territorians, as the locals are referred to, are keen to project Darwin's reputation as a frontier town populated by swaggering Crocodile Dundees, it is in fact a pleasant, civilized place, with pastel coloured buildings, wide tree-lined avenues and a slow pace perfectly adapted to the usual 40°C temperatures.

As I planned to leave the boat for several weeks in Darwin I hauled her out at Sadgrove Quay boatyard, whose owners George and Penny LaSette had been generous supporters of the round the world rallies. Throughout the voyage I tried to leave Aventura in a safe place and return to our home in Provence during May and June. This time I was going to be later than usual as we only arrived in Darwin on 29 May, almost exactly three months and 4000 miles since leaving Auckland. It had been a busy but highly enjoyable three months, and the stops in Vanuatu and the Louisiades were already etched in my mind as highlights of the voyage.

Into the Indian Ocean

As the closest Australian port to Indonesia, Darwin is also the ideal starting point for a cruise to that archipelago of ten thousand islands, amongst which Bali continues to be the preferred destination for most sailors. Benign weather conditions for the one thousand mile passage across the Arafura and Timor Seas gave us one week of glorious sailing, all of it under spinnaker. In Darwin I had a change of crew as Dieter had to return to his architectural practice in the German city of Zwickau, and I was joined by an acquaintance who had recently acquired a boat and was keen to do some offshore sailing.

The only hiccup on an otherwise perfect passage occurred right at the end when a strong contrary current slowed us down so that it was already dark by the time we arrived off the entrance channel into Benoa harbour. As I knew the harbour I decided to enter but only narrowly avoided running aground when a strong current pushed us out of the channel as described in chapter 6. Ten minutes later we were tying up at Bali marina.

Although the marina was full of cruising boats, the number of other tourists had gone down considerably after the bomb explosion of 2002 and even two years later most hotels were half empty. Having been to Bali on many occasions, both by boat and aeroplane, I knew the island quite well and could never understand how such an atrocity could happen amongst what I regard as one of the most peaceful and gentle people in the world. In spite of the massive impact of tourism, traditions are still very much alive and the Hindu religion, to which most Balinese belong, plays an active part in their day-to-day lives. Each home has a shrine dedicated to its patron god, and, to appease the gods, small square baskets are put out every day in front of shops and offices, usually right on the pavement. Every taxi that I took had a similar offering on its dashboard.

While having breakfast at the marina restaurant one morning I saw one of the waiters set a small offering in front of the statue of a deity overlooking the marina. I later noticed that the offering was renewed throughout the day, the small basket containing rice and food as well as flowers. Statues of various deities, usually shaded by a dainty umbrella, could be seen everywhere, their lower half prudishly swathed in a black and white checked sarong. Even a sacred banyan tree, which I saw while driving across the island, had its lower part covered by such a sarong.

The day before we arrived in Bali, news reached my crew that his former wife had

Women take their offerings to a temple on Bali

died after a long battle with cancer. As his son had been living with his mother, my crew decided to return home for a week to help sort things out. I told him that in view of the changed circumstances it would be better if he stayed with his son as I would have no problem finding replacement crew, but he refused telling me that he was keen to continue the voyage.

With one week to kill on my own, I spent much of the time visiting the interior of the island. What I found amazing was that in spite of the large number of tourists that had made Bali one of the most popular holiday destinations in the world, all that influx was confined to the beach resorts. In the interior life continued at a pace that had hardly changed for centuries, with people tending their fields and buffalo drawn ploughs scouring the deep mud of terraced rice paddies. On narrow lanes I came across women walking to the nearest temple with layered piles of offerings precariously balanced on their heads. On our first visit with Aventura I we had spent some time in Bali's interior visiting various temples and the sacred Gunung Batur Mountain, and I was happy to see that virtually everything was just as I had remembered it. As we were preparing to leave Bali and head west into the Indian Ocean, I set my own little basket of offerings in front of the god overlooking the marina, and asked him to bless Aventura and those who sail in her.

An Indian Ocean hideaway

That Balinese deity must have taken notice of my prayer because we had the most perfect sail to Cocos, with only two noticeable occurrences during the week long passage. One night I saw what I first thought to be a bright white flare to the east but as it kept growing larger and plummeting fast towards the sea I realized that it could only be some space debris burning up as it entered the atmosphere.

A rich harvest of flying fish landed on Aventura's deck during the night

That same night we were bombarded by aliens of a more friendly kind as an entire school of flying fish landed on Aventura's deck. Some managed to wriggle their way to freedom but in the morning I still found in the scuppers a total of twenty-two large flying fish. I arranged them in a line to photograph them and then emailed the photograph to Gwenda, Doina and Ivan. Although I was very happy to be sailing in the middle of a huge ocean and had no feelings of remoteness or isolation, I also appreciated being in constant touch with family and friends. Being able to send a digital photograph via satellite phone to the other side of the world seemed a miracle.

Direction Island in North Cocos is unique in that it feels as if it belongs to cruising sailors. Because of its remoteness this Australian outpost in the South Indian Ocean has gained the affection of all long distance cruisers who call there. The authorities welcome sailors, having cleaned up the island, installed a barbecue pit, toilets and built an open sided hut with tables and benches. There was even a phone for free local calls, and two large water tanks to use for a shower or to do one's laundry. The so-called clubhouse was

adorned with hundreds of mementoes of boats that had passed through, among them some famous names. Sailors had given free rein to their artistic talent whether in the form of carved name boards, inscribed fishing floats, decorated pieces of driftwood, a stuffed puffer fish, signed country or club flags, even a couple of quite beautiful paintings that reminded me of the wall paintings of Horta in the Azores.

There were nine other yachts there when we arrived and tied to the yellow quarantine buoy. An Australian police officer came over in a boat from the main settlement on West Island and quickly dealt with all formalities. Kindly ignoring the strict quarantine rules, he allowed us to keep all our fresh provisions provided they were consumed on board and made us promise that any garbage that was taken ashore would be burnt. Later that

Completing formalities on Cocos Island

afternoon we joined the other sailors for the daily happy hour ashore, everyone bringing their own drinks and snacks. A hurricane lamp was lit when it got dark and the party continued late into the night. 'This is what I always dreamt of as being the true cruising life,' my crew told me as we made our way back to the boat.

Practical Aspects of Offshore Cruising

There is now an internet café on every rock.

Michelle LaMontagne

Tongan immigration, customs, health and agriculture officials come to clear us in

Dealing with formalities is an unavoidable aspect of cruising and especially for newcomers it can be both daunting and irritating. Whereas in most countries that are used to cruising yachts formalities are simpler than in the past, there are still many more restrictions imposed on cruising sailors than on ordinary tourists arriving by air. Formalities were not any simpler in the days of Columbus and he was arrested when he reached Lisbon on his first return from the New World. Admittedly he wasn't flying a yellow Q flag so no wonder he was treated with suspicion.

Formalities and documents

There is a certain routine, almost an etiquette, which must be observed whenever clearing into a new country. The first rule is to make for an official port of entry and show your intentions by flying the yellow Q flag as well as the courtesy flag of that country as soon as you enter its territorial waters (usually three miles). Never stop and go ashore anywhere before having cleared in first. It is important to remember that it is the intention that counts. Sometimes it is sufficient to make a call to customs whether on VHF or, as in the USA, from one of the special telephones installed on arrival docks. By clearly stating your

intention no one can later claim that you had tried to sneak in. Some countries insist that they are warned 24 hours in advance of one's arrival, while Australia has the most stringent rules requiring 96 hours advance notification. On arrival, follow VHF instructions and only dock where advised. Normally one can ascertain by VHF whether officials will visit the boat or alternatively the skipper may be required to attend offices ashore. Arriving boats are usually visited by officials from customs and immigration, but in some countries yachts are also visited by plant and animal quarantine officers, port officials, security and even secret police. To complete the clearance procedure some, and occasionally, all of the following documents may be needed:

- Ship's registration certificate
- Passports of all crew
- Captain's licence or certificate of competence
- Crew lists
- Vaccination certificates
- Licences for equipment that may need it: radio, amateur radio, even diving in some countries

- Gun permit
- Fishing licence
- Cruising permit
- Insurance policy

Other documents to be carried:

- Driving licence
- Diving and dive tanks certificate
- If planning to work: professional diploma(s), CV and references from previous employers.

Some countries are very strict about boats stopping anywhere before clearing in (Fiji, New Zealand, Australia) so this matter should not be taken lightly as many sailors have got themselves into serious trouble for ignoring this rule. A few years ago a British yacht stopped briefly at St Thomas in the US Virgins to drop off a crew who had to catch a flight. When he got to the airport with minutes to spare the immigration officer asked about his entry stamp and soon realized that he had come off a boat that had not cleared in. The crew was immediately arrested and it took several months of legal wrangling and a fine of $5,000 before he was released from prison.

A number of countries now insist that arriving yachts advise the relevant authorities of their impending arrival well in advance of their ETA. Several foreign skippers were fined heavily in Australia in 2006 for failing to give adequate notice 96 hours before their arrival.

The European Union is a special case and EU boats and nationals can move freely within the EU area without the need to complete any formalities. If non-EU citizens are on board, the skipper is required to inform immigration officials. Non-EU flagged boats need to clear in to the first EU country whose waters they enter and nationals that need visas for the EU must have acquired these in advance. Regulations still vary slightly from country to country, so while in some countries non-EU boats have freedom of movement once cleared in, in a few countries such as Greece, all boats, both EU and non-EU, have to clear in and get a cruising permit as well as contacting port authorities in every major port or marina.

Special requirements

Some countries require that passports must be valid for at least six months beyond the date of arrival. Passports should have sufficient blank pages for visas as many use up an entire page. When getting a new passport it is advisable to try and get one with more than the usual number of pages.

- Visas must be obtained in advance for some countries where the crew of yachts cannot get a visa on arrival. Although the USA has a visa waiver scheme with some countries for air travel, a visa must be obtained in advance if arriving by yacht and that includes not just mainland USA, but also Puerto Rico, the US Virgin Islands and Hawaii. This does not apply to Canadians.
- Any crew joining the boat should have a letter signed by the skipper so that it can be shown at check-in at the airport of departure or immigration on arrival. The letter should state the name of the boat, give details of the crew and mention that he or she is joining the boat and will leave the country on a given date. Occasionally such a letter may be sufficient to allow the crew to arrive on a one-way ticket.
- Having two passports can be very useful if visiting such countries as Israel as

Australian quarantine official disposes of prohibited products in special bins

and can be purchased on arrival.

■ Diving tanks need to have a certificate showing when they were last tested or they may not be refilled.

■ If planning to work underway it is essential to be able to show to a potential employer any professional qualifications, diplomas or degrees. It also helps to have an attractively produced CV and recommendations from your last employer(s). In most countries working without a work permit is illegal and may lead to deportation. In the USA even expressing an intention to work, unless one has a green card, may lead to penalties. Similarly, if trying to sell a yacht in the USA and customs finds out, they may impose import duties based on that intention alone.

■ If a crew intends to fly out of the country, his or her ticket may have to be shown to immigration. The skipper must make sure to sign off the crew before his or her departure.

■ In some countries yachts in transit are allowed to keep a certain amount of duty-free drinks on board, although they may have to be sealed in a special locker.

Regulations and requirements differ from country to country and this must be born in mind as ignorance is no excuse. In many countries different restrictions apply to the yacht as to the crew. In French Polynesia a yacht is allowed to stay for 12 months, but non-EU nationals only for 90 days. Some sailors found a solution to this by flying to one of the neighbouring countries, like the Cooks or Easter Island, and obtaining a new visa on their return. In some places leaving a boat unattended between seasons must be cleared with local customs

arriving in some Muslim countries with an Israeli stamp (Saudi Arabia) is prohibited or can lead to complications. Having a second passport is also good if it needs to be sent off to get a visa.

■ A cruising permit is required in a number of countries (Indonesia, Venezuela, Palau, Vietnam) and usually must be obtained in advance.

■ Although the yacht insurance policy is rarely requested when clearing in, nowadays most marinas will not accommodate a boat that is not insured.

■ Guns and ammunition must be declared on arrival and will usually be impounded for the duration of one's stay. It becomes more complicated if one intends to leave the country from a port that is different from the port of arrival as a custom officer will have to accompany the gun and skipper to the boat and seal it until departure. In spite of all these problems it is very unwise to hide a gun as penalties for this are very severe.

■ Fishing licences are compulsory in a number of countries (Bahamas, Canada) as the yacht may have to be sealed and put in bond.

In some countries (South Africa, New Zealand) visiting yachts may buy equipment either tax-free or the tax paid will be returned on one's departure. Similarly in the European Union, VAT (value added tax) may be redeemed if locally bought equipment is exported. If having a major overhaul done it is worth asking the yard to get permission from customs not to charge any local taxes on any of the equipment that will leave the country with the yacht. Consumables such as antifouling paint are usually excluded, and so is labour.

Quarantine regulations are very strict in some countries, Australia and New Caledonia being the strictest, as most food will be confiscated and destroyed. It is therefore advisable to arrive in such countries with no fresh produce nor any prohibited items (honey, tinned pork, souvenirs containing feathers or bones, etc). Arriving in Australia should be avoided at weekends and on public holidays when the already high quarantine charges are doubled.

Transit formalities for the Panama and Suez Canals are time consuming and, especially in the case of Suez, are best done via a local agent. The use of an agent is not absolutely necessary in Panama although the agent will not only handle all formalities but, if booked in advance, will considerably shorten the waiting time for a transit. Similarly in Galapagos, where a skipper can handle the entry formalities, the agent will also secure fuel, provisions and water. The Indonesian cruising permit (CAIT) is best obtained via the Bali International Marina.

In some countries it is much easier to arrive as part of a rally whose organisers take care of all these necessary formalities including cruising permits. The annual rally from Darwin to Indonesia will secure the compulsory cruising permit, while the annual rally from Phuket to the Andaman Islands will do the same for that Indian territory. The annual EMYR (East Mediterranean Yacht Rally) visits a number of countries (Lebanon, Syria, Northern Cyprus, Israel, Egypt) where not only are formalities eased by the organisers but one has the rare chance of visiting some ancient sites safely where access is otherwise quite difficult.

www.noonsite.com has details on formalities and practical information on all maritime nations of the world and was set up to assist cruising sailors planning to sail in foreign waters.

Email and internet

Most cruising sailors nowadays have some email arrangement on their boat, but before leaving home it is advisable to set up an additional internet based address that can be easily accessed underway, such as yahoo, hotmail or wanadoo. Although there are now cyber cafes in the most unlikely places, one should not count on finding internet access everywhere. For example, in Sardinia it is almost impossible to find a cyber cafe while in Tunisia they are to be found everywhere. Some marinas and yacht clubs allow visiting sailors to use their computers but usually insist that this is done in moderation and if at all possible only use their facilities for mail. Needless to say, some cruisers abuse this hospitality and this makes life difficult for anyone following in their wake. It happened to me at the Royal Cape Yacht Club that had thoughtfully set up a computer with 24 hour internet access. Even in the middle of the night there were visiting sailors

Open air internet café in a Dubrovnik alley

points concerning travel while leaving the boat unattended are discussed in chapter 34. There are also a number of aspects that must be born in mind when booking flights.

Crew or family planning to join the boat on a one-way ticket may not be allowed to board at the airport of departure, as airlines are responsible for the repatriation of passengers if they are denied entry at the airport of arrival. In many countries passengers are only allowed entry if they have a return ticket or a valid onward ticket. As in many cases crew may arrive with what is called in the airline business an open-jaw ticket (for example: flying from Los Angeles to Tahiti and returning from Auckland to Los Angeles), immigration at the airport of arrival may insist that the crew buy a ticket for the missing section. If this cannot be avoided the best solution is to buy such a ticket from a better airline and make sure that it is fully refundable so the fare can be redeemed later if the ticket had not been used.

If booking flights online some airlines (British Airways, Virgin) will only accept payment by credit card if the account is registered in the country where the flight originates. One solution to overcome this is to use a local travel agent. It is tempting to buy the cheapest tickets but as they are usually unchangeable and as often plans change, it is more prudent to either buy a flexible ticket or to ensure that the airline in question will allow changes to be made on payment of a penalty fee.

who would hog that computer for hours surfing the internet selfishly ignoring those waiting to check their emails.

The internet is the best source of information both at home and once underway, and should be consulted regularly on countries to be visited, their visa and entry requirements, marina and repair facilities, etc. Our website www.noonsite.com was set up with this very aim in mind and is now the most visited site by cruising sailors seeking this kind of information. It has been designed so that low bandwidth text can be accessed over slow links and all material on noonsite can be retrieved by email.

Travel

Many cruising sailors travel widely away from their boats and there are very few who do not take this excellent opportunity to see more of the world. Some specific

An easy matter to overlook, and which can have annoying or even serious consequences, can occur in some countries, such as South Africa, where the crew of an arriving yacht gets a different visa from that of a normal tourist. This is a seaman's landing permit, which in principle restricts movement to the port of arrival.

Those who leave by air must first clear out with the port immigration office and have their passport stamped accordingly. These formalities are essential or the crew may risk being stopped at the airport and miss their flight.

Finally, if travelling extensively away from the boat, it is important to have a comprehensive travel insurance that covers not only flight cancellations but also personal health. Obtaining this type of policy may be difficult for those who are

west and thus all around the world, I wanted to return to Europe but taking the eastern route would have taken probably just as long. My doubts came to an end when I heard about the Dutch company Dockwise Yacht Transport that had regular runs between Vancouver and the Mediterranean. They use ships that are specially designed to transport yachts and are similar to a floating dock. The ship's lateral airchambers are filled with water so the ships sinks to allow

Yachts being loaded onto a transporter ship in Vancouver harbour

already underway, so it is advisable to start buying such insurance before the planned voyage in the hope that it can be renewed more easily once underway.

Yacht transport

In today's world there seems to be a solution to everything as I found out when Aventura III reached Vancouver in British Columbia after the transpacific marathon that had taken us from Antarctica to Alaska in only four months. Rather than continue

access to the yachts. Once the loading is completed the airchambers are pumped dry. The yachts, whether sail or power, sit on their own keels and, on arrival, the ship is sunk again and the operation is repeated in reverse. Six weeks after we had loaded Aventura in Vancouver she floated off in Toulon, France, and I had my boat where I wanted her to be. Dockwise have now expanded their operations to reach the most popular cruising destinations and are used regularly by owners who are short of time or sailors who are not keen on long ocean passages.

Languages

Although English is now almost universal and widely spoken in any of the former British territories as well as in many other countries, speaking another language or trying to learn at least a few useful words of the local language can be a great advantage. Learning a few basic words is not very difficult and one should at least learn two expressions: hello and thank you, so you can greet a local in Tahiti with iaorana (apparently a derivation of 'your honour' which the Tahitians heard their early English visitors use frequently), salaam aleikum in Arab speaking countries, bula (pronounced mbula) in Fiji, hola in Spanish speaking countries and g'day in Australia. Last time I arrived at Sydney airport I greeted the immigration officer with the most Ozzy sounding 'g'day mate' (he was younger than me).

The officer didn't reply, just looked at my passport and asked, 'have you got any convictions?'

'Is that still necessary to enter Australia?' I asked politely. This time he did burst out laughing.

Australian is only one of the languages that I speak. I never have great difficulty picking up the basics of another language having grown up with Romanian (father), Hungarian (mother), German (school), Russian (compulsory in communist Romania, now mostly forgotten) and then added English (university), Spanish (working in the Canaries with the ARC), French (mostly thanks to Erick and Muriel). The various Romance languages that I am familiar with help me get by in Italian and Portuguese.

Before our first arrival in Indonesia I spent some time trying to learn some basic Bahasa Indonesia. Developed from basic Malay this language has now become the official language of Indonesia and it is also spoken and understood in Malaysia. In Vanuatu I tried to do the same with often unexpected results. Both in Vanuatu and Papua New Guinea there is a local language, basically pidgin English, developed by the early traders and plantation owners. It is called Bislama in Vanuatu, a derivation of the French beche-de-mer that refers to the times when sea slugs were a main export item of the area. As most words have some semblance to English it is possible to understand the gist of it, even if every second word is "fela" introduced by Australians planters who called everyone a fellow and also used some much more juicier expressions. Basically the language is simple and quite logical. A sign outside an electricity substation read: "Yu go in yu ded!"

One of the best reads is the Bislama New Testament in which Jesus tells the devil off, 'yu no bagar ap mi church'. Bugger up, a favourite expression used by those colourful Australian planters, means to spoil in Bislama. There are many other such gems like titibasket for a lady's bra, meri (Mary) for woman, numbawan (number one) meaning the best or very important, while mifela means I, yumi means we (you and me), weit smol is a short delay, dipsea is the ocean, bel blong mi soa (my belly is sore) meaning stomach ache, hamas (how much), yu save (do you know?), mi no save (I don't know), mi glad tumas (I am happy), ale mi go (I am leaving, from French aller).

Sori tumas, mi ask, how can anyone not be interested in languages?

I had a rather unexpected experience in Argentina where I caused great hilarity among the guests at the hotel I was checking in at Buenos Aires when I called across the lobby to the porter waiting at the lift, 'Por favor cogen mis maletas a mi habitacion'. I simply could not understand what was so funny about asking the porter to take my luggage to my room, especially as I was sure that it had been said in what I thought was good Spanish. However much I insisted to be told what I had done wrong, the receptionist just looked embarrassed and kept saying that I had done nothing wrong really. As soon as I got into my room I called my friend JuanFra and he told me 'Jimmy, never ever use the word "coger" south of the Rio Grande as it doesn't mean to take or fetch as in proper Spanish but something much worse and very rude.'

'Even if you do it to your own luggage.'

'I hope you didn't. Was it in public?'

'I am afraid, yes.'

'And you are still alive to tell the tale? Lucky you!'

In Egypt I only got as far as learning to read the numbers but that also helped. I even tried to get by in Japanese and was puzzled that every time I asked a taxi to take me to the railway station the driver always dropped me at the back of the station. After three such incidents I realised that I was saying something wrong and asked a Japanese friend for his advice. When I told him that I was telling the taxi driver 'iki mae' he burst out laughing, because they were doing exactly what I had asked them to: go behind (iki) the railway station (mae).

During the initial two seasons we spent in Greece I managed to learn a number of essential words and expressions which made our life a lot easier and more enjoyable especially in markets and restaurants. I had a good reason to improve on my Greek because shortly before we sailed there we had been camping on a beach and on that occasion my limited Greek almost landed me in prison. A local man who had befriended us invited me to the local bar for a drink. Trying to amuse him, I started telling him a joke about the large Greek Cypriot community that lives in a suburb of London called Kentish Town. As the joke went, when the leader of the Cypriot community, Archbishop Makarios tried to convince the British government to grant independence to Cyprus, that at that time was still a British colony, Makarios said, 'if you give us Cyprus we will give you back Kentish Town'.

The problem was that I only got as far as the term British Prime Minister, which my local friend did not understand and could not work out what I was talking about. By way of explanation, I blurted out, 'Prime Minister is like Colonel Papadopoulos, the head of your government.'

I had hardly pronounced that name when all the customers of the bar including my friend just melted away and left me on my own. This was at the height of the Greek military dictatorship and everybody must have thought that I was trying to make a political joke against the regime.

I ought to point out that these modest, and often hilarious, linguistic achievements have deeper roots as I have always been interested in languages. One consequence of speaking or trying to speak so many languages is that people have difficulty in placing me. While in the Pacific I was constantly asked where I came from. 'From east of Fiji,' I would invariably reply and that would usually shut them up.

At the insistence of my parents, and especially my father, who was fluent in several languages and believed that being able to communicate with other people in their own language was the best way to achieve harmony in the world, at the age of nine I was enrolled in a German school where I arrived speaking not one word of that difficult language. I somehow muddled through the first year at the end of which we had to pass some exams. In preparation for my German exam I had learnt by rote a few details about the lives of Karl Marx and Friedrich Engels. My German master received me with a smile and told me to pick a folded paper from the desk. I looked at it and all I could understand was that it had something to do with Goethe. I read out the question as well as I could then quickly added, 'Goethe lived in the century before Karl Marx who was born in Trier in 1819, his father was...' and trotted out some other trivial details.

'Very good, very good, Cismasiu. So what else do you know?'

'Friedrich Engels lived around the same time, he was born in 1821 in Barmen...'

'That is even better,' he said and passed me with a sour grin. The poor guy had no choice. How could he not reward a pupil who had so diligently learnt the biographies of the two venerated founders of communist dogma?

Official incidents

As long as I can remember I always had a deep aversion for uniforms. In my early days of cruising this aversion probably showed, but I gradually learnt to control it especially as most officials I met were decent people. Over the years I usually had only good experiences with the officials that I had to deal with in nearly one hundred countries that I visited by boat. Unfortunately there were a few bad apples among them and it annoys me that it is those that I remember more easily than the much more numerous nice officials.

While in Greece, my radio work almost landed me in serious trouble on a couple of occasions. To celebrate Doina's birthday we had picked a quiet anchorage close to the line dividing the Greek from Turkish territorial waters but still well inside Greece. While Gwenda was baking a cake and the kids were messing about in the dinghy, I set up my two UHER reel to reel tape recorders and started editing my latest programme. Suddenly Gwenda shouted.

'Put everything away, a patrol boat is approaching.'

It was alas, too late, as my ad hoc studio was occupying the entire navigation table. As the boat came alongside I went up and greeted the crew in my basic Greek with a wide smile.

'What are you doing here?' asked one of the officers.

'Nothing really.'

'You can't stay, don't you know this is a prohibited area?'

'Sorry, but it does not say anything of that sort on my chart. Do you want to see it?'

'No. I tell you this is a prohibited area and you must move. Now!'

They stayed to watch us move away but fortunately did not come on board or we would have been in very serious trouble indeed. This Greek obsession with security, and primarily their deep aversion for anything to do with Turkey, was one of the things that annoyed me and still does in this otherwise admirable nation.

There had been other occasions where I had fallen foul of this unhealthy suspicion but never as serious as on the island of Samos. In common with other cruising boats that summer we were regularly commuting between the Greek islands and the Turkish mainland coast only a few miles away. When we returned to Samos from yet another brief foray into Turkey, I was hauled in to see an officer. It soon became clear that he was no ordinary police or immigration officer but something more sinister. He looked, behaved and sounded just like a Securitate clone of whom I had seen plenty.

'What business do you have in Turkey?'

'None, just sightseeing.'

'Rubbish. Out with the truth! This month you have been across three times, you call that sightseeing?'

'What else can I call it? Is it illegal?'

'Don't be cheeky or I'll soon put you in your place. What's your job anyway?'

'I am a sailor.'

'Yes, yes, but what do you do to earn a living?'

'I am a journalist.'

'Oh, a journalist, that's interesting. And who do you work for?'

'Freelance really, but mostly for the BBC.'

'Did you say BBC? Now that's really interesting.'

He proceeded to grill me more and more and I realised that this guy was not going to give up until he found something to nail me with.

'Look, officer, I understand your concern. I know enough about Greek history to understand your suspicions. Furthermore as we Romanians, who have suffered just as much from the Turks in the past as you Greeks, I have only the deepest sympathy for the sufferings of your people. But a spy I am not and I swear it.'

'Why did you not tell me you were Romanian from the beginning?'

'Well, you didn't give me a chance.'

'OK let's leave it at that, but no more trips to Turkey or I'll be forced to act.'

Not all my encounters with Greek officials were as potentially dangerous as this one. Having decided to set off on our voyage in 1975 come what may, I had resigned from the BBC while still waiting for my naturalisation. The previous year, exactly the required five years after my arrival in the UK, I had applied for British citizenship but by spring 1975 it had still not been approved. As Aventura was by then ready to go I decided to leave London with my old and trusted stateless document which I could use in Europe as long as I got the necessary visa for each country visited. In the summer of 1976 while in Crete, I got a call from a friend in London who was looking after our house to urgently call Detective English at Scotland Yard who had some good news for me. I went to the Iraklion post office and trying to save money I booked a person to person call, telling the operator that I wanted to speak to Detective English. The call came through but I was told that Detective English was out and that I should call again in one hour. I went to the counter to redeem my deposit.

'Why?' asked the operator.

'Because I haven't been able to speak to Detective English.'

'But you did, you spoke to English detective, so you must pay.'

'No, I spoke to an English detective, but I did not speak to Detective English.'

He looked at me as if I was mad. 'Are you making fun of me?'

'No, please let me explain. English is ... an English surname. It is not very common, but the person I need to speak to is called English.'

'But he is English, the man you spoke to. What is the difference?'

I decided to give up on my deposit and one hour later I was back.

'And who do you want to speak to now?' the operator asked sourly.

'You may not believe it, but to Mister Detective English and please if you don't trust me, you put the call through and say that Jimmy Cornell wants to speak to Detective English at Scotland Yard and not any other English detective but only the one whose name is Mr English.'

Fortunately it was Detective English who came on the line. He told me to come to London as soon as possible to swear my oath of allegiance to the Queen as the final step to becoming British.

'And by the way, what are you doing in Crete of all places?'

'Oh, I'm cruising on my yacht.'

'On your own yacht?' he asked with a noticeable change of tone. 'In that case I see no reason why we should rush you. Just come over in your own time and give me a call when you are here. I'll put the papers on hold for you.'

'That would be wonderful. I'll come at the earliest opportunity. Thank you.'

'Well, so it was an English detective after all,' the operator confronted me. 'And you have made a fool of me. You foreigners are disgusting.'

'Not a foreigner, British!' I replied firmly and paid the full whack.

The worst incident happened in Peru where we arrived shortly before Christmas 1977. We were warmly welcomed at the Callao Yacht Club near Lima and were assured that Aventura would be safe on its mooring while we left on a planned tour of the neighbouring countries. A bone-chilling two day ordeal took us on a rickety bus over the High Andes to Cuzco and the ancient Inca remains at Machu Picchu. Our trip continued by train to Lake Titicaca from where we had to cross on foot into Bolivia. The border guard took a look at our passports and shook his head.

'You should not be here at all. You have a seaman's shore pass, not a visa. You must go back to Callao and sort it all out.'

When we had arrived from Panama I thought I had completed all necessary formalities but it never occurred to me that we needed to obtain special permission to leave the port area. I begged and argued, but he was adamant: we had to go back.

'Señor, I see that we have done wrong, and as such we should be punished. Why don't you fine us, say twenty dollars, so we learn the lesson and never do it again.'

While saying this I slipped a $20 note between the pages of my passport.

His eyes lit up. 'That sounds better. Let me have those passports and see what I can do... In fact, to help you, I will alter the date and place of entry and give you the proper entry stamp as well.'

'That is ever so helpful, señor, thank you.'

This was the first and only time I ever bribed an official as it is something that I am very much against. He put all the necessary stamps in our passports and waved us on our way. Over the next six weeks we visited by train, bus and taxi some of the highlights of South America, Bolivia's stunning interior, carnival in Rio de Janeiro, the Iguazo Falls in northern Argentina. From Paraguay we flew back to Lima and started preparing Aventura for the passage to Easter Island on which we were to be joined by Alan Sitt, a young American friend who was living in Lima and who had kept an eye on Aventura during our long absence. The morning of our planned departure I went to do the usual clearing out formalities. As I stepped into the immigration office, the official who had cleared us in on arrival, looked at me and said 'Aren't you from that English boat?'

'Yes, Aventura.'

'And where have you been all this time? Didn't I tell you to come and see me to get your proper visas?'

'I am sorry I must have misunderstood, but, anyway, we are now ready to leave.'

'OK, let me have those passports.'

He suddenly looked up and said, 'What on earth have you done? You have not only left the port without express permission, but have also faked your visas. This is a serious offence.'

I tried to explain what had happened but he was adamant.

'This is no joke. This is very serious. I must take it up with my superiors.'

I knew that he meant it and I also knew that I was in very serious trouble.

'Can I please make a phone call?'

'You can call God if you want but it won't help you!'

Alan's father, who everyone referred to as Colonel Sitt, had been an officer in the US Army and had retired to Peru where he had a small factory. I somehow felt that there was more to it than that so I called Alan and briefly described my problem.

'Alan, please talk to your father, maybe he can help.'

'OK, I will, what is your number there?'

The officer told me to wait outside. Even compared to some of my troubles in Romania I felt that this time my luck had run out. Worse still, on our return we had been told that the crews of two yachts that had arrived during our absence had all been thrown in jail after cocaine had been found on one of them. I was sure that I would probably share their fate. After a while the officer called me in.

'Mr Cornell,' he addressed me in a surprisingly friendly manner, 'why did you have to involve other people in this simple matter that could have been easily resolved by the two of us? I agree that you have made a mistake, but, after all, we are human, aren't we?'

I could not believe my ears.

'Yes, and believe me I am very sorry for being so stupid... but I only made that call because my friend is going to sail with us to Easter Island.'

'I am glad to hear that you have such an important friend in our country. You must have got him worried, so why don't you call him to say that it was, as it were, only a storm in a teacup. Please use the phone.'

I called Alan to say that it all seemed to have been sorted out in a satisfactory manner.

'I am glad to hear that, even if my dad had to revert to some really heavy guns... but he is very good at that.'

'Here are your passports,' the official said as he handed them to me, 'You will see that I have retroactively granted you the necessary visas, so now you are in perfect order.'

'Thank you so much.'

'That's OK, but don't do it again as in other countries you could get into some serious trouble. Fortunately here in Peru we are much more tolerant.'

I have remained in contact with Alan ever since and visited him in Hawaii when I stopped there on the way to Alaska. He lives on Oahu with his Peruvian wife and works as a pilot. I never asked and he never told me what Colonel Sitt's real role was but it didn't really matter. What mattered was that he managed to save my skin.

Soon after the end of our first voyage I reluctantly decided to sell Aventura. The new owner, a famous international rugby player, flew out to Greece to take over the boat and I generously offered to take him on a cruise to show him all the ropes. To make the trip more interesting I decided to make a detour to Kusadasi in neighbouring Turkey. On the morning of our departure from Kusadasi I went to the port captain's office to clear out. After looking at my various papers he asked, 'Where is your captain's licence?'

'I don't have one. You don't need one in England.'

'This is Turkey, not England, and no one is allowed to handle a yacht or ship without proper qualifications.'

'But I have just completed a six year voyage around the world, what better qualification do you need?'

'You could have flown to the moon as well, but what I need is a proper licence, do you understand?'

'But what can I do if I don't have one?'

'Then you cannot leave.'

'But my crew have to catch a flight out of Athens tomorrow evening, we must go.'

'Then you need to get a properly licensed captain to accompany you. Otherwise the boat stays here.'

'I hope you realize that this is a very serious matter. This is a British ship that you intend to seize. I will have to call the British embassy to inform them.'

'You call who you want,' he said and dismissed me.

I went to the telephone office and called the British embassy in Ankara but as it was a Saturday the officer on guard told me to call back on Monday morning. I explained the seriousness of the situation, mentioned the BBC as I knew that it usually helped and he eventually agreed to put me through to a secretary. When he came on I explained the fix I had landed in, told him about my recently completed voyage, my famous crew, and the fact that captain's licenses were not required in the UK. He sounded quite sympathetic and asked me to call him back in two hours. When I did he told me that the matter had to be taken up by His Excellency who happened to be a keen sailor himself so he understood my predicament. He called the Minister of Foreign Affairs at his home and the matter was settled.

When I returned to the port office, the official looked even angrier than when I had left.

'You British are real bullies. Because of you I had a dressing down from the Minister himself.'

'I am really sorry, but what else could I had done?'

'Have proper papers, that's what. Anyway, I will let you go, but don't ever dare come back without proper documents. This is Turkey and we respect the law here.'

Needless to say I have not been back to Turkey by boat since, neither to Kusadasi nor anywhere else, but I have acquired a Certificate of Competence, which is asked for nowadays in several countries.

There are two more trivial incidents that I'd like to mention. When we arrived in Fort Lauderdale with the first Aventura, one of the many officials who inspected the boat, rummaged through all our lockers and came up with a bunch of garlic.'

'What is this?' He asked.

'Garlic. Do you want some?'

He looked at me as if I were mad.

'This is a prohibited import and you should have declared it, not hide it out of sight.'

'It was not out of sight, but out of light.'

'You boat people have an excuse for everything. I'll confiscate it and I could fine you as well but I let you off... this time.'

Many years later I arrived in New Caledonia with a lot of fresh food from New Zealand not realizing that this was not allowed. To my shame I should have known as it is mentioned clearly in World Cruising Handbook. The plant quarantine officer went through every locker, emptied our fridge and vegetable baskets and started putting everything in a large rubbish bag. I saw her pick up a box of eggs.

'Do you have to take those as well?'

'They are fresh so they must go.'

'What if they are broken? Are you worried about their contents or the shells?'

'The shells really.'

'Then let me deal with them myself,' so I broke the whole dozen into a bowl and handed her the shells. For lunch we had the largest omelette south of the equator.

These examples are some rare exceptions as there were many more situations where officials had been more than friendly and helpful. When we arrived in Cocos Keeling from Bali with Aventura III loaded with fresh provisions that were to last us the month it would take us to sail via Chagos to Mauritius, the Australian officer understood our situation and allowed us to keep all fresh produce provided none of it was taken ashore. Just as helpful was the US immigration officer in Honolulu where Ivan arrived without a passport that he had somehow lost while in Bora Bora. American officials are known to be absolute sticklers for rules but this one was a gentle older person who made no fuss at all. He only fined Ivan $170 and granted him a one month waiver that allowed him to get to Alaska and wait there for a new passport.

While I may remember some of the more troublesome officials, my lasting memory is not of them but of the warmth and friendliness we encountered everywhere we stopped. My firm conviction after all this voyaging is that most people are kind and generous and that bad ones are a tiny minority. So nothing will ever make me change my mind that the world is full of wonderful people and it has been my great fortune to meet so many of them.

Tips

- Fly the yellow Q flag as soon as you enter a country's territorial waters and head directly for the nearest official port of entry. Never stop anywhere before properly clearing in.
- Contact the relevant authorities by radio, phone or email in countries where advance notice of arrival is compulsory.
- Respect the dress code of the country you are visiting and never go to an office unsuitably dressed. Treat officials with respect and courtesy and whatever happens never allow yourself to lose your temper.
- Try having two passports if planning to visit sensitive countries or to have one as a backup if a passport needs to be surrendered or sent off to get visa.
- Check the validity of your vaccinations and get any vaccinations that are needed in the countries that you plan to visit before leaving home as it is both easier and safer.
- Produce and print or photocopy several crew lists with all personal details so they can be handed out when clearing in.
- Crew joining the boat should have an official letter from the skipper/owner of the boat to be shown at check-in at departure or to immigration on arrival.
- Have a boat stamp that, for some strange reason, is appreciated in some of the more bureaucratic countries.
- Prepare a complete list of all electronic equipment on board as in some countries this is required by customs.

South Indian Ocean Landfalls

The south-east trade winds that I described as balmy on the leg to Bali steadily increased the further west we moved into the South Indian Ocean and on the leg from Cocos to Chagos never fell below twenty knots. We also had frequent

after midnight I slowed down. Every quarter of an hour I checked with the radar as none of the hazards were lit and I had already worked out that we had a strong current pushing us westwards. The low islands of Salomon Atoll had still not shown up on the radar when I estimated that we only had another ten miles to go and they only appeared on the radar at four miles. By now it was dawn and the islands were also visible in the half light with the naked eye. We entered the large lagoon through

Aventura has all of Egmont Island to herself

squalls, usually at night, so the spinnaker was confined to the cockpit locker and most of the time we sailed with two reefs in the mainsail and a poled out yankee rolled up to half or even one third of its surface. Even so we moved at a fair clip and covered the 1500 miles to Salomon in a little over nine days.

As always seems to happen at the end of a long ocean passage, at the rate we were going we would have arrived at our destination in the middle of the night, so

Centre Pass and dropped the anchor in 21 metres off Fouquet Island in the SE corner of the large lagoon.

Paradise lost?

A small dinghy with a young boy at the helm made his way towards us and asked permission to come on board. He told us his name was Janni, that he was Austrian, sailing with his parents and that they were now on their fourth circumnavigation. He proceeded to give us the local lowdown as well as some fishing tips and suggested that if we wanted to have more privacy we should anchor off Takamaka Island near their yacht Mapopo, that stood conspicuously apart from the others. There were altogether nine yachts anchored in the lagoon but as it was still early in the morning there was no sign of life on any of them.

It didn't take long to realize that the atmosphere among the sailors anchored around us was very different from our experience at Cocos. Whereas those who called at Cocos could best be described as birds of passage, those whom we met at Chagos had grown roots there. In recent years the uninhabited islands of this small British colony had become a semi-permanent base for some cruisers who spent months or even years there. A British patrol vessel made the rounds of the islands on a regular basis, charged an anchoring fee, but generally left people alone provided they observed some basic rules: no spear fishing, no collecting of shells, coral or coconut crabs, no living ashore. The largest island of Diego Garcia, that the UK had leased to the US as a military base, was strictly out of bounds.

Among the three atolls: Salomon, Peros Banhos and Egmont, the former has the best anchorages. It was also here that the original Ilois inhabitants had some of their settlements until the early 1960s when all Ilois were moved by the British authorities to Mauritius. All settlements on Salomon and Diego Garcia had to be vacated to clear the entire area for the military base. Recently the Ilois have won a court case against the British government that gives them the right to return to their ancestral lands but I suspect that, as Diego Garcia is such a strategically important base, they may only end up with a more generous

Abandoned church on Boddam Island

compensation deal rather than be allowed to resettle the islands.

Late in 2006, the previously laissez-faire attitude of the British authorities towards cruising yachts underwent a drastic change with the introduction of draconian measures that will probably keep most cruising yachts away. Chief among the new requirements is that access to the islands is only allowed if in possession of a permit that must be applied for in advance from BIOT (British Indian Ocean Territory). The new regulations are described on www.noonsite.com under Chagos.

During the week we spent at Salomon we moved between Fouquet, Takamaka and Boddam Islands, all of which used to be inhabited. The largest Ilois settlement was on Boddam, where there was a roofless church, several ruined houses and a cemetery. The latter looked as if it had been cleaned up recently, as occasionally Ilois are allowed to visit the graves of their families, but the rest of the island was an almost impenetrable jungle. With little else to do on the island, we took the dinghy to a tiny islet on the windward reef and snorkelled on a nearby coral patch. It had some of the most beautiful underwater scenery I had seen in years with lots of fish and brightly coloured coral.

On our return we moved to anchor close to Mapopo, whose crew Hans and Karin invited us to join them ashore as they were baking bread in an oven they had built. They had been there six months and it was their fourth visit on as many circumnavigations in the last twenty years. Hans opened some green coconuts to drink and made us quite welcome. This was quite a contrast to the attitude of some of the others we had met and who obviously did not like company. Indeed, some of the long stayers were quite strange people, they rarely went ashore, and a few never left their boats during the week we spent there. Hans explained that

Barbeque on Takamaka Island in Chagos

some people would do a trip every six months or maybe once a year usually to the Maldives to stock up on staple things, but as there were water wells and plenty of fish in Chagos they could easily survive there as long as they wanted. Having met some of those people I could not make up my mind what made them tick... all I knew was that they ticked very slowly.

In one of the deserted houses on Boddam Island someone had spray painted a graffiti which summed up Chagos better than I could ever do: "Welcome to the yachtie hangout par excellence". Unfortunately that is no longer true and I wonder if that unique cruising destination is not just another victim of the British government's involvement in the Iraqi war.

An overnight sail mostly in the lee of the extensive Chagos Bank took us to Egmont, one of the least frequented spots in the Chagos archipelago. Navigation through the lagoon was not easy as it was peppered with isolated coral heads but with the help of the forward looking sonar we managed to make our way slowly into the far SE corner where we anchored off a beautiful golden beach. In my long cruising life I had anchored in many attractive spots but none came close to Egmont. Knowing that this was going to be my last anchorage in the tropics, I was hoping to stay for a few days but an unexpected spell of easterly winds cut short our highly enjoyable stop. However tempted I might have been to stay longer in that lovely place the prospect of a fast passage to Mauritius quickly wiped out the temptation. Both in Bali and Cocos whenever I mentioned the fact that I planned to sail to Chagos and from there to Mauritius the reaction had been the same. "You'll have a hell of a hard time beating all the way to Mauritius," I was invariably told. I had heard this so many times that I had almost started to believe it myself, but I still decided to sail to Chagos come what may.

The prospect of a tough windward leg from Chagos to Mauritius seems to be the reason why most boats crossing the South Indian Ocean choose one of two routes: either the traditional route from Cocos to

Caudan Marina at Port Louis in Mauritius

Mauritius, Reunion and on to South Africa, thus forsaking a stop in Chagos altogether, or a more northerly route that took in Chagos and then continued to Madagascar and on to South Africa via the Mozambique Channel. The former was the quicker and more straightforward route, whereas the latter was more attractive from the cruising point of view as it offered several alternatives including a possible detour to the Seychelles. Being equally attracted by both options, I eventually compromised for a combination of the two.

The 1200 mile passage from Chagos to Mauritius can often be quite tough, especially later in the season when there is more south in the trade winds. But in sailing, as in everything else in life, one can do with a good dose of luck. Once again fortune was on my side and we had a perfect eight day passage to Mauritius, mostly close-hauled but comfortable none-theless. Meanwhile the news on the daily radio net that acted as a forum for boats heading west was going from bad to worse. While we enjoyed almost perfect conditions, further east the weather

sounded atrocious with gale force winds and a nasty cross swell that caused a lot of damage. The winter trade winds in the South Indian Ocean are usually more potent than elsewhere and the strong winds combined with a big swell rolling up from the Southern Ocean often resulted in tough and unpleasant sailing conditions.

Old and new in Port Louis

After the tranquillity and slow pace of Chagos, the noise and constant traffic of Saint Louis, the busy capital of Mauritius, was almost too much. A major development programme had given the once rundown waterfront a welcome facelift with a neat little marina huddled among the tall new buildings. Not far behind this picture postcard image, the bustling street markets of the old town retained the true character of this ethnic melting pot where Asia, Africa and Europe had come so harmoniously together. When the writer Joseph Conrad described Mauritius as the "sugary pearl of the Indian Ocean" he probably meant the crop that has shaped the island's history and contributed to its prosperity. While sugar continues to play an essential part in the local economy, its importance has been supplanted by tourism. Mauritius is now a trendy holiday destination with new resorts mushrooming among the old plantations but has little to offer as a cruising destination.

The crew, who had sailed with me from Darwin, left in Mauritius and I was joined by Gwenda but as she was going to stay on board only as far as Reunion, I had already arranged to be met there by my friend Antti who had kindly agreed to join me at short notice for the long trek to Cape Town.

A French enclave

In spite of their shared history, as both islands were originally colonised by French settlers who started the sugarcane industry, neighbouring Reunion could not be more different from Mauritius. For some strange reason, Reunion was declared a department of metropolitan France, an administrative legerdemain that ensured that this island in the midst of the South Indian Ocean remained a remote corner of France. Rather than opt for the new marina at Les Galets, near the capital St Denis, where most visiting boats go, I decided to head for St Pierre, a small town on the south coast.

The entrance into St Pierre marina is quite tricky as it is constantly silted up by a river that empties into the ocean. When we arrived after an overnight passage from Mauritius, a high swell was breaking on the beach by the harbour to the obvious enjoyment of local surfers. Having been assured that the swell in the harbour entrance looked worse than it was, somewhat reluctantly, I decided to have a go. The channel was buoyed and we made it through safely at the cost of nothing

more than a few more white hairs. The small marina was located right in the middle of the lively town, with dozens of restaurants and bars within walking distance. As I have said before, and will gladly repeat, the French do know how to enjoy life and eating well is not just part of this "joie de vivre" but absolutely central to it. St Pierre is a case in point.

The mountainous interior of Reunion is dominated by three remains of huge craters called "cirques" whose sheer walls rise to well over 2,000 metres. The volcanic scenery is quite breathtaking and the best way to appreciate it is to go on one of many walks, the island being crisscrossed by several marked paths.

As I had committed myself to the southern route and the season was by now well advanced, a detour to Madagascar was no longer feasible. However, being so close it was a shame not to see this fascinating island, so Gwenda and I left the boat in St Pierre, and flew to Madagascar. We hired a 4WD car with a local driver and explored the island from north to south stopping at several of the nature reserves for which Madagascar is famous. Having been isolated from neighbouring Africa for millions of years, its flora and fauna are unlike anywhere else on earth. Hundreds of species of plants and animals are unique to the island, perhaps none more distinctive than the lemur, a primate of which several species survive.

African landfall

Oh, the joys of cruising! We were motoring in a flat calm some 300 miles from the South African coast when just 24 hours previously it felt as if we were in a boiling cauldron with waves crashing, thunder cracking and lightning exploding as if Armageddon had descended upon our poor heads. It is almost impossible to say what was the worst: the wild breaking waves, the wind gusting at over 40 knots, or the awesome thunderstorm that even the forecast had described as "severe". The same forecast broadcast on Inmarsat C had warned of a large log that had been seen afloat posing a serious hazard to shipping. The reported coordinates put it south of Madagascar, close to our intended track. With night approaching there was little we could do, except keep our fingers crossed. Before we were hit by the front that brought with it all the above ingredients, we had been sailing along nicely in 25 knots. As the sky darkened and the wind kept rising, I rolled up the yankee and continued

Rhinos at a nature reserve near Richards Bay

with two reefs in the main. Broad reaching like this I had often sailed in winds over 30 knots on previous occasions, so there wasn't much to worry about... or so I thought.

During my night watch, with the wind steady at 35 knots, sometimes gusting more, and our speed never going below 9 knots, the pattern of the waves changed and the swell started to look menacing. As I described on page 195, we hit something that night, quite likely a log or other debris that had floated off Madagascar. Whatever

it was, the boat had ridden over it and, as the centreboard was up, there was nothing under the boat to stop it, it ended up hitting the rudder. Thanks to its design, the rudder had absorbed the shock without suffering any obvious damage, although later I did discover a crack in the rudder so the collision must have been more violent than it had felt at the time.

The rest of the 1370 mile passage was uneventful and we reached Richards Bay nine days after leaving St Pierre. The small marina was full with visiting yachts some of whom had spent at least one year there. While the port and nearby town had few attractions, the proximity of Hluhluwe-Imfolozi Nature Reserve, one of the largest game parks in South Africa, was a great temptation. After the clearance formalities into South Africa had been completed, we planned to spend a couple of days touring the large park but Aeolus had other ideas for us. The promise of two days of favourable weather sent us racing out of Richards Bay and, as the weather looked like holding, I also decided to bypass Durban and try to make it as far as East London. I knew that in this notorious part of the world if conditions look right, you go, so that's what we did, even if there were a few raised eyebrows among our neighbours seeing us leave in a hurry when we had hardly arrived.

The section between Durban and East London is the most difficult stretch along the entire South African coast: 250 miles with absolutely no shelter along the aptly called Wild Coast, and the Agulhas current running parallel to the coast at a rate of three to four knots. This is most certainly no place to be caught out by those infamous SW winds that are generated by lows coming up from the Southern Ocean and, combined with the strong current flowing against the wind, cause horrible seas that can overcome yachts and occasionally huge tankers as well.

The nice NE wind held the whole of the second day and we made excellent progress with a welcome boost from the current. By midnight the wind had dropped to almost nothing, so with only seventy miles left, on came the engine and we continued, hoping to arrive in East London by early afternoon. Suddenly the engine slowed down and stopped. After checking everything as described in chapter 14, I found the culprit was the starter motor, the only engine spare I did not have on board.

We eventually made it into East London where it took us several hours and probably one hundred short tacks to make headway

Closing with Cape Agulhas at the southern tip of Africa

up the narrow Buffalo River and into the inner harbour where we ended up tied alongside the local police launch. With my usual luck, I tracked down a starter motor and with the engine working again, there was nothing to keep us in East London.

As soon as the weather looked right we left and made a beeline for the axis of the Agulhas current. The strongest rate is along the two hundred metres line, which we found about fifteen miles offshore. Soon we

had the thrill of having three knots in our favour but the excitement was short lived as during the night the wind started to shift into the SW foretelling a blow from that direction which the forecasters seemed to have missed. The first thing to do in such a situation is to move as quickly as possible inshore, into shallow water, so as to be out of the current before the wind gets too strong. Even winds of 25 knots against that mighty current can create hellish conditions with huge breaking waves. We made it into shallow water before the wind got too strong and spent the rest of the night taking short tacks and making painfully slow progress.

Sailing around the bottom of Africa is very much like a game of snakes and ladders as you depend entirely on the weather dice. If you are unlucky and conditions are not right you simply won't get anywhere. The one redeeming factor is that while the weather can indeed be worse than almost anywhere else, it is generally fairly predictable. On a synoptic chart, the lows and accompanying fronts marching up from the south-west look like beads on a string. As the system gets closer, the wind swings into the SW and the barometer starts to rise. Once the front had passed, the wind backs into the SE and continues to back slowly to NE. When the barometer starts falling again, you know that the next front is on its way, so it's high time to look for shelter. The gap between lows can be anything from 36 hours to five days.

By the morning the wind had gone into the SE, so up went the ParaSailor and I plotted a course that wasn't too far offshore but would still benefit from a favourable current. Listening to the next forecast, the weather appeared relatively settled for the following three days so I decided to push on rather than stop at one

The Cape of Good Hope

time I had seen so many birds had been off Cape Horn. I wondered what made them congregate at such significant locations.

It took us all day to reach the more famous Cape of Good Hope. Initially called Cape of Storms, it was on Prince Henry the Navigator's insistence that it was changed to the current more positive sounding name. True to form, by nightfall the wind came up stronger and stronger from the SE and was soon blowing at over 30 knots. It was also bitterly cold with a true whiff of the Antarctic in it. Even with three reefs in the mainsail Aventura was romping along at over eight knots and my planned dawn arrival at Cape Town now looked more like an ETA of 2 a.m., yet another night arrival in an unfamiliar port. For all of two seconds I thought of heaving to and wait for dawn, but the temptation proved irresistible and I called Port Control. Permission to enter the harbour was granted and we crossed the huge port past several sleeping ships all the way into the far corner where the Royal Cape Yacht Club has its base. Having phoned the club the previous day we slowly crept in and tied up to our assigned berth. I had a feeling of deep satisfaction but also of great relief to be there having covered close to 12,000 miles in the six months since I had left New Zealand. A bottle of champagne, which I had bought in Reunion with this very celebration in mind, was duly popped and Antti and I drank a toast to our safe arrival. Happiness is made up of small moments like this. Small maybe, but unforgettable.

of those tempting places along the way: Port Elizabeth, Knysna or Mossel Bay.

At dawn the third day after our departure from East London we could make out in the distance the low outline of Cape Agulhas, the southernmost point of Africa. Agulhas means needle in Portuguese and the early navigators had given it this name because the compass needle showed true north when their ships were level with the cape as, in those days, there was no magnetic variation in this area. In the intervening years the magnetic north pole had shifted a long way and the current charts now show a hefty 25°W variation.

The featureless headland is a highly significant landmark as it is the point where the waters of the Indian Ocean meet those of the Atlantic, and I felt a great thrill to sail past it. The low cape may not have looked very dramatic but the sea life around it was quite prolific. Earlier we had seen dolphins and whales but it was the countless seabirds that held centre stage: white and painted petrels, gannets, and several kinds of albatross, the majestic wandering albatross among them. The last

Financial Matters

Don't flaunt money, overpay or overtip as in most third world countries people will only feel that you don't care about money. Be fair, but keep within the local custom of costs and tipping. Many cruisers have ruined local economies by trying to "improve" the lifestyle of local people.

Michelle LaMontagne

I totally agree with Michelle's views who, as a singlehander and woman travelling on her own, has been able to observe the world from an even wider angle than most other sailors. Although I stated elsewhere that problems with crew are a common reason for ruining a voyage, I must add that not having sufficient funds and the problems associated with this can be just as bad, with some voyages being abandoned for this reason. The likely explanation is that most people are unable to set a realistic figure for their proposed expenditure. I know this only too well because we set off in 1975 without the slightest idea of what to expect and if it had not been for our tight budgeting and an absolute determination not to give up we could easily have come back home after one season in the Mediterranean.

At the start of our voyage we left London with only £50 ($100) in reserve, which even then was very little. From the start we had to survive, maintain the boat and pay any charges on the £28 ($56) I was earning for my weekly radio programme. It was tough but we managed. During the six months we spent in the Eastern Caribbean we could only afford to eat out once, and that was a modest hamburger in Bequia.

We easily adapted to this kind of life, which continued for another two years until I started earning more from my additional freelance work. Even then we never allowed ourselves to be extravagant.

At the start we tried to live off the land and sea as much as possible. While in Greece I became very proficient with my speargun and fish continued to be our main source of food throughout our six year long voyage. I became quite ingenious at finding new sources of food such as grating green papayas, which grow widely in the Pacific, and made a tasty salad, not to speak of eating coconuts in all their stages of development, although I never managed to master the skill of opening them as easily as Pacific islanders do.

Some thirty years later it is interesting to see what kind of effect our lifestyle has had on Doina and Ivan. Already as teenagers they impressed us with their thriftiness and we noticed that when Ivan got a birthday cheque from his grandmother, weeks later it still had not been cashed. Even today he is simply not interested in money. Doina is the same and even when she started earning money, she still preferred to buy her clothes at the Oxfam charity shop. I will never forget the hilarity she caused at one of my lectures. I had been invited by Cruising World magazine to give a series of lectures in various US cities. As Doina had just finished her studies I asked her to accompany me on this tour. At one lecture a lady in the audience put a question directly to Doina.

'What is the most memorable occasion in your six year long voyage?'

'The day I had TWO ice creams at a place in Greece!' she replied without a moment's hesitation.

For an American audience this was quite incredible as was clear from their reaction. Instantly Doina became the star of the show among the four hundred people filling that hall.

Financial surveys

The cost of cruising? It's something that I've been afraid to really find out!

David Hersey

The simple life we led on our first voyage had one great advantage in that almost everyone else was in the same boat, cruising on a limited budget, and as a result people were much more sociable and helpful to each other than seems to be the case today. Meeting so many sailors was also a great source of information and not surprisingly this is what led me to my first cruising survey in 1978. I remember vividly the remark made by a retired French Police officer whom I interviewed for one of my cruising surveys, who, when asked if he had a fixed budget, replied 'There is no real need for a budget as we only spend what we've got. There is no better way to budget your finances than by paying cash. We always know the balance.'

We were in exactly the same situation and we certainly had no need to have a budget for the simple reason that we could only spend what we happened to have at the time. I was naturally interested to find out how other cruising sailors managed their affairs and investigated this matter in several surveys. Most of them seemed to have a similar easy going attitude as we did, living, as it were, hand to mouth, and not worrying too much about the future when the present was there to be enjoyed.

The financial surveys dealt not only with budgeting but also with such subjects as the cost of provisions, maintenance, repairs, spending ashore, insurance, unforeseen expenses, docking and other fees. The most common point made by people was that they had failed to allow enough for maintenance and repairs. Many had in fact not allowed anything at all. The reason

was simple: many had left home in well prepared boats and the early maintenance and repair bills were quite reasonable, but these increased dramatically as the boats started covering lots of miles. As a result, keeping up with wear and tear starting eating into the reserves. Furthermore as most of those sailors were still quite inexperienced and the voyage was more strenuous than any sailing they had done before, they broke more gear, one more reason why the financial consequences surpassed their expectations.

Another problem, which I considered even then quite serious, was that the early cruising literature was awash with fairly irresponsible advice suggesting that one could drop everything and set off

Interviewing a skipper for a survey

immediately on this carefree life where one could live off the land and be welcomed by friendly natives. I am talking about the period immediately after the hippy years of the 1960s when many saw the world in a rosy light usually through a thick curtain of smoke. Some people continue to maintain this kind of wishful thinking to this day but most are realistic enough to admit that those days are well and truly over. I was horrified recently when I saw a picture of myself from those days with a big beard and long hair down to my shoulders held in place by a headband.

Financial matters have become much more important nowadays and so just before the finish of the Millennium Odyssey I conducted a survey among the forty crews who had taken part in the two year long event. The full results of the survey are published in World Cruising Essentials, which also mentions the results of some of the earlier surveys, so I will repeat here only the most significant findings. Once again the highest costs were those of maintenance, repairs and unexpected expenses with a top figure of $2,000 per month quoted by one owner. This was neither the average cruising boat nor the average cruising sailor, but even looking at the figures quoted by those sailing on some of the smaller boats I was still surprised to see how high their maintenance and repair costs were. This can only be explained by the nature and duration of the event, which must have been quite tough on their boats. Some of those who could not give specific figures for maintenance and repair were nevertheless able to quote their overall expenditure over the two years of the rally. Thus a couple sailing on a forty foot boat gave a total figure of nearly $60,000, which included all expenditure over two years. A couple on another Millennium boat estimated their total costs to have amounted to $42,650. As they were both accountants by profession it is not surprising that they could provide me with itemized figures for all expenses during their circumnavigation. Before anyone takes those figures as a useful yardstick to plan one's own expenditure on a similar voyage I should point out that those boats were sailing

in an organised rally in which such costs as docking, formalities and Panama Canal fees were included in the entry fee.

A large proportion of long term cruisers are retired with a fixed income that has the advantage of being regular and reliable, as was the case of Michael Frankel, who sailed as a crew on one of the Millennium boats and shared equally in all the costs of the boat he was sailing on. He estimated his total costs for the rally at $19,900 (or $1,200 per month) itemized as follows: his share of the rally fee $1,600, food and fuel share $2,100, communications $3,200, mail forwarding $900 and shore activities $12,300. In Michael's view it was money well spent. 'I think my expenses were reasonable. It was much cheaper than living on land for sixteen months, and a lot more fun.'

At this point I asked Gwenda, if she could help me work out how much money my recently completed voyage had cost.

'Down to the last penny if you are interested. But are you really interested?'

I smelt a rat that might get me into trouble as I hadn't been my usual thrifty self, but it was too late. Ever since we launched World Cruising Club Gwenda had been running the financial side of things, or put simply, she manages our money while I spend it, which I must recommend as the perfect solution to the controversial subject of labour division in a marriage, whether afloat or ashore.

When Gwenda produced the figures for the years 2001 to 2006, I found them quite realistic bearing in mind all the work that had been done on Aventura during those years with the result that she completed her circumnavigation in better shape than when she had started. The annual average for the five years was £10,000 ($20,000) per year and included all the boat and living expenditure. The most expensive items were maintenance and regular servicing as well as the purchase of new items, such as a mainsail, cooker, 120 AH alternator, battery charger and gel batteries in New Zealand. Also included were various alterations such as a new charging system (Auckland) and the replacement of all running rigging (Cape Town). Not included is the cost of my flights to and from the boat, which I estimate at around £10,000 ($20,000).

Generally, a lot depends on how much one has to spend on the boat as those are the costs that are most difficult to estimate in advance. Having a well prepared boat will certainly keep costs down, especially as most of the higher costs will have been incurred before the voyage begins. Once underway, a lot depends on the style of each individual, but there are some basic costs to be budgeted for such as the cost of docking in marinas, most of which cost less than their equivalent in the USA or Western Europe. In some areas marinas are still few and far between and it is more common to be at anchor, for which there is rarely a charge. In most countries the price of fuel, which has increased everywhere in recent years, is about the same as in the USA but lower than in Europe. The same is true of food, with similar or lower prices in most countries, but higher in the Caribbean. The cost of food generally goes down the further one moves from home, especially in those remote cruising destinations.

For many people setting off on a long voyage their cruising life often starts in earnest in the Caribbean, which currently is one of the more expensive cruising areas. Some people find it difficult to change the style of spending they had while still in permanent employment and continue spending as much or even more than before. What struck me on my last visit to St Lucia was that all the boats in the marina were deserted at night while the crews were having a meal ashore. On a regular basis such expenditure can turn out to be a heavy burden on one's budget. While this may have been all right when one's bank account was replenished punctually at the end of each month, many come to realise that the hole is no longer so easily refilled. Cruising sailors also spend money on rental cars, flights home, sightseeing and excursions to neighbouring countries, so there are quite a few items that may affect one's finances unless proper allowance has been made for this added expenditure.

Practicalities

Soon there will be an ATM under almost every palm tree.

John Ellis

The financial side of a voyage plays a most important part in one's long term preparations. It is wise to discuss plans with your bank before your planned departure as some of the accounts may have to be changed. It is also essential to make arrangements to be able to check your accounts on the internet. It is useful to keep an account with a reliable chandlery that is used to shipping goods abroad, and possibly also with a known international courier company in case their services are needed. The most common breakages in all round the world rallies were those to automatic pilots. In almost all cases the skippers had great difficulty getting repairs done in the countries visited so it is highly advisable to set up an arrangement that will allow essential spares to be shipped out at short notice.

The wide use of credit cards is one of the greatest improvements for anyone travelling today and virtually everywhere in the world withdrawing money with a card is now the accepted way and as a result people travel with little cash. Not that long ago getting cash or money transfers from your bank by anyone travelling in remote places was a nightmare. I remember the frustrating hours I used to spend in some obscure bank trying to get my British bank to transfer urgently needed funds. Once, while in Peru, I spent a long time on the telephone, at a cost in those days of around $5 per minute and the conversation with the bank clerk in England went like this:

'Where did you say you were?'

'In Lima, Peru.'

'Where did you say, Roma?'

'No, no, Lima... Lima... in darkest Peru, where Paddington Bear comes from!' I shouted exasperated.

'Oh, Peru, why didn't you say so?'

For those who may not be familiar with Paddington, I must explain that this delightful character of a little bear was found wandering on Paddington railway station in London and was adopted by a kind English family. He hailed, as you may have guessed, from Peru, and is a popular fictional character for English children. Doina and Ivan were his fans and while in 'darkest' Peru we visited the ancient remains at Macchu Pichu. Ivan was wearing a Paddington Bear t-shirt when we met an elderly gentleman, who noticing Ivan's shirt, told him, 'Are you looking for Paddington? Just carry on along this path as I think I caught a glimpse of him.'

If the source of payment will be by credit card make sure that you have more than one and that each has a generous credit limit. The most accepted card worldwide I found to be Visa followed by Mastercard. Diners Club and American Express are less popular in some countries and AmEx is sometimes not accepted because of the high commission they charge the trader. If using a debit card for payments or to withdraw cash make sure that there is not too much money in your account so it cannot be emptied in case of card fraud, if your PIN number is stolen or you are forced to disclose it. For similar reasons agree with your bank not to top up your account automatically, except to cover monthly credit card payments or other direct debits, but only after receiving specific instructions from you. If payments are done by direct debit make sure to check the statements regularly by internet. It is highly recommended to have the various accounts linked and accessible by internet, so that funds can be transferred on line from one account to another.

A major concern nowadays is that of identity theft and therefore one must never let one's card out of sight. While in Puerto Rico I had invited some friends to lunch and when the bill came I gave my card to the waiter who took it to the cash desk. After a while I got suspicious as he seemed to take too long, so I walked over to the cashier and was surprised that neither the waiter nor my card were there. When I asked the cashier she looked flustered so I insisted that she produced my card immediately and she sent someone to look for the waiter. He did appear with my card saying he had been delayed in the kitchen but it sounded to me like a very limp excuse, and I am convinced he was about to extract my card details. I immediately contacted my bank to alert them but was later told that nothing untoward had happened. Now I make sure that either the PIN machine is brought to the table or I take the card myself to where I need to sign. This may sound like paranoid behaviour but, as the joke goes, just because I think that everybody hates me doesn't mean that I am paranoid!

Working as a film extra in Bora Bora was one of the pleasantest ways of earning money while cruising

It is also a good idea to have all your card numbers listed somewhere easily available if they are lost or stolen, but not with their PIN numbers, and also the phone numbers of whom to contact to stop the card. Finally, it is also advisable to insure the cards for loss or theft with a limit of liability. As credit cards are not accepted everywhere and by everyone, it is still necessary to always have some cash available. In Europe and increasingly more countries the euro is widely accepted, while worldwide the US dollar is still the preferred currency. In both cases one should have mostly notes of a smaller denomination as, for example, $100 bills are often not accepted as there are many counterfeit bills in circulation. Similarly, large denomination euro bills (such as €200 and €500) are often not accepted.

Earning a living while cruising

During my recent voyage I noticed that, judging by their yachts, equipment, large RIBs and their attitude generally, my fellow cruisers looked much more affluent than the sailors of even the recent past. From what I gathered most had a healthy financial situation, whether from a regular retirement pension, savings, investments, rented property or a combination of these sources. Some were still active in playing the stock market while a few had franchised their companies in exchange for a regular income.

Gone were the crews of home-built boats cruising on a shoestring and on my modest 43 footer I was occasionally made to feel that I didn't belong to that opulent cruising club. As I came to more remote or difficult to reach places, the situation gradually changed as most of those more expensive yachts seemed to prefer the well-trodden route where the crew had no problem going out for a meal every evening. It was in those out of the way places that I came across the sailors that are closer to my heart and whose outlook I still share. I was relieved that they had not disappeared altogether but were just keeping their heads down while doing their own thing.

Not everyone manages to leave home with a solid financial background and there are still many sailors who set off in the hope that they'll manage to get by somehow. While this may not be all that easy, over the years I have come across a number of people who either had a useful profession or were willing to do anything to earn money. Among the professions of those who managed to find local employment were doctors, dentists, nurses, truck drivers, qualified divers or diving instructors, sailing monitors, car mechanics, diesel or outboard engineers, electrical or electronics engineers, qualified pilots, accountants, teachers, builders, a building surveyor and even a butcher. To this list should be added people who saw a business opportunity in one of the countries visited and either interrupted their voyage or returned later to pursue that idea, and I know of several examples of successful tourist resorts or other businesses that came about in this way. Some of the friends I met again during my latest voyage had stopped briefly for a temporary job... and thirty years later they were still there.

If planning to get a job while underway it is essential to carry all qualification papers with you and also a good recommendation from previous employers, both from back home and from those met on the way. One important consideration to be aware of is that such temporary jobs are rarely covered by insurance, either health or liability, and also that in most countries working without an official work permit is usually illegal and may be stipulated as such on your visa.

From my earliest days I had to find ways to earn a living and looking back over the years I see that the range of jobs I had in Romania was quite varied: vegetable porter and church bell ringer in my childhood; commercial photographer, interpreter and professional rugby player in my late teens; bodyguard, hotel receptionist, tour conductor, barman and budding film producer in my twenties. The range considerably narrowed when I got to England but while waiting to find a permanent job I worked as a night porter at a large London hotel. My BBC job sealed my fate as a journalist, which I still regard as my profession. Later in life I found an occupation that I believe best suited my talents and which had always been my true aim besides that of being a sailor, namely to run my own business, to deal with people myself and to be my own boss. From this point of view the fifteen years I

spent running World Cruising Club had been the most satisfying of my life.

All those early jobs stood me in good stead during our first voyage, when I worked mostly as a radio reporter then ended up writing for various magazines and taking photography seriously. Although I had not set off with the intention of finding paid work while cruising, I knew that if the worst came to the worst I would probably find a way. My weekly half hour radio programme remained our main source of income throughout the six years of our voyage but I also tried to branch out by sending taped reports to other sections of the BBC. The earliest success happened in the winter of 1976 soon after our arrival in Barbados. While there I visited the local radio station looking for a suitable subject for a report. The studio was recording an interesting sounding song, which I was told was of African origin having been preserved from the early days of slavery. I got my portable tape recorder and taped the song then asked the leading singer to explain the story behind it. He got into quite a stride and was soon digressing into the heartrending story of his ancestors, how they had been cruelly snatched away from their roots and transported in the most inhumane conditions across the Atlantic. Back on board I made a rough edit with the help of my second tape recorder and then sent the tape to a friend with whom I had been on a BBC training course and who was now editing a programme called Good Morning Africa. When my report was broadcast to the African audience it was an instant success as they knew about the history of African slaves in America but knew little about the Caribbean. That was the beginning of one of my biggest journalistic successes, my regular reports becoming part of a long running series

Princess Pilolevu at her office in Nuku'alofa

called The African Connection. My initial contact in Barbados gave me a list of people in the other islands who helped me find new sources of original material. The African Connection turned out to be a never before explored treasure trove of original material: bush medicine, folk tales and legends, traditional dances, working songs, lullabies, wedding songs and much else besides.

The series continued to Panama, Peru and all the way to Fiji where my African Connection finally fizzled out. By then I was more involved in a different kind of BBC programme called Hello Tomorrow that dealt with practical subjects in developing countries. The programme was produced in London and was sent by the BBC to be broadcast by various national radio stations around the world, from Sri Lanka to Zimbabwe, Samoa to Jamaica. Often an interview that I had recorded at some previous stop preceded me and had already been broadcast in the country where we had just arrived. It happened in Fiji where people had already heard my reports and recognised my name and voice. This made my life much easier and I had no problem finding new material everywhere: visiting an experimental farming station in the jungle

of Panama, the Potato Institute high in the Peruvian Andes, a pig farm in Tonga producing methane gas from manure which was then used by the villagers as cooking fuel, a fish farm in Fiji, a rubber plantation in Malaysia and later a tea plantation in the highlands of Sri Lanka.

While spending the cyclone season in New Zealand I visited the Maori and Pacific Island Section of Radio New Zealand in Auckland and was received by its Maori boss who asked me to be their roving correspondent and send back recorded interviews with island people of interest. By now cruising had almost taken a back seat to work and I must have been a sight riding my bright red folding bike with a large black tape recorder strapped to my back while going to make a rare recording of the haunting tune played on a nose flute to wake up the King of Tonga. Although recording music continued to be my passion, it was the personal interviews from this period that stand out. While in Tonga I had gone to visit the King's daughter HRH Princess Pilolevu, who was the head of the Tonga Tourist Board. After recording an interview with her, I asked if I could take her photograph as I was also sending regular reports to the magazine Pacific Islands Monthly. Just as I was about to release the shutter, I saw through the viewfinder a photo of Colonel Gaddafi on the shelf behind her. The Libyan leader had given substantial financial aid to Tonga and obviously his signed photograph as well.

'Your Highness I feel that photo might give the wrong impression.'

'Oh yes, of course,' she said and turned the photo around.

That inspired impulse had made me a friend and we always had a good laugh about it on my subsequent visits to Tonga.

As we moved west I landed a major job with the Australian Overseas Service to report on the 1980 South Pacific Festival of Arts, which brought together hundreds of artists, singers, dancers and craftsmen from all over Polynesia, Melanesia and Micronesia for a fortnight of music, dance and stupendous displays of traditional dress. As we had heard that a large fleet of canoes was going to gather off the south east coast of Papua New Guinea and then sail in company to the capital Port Moresby for the start of the festival, we sailed over from Australia to join them. As we sailed along the Papuan coast the fleet of traditional sailing canoes got larger and larger as more and more boats arrived from the outlying islands. By the time we reached the capital we were in the company of an armada of over two hundred traditional craft, yet another unforgettable highlight of our voyage.

Throughout the festival I recorded everything I could thus swelling my burgeoning music collection which already included such songs as the haunting tune played by Pitcairners for departing ships, the harmonies sung by Easter Islanders, a traditional Fijian kava ceremony, a shark calling tune from the Koro Sea, stomping music from Tuvalu and Kiribati and a whole tape of moving songs by the royal choir of Wallis Island with whom we had spent an entire night listening mesmerised to their harmonious voices. My collection made even the known musicologist and composer David Fanshawe jealous when we met him by chance in Fiji.

My work for Radio Australia was so highly appreciated that when we hired a car and drove 5000 km from Cairns to Melbourne, the boss offered me a permanent job. He promised to keep the offer open until we

finished the voyage the following year and I agreed to return from London to Australia. However, by the time we arrived in England and I started making preparations to return to Melbourne, the children had settled in at school and as I had been offered my old job back at the BBC with all the increments that I had missed during my absence, my previous employer took precedence and we stayed in England.

Those busy three years in the South Pacific was also the time when I started my cruising surveys. However informative I had found the many books I had read in preparation for our voyage I disliked the fact that virtually every author was only presenting his own point of view. For this reason I found that most of those books lacked breadth and the opinions expressed sounded too one-sided. This was the exact opposite to how I had been trained by the BBC and I was very tempted to put this right. I felt that other sailors in my situation might prefer to be presented with a wider perspective and ideally a wider choice of options, so that they could make up their own minds which of those options suited them best.

With this in mind I devised a comprehensive questionnaire, whose many subjects attempted to cover all essential aspects of cruising, from boat design to life on board. Over a period of many weeks while cruising in the Central South Pacific I interviewed fifty skippers on their boats and duly recorded their answers and comments. The results formed the basis of my first in depth cruising survey, something that had never been done before. I sent the finished article accompanied by a selection of photographs to an American sailing magazine and not long afterwards while in Fiji received a cable saying, "Excellent stuff. Publishing next issue. Paying top rates." Similar reactions followed from magazines in other countries that had received the same article. I was over the moon... and eventually so must have been my bank manager. Having left London in 1975 with a meagre £50 in our account, by the time we returned six years later our reserves had grown to several thousand, not to speak of the money we had openhandedly spent during the final highly enjoyable months of the voyage when we could hire cars, travel inland and generally do all the things that we could never afford in the earlier belt-tightening days.

In the next thirty years that first survey was followed at regular intervals by eighteen more surveys. My initial approach to investigating matters of interest to fellow sailors also defined my writing style and the resulting books that I wrote later. It was a straight reporting style in which I attempted to present the reader with all the facts I could gather, keeping my own views in the background and let the reader draw his or her conclusions. This book is an exception because, as I said in the introduction, I decided to set aside that well tried method and write about things the way I see them. Over the years many readers of my books have written to me asking for my point of view on certain subjects and while occasionally I did allow myself to make the odd personal comment, I always made sure it was backed up by how others saw that same subject and which often differed from my own view. This book is a conscious departure from that well tried approach.

Luc Callebaut

Over the years I have met many sailors who were cruising on a limited budget but managed to keep going by picking up a variety of jobs in whatever place they happened to be. By far the most ingenious and versatile sailor in this respect is Luc Callebaut with whom I have been in regular contact since the early days of noonsite. I finally met him and his wife Jackie when I passed through the Tuamotus. By the time I met them, Luc and Jackie had been gone from their respective homes, Belgium and

Jackie and Luc Callebaut on board Sloepmouche in Bora Bora

California, for a very long time and were leisurely cruising through the islands of the South Pacific on their 46 foot Norman Cross trimaran Sloepmouche. Since 1995, when they bought their current boat in the Caribbean, they had only sailed some 20,000 miles but as Luc pointed out, 'We have probably anchored in more places than anyone else except perhaps someone writing a cruising guide. We may also be able to eventually complete a circumnavigation of the globe but at the rate we are going don't bet on it.'

As both of them are qualified divers, as they made their way around the world they have worked as diving instructors, underwater photographers, video producers and sports directors on cruise ships. They have also done much volunteer work in the islands such as managing the Seafarer Center in Pago Pago, American Samoa or promoting tourism in Tanna, Vanuatu. More recently Luc has been selling and installing electronic equipment on other boats, writing reports for sailing magazines and local newspapers. For the last few years Luc and Jackie have been roving editors for noonsite and, with their wide experience and knowledge of the current cruising scene, have made many valuable contributions to our website.

While in Tahiti, Luc was employed by a local tourism agency as driver/guide on a bus taking tourists on day trips around the island. On his days off he would walk around the waterfront in Papeete and invite any sailor to join him for a free ride around Tahiti.

To a seemingly never ending list of odd jobs Luc added the following comment, 'There were also a lot of small jobs that were fun and brought money at the same time like working on pearl farms, doing salvage operations and mooring construction, being asked to do a promotional movie for a resort, giving cruising seminars, or chartering our own boat.'

The last I heard from Luc and Jackie was that they were planning to get a partner for their Schipperke dog so they could start breeding them. Schipperke are barge dogs that make excellent guard dogs as they are very alert and intelligent, and have a loud bark entirely disproportionate to their small size. But the thought of starting a dog breeding business on a trimaran is hardly one of the solutions I would

recommend for earning a living while cruising. However, knowing just how ingenious and original a man Luc is, he will probably turn even that crazy idea into a success!

Tips

- Discuss your plans with your bank before leaving and make arrangements for internet banking.
- Have an account with a reliable chandlery that is used to shipping goods abroad and possible with an international courier company.
- Have more than one credit card, each with a generous credit limit. If using a debit card make sure that there is not too much money in your account so that it cannot be emptied in case of card fraud or if your PIN is stolen.
- Have all card numbers listed somewhere and also the phone numbers of whom to contact to stop the cards.
- Insure the cards for loss or theft with a limit of liability.
- Always have some cash in smaller denominations as credit cards are not accepted everywhere.
- Never carry more than one card with you when going out and if you are mugged don't try to resist but hand over your cash.
- Have a copy of your qualifications, a CV and some references if planning to find paid employment while cruising.

South Africa to the Canaries Direct

The tough leg around the bottom of Africa made me appreciate even more the warm welcome we received on arrival at the Royal Cape Yacht Club. Throughout the dark days of apartheid this well endowed club tucked away in a corner of Cape Town's huge harbour had hosted cruising and racing sailors from all over the world. The open-mindedness and hospitality of its members had ensured that the club never lost its royal warrant, as happened elsewhere. The club's active racing community is supported by a wide range of repair facilities of which Aventura took full advantage. In the six months since leaving New Zealand we had clocked up a lot of miles of often hard sailing, so I wanted to make sure that everything was properly checked and serviced before taking on the Atlantic Ocean. One of Cape Town's great advantages was the relatively low cost of specialized labour, marine equipment and spares. By the time we were ready to leave, Aventura was in tiptop condition and that included a replacement of all the standing rigging.

Two French friends, Marc Martinez and Patrick Canut, who have their own boats in the Med but had never done any serious offshore sailing, joined me for the leg to the Canaries, over 5,000 miles of mostly empty ocean. As we sailed out into Table Bay on a sunny Saturday morning, the ocean was anything but empty as scores of racing yachts were piling on the canvas in the unusually light breeze while several large catamarans full of sightseers were chasing whales. We joined in the fun, zigzagging among the countless dolphins, seals and pods of whales, which congregate in this sheltered area to breed and nurse their

Marc and Patrick proudly display the day's catch

young. One large humpback gave us a fright when it surfaced a few feet from Aventura and for a few seconds it looked as if we were going to collide. Two weeks later we heard that in the same area Shosholoza, the South African America's Cup contender, collided with a whale while sailing at 14 knots. The violent impact caused extensive damage to the boat, threw one crew overboard and injured several others but not the whale, which swam away without even a glance at the commotion caused.

As the distinctive shape of Table Mountain faded into the far distance, we were finally on our own, surrounded by the vastness of the South Atlantic. The solitude embraced us like a velvet cloak as day after day and night after night we ploughed the waves on our way north, the only sign of life a lonely albatross. Three days after leaving Cape Town, the south-east trade winds set in, so up went the spinnaker and it stayed there all the way to St Helena. The weather on this stretch of ocean is among the most benign and reliable in the whole world. The trade winds blow throughout the year and although the first recorded tropical storm tried to spoil this picture of perfection when it formed off the coast of Brazil early in 2004, hopefully it was an exception that will not occur again.

The weather was so settled and the sea so calm that we had every meal at the cockpit table. One evening, in the middle of dinner, this dream-like routine was shattered when a tanker passed us at what seemed like hailing distance. Our own tricolour masthead light was on but the large ship had no running lights and it glided past like a ghost ship. All three of us were so shocked we could hardly speak, and after that we made sure that whoever was on watch scanned the horizon every few minutes, but no other ship was sighted until we reached St Helena.

Napoleon's exile island

St Helena is a truly fascinating island, not least because its most famous visitor arrived by force, spent nearly six years of exile there and ended his life on this remote speck of land. Its very isolation is probably St Helena's main attraction and the lack of an airport means that only determined travellers actually set foot on this island lost in the vastness of the South Atlantic. Its most regular visitors are cruising sailors, most of whom stop here on the way from South Africa to Brazil or the Caribbean. It is always such a good feeling to arrive in a place where visiting sailors are not only warmly welcome but their presence makes a visible contribution to the local economy. The large number of yachts is in contrast to the ever diminishing number of passenger ships for whom St Helena was once a favourite port of call on the Europe to South Africa run.

St Helena's checkered history is reflected in the island's three thousand inhabitants called Saints, a rainbow mix of colours and races: African, English, Irish, Portuguese, Indian and probably a lot more. In this small place, everyone greeted us warmly in the street, so it was not just the language that made me feel immediately at home. Quaint is the term that springs to mind whenever I think of St Helena, from the name of her inhabitants to those of some landmarks, such as Longwood, Levelwood, Deadwood or Alarm Hill where a canon was placed in wartime to sound the alarm if an enemy vessel was sighted.

One day we hired a taxi to take us on a tour of the island, which measures some six by ten miles, with steep roads and a hilly interior that rises to 800 metres. Some of the interior was surprisingly lush, with grassy meadows sprinkled with all kinds of wild flowers, whereas the western, lee side was parched brown. A winding road led to Longwood, Napoleon's residence, now a museum set in a landscaped garden that had been declared sovereign French territory. Ever since Napoleon's death the British have tried to make amends for the rather awful way they had treated their

Jamestown, the main settlement on St Helena

unwanted prisoner. The house where he spent his exile, and where he died of stomach cancer at the age of fifty-one, is now in much better shape than it was when the former emperor and his entourage lived there. Then it was a draughty, damp, rat-infested place with sagging floorboards, dripping walls and smoking fireplaces. As we walked around on the squeaky floors, Napoleon's presence was almost palpable, a feeling that was helped by the fact that some of the original furniture had been preserved: his desk and chair, an ornate mirror, the large zinc bath in which he spent endless hours feeling sorry for himself.

In some ways it felt like a pilgrimage and I was quite moved, as I had always felt sorry for the way Napoleon had been treated, but my French friends were unimpressed and clearly did not share my enthusiasm for visiting Napoleon's last residence.

'Nothing to get too excited about. Just another megalomaniac who was responsible for the deaths of a lot of innocent soldiers,' was Patrick's verdict as he took a quick look around and then went outside to walk in the garden.

Just before flying to Cape Town to resume my voyage I had spent a few days in Paris where I went to see a special exhibition to mark the bicentenary of Napoleon's coronation as emperor of France. The final room of the exhibition was dedicated to his stay on St Helena and one of the most interesting exhibits was an exercise book in which the great Frenchman had carefully copied out his English lessons. Napoleon trying to learn English! Quelle horreur!

The 700 mile run from St Helena to Ascension was among the most enjoyable passages of my voyage, a pleasant spinnaker run in dream-like trade wind conditions. The night before our landfall, we were overtaken by RMS St Helena, a cargo ship that makes regular runs between the UK and South Africa. Besides mail and supplies it also carries passengers to the few remaining outposts of the former British Empire: Ascension, St Helena and Tristan da Cunha. The ship overtook us on my watch, so I had the opportunity to have a long chat on the radio with the officer on duty. He told me that they had first picked us up on radar at 11 miles and saw our masthead light at 9 miles, both of which I found quite reassuring. He also said that earlier in the evening they had passed another sailboat that showed no lights and there was no sign of anyone on watch. They passed so close that they shone a searchlight on the yacht expecting to get a response on the radio, but to no avail. I knew immediately whom he meant: a South African yacht that had left St Helena at the same time as us with three young men and one woman on board who, I believe, were delivering the boat to Brazil. The officer sounded quite irritated by such irresponsibility and echoed the remarks made to me earlier by the port captain in St Helena, who had had complaints from several ships' captains that sailing boats often failed to keep a watch at night, and many didn't show lights either. This reminded me of a survey I once did among ARC participants, when they were asked what watches they kept, if they showed lights at night and how many boats they had seen during the Atlantic crossing. When the results were processed it became clear that boats with large crews, especially those in the racing division, where watches were kept on a regular basis, reported seeing several boats, whereas boats with smaller crews rarely saw any boats at all. As one of the interviewed skippers remarked, 'It's only those who don't keep watches who never see other boats. We see them all the time.'

Miracle on space-age island

Compared to sleepy St Helena, where people lead a normal life, running shops, tending small farms or fishing for a living, Ascension is firmly set in the space age. The island bristles with antennae of all shapes and sizes, gigantic dish aerials, satellite tracking gizmos and communications towers. The US Air Force has a sizeable presence here as does the British Royal Air Force, the European space program has a tracking station, and the BBC maintains several antennae to relay its international radio broadcasts. There is a military airport used also by the twice-weekly flight between England and the Falkland Islands.

Cruising boats are welcome to make a short stop provided their crew keep out of the restricted areas and do not spend the night ashore. Getting ashore was a serious test of stamina as landing on the slippery steps with a violent surge breaking against the high wharf was a major feat. Entry formalities were quickly completed at the police station, then we were free to do what we liked, which wasn't very much until we found a small hotel that also rented cars, so we hired one for the day.

The interior was rather barren and less attractive than St Helena but there was a surprising amount of wildlife, mostly formerly domesticated animals that had been let loose. A couple of wild donkeys ran over when we stopped the car expecting to be fed and looking very disappointed when it didn't happen. Shaggy sheep walked around in a daze obviously very uncomfortable in the 36°C heat as no one bothered to shear them. No Aussie yachties around here, I thought. Back in Suwarrow I had met an Australian couple who had a farm in South Australia with several thousand sheep. Every year they had to return home in October to round up and shear the sheep, then back they went to their small boat to continue their voyage. When we met them they had been doing this for some ten years and were close to completing their circum-navigation.

One of the great pleasures of cruising, especially after a long passage, is treating yourself to a nice meal ashore. The hotel where we had hired the car also served lunches so, full of anticipation, I asked for the menu.

'What can we have?' asked my crew, who, being French were probably expecting a three course gourmet meal with local specialities.

'Hamburger and fries,' I said meekly.

'What, no other choice?' Patrick asked visibly shocked.

'Oh yes. Cheeseburger.'

Marc is the owner and chef of the best restaurant in our village and Patrick runs the local patisserie and bakery so both of them know a thing or two about food. As we were digging into our dessert of apple crumble and custard, Patrick exclaimed,

'Jimmy, don't you ever tell my wife and kids that you saw me eat this awful Anglo-Saxon grub or I'll be compromised for life!'

A few months after we got home I received a call from Patrick.

'Jimmy how could you do this to me?'

'What have I done?'

'You promised me not to mention that meal on Ascension and now the story is in a French sailing magazine.'

'Patrick, I'm sorry. I sent a report to an American magazine where I didn't think you'd be worried if it was published, but I forgot that my reports were occasionally translated and published by a French magazine.'

'Whatever. The damage is done.'

'I will explain it all to Marie-France personally'

'Oh, it's not Marie-France that I'm worried about, but my customers...'

'Come on Patrick, nobody reads that magazine in our village. It is not even sold within 50 km of here.'

'Don't you believe it! I've already had two customers at the bakery who told me how amused they were to read about my culinary adventures among the enemy.'

'From the way you said that I feel it can't have been all that bad... after all, any publicity is good publicity.'

'Maybe, so I suppose I can live with it.'

In fact not only did Patrick manage to laugh over the entire incident but gradually came to enjoy his unexpected notoriety.

We all live in a small medieval village in the hills above the French Riviera. I had met Patrick and his wife Marie-France on many occasions in the twenty years since we bought our house there but we never went beyond the normal pleasantries. One day when I went to buy bread Marie-France took me by surprise when she asked if Gwenda and I would like to join them for lunch adding that there was another local sailor who was keen to met me. On the agreed day we met at a local restaurant which we often frequented but had no idea that the friendly couple who ran it had anything to do with sailing. Over lunch Patrick told me that he had been on a navigation course and when the tutor had heard the name of his village he had asked Patrick whether he knew Jimmy Cornell who also lived there. Although Patrick knew my name, and even had bought some of my books, he had never put two and two together so as soon as he got home he asked Marie-France to talk to me next time I came to the bakery. What I found even stranger was that Marc and Corinne, the owners of the restaurant, were also keen sailors and kept their 40 foot yacht in a nearby marina in Marseille.

'I cannot believe it,' I said, 'three sailors in such a small mountain village.'

'In fact not three but five,' pointed out Marc, 'as the previous owner of this restaurant also has a yacht and so does a retired Belgian.'

'With so many sailors we might as well found a yacht club,' I suggested more as a joke.

'Let's drink to that,' said Patrick, 'and let this be the first general assembly of the smallest yacht club in France!'

We met on several other occasions so when I started looking for crew for my onward voyage from South Africa I immediately thought of Patrick and Marc.

The timing was perfect as February and March is the idle season for both of them and, as they had repeatedly told me that they were very keen to gain some offshore sailing experience, the long passage to the Canaries was the ideal opportunity.

By the time we got back to the dock after that unmemorable lunch on Ascension Island the swell was even worse than when we had arrived, but we launched the dinghy and managed to cast off without being swamped. Having cleared the long mooring lines holding various launches, I pulled the cord of the outboard motor and, as often happens in such situations, it failed to start. Pushed by the strong wind we started drifting quickly in the direction of Brazil and rowing an inflatable under those conditions seemed futile. To my utter horror I noticed that while we had been ashore, a huge pipeline had been floated from the quay to a tanker lying one mile offshore, and the only way to reach Aventura was to go all the way around the tanker, which I knew was quite impossible without an engine. We managed to grab a mooring as we drifted past it. While Patrick and Marc held onto the mooring I tried desperately to get the outboard started but with no success. Somebody ashore must have observed our antics because a big launch detached itself from the quay and zoomed in our direction, on board two St Helenians wearing overalls with badges of the US Air Force. They took one pitiful look at us, threw us a line and drove us at what felt like thirty knots all the way around the tanker and its pipeline, and deposited us safe and sound on Aventura.

'Hang-on guys,' I said and I dove below to put some cold beers in a plastic bag, which they accepted gratefully. Long after they'd left I was still trying to take it in. Saved by two Saints.... on Ascension Island! Does it rate as a miracle?

In Neptune's role

For many years the accepted tactic for anyone planning to sail from South Africa to either Northern Europe or the Mediterranean was to stay with favourable winds as long as possible by making a long detour via the Lesser Antilles. The alternative route via the Azores is considerably shorter but entails being hard on the wind for some 1500 miles north of the equator. I decided that there was little to lose by trying out a third alternative and sail the shortest route from the South Atlantic to the Med. Two groups of islands, the Cape Verdes and Canaries, sit temptingly astride this route and would allow the long passage to be broken into shorter sections.

The start from Ascension was very encouraging as we held the steady south-east winds all the way to the equator which we crossed at 17°30'W. Up to that point, ideal trade wind conditions had given us several days of perfect sailing, with gentle seas, the most wonderful skies at night and excellent fishing. As we were busy preparing for the traditional celebration of crossing the Line, and not paying much attention to the weather, we were hit by a most violent squall. Too late to take down the spinnaker all I could do was pray that, as on one memorable previous occasion, the ParaSailor would hold. I disengaged the autopilot and although the centreboard was up, as it normally is when downwind sailing, I found that steering was quite a struggle. With the wind gusting at 27 knots I tried to point dead downwind thus keeping the apparent wind to a reasonable level which was helped by us surfing at over ten knots. My two friends were watching wide-eyed from the corner of the cockpit, their eyes darting between the spinnaker and the instruments. Both were visibly

Fish market at Praia in the Cape Verde Islands

awed... or perhaps just worried. Maybe this is what is meant by the term shock and awe.

As the wind started abating, the heavens opened and the most awesome deluge broke over us. Solid water washed over us in cataclysmic quantities while the skies were rent asunder by blinding rods of lightning accompanied by ear-shattering thunder. Streaking flashes were bombarding the sea all around and I expected to be struck at any moment. I told my crew to go below and keep away from any metal, while waiting for final confirmation that an aluminium hull was indeed safer when hit by lightning. Fortunately it did not come to pass, the rain stopped and when the GPS finally displayed all those zeroes we opened a bottle of champagne to celebrate not just my crew's first crossing of the Line but also surviving unscathed that mother of all squalls – an unforgettable farewell from the South Atlantic. A dram of 12 year old whisky was poured into the ocean to thank the gods, both Neptune and Aeolus, for the perfect winds they had given us for the 3,000 miles from Cape Town.

As this was my eighth crossing of the Line, I had dressed up as Neptune, sporting a cardboard trident attached to a deck brush, and a crown made from an empty box of cornflakes, which fitted snugly over my head. Around my neck I wore a Swedish Cruising Association tie, which I felt to be suitable for the occasion as it was adorned with tridents. To complete the picture, I draped myself in some netting because I had always wondered why mermaids wore it. Seated on my throne, I had my crew prostrate themselves at my feet and performed their baptism by smearing their faces with shaving cream and dollops of ketchup.

I have often wondered why crossing the equator has had such a mystical significance for sailors and now I felt that I had the answer. For sailors from northern countries crossing the equator on their way south meant that they were well and truly on their way to whatever destination they were going to. Coming north, as in my own case, they knew they were getting closer to home and the safe completion of their voyage. Besides that, the equator is a permanent marker where weather systems change and you feel you are entering a different world and this is exactly what happened. While we were still celebrating, the wind died completely, the skies turned into a menacing grey, punctuated by massive electrical discharges, like silent lightning. The sea was dull, ugly and black, no wonder the French refer to the doldrums as 'pot au noir' – a black pot.

Cape Verde landfall

The additional fuel we had loaded at Cape Town and had hardly used so far came into its own and we could motor out of this nightmare. Around 5°N we started having some north-east wind but it was too light and also from the wrong direction, so our progress became frustratingly slow. We tacked and tacked again, and on some days only managed to cover 60 miles in a straight line. But even the slowest passage eventually comes to an end and we finally crept into Praia, the capital of the Cape Verde Islands. The port captain directed us to tie up alongside a tug, a rust covered monstrosity that looked as if it had not seen a paintbrush for half a century.

Even by African standards this former Portuguese colony is a poor country, but the Cape Verdians more than make up for it by their sunny attitude. Provisioning the boat for the next leg was a delight as the market was overflowing with a most amazing range of fresh fruit and vegetables. But it was the fish market that left us with our mouths gaping: never in my life have I seen such a profusion of fish of all species and sizes, proof that this area is one of the richest fishing grounds in the world. Poor the Cape Verdians may be but I am sure that nobody goes hungry.

Closing the circle

After the short stop in Praia, the rest of the passage to the Canaries was more or less the same as we kept taking short tacks trying to stay close to the rhumb line in the hope that a change of wind would give us a better sailing angle. It was a tactic that seemed to work and in some 24 hour periods we managed to make as much as 120 miles in the right direction. On the eighth day after leaving Praia, Aventura crossed her outward track when she had set off from the Canaries for the Caribbean in December 2001. For the third time in so many decades, I had safely closed the circle.

On my last night watch, as we were closing with the island of La Gomera, I thought I saw a dark shape to the east but was not sure if it was a small vessel. As it was showing no lights I switched on the radar and picked up a definite signal moving in the same direction as us. I didn't give it another thought and, as we were faster, we pulled ahead and lost it.

Shortly after midnight we crept into San Sebastian de la Gomera and tied up in the new marina. It had taken us eight and a half days to cover the 880 miles from Praia, although with all the tacking we must have covered close to 1100 miles. I was relieved that my gamble had paid off but even happier to be back in a familiar place.

A few months later, when reports of the thousands of African asylum seekers arriving in the Canaries started making the international news, I realized that what I had seen that last night must have been one of those ramshackle boats filled with refugees. My heart went out to those desperate people as many of them had lost their lives in totally unseaworthy boats. I knew how they felt as I had similarly tried to escape from my native country in the hope of finding a better life elsewhere.

Where do all the Yachts Go?

Cruising around the world is not as difficult as it sounds. People should spend less time worrying about it and just do it.

Michael Frankel

Returning to the Mediterranean after an absence of five years I found it rather too crowded for my taste, but when I complained to a friend, who has kept his boat in Croatia for many years, he seemed quite irritated.

"It's not as bad as it looks, and you'll get used to it. But if you find it so bad why did you come back or is the whole world getting just as crowded?"

"Yes, I keep asking myself why I came back. But the oceans are definitely not getting more crowded. If anything, in many of the places that I visited during my voyage the number of cruising boats appeared to have gone down."

The first time I became aware of this was when we arrived in Tahiti and although it was July, and the height of the cruising season, the visitors' dock in Papeete was half empty. The customs officer agreed that after a couple of bumper seasons when a lot of yachts had passed through on their way to New Zealand to watch the America's Cup, the number of visitors

Yachts dressed overall before the start of the ARC in Las Palmas

had fallen sharply. I heard the same story repeated everywhere we stopped, from Fiji to Bali, but still found it hard to believe, so I decided to compare the current figures with the findings of a survey on global yacht movement that I first conducted in 1987 and updated in 2001.

Just as on previous occasions, I contacted a number of officials in thirty of the most significant ports on the world cruising

387

circuit and obtained the number of yachts that had passed through each of those areas in 2006. Compared to twenty years previously, in some places there had been an increase in the number of visiting yachts but certainly not as dramatic as expected. After the millennium rush the numbers seemed to have stabilized and in some places had actually decreased.

The Atlantic circuit has seen little change over the years, with the majority of boats crossing from the Canaries to the Caribbean after the middle of November, and returning the following year in May or June to the Azores, either direct or via Bermuda. Las Palmas de Gran Canaria continues to be the main port of departure and the Port Authority estimates that from the 1024 yachts that called at Las Palmas during 2006, approximately 60% crossed the Atlantic that same year. By adding to this figure the boats that left from other ports and islands in the Canaries it can be estimated that between 1000 and 1200 boats cross the Atlantic along the NE trade wind route every year. It is interesting to notice that even in Las Palmas the numbers have gone down as 1122 yachts had passed through there in 2005. One other significant change has been in the national make-up of the yachts passing through Las Palmas as among the 2006 boats the leading nation was France (207), followed by Germany (195) and UK (173). This is in contrast to twenty years previously when France was in the clear majority (318), followed by the UK (157) and Germany (110). By 2000 British yachts had moved into the lead (235) compared to 188 French and 148 German yachts.

The preferred landfall islands in the Caribbean are St Lucia, Antigua and Barbados, while French sailors usually make for Martinique or Guadeloupe. Mainly thanks to its association with the ARC,

St Lucia saw 560 arrivals from overseas in 2006 compared to 536 in 2000.

The number of boats sailing across the Atlantic from west to east along the northerly route is reflected in the figures obtained from Horta Marina in the Azores, which in 2006 recorded a total of 1178 arrivals, of which approximately 1000 had arrived from the Caribbean. The number of arrivals in Horta has been quite constant in recent years: 729 in 1987 and 1144 in 2000. The situation was similar in Bermuda with 998 arrivals in 1987, 1160 in 2000 and 1137 in 2006.

The number of boats that spend the winter season in the Caribbean has remained stable in recent years but one area that has seen a significant increase is Cuba. It is reported that a total of 472 yachts had cleared into one of the nine designated international marinas where all arriving yachts must report first. Most of the yachts flew the flags of European countries or Canada, as American boats are prohibited to visit the island by the US authorities. As most boats would have cleared into more than one marina, it is estimated that Cuba was visited by approximately 160 yachts in 2006. The most popular marina was Hemingway International Marina near Havana.

Over half the boats that arrive in the Caribbean from either Europe or America plan to spend at least one season there. The largest number of boats spending the hurricane season in the Eastern Caribbean go to Trinidad, where a total of 1845 boats were based during the critical summer months in 2006.

The Panama Canal continues to be the most valuable indicator of yacht movement between the Caribbean and Pacific as the administration keeps detailed records of all yacht transits. The Canal is currently working at full capacity so handliners (as yachts are referred to) normally transit with large ships, being docked behind the ship in the uplocks and in front of the ship in the downlocks. The operation is usually completed over two days, with the night in between being spent at anchor in Gatun Lake. The peak transit time for yachts is March (150 yachts in 2006) while August saw only 23 transits. Waiting time on the Caribbean side can be as long as two weeks but this can be speeded up by using a local agent. The docking situation has been greatly improved on the Caribbean side with the opening of Shelter Bay Marina, and two more marinas are planned, but on the Pacific side matters are worse than in the past. As a result some yachts do all their provisioning and the necessary clearing out formalities while in Colon and do not stop in Balboa after having completed the transit.

The number of yacht transits shows only a slight increase compared to 2000 and the proportion of boats turning north or south after the transit was virtually unchanged. In 2006 there was a total of 870 yachts transits compared to 790 in 2000 and 568 in 1987. Of the 552 transits between the Caribbean and the Pacific completed in 2006 about two thirds of the boats turned north, towards the west coast of Central and North America, while approximately 180 turned left, bound for the South Pacific. Although the majority took the traditional route to Galapagos, about one third sailed first to the South American mainland. The marina of Puerto Lucia Yacht Club in La Libertad, in mainland Ecuador, reported 71 arrivals during 2006. The small marina is a convenient and safe place to leave the boat while exploring the interior of Ecuador, with the High Andes and Amazonia within easy reach.

The restrictions applied to visiting yachts in Galapagos have not changed much and so-called emergency stops of one to two weeks continue to be granted by the port captains in the two main ports of entry: Baquerizo Moreno (Wreck Bay) and Puerto Ayora (Academy Bay). Compared to 180 yachts in 2000, only 120 cruising yachts were reported to have passed through Galapagos in 2006. One interesting final stop is at the westernmost island of Isabella, where the port captain usually allows a brief stop and we spent an enjoyable few days there with Aventura III before the long passage to the Marquesas.

While the majority of yachts continue from Galapagos along the classic trade wind route to the Marquesas and beyond, in recent years a number of boats have made a detour to Easter Island and sailed to French Polynesia via Pitcairn Island. About half the boats that called at Easter Island sailed from there towards Chile and Patagonia. A total of 18 yachts called at the island of the mysterious giant statues in 2006, compared to 22 in 2000.

Arrivals in the Marquesas have remained steady in recent years, with 235 yachts arriving in 2006 compared to 253 in 2000. Most boats arrive there from Galapagos and were joined by North American boats that had sailed directly from either California or the west coast of Mexico. Whereas in the past boats would bypass the Tuamotus on their way to Tahiti, thanks to GPS and electronic charts the Tuamotus are now often visited by yachts.

The number of arrivals in Tahiti is the best indication that the total number of yachts undertaking a world voyage is definitely decreasing. Compared to the 442 yachts that passed through Papeete in the bumper year 2000, the port authority recorded only 350 arrivals in 2006, which is not very different from the 328 yachts that had called there in 1987.

Whereas in the past most cruising boats used to leave the tropics during the cyclone season, normally to sail to New Zealand or Australia, on my last visit I noticed that a significant number were prepared to take a chance and remain in the area. Even so, New Zealand and, to a lesser extent, subtropical Australia, continued to attract the bulk of cruising boats during the critical period (November to April).

While the global movement of yachts may point to a slight decline compared to the past, the survey showed a definite increase in the number of local yachts engaged in regional cruising. Whereas in past surveys the proportion of New Zealand or Australian boats cruising in the South Pacific was always lower than that of European or North America boats, nowadays boats from downunder appeared to be in the majority. This observation was born out by the figures obtained from Australia, where a total of 762 cruising boats arrived in the country during 2006, of which only 240 were foreign flagged vessels. The figures for New Zealand told a similar story with a total of 298 Kiwi boats returning home compared to 342 foreign yachts spending the 2006/2007 cyclone season there.

While the South Pacific continued to attract most of the yachts undertaking a world voyage, the North Pacific is rarely visited by long distance cruising sailors, with only 25 foreign flagged yachts calling at Hawaii in 2006 compared to 31 in 2000. Most of the yacht movement in the eastern part of the North Pacific continues to be made up by US and Canadian boats commuting between the mainland and Hawaii. Very few yachts continue west from Hawaii through Micronesia and even fewer make a detour to Japan, although some North American yachts sailed south from Hawaii to Tahiti and the South Pacific.

Having left the South Pacific via the Torres Strait, cruising boats normally stop at Darwin, on Australia's north coast, which in 2006 saw the arrival of 246 yachts, of which 78 were non-Australian. The most significant gateway in the Indian Ocean is Bali marina as practically all boats stop there, regardless of whether they are planning to continue to SE Asia and the Red Sea or sail the Cape of Good Hope route. In 2006, a total of 174 boats arrived in Bali from the east, with roughly half of them continuing into the South Indian Ocean. The latter estimate was confirmed by the 67 yachts that stopped at Cocos Keeling most of which continued from there to either Chagos or Mauritius.

Many of the foreign yachts that arrived in Mauritius in 2006 flew the South African flag. This was another instance of a regional increase as many South African yachts are now cruising in their own backyard by planning to complete a round voyage during the favourable winter season (May to October) that allows them to visit Madagascar, Reunion and Mauritius before sailing back home.

The Cape of Good Hope route has been gaining in popularity mainly because of the perceived risk of piracy attacks on the northern route from SE Asia to the Mediterranean. In fact, 2006 was the first year for a long time when there were no reports of such attacks on yachts on that route. The early part of 2007, when most boats sail west across the Gulf of Aden, was also incident free. This is undoubtedly thanks to the more active presence of the coalition forces' ships and their determination to rid the waters around the Horn of Africa of this menace, most of which originates from neighbouring Somalia.

The number of cruising boats visiting SE Asia seems to have remained stable.

Antarctica continues to be off the beaten track

The 2004 tsunami does not seem to have significantly affected the number of boats visiting the area and Phuket is showing an actual increase of some fifty percent in 2006 (150 yachts) over the estimated 2000 figures (100). Where the numbers have definitely gone down is among the northbound boats transiting the Suez Canal, with only 103 boats reaching the Mediterranean by this route in 2006 compared to 160 in 2000. The main change has been in the other direction as more boats head south from the Mediterranean to spend the winter in the Red Sea.

Over the years, Cape Town has seen a steady if slow increase in the number of visiting boats, from 80 in 1987 to 120 in 2000 and 128 in 2006. These figures tally with those supplied by the harbour master of St Helena, yet another important gateway on the world cruising circuit. Because of its strategic location in the South Atlantic, very few yachts bypass St Helena without stopping there. The impression that the global movement of yachts is actually on the decrease was confirmed in St Helena where a total of 122 cruising yachts called there in 2006 compared to 184 in 2000.

The destinations after St Helena were quite interesting as they differed significantly from previous years. While the main destination continued to be Brazil (57 yachts), 14 yachts sailed directly from St Helena to the Caribbean and 35 to Ascension. Only five yachts took the traditional route to the Azores and Northern Europe. As many as eleven yachts left St Helena planning to reach the Mediterranean by the direct route via the Cape Verdes and Canaries. This must be a new trend as, when I sailed that way myself in 2005, Aventura III was the only boat to take that route.

Two high latitude destinations that are now regularly visited by cruising yachts, even if in limited numbers, are Antarctica and Spitsbergen. In 2006 a total of thirty yachts visited the Antarctic Peninsula but as some of those boats were engaged in charter work, the number of actual cruising yachts was only eighteen, with two among them being powerboats. The number of visiting yachts seemed to have stabilized as in 2000 the Antarctic Peninsula was visited by a total of 31 yachts, of which sixteen were cruising boats, and only a total of eight yachts in 1987. While the number of yachts sailing to Antarctica appears to be stable, the total number passing through Ushuaia has gone down. Compared to an estimated 30 yachts in 1987, Ushuaia saw 105 yachts in 2000 but only 67 in 2006. This busy Argentine port lying on the Beagle Channel is a major port of transit and reprovisioning both for yachts striking out across the Drake Passage to Antarctica and those heading north through to Chile. Chilean customs estimate that around 90 yachts visited the country in 2006.

Compared to Antarctica, the number of visiting yachts reported from Spitsbergen show a significant increase: 37 yachts in 2006, compared to ten in 2000 and only four in 1987.

A trend that was started by large private yachts being shipped at the end of the season from the Caribbean to the Mediterranean and vice versa is now popular among smaller cruising boats too. For me it was the best solution when I shipped Aventura from British Columbia to the Mediterranean on completion of a transpacific voyage from Antarctica to Alaska. Dockwise Yacht Transport now operates a number of specially designed ships that run regular services between the most popular cruising destinations of the world: the US east and west coasts to the Mediterranean, Northern Europe, Eastern Caribbean and South Pacific. The schedules coincide with the end or start of the favourable sailing seasons in the North Atlantic, Mediterranean and South Pacific and provide an attractive solution for owners who prefer to reach their favourite cruising destination in the shortest time and most convenient way. DYT carried a total of 1200 yachts in 2006 with the South Pacific being the most popular destination.

The largest increase in yacht movement occurred in the Mediterranean as reflected in the number of yachts that passed through Gibraltar where there has been a threefold increase from approximately 5,000 yachts in 1987 to 16,269 in 2006. There has been a similar trend in the Bahamas, even if the total numbers do not show such a drastic increase. Neither the Mediterranean nor the Bahamas appear to bear any significant reflection on the global movement of yachts. Far more telling are the figures obtained from such places as the Panama and Suez Canals, Las Palmas, Bermuda, Tahiti, Bali, Cape Town and St Helena, which are gateways that are missed only by boats sailing nonstop around the world. Taking into account the number of boats passing through those strategic gateways, my estimate is that between 60 and 80 yachts complete a circumnavigation in any one year, with the lower figure probably closer to the truth. For many sailors completing a circumnavigation seems to have lost its aura and whereas in the past many set off on a world voyage with the stated aim to eventually sail around the globe, in recent years such an achievement has become so common that only the most determined find the motivation to go all the way.

The above statistics also show that whereas popular cruising areas such as the Bahamas, Eastern Caribbean, Croatia, the Balearics, the west coast of Mexico, have witnessed a steep increase in the number of visiting yachts, on a global level the figures for 2006 indicate a slowdown compared to 2000. The North Atlantic is the only ocean where there has been an increase of around twenty per cent compared to twenty years previously. Elsewhere, and especially in the more remote parts of the world, the numbers have remained stable or have even gone down. It is something that I noticed during my recent circumnavigation and is good news for anyone planning to set off on a world voyage.

Return to the Mediterranean

At the end of the voyage from South Africa, rather than continue immediately to the Mediterranean, I decided to keep Aventura for a while in the Canaries, a group of islands that I knew well but where I had done little actual cruising. I was as guilty as most owners of the many boats that pass through the Canaries every year and regard the Canaries just as a convenient stepping stone on the way to somewhere else.

I made my base on the island of La Gomera, one of the smallest and least developed in this archipelago of eight inhabited islands. Determined not to repeat the mistakes of their larger neighbours, for many years the gomeros resisted all attempts to develop a tourist infrastructure and until recently was the only island not to have an airport. But change is underway, there is now a small airport in the south of the island, and a new marina in the capital San Sebastian.

Maybe because of their attachment to a traditional life style, the gomeros are the butt of countless jokes, like: 'Why do the people of La Gomera look up in the sky at midday and smile? Because this is when the weather satellite is taking pictures.'

Slow they may be, but there is a certain wisdom in that slowness, as shown by the way they have chosen to adapt to modern life on their own terms. Among all canarios, the gomeros are closest to the original Guanches, who had inhabited these islands at least since Roman times, and who were ruthlessly decimated by the Spanish conquistadors. From their

Strong winds in the acceleration zone while sailing past Tenerife's Pico de Teide

ancestors the gomeros have retained a unique whistling language that made it possible to communicate over long distances in the island's rugged interior. Although not much used nowadays,

393

Typical Canarian balconies on the island of La Palma

but I knew that it wouldn't last. The Canaries may boast having one of the best climates in the world with benign winters and pleasant summers, but local sailing conditions are not to everyone's liking. The high islands generate their own weather similar to that encountered in Hawaiian waters with wind acceleration zones in the channels separating the islands. We had a taste of this at the start of our 40 mile trip to La Palma, when the wind went up from 10 to 30 knots in a matter of seconds and I understood why local sailors call these sudden gusts 'mosquitoes' as you only hear them when they bite.

The development of marinas on every island has been the policy of the regional government which is determined to exploit the so far untapped potential of making the Canaries an attractive cruising destination rather than just a convenient transit point. Until recently yachting facilities in the western islands were non-existent but this has changed as first La Gomera and in the summer of 2005 La Palma and El Hierro also built marinas in their main ports. Ever since we first stopped at Santa Cruz de la Palma in 1976 finding a place to dock had been a problem so it was a great relief to be one of the first yachts to tie up to a temporary pontoon in the half-finished marina.

The capital Santa Cruz de la Palma is one of the most attractive towns in the Canaries and its main cobbled street, named Calle O'Daly after a local dignitary of Irish origin, has preserved many of its ancient buildings. Many houses have the attractive enclosed balconies that are a

the language has not been lost and, at a demonstration, I was amazed to see what complex messages could be transmitted between two whistling men.

The centre of the island is dominated by the sacred Mount Garajonay where an ancient stone circle has been discovered that was used for worship by the ancient Guanches. There are stupendous views from here on a clear day, with the peaks of the islands of La Palma, El Hierro, Tenerife and even Gran Canaria, at over 100 miles, visible above the clouds. It was easy to see why the gomeros keep telling you that they have the best views, and although the tinerfeños possess the imposing 3700 metre high Mount Teide, the actual view of it belongs to them.

The Western Canaries

One morning we left San Sebastian to sail to the two westernmost islands: La Palma and El Hierro. The wind was unusually light special feature of this island. Most buildings date from the 16th century when Santa Cruz was a prosperous town as all Spanish ships heading out to the Americas were obliged to stop there to register before crossing the Atlantic. In later years La Palma continued to trade directly with the outside world and was regularly visited by British ships and merchants.

The interior of La Palma is dominated by a huge extinct crater, the eight km wide Caldera de Taburiente, the largest of its kind in the world. The enormous circular bowl is surrounded by sheer rock walls that soar to over 2,000 metres. The only opening is a wide crack called the Gorge of Fear (Barranco de las Angustias).

One of La Palma's prime attractions are the various walks and the island is crisscrossed by many treks. One morning Gwenda and I took a taxi to the starting point of the so-called Ruta de los Volcanes, the route of volcanoes, a long trail that runs along the crest of the island and passes a string of extinct volcanoes before it ends at the southern tip of the island. As with any special treat, the last bite is supposed to be the tastiest and so the very last volcano Teneguia is only dormant. The last time it erupted, in 1971, it changed entirely the shape of the southern end of La Palma and left behind a large area of devastation that still looks as fresh as if it only happened recently.

When we arrived at El Hierro's main port of La Estaca we landed in the middle of a building site. The promised marina was still a twinkle in the eye of the architect and the inner breakwater was just about taking shape. Fortunately my good friend JuanFra had phoned the port captain who had thoughtfully arranged for Aventura to be docked in the only available space.

Until 1492 the boomerang shaped island was considered the end of the world. Even today El Hierro feels more remote than any of the other Canary Islands, its unique landscape and climate making it a UNESCO biosphere reserve. The south of the island is a barren area covered in volcanic badlands, deeply eroded lava fields that are pierced by tunnels and small caves produced by volcanic bubbles. Even the vegetation has a tortured look about it, the gnarled trees having been twisted by the wind into odd shapes. The shoreline is just as rocky and rough with the only exception the island's protected south coast aptly called La Costa Calma.

An old lighthouse stands on the wind-swept headland of La Orchilla at El Hierro's westernmost point. As I looked out over the grey Atlantic waters, my thoughts went to that great sailor whose deeds had done so much to bring the world closer to how we know it today.

Admiral of the Ocean Sea

Five hundred years after his death, the shadow of Christopher Columbus still lingers over the small port of San Sebastian de La Gomera. Still standing after all these years is the church where the great navigator and the crew of his three ships prayed on the eve of their historic voyage. Locals proudly point out the small house where he stayed, while in a nearby courtyard is a deep well with a plaque which states that "with water from this well was America baptized." The most impressive remnant of that era is El Torre del Conde, a massive red stone fortress that is now a museum dedicated to that first transatlantic voyage. A copy of the world globe drawn by the German cartographer Martin Beheim in 1492 shows Chipango (Japan) approximately in the location of the Lesser Antilles. This was the first time that the earth had been depicted in three dimensions as a sphere. As the globe was produced a few months before Columbus left Spain, he might have been familiar with Beheim's work and there is speculation that he did not sail entirely blindly into the unknown.

Columbus stopped in La Gomera on three of his transatlantic voyages and although the sheltered harbour and fertile island were probably the main reason for his

Well on La Gomera where Columbus drew water before his voyage of discovery

repeated visits, the presence of beautiful Beatriz de Bobadilla might have been the deciding factor. She was the widow of the Count of Peraza and governor of the island and on her husband's premature death Beatriz took over the running of the island. By the time of Columbus's first visit in late August 1492 she was in her late twenties and famous throughout Spain as a great beauty. Their romance has fired the imagination of Columbus fans ever since.

On that first transatlantic voyage, Columbus called first at Las Palmas de Gran Canaria. Some of his three ships needed repairs after the voyage from mainland Spain but what is puzzling is that while in Las Palmas, Columbus ordered the smallest ship, La Niña, to have its traditional lateen rig changed to square sails. This fact has puzzled historians ever since because by doing this Columbus must have known that he could expect following winds on the subsequent portion of his voyage. This was indeed the case as north-east winds are a regular feature in the tropical North Atlantic and ensured the small fleet a favourable passage across the ocean to their historic landfall in the Bahamas.

This small fact coupled with the existence of the Beheim globe have been mentioned ever since as a probable indication that Columbus knew more about the North Atlantic than he admitted. Be that as it may, no one disputes the fact that Christopher Columbus was a great navigator, and he proved it not only by bringing to a successful conclusion that first voyage, but by his three subsequent Atlantic crossings when he took larger fleets across the ocean guiding them precisely to safe landfalls in the New World. Even more remarkable were his return voyages to Europe, and especially the very first, early in 1493, when, on his return from the Caribbean, he decided to first sail a north-easterly course as if knowing that he would find favourable westerly winds in that area, then having found those winds, turned east and made landfall in the Azores. This is exactly what contemporary sailors still do on their return from the Caribbean to Europe – more than five hundred years after the Genovese navigator pioneered that route.

Having managed, against all odds, to get the Catholic Kings Ferdinand and Isabella to finance his expedition, Columbus also persuaded them to agree to his various demands which included a share of all the riches brought back from the newly discovered lands as well as a noble title for him and his descendants. Few of those promises were fulfilled and when he died in Valladolid on May 20, 1506 Columbus was virtually destitute. But his travels were far from over. In 1509 his remains were transferred to the family grave in Seville and later to the cathedral in Santo Domingo. In 1795, when Santo Domingo became a French territory, his remains were taken to Cuba but when that Spanish colony became independent in 1898 back went the bones to Seville cathedral in mainland Spain, where they now rest.

Much was written and said in 1992 on the 500th anniversary of Columbus's historic voyage but very little was done on the 500th anniversary of his death, and May 20, 2006 passed almost unnoticed. Sadly, that seems to have been the fate of this great mariner who ended his life ignored and almost forgotten. By way of an epitaph, I wish to repeat the heartfelt words of Samuel Eliot Morison, the author of what I regard as the best biography of Columbus and his four voyages to the New World. "Waste no pity on the Admiral of the Ocean Sea! He enjoyed long stretches of pure delight such as only a seaman may know, and moments of high, proud exultation that only a discoverer can experience."

Volcanic moonscapes

Carved into a black marble slab overlooking Las Palmas marina are the names of the 146 yachts that sailed in the America 500 transatlantic rally commemorating Columbus's original voyage to the New World. Where else in the world would local authorities take cruising boats so seriously as to erect a monument in their honour? In fact, this is not at all surprising as throughout the history of these islands, ships and sailors have been the lifeblood of their existence. A small settlement surrounded by a palisade of palm trees (hence Las Palmas) stood on the shores of this bay when Columbus called here in August 1492. Some medieval buildings still survive in the oldest part of town, called La Vegueta, where narrow cobbled streets are flanked by beautiful homes built around cool central patios. To the north, the modern town prosaically called El Puerto has developed around what is now one of the busiest ports in Spain thanks to its strategic location astride the shipping lanes between Europe, Africa and South America. Las Palmas is also a great favourite among yachts on their way from Europe to the Caribbean with over one thousand yachts calling here every year attracted by the wide range of repair facilities and excellent provisioning.

Bucking the westward trend, one fine morning Aventura set off in the opposite direction on the first stage of a long delayed return to the Mediterranean. As we rounded the massive breakwater that protects the large port of Las Palmas, I set a course for Lanzarote about one hundred miles away. On cue, having blown from an easterly direction for a couple of days, the wind turned into the NE and was now smack on our nose.

'Here we go again,' Gwenda exclaimed bitterly, 'as soon as I get on board, the winds start blowing from the worst possible direction.'

'Don't take it so personally. After all, this is their prevailing direction,' I commented rather meekly.

'OK, if it's not the wind then it can only be Aventura who doesn't seem to like me.'

'It's neither one nor the other... just bad luck. There is no need to exaggerate.'

'I still find it strange that as soon as I join you, all your talk about balmy winds and perfect passages turn to nothing. So who is exaggerating? Let me just mention recent longer passages that we did together: Bora Bora to Suwarrow, lousy weather almost all the way; winds of over thirty knots for most of the passage from Fiji to New Zealand; strong headwinds even on that shortest of trips between Mauritius and Reunion. So am I really exaggerating?'

Gwenda was absolutely right and as we were in no great hurry, I eased the sheets and altered course for the southern end of the nearer island of Fuerteventura. Just before nightfall we crept into the port of Morro Jable, where the local council had provided a number of floating pontoons for the use of visiting yachts of which there were about a dozen enjoying this nice touch of local hospitality.

Next morning we left at crack of dawn for the sixty odd miles to Lanzarote. The strong winds that are a local feature and have given Fuerteventura its name, making it a windsurfers' paradise, never rose above a gentle breeze so it took us all day to motorsail along the island's eastern shore. While the western Canaries are mostly lush and green, their eastern sisters are barren and sun-scorched, a constant reminder that Africa is only fifty miles away. As we got closer to our destination, the scenery in neighbouring Lanzarote looked even starker, its skyline punctuated by a panorama of brooding extinct volcanoes. The last few miles found us negotiating the channel between the two islands under a brilliant full moon. Having identified the flashing green light of the marina breakwater among the confusion of dazzling shore lights we made our way into Marina Rubicon.

The marina is the centrepiece of a large resort that has sprung up close to the old port of Playa Blanca on Lanzarote's southern shore. Both the marina and adjacent tourist complex are surrounded by bleak lava fields that are a legacy of the island's volcanic origin. Nowhere is this more obvious than at the nearby Montaña del Fuego (Fire Mountain), now a nature reserve, where volcanic magma still bubbles close to the surface and the temperature at a depth of only thirty feet is 600°C. The chief attraction of the restaurant at the summit is a grill where the food is cooked over a hole in the ground. All around the

Lunch grilled over a volcano on Lanzarote

earth is so hot that it can scorch the soles of your shoes if you stand still. This is the result of a catastrophic volcanic eruption in 1730 that lasted six years and completely devastated nearly half the island covering it in a thick gnarled crust of black lava suitable called malpais (badlands). This moonscape quality was used to full effect in Stanley Kubrik's "2001: A Space Odyssey", which was filmed there.

A local artist whose work was greatly influenced by these surroundings and whose mark is evident everywhere on the island is Cesar Manrique. Having achieved international fame as a painter and sculptor he returned home and set about applying his vision to his native land. By the late 1960s the island's tourist potential had started a development boom that threatened to scar forever the island's unique environment. Manrique skilfully managed to persuade the local authorities to draw up a set of wide-ranging standards, such as a strict control on the height and style of buildings, a ban on roadside hoardings, and the highly effective edict, probably inspired by Henry Ford, that houses and hotels can be of any colour as long as it's white. The eye-catching white houses, dotted about the black landscape, have a definite charm, and as a result Lanzarote is architecturally the most attractive island of the entire archipelago. Unfortunately, later tourist developments have managed to circumvent Manrique's edict and as a result look as uninspiring as similar resorts all over the world.

Ivan helming Aventura in a stiff breeze

Cesar Manrique, who died in 1992, did a lot more for his island than just trying to preserve its uniqueness. By applying his fertile imagination to some special features of his island he created a number of highly original projects, such as an auditorium with excellent acoustics in an underground cave, an exquisite cactus garden with scores of species unique to these islands, a modern art gallery inside a medieval fort, to name just a few. Nowhere, however, is Manrique's bold style and faultless taste more noticeable than in his own home and studio, built in a series of volcanic bubbles in the middle of one of Lanzarote's badlands, and now open to the public. This special island has one more attraction: a tasty white wine produced from grapes that miraculously thrive in the black volcanic soil. It is the perfect accompaniment to freshly grilled seafood prepared as close as one can get to the devil's own cuisine.

A windy passage

Two days before our planned departure for Gibraltar a depression forming in the North Atlantic close to the Azores started tracking east towards the Iberian Peninsula producing SW winds in the area we were going to sail through. As I had expected to have strong headwinds on this passage, rather than risk exposing Gwenda to more misery, I had asked Ivan to sail with me from the Canaries to Southern Spain.

Ivan is an excellent sailor, which is not surprising as he grew up on a boat and had completed his first circumnavigation before he was twelve. He has done a lot of sailing

A Barbary ape keeps guard over Gibraltar

since, two Atlantic crossings in his gap year as a teenager, skippering Aventura II from Fiji to Darwin and a 60 foot boat from Brazil to the Caribbean in a round the world rally as well as a circumnavigation of the British Isles in one of the two boats he has owned. Sailing seems to be in the blood of both my children. Although recently Doina has had fewer opportunities to sail with me, before she had children she often accompanied me and we had a great time together sailing on Aventura II in the North Atlantic, and later from Bora Bora to Fiji. I am now happy to see that Doina's children Nera and Dan also seem to have an affinity for sailing and, when they joined Aventura in the Canaries and later in Croatia, they behaved just like Doina and Ivan at that same age, spending most of the time swimming around the boat or rowing the small dinghy.

When Ivan and I set off from the Canaries, the south-west winds were quite strong, often gusting in the low thirties, but it was still better than having to beat into the north-east winds that normally blow in this part of the world. Broad reaching with the staysail and three reefs in the main we rarely went below eight knots. It was an exhilarating sail and only four days after leaving the Canaries we picked up the light on Cape Espartel, at the NW point of Africa. By dawn we were greeted by the unmistakable shape of the Rock of Gibraltar bathed in blushing pink by the rising sun. As the gateway between the Atlantic and Mediterranean, Gibraltar has always had an enormous significance for sailors quite unrelated to its small size. Whenever I call there, I have a strong feeling, almost a tingle in my bones, of being in a very special space, a famous landmark that means so much to seafarers.

Gibraltar was undergoing a wide-ranging makeover with lots of building going on and every one of its three marinas being refurbished. The biggest change was the complete rebuilding of the old Sheppard's Marina now being turned into a residential complex under the new name of Ocean Village. Sheppard's used to be the favourite hangout of a large colony of liveaboards. Many a dream came to an end there, with several boats left unvisited for years, their owners probably traumatized by a rough trip across the unforgiving Bay of Biscay.

Several boats looked in no state to go anywhere, and so I asked the manager Miko Sheppard what would happen to them now that the new marina owners intended to create a new image.

'All of the owners have been given notice, so if they don't take them away, the boats will be towed out into the Strait and sunk. An artificial reef could be thus created for the benefit of divers and at least the old hulks will be recycled for a better use.'

Balearic sojourn

Although I love being on the ocean and cruising to remote places, for the sake of marital harmony I had decided to return to Europe as quickly as possible in the hope that cruising in the Mediterranean would be a suitable compromise. Distances between places are relatively short, the weather is quite predictable, there are plenty of good ports, and there is a lot to see and do ashore.

I cannot think of any other place that concentrates all those attractions better than the Balearic Islands. After a quick change of crew at Moraira in Southern Spain, where Ivan left and Gwenda took his place, we set off for the Balearics. It took us only a day's sail to reach the well-sheltered port of San Antonio on the north-west coast of Ibiza. Away from the tourist hot spots, Ibiza still has some charming corners, most of them along the less developed north coast. As in all other Balearics, the high cliffs are interspersed with deep fiord-like inlets but wherever there is a beach, hotels have mushroomed around it like flies on a pot of honey. What was worse was that even the smallest bay is jam packed with fixed moorings laid down by the hotels for their customers' diving boats, water scooters and sailing dinghies, so finding an anchoring spot is often difficult if not impossible.

Another day's sail took us across the fifty odd miles to Mallorca and as I had to have some work done on the boat we headed for the capital Palma. Although the large bay is peppered with marinas, it was with great difficulty that we found a free space. The port of Palma has probably a higher concentration of yachts than any other place in the world, with the entire waterfront being taken up by marinas. Palma itself is an attractive town whose medieval core is dominated by a huge cathedral but the most impressive building is that of Castell de Belver, a fairy tale citadel from the 14th century standing in splendid isolation on a hill overlooking the city.

Before crossing over to the easternmost island of Menorca we called at Porto Cristo, best known for the nearby underground Coves del Drac (Caves of the Dragon). Reputed to have the best stalactite formations not just in Spain but possibly in the entire world the extensive caves are indeed a sight to behold. There are no words to describe the beauty and perfection of what nature has created here. To round off the unforgettable visit, as we sat down in a natural amphitheatre by the side of an underground lake, a small boat glided out over the still waters and a quartet played some haunting music by Mahler and Schubert.

Quite apart from their size, Mallorca and Menorca are very different in most ways as Menorca has maintained much of its rural character and most of its interior appears to have been left largely untouched by the modern world. Menorca's main attraction is the numerous pre-historic remains, large stone structures built by a mysterious people over three thousand years ago. The two main ports of Mahon and Ciutadela are almost as old themselves, their perfectly sheltered deep inlets being used as staging posts by the early Phoenician navigators who were sailing in these waters one thousand years before Christ.

The stone beehives of Sardinia

A blustery mistral gave us a fast passage from Menorca to Sardinia, the strong wind staying with us until the mountainous outline of Sardinia punctured the eastern horizon. My old chart showed that we had made landfall in the wide bay of Oristano smack in the middle of the island's west coast. It was certainly a more successful landfall than thirty years previously when we had sailed almost exactly the same course but when we had reached the same spot, Sardinia was nowhere to be seen. While tidying up the boat in Menorca Gwenda had moved a portable radio into a locker located under the main compass. The radio's speaker had a powerful magnet that had affected our main compass and so we had sailed unknowingly past the large island.

Fortunately Sardinia was there this time and was certainly worth waiting for all these years. In recent years many marinas have been built and the island is now surrounded by some fifty marinas that are used as a year-round base mostly by Italian yachts. The best known is Porto Cervo, the playground of millionaires, with prices to match. Municipal marinas, like that at Torre Grande, where we made our landfall, are more affordable.

Even more than in the Balearics, Sardinia's main attraction is its interior, a wild area of craggy mountains and remote villages. It is here that Sardinia's once feared reputation as an island of outlaws and bandits was born. The most interesting feature of the interior are the pre-historic remains of the nuraghe people. Nuraghes are large stone structures that date back to the time of the Egyptian pyramids. Several hundreds of these strange towers dot the Sardinian

A well preserved nuraghe in Sardinia's interior

landscape, some going back as far as 800 BC. The beehive-shaped buildings were constructed from massive slabs of basalt to intricate designs. The technical solutions that were used to erect such massive stone structures were so ingenious as to make it almost impossible to believe that they were perfected by a bronze-age people. How advanced their civilisation must have been is shown by the bronze statuettes found at some of the sites and now exhibited in the archaeological museum in the capital Cagliari. The quality of that art is simply astonishing and certainly makes the effort of getting to Sardinia worthwhile. If you can find it, that is!

Cruising In Stages

Cheaper travel and more places to leave your boat safely between seasons have made cruising more enjoyable as it is now possible to return home more frequently than leaving on a voyage of several years.

Amanda Neal

During my first circumnavigation between 1975 and 1981 Aventura covered some 68,000 miles and we spent the entire six years away from home. Flights in those days were very expensive and there was no real reason to return home as we were sailing as a family. My voyage between 2001 and 2006 totalled 38,000 miles at sea in addition to which I flew 148,000 miles on the twelve return trips between the boat and home. Now that the buzz is all about carbon emissions and global warming I am quite embarrassed by this, especially when it is associated with what is the most non-polluting means of travel: sailing.

Some of my absences from the boat were as short as two months, while the longest was ten months when, for family reasons, I could not rejoin the boat at the appointed time, thus missing an entire favourable season in the South Pacific. Whenever I left Aventura somewhere I made sure that she was safely laid up, usually ashore, in a secure place and always outside the tropical storm areas. The wide availability of such safe places is another feature that was almost absent thirty years ago.

I am certainly not alone in this new approach to cruising as in recent years I have come across more and more people doing just that. In many ways it is the best and probably safest way to cruise and see the world. If I ever set off again I would do

the same but I would try to fly less. As often happens, the worst problem that may occur is that of crew. Friends will enthusiastically commit themselves to join certain legs when the intended voyage is described but as destinations become more remote and flights more expensive they often start finding excuses and back down. Unfortunately I have witnessed plenty of such cases.

Choosing a place to leave the boat

There is now a wide choice of safe places strategically located along the main world cruising routes. Whether planning to leave the boat in a marina or boatyard, such a place must meet a number of criteria: good security, properly prepared area for storing boats ashore, good range of repair facilities, availability of spares and equipment, reasonable shore facilities, closeness to an international airport. Finding a place that incorporates all these features may not prove to be easy and this is why I stress that careful forward planning is much more important when cruising in stages than on a continuous voyage when one can improvise and change plans at short notice.

In order to help would-be voyagers plan the individual stages of a proposed voyage and select potential destinations, I wrote World Cruising Routes and its companion volume World Cruising Handbook. To complement these two books our website *www.noonsite.com* also has all the necessary information on specific places and can help both in the planning stages and later, when details of new destinations need to be found.

The internet is a helpful source to find out what is available locally, but as with almost everything in life the best advice is usually by word of mouth. As one sails closer to an intended destination one starts meeting people who may have first hand experience of such a place or be resident of that country. The research should start well in advance and once you have drawn up a short list of potential destinations you should start contacting some of marinas or yards by email. Part of this pre-selection will be done for you as some marinas reply promptly with plenty of detail while others may not answer at all. Facilities available and costs should be discussed at this stage but a firm decision based on cost alone should not be made, however tempting it may be, as a lower than average price might mean that the marina is in a remote area with substandard facilities or the yard is running on a shoestring.

Three circumnavigations in stages 1975 – 2006

Cruising in stages is dictated primarily by seasons, and this is best reflected in the way I planned my own voyages. From my very first foray into the tropics I always planned my route carefully so as to avoid being in a critical area during the next tropical storm season. Our first arrival in the Caribbean was planned for December 1976, shortly after the end of the hurricane season. We then cruised all the way to Maine, in the USA, where we turned around in July 1977, always staying ahead of the hurricane season to the south of us. We left Beaufort, North Carolina early in November 1977, soon after the start of the safe season, and sailed via the Bahamas to Panama, then continued down the coast of South America to Peru and on to Easter and Pitcairn Islands.

On that first voyage into the South Pacific, early in 1978, we delayed our arrival in French Polynesia from Peru so as to get to the Gambier Islands, on the verge of the cyclone belt, in April. Thus, from there on we would have a complete safe season at our disposal to explore the delights of the South Pacific at a leisurely pace. By late October we were in Fiji and sailed from there to New Zealand, where we spent the entire summer, returning to the tropics and Tonga the following May 1979, at the start of the safe season. Once again we had a complete safe season for leisurely cruising that saw us roaming far and wide including a detour to Kiribati, north of the equator. In November, close to the onset of a new cyclone season, we sailed to Papua New Guinea, which is outside the cyclone belt so we could spend the critical period in that interesting country until the following April. Only when the cyclone season had ended did we sail to Australia, but returned to Papua New Guinea for the South Pacific Festival of Arts in June 1980. We passed though the Torres Strait in August, well before the onset of the new cyclone season, then sailed through the entire Indonesian archipelago, all the way from its eastern end to Singapore, which was still possible in those days, and arrived in Malaysia in November.

The onward voyage across the North Indian Ocean took place during the safe and favourable NE monsoon (December to April). We left Malaysia in January 1981, crossed the North Indian Ocean in perfect weather and continued with favourable winds to Port Sudan. In the northern half of the Red Sea we had, as expected, strong head winds, but managed to arrive unscathed in the Mediterranean in early April 1981 at the start of the safe summer season.

This concern to be in the right place at the right time was similarly applied to the voyage of Aventura II, which completed a

Puerto Lucia Yacht Club in La Libertad

circumnavigation as part of the first round the world rally. Tropical storm seasons were avoided by careful planning and the same concern for safety dictated the route and timing of Aventura III's voyage. As I mentioned in chapter 4 this is probably the reason how I have managed to avoid really bad weather for these last thirty-two years.

Aventura III's schedule

Aventura III's route was chosen so as to benefit from the best sailing conditions. The stopover ports were dictated by the need to avoid the bad seasons in the various oceans. This is the schedule followed, where she was laid up during that time and some essential details of the stopover places.

■ March 2002 – late January 2003, laid up ashore at Puerto Lucia Yacht Club in La Libertad, Ecuador. The entire west coast of South America is free of tropical storms.

Airport: Guayaquil (150 km/90 miles/ 2 hours): flights to Miami, New York, Los Angeles, Panama, Amsterdam, Madrid, main South American destinations, Galapagos.

■ May – July 2003 afloat at Tahiti Yacht Club in Papeete. This is the safe season in the South Pacific.

Airport: Faaa (6 km/4 miles/15 minutes): flights to Los Angeles, New York, Auckland, London, Tokyo, all main French Polynesian islands.

■ Early October 2003 – late March 2004 laid up ashore at Halfmoon Bay Marina, Auckland, New Zealand. The tropical cyclone season is November to April, but tropical storms rarely reach as far as Auckland.

Airport: Auckland (20 km/12 miles/ 30 minutes): flights to Los Angeles, New York, London, Hong Kong, Singapore, all main Australian and South Pacific destinations.

■ May – July 2004 laid up ashore at Sadgrove Quay boatyard in Darwin,

405

Australia, during the safe season in the South Indian Ocean.

Airport: Darwin (5 km/3 miles/10 minutes): flights to Los Angeles, New York, Singapore, Hong Kong, Bali, Djakarta, all Australian destinations.

■ Late October 2004 – late January 2005 laid up afloat at the Royal Cape Yacht Club in Cape Town, South Africa. Although this is the cyclone season in the South Indian Ocean, Cape Town is not affected.

Airport: Cape Town (10 km/6 miles/15 minutes): flights to New York, Los Angeles, London, Rio de Janeiro, Perth, Singapore and all main South African cities and some African capitals.

■ Late March – early July 2005 laid up afloat at Pasito Blanco Marina on Gran Canaria.

Airport: Gran Canaria (15 km/9 miles/20 minutes): flights to London, Madrid, both with onward connections to many US destinations, and all major Spanish cities, Madeira, Cape Verde, many European destinations. Until Hurricane Delta early in 2005, the Canary Islands had been considered to be entirely out of the tropical storm belt.

■ October 2005 – January 2006 laid up afloat at Rubicon Marina on Lanzarote, Canary Islands.

Airport: Lanzarote (15 km/9 miles/20 minutes): flights to London, Madrid and all major Spanish cities, many European destinations (charter).

■ January – March 2006 laid up ashore at Las Palmas Marina, Gran Canaria.

Airport: Gran Canaria (20 km/12 miles/30 minutes): flights to London, Madrid and all major Spanish cities, Madeira, Cape Verde, many European destinations.

■ May – July 2006 laid up afloat at Marina Monastir in Tunisia.

Airport: Monastir (5 km/3 miles/10 minutes): flights to Paris, Nice, both with onward connections to US destinations, and many European destinations (charter).

■ October 2006 – June 2007 laid up ashore for the winter at Marina Kremik, Croatia.

Airport: Split (20 km/12 miles/25 minutes): flights to London, Rome, Frankfurt, all with onward connections to US destinations, other Croatian and many European destinations.

Global weather

The early passage from New Zealand to the tropics (early April) could have turned out to have been a bad decision as late cyclone Gina passed over Vanuatu in June, much later than what is considered the end of the dangerous season. Fortunately by that time we were already in Papua New Guinea and well to the north of the affected area. The late cyclone Phoebe that formed close to Cocos Keeling in August 2005, while we were 1,000 miles to the west in Chagos, took all meteorologists by surprise as it came some three months after the start of what is considered to be the safe season in the South Indian Ocean. The passage north from Cape Town into the South Atlantic was also planned for the safe season. Catarina, the first ever recorded hurricane in the South Atlantic, formed off the Brazilian coast in late March 2004 exploding the long held view that the South Atlantic is entirely free of tropical storms.

There have never been hurricanes in the Canaries so no precautions needed to be taken while cruising there, but all this changed early in December 2005 when Hurricane Delta wrought havoc in the Canaries, the first tropical storm in their recorded history.

Gina, Phoebe, Catarina, Delta were all unpredicted tropical storms occurring either at the wrong times of year or in the wrong places. Four such rogue tropical storms in two years could be just an unfortunate coincidence, but I doubt it. They probably mean that changes in world weather are actually happening and ignoring these harbingers of worse things to come is simply mimicking an ostrich. Therefore careful planning in the future will be even more important but also more difficult.

Around the world in eighty minutes

I will attempt to go on a quick round the world trip passing through some of the marinas and yards I have visited or used myself during my own voyages so whatever I say is based on personal experience. In order to present as comprehensive a picture as possible of what is currently available along the main globe-girdling routes I will mention most relevant marinas, even if they may not meet the criteria of a cruising in stages project.

North Atlantic

For voyages that start in the Eastern North Atlantic, or the Mediterranean, the first offshore marina is at Caniçal on Madeira Island. There is also a smaller marina on the neighbouring island of Porto Santo but it is only recommend for brief stops. I would not consider Madeira for long stays either mainly because the point of departure for an Atlantic crossing will probably be from somewhere in the Canaries. There are now marinas in every one of the eight Canary Islands. The smallest island of La Graciosa, the first landfall coming from the north, has a small municipal marina at La Sociedad. There

are two marinas on nearby Lanzarote at Puerto Calero and Marina Rubicon, both are of a high standard and have good repair facilities. Neighbouring Fuerteventura has two marinas at Puerto Castillo and Morro Jable, neither of which is recommended for long stays. Gran Canaria has four marinas, three on the sheltered south coast (Pasito Blanco, Puerto Rico and Puerto Mogan) and in Las Palmas itself Puerto Deportivo, a 2000 berth marina and starting point of the annual ARC. Repair facilities in this thriving port are of the highest standard, so it is really the best choice for a temporary base. Over the years mainly due to the ARC repair facilities have greatly improved and there is little that cannot be fixed here. There are several supermarkets that deliver to the yachts and also several fresh produce markets. Although part of the European Union, the Canaries are a duty free zone (VAT exempt) so everything is cheaper than in mainland Spain and technical goods are a bargain.

One possible drawback of Las Palmas is that the marina being part of a commercial harbour is less private and leaving a boat unattended for longer periods may be better elsewhere. It is therefore better to get all necessary work done in Las Palmas and if the boat needs to be left unattended for a while one should try getting a place at Pasito Blanco. This is the nearest marina to Gran Canaria airport, has good security and a small but efficient repair yard.

Neighbouring Tenerife, the largest of the archipelago, has five marinas with more in the planning stages. There are two marinas in the capital Santa Cruz (very confusingly called the same as the capital of neighbouring La Palma). For short stays I would recommend Marina del Atlantico in the centre of the city, close to shops and restaurants. For any repairs one needs to go to Marina Tenerife three miles north of the capital, which has good facilities. Marina Tenerife is also good for longer stays as is Marina Radazul just south of Santa Cruz and within easy access to the capital.

Marina La Gomera occupies part of the ferry port of San Sebastian similar to the new marina in La Palma that is located in a corner of the port of Santa Cruz. The westernmost island of El Hierro has a similar arrangement with a small marina carved out of the commercial harbour of La Estaca. Good provisioning is possible everywhere but repair facilities are limited.

Before crossing the North Atlantic it is worth mentioning two popular stopover places on the west to east circuit: Bermuda and the Azores. Bermuda has several protected places and one large marina where boats can be left unattended. Repair facilities are good and there are flights to both the USA and UK. The Azores are a useful stop for boats arriving from the west and bound for either the Mediterranean or Northern Europe. There are now several marinas on the various islands but by far the most popular continues to be Horta on the island of Faial, which during the peak time of May and June will see as many as one thousand arrivals. The marina is currently having its capacity doubled.

Also worth mentioning are the Cape Verde Islands, which are close to the trade wind route from the Canaries to the Caribbean so they can be a convenient stop in emergencies. Every year ARC yachts stop at Mindelo, on the island of Sao Vicente, to drop off crew or buy fuel.

Caribbean Sea

The Eastern Caribbean islands can be quite bewildering in their wealth of choices. Furthest east, Barbados is not recommended as a first landfall, as with the exception of a very expensive and small marina, it is entirely unsuited for long distance yachts. Personally I feel that having sailed 2,700 miles from the Canaries one might as well continue another hundred and end up in a proper marina, such as those in Grenada, St Lucia or Martinique. Some skippers prefer to make landfall further north in Antigua, then cruise south.

Normally boats arrive in the Eastern Caribbean before Christmas at the beginning of the safe season and most stay until May or June. Those who do not plan to either sail home to the USA or Europe, need to head for a safe place where the boat can spend the impending hurricane season. As stipulated by the insurance companies, such a place must be south of 12°40'N, the only exception being Rodney Bay Marina in St Lucia. Most boats make for Trinidad, where there are several places specializing in looking after boats during the critical period. Although Trinidad and Tobago are widely considered as lying outside the hurricane belt, this is not really true as several hurricanes have devastated the islands in historical times (1790, 1847, 1921, 1963, and three more hurricanes between 1980 and 2000). Bearing in mind the current changes in world weather as well as the intensity of recent hurricanes, I am convinced that it will not be long before one of these tropical storms descends upon Trinidad. If it happens, the havoc caused among the tightly packed boats will be beyond imagination. Neighbouring Venezuela, although south of the stipulated latitude, is not a viable option because of the number of violent robberies involving cruising boats that were reported there recently.

As I have never spent a hurricane season in a critical area my advice is to avoid it if at all possible. Even if one decides not to stay in the Caribbean and leave for Panama in June half of the safe season in the South Pacific will have been missed. So, if I were on a Pacific-bound voyage I would only spend two or three months in the Eastern Caribbean, which is plenty of time to see more than just the highlights, then head for Panama. Some may be surprised when I suggest to compress the Eastern Caribbean into such a short time but the Caribbean is certainly not what it used to be and, in my view, a longer stay is hardly justified when so many more attractive places are waiting beyond the horizon. Furthermore, sailors who plan to set off on a round the world voyage will most likely end up in the Caribbean on their return, when they can easily catch up on everything they may have missed on their previous visit.

In the Western Caribbean there are a few marinas worth mentioning briefly. In the Bahamas I have visited recently only two marinas, the small marina in George Town on Great Exuma and the even smaller marina on San Salvador. The latter has the advantage of being close to the direct route from the east coast of the USA to Panama. Jamaica has a marina and yacht club close to its western end at Montego Bay, which I have used on a couple of occasions. It is conveniently located, safe for longer stays and good for crew changes, as there are frequent flights from the nearby airport to Miami, New York and other US destinations as well as to London. A possible place to head for the summer season are the well protected marinas on the Rio Dulce in Guatemala. Another possibility is Cartagena in Colombia, which is the only place that can be safely visited in that troubled country. Cartagena has two good docking facilities and as an old Spanish colonial city is an attractive place to visit.

The Bahamas, Jamaica and Guatemala are all affected by hurricanes and may not be safe during that season but the area of Cartagena and all of neighbouring Panama are free of hurricanes. Until recently the docking situation on the Caribbean side of the Panama Canal was far from satisfactory but a new marina at Shelter Bay has been opened near Colon and other marinas are promised to follow. On the Pacific side of the isthmus the situation continues to be as bad as ever and although there are now two marinas, the one near the centre of Panama City is shallow and in an unsuitable place, while Flamenco marina near the Canal exit is usually full. The only other option at the moment is to get a wet mooring at the Balboa Yacht Club but this needs to be arranged in advance. One solution is to do all provisioning and sightseeing from the Colon end, as well as the necessary exit formalities before the transit and leave once the transit is completed.

South Pacific Ocean

For those who may have transited the Panama Canal too late in the season and need a safe place to leave their boat the best option is Puerto Lucia Yacht Club, a small marina in Ecuador, where Aventura stayed not for the two planned months but ten. This is why it is so very important to choose such a place carefully as the only firm date that you know is when you leave the boat. The return can be affected by many unforeseen causes and it is this very flexibility that what makes this kind of cruising in stages so attractive.

From South America, the route will probably head west to the Galapagos but as cruising yachts are only allowed to spend a limited time there, and with a total

Visitors' dock in Papeete

absence of docking facilities, they cannot be considered for longer stays.

There are no marinas in the Marquesas or Tuamotus but there are some in the Society Islands. Marina Taina in Tahiti is usually full with local yachts and because protection is not good, it cannot be recommended as a safe place during the cyclone season. The better protected Tahiti Yacht Club in Arue is also normally full with members' yachts but a place may be found if approached in good time. Another alternative is to have the boat hauled out in the commercial port of Papeete and stored ashore. There are two marinas on the island of Raiatea, at Uturoa and Apoiti, both of which are used by visiting yachts during the cyclone season. Boats are also stored ashore at the boatyard next to Marina Apoiti.

A new marina is being built at Rarotonga in the Cook Islands and may be a useful stop once finished. Going west the first proper marinas are in faraway Fiji, and are located on the west coast of Viti Levu. The marina at Vuda Point offers good protection in a circular basin that can be entirely closed off by an anti-surge barrier. Boats left on the hard have their keels dropped into a trench for added protection. Another marina is being developed nearby. A cyclone shelter has also been created in a completely land-locked basin at Musket Cove on the island of Malololailai. All of these places are within easy reach of the international airport at Nadi.

Those who do not wish to spend the cyclone season in the tropics normally head for New Zealand towards the end of the safe season (October). New Zealand has so much to offer and there are so many marinas that it would be impossible to list them all here. Repair facilities are also mostly of good quality especially in the Auckland and Whangarei areas.

From New Zealand Aventura's route went north-west to New Caledonia, whose capital Noumea has a good marina, Port Moselle. There is no marina in neighbouring Vanuatu, there is however a good one in Port Moresby, the capital of Papua New Guinea. The marina is run by the Royal Papua Yacht Club and is considered to be a safe place both for security and weather as the entire country is outside the cyclone belt.

Australia's long eastern seaboard, both in the tropical and subtropical areas, abounds with cyclone proof marinas, most of them with good repair facilities. Those used by visiting yachts for long stays are concentrated around the Brisbane area and are considered safe during the cyclone season. Finding a suitable place during the safe season is easy as there are marinas with good facilities all the way from Sydney to Cairns.

North Pacific Ocean

Mexico has a number of good marinas on its west coast. This area is affected by tropical storms, but not as badly as the Caribbean. Sailing west from there the first logical stop is Hawaii, which is rarely affected by cyclones and also has a large number of marinas as well as excellent repair and shore facilities. The entire area between Micronesia and Japan is affected by tropical storms for virtually all months of the year, although January to March are usually the safest. The only marina along the tropical route is at Guam. Japan being used to frequent violent typhoons has many sheltered ports and marinas. The situation is equally good on the western side of the North Pacific, in Hong Kong and, less so, in the Philippines. There are no marinas, as yet, in Vietnam, but there are some on the north coast of Borneo.

South Indian Ocean

With that significant waterway, the Torres Strait, safely behind, the first logical stop is on Australia's north coast at the port of Darwin. There is a good marina, Cullen Bay, but most repair facilities, which are excellent as Darwin supports a large prawn fishing fleet, are concentrated around the Town Basin. This marina type facility is normally used by fishing boats but visiting yachts will be accommodated if there is space.

Indonesia for all its size has only a few marinas worth mentioning. The most useful for yachts in transit, but only for shorter stops, is Bali International Marina

Aventura at the Royal Cape Yacht Club with Table Mountain covered with its tablecloth

in Benoa harbour. For most sailors Bali is the one and only stop, whether en route to South Africa or South East Asia. The small marina is often full and there are only basic repair facilities. Conveniently close to

411

Singapore, but still in Indonesia, is Nongsa Marina, which is often used by visiting yachts for long stays.

North Indian Ocean

Singapore has at least three suitable places for long stays: Changi Yacht Club at its eastern end closest to the airport, Republic of Singapore Yacht Club, closer to the centre and Raffles Marina, at the city's western end. Singapore is a good place to stop even if marinas are more expensive than in neighbouring Malaysia. For this and other reasons many live-aboards prefer Sebana Cove Marina.

On Malaysia's west coast the nearest marina is at Port Klang close to the capital Kuala Lumpur, home of the busy racing club Royal Selangor Yacht Club and thus having good repair facilities. The most popular base is at Langkawi, right at the top of Malaysia, close to the border with Thailand. There are two marinas here: the Royal Langkawi Yacht Club and Rebak Marina. Langkawi also has the advantage of being a duty free area, so equipment can be bought at attractive prices.

The next stop is the popular island of Phuket, which has a number of marinas for long stays: Royal Phuket Marina, the Boat Lagoon and Yacht Haven Marina. There are no marinas in neighbouring Myanmar (Burma), which is slowly opening up to visiting yachts. Sailing west from Phuket the port of Galle at the southern tip of Sri Lanka has only basic docking facilities so only a short stop should be considered. There are no proper marinas in the Maldives, nor in Southern India, although Cochin is a convenient place to visit more of this interesting country.

Rather than sail non-stop across the entire width of the North Indian Ocean many boats bound for the Red Sea make a diversion to Oman where Marina Bander al-Rowdha is a useful place to provision and prepare the boat for the forthcoming voyage to the Red Sea and Mediterranean. The route through the Gulf of Aden has caused more anxiety among cruisers than any other area in the world as there have been piracy attacks on cruising yachts. After a number of ships have been attacked, some of their crews killed and the ships ransacked, the coalition forces decided to tackle this ongoing problem. Something must have happened because at noonsite, where we keep an update of all piracy attacks on yachts, we had no reports of any incidents involving yachts in 2006 and the early part of 2007 was equally quiet.

Close to the entrance to the Red Sea, there are two stopping possibilities: the port of Aden in Yemen and that of Djibouti on the African side. Aden has only an anchorage in the commercial harbour and is definitely to be used for short stops only. Djibouti has a small yacht club with some docking and a protected anchorage. There are only basic repair facilities, good provisioning and an international airport with direct flights to Cairo and Paris among others.

Once in the Red Sea proper, a stop in Eritrea's Massawa or in neighbouring Port Sudan is possible, but neither is suited for anything more than a brief stop. In Egypt there are now three marinas in the Hurghada/Safaga area, Abu Tig Marina is probably the best as it is also an official port of entry. This is a good place to relax after the long slog up the Red Sea. The other advantage of these marinas is that they are within convenient distance to the ancient remains of Luxor and the Upper Nile. At the southern end of the Suez Canal, the Suez Canal Yacht Club has a few moorings for visitors and is a useful place to await the transit or visit Cairo. Such a side trip can also be made at the north end of the Canal where the Faoud Yacht Club in Port Said will look after a boat while its crew visit the interior.

The Mediterranean

That brings us to the Mediterranean and the greatest variety of marinas anywhere in the world. At its eastern end Israel has several marinas with good repair facilities. Neighbouring Cyprus has two marinas used by visitors: Larnaca and Limassol. There is also a marina at Girne in Northern Cyprus.

Sailing west, Turkey has several useful marinas strategically located along its attractive coastline. Turkey is a favourite place for long stays. In neighbouring Greece most marinas are concentrated around Athens. All of these marinas have their own boatyards and repair facilities are good. One very useful marina is at Aghios Nikolaos on Crete's NE coast. This is a good place to leave the boat while visiting the interior of this interesting island.

An attractive detour is Croatia, which has seen a substantial boom in yachting and there are now many marinas in what is currently the most popular cruising destination in the Mediterranean. On the direct route west Malta has always been a stopping layover place and its docking and repair facilities are of a good standard. Neighbouring Sicily and Sardinia as well as mainland Italy have too many marinas to mention. Corsica has many marinas as well but while they are always full in summer, in winter places are available and prices come down. The French Riviera may have some of the most beautiful ports in the world but also the most crowded, so in spite of its many attractions, I would rather visit this area overland.

Back on the direct route, Tunisia is one of my favourite places in the Mediterranean. It has three marinas on its east coast, prices are very competitive and Tunisia has the great advantage of being outside the European Union and thus free of EU restrictions. The same applies to Turkey and Croatia neither of which is in the EU. Being able to leave a boat in any of these three countries is an attraction for non-EU boats, which may need to spend time outside the EU.

The Balearics are the Med's busiest yachting centre with repair facilities of a high standard and many marinas in all three main islands (Mallorca, Menorca and Ibiza). Most marinas are often full but it is worth looking around for a free space provided it is done in good time. Marinas are dotted about all along the Spanish Mediterranean coastline and the berthing situation is similar to that in the Balearics: perseverance pays.

Finally, Gibraltar as a traditional layover port has two marinas, Queensway and Marina Bay Marina. Gibraltar has good repair facilities, duty free provisioning and daily flights to London for onward connection to anywhere in the world.

South Indian Ocean

Heading west from Bali the first place with good docking facilities is Port Louis in Mauritius and the well protected Caudan Marina. There are direct flights from there to London, Paris, South Africa and other international destinations. Neighbouring Reunion has two good marinas, St Pierre on the south coast and Port des Galets on the island's west coast. There are adequate repair facilities and both marinas can be used for longer stays. There are flights to Paris and other international destinations

Marina Kremik on Croatia's Dalmatian coast

from the airport on the north coast. Rather than sail to Madagascar, where I knew that facilities were practically non-existent, I decided to leave Aventura in St Pierre and visit Madagascar by air and land.

The long leg to South Africa normally ends at Richards Bay, which is a convenient port of entry. There are two docking possibilities for visitors, a small marina in the town basin and the local yacht club. Richards Bay has frequent flights to other cities in South Africa and is located close to one of the country's best wildlife reserves, which can be easily reached by car. Not far to the south is the commercial harbour of Durban with its yacht club where visiting yachts are always welcome.

The leg to Cape Town is regarded as one of the most challenging in the world. There are well protected ports dotted along the coast where shelter can be sought if bad weather is predicted. Cape Town itself has two useful facilities: a marina at the new Waterfront development and those of the Royal Cape Yacht Club. The Waterfront marina has no repair facilities for which the yacht club is the only alternative. As a very active racing club, the Royal Cape Yacht Club marina is usually full but with advance warning a free place can usually be found.

All yachts are stored in the water but the club has an overspill area in the commercial harbour where boats are stored on land. The adjacent boatyard has a good chandlery and deals with all usual maintenance jobs, haulouts and hull repairs.

South Atlantic

With the exception of Cape Town, there are no marinas on the African side. At the first logical stop, the remote island of St Helena, there is a protected anchorage by the main settlement of Jamestown. As the island has no airport and facilities are basic most yachts only spend a short time here. From St Helena the choice of routes multiplies as from here boats have the choice of heading for Brazil, the Eastern Caribbean or Europe. An interesting detour is the Brazilian port of Salvador da Bahia, a highly colourful place, which overflows with life, dance and music during the annual Carnival. A stop there around this time can be easily accommodated as the best time to sail north from Cape Town (January) makes it possible to be in Salvador in time for its famous Carnival. From there favourable winds ensure a fast passage to the Eastern Caribbean, and this brings me to the end of this hypothetical circumnavigation.

Costs

As a rough estimate I guess that, over the five years of the voyage, my own costs averaged £10,000/$20,000 per year. This included marinas and laying up fees, insurance, maintenance, repairs, spares and servicing, fuel and provisioning, car rental, the occasional hotel, eating out, charts, cruising guides, communications. Not included was the cost of flights, nor that of trips inland. The annual cost may seem high but is only about twice what it would have cost in docking fees alone if the boat had spent all that time sitting in a marina in the South of France. Whichever way I look at it I feel that not only was it money well spent but that it was actually less than I had expected.

Flying in stages

This is another aspect of this cruising in stages phenomenon as not only can long voyages be broken up into convenient stages, but family or friends may also join the boat in similar fashion. Cruising in stages seems to suit some wives who are not keen on long passages but who are happy to join the boat to cruise in attractive areas. Some men, keen to realize their dream voyage and not wishing to risk the harmony of their marital life, have found this solution to be a truly win-win situation.

Tips

Although some of the following suggestions may have been made in other parts of the book, I will try to summarize the most relevant ones here.

- Choose the marina or boatyard carefully especially if it is in a tropical storm area. Have the boat well supported with strong props. Try to have it stored away from other sailing boats whose masts will cause serious damage if they fall over.
- Even if the marina or boatyard promise to look after the boat as part of the contract, it pays to make a private arrangement with a reliable local person to keep an eye on the boat and occasionally give it a wash. Inform the marina of such arrangements.
- Ask the marina or boatyard to draw up a proper contract and take a copy to have in case the authorities ask to see it at the airport.
- Always pay for a longer period than the intended length of stay as delays do happen and most marinas offer a better deal if fees are paid in advance.
- Complete necessary formalities with customs if the boat needs to be left in bond (as in many countries unattended boats are).
- If sending or taking parts overseas to be repaired and returned, clear this with customs so as to avoid paying import duty when they are returned. Take a copy of such a letter to be able to show it to customs at the airport.
- Bring back essential spares that are not available locally.
- Order antifouling paint, charts and any essential parts before departure so they are available on your return.

Golden Sands and Black Mountains

Over the years I have visited every corner of the Mediterranean but somehow never stopped in Tunisia. This time I was determined to put this right, and, after a windy crossing from Sardinia, at sunrise we made landfall at Cape Bon, the historic landmark where Africa juts into

purpose-built marinas from among which we chose Cap Monastir, which was Aventura's base for three months. The small town of Monastir is the birthplace of Habib Bourguiba, Tunisia's national hero and father of modern Tunisia. His mausoleum is opposite the Ribat, a fairy tale medieval citadel whose massive walls rise above the marina.

The marina is the centrepiece of a tourist complex of shops, restaurants and apartments. On summer evenings, as the temperature started cooling

Aventura at Cap Monastir marina with the medieval Ribat in the background

the Mediterranean. As we turned the corner, the strong wind petered out and out of nowhere we were suddenly surrounded by scores of small boats rushing home after a night of fishing.

Considered one of the most stable Muslim countries, Tunisia has seen a massive tourist boom in recent years. In parallel with the development of holiday resorts a number of marinas have also been built, usually as part of a large tourist complex. The east coast has several

down, locals would descend on the marina to walk up and down, look at boats, chat with friends or stop for coffee. What struck me most was just how pleasant and relaxed people were; groups of friends walking together, or entire families, from a grandmother wearing the traditional veil, accompanied perhaps by a married daughter whose attire was usually more modern, while the teenage granddaughter might sport a bare midriff. Boys walked in their own groups, and what impressed me most about those teenagers was just how well behaved and well disposed they were, greeting each other with a smile and

Ulysses and his crew on a Roman mosaic from the third century AD

a handshake, never being loud and brash as boys of their age often can be.

Everywhere we went in Tunisia, we were impressed by the friendliness we encountered. Maybe this easy-going attitude has something to do with the country's tumultuous history and the many waves of people who have landed and settled here: Phoenicians, Greeks, Romans, Arabs, Turks, French, all of whom have left their mark on the national character. After independence from France in 1963 Tunisia continued to look to Europe for inspiration and today it is the Muslim country closest both economically and politically to Europe.

History is a permanent feature of the Tunisian landscape where several civilizations have left their mark and it is this rich diversity that makes Tunisia such an interesting place to visit. Most impressive are the late Roman remains, mostly from the third and fourth century AD, when this was a prosperous Roman colony. The Romans built themselves some magnificent villas, most of them adorned with intricate mosaics, hundreds of which are perfectly preserved and are now on display in various museums. It is a unique experience to see those mosaics and to realize from their artistic quality and

the obvious comfort of the villas the kind of civilized life those people must have been living. Besides the villas and mosaics there are many other remains from the Roman and Byzantine eras: well preserved temples, early churches, amphitheatres and a large Coliseum. The oldest remains are the very early Phoenician sites of Carthage and Kerkouane. Just as interesting are the medieval quarters of the walled Arab towns with their narrow alleyways and vibrant markets.

While some of the older ports, such as Bizerte or Sousse, are quite attractive, it is the interior that makes Tunisia such an interesting country to visit. Life here proceeds at a very slow pace, farmers tend their vegetable fields and orchards, just as their forefathers had done, with hardly a modern implement in sight. But it is the olive groves that dominate the landscape and the production of olive oil has been for centuries this country's main source of wealth. After the fall of Carthage this was Rome's most prosperous colony, primarily due to the wealth generated by the export of olive oil, and the luxurious villas that have survived are a constant reminder of that period's affluence.

From the cruising point of view, Tunisia's main drawback is that its coast is rather featureless and there are no quaint little harbours so, by force rather than choice, one ends up being marina based. While some ancient sites are within easy reach of one or other of the marinas, it was the deep interior that attracted us. We overcame this by bringing our own Jeep across from France by ferry and made a complete circumnavigation of Tunisia that included all major sites of this truly fascinating country.

Meeting a camel caravan in Ksar Ghislane oasis

We were pleasantly surprised to find excellent roads everywhere and little traffic away from the main towns. Cruising on four wheels was a real pleasure. The ancient villages looked straight out of a film set, and in fact some were just that, as some troglodyte dwellings typical of an area in the south of the country had featured in an early Star Wars film. A long detour took us to the Grand Erg, the Sand Sea of the Sahara, which, for the real adventure seekers is Tunisia's foremost attraction. Our four wheel drive Jeep proved its worth as it allowed us to drive some 60 km across the desert to the oasis of Ksar Ghilane. With only the help of the car's compass we got lost only once and had to retrace our tracks through the sand. As we reached the oasis, a camel train hove into sight, a stark reminder that we had entered another world. As a sailor I could easily understand how people can get hooked on the desert and its sea of sand.

Summer cruise in the Black Mountains

I need to confess that I have a serious weakness: I like catching fish. Let me make it clear: it is not fishing as such that I like but catching those creatures and even more enjoy eating them. The way I go about it is far from an art form because all I use is a selection of lures, a very non-sporting heavy-duty line and a reel clamped to the aft pulpit. Over the years I have been fairly successful in all the oceans but was doubtful about the Mediterranean so it was a great thrill when shortly after dawn while on passage to Montenegro, I caught a large tuna. As it lay on Aventura's stern platform, its large eyes seemed to look at me full of reproach for having terminated its carefree life. Having just entered the Adriatic I felt a tinge of remorse or maybe foreboding, and hoped that it was not a bad omen. Well, it probably was, because not long afterwards I noticed a menacing black cloud chasing us from behind. Realizing that we were going to be hit by a squall, I quickly reefed down and headed for an area where the sky was clearer. Within minutes heavy rain had caught up with us, and with it came lightning and thunder. With fully rolled up headsails and deeply reefed mainsail we were skimming the waves in near zero visibility. By now the interval between the flashes of lightning and the crack of thunder was so close that the storm must have been overhead. I quickly disconnected all electronics, computers, satellite phone and anything else that I could think of. I was convinced that we would be hit any moment as tremendous bolts of lightning crashed into the surface of the sea closer and closer to us.

As always with such sudden storms, the turmoil ended just as quickly, the skies cleared and the wind dropped. Ahead of us, shrouded in mist, rose the dark coast of Montenegro, the serrated ridges of the high Black Mountains reaching to the sky. Soon afterwards we reached the port of Budva over whose medieval citadel proudly flew the red-orange flag with a black eagle, symbol of the newest of the world's independent nations: Montenegro. As we tied up to the dock in the small marina, the attendant welcomed us to "Charna Gora". With my limited knowledge of Russian I understood those basic Slav words and suddenly the penny dropped: charna gora = black mountain = Monte Negro! Or, as Sherlock Holmes would

welcomed and formalities have been kept simple. Visas are granted on arrival and there is a cruising fee to be paid which varies from just under 100 euros for a ten day stay to about 300 euros for a whole year. Although not part of the European Union, Montenegro had decided to adopt the euro, which is now the official currency.

Budva is a delightful small town, its older part, enclosed by the medieval city walls, is a warren of cool narrow streets. The central citadel had been converted into a maritime museum with an astounding library of old

Budva nestles at the foot of the Black Mountains

certainly have said: 'Elementary, my dear Watson!'

The latest of the component parts of former Yugoslavia to take its destiny in its own hands, Montenegro is also the smallest, with a population of just over six hundred thousand people. Blessed with a beautiful coastline and a scenic interior, Montenegro's economy depends heavily on tourism and sailing plays a major part in that field. Visiting boats are warmly

books among them an original first edition of Richard Hayklut's "The Principal Navigations, Voyages and Discoveries of the English Nation made by Sea or over Land". Published in 1589 it contains the best description of the early voyages of discovery especially those to America.

Early maritime history is present everywhere in this part of the world where some of Europe's best navigators were born and bred. Nowhere is this more obvious than in the picturesque Bay of Kotor, a large land-locked bay that is one of the most attractive natural spots in the entire Mediterranean. Surrounded by a ring of mountains over one thousand metres high, its shores are lined with old villages, each with its pointed steepled church. The small port of Perast, lying in the innermost part of the bay, has several substantial stone houses that belonged to sea

Medieval ramparts surround Dubrovnik's old port

captains. Local seafarers ranged far and wide over the world's oceans and were taught in the sixteenth century nautical school that was founded here.

Opposite Perast are two small islands, one of which was built by the people of Perast after two sailors had found an icon of the Virgin that had miraculous powers. With stones carried over from the mainland, in 1630 the locals started laying the foundations of a small island and on it erected a church they called Gospa od Skrpjela, Our Lady of the Rock. The interior of the church is richly painted and adorned with over two thousand votive plaques donated by grateful sailors. There are also many paintings depicting scenes of violent storms, shipwrecks, battles with Turks and pirates, from which the Lady of the Rock had saved them all. Before we left, I gave my own thanks to the Lady of the Rock and prayed that she extended her protection to Aventura and her crew.

Dalmatia without spots

For boats arriving from the south Dubrovnik is the perfect gateway into Croatia. Declared a world heritage site by UNESCO, it is considered one of the most beautiful and well preserved medieval cities in the world. All this almost came to an end in 1991 at the height of the war that marked the break-up of Yugoslavia when Dubrovnik was besieged and heavily shelled by Yugoslav forces. After the end of hostilities, in a rare example of international solidarity, enough funds arrived from abroad to repair all damage in record time and restore the old city to its former splendour.

As we sailed up the coast from neighbouring Montenegro, we passed the ancient walled harbour of Dubrovnik but could not enter as the port is now reserved for the use of local excursion and fishing boats. We continued to the nearby commercial port of Gruz where all port activities are concentrated and where Aventura completed entry formalities into Croatia. Visiting boats then have the choice of either taking up a stern-to mooring alongside the main quay in Gruz itself or move two miles up the Dubrovacka River where Dubrovnik Marina is located. We chose the former option as Gruz is almost within walking distance of the old city, although for longer stays the marina is definitely a better choice.

The independent Republic of Ragusa, as Dubrovnik was formerly known, was once an important mercantile centre that traded worldwide and maintained consulates in such faraway places as Constantinople and Lisbon. At the height of its power, Ragusa had some 180 trading ships and Dalmatian captains and seamen were among the most sought after mariners in the sixteenth and seventeenth centuries. The republic had a unique democratic system of government and its old people's home, pharmacy, orphanage and city sewage system were among the first in medieval Europe.

The city is enclosed by massive ramparts and there is a tradition that anyone who visits Dubrovnik must walk the entire perimeter. Inveterate travellers that we are, we got up early one morning before it got too hot and walked around the whole city savouring the stupendous views. Inside the walls perfectly preserved medieval buildings vie for attention: churches, convents, colonnaded markets, but, for me, the most memorable impression was that of an exhibition at the maritime museum showing photographs taken by a young local photographer during the infamous siege of 1991. Nothing could better reflect the horror and insanity of that futile war than those stark black and white images of burning buildings, frightened people and boats on fire in Gruz where Aventura was moored. Poignantly, the photographer himself was killed by a shell as he was recording this mayhem. He was only twenty-one.

All that is now history. Dubrovnik is firmly back on the tourist circuit and Croatia is now the hottest cruising destination in the Mediterranean. Having spent a couple of months there in the summer of 2006 I could easily see why. Croatia has a most attractive coastline with hundreds of islands and unlimited cruising opportunities, small ports and well appointed marinas. For non-EU sailors is has the added advantage that as Croatia is not a member of the European Union, EU restrictions do not apply and boats can spend as long there as their owners wish. The cost of living is below that of the European Union, as are labour costs, although due to demand, docking fees are slowly catching up. More than in any other country, and certainly in obvious contrast to Greece, the Croatian authorities have encouraged a wide-ranging programme of infrastructure development. There are now dozens of marinas, most with their own repair yards, and every port has an area set aside for visiting boats. Gwenda much appreciated the young men on duty everywhere to hand over the mooring and help dock the boat. Formalities have also been greatly simplified and many previous restrictions lifted.

Croatia however has become a victim of its own success. There is a profusion of charter companies, offering a wide range of boats, from bare monohulls and catamarans to large motoryachts as well as the ubiquitous flotilla holidays. As a result, during the peak summer months of July and August ports, marinas and popular bays are full of boats, although the situation is much better earlier or later in the season that lasts from late April to early October.

Fortunately there is such a choice of ports and anchorages that however crowded it may be, it is nearly always possible to find a sheltered place within a reasonable distance. After a couple of overnight stops we reached our first target: the island

The popular harbour on the island of Vis

of Korcula which had been high on my list of priorities for a long time not least because its attractive capital is reputed to be the place where Marco Polo was born. The old port, which shares its name with that of the island, once played an important role when the Venetians ruled this part of the world and the house where that greatest of medieval travellers first saw the light of day still stands in a narrow side street.

In about 1270, when Marco Polo was seventeen, he accompanied his father and uncle, who were Venetian merchants, on an overland voyage to China, which they reached after three years. There, Marco Polo entered in Emperor Kublai Khan's service and during the next seventeen years visited many parts of the far-flung corners of the Khan's empire. Twenty-four years after their departure, the Polos returned to Venice laden with gold, jewels and spices. A few years later, as a captain in the Venetian fleet, Marco was taken prisoner after a battle with the rival Genovese and imprisoned in Genoa. While in prison he dictated his memoirs to a fellow prisoner who later published a book describing Marco Polo's voyage. Although successful, contemporary readers suspected him of having grossly exaggerated what he had seen, and it was only much later, when other travellers to those areas confirmed his observations, that Marco Polo's achievements were finally recognized. It is said that both Vasco da Gama and Christopher Columbus were among those inspired by that incredible voyage.

After being ruled for more than forty years by a communist regime as part of Yugoslavia, whose long term leader Iosip Broz Tito was himself a Croat, Croatia has undergone an amazing change in the relatively short time since it broke free and became independent. What is remarkable is how people managed to switch so quickly to a market economy. The fact that Croatia's main income derives from tourism has no doubt helped this smooth transition. Private enterprise is flourishing with guesthouses, small hotels and restaurants mushrooming everywhere. Visiting sailors have greatly benefited from this changeover that has made cruising so much more enjoyable.

Compared to other former communist countries Croatia has also been fortunate that most of its ancient towns and buildings have survived both communism and the latest war generally intact, and even those that had been damaged have been carefully restored. Besides Dubrovnik, which is an architectural jewel in its own right, many of the ports along the Dalmatian coast and on the offshore islands date from medieval times, places like Trogir, Hvar, Vis and many others.

Until the break-up of Yugoslavia Vis was off limits to foreign visitors. The military must have been quite paranoid about a possible invasion as much of the Dalmatian coast was fortified, there were submarine pens dug into the cliffs and several offshore islands were barred to foreigners. Vis was one of them, but now its sheltered main harbour is a popular and much frequented place by both charter and cruising yachts. One of Croatia's attractions are such ports where the town quay has been turned over to visiting yachts, with restaurants and bars lining the welcoming waterfront. Even the smallest place has a well stocked supermarket and locally grown fruit and vegetables are sold in markets or from stalls set up on the quay.

Lest I paint too rosy a picture I must admit that there was a downside. The large number of boats made it often impossible to find a free space on a quay, and even some of the more popular bays were too crowded for my taste. Much worse was the inexperience of many sailors, especially on charter boats, whose actions were occasionally dangerous. One evening we anchored in Okruk Bay, near Trogir, that was protected from all sides except the north-east. Around 0330 we were hit by a strong squall with the wind quickly climbing up to 35 knots. As luck would have it, the wind was blowing straight into the anchorage and within minutes it had set up a short chop. As we were well anchored in a depth of five metres with thirty metres of chain out, there was nothing to fear, but even if I had tried to leave the anchorage, as I often do under such circumstances, a large yacht that had come in after us had anchored right in front of us so that our anchor was now somewhere underneath it and trying to retrieve it would have only made things worse. With things apparently under control and our anchor holding, I sat in the cockpit waiting for the squall to blow itself out. Two of my neighbours unfortunately had other ideas as first one and then the other, started their engines and kept motoring into the wind towards their anchors, then fell back pushed sideways by the strong wind. Every time they came to the end of their chain, they repeated the manoeuvre, passing perilously close to Aventura. Not being able to get up my own anchor, I had no choice but to stay put, hoping that neither of the slaloming boats would smash into us. As both their anchors seemed to be holding, their action was both useless and stupid, and in fact one of them did trip his anchor on one of his misjudged upwind drives. With no small effort he eventually managed to re-anchor further back. As I was watching all this activity around me, with yachts anchored further ahead also dancing about their anchors, I was struck by one thought: "do I really need this?"

Having spent several weeks among the offshore islands we decided to end our summer cruise with a visit to the Krka National Park. Set on the upper reaches of the Krka River, the main feature of the nature reserve is an impressive range of waterfalls. The river mouth is guarded by a large fort so we anchored Aventura nearby and landed from the dinghy on a pontoon by the fort entrance. A drawbridge led to the massive gates which, to Dan and Nera's delight, were open. Ever since he could walk, Dan has been obsessed with knights, swords and armour, and he carried a sword (plastic) everywhere he went, just in case. The role of the fort was purely military and although there were no longer cannons in place, the narrow embrasures gave a commanding view over the river entrance. Sited in such

Gwenda, Dan, Nera and Doina at Krka Falls

a strategic location the fort could repel any attacks from the sea on the city of Sibenik set on the left bank of the river about one mile upstream.

Sibenik's attractive waterfront is overlooked by St Jacob's Cathedral built in the fifteenth century under the supervision of Juraj Dalmatinac, who was not only a great architect but also a skilled stonemason. The cathedral's dome and roof complex are a permanent legacy to his ingenuity as they are made entirely of precisely cut stones that fit perfectly together, the large interlinked slabs being totally unsupported.

The navigable section of the river ends about ten miles above Sibenik at the small town of Skradin. Its marina is conveniently located for visiting the nearby nature reserve access to which is permitted only by excursion boat. Even in the relatively dry summer season, the first set of waterfalls was impressive. A smaller excursion boat took us to the upper reaches of the river and another waterfall. As we made our way up the slow flowing river, we came across all kinds of water birds nesting in its reed covered banks.

This image of peace and tranquillity was somewhat marred by a walk we took on our return through the back streets of Skradin. As we passed the Serb Orthodox Church we found it had been bombed and torched. What I found puzzling was that there was only an open grill closing off the entrance through which the debris strewn interior of the church was visible for all to see. This was quite clearly the intention as the entrance could just as easily have been boarded up.

Later, when we took a long drive through the interior, we passed several villages where one section looked well tended and clean while all buildings in another part of the same village had been bombed, and were without roofs, doors and windows. The latter had obviously belonged to Serbs, of whom few, if any, had returned after the war. From what I was told, the ruined houses had not been bombed during the war but were deliberately blown up later so as to make them uninhabitable.

424

As Transylvania, where I come from, is a similar cocktail of nationalities, I found the various wars between the peoples of Yugoslavia and their consequences hard to understand. Having grown up in a mixed society of Romanians, Hungarians and Germans, with many mixed marriages and friendly relations between people regardless of their nationality or religion, the

View of Hvar Harbour from the Citadel

senseless tragedy that befell Yugoslavia was something that I could never come to terms with. I realize that the divisions, both religious and ethnic, between Orthodox Serbs, Catholic Croats and Muslim Bosnians, ran much deeper than in my own country, but I could still not understand how, after living in harmony, however superficial it might have been, neighbour could kill neighbour. Some of the blame can be attributed to irresponsible politicians, like Slobodan Milosevic, but the main burden of guilt must rest with the people themselves. When the Romanian dictator Nicolae Ceausescu tried to inflame the Romanians against other minorities, people shrugged off his inflammatory pronouncements as the rantings of a deranged megalomaniac, and nothing happened. I wish the Yugoslav people had done the same.

The Croats are making a great effort to put all that behind them and concentrate on the present. In spite of the large number of boats, Croatia is undoubtedly a most attractive cruising destination. Weather conditions in the summer of 2006 had been quite disappointing, with at least one violent thunderstorm each week, although I was assured by some old hands that this was unusual, something that I take to

mean, it happens more or less all the time. Aventura was well prepared to deal with sudden wind increases, even if I found it boring to have to quickly swap the spinnaker for the staysail and three reefs in the mainsail, but others fared worse with blown sails and boats out of control a common occurrence.

By early October the weather had got unexpectedly cold so we headed for Kremik Marina where we had arranged to leave Aventura for the winter. Set in a narrow fiord-like inlet, the marina is perfectly sheltered from all directions and its facilities are of a high standard. The boatyard can handle repairs of any kind as it caters for a large charter fleet that is based there. Having gone through the well tried procedure of laying up Aventura for a long period of inactivity, she was hauled out and stored ashore. She spent the winter of 2006/2007 waiting patiently while I was writing this book and no doubt looking forward to more sailing. But that is a different story.

Laying up the Boat Ashore or Afloat

It never fails to amaze me to see how some boats are left by their owners even if they go away and leave the boat unattended for a long time. One of the worst examples was a boat berthed next to us in St Lucia, whose owner had just left and was not going to return until the end

Boats left unattended for the cyclone season

of the hurricane season six months later. Not only was the furled genoa left on with its sheets but so was some deck gear and even a large inflatable was hanging in the davits. Such a boat would have got into serious trouble in a hurricane, as one of the most vulnerable items in such situations is a furled sail that gets unrolled by the strong wind causing untold damage.

I am exactly the opposite and have almost an obsession about leaving the boat as tidy and well prepared as possible. Usually for anything more than six weeks,

Aventura is left entirely bare with all gear, sails and running rigging neatly stowed away. This is not just a safety measure but also a good opportunity to check everything over so any broken equipment can be put right before my return and the start of another cruising period.

To make sure I do not forget anything important, I have drawn up a list of jobs, which has been thoroughly honed over the last nine years during which time I must have laid up Aventura on at least a dozen occasions. The procedure is almost the same whether the boat is left afloat or ashore but if possible I prefer to leave the boat ashore. I realized the benefits of leaving the boat ashore even for relatively short periods with Aventura II, which was made of steel, and needed special care when left afloat unattended. Having her hauled out ashore was very useful as I was able to inspect all systems, clean and antifoul the hull before she was put back in the water. Although an aluminium hull needs less attention than steel I continued with this practice with my current boat. Having sailed nearly 70,000 miles since she was launched in 1998, Aventura III looks half her age and this is not so much due to my constant care but to the simple fact that she has only spent a total of some four years in the water. This practice is beneficial for a boat made of any material that is to be left unattended. As normally the boat will have to be hauled out on one's return to apply a new coat of antifouling paint, it makes sense to have the boat stored ashore. Furthermore, the cost is often similar and, in fact, in some busy places, leaving the boat in a wet berth is more expensive than on land. For all the above reasons, when I start looking for a place where to leave Aventura unattended for a longer period, the first priority is to find a place where she can be hauled out and left ashore safely.

Watermaker

Normally I prefer to tackle the most difficult job first, so I know it is out of the way and I can continue with easier or more pleasant tasks. The most time consuming job on my list of things to do when I lay up Aventura is to "pickle" my watermaker. If the watermaker is not going to be run for any period longer than two weeks it is supposed to be rinsed and preserved. On my older HRO model it is a complicated and lengthy procedure that I am sure has given me grey hairs. Later models are more user- friendly, but as in all other respects my watermaker works well, I have to put up with it. As this job can be done in advance of actually laying up the boat I always try to find a nice anchorage where I can relax and do a number of jobs that need not wait until I arrive at the chosen marina or boatyard for the haul out. Being in an anchorage has the added advantage of being able to make water (I never make water except offshore or in clean uninhabited bays) as I need at least eighty litres for this procedure. The watermaker is first rinsed out with half of this made water. The next step is the difficult one as a chemical preservative needs to be added to the final rinsing water and for this the system has to be bled, and this is where the fun starts as sometimes it

can take me several hours to get the thing to work. If freezing temperatures are expected, glycol or food-quality anti-freeze also needs to be added at this stage. Once the final rinse is completed the watermaker can be shut down, its seawater intake seacock turned off and the electricity supply switched off. In Croatia, where winter temperatures can go below freezing, I also lagged the unit.

Sails, sheets and halyards

Once we are berthed in the marina where Aventura will be hauled out, the laying up procedure can start in earnest. The yankee and staysail are always the first to come down, be rinsed, dried and folded neatly. I usually hand them over to a local sailmaker to do a thorough inspection and

Washing the sails before storing them between seasons

any necessary repairs. Every time I am surprised at what a sailmaker's keen eye can discover on a sail that I could have sworn was in perfect order. On a couple of occasions in the last nine years I had the

427

anti-UV strip replaced on the two foresails when it started showing signs of wear. I am pleased that after all the miles sailed I still have the original yankee and staysail and they look almost like new. I am just as pleased that I have never blown out a white sail on any of my boats, and even damage to spinnakers has been minor and easily put right.

When laying up the boat in the past I usually took off the mainsail as well, a lengthy and difficult procedure that also entailed taking off the battens, reefing lines and blocks. For a while I only did it for longer stays, but then realised the futility of the operation as the mainsail is perfectly protected by the lazybag. Now I usually leave the mainsail on the boom and it saves me about half a day's work when the boat is recommissioned.

All sheets, guys, jackstays and the boom brake are taken off, rinsed in fresh water on the dock, dried, coiled up and stowed. I always stow the various lines in such order that the first things to be needed on my return are stored on top and vice versa. With the exception of the topping lift, all halyards are taken off, rinsed and stowed. Every line is replaced by a messenger, a strong thin multi-ply line, which I usually buy in fishing shops where they cost a quarter of what is normally charged in a chandlery. Each messenger is marked with the name of the halyard it is replacing. The two ends are tied to one of the granny bars, well away from the mast, to stop them banging or chafing against the standing rigging. At first I used the lines again and left the labels on so I didn't have to guess their length but after losing one messenger that had chafed through having been caught between a spreader and a cap shroud, I now use new lines every time. For labelling I use masking tape doubled over the line and an indelible marker pen. The most useful messenger is the one replacing and following the track of the mainsheet, whose blocks I leave in place, so that on my return I don't have to guess the correct way the sheet runs over all those blocks.

Deck gear

All loose deck gear is taken off and stowed: danbuoy, horseshoe buoys and their lights (all batteries are taken out so they don't get discharged if the light falls over and is activated), fishing reel, helmsman's seat, steering wheel. I used to even stow away the liferaft but it seemed an unnecessary precaution and now I leave it in its place in a recess by the stern platform. As regular inspections are always best dealt with during such long absences, I normally arrange for the liferaft to be collected by an approved agent and only returned serviced when I come back so I know it was stored in a dry place.

Spars

As the main boom is open-ended I block it with rags so as to stop birds getting in and making a nest, as happened to me twice, the last time with serious consequences. On my return to the yard near Athens where I had left Aventura during the winter of 2000, I found a nest halfway inside the boom but managed to get it out and clean up the mess. In Cape Town it was only when a local rigger was trying to sort out my reefing system that he realised that something was amiss. A bird had built itself a nest far inside the boom that completely blocked all lines and blocks and could not be cleared. The rigger had to take the boom to his workshop to sort out its insides so now I make sure

Aventura laid up ashore at Marina Kremik

Plastic cable ties make good chain markers

the end of the boom is always sealed with rags.

In places where I had doubts about safety I used to stow away the two spinnaker poles as well as the aluminium boarding ladder. I still do and they are among the last things to be put inside the boat but not so much for their safety as to leave the decks entirely clear.

Masthead unit

While in Ecuador I noticed a large black bird perched on the top of the mast of an unattended boat. It suddenly took off, making the whole mast and rigging shake. It was an adult frigate bird that can easily weigh more than 5 kilos. It flew a few circles then landed clumsily on the same wind indicator arm, which I expected to snap under its weight. I had seen enough, so I put on the harness, climbed to the top of the mast and removed the wind indicator masthead unit. This was also a good opportunity to have a visual check of the rigging as I passed close to it. I have been removing the unit ever since. It may be

primarily an anti-bird measure but it also means that on my return I need to go aloft to replace the unit when I can also check the masthead lights, rigging, spinnaker blocks and the top of the yankee furling gear.

Anchor and chain

After the boat has been hauled out I drop the main anchor and all chain onto the ground, rinse and leave it spread out neatly under the boat. Worn chain with some of its galvanising missing can easily start rusting during a wet winter and may end up in a solid heap that could only be loosened with a hammer. Having to reach into the chain locker, which on some boats is inaccessible, is another good reason for this precaution. Not only does this prevention help protect the chain, but is also useful on my return when I can replace any missing length markers on the chain. For markers I use coloured cable ties inserted at five metre intervals.

Bilges

If there is any water in the bilges they are emptied, dried and thoroughly cleaned. I wonder if there is a boat that doesn't have any water in the bilge? Ever since new Aventura has had a maddeningly mysterious leak and although I managed to discover the worst source, a tiny trickle has continued to mar my life. Recently I discovered a faulty safety valve on the hot water tank, which opened when the water overheated and discharged some water into the bilge. Having replaced the safety valve the leak has still not entirely disappeared but it is now much reduced and I am resigned to it.

If the boat is left in a tropical country, once the bilges are clean and dry, I sprinkle some anti-cockroach powder especially in the galley area.

Seacocks

Whether the boat is left ashore or afloat I normally turn off all seacocks. As on Aventura III the seacocks are made of plastic they don't need to be serviced or greased but this must be done on boats with bronze seacocks which should be inspected regularly. In case I have work to be done on the boat during my absence, or the engine has to be run if the boat is left in the water, I clearly mark the location of the seawater intake. I also leave a sheet of paper that is placed on the steps by the companionway so that it cannot be missed: Engine intake seacock OPEN.

Batteries

What to do with the batteries during one's absence is a difficult decision, whether to leave them as they are and not charge them, disconnect and separate them, or leave them on a trickle charge. It all depends on the type of battery. Lead acid batteries are the worst in this respect as they cannot be left uncharged for long periods or they will be ruined. Gel batteries are much easier to manage as they can be left charged up and, if they are in a good state, will keep their charge almost indefinitely. In the past I left my gel batteries without being on charge and also disconnected the cables linking the separate batteries. On my return I measured their respective voltages and was surprised to see how much better some were than others after an absence of several months. It was a first indication that the batteries were no longer in their best state. By the time I reached Croatia the batteries were three years old and appeared to be nearing the end of their lives, so I decided to leave them connected to the solar panel. They are on a permanent trickle charge, which should do them no harm as they are charged via a regulator.

Mainly for this reason I feel that gel or similar maintenance free batteries are better suited for cruising in stages. In my own case the choice was easy as one cannot have lead acid batteries on an aluminium boat in case of a capsize and the risk of spilling sulphuric acid into the bilges which can have disastrous consequences and possibly a lost boat once the acid has eaten its way through the hull. Even without capsizing I feel that however well the batteries are strapped in the danger of an acid spill remains. So my advice is to avoid lead acid batteries if planning long passages not just for aluminium boats but for any hull material.

Whichever type of battery one has, they should be checked and cleaned before leaving and if they are of the lead acid type they should be topped up. Gel batteries must not be opened or they will be ruined, as happened to two of my new batteries when the New Zealand electrician who had installed them unscrewed their tops while looking for the source of some spilt liquid. The batteries were ruined and had to be replaced. What was amazing was that the electrician had never heard that this type of battery must remain permanently sealed or they lose the pressurized hydrogen inside.

Boat cleaning

This routine was added to my list by Gwenda and can be easily done while lockers and other things are being sorted out prior to packing up the boat. Gwenda also discovered that wiping the insides of drawers and hanging lockers with vinegar will inhibit the growth of mould or mildew and the development of the typical stale boat smell.

This is also a good time not only to give the heads a good clean, but also to check the state of their discharge hose to see if it empties satisfactorily. If it does not, it probably means that the hose is partly blocked with lime scale deposit and during the long period of inactivity may seize up completely. This may mean having to replace the entire hose which, as a precaution, should be done every five years or so. When I arrived in the Canaries I found that the discharge hose on the forward toilet was completely blocked. As it would have been very difficult to replace it I bought from a shop supplying professional plumbers a bottle of hydrochloric acid. Handling it is very dangerous as it is extremely corrosive and it should be treated with utmost caution. The acid does not react with plastic hoses nor with the toilet material or usual components but I was warned that the reaction would be spectacular and so it was. As soon as I poured some acid into the toilet bowl and started pumping there was an immediate reaction with rumbling and hissing and choking plumes of gas pouring out. The hose got increasingly hotter as the acid made its way slowly along towards the grey tank. A few minutes later, while I continued pumping, the acid had reached the end of the hose and pieces of solid grey lime scale started falling out. Some pieces fitted neatly together, having the shape of the pipe with a tiny half inch hole in the centre (in a two and a half inch hose) which explained the restriction I had been experiencing. When I repeatedly rinsed the system with clean water I was amazed how easy it was to pump, just as it was when the boat was new.

The tidying up blitz is also the best time to get rid of any useless stuff, books that are no longer wanted, old magazines, etc. The galley and provisions are also gone through and any opened bottles or containers, or those whose expiry date will pass soon, are thrown out. Unless there is a book exchange system I normally put my old books on top of the marina garbage containers, and line up next to the garbage container any expired cans, bottles or food cartons that may be useful to others. Invariably they disappear within minutes as happened in Croatia when Gwenda insisted on getting rid of everything that looked out of date or doubtful (our views never coincide in this respect as I always keep things "just in case"). So out went my collection of unopened colourful beer cans from Tahiti, Australia, Mauritius, Bali and South Africa. At least I had the satisfaction that somebody else picked them up as soon as I left them, probably attracted by those exotic labels than by their out of date contents.

Finally, I tidy up my navigation desk and chart locker and go through my cruising guides and take home those that I will not be using again. I make a detailed list of all guides and charts that I leave behind. I also go through the chart catalogue and write down the names and numbers of charts I may need on my return, all the way to my next destination. In some countries navigation charts can be purchased locally and often at better prices than back home. I normally try to buy or order before leaving anything that I may need on my return such as charts, antifouling paint, as well as spares and consumables.

I usually take my main laptop away with me, and also the logbook, as I often need to refer to it. All loose or easily removable items that are of value I hide in a suitable place. Having had Aventura II broken into in Gibraltar when all such items were stolen as well as the SSB radio and an early GPS model, both of which were ripped off their mountings, I regard this as a simple precaution.

Timing

Dealing with all the above jobs sounds like taking a long time to do but some of them need not be left until the last moment. As the laying up operation is repeated and becomes routine, it ends up taking less time to complete. Initially I allowed two days for the entire laying up operation, but it often took less because I had done some jobs earlier. Usually I look for a nice last anchorage close to the marina where I can deal in my own time with the watermaker, boat cleaning and other jobs such as removing all spinnaker sheets and blocks. Tidying up the boat and putting everything in its place is better

The List

The following list is a personal aide-memoire that includes all essential jobs to be done when laying up Aventura III but it can be easily adapted to any boat.

- Rinse, preserve and winterize watermaker.
- Lag watermaker and hot water tank; add food grade glycol if freezing temperatures are expected.
- Defrost and clean fridge/freezer.
- Check fridge anode.
- Empty and clean bilges.
- Test automatic bilge pump(s) if left afloat.
- Service engine, change oil and filter, replace main fuel filter, check, empty and refill bowl on fuel filter, clean seawater trap, check engine coolant, winterize engine.
- Service and winterize outboard(s).
- Check batteries, clean terminals, top up lead acid batteries. Arrange for lead acid batteries to be checked and charged regularly. Disconnect and separate batteries if they are not being charged while away.
- If the boat is left afloat sink anodes if in a doubtful situation.
- Take down sails and sail covers, rinse, dry and fold; have sails serviced if necessary.

done earlier and not left until the boat has turned into a storage depot and some places become inaccessible. Also, there is often something unexpected that may crop up and the only thing you don't have with a booked flight approaching rapidly is any extra time.

After arriving in Ecuador, having been away from home for a long time, I was so keen to leave immediately, that I had booked, rather optimistically, my flight to London for the following evening. Although I only had 24 hours to do everything, I worked late into the night of my arrival,

- Cover well and secure mainsail, stow reefing lines inside sail cover if the sail is left on the boom.
- Secure boom if open-ended and block its end as an anti-bird measure.
- Take down wind masthead unit.
- Take in all sheets, guys, jackstays, rinse, dry and stow.
- Power rinse furling gear(s), genoa and mainsail travellers.
- Take down all halyards, replace with messengers, rinse, dry and stow.
- Secure messenger lines well away from the mast to stop them banging in strong winds.
- Take in mainsheet, replace with messenger, rinse, dry and stow.
- Take off selfsteering lines, windvane and servorudder.
- Take down cockpit dodger and bimini, check for tears, rinse, dry and stow.
- Stow outboard(s), danbuoys, horseshoe buoys, fishing reel, all loose deck gear.
- Take in boom brake, rinse and dry lines, stow.
- Take off steering wheel, helmsman seat, cover instruments and steering console.
- Cover or close all dorades.
- Take down running backstays and stow.
- Release backstay tensioners.
- Stop wind generator.

- Disconnect solar panel (take out fuse) if not in use during absence.
- Empty and rinse all water tanks.
- Flush out, rinse and clean toilet(s), use strong disinfectant for final flush, close seat lid, rinse out and empty grey tank.
- Release main anchor and all chain, rinse, lay out neatly under the boat.
- Turn off gas at the tank.
- Wipe the insides of lockers with vinegar. Leave all lockers and drawers open for air circulation.
- If leaving the boat in warm countries set cockroach poison in critical spots and sprinkle some in the bilges.
- Take in the solar cockpit light.
- Pump up centreboard and rudder (if applicable).
- Close all seacocks except the seawater intake if engine is to be run while away.
- Mark clearly the location of the seawater intake seacock and main electrical switches.
- Hide in a secure place small items, VHF radios, portable GPS, laptop, binoculars, cameras.
- Take home logbook, any other reference material, used guides and charts.
- Take in flags.
- Turn off power.
- Lock up boat and all lockers. Leave set of keys with marina/yard.

A quiet anchorage to prepare Aventura for laying up at Marina Kremik

something I had never done before, as after a long passage I normally prefer to relax over a nice dinner cooked by somebody else. That time, having singlehanded to Ecuador, I was on my own so did not have anyone to take out nor was there anyone else to invite me to dinner. I finished all the work at noon the following day and I was very pleased with myself as it had taken me less than 24 hours to tick off all boxes on my list. So nowadays if I am short of time I only allow one day for the laying up operation.

The last things to be taken in, when I am ready to leave and no longer need to go below, are the ensign and courtesy flag. I used to leave the latter up as a courtesy to the host nation but it never outlasted my absence so now it comes down too. A final check, a last look and farewell caress to my faithful companion and I'm off, invariably with a heavy heart as I always feel when I part from a good friend for a long time.

I have two sets of keys, one for every lock, which I take with me, and one that has the engine key and only gives access to the main companionway that I leave with the marina office or with the boatyard if they will be doing any work in my absence. I usually try to avoid this as I have had a few bad experiences and prefer to be around when any work is done, but I am occasionally forced to compromise when some essential job needs to be done. When I left the boat in Croatia, and as for the first time in many years there could be frost during winter, I arranged to have the engine winterized. As I was about to leave, the mechanic, who had already started working on the engine, asked me to come back and have a look at something. He took hold of the propeller shaft, shook it, and pointed to a serious play that could only mean a worn stern bearing. But that was not all. He then grabbed hold of the MaxProp and it also showed an unnatural play. Although I had had some suspicion because the boat seemed to be slower under power than before, I had actually missed both faults when the boat was lifted out of the water, so I knew I was dealing with a good professional and that Aventura was left in the best hands possible.

How Safe is Cruising?

While on night watch between Sardinia and Tunisia, the persistent beep of the Inmarsat C alarm broke my reverie. I switched on the computer and read the emergency message: a cruising boat on passage from Brazil to French Guyana with a couple and child on board was overdue. It is quite rare that such messages are broadcast, so does this mean that the oceans have become safer? This thought had occurred to me several times during my recent circumnavigation. This gave me the idea to try and compare my latest observations with my early days of cruising when boat losses seemed to be much more frequent. During the three years we spent in the South Pacific in the late 1970s we had a few close shaves but nothing dramatic. Others were not so lucky and I knew of several boats that were lost, usually hitting a reef at night, often sailed by a singlehander. This was long before satellite navigation, when position fixing was still an imprecise art and astronavigation the only recourse on offshore passages. During that period I conducted a survey among my fellow cruisers and compiled a list of forty boat losses and their causes. In any one year there were probably around half a dozen boats lost or seriously damaged in the South Pacific and most of these disasters were caused by errors in navigation.

During my latest voyage I kept a record of all boat losses I heard of, but ended up with a much shorter list. Taking just the South Pacific as an example, I heard of two boats lost in the Tuamotus, one each in Vanuatu and Tonga, and a singlehander and his boat that disappeared somewhere between Tahiti and New Zealand. Thirty years earlier I would have ended up with at least double that number, so my first reaction was that cruising must have become safer. However, when I started researching the matter more thoroughly, and on a global level, some doubts started creeping in.

I started my research in April 2006 and soon the bad news started rolling in: a singlehander was missing at sea and his dismasted boat had been found off the Azores, a French catamaran had capsized in the Mediterranean in bad weather, four crew had lost their lives but two managed to cling to the upturned hull and were eventually washed onto the Spanish shore. Two separate incidents involving catamarans were reported from the US west coast. In both cases the boats had been washed ashore and their crews had lost their lives. The most tragic case involved a stolen steel sailboat that was found drifting off Barbados with eleven dead men aboard. They were African asylum-seekers who probably had attempted to land in the Canaries but had perished while their dismasted boat drifted slowly across the Atlantic. This case is worth mentioning because it shows how a well-built boat can cross an ocean, even without a mast and no one at the helm.

As my main concern was to assess the overall safety of offshore cruising, I decided to deal only with boats lost while cruising and discount those lost or damaged in coastal waters or by tropical storms while stored afloat or ashore. As no maritime authority or insurance company seems to keep an accurate record of global boat losses, I conducted an ad-hoc survey among a number of sailors who were cruising in faraway places, from Antarctica to the North Pacific, the Caribbean to Indonesia and Australia. A number of officials in key locations, such as Phuket, Bali, Cape

Town, Tahiti, Auckland, Azores and Suez also contributed to this survey that slowly coalesced into a global picture. One of the main questions that everyone was asked was to estimate the number of total boat losses that had come to their knowledge in their part of the world. In most cases my correspondents

A large humpback whale passes Aventura in Antarctica but such close encounters are not appreciated on the high seas

could only name one or two cases of total losses per year and as they also described the causes, when known, I decided to list them here as well as describe some of the more significant incidents.

Perhaps the greatest surprise came in an email from Skip Novak, who has been running charter cruises to Antarctica and in the area of Cape Horn for the last fifteen years. 'I have never heard of any yachts lost in the Antarctic or in the Drake Passage, which is quite amazing given the situation. You can take this as fact as we would have all been aware of an incident if it had happened.'

Groundings

In spite of the much improved precision of navigation, the major cause of boat losses continues to be groundings and, in my survey, this still accounted for more than half the total losses. The main reasons for groundings are: navigational error, crew error and being caught on a lee shore.

Several of the reported losses gave the reason as navigational error. Two boats were lost on a reef on the north coast of Tahiti within one week of each other, in both cases their navigators relying on outdated charts. Similar cases were reported from the Caribbean and South Indian Ocean. Crew error was mentioned in a number of cases, either the crew failing to steer an accurate course, or taking the wrong decision in a critical situation usually leaving it too late to call the skipper. Finally, being caught on a lee shore has always been a seaman's nightmare and unfortunately it still happens. Two multi-million dollar superyachts were grounded in the Mediterranean and having the latest equipment on board proved of no help when a change in wind direction drove them aground. Boats are lost or damaged every year in tropical anchorages when a sudden squall or passing depression puts them on a lee shore.

Collisions

The second most common cause of boat losses is collision whether with ships, whales, containers or other debris. Some of the mysterious disappearances of yachts on passage were probably caused by collision with an unidentified object. A French aluminum cutter of the same design as my own Aventura disappeared between Tahiti and Tonga, without a trace of it or its crew ever being found. Aventura could have shared that fate after a collision in the South Indian Ocean that damaged her rudder and steering system. In the South Pacific, a cruising trimaran with a couple on board disappeared in 2005 while en route from New Zealand to Tahiti. Remains of their yacht were found one year later washed ashore in the Cook Islands. A collision was probably to blame for the disappearance of Pierre Ribes, a French singlehander, whose 36 foot Sphinx vanished while crossing the Bay of Biscay.

Several collisions with whales have been reported over the years and a few had resulted in the boat being sunk. Deliberate attacks by whales are very rare, whereas collisions, often with a sleeping whale, are quite common, and it all depends on the strength of the boat which of the two suffers the more serious damage.

Structural damage

Several of the reported losses were as a result of structural damage, often caused by rudder failure. On some occasions this may have been the result of collision, and unsupported spade rudders seem to be particularly vulnerable. Over the years, five boats taking part in the ARC were abandoned after losing their rudders. In most cases this seems to have been a result of a design fault or inherent weakness. Although some of the crews believed that the rudder might have been lost as a result of a collision, the very fact that they could not be sure that they had actually hit something probably means that those rudders were not up to the job.

Two other total losses were reported to have been caused by fire and subsequent explosion. While on passage from the Andaman Islands to Thailand, a lightning strike caused a boat's 240 Volt system to catch fire and the boat had to be abandoned. The crew were picked up by a passing freighter. A boat sailing off the coast of Nicaragua with a large quantity of gasoline onboard caught fire and exploded. The crew was saved by another yacht.

Weather

Boats continue to be lost while caught on a lee shore or while anchored in an unsafe place. I came across two such cases during my recent voyage: a boat dragged its anchor and broke up on a reef in Chagos during a sudden squall. A boat anchored in Vanuatu, tried to leave at night when the wind changed direction and they were being pushed onto a lee shore. As they were leaving the bay in the dark, navigating by GPS and radar, they clipped the corner of a fringing reef and the boat ended up being smashed to pieces. The crew walked ashore.

The best documented weather damage suffered by cruising boats while on passage occurred during the so-called Queen's birthday storm, in June 1994, when a group of boats sailing from New Zealand to Tonga were caught by a violent storm. In spite of the severity of the storm only nine of the thirty-five boats closest to the center of the storm suffered serious damage. One boat and its crew of three were lost, and eight other boats had their crews saved and were abandoned. The high seas caused some boats to pitch-pole or roll over repeatedly and seven boats lost their rig. With the help of a Royal New Zealand Navy ship and helicopter seventeen crew were saved. What was quite remarkable was that in spite of the damage suffered, all the boats whose crew were saved were still afloat when they were abandoned and looked as if they may have been able to survive the storm if left to their own devices. Never was the old wisdom more true that you should only abandon your boat when you have to step up into the liferaft!

The above boats were sailing in company with other boats as part of an organized rally, so it was tempting to try and find out if there is any safety in numbers. Among the approximately two hundred boats that took part in the four round the world rallies that I organized between 1991 and 2000, there was only one total loss, the Hungarian Jolly Joker, that ran aground on a reef in the Torres Strait. Besides that incident, the round the world rallies produced little drama with only two dismastings and a few groundings, none with serious consequences. What is quite remarkable about those round the world rallies is how very few serious breakages the boats experienced, which shows, as in my own case, just how trouble-free a circumnavigation can actually be – if one is well prepared.

Several correspondents contributed to my survey not just with figures on total losses but also with comments on near losses. Several stressed the vulnerability of unsupported rudders, and pointed out that losing the rudder often led to the yacht being abandoned. It is interesting that there was not a single example of a boat being abandoned after it had been dismasted apart from those in the Queen's birthday storm.

By looking closely at recent boat losses what is striking is that in many of the cases in which boats were lost as a result of grounding, this appears to have been caused, just as in the old days, by a navigational or human error. Looking at a number of incidents of near or total losses, I was tempted to draw the conclusion that whereas in pre-GPS days boats were often lost because sailors didn't know where they were, nowadays boats are lost because skippers know where they are. Or so they think!

In several recent cases, a boat ended up on a reef because the skipper, by knowing where he was, had plotted a course that passed too close to a known danger. This included the loss of my friend Antti's Pegasos as described in chapter 6. Maybe the crew didn't steer an accurate course, or a current had swept them sideways, but they somehow clipped the reef and the boat was a total loss. GPS can be a false friend indeed!

To add some weight to my research I contacted Falmouth Coast Guard in the UK, who, alongside the US Coast Guard, is one of the leading search and rescue authorities in the world. Colin Struman is the Area Manager and for the last eight years has been dealing with boats in distress, not only in British waters but all over the world. He was of the opinion that, bearing in mind the number of boats sailing the world's oceans, very few boats were lost cruising offshore. On average, he believed that one or two boats got into some kind of trouble every month, but very few of them were sailing in the open ocean and most incidents occurred in coastal waters. As Colin Struman emphatically pointed out, 'The real problem are what we call the "rockhoppers", inexperienced people who set off in unsuitable boats and get into trouble while coastal cruising. Offshore, many more racing boats get into serious trouble than cruising boats... probably because cruising sailors going offshore are usually well prepared and know what they are doing.'

Sunset over Refuge Harbour, one of the
safest natural ports in the South Pacific

Those comments were reinforced by the statistics obtained from the search and rescue authority in Gran Canaria, which, in the previous twelve years, had recorded a total of 24 pleasure craft losses in its area. The majority of the total losses (16) had occurred in coastal waters close to the Canaries and three of those had been caused by fire. Eight other boats had been lost further offshore, six of which had sunk while two had been abandoned. In all cases the crews were saved with the exception of the Italian yacht Valvode which foundered SW of the Canaries. Only two of its crew of five were saved.

So is cruising safer? Personally I believe that cruising generally is safer, and I am relieved that the findings of my admittedly subjective survey bears this out. Boats still get lost but certainly not as frequently as during the days of astronavigation. What I found, however, is that whereas offshore cruising is indeed safer, the situation is not so good when it comes to coastal cruising or navigating close to land. Although there are more boats on the world's oceans than in my early days of cruising, the comments from some of my contacts were very encouraging when most stated that they could only think of maybe one boat lost in their part of the world every year. Bearing in mind the thousands of miles travelled by cruising yachts, sailing in distant waters is probably the safest way to see the world.

A Boat for Offshore Cruising

Accept nothing as nearly good enough.

Sir Henry Royce

The choice of boat and its various features lies at the very core of a successful voyage. In previous chapters I have tried to deal with some of the other factors that might affect the success of an offshore voyage, such as crew, finances, safety, weather and practical considerations. In this chapter the boat itself takes centre stage and the most important features on a boat chosen for an offshore voyage will be examined. In search of that elusive "ideal cruising boat", I have conducted various surveys over the years, from questioning the two hundred skippers taking part in the first ARC to the most recent Global Cruising Survey, which was the basis of my book World Cruising Essentials (USA) or World Cruising Survey (UK). The obvious conclusion from all these surveys is that while a particular boat may be ideal for one sailor, it might be totally wrong for another.

Although drawing primarily from my own experience, I also tapped the concentrated wisdom of the forty long distance sailors who took part in the Global Cruising Survey and gave their views on the essential features of an ideal cruising yacht. Their views differed widely but they all agreed on one point: the choice of a suitable boat for an offshore voyage is of such paramount importance that the final decision should not be taken lightly. This is echoed in the advice quoted above of Sir Henry Royce of Rolls Royce fame, who should know that only the best is good enough.

With the wisdom of hindsight, I can say that I am happy with my three choices of boat, which were right for my circumstances, experience and plans at the time of choosing. In contrast, among the 3,000 yachts that have sailed in the transatlantic or round the world rallies that I was involved with, I noticed many quite obviously unsuitable choices. Some were so bad that their owners were eventually forced to abandon their voyage. Although I could probably fill a book with examples of bad choices that I have encountered I will limit myself to only two.

An acquaintance asked me one day to come and look at his new boat. He was obviously very proud of his choice and asked me to comment. I tried as diplomatically as I could to avoid the question, as only one look told me that he had picked about the worst built boat currently on the market. As he didn't have any sailing experience, I wasn't entirely surprised.

'I hope you agree that she looks good to go anywhere.'

'Well, it all depends where you plan to go.'

'Oh, eventually around the world!'

'If I were you I'd cut my teeth first in the Med, then maybe upgrade to something more... ocean-going.'

'Funny you say that because the salesman told me the opposite, that this is a true ocean-going boat that will take me anywhere I want to go.'

'Lucky you. But tell me, how did you decide on this particular boat?'

'Oh, I liked her looks.'

'Is that all?'

'What else? What's the point if you don't like her looks? After all, isn't a boat supposed to be like a woman?'

Coming from a guy who had been through a number of marriages, I could say no more. Later, after having sailed to Mallorca and back, he confirmed my doubts when he reluctantly admitted that the boat was flimsily built and inadequately rigged, with the coachroof flexing visibly when a sheet was winched in. Even worse was that when the rigging was tightened she took on a banana shape and the deck came apart from the hull, with water pouring into the bilges through a gap that opened at the stern where the two halves were lightly joined. He also agreed with a point I had made on my first visit when I mentioned that I didn't like the idea of having the spreaders swept right back making it possible to do without a backstay. It may be all right on a daysailer, but is simply not a solution that I considered adequate for a long offshore voyage.

The reason he gave me for his choice reminded me of a couple who had joined one of the early ARCs with their brand new 49 foot boat and were so proud of their acquisition that I asked them what made them choose exactly that boat, as it was a poorly built cheap production boat.

'Basically my wife liked the coordinated upholstery and curtains.'

I thought he was joking.

'Really? Is that all?' I asked, unable to believe that people would trust their lives to a boat chosen on such flimsy grounds.

'Well the price was also right so we did get a lot of boat for our money.'

For family reasons they missed the start of the ARC, which was maybe just as well and I never saw them again. I wondered if I shouldn't have followed my first impulse, which was to refuse their entry into the ARC, as we sometimes did on safety reasons, and thus indirectly make them understand what they had got themselves into. As I gained more experience with rallies, I was less shy about making my opinion known, but it rarely went down well and occasionally I ended up upsetting people.

Overall length

Too many of my friends follow the erroneous belief that a yacht should be as long in feet as the years of your age.
Bill Butler

Deciding on the size of a boat is not only the most important but also the most difficult of the entire decision making process and it is here that most serious mistakes are made. More often than not people choose a boat that is too large for their requirements, difficult to handle shorthanded and more expensive to run and maintain. The temptation is hard to resist, as the same money nowadays will buy a much larger boat that it did ten years ago. Also equipment such as electric winches, powered furling gears and bow thrusters have made even large boats much easier to handle. The used boat market is awash with excellent offers and, as more and more used boats become available, prices become proportionally even more attractive. If there is one single aspect to be borne in mind and stuck to firmly before any decision is taken is to ask, 'Can I sail this boat with just my partner or a small crew?' As I explained elsewhere finding suitable crew can be a serious problem and is often a source of frustration so that if the boat will be sailed most of the time short-handed, it should be of a size that can be easily handled by that crew. The situation is, of course, very different for a fully crewed yacht, in which case the sky, or more likely one's wallet, is the limit.

I would like to quote here my good friend Arthur Beiser, author of the highly successful classic book 'The Proper Yacht',

Aventura II incorporated all four essential features listed by Arthur Beiser

who points out, 'there are four essentials for a proper yacht. These are, not in order because all four are needed, that the boat be (1) beautiful; (2) fast under sail and under power; (3) able, well-designed and engineered, strongly built and well equipped and (4) comfortable at sea and in port, on deck and below.'

The boats currently sailing in the ARC are a good indication of the size preferred by most people. Leaving aside the very large and fully crewed yachts, about half the boats are in the 40 to 50ft range, showing that this continues to be the most popular size among long distance cruisers. In the Millennium Odyssey where the boats ranged from 37 to 73 feet, with only a couple of exceptions all family or shorthanded boats were between 40 and 50 feet. The smallest boat was a 37 foot catamaran sailed by a couple with their young child. The apparently optimum size was confirmed by the figures obtained from Cape Town showing all the cruising boats that had passed

through there the previous year and whose average overall length was 42.8 feet.

This important subject was also examined in a survey I conducted in 2002 among a selection of long distance sailors of which at least half had completed a circumnavigation. Although the ideal size had moved up considerably I understood that these were highly experienced sailors, for whom speed and comfort were of importance and who would probably be able to handle a boat of up to 60 feet even with a small crew.

Skip Novak, who had sailed in several Whitbread (now Volvo) round the world races and now runs a successful charter operation in the Antarctic with his 55 foot steel Pelagic and the 80 foot aluminium Pelagic Australis, gave the following advice, 'The length depends entirely on the purpose of the boat and how many will sail on her. For a couple or maybe four people, and your goal is to explore remote areas rather than make long ocean passages, then the boat should not be longer than fifty to fifty-five. If you are interested in making fast passages, I would say a slightly bigger boat, which can easily sail at ten knots, would be preferable. At 55 feet a boat is big enough for comfort and yet small enough to be easily handled.'

Skip's ideal size might be too large for most short-handed crews, especially if they are not experienced. Both in the rallies and during my recent voyage I came across several couples sailing 53 foot yachts which they found difficult to handle on their own and ended up being forced to take on extra crew, a solution that they didn't like at all. As Ian Allmark advised, 'don't go for a bigger boat than you need just because you can afford it.'

While all my previous surveys had shown that most owners were happy with their choice, whether large or small, in every survey there were also a few disgruntled skippers. A few complained that their boat was too large to handle, but the majority of dissatisfied owners complained about their boat being too small. The feeling of being overcrowded or the lack of space or privacy can have a negative effect on morale and lead to friction among members of the crew. Another cause of complaint was not having enough space to store all the gear necessary for a long voyage. Often this meant that surplus gear was stowed on deck, which can lead to a potentially hazardous or unseaworthy situation. Having been on the dockside watching the ARC boats coming in after their Atlantic crossing, I have been amazed at the clutter on the stern of some boats, as the person throwing the line struggled to clear a forest of obstructions from wind generator mast to danbuoy, radar, fishing rods, flag pole, spare anchor, whip aerial, outboard motor, barbeque and even a bicycle. I am not even going to mention what their decks looked like. I wondered how in a real emergency one would be able to throw a line to a man overboard or launch the liferaft past all such obstructions.

I'd like to leave the last words on suitable size to Arthur Beiser who with his wife Germaine have owned everything in the last fifty years from dinghies to a 72 footer. 'I will never have a boat so large and complicated that I cannot with my own eyes and hands check everything regularly and be able to fix almost any defect that may arise.'

Monohull versus multihull

I was very happy with the performance of our catamaran during our circum-navigation. I believe that it was the ideal boat for that voyage, for that route and also for our budget. In spite of which, I feel that if you want to sail in the Southern Ocean, a monohull would be better but not just any monohull.

Javier Visiers

To go for one or more hulls is just as difficult a decision as that of size. In my view trimarans are unsuitable for an offshore ocean passage as over the years there have been several fatalities involving trimarans, so I am not going to discuss them here. In the early days there were serious doubts about the suitability of catamarans for offshore sailing as well, and I had felt some relief when the decision was taken out of my hands when two catamaran builders refused to sell me a bare hull. Since then catamaran design has improved dramatically, architects have put a lot of thought into their safety while builders have done their best to produce strong seaworthy craft. Their ever-increasing popularity among long distance cruisers is the best proof and I know of many safely completed circumnavigations in a cat. As catamarans have many advantages over a monohull of the same length I have an open mind on this subject yet I do know that many sailors still have doubts about their ultimate safety. Just as I started writing this book I heard of the tragic loss of a singlehander whose upturned mastless 50 foot catamaran had been found off the coast of Oregon. A few days later another mastless catamaran was found washed ashore in the same area of the Rogue River, the three crew, who were finishing a delivery from South Africa to Seattle, were all lost. In all fairness to catamarans it must be said that both incidents happened in December when there can be a large swell in that notorious area. Also they may have been caught in the breakers while attempting to approach the coast and had strayed into shallow waters. Such conditions are entirely unsuitable not only for a catamarans but for monohulls as well.

Those who plan to set off in a catamaran on a long voyage must choose their route carefully to minimize the risk of dangerous weather, observe the safe seasons and always be aware of a catamaran's weak points. Catamarans are much less forgiving than monohulls when conditions deteriorate and things start going wrong. Whereas a catamaran needs to be helped to overcome extreme conditions, a well-found monohull can be battened down and left to its own devices. It may capsize and lose its mast but it will probably survive upright.

Javier Visiers, who is quoted above, is a well-known Spanish naval architect, who designed the highly popular Fortuna range. He took many by surprise when he chose a catamaran for the Millennium Odyssey round the world rally. Javier did in fact what many other sailors do and chose what he thought was the most suitable boat for a particular voyage, a pragmatic attitude that I fully share. Other sailors may consider a

catamaran, even if with some provisos, as in the case of David Beauchamp. 'I am considering a catamaran for cruising, as a catamaran over 12 meters can be handled by a couple with, on most occasions, more ease than a monohull. I have spoken to owners of large cats. They are best kept between 30 degrees north and 30 degrees south for safety's sake.' John Ellis agreed. 'A cat is a perfect boat for destination cruising. Long ocean crossings on a multihull are probably OK in some areas, although I still prefer a monohull for this.'

As a final word on the choice of a suitable catamaran, having looked at a few of them at recent boat shows I came away with the distinct feeling that most were designed for the charter market not passage-making. How well built they were I couldn't say, but I just felt that some of them simply didn't look right to go on a long offshore voyage. This is one more point to bear in mind but it can be overcome by talking to the architect who designed the boat. I am convinced that if you outline your cruising plans to the designer, and ideally also to the builder, they would not recommend something unsuitable for the voyage you have in mind.

Rudders

As my knowledge of naval architecture is rather superficial I always prefer to leave such matters to the experts. An amateur sailor can hardly improve on a professional's well thought out design, so one shouldn't even try. However, it helps to be aware of some important design features that should dictate the choice of boat in the first place. Chief among them are those to do with safety, such as suspended rudders. Unprotected by at least a partial skeg such rudders are extremely vulnerable and have gradually crept from racing to cruising boats. If one cannot avoid a boat with this kind of rudder, at least insist that the lower half of the rudder is made to be sacrificial, as this is where it is most likely to be hit by debris or damaged if making an accidental hard landing.

Two worlds apart: a vulnerable spade rudder and a sturdy old fashioned version

Regardless of the type of rudder, an adequate emergency system should be prepared in the event of the loss of the rudder and steering. Such an emergency backup should be easy to set up and known to all members of the crew.

My concern over vulnerable rudders was confirmed by a number of incidents that happened to yachts that were crossing the Atlantic in December 2006, when two boats sailing in the ARC lost their rudders. One of them was a Bavaria 35 that lost its

rudder in a collision, possibly with a whale. The crew tried to steer the boat with a drogue and emergency rudder but could not manage and after 48 hours were taken off by another ARC boat. The boat was abandoned. The other ARC boat to lose its rudder in mid-Atlantic was a Contest 46. The crew managed to improvise an emergency rudder and sailed the boat without outside help to St Lucia.

By strange coincidence there was a similar situation involving a non-ARC boat, a 43 foot Jeanneau that lost its rudder at about the same time. The crew managed to steer the boat for one week but eventually decided to ask for help. The Maritime Rescue Coordination Centre in Martinique contacted the British sail training ship Tenacious whose skipper altered course and picked up the crew. The crew was saved but the rudderless yacht was scuttled. Tenacious was involved in the rescue of another ARC crew in 2003 when a Hunter Legend 450, had broken its rudder stock and was left without a rudder. On that occasion the engineers on Tenacious managed to manufacture a new rudder but after one week in worsening conditions this rudder broke too, the crew had to be evacuated and the yacht abandoned.

The fact that over the years five ARC boats have been abandoned as a result of rudder failure speaks for itself. Besides the three incidents mentioned above, Chaot reported a broken rudder stock in 1990 and was subsequently abandoned, while in 1998 a Dehler 41 was abandoned also as a result of a damaged rudder stock. ARC yachts have also been involved in rescuing crews from non-ARC boats that sank because of rudder problems: Cap d'Ambré in 1993 and Sagitar in 2001.

In some of the above cases, the crew reported the cause as a possible collision although they were not entirely sure. I have been aware of this potential problem ever since I noticed the trend borrowed from racing yachts to fit cruising boats with unsupported spade rudders. While working on Aventura III in preparation for the 2007 season, I walked around the yard in Croatia where there was a large number of boats stored ashore for the winter. Most were recent production boats and, without exception, all had spade rudders. There were also a few older cruising boats so I could easily compare their rudders and keels with those of the yachts built only a few years later, and the only conclusion that I could draw was that the situation was even worse than I had expected. It certainly explained the rudder failures that had occurred in the ARC, where all damaged boats were of recent construction, as well as other similar incidents that have come to my knowledge in recent years.

Keels and draft

Keel configuration and ideal draft were examined in earlier surveys when many skippers expressed their concern over the vulnerability of a fin keel on a cruising boat, several skippers stressing that fin keels should be matched with well supported rudders protected by strong skegs. Several skippers qualified both their choice of keel and maximum draft by pointing out that a final decision would depend on the particular cruising area they would spend most time in.

In all surveys dealing with the subject of ideal draft there was a consensus that a fixed keel was best suited for ocean passages whereas shallow draft, whether with a shorter keel and bulb or a centreboard arrangement, was ideal when cruising. Skip Novak spoke for many when he commented, 'if your priority is to explore, rather than see from a distance, then some lifting appendage is necessary. A centreboard allows you to get into shallower places. However, if you are cruising in deeper well charted waters, and staying in marinas, then a fixed keel would be better.'

One skipper who went the opposite way was Alastair Duncan, who switched from a centreboard aluminium boat to a deep drafted fibreglass yacht. 'There are times when I regret not having the ability to slip into those shallow sheltered anchorages, but all this is blown away as soon as I realize that going to windward is no longer the trial it used to be and is indeed something to be enjoyed.'

As to actual hull shape the only general comment I am prepared to make is that a fine V entry makes for a more comfortable ride when going to windward. I know this only too well because the pounding of Aventura's flat bottom when sailing hard on the wind, especially in a swell, can be quite tiring. When I can't stand it any longer, I ease the sheets and go a few degrees off the wind, which usually reduces the slamming. In fact Aventura has a modest V entry, which does help a little. This pounding can be a serious problem not only on flat-bottomed monohulls but on catamarans too. On some catamarans the bridge decks are designed too low, but more often the boats are overloaded, their owners not able to resist the temptation to fill all those empty spaces, with the result that such boats slam hard into the waves as they bash their way through the swell.

Displacement

*What fun can anyone get from sailing
in a floating safe?*

Erick Bouteleux

Erick's barbed comment was addressed at those sailors who copied Bernard Moitessier's Joshua and built themselves massive steel boats that used to be regarded not only the safest option but also best suited for cruising. Fashions do change and nowadays it is rare to see heavy displacement boats while homebuilt boats are even less common.

Displacement should be a serious consideration, as I know too well from personal experience. At 9 tons for her 36 feet, the first Aventura was on the heavy side and, having a rather short main mast, was an indifferent performer in light winds. After my first voyage, when I had come across a number of groundings, I was also attracted to the idea of a strong steel boat and ended up with Aventura II, although compared to a Joshua it was certainly a case of beauty rather than the beast. My intention was to have a strong steel boat of reasonable displacement but while the designer followed my suggestion, the builder had other ideas and Aventura II ended up with a displacement of 17 tonnes rather than the 12.5 tonnes envisaged by the architect Bill Dixon. While Aventura II sailed well in moderate winds, in light winds she was a source of continuous frustration. So I was determined to get a boat with a lighter displacement for my third Aventura. Indeed Aventura III's designed displacement of 9 tons for a beamy 43 footer is in my view as close to perfect as possible and I have always made sure to keep the boat's weight down to a reasonable level. A good point to stress is how important it is not to overload your boat, whether catamaran or monohull. Many cruisers ignore this factor and I am amazed to see the amount of useless junk some people are prepared to carry.

Hull material

*There is no good or bad construction
material, but unfortunately there are good
and bad boat builders!*

Javier Visiers

As in the case of displacement, this is another decision that may very well be taken out of one's hands, unless hull material is put at the top of the list of priorities or one orders a one-off. In most cases the boat of one's choice is built in the most suitable material the architect and builder have agreed upon. For a long offshore voyage the builder might be persuaded to put some additional strength in critical areas (bows, along the waterline, rudder area) so it is worth discussing this early with the builder so that such modifications can be done in the initial building stages and not as an afterthought.

Having sailed around the world in a fibreglass yacht, Carlton DeHart found it difficult to make up his mind on the ideal material. 'An alloy boat would be much stronger and take hitting a container better than most materials. The downside is being ever mindful of electrolysis. I don't really think that there is an ideal material. It is a compromise at best. Every material has good points and bad.'

Steel or aluminium both have advantages and disadvantages, their intrinsic strength being their main advantage. As for the disadvantages, in the case of steel it is the need for the best possible preparation of the hull and decks for painting, which must be followed by careful maintenance.

Efficient cutter rig with furling yankee and staysail

past, many production boats continue to be rigged as sloops, probably because of the concern for saving costs shared by most builders. A recent survey among the boats taking part in the ARC showed that 92% of them were one-masted. Eventually some cruising skippers come to realize the advantages of a cutter rig and convert their sloops, either by adding a permanent or a temporary inner forestay. In a survey I did among a large group of cruising boats in the Bahamas, I found that among 115 boats there were 68 sloops, 28 cutters, 17 ketches and 2 schooners, with several of the ketches having a staysail on an inner forestay. Although the proportion of one-masted boats was lower than in the ARC, the trend away from ketches, and certainly schooners, was quite evident.

In the case of aluminium hulls some people are concerned about the risk of electrolytic reaction but this is quite unjustified. Modern alloys have taken care of that, as do sacrificial anodes. This aspect was discussed in chapter 18.

Rig

A cutter rig is ideal as when the going gets rough our little staysail gets tough

Don Babson

Don's view was shared by Dave Beauchamp. 'A cutter rig with furling jib and staysail gives as much sail as is possible to handle shorthanded, while being increased or reduced easily.' Arthur Beiser has no doubts that a cutter rig is best for long distance cruising. 'No other rig makes sense these days except in very small boats when a simple sloop might be OK.'

Whereas ketches and schooners under fifty feet are now mostly a thing of the

Rigging

My ideal boat would have an efficient rig backed by strong reliable rigging.

Luc Callebaut

The first thing to consider whether on a new or used boat is if the rig gives an impression of strength and reliability. In recent years some boat builders have tried to get away with the minimum strength rigging. Several new production boats, at the lower end of the market, have lost their masts in the ARC, often on the way to the start in the Canaries, the unforgiving Bay of Biscay having a perverse way of finding weaknesses in newly launched boats. I saw a spectacular dismasting of a new 49 foot boat in 25 knots at the start of a rally from Madeira when the mast crumpled like an overcooked spaghetti. Several ARC boats have arrived in St Lucia with badly compressed masts, or lost forestays, only luck and the vigilance of the crew saving their masts. So, if one has any doubts about the rigging, one should ask the builder to upgrade it or do it oneself if buying a used boat.

When inspecting a used boat a climb to the top of the mast is always a good idea not just to have a general look at the state of the mast, standing rigging and terminals, but also the spinnaker blocks and top end of the forestay furling gear. On deck level, look if the turnbuckles are in good state, check their colour and state if made of bronze. The forestay turnbuckle should be easily accessible to inspect, service and to put more tension on the forestay if necessary. Also the installation and state of the furling gear and its ease of operation should be checked. Sight along the profile to see if any grub screws holding the separate sections together are missing or have come unscrewed. Even if satisfied with this initial inspection, when buying a used boat it is advisable to have the rigging checked by a professional rigger who should inspect all terminals, turnbuckles, radio antenna backstay connectors, as well as the furling gear(s) and their aluminium profiles.

Some of the above suggestions are just as valid for new boats. Other points to consider if ordering a new boat is to ask the builder to fit protection hoses on all rigging by the side of the mast as well as the backstay(s) as this is easier to do before the terminals and turnbuckles are fitted. This makes getting hold of the rigging more comfortable to the hands and protects the sails from chafe if they rub against the rigging. On long runs if the mainsail is fully let out it will usually chafe against the rigging and possibly the spreaders too. To avoid this on the current Aventura I taped a split length of half-inch clear hose to the trailing edge of the spreaders that were sharp to the touch. Such preventative care pays in the long run and I never had any chafe problems after our first voyage when, from lack of experience, I had a lot.

As to the running rigging there is little to say except that it should be adequate for the job. If most lines come to the cockpit it is essential to have them colour coded and brought to individual jammers. If the ropes are of good quality they should last for many years. As synthetic ropes have got stronger, I don't like the current trend of using thin lines for sheets as I prefer them of adequate diameter to be comfortable to the hands. Fitting a boat with insufficiently powerful winches is another trend dictated by the need to save costs. On Aventura III the standard cockpit winches were upgraded and I also fitted a powerful electric winch, one of the best decisions that I made.

While checking the running rigging it is recommended to have a good look at the general deck layout and the run of the various sheets and halyards. These should have a clear unobstructed run back to the cockpit and be helped by sheaves or turning blocks at critical points The same goes for the control line(s) from the furling gear(s) to the cockpit.

As to the halyards, the mast should have enough dedicated channels for spinnaker and genoa halyards and their backups. On Aventura, the main halyard is of a strong non-stretch material and I decided to have the mainsail topping lift from a similar material so as to have a permanent backup for the main halyard. I have two spinnaker halyards so they can be used on the relevant side of the boat.

On Aventura all lines lead back to the cockpit

Deck layout

A well-thought out deck layout makes it possible to sail the yacht singlehanded and preferably without leaving the cockpit.

John Ellis

A functional deck layout is essential and should be adapted to one's own needs and preferences. This subject was dealt in detail in chapter 2 where I described Aventura III's deck layout. Clear unobstructed decks are of paramount importance on an ocean going yacht and due thought should given to an efficient deck layout. Some production boats fail badly in this respect, their builders trying to get away with the minimum. This will have to be put right by the new owner and I shall try to point out a couple of features that I consider essential. As a swinging boom can cause a serious or even fatal injury, a way to prevent this is one of the first jobs to be tackled. Temporary preventers help

but it is much better to use a permanent arrangement such as a boom brake like the one made by Walder.

Another point to consider if a spinnaker will be used frequently is to have sheets, guys and blocks permanently set up. I once went on an afternoon sail on a large yacht used for crew training. Out of the marina, the skipper decided to put up the spinnaker but as the decks were absolutely bare, all blocks and sheets had to be retrieved from lockers. As we were sailing in the Mediterranean, by the time everything was ready, the wind had died so all those lines and blocks were neatly gathered and stowed safely away, the whole procedure being probably repeated next time the skipper deemed conditions to be right to hoist a spinnaker. I couldn't help wondering what those paying crew were going to learn from such a traditionally minded skipper.

Interior comforts

Comfortable sea berths at any angle of heel are an absolute must.

John Wicks

Comfortable sea berths are essential on an offshore passage and there should be at least one all-weather bunk for the person off watch. Comfort on passage is of utmost importance as one normally spends most of the day sitting, so serious thought should be given to comfortable seating both in the main cabin and cockpit. One aspect that is easily neglected if planning to sail with crew is to have two toilet compartments.

Good insulation as well as adequate ventilation with sufficient hatches and dorade boxes for rough weather are features often missing on production boats built in and for temperate climates. They are vital for cruising in the tropics. Essential provisions for the engine room are good ventilation and sound insulation.

A safe, well thought-out galley should be a priority. On many production boats that are most likely to be used for charter in sheltered waters, the galley is quite inadequate if used on passage or in rough seas. Compact, U or L shaped galleys are to be preferred over open plan ones which are unsuitable on an offshore cruising boat. There should be sufficient storage space in the immediate area of the galley so that all essential provisions and cooking utensils are within easy reach.

As comfort is so important on a cruising boat, everything should be done to make the boat as liveable as possible. However, there is a limit to how far one can go, especially on a smaller boat, so, as Anne Hugget suggests, 'one must be prepared to do domestic chores as one would have done them fifty or a hundred years ago, such as washing laundry by hand. If one is not prepared to give up some shore comforts

it's better not to go at all.' Straight advice from someone who has lived on a cruising boat for many years.

Cockpit protection

The ideal yacht should provide total shelter to the cockpit and to be able to navigate and manoeuvre as much as possible from inside with good visibility.
Antti Louhija

Good cockpit protection was one the main items mentioned by the surveyed

Excellent cockpit protection was highly appreciated on Aventura II as we beat our way up the Red Sea

skippers when questioned about essential features on an offshore cruising boat. Carlton DeHart commented, 'Because I wish to go to high latitudes, I would like to have a pilothouse with inside steering capabilities.'

A number of production boats have a raised deck salon that greatly contributes to their comfort. Some even feature an inside steering position, although both these features are normally found only on larger yachts.

Sails

I do like a fully battened mainsail but if I were a little older I would consider in-boom furling.

Don Babson

So many books have been written on the subject of sails that I will focus only on the very essentials. This is an area that has seen great improvements and nowadays even standard production boats have well cut sails. For a long voyage one should make sure that the mainsail is made as strong as possible, with double, ideally triple UV resistant zigzag stitching. The furling foresail(s) should be provided with anti-UV strips. Spinnakers should be provided with adequate dousers or it will be difficult to douse them in strong winds when this needs to be done quickly. While there isn't much to choose between well-cut spinnakers, some dousers are better than others. Ideally, as on the ParaSailor, the collar should be rigid and not be made of a soft material. The douser collar should also have a wide enough mouth to snuffle the spinnaker easily. To be on the safe side, the sailmaker should be asked to strengthen the corners and top panel of the spinnaker.

Engine

As I get older the ability to hang upside down into a dark cavity to reach an oil filter is both more difficult and less fun.

Alastair Duncan

The engine location and general accessibility are features that can be easily overlooked although they should be a high priority. All points that need regular inspection or maintenance should be easily accessible so there will be no good reason to neglect it. Equally important is easy access to the main components: alternator(s), belts, starter motor, seawater pump, injectors, oil changing system, oil and fuel filters, engine intake seacock, seawater trap, transmission, stern gland.

The first Aventura's Perkins 4108 had been thoughtfully provided with a dedicated sump pump that made oil changes easy and clean. My current Volvo MD22 has no oil changing provision. To empty the oil one has to do it via the

Easy access to the engine room on Aventura II

dipstick tube by feeding a thin plastic hose through it. The oil is then emptied with the help of a manual or electric pump. It is a messy job and I hate it. Other regular maintenance jobs on Aventura III are not necessarily easier because Volvo, like most other engine manufacturers, try to compress the engine into the most compact shape. This is then made worse by the boat builders, who try to fit the engine into the tiniest space possible so that those essential parts are then truly inaccessible. At least Aventura's builder thought of cutting access panels opposite all such parts so that they can be reached. Therefore my advice is to look not just at easy accessibility for regular maintenance jobs on the engine but whether it will be possible to dismantle and remount an alternator, solenoid or starter motor on a dark and windy night at sea.

Optimum power

Engine power is never enough.

Skip Novak

For various reasons, most cruising sailors, and that includes me, never seem to be satisfied with the power provided by the designer and, if given the choice, would choose a more powerful engine. Aventura III's engine is a standard Volvo of 50 HP. Initially I insisted on a more powerful engine of 62 HP but the engine room was too small for it and reluctantly I gave up. I am now glad I didn't insist as I cannot think of many occasions when I would have needed that additional power and, in exchange, I would have paid with proportionally higher fuel consumption.

This subject was examined in several of my surveys and the conclusions were always the same. Most recently, in the Global Cruising Survey, the consensus was similar: while some skippers agreed that there is nothing to beat the old yardstick of one horse power per foot of length, others would have preferred a slightly higher ratio of 1.2 HP per foot of length. Other skippers suggested a different yardstick by aiming for 5 HP per ton of displacement.

For Don Babson there was a very valid justification for having a more powerful engine. 'Bigger is better. In the Millennium Odyssey, if we had more horses, we could have made it to the parties before all the goodies and grog were gone.' Matt Rollberg, who sailed in the same rally, shared that view. 'We wouldn't do another round the world voyage unless we had a bigger boat and a bigger engine.'

Optimum fuel capacity

Ideally the boat should have sufficient fuel capacity to be able to motor for at least one third of a given passage.

Antti Louhija

Fuel capacity and range under power were also examined in various surveys. In an earlier cruising survey, the average fuel capacity was 400 litres (100 US gallons), although several skippers pointed out that additional fuel was taken for longer passages or when cruising in areas where diesel fuel was difficult or impossible to obtain. The average range under power, when motoring under calm conditions at medium revs, was 750 miles per boat. Motoring or motor sailing under such conditions, the reported average consumption was 2 litres (half a gallon) per hour. Asked about the ideal amount of fuel to be carried, some skippers suggested that when setting off on a long passage, one ought to have enough fuel to be

Extra fuel was taken in jerrycans for the trip to Antarctica

market for those who are interested in better efficiency and also wish to reduce drag. There are so many different types and models available that I prefer to limit my comment to the make I know best. Having had a Max-Prop on both my previous and current boat I can vouch for the quality of this well engineered product whose performance will be considerably extended if the propeller housing is filled with the recommended grease at regular intervals.

Ideal features

My ideal is a sound, well-found hull and well-conceived deck. Well designed and easy to use rig and rigging. Enough storage space to stow all those items that make life comfortable, not just bearable.

Dave Beauchamp

able to motor between one quarter and one third of the entire distance should there be a serious emergency. Aventura's fuel capacity is almost exactly the average mentioned above (380 litres) which provides an autonomy of about 800 miles under power. On a few occasions, such as when cruising in Antarctica or Chile, I carried an additional 120 litres of fuel in jerrycans.

Propellers

A fixed propeller on a modern sailing yacht is like a Model T Ford, reliable but boring.

Tom Williams

Although most production yachts continue to be fitted with fixed blade propellers, there is now a wide range of folding or feathering propellers on the

This subject was examined in detail in the Global Cruising Survey when I asked the forty skippers to name the most important features they would have on their ideal cruising boat. The five most quoted items were a powerful electric anchor winch, watermaker, dependable reefing system, a powerful and reliable autopilot and an electric cockpit winch. To narrow down their priorities the skippers were asked to limit their choice to three items they considered as absolutely essential. Perhaps not surprisingly by forcing them to focus on the crucial aspects of their ideal boat, the priorities changed, with seaworthiness now becoming the number one priority, as summarized by Antti Louhija whose ideal would be 'a solid, sturdy and comfortable boat even if it means sacrificing some speed. If you are comfortable you gladly spend more time on passage.'

Steve Dashew considered as essential features 'water tight bulkheads, the ability to hit the ground at slow speed without having to go into a boatyard and a good turn of speed when one needs it.'

Several skippers stressed the importance of good sailing capability such as for the boat to be able to point high. Beside their logical concern for safety and performance, several skippers stressed the importance of comfort. As many as one third of the skippers specified a permanent structure, that provided shelter to the cockpit, as an essential feature. The full results of the Global Cruising Survey, including a complete list of essential features on an ideal yacht, as specified by the forty skippers, are published in World Cruising Essentials.

Safety

Safety and seaworthiness are the most important features followed by comfort and easy sail handling.

Bob Hall

Whenever I visit a yacht and am asked by the owner to express an opinion, I always start by looking at the boat primarily from the safety point of view. How well protected is the cockpit? How exposed is the person at the helm? How safe is it to work at the foot of the mast or on the foredeck? Are there sufficient handrails provided? Do stanchions and lifelines look strong and reliable? How dangerously low does the boom pass across the cockpit? How easily accessible is the main bilge and is it provided with a good pump as well as an emergency backup? How accessible is the steering mechanism and what provision has been made for an emergency? Is the liferaft stowed in an easily accessible place from where it can be launched by the weakest member of the crew? How can the

dinghy be stowed safely while on passage? How easily accessible is the anchor chain? How easy it is to board the boat or retrieve an overboard person?

I must admit that I rarely get the desired answer to some of these questions but I believe it is my obligation to point out any shortcomings to the owner. My remarks are rarely accepted graciously but nowadays I prefer to be honest, even if my frankness is not necessarily appreciated.

Final decision

Know your boat and your abilities. Think of the worst case scenario and how to cope with that in the worst situation. For world cruising self-reliance is the key and part of the pleasure.

Skip Novak

Because my friend Erick Bouteleux had played such an important part both in the choice of Aventura III and in fitting her out for my planned voyage, after I had finished writing this chapter I asked him if he had any advice to give to anyone faced with the decision to choose and equip a boat for a long voyage. He replied that he was reluctant to be too specific as nowadays there was such a choice of boats and equipment that finding a suitable boat should not be at all difficult provided one knew one's priorities. Knowing just how opinionated he can be on any subject that is of interest to him, I was taken aback by his reluctance, and said so. Erick had an answer to this too when he said, 'We have the great advantage of having sailed on simple boats with no sophisticated equipment. Once you have sailed on such a boat you can easily adjust to a more sophisticated boat, but not the other way around. Current sailors planning to set off on a long voyage have a much tougher job, mainly because there is so much to choose from. This is why it is so important to decide first on one's main priorities. For us it was dead easy as the choices were so limited that most people like us left in whatever they could afford, and, with very few exceptions, we all managed to complete our voyages.'

So the choice of a boat that incorporates one's main priorities is crucial but, as I pointed out earlier, crew and finances are two other equally important factors that affect the success of a voyage. There is, however, an even more important factor and this is why I left it to the very end: one's attitude to sailing in particular and to cruising life in general. Setting off for a life on the ocean is a huge leap that entails a complete change of both life style and mentality, something that many people have not considered in depth. I have come across this frequently among rally participants many of whom were unwilling or unable to make the transition from a shore-based person to a sailor. This is not too much of a problem on a relatively short voyage, such as the ARC, but can and did have serious consequences among those who left on a longer voyage. Leaving on a cruise in a sailing yacht just because it is a convenient way to see the world is not a good enough reason. Those who do not honestly enjoy sailing and do not feel comfortable or at ease on the ocean, would do better to think again. I say all this because I know just how I feel about the sea and sailing and I have absolutely no doubt that it is because of this attitude that Mother Ocean has treated me so kindly.

Tips

- Resist the temptation to buy a larger boat just because you can afford it. The deciding factor should be ease of handling by the proposed crew.
- Avoid a boat with a vulnerable unprotected rudder that is unsuitable for offshore cruising.
- The rigging should make no concession to safety in favour of convenience.
- The engine and essential components must be easily accessible for routine maintenance and emergency repairs.
- The boat must have adequate engine power and sufficient fuel capacity for the planned voyage.
- A functional deck layout is essential.
- The boat must have a well thought-out mainsail reefing system that ideally can be handled from the cockpit.
- There must be backups for all halyards.
- The cockpit must have good protection for both safety and comfort.
- A well planned compact galley that is safe to use in rough weather.
- There must be at least one comfortable all-weather berth for the off-watch crew.
- The boat must have sufficient storage space for a long voyage.
- The liferaft should be easily launched.
- There must be adequate man overboard provisions: stern platform with boarding ladder.

Rallies and Races

The Atlantic Rally for Cruisers (ARC)

We used to have four seasons in the Canaries but now we have five: spring, summer, autumn, winter and the ARC.

José Manuel Fernandez

The most significant decision for us was to join a rally. Had we not joined America 500, there would have been no Atlantic crossing for us in 1992. Without that experience, and without the Millennium Odyssey, there would have been no round the world voyage for us either. Without those rallies the friendships amongst the whole fleet, which will last for many years, would have never developed. The shared accomplishments will live in each of us forever.

Don Babson

The launch of the first transatlantic rally in 1986 is one of the main achievements of my life. The immediate success of the annual ARC inspired similar rallies all over the world and I am now credited with having conceived the format of such cruising rallies. One of the main advantages of cruising rallies is that the organisers take care of everything: formalities, docking, weather and routing information, transits of the Panama and Suez Canals. There is also the safety in numbers factor and being able to get help or advice in an emergency from fellow participants. Another advantage is that there is a fixed schedule, which imposes a certain discipline. As many of the participants are business people, retired or close to retirement, they seem to appreciate this aspect and also the fact that they can delegate responsibility, which is what they normally did in their professional lives. But rallies do not suit everyone's taste and requirements, so my advice to anyone who is considering joining one is to carefully assess the advantages outlined above.

Memorable words from the President of the Las Palmas Port Authority at the festivities marking the tenth ARC in 1995. Twenty years after its inception, the ARC (Atlantic Rally for Cruisers) has become a local phenomenon in Las Palmas de Gran Canaria and the annual arrival of over two hundred boats and their crews is eagerly awaited by most canarios. Besides its attraction as an international sailing event, the ARC plays a major economic role in the life of this busy port as the ARC crews spend several million euros on provisions, equipment, repairs, hotels and restaurants.

Walking down the main dock in November 2005, shortly before the start of the twentieth ARC, what I noticed immediately was the higher proportion of really large boats. In earlier ARCs there were perhaps half a dozen boats over 70 feet, now there were dozens. Perhaps the best person to give an objective assessment of the changes that have occurred over the years is Tony Mark, who for many years was the safety inspector of the ARC. He made the following comment. 'There is no doubt that boats are getting bigger every year and there is also a much higher proportion of new boats. In the early ARCs there were a lot of old boats, whereas now the average age is one or two years. Also there are more proprietary brands such as Swan, Oyster, Hallberg Rassy, Beneteau, and hardly any boats from small builders. What has not changed is the amount of breakages reported. The range of electronics on these boats is truly amazing. Because of

The crew of a Spanish warship watch the
start of the ARC in Las Palmas

all the equipment the boats are carrying,
there is a much higher percentage of
breakages.'

Among the 2005 participants, sailing
on one of the most attractive boats, was
Tim Aitken who had sailed in the first
ARC in 1986, and was now doing his fourth
ARC, this time on the 75 foot Braveheart
of Sark. Tim was a good person to ask if
the ARC had indeed changed and while
he agreed that the spirit of the rally
might have remained the same, he felt
that the participants were quite different
from those he remembered from the early
ARCs when long term cruisers were the
norm. As he pointed out, 'Now there seems
to be a lot more boats crewed just by men
and because of this some of the family
atmosphere of early ARCs appears to have
been lost.'

Tony Mark agreed that there have
been some notable changes among the
participants themselves. 'There seem to
be fewer family crews, such as couples
with kids, dogs and cats. There are now
many more men sailing with their friends,
and there are also fewer young people
overall. What is noticeable is the large
proportion of retired people who have
sold their businesses, bought a smart
boat and set off. Most plan to stay in
the Caribbean and North Atlantic, and

Over the years Manfred Kerstan has sailed
his Albatross in fourteen ARCs

compared to previous ARCs only a few
plan to carry on around the world. What is
also striking is how much more interest
there is in safety features. People want to
know that their boat is perfect and will

458

spare no money to get everything just right. This is mainly among owners of medium and small sized boats – owners of larger yachts are more nonchalant about safety and believe they can get away with it.'

From the very beginning, one of the primary aims of the ARC was to provide a framework of safety and support to sailors who lacked offshore experience and, in spite of the changes mentioned above, this continues to be one of its main attractions. A series of lectures and practical demonstrations held during the week before the start focussing primarily on safety have laid the foundation of the ARC's good safety record. Communications have always played an equally important part and in recent years there has been a dramatic shift to satellite communications. In the past most boats had a SSB radio and this continues to be the main means of communication among ARC boats at sea, even if the number of SSB radios has gone down as increasingly people prefer to communicate by email or satellite phone. Every boat is expected to check into the ARC radio net once a day to give their position. This is then emailed back to base and posted on the rally's website (www.worldcruising.com).

In order to accommodate both those who join a cruising rally for its safety aspect, and those who are looking for a challenge and some competition, the ARC as well as the round the world rallies include a racing division. Using the engine in this racing class is not allowed, but in the cruising division a limited of engine use is allowed, must be declared and is penalized when results are calculated.

I shall never forget what happened shortly after the start of the ARC in 1992, when I had to fly from the Canaries via London and Miami to be in the Bahamas in time for the arrival of the first America

500 yachts while Gwenda headed for St Lucia to look after the ARC finish. While flying over the Atlantic, the British Airways pilot asked anyone interested to come to the flight deck. I jumped at the opportunity and after the captain had explained the various controls he asked me where I was going.

'To the Bahamas.' I replied.

'On holiday I suppose?'

'No, not at all... to supervise the arrival of a transatlantic race commemorating the anniversary of the Columbus voyage. In fact, at this very moment there are some two hundred and forty of my yachts spread out on the surface of that vast ocean beneath us.'

Doina's entry in the 1989 ARC painting competition

As I said those words I was suddenly struck by the enormity of my undertaking but even more so by the huge responsibility that I had taken on without ever giving it a second thought. Fortunately both events finished without any serious problems.

Round the world rallies

Symbolic historic events or anniversaries have a special fascination for me, so when I started organising international sailing events I had a readymade vehicle to promote and celebrate some of the most significant dates of our times. The success of the ARC served as an inspiration for the first round the world rally, something that had never been done before. Having briefly mentioned the idea to a number of ARC participants, by the late 1980s I knew that such a rally was feasible. This was instantly confirmed when the project was launched and the maximum number of participants (40 yachts over 40 foot LOA) was quickly reached and a waiting list started. Being a great believer in the European concept I had decided to call the first round the world rally Europa 92. I contacted the sports and special events department at the European Community headquarters in Brussels and was invited over. Unfortunately my enthusiasm left the various narrow-minded bureaucrats visibly cool and I came back empty handed. But I still wanted to do something to celebrate this burgeoning political union that promised to bring peace and prosperity to a continent that had been divided and at war for so many centuries. Furthermore this was the height of the Yugoslav conflict and so I decided to go ahead with my chosen theme come what may.

Europa 92 started from Gibraltar at the beginning of January 1991, Gibraltar's far seeing government doing everything possible to support this international event, whose aims coincided so closely with Gibraltar's own endeavours and hopes. A Gibraltar start was both logical and convenient. The weather was acceptable for a winter start, it was perfectly located for both the start and finish and was easy for the participants to get to. Some arrived earlier and docked their boats in a secure marina until the start. The route and timing of the rally had been chosen carefully to take advantage of favourable seasons as well as winds throughout the projected route. Also, knowing that most participants wanted to accomplish a round the world voyage in the shortest time possible and were not interested in dallying too long en route, the rally was to last only a total of seventeen months. This was rather a tall

Rally yachts transit the Panama Canal as a group

order but in the end proved to be the ideal solution and it was not altered in the following rally.

Choosing the route was almost as simple as the timing. After stopping in the Canaries, the rally crossed the Atlantic, passed through the Panama Canal in February and, via the Galapagos, headed for the South Pacific, which was reached at the start of the safe winter season. Stopping at a number of island nations en route, the rally reached the Torres Strait and entered the Indian Ocean. From Bali the

Europa 92
round the world
rally yachts in
Tahiti

route turned north to Singapore, before crossing the North Indian Ocean during the favourable north-east monsoon that blows constantly in the early months of the year. A final stage through the Red Sea brought the fleet into the Mediterranean and eventually to a grand finish in Gibraltar.

The fleet that left from Gibraltar was joined in the Eastern Caribbean or Panama by a number of US boats. Everywhere it stopped, the rally, which was the first of its kind, was received with great enthusiasm, local people and officials welcoming the participants with open arms. Cruising stages of adequate length had been carefully planned inbetween the legs, giving participants, their crew and families who were joining underway, a perfect opportunity to visit some of the most attractive cruising grounds in the world.

One of the main attractions of such a rally was the safety it offered to participants, especially those who were rather inexperienced and drew comfort from being able to draw support from other more experienced sailors. Safety in numbers had probably never been more true. The overall safety record of all the five round the world events that I organised is quite outstanding, although unfortunately

it was in that first round the world rally that there was one fatality and one boat lost. A young Finnish sailor was lost overboard on the long leg from the Galapagos to the Marquesas when the 53 foot Cacadu went into an uncontrolled gybe while flying a spinnaker at night. In spite of frantic efforts by the crew who were joined by eleven other rally yachts, he was never found. The only loss involved the Hungarian 43 foot Jolly Joker, whose skipper had handed over the control of the boat to his young crew, having to return home for urgent family reasons. Jolly Joker ran aground and broke up after it had strayed from the main navigation channel in the notorious Torres Strait. The crew were saved almost immediately by another rally yacht.

As in all other rallies of this kind, competition played a certain part, which was taken to heart in greater or lesser degree by the participants. There were two divisions, racing in which the use of engines was prohibited, and cruising in which the hours of motoring had to be declared so that a penalty could be applied when the results were calculated. Competition was keen in both divisions and added a special zest on long ocean passages. The boats were in constant contact with each other and in regular links with the organisers,

461

Warm welcome to a rally participant
on arrival in Papeete

initially by SSB radio and in later rallies by
Inmarsat C or email. Eventually the arrival
of satellite phones made communications
instant.

Europa 94

The unquestioned success of
that first round the world rally
proved the validity of its basic
concept and, not surprisingly,
was followed three years later
by a similar event along a
similar route. Having been
unable to elicit any response
from Brussels even after its
successful completion, I gave up on the
suits in Brussels but not on Europe and
as I could not think of a better name, the
second rally also ran under the generic
name Europa.

The various difficulties encountered in
the first round the world rally were mostly
ironed out in the second, chief among them
an improvement in communications
between the shore-based rally staff
and participants, and also among the
participants themselves.

The rally attracted a number of boats
crewed by fee paying guests, a new
phenomenon which was to become
widespread in the ARC too and was not
entirely to my liking. Overall, though,
Europe 94 was as successful as Europa 92
and, apart from one dismasting on the leg
from Madeira to Gran Canaria and one
boat running aground off the coast of
Brazil, also fraught with less problems.

Compared to the first rally, participants in
Europa 94 were more competitive. With this
in mind, some of the legs were rescheduled
while the final leg from Malta to Gibraltar
was split into two, with a final stop in Palma
de Mallorca, so that the shorter final leg
kept the fleet close together. Such interest
in competition, which was also becoming
evident in the ARC, showed the need for a

Start of the leg from Fiji to Vanuatu in
Europa 94

round the world race for amateur sailors
that eventually led to the Hong Kong
Challenge.

America 500

Long before the first round the world
rally took off I became intrigued by the

imminent approach of one of the most important nautical anniversaries of the twentieth century, that of Christopher Columbus's voyage to the New World in 1492, whose quincentenary promised to be celebrated in unprecedented style. There were to be several major sailing events to follow the historic route from Spain to the Bahamas and I could not resist the temptation to make my own contribution. The idea of America 500 was soon born, a rally for cruising yachts that would follow Columbus's original route and would hopefully attract the symbolic figure of 500 yachts. The initial enthusiasm with which America 500 was greeted by the international sailing community made this figure a real possibility. Unfortunately negative press in the USA highlighted all the bad things that had followed Columbus's arrival in the New World and this dissuaded many potential participants from joining. Even so, half of the 146 yachts that took part came over from all over the New World, with the largest national contingent from the USA, but also yachts from Canada, Mexico and Argentina.

From the moment I launched the idea and then went to Madrid to discuss it with the 1992 commission I found I was hitting my head against a brick wall. Not only were the officials both there and in Miami where I initially intended to finish the rally, not interested in what I proposed to do, but were actually obstructive as they regarded my event a potential threat to their own grandiose plans. By various means they tried to kill the event in the bud and to my chagrin they almost succeeded by raising objection after objection, putting pressure on the authorities en route, and doing their best to thwart this beautiful idea. Instead of simply giving up, their negative and arrogant attitude made me even more determined to carry out my plans. I can be extremely stubborn and feeling a great empathy for Columbus and the problems he had in organising his own voyage, I

America 500 briefing in the same room of La Rabida Monastery where Columbus briefed his own captains

refused to give up. America 500 became too big to be ignored.

Columbus and his small fleet had left from the small Andalucian port of Palos at dawn on August 3, 1492. Following in Columbus's footsteps I had managed to obtain permission to bring our own skippers to the same room in the ancient La Rabida monastery, where Columbus had briefed his captains. Just as had happened on the eve of their own departure five hundred years earlier, the America 500 skippers had their briefing in the very same room as their illustrious predecessors. The highlight of the festivities was an unforgettable flamenco opera based on the Columbus story and played in an amphitheatre below the walls of the monastery attended by thousands of people and all our participants.

At dawn on 3 August 1992, the America 500 skippers and some of their crews attended a special mass and blessing in the small church of St George where Columbus and his crews had worshipped on the morning of their departure. We even left by the same rarely used side door and made our way to the boats floating on the river Odiel nearby.

After all the bad blood and strong opposition, Madrid's ambitious plans came to almost nothing and America 500 was hailed as the only international sailing event of the 1492-1992 celebrations to accurately reflect and observe the historic significance of the Columbus anniversary. King Juan Carlos and Queen Sophia flew over from the Olympic Games in Barcelona and gave the start of America 500 as the fleet floated on a falling tide on its long way to the New World. As the director of the event I had been invited to be presented to Their Majesties on the day of the start but I felt that my right place was on the start line. Do I have any regrets? Not really. America 500 was one of the happiest moments of my life that even such an audience could never have matched.

The start off Palos was followed by a stop at the island of Porto Santo where Columbus had spent some time with his wife Maria de Perestrello, the daughter of the Portuguese governor, while planning his intended voyage. The America 500 fleet then sailed to neighbouring Madeira and from there to Las Palmas in Gran Canaria.

While Columbus had unknowingly crossed the Atlantic at the height of the hurricane season (September) it would have been irresponsible for us to do the same. For this reason I had to plan that the Atlantic crossing be done later in the

America 500 crew plant their Canarian palm tree on arrival in the Bahamas

season when the risk of a late tropical storm would be minimal. Also as the long total duration of the rally did not suit many participants, most of whom were still in employment, a second start from Palos had been planned for the equally symbolic date of 12 October. On that date a second America 500 fleet gathered on the river Odiel and enjoyed the same festivities as the first group had done two months earlier.

The two fleets, as well as a number of boats that had taken part in a special rally around all the Canarian Islands, came together in the large port of Las Palmas. On the eve of the start of the transatlantic leg on 15 November 1992 every boat was presented with a two foot high sapling of a Canarian palm tree to be planted on arrival in San Salvador. Before embarking on the 3000 mile passage, a two hour stop was made at the small island of La Gomera where Columbus himself had left from on 6 September 1492. After the skippers had had their special souvenir logbooks signed by the mayor of La Gomera they walked to the nearby church of the Assumption where Columbus and his sailors had prayed all those years ago. A final gift of a large specially baked loaf of bread stamped with the logo of America 500 was given to each yacht and they were finally on their way.

By late November the hurricane season had come to an end and the fleet made a fast and generally uneventful passage all the way to the small island of San Salvador in the Bahamas. There the crews were welcomed by the local governor, who signed their logbooks, they planted their trees next to the Columbus monument, then sailed over to George Town in Great Exuma. Its large protected harbour was the only place capable of sheltering such a large fleet, which was the reason why it had been chosen in preference to San Salvador. It was there that the final America 500 celebrations took place, an unforgettable finale to a unique event.

Hong Kong Challenge

Never at a loss for inspiration, the rapidly approaching date of the handover of Hong Kong to China in 1996 provided the theme of yet another special event. Because of the location of Hong Kong as well as other practical considerations I soon realised that this was not to be another cruising rally. The route and weather conditions were much tougher and could only suit larger yachts sailed by experienced crews. For all these reasons the Hong Kong Challenge was a

proper round the world race for ocean going yachts. Once again the idea was greeted with enthusiasm and eventually a dozen yachts sailed in the event. From the start in London where the famous Tower Bridge was specially opened for the fleet to commence its passage down the river Thames, the yachts sailed via the Canaries

Start of the Hong Kong Challenge through London's Tower Bridge

to Panama, transited the Canal, proceeded to Hawaii and Japan before arriving in Hong Kong. The return voyage took the yachts via the South Indian Ocean around the Cape of Good Hope and to Brazil, then finally back to England.

The race marked several significant firsts and will be remembered as such: the first round the world ocean race to transit the Panama Canal, the first such event to visit Hawaii, Japan, Hong Kong and Singapore. It also pioneered an entirely novel route, which is still followed by the Clipper Race, which the Hong Kong Challenge had inspired. In spite of its toughness and length the Hong Kong Challenge was completed without serious mishaps by

465

all yachts, sailed mostly by amateurs. The overall winner was the Hungarian yacht MOL Hungaria whose victory gave me great pleasure as I had set the London start for 23 October 1996 exactly forty years to the day since the revolution of 1956 had exploded on the streets of Budapest, which may have marked the beginning of the end of East European communism.

Expo 98 Round The World Rally

Soon after the end of the second round the world rally, I started planning a third one and, having drawn a blank with getting any support from Europe, was now actively looking for a suitable theme. One day I read a long report in a London newspaper describing the ambitious plans that the Portuguese government was drawing up for the anniversary of Vasco da Gama's voyage around Africa in 1498. The planned celebrations were to be incorporated in a big world exhibition to be built on a derelict site on the banks of the river Tagus in Lisbon. The theme of Expo 98 was "The Ocean, a Heritage for the Future". I knew instantly that there couldn't be a more suitable theme for my rally, so I started making overtures to my Portuguese contacts. I flew to Madeira where my generous supporter Joao Carlos Abreu, Director of Tourism, had worked wonders in 1992 when America 500 had passed through his island. He welcomed me warmly, listened carefully to what I had in mind and immediately picked up the phone, called Lisbon and asked to speak to the Minister of Commerce, who was responsible for Expo 98. After a short conversation, he turned to me, 'OK, all done, but you must go immediately to Lisbon as the minister is very busy and he can only see you tomorrow at 6 am. He is an old

friend and he is coming to the ministry early just to see you.'

Punctually the following morning I was at the Ministry, but the guard refused to believe what I told him and told me to wait outside. A few minutes before six an official car pulled up and a smartly dressed man of my age stepped out. He realised who I must be, shook my hand with a strong manly grip and invited me into this office. I briefed him on America 500, of which he knew more than I imagined and also the success of the previous two round the world rallies. I then told him that the theme of the forthcoming world exhibition was so attractive that I was very keen to be associated with it.

'OK, that's no problem at all. What can you do for us?'

Not knowing what to expect I had come without my usual wish list, so I decided to play for time.

'For Expo 98 to be the title sponsor of the rally we would expect your full support throughout the event.'

'No problem,' he replied.

'Bearing in mind the dates of the proposed exhibition we could easily plan to start and finish the rally in Lisbon. In fact we could adjust the timing in such a way that we could be back in Lisbon for the grand opening in May 1998.'

'That sounds interesting, but could you include any current or former Portuguese territories on your route?'

I thought for a moment and then said, 'Stopping in Madeira at the start is no problem. After we have sailed through the South Indian Ocean we could pick up the traditional Portuguese route at the Cape of Good Hope.'

'Excellent.'

'From South Africa we could make a detour to Brazil, then sail to the Azores for a final stop where we can organise a rally around the main islands before the final leg to Lisbon.'

He was now all smiles.

'It sounds fantastic! Anything else?'

I hesitated for a diplomatic moment.

'Well, yes, and I hope won't you mind a final request, but with an event of this scale and nature, which is going around the world on a totally new route, the entry fees will not be able to support the budget on their own.'

'How much?'

'150,000 pounds sterling.'

He thought for a moment, then said simply, 'Done. And thank you for thinking of us. I like the idea very much and can guarantee that you have made the best decision.'

'I know and I am very grateful.'

We shook hands and when I walked out of the ministry I realised that it wasn't even 6.30 am. I had secured my first ever commercial sponsorship in record time. I was on cloud nine.

Christmas 1996 found our 36 yachts tethered to a couple of pontoons in a commercial dock on the Tagus close to the most famous Portuguese yacht club, Asociação Naval de Lisboa. Its prime location was in Belem next to the imposing statue dedicated to Prince Henry the Navigator and the explorers and sailors who had pioneered the modern era of maritime exploration. We were in excellent company. On the eve of the start the President of the Club, Carlos Ferreira, had invited all rally skippers and the most prominent club members to a special farewell dinner. Carlos hails from the famous family of Pedro Alvares Cabral, the discoverer of Brazil, whereas his wife is a Perestrello, the family of Maria Perestrello, the wife of Columbus. At the end of the meal, Carlos asked me to make a speech, which normally I don't find too difficult. However I wanted to end this evening on

Expo'98 rally fleet on the eve of the start in Lisbon

a special note, so I concluded with the following words.

'Many years ago a foreign sailor came to this city looking for support and sponsorship for a special voyage that he had in mind. Unfortunately he was shunned so he did the best next thing, went next door, presented his idea to the King and Queen of Spain... and the rest is history.'

Having been reminded so bluntly of one of the greatest blunders in their otherwise glorious maritime history, when their King Joao had flatly refused to support Columbus's plans, the smiles of my

Portuguese audience had by now disappeared, while Carlos looked painfully embarrassed. But they were soon smiling again when they heard my conclusion.

'I am happy to say that history does NOT repeat itself and this foreign sailor has secured all the support he needs for an endeavour that will surely make a great contribution to the lasting glory of Portugal. Thank you.'

The following day all yachts headed for the start line in front of Henry the Navigator's monument, being helped both by a favourable wind and tide. Four of the yachts were flying the Portuguese flag and not surprisingly we were welcomed warmly in all the Portuguese territories. The first stop in Madeira was an excellent foretaste of things to come. The Expo 98 official, Joao Gonçalves, who had been seconded to the rally, joined us in a number of significant stopovers, such as Cape Town and Salvador da Bahia, where he put on large receptions for local dignitaries and rally participants. On our arrival in South Africa at Richards Bay, the rally was welcomed by the King and Queen of the Zulus, who presented all participants with exquisite carvings of wild animals.

The stop in Salvador da Bahia was timed to coincide with the colourful carnival and the famous samba groups were joined by our participants with great enthusiasm even if less dancing skills. The long leg from Brazil to the Azores finished in the picturesque marina at Horta. From there we sailed to the Azorean capital Ponta Delgada and on to Lisbon. With perfect timing we sailed up the River Tagus on the day of the opening of Expo 98 and the yachts were docked in a special pool inside the large exhibition. Our crews, including the scores of friends and families who had joined them, had the run of the place as they could roam freely around the exhibition, night and day. It was a wonderful atmosphere that kept some of them there for weeks. The end was not too painful as I knew that we would be back with the Millennium Odyssey before Expo 98 closed. And so we were.

Millennium Odyssey

The Millennium Odyssey proved that rich people can sail around the world.
                                    Fabio Colapinto

Less affluent people can do it too!
                                    Michael Frankel

The impending new millennium and its huge potential had my mind already spinning in the early 1990s long before even the idea of the Hong Kong Challenge had been born. Not only was I keen to organise something unique and original for this very special occasion but the year 2000 coincided also with my own 60th birthday when I was determined to retire and therefore had one more reason to try and leave the rally scene with a big splash. A round the world rally was quite obviously the logical answer but, for the first time, I was stuck for a suitable theme. I mulled over the millennium's historic significance, international implications and its religious foundation... and still could see no light at the end of the tunnel. But gradually those very elements started to coalesce, come into focus and the idea started to take shape by itself. This would be an opportunity not only to celebrate the arrival of a new millennium, but much more important, to mark a milestone in the history of humankind that after the fall of communism promised to usher in an age of peace, international harmony and understanding. Looking back into

The Millennium lamps are lit at the Church of the Holy Sepulchre in Jerusalem

the early history of man I saw that the gift of fire to another clan or tribe must have been the original symbol of peace, an early instance of man stretching out his hand in help to a fellow human being. My idea therefore was for a symbolic Millennium Flame to circle the globe and bring everywhere a message of hope, understanding and, above all, peace.

The true meaning of the millennium celebrations imposed its own parameters and, in spite of a certain reluctance, the Christian dimension could not be ignored. The rally, therefore, had to have a symbolic start in Jerusalem and an equally symbolic finish in Rome – with the wide world in between.

A small fleet of Millennium Odyssey yachts gathered in the Israeli port of Ashkelon early in August 1998 for the start of the most ambitious project I had ever undertaken. One morning we all drove to Jerusalem to the Church of the Holy Sepulchre, where the Orthodox Church who had administered this holy place throughout its turbulent history, had agreed to put on a special ceremony for the lighting of the Millennium Lamps. These had been specially designed and

each participating yacht was to carry a lamp and its flame around the world. At every stop the flame was to be handed over to local dignitaries in a special ceremony.

Gathered in the smoky gloom in front of the tomb of the Saviour the venerable Russian Patriarch emerged from the narrow tunnel leading to the holy Sepulchre and, from a blazing torch that he had lit from a candle on the tomb, transferred the flame to the expectant skippers. The moving ceremony having been completed we all went into a neighbouring side chapel where the Papal Nuncio, Monsignor Pietro Sambi, blessed us, prayed for the safe completion of our endeavour and then ended with a statement that filled my eyes with tears.

'My heart is filled with joy that your very special event has already borne fruit because as far as I know this is the very first time in the 2000 year old history of this venerable place that our two religions had actually agreed to give their support and cooperation to one project. Thank you all, but above all thank you Jimmy Cornell.'

While the Jerusalem fleet made its way across the Mediterranean with a

Millennium yachts at Anakena on Easter Island

first stop in Crete, a similar fleet had left London for the rendezvous in Lisbon. Having opened Expo 98 in May, the organisers of the international exhibition had enthusiastically agreed to host the Millennium Odyssey fleet inside the exhibition. With perfect timing our world voyage departed just as the curtain fell on Expo 98. Sailing down the River Tagus on the last day of the world exhibition the rally made its way towards Madeira and Gran Canaria. The merging of the two fleets in Lisbon was a joyful occasion made even more enjoyable by the many families joining the crews during the exciting last days of the highly successful show.

In Las Palmas the fleet split in two as in order to cover as much as possible of the world I had devised two very different routes: a warm water route that went through the Panama Canal and the tropics, which attracted the bulk of the fleet, and a cold water high latitude alternative via Cape Horn and the Cape of Good Hope.

One unique feature of the rally was the special souvenir logbooks that had been produced for each yacht. Each log had the usual pages for daily entries and notes to refresh the memory. Specially designed pages were inserted at the relevant points that were meant to be signed by a high official at each of the flame handing

over ceremonies. Among those who signed were the Papal Nuncio in Jerusalem, the President of Panama, the Mayor of Rio de Janeiro, the Governor of the Falkland Islands, HRH Princess Pilolevu of Tonga and many others. The pages that I treasure most in Aventura's logbook are those signed by all the scientists of the Ukrainian Vernadsky station in Antarctica, the distinctive stamp added by the keeper of the lighthouse at Cape Horn, and the signatures of some of my Pitcairn friends.

While the warm water fleet was to head west via the Panama Canal, seven of the more daring yachts set sail south from the Canaries towards Brazil, Argentina, the Falklands and Southern Chile. Nowhere was the symbolic gesture of the handing over of the Millennium Flame appreciated more than in Mar del Plata, where the Bishop gave us a message of peace and friendship from the people of Argentina to take to the Falkland Islands. The Millennium Odyssey was the first international event to link the two previously warring communities since the tragic conflict that had marred lives on both sides. Equally impressive had been the flame ceremony at the Cathedral of Rio de Janeiro where a famous Brazilian sculptor had created a huge frame to hold the tiny millennium lamp that was guarded by a Republican Guard in full ceremonial uniform.

At Puerto Williams on the Beagle Channel the small fleet split into two with four yachts crossing the Drake Passage to Antarctica while the other three took a leisurely cruise through the Chilean Canals. The fleet was reunited in the Chilean port of Valdivia where we proceeded via Easter, Pitcairn and the Gambier Islands to Tahiti.

The tiny population of Pitcairn, where our arrival had been eagerly awaited, gathered in the small church to receive the flame. The rally sailors were very moved to be on this island whose turbulent history had always been closely linked to the sea. In Tahiti the cold water fleet was reunited with those that had transited the Panama Canal and who earlier had been joined by a number of American yachts, that had started from Florida.

After a moving ceremony in the Catholic Cathedral in

Ecumenical service for the safe arrival of the Millennium fleet in Mauritius

Papeete the rally proceeded westward to Tonga, where the skippers were received at the Royal Palace by HRH Princess Pilolevu, who gave participants a warm welcome, something that our royal hosts had done on every previous rally. Princess Pilolevu's interest in the current rally went back to the very first round the world rally when she had graciously agreed to come to Gibraltar to give the start of Europa 92.

Special ceremonies, combined with cruising interludes marked the rally's passage through the rest of the South Pacific with the highlight at the resort of Musket Cove, an unforgettable traditional Fijian welcome ceremony. In Bali it was time for the two fleets to go their separate ways again. A smaller fleet headed along the more difficult route across the South Indian Ocean and the Cape of Good Hope while a larger group pointed their bows for the Red Sea and Mediterranean. What stood out in this part of the world was the enthusiastic welcome the flame ceremony received everywhere from Buddhists, Hindus and Muslims just as in previous countries we had been warmly welcomed by various

Christian denominations. In Mauritius the ceremony was attended by each of the island's three main religions, a unique occasion that marked yet another first for the Millennium Odyssey.

While the main fleet spent some time in South East Asia, the smaller fleet sailed across the South Atlantic to Salvador da Bahia in Brazil, where, once again, the arrival coincided with that city's unique carnival. From Brazil, the fleet continued to the Eastern Caribbean and in Antigua it was time to bid farewell to the American participants who were sailing home from there. Among them there were some old friends who had also sailed in America 500. The other yachts, that were going to sail either to the Mediterranean or to Northern Europe, set sail from Antigua for the Azores.

Handing over the Millennium Flame to Pope John Paul II on the successful completion of the rally

Meanwhile, after stops in Singapore, Malaysia and Phuket, early in 2000 the larger Millennium fleet sailed across the Indian Ocean to Djibouti and then via Eritrea and Sudan to Egypt. Being docked in a marina south of the Suez Canal gave participants the opportunity to visit the ancient sites of Luxor and the Valley of the Kings before finally reaching the Mediterranean. After a final stop in Crete the fleet arrived in Rome's ancient port of Civitavecchia where in the following days we were joined by scores of families and friends that had flown in from all over the world.

Millennium Easter Monday had been set aside for a large outdoor ceremony in St Peter's Square where the Millennium Odyssey contingent had been reserved places in a special enclosure among the 100,000 pilgrims from around the world. I had the great honour to hand over the Millennium Flame to Pope John Paul II, an occasion which filled me with awe but also with immense pride and satisfaction for what I consider the single most important achievement of my life. I was very moved to hand over the Millennium Lamp to this frail but remarkable man, who had done so

much to shape the closing years of the twentieth century. With a warm smile on his face he asked about our rally and, with a trembling voice, I explained very briefly how the flame had reached him and how our message of peace had travelled around the world.

Having had serious difficulties in securing the cooperation of the Vatican, difficulties that had plagued me to the very last moment so that even the meeting with the Pope was only confirmed on the morning of Easter Monday, I had decided to play it safe and, in order to avoid disappointing my participants in case all my efforts with the Vatican fell flat, I had made arrangements for a backup ceremony with Cardinal Carlo Furno, the Grand Master of the Order of the Holy Sepulchre, whose magnificent headquarters were also in St Peter's Square. With the help of a Roman friend I also managed to secure an appointment with the Mayor of Rome. As fate would have it, not only were we received by the Pope but we also had the added satisfaction of attending those two other special ceremonies as well. Our reception at the Campidoglio Palace with the President of the Rome Municipal Council took place in the ancient Roman Senate overshadowed by a statue of Julius Caesar who had once presided over proceedings in that very spot. We were then taken on a private tour of this famous building that overlooks the Forum and is not open to the general public. The participants were quite blown over by the setting and I'm sure that all that happened that day will be remembered by them to the end of their days.

A final ceremony awaited the few yachts that had decided to end the rally where they had started – on the Greenwich Meridian in London. Once again I was

well crystallized my own hopes for this truly unique event. 'The idealism of the journey takes visible form in the people we encounter. Only through meeting people one to one can we hope to find peace. A big dream of Jimmy Cornell's, an adventure for all of us and maybe, just maybe, understanding can grow between people through encounters like these.'

The Grand Finale

The successful finish of the Millennium Odyssey also marked the end of my career as a rally organiser. Shortly before the Rome ceremony we sold World Cruising Club, which Gwenda and I had founded in 1986

Millennium Odyssey participants in St Peter's Square

fortunate to find just the right place, the 15th century chapel set in the grounds of the Tower of London, where the Millennium Lamp now rests not far from the remains of the martyred St Thomas More.

From among the many comments made by the Millennium Odyssey participants I wish to conclude with the words of Saundra and Charles Gray as they so

when the first ARC was taking shape. The new owner of the company Chay Blyth of the Challenge Business already had a number of sailing events on his books and so seemed a suitable person to take over. Eventually I came to regret not so much the actual sale of World Cruising Club as it gave me the long delayed opportunity to do what I like best and go sailing, but the

Patrizia, Alexander, Klaus and Renate Girzig
receive their Millennium Odyssey award
from Sir Edward Heath

direction the ARC took after my departure. Of all the rallies the ARC remains closest to my heart as it is in every respect 'my baby' and, as any loving parent, I wished the very best for it. I had therefore hoped that the ARC's nature would not be altered by the new owner but I soon realised that my worst fears might come true. Whereas throughout the fourteen ARCs that I ran between 1986 and 1999 I had done my best not to stray from the original concept, that of a cruising rally for cruising sailors, the ARC's commercial potential proved to be too tempting to the new owners who kept putting up the fees thus turning off many of those for whom the ARC had been initially intended. Gradually the ARC started attracting increasingly larger and larger yachts, many of them racing boats and just as many operating as charter boats, two aspects that I had strenuously resisted while still being in control. In spite of this, or perhaps because of its solid reputation, the ARC continued to be successful, at least on the surface, and judging by the constant large numbers of participants, my comments may sound like sour grapes. What I found most surprising was that having handed over the operation to the

Challenge Business and in spite of the firm assurances and promises I had been given I ended up entirely sidelined, my presence being obviously no longer welcome in Las Palmas. It went so far that Gwenda and I were not even invited to attend the special celebrations marking the twentieth ARC in 2005, this deliberate insult being graciously put right by my long time supporters, the Tourist Board of Gran Canaria and the Port Authority of Las Palmas, who insisted that we joined them for the final days of the celebrations.

To my great satisfaction early in 2006 the ARC changed hands again and was taken over by Andrew Bishop and Jeremy Wyatt who had managed the ARC throughout the intervening years. Andrew and Jeremy had worked for me since the early 1990s and were responsible for maintaining much of the original spirit of the ARC under its new ownership, so my baby seems to be in good hands again and I wish it all the best for the future.

In spite of the occasional regret, I am actually quite happy that my rally days are over and that my priorities are now of a very different nature, this book being the first in a number of projects I would like to complete. Much of my time is now taken up by our website which is going from strength to strength and incorporates all the basic ideas that led to the success of the ARC and other rallies. Launched in 2000, noonsite is a non-commercial venture whose main aim is to provide an unbiased free service to cruising sailors. By early 2007 noonsite was averaging over one million hits per month and is now a prime source of information for cruising sailors everywhere.

Highlights of a Sailing Life

Robert Louis Stevenson, who was an inveterate traveller and whose sailing adventures took him right across the Pacific Ocean, wrote: "I travel not to go anywhere, but to go; I travel for travel's sake." If "travel" is replaced by "sailing" it should become immediately clear why the title of this book is "A Passion for the Sea". Besides the sheer joy of sailing, my voyages were also rich in new experiences, most of them well off the beaten track. Few, if any, were due to chance but mainly to my insatiable journalistic curiosity which led us into some lengthy and ambitious detours. This willingness to put up with some inconvenience was the price both Gwenda and I were ready to accept as the unavoidable sacrifice that committed travellers have to pay. From among a long list of unforgettable highlights I will mention some of the more significant ones as they illustrate not just the beauty of cruising but also the abundant rewards that we have been fortunate to reap.

Aventura I

When we stopped on our first voyage in Easter Island we met by chance Tom Layng, the British Commissioner of the Ellice Islands. When he heard about our cruising plans and our intention to spend the next two or three years in the South Pacific, he urged us not to miss the forthcoming independence celebrations of those islands, one of the smallest countries in the world, soon to be renamed Tuvalu. Later that year we made the long detour towards the

equator and Tuvalu, a decision we never regretted, as it turned out to be one of the most memorable experiences of our entire voyage. When we arrived in Funafuti we were amazed at how small a place it was. The strip of land it was built on was maybe half a mile long and about two hundred metres wide. A landing strip had been

Talofa, Welcome toTuvalu

cleared but it was normally used as a village green and the one and only local policeman had to cycle all over the strip to chase children, dogs and chickens away when an aeroplane came in to land. Tom Layng welcomed us warmly at his residence and asked us if we wanted to take a shower. 'Oh yes,' we all exclaimed enthusiastically, so Tom turned to his secretary and told her, 'Get a prisoner, will you?'

I thought I had misunderstood, but a while later there was a knock on the door

475

Doina and Ivan with Tuvalu's Prime Minister Toalipi Lauti awaiting the arrival of Princess Margaret

and a man in what looked like prison garb stood there expectantly.

'Semisi, you go pump water for these people who want take shower. OK?'

'Yes sir.'

We took our turns to stand in the shower cubicle while Semisi was busy pumping on the outside. I somehow felt that I was back in ancient Egypt.

The nine thousand strong population had pulled out all the stops to celebrate in style their impending statehood and various dignitaries, foremost among them Princess Margaret, Queen Elizabeth's sister, started flying in. There were plenty of naval ships too, from a US destroyer to ships from New Zealand, Australia, France and Fiji. One ensign that was glaringly and surprisingly missing was the one bearing the Union Jack of the departing colonial power. One of the events in the celebration programme took place at the Philatelic Bureau as in those days Ellice Island stamps were sought

after by collectors. I was reporting on the event for a British newspaper and when, after all the VIPs as well as the ship captains had received their special souvenir collection, I piped up from the back and said, 'How about an album for the captain of the only British ship to attend these celebrations?'

There was a moment of embarrassed silence followed by loud laughter. I was called forward and was duly presented with an album containing a collection of Ellice Islands stamps. The biggest laugh however came the following day when the correspondent of the prestigious The Age newspaper of Melbourne told me that my story headed the front page as "Ex-Romanian Yachtie Represents British

Sitting dance during Tuvalu independence celebrations

Navy at Tuvalu Independence Celebrations." It was just the kind of story Aussies relish – any chance of putting down the mother country. I was later sent that front page

many remote corners of that fascinating country both by boat and on land. While driving in the Highlands we caught a glimpse of a man with an amazing headdress as he disappeared in the dense bush by the side of the road. We quickly stopped and followed him into a

which now occupies a prominent place in my collection of souvenirs as does that special stamp album.

If I had to pick one country that stands out more than any other in all my voyaging it is Papua New Guinea. We spent half a year there during the 1979/1980 cyclone season and explored

clearing where hundreds of men and women from the surrounding villages had gathered for a traditional singsing. That unique experience and the photographs that I managed to take were another highlight of our voyage.

A floating market as Aventura is surrounded by outrigger canoes whose occupants have come to trade

A place where time had stood still were the Trobriand Islands off the coast of New Guinea, famous for their trading voyages in traditional craft. Doina and Ivan attracted a lot of attention as white children were rarely seen there, while we were equally fascinated by aspects of village life such as making pottery without a wheel.

Ivan, Gwenda and Doina in a Trobriand village

A canoe from the Amphlett Islands with a sail woven from pandanus leaves is making its way to the mainland for a load of pottery clay

In July 1980 Papua New Guinea hosted the quadrennial Pacific Festival of Arts. To coincide with the opening ceremony, sailing canoes from all over the country made their way to a meeting point and then sailed in company towards the capital.

Aventura was the only non-traditional sailing craft to accompany the ever growing fleet which by the time it reached Port Moresby had grown to an armada of over two hundred canoes of all types, shapes and sizes.

These two canoes had sailed several hundreds of miles from Manus in the Admiralty Islands to join the Armada

The armada of canoes were welcomed by dancers and music at every stop along the Papuan coast

The opening ceremony of the Festival was a wonderful finale to the three years we had spent in the Pacific as each island group had sent their best performers to Port Moresby. Polynesia, Micronesia and Melanesia tried to outdo each other in flamboyance and originality. It was an excellent opportunity to see again islanders that we had met before and also to become acquainted with the culture and art of the few islands that we had not visited.

Aborigines from Arnhem Land

Group from Western Province of Papua New Guinea at the opening ceremony of the South Pacific Festival of Arts

Dancer from Ponape in Micronesia

Papuan boy at the children's singsing

The beauty of the costumes seen at the Pacific Festival were probably equalled by a spectacle we witnessed on the Greek island of Patmos right at the end of our voyage. The biblical scene of the washing of the feet is re-enacted every Easter by the monks of the monastery on Patmos who have been performing this ceremony since immemorial times. It was a most suitable occasion for the completion of Aventura's six year long voyage.

Aventura II

A highlight of my voyage on Aventura II was a summer cruise that I undertook with Doina from the Azores to the Canaries. Although hundreds of boats stop in the Azores every year, most of them arriving from the Caribbean, very few sailors take the time to see more of these beautiful islands. I tried to put this right by writing a cruising guide to the Azores, and while gathering material for the guide I visited every one of the nine islands of the archipelago. Life there moves at a tranquil pace and their beauty makes them some of the most attractive islands in the world and one of my favourite destinations.

Aventura II in Horta
Marina with a flying
saucer cloud above
the island of Pico

The picturesque
fishing village
of Camara de Lobos
on Madeira

On our way south, we stopped at Madeira and its outlying islands. The Portuguese, who discovered and populated these islands called Madeira the "wooded" island which, alas, is no longer the case but they were quite prescient when they named the nearby islands Desertas as they are still deserted, while the Selvagems are just as "wild" as when they were first stumbled upon.

As we headed south we felt quite privileged as we were in possession of a rare permit to stop and land at the Selvagem Islands. The two islands (Grande and Pequeña) are protected nature reserves and boats are normally only allowed to stop in real emergencies. Anyone else will be politely chased away by the wardens who are stationed permanently there to protect their fragile environment from further deterioration. The Selvagems are the breeding ground for a variety of sea birds, most common among them the shearwater. Thousands of birds nest on

A solitary wild flower on Ilhas Desertas

the bay in every direction. When we landed we were shocked to see the decaying carcass of a small sperm whale which had grounded on the narrow beach. Doina was in tears at the sight of this beautiful animal that had come to its end in this quiet corner of the Atlantic. Back on board she penned this poem:

A sperm whale not yet full grown
at his last breath, storm cast
onto this land no flourished tail
would yield a welcome;
he lies silent as a dead king,
under dry eyed turtle stare,
eternal sentinel-pair - or guardians of the rot,
skin split, flesh yellowed,
teeth stolen & eyes gouged,
rock pools ooze black & stinking;
no princely treasures nor tool-scratched story
no Valley of the Kings
suffice a sky-blown, depth-sounding tomb
only his spirit swims the luminous waters of Atlantis.

the islands and even those visitors fortunate to stop there, such as ourselves, may only walk ashore accompanied by the resident warden. There are more birds on the larger of the two islands but after a brief stop we moved to its smaller neighbour, even if finding a suitable anchorage proved to be a hair-raising experience as we carefully wove our way between the menacing rocks that surround

Aventura III

There were many highlights during my voyage on Aventura III and most of these have been described in the preceding pages of this book.

Photography has played a significant role in capturing the high points of my voyaging so I would like to end by including some of my favourite photographs of animals and children, and also of Ivan, Doina and Gwenda with whom I shared the happiest moments of my life, on both land and sea.

My reflection caught in the eye of a mighty elephant seal

A lone penguin taking an afternoon stroll on the shore of the Lemaire Channel

The Loch Ness monster is alive and well in Antarctica chased away from his native Scotland by global warming

Children from Polynesia, Melanesia and Micronesia

Waiting for
the supply
boat to come
in at Roviana
Island in the
Solomons

Having fun being
photographed
on Ua Huka Island
in the Marquesas

Camera shy children in
the Trobriand Islands

Fanning, a traffic free
island where children can
play in the middle of the
road

*Great Barrier Island,
New Zealand*

*Gran Canaria,
Canary Islands*

*Komodo Island,
Indonesia*

*Two wandering
albatross bid us farewell*

The most beautiful moments in life are those
that are still to come.

Jimmy Cornell
Aventura III, August 2007